TOUR DE FRANCE

www.transworldbooks.co.uk

Graeme Fife is a full-time writer with numerous books published in the UK, Holland and the USA. He has broadcast on the six main BBC Radio networks and has written plays, stories and features for radio and stage, as well as directing and performing. A keen cyclist, he has ridden all the celebrated cols of Tour legend.

TOUR DE FRANCE

THE HISTORY, THE LEGEND, THE RIDERS

GRAEME FIFE

MAINSTREAM
PUBLISHING

EDINBURGH AND LONDON

For Lucy

TRANSWORLD PUBLISHERS
61–63 Uxbridge Road, London W5 5SA
www.transworldbooks.co.uk

Transworld is part of the Penguin Random House group of companies
whose addresses can be found at global.penguinrandomhouse.com

Penguin
Random House
UK

This edition first published in Great Britain in 2015 by Mainstream Publishing
an imprint of Transworld Publishers

A CIP catalogue record for this book
is available from the British Library.

ISBN 9781910948026

Typeset in Sabon and Garamond
Printed and bound by Clays Ltd, St Ives plc.

Penguin Random House is committed to a sustainable
future for our business, our readers and our planet. This book
is made from Forest Stewardship Council® certified paper.

CONTENTS

Author's Note   7

Foreword   9

Preface   10

Jerseys of the Tour de France   29

1 L'Alpe d'Huez   32
   Fear, Moral Strength and Eddy Merckx

2 Col du Glandon   52
   Hinault and Fighting Spirit

3 Col du Télégraphe   78
   Tours of the 1920s

4 Col du Galibier   104
   The 1930s

5 Col d'Izoard   129
   Coppi and the Modern Era

6 Col de Vars   151
   Drugs in the Sport

7 Mont Ventoux   180
   The British Riders

8 Tour '98   201
   The Tour is Dead, Long Live the Tour

9 1999   211
   The Tour of Renewal

10 2000   227
    Answering the Cynics
11 2001   241
    Armstrong v. Ullrich
12 2002   259
    Armstrong's Four-Square Triumph
13 The Centenary   279
14 2004   300
    A Historic Sixth
15 2005   322
    Seventh Heaven: Armstrong's Last Tour
16 2006   345
    The Crazy 'Bottle of Ink' Tour
17 2007   371
    Sunshine in London . . . Squalls into Paris
18 2008   397
    A Clean Start?
19 2009   414
    The Comeback Tour
20 2010   437
    Hail and Farewell
21 2011   458
    Racing, Old Style
22 2012   483
    First British Winner
23 2013   507
    100th Edition
24 2014   535
    The Sicilian Shark

    Afterword and Mythology   561
    Index   573

AUTHOR'S NOTE

Wherever possible I have based this account of the Tour de France on original testimony: the riders' memoirs – Bidot, Anquetil, Merckx, Hinault, Robic, Maertens, Lemond, Simpson and others; the specialist French journals, magazines and books; and my own recollection garnered over a period of some 25 years of addiction to this unique event. It is not a comprehensive history. Such a tome would probably be unreadable and certainly too heavy to read other than from a lectern. My aim, rather, was to get inside the mystique of the Tour.

I have checked and cross-checked information but am aware that factual errors may have strayed into the text – sources tend to be contradictory. I cheerfully acknowledge the sterling help of two fellow enthusiasts and friends of mine, John Partington and Nick Flanagan, who have helped me with statistics, sharpened my knowledge of the more arcane workings of Tour methodology and given unflagging support in the enterprise, not least in fielding my opinions on and joining discussion of tactics, the evaluation of riders and exploring the peculiar allure of the race itself. If any errors have survived a painstaking scrutiny, the fault is mine alone.

Anthony Wood, as ever, gave me invaluable help in shaping the text; and John Partington's editorial advice in streamlining the original manuscript was as spot-on as his wheelbuilding.

My thanks to Nigel Dick for his peerless insight into what it's like to be a *domestique*/water carrier in the *peloton*. Many thanks to my friend Luke Edwardes-Evans for supplying material for the

Moto-camera Diary. Graham Watson, whose photography has, to my delight, graced the book from the start, has supplied six more trademark images for this new edition.

To everyone at Mainstream who has been involved in the shaping and production of this book since it was first published, high professionals all, long overdue thanks and acknowledgement, particularly Ailsa, Claire, Emily, Graeme and Kate, whose help and contributions latterly have made my job so much easier.

Henri Desgrange, the 'father of the Tour', was all for simplicity. Set aside the Byzantine complexity of his rules, his undimmable idealism, his fanatical resistance to technological innovation, his misogyny – sex and cycling in his view did not mix – his restless search for more arduous challenges, and the imperative was direct: to win the Tour, he said, requires two things – *tête et jambes* . . . head and legs.

This book has much to do with both.

Here are the stories, epic, tragic, comic, bizarre, incredible, fascinating, of the riders who have won, lost or simply ridden the Tour de France.

FOREWORD

BY CHRIS BOARDMAN MBE

When I first entered the Tour I didn't really know what to expect. I had no idea what I was going into. It was our plan for me only to ride the first ten days, up to the Pyrenees, to see how I went and as preparation for future rides. Winning the Prologue was something I'd thought about, obviously – it's my specialist event – but I was so new and inexperienced I hardly knew it had happened. Even standing on the podium, receiving the yellow jersey that every cyclist dreams of wearing, I could hardly grasp the importance of it. I was really hyped but it felt as if that victory had just landed on my plate. It was only later that it really dawned on me just how big the event was, how important, and riding the other Prologues, knowing what it took to win, trying to emulate that first win, was much harder than anything else I had ever done. That first year I went to see the finish in Paris; it was thrilling to see the *peloton* ride the final lap. It was when the manager drove me up the Champs-Elysées that morning that I fell in love with the Tour. I don't take my Prologue wins for granted in the least as they are only part of my goal, a goal I am pursuing as hard as I can.

The Tour is, without doubt, the biggest single sporting event in the world. You have to see it in person – standing at the side of the road, behind the barriers at the *Arrivée*, perched by the side of the mountains – to believe the impact it has. When the Tour comes to town it's like the Olympics arriving. There simply is nothing else like it. And, as a test of physical and mental endurance it has no equal. Other sports may be as intense, as pressurised, as hard for short periods: but the Tour goes on day after day after day. They say it's the only race in the world where you have to have a haircut halfway through.

Graeme has written a terrific account of this amazing race, from the early days. It's a book tailor-made for bike fans as well as for the casual fans who see the Tour on Channel 4 every year. The Tour de France *is* a legendary race and here is a great read to go with it.

PREFACE

Millau, 15 July 1995

The Tour de France is due to pass through here around noon. Metal barriers lining the streets have been in position since 9 a.m. Last night, the town was *en fête* for Bastille Day: fireworks, accordion bands, thronging crowds and dancing in the town square. The same crowds are beginning to flock into town now. The accordion band, eight-strong, is back on the makeshift stage in the Place de Ville, zipping through a medley of boulevardier tunes, quintessentially French. Mid-morning, the municipal brass band, in maroon uniform with silver brocades and swagging, struts and oompahs its repertoire up and down the main street – cornets, trumpets and euphoniums, cymbals, tubas and drums . . . *Allons enfants de la Patrie, Le jour de gloire est arrivé.*

We stroll round the shops, but everyone is at the same game this morning in Millau: filling in time. There's an air of expectancy as if the whole town was waiting with bated breath, and sudden silences pervade the streets and pavements. We wait, nerves taut, listening for the whisper from way off that the Tour has hit the outskirts; but it is a false alarm. The low murmur of meandering citizens at leisure and desultory business resumes, Saturday-morning errands, window-shopping and rendezvous. The cafés and bars do slick trade in the lazy sunshine.

By 11 a.m. the barriers are pretty well lined with spectators, there's some good-humoured jostling for a better view: on the cusp of a bend, maybe, or with a long view of the straight, even if slightly obscured by plane trees to either side. Some old hands keep their seats at the pavement tables, time enough to move in before the action proper begins. A flurry of applause, cheers, laughter, as a young bride in white silk and lace, hoisting her dress up round her calves, is tiptoeing across the street and through a gap in the hurdles, picking her way to the church to be married. The Tour rules: thou shalt walk to thy wedding. She beams with mirth at the public congratulation on this doubly auspicious day.

At 11.30 a.m, a raucous fanfare of klaxons in the distance heralds the Tour vanguard: radio and television cars, Commissariat, publicity cavalcade – soda cans on wheels, motorised Coca-Cola bottles, petrol-driven bonbons – team wagons topped with serried ranks of spare wheels spinning fast in the slipstream. A maroon saloon draws up alongside the barriers where I'm standing. Out steps Raymond Poulidor. Blimey. The great Poupou, suntanned, fit, smiling. Poupou, the 'eternal second', still in the Tour promoting Poulain chocolate. He never promoted himself half as successfully; one reason, perhaps, why he never won the Tour, never even wore the *maillot jaune*, albeit he had the class, and class to spare. His *bête noire*, Anquetil, was the first to win five times, and when he retired Poulidor met another *bête noire*, Merckx, the second man to win five times. What luck. Poulidor came to terms with defeat; Anquetil never could. But here is Poulidor while Anquetil is eight years dead, mourned by none more than his old adversary. Someone taps him on the arm; he scrambles back into the car. Apparently a break of five riders has jumped clear of the main field and will be through 15 minutes ahead of schedule. The chocolate saloon roars off. I remark to a bystander, a local: 'Poulidor, eh? Such a pity he never won.'

'Yes; still, he's got more money than he can spend, and he's still alive. Anquetil had no heart; he was always for himself. Poulidor? A gentleman; too much a gentleman, maybe, but that's past and he's as popular now as he ever was.'

Anquetil enjoyed not an iota of that: indubitably the best, but he never won their hearts.

Hush again like a blast of heat. They must be close and, in a sudden intense silky hiss of ultra-lightweight racing tyres on hot tarmac, a windrush of whirring spokes, a flash of colour, the escapers are there and past us. The American Lance Armstrong, ex-world champion, the prime mover, evidently. He's controlling things from the middle to the side, gesticulating urgently with his right arm, wagging a finger at the road, glancing over his shoulder at his *directeur sportif* (team manager), maybe, but why? Food? Drink? An update on the lead time? Mechanical adjustment to the bike while on the move? Such tiny snippets of drama; the Tour is replete with them. But, most of all, 'escape' sums it up. These fugitives are riding as if they were aristocrats and the bunch were a Jacobin mob howling for their blood.

Ten minutes later, the Tour is on us; the *peloton*, en masse, a multicoloured polycycle, 150 rider-strong express engine moving at such a lick you can't believe the attack will ever have the speed and stamina to hold them off. The sensation of raw power makes you shiver; the thrill of the colour; the noise of the generator whirring – wheels, cranks, chains – is abrupt but exhilarating. Spotting faces in the pack is well-nigh impossible: too dense, they're riding tyre to tyre, elbow to elbow; and too many splashes of yellow in the team jerseys to pick out *the* yellow. But wait, there he is, Indurain, six feet plus of him, crouched like a big cat on the bike; effortless power, fluid action, ball-bearing-smooth tempo. Not all of them have that, the supple grace that only changes as the stage finish approaches and the break is still out and they charge up to crisis acceleration. Merckx was a bruiser in style.

And, like a daytime comet blazing across France by small ways and highways in garish pageant, they are gone, west. Millau's sudden moment of regal blessing has passed. *Ville d'étape*, a singular honour the town has enjoyed before. Within 15 minutes all the cordons have been dismantled, cars and pedestrians are soft-shoeing the market-day shuffle in the four roads leading to the central roundabout, and we head for lunch in a tiny restaurant down the road leading north which the Tour did not touch. It is markedly darker, cooler, quieter, lonelier without that heat of the race and the elation of the crowd when the leading bikes burst out of the mirage. I commiserate with the *patronne* who couldn't watch the race go by because she was busy serving lunch. And who, please, was eating *lunch* when the Tour came by? French who didn't *care*? Tourists who didn't *know*? *Imagine*.

One and a half hours later and the pack of eastbound traffic, which concertina-ed up along the Gorges du Tarn till the Tour had passed on closed roads, is still overheating on the outskirts of town. We drive past the jam in the opposite direction; I scan the verges for sight of a discarded water bottle, but they've all been snapped up. And as we wind up the twists of the gorge roads which the riders flew down, I wish I were on a bike, not cooped up in a car. The rest of the day's action we'll see on television. Armstrong missed out by a few wheel lengths. He had his victory later.

✶

The Tour de France is, and always has been, one of the hardest endurance events in the professional sporting calendar. And the roads of France are free, year round, to be ridden in the wake of the Tour itself. For the fanatic, the Étape du Tour follows the route of one stage each year, special tours allow amateur riders to cover the route of the day's race, starting long before the Tour rolls out; and the *Tour Routier*, an event for club cyclists, ghosts the race a month or so after the final *Arrivée* in Paris. Organised sallies apart, France is a fine country beckoning to any cyclist. While there may be no real feel of the race, the long flat coast roads in the Landes of the Atlantic coast beckon us, or the brutal cobbles of the 'Hell of the North' which may simply amount to masochism on a grand scale, as unkind to the metal frame as to the human. Spin the twisting lanes of Champagne, follow the sweep of the big rivers – Loire and its châteaux, the rocky defiles of the Gorges du Tarn, the baking hot ups and downs of the lower Rhône – and you will be tracing the route, this way or that, of one *Grande Boucle* or another. But the one place you will get as close as any non-participant can to the emotion, the physical stress and distress, the elation, the frustration and the punishing effort of will which animates the still photos and the moving pictures of the Tour de France riders, at one extreme or another, joy or despair, is in the mountains. The mountains almost invariably form the crucial battlefield of the Tour.

Many images of the Tour, caught in still photos, encapsulate the drama, the forum of its rivalries, its cruelty, its essential magic and the peculiar fascination of cycling and might, perhaps, appeal to few other than cyclists. However, there is a generosity about cycling rooted, I believe, in its very equality. Where high-performance machines are in competition, their drivers will always have to concede some of their triumph to the machine; or ought to; there are some disagreeable exceptions. But the bicycle can never make so much difference that we will all call 'Foul' because one rider has a demonstrably, an intrinsically, superior machine to another. On the road, at any rate.

★

SNAPSHOT: Coppi and Bartali, big rivals in their day (the duel between them talked up, of course, by journalists to sell newspapers, but neither was disposed to do the other any favours in the pursuit of victory), are here, riding a mountain road. The sun is evidently beating down, not a breath of wind, air burning hot, both of them sweating profusely, both wearing that gaunt expression which portrays effort at the limit. Coppi, slightly in front, Bartali stuck to his wheel, stares fixedly ahead and reaches behind to take the drinking bottle his adversary is handing him.

★

I want to see the mountains the Tour crosses, to ride them, to seek out the compulsion of this majestic, crazy, perdurable, inspiring, heroic cycle race which started as a publicity stunt, was written off as a grotesque absurdity almost as soon as its first edition ended and yet has continued to astonish ever since.

They call the high mountains *les juges de paix* : 'conciliation magistrates' who arbitrate in disputes. In the mountains, the man who weakens will be eliminated; men who were in command one day may falter the next and sustain crippling losses, even abandon the race. The mountains preside without pity.

Above all, this is a record of courage: the courage of all the riders who have ridden the Tour, every rider in the bunch. And, ever present, surging through the mêlée, the metronomic, unyielding momentum of the strongest men who devour punishing mileage and competition day after day – in French the *train-train* – the ceaseless treadmill of stage racing; the men of herculean constitution and will, those who somehow find the wherewithal, mental and physical, to launch an all-out attack when they're at their limit, ill with fatigue, knowing that even if their rivals aren't suffering as badly yet, they soon will be. The Tour is a test of nerve, audacity, stamina, competitive instinct and generosity without equal. Three weeks of punishment and nowhere to hide. Everyone has a bad day; it's the mark of the champions that not only can they keep their bad days secret from the others but even ride through them at cruel speed. Hinault said it: 'When I feel bad, I attack; that way no one can find out just how bad I do feel.'

Naturally, there comes a day when the champion can't do it any more; when, however strong the mind is, the legs are not capable. So often that fatal onset of weakness, *défaillance*, can be pinpointed to a moment when the young wolves cast off the old Akela: 1990, on the Tourmalet, when Lemond watched the leading group move ineluctably ahead of him; he had nothing to counter with and Indurain rode to his first victory. Six years later, Big Mig took his own long stare into defeat's same telescope as the leaders vanished into the distance without him.

Marcel Bidot, a pro during the '20s and '30s and, later, manager of the French national team, said: 'In this business you cannot afford sentiment or else you'll be flattened.' You need mental and physical toughness, plus the supereminent courage that surpasses both, and courage day after day after day. Bravery, as the Spanish say, must be judged again and again on performance, not reputation.

In 1893 the French government imposed a yearly tax on bicycles and official census figures show that by the close of the century over a million cyclists were paying it. Men and women clamoured to own the new freedom machine: it was relatively cheap, it was fast – *vélocipède*: 'fast walker'. The basic 'ordinary', nicknamed penny-farthing, had been superseded by vital technological advances, in particular, the invention of the chain which made efficient transmission possible and pneumatic tyres for a smoother ride. The new bike with its diamond frame was called a safety. Penny-farthings were ungainly and perilous, especially downhill:

no brakes, feet off the fixed pedals. Accidents, some fatal, were frequent.

It was an age of astonishing ingenuity and invention: the steam engine, telephone, telegraph; advances in science of major significance. But two revolutionary machines actually paved the way for the great social upheaval of the twentieth century: the 'pernicious sewing-machine', as one apopleptic male diehard called it, emancipated women from the domestic prison of the needle-room where not the sneakiest devil would find idle hands. And the bicycle gave all who could afford it – and large numbers of a hitherto disadvantaged populace could – independent transport, the freedom of the road. From the start, it was a clean machine, in contrast to the railway (whose impact on towns and landscape was roundly rebuked by Dickens in England and Zola in France). On bicycles, anyone could ride out from town to countryside to partake of *la vie au grand air* ('the fresh-air life') – a phrase used to publicise the first Tours.

The French army saw another more sinister potential. Obsessed since 1870 with the idea of reclaiming Alsace-Lorraine from the Germans, to whom it had been ceded in the Franco-Prussian war, the military Staff formed a regiment of bicycle soldiers – *pioupious à bécane* – stationed at Longchamp, in 1901. They would head the dash across the border:

> *Les cyclistes nouveaux soldats*
> *S'ront les premiers aux combats,*
> *Pour nous votre baïonette*
> *Sera sera sera la bicyclette.*

> A new sort of warrior,
> soldiers on bicycles,
> first into battle,
> the bike as bayonet.

In a blatant gesture of patriotism, the first time the Tour crossed the border out of France it was into German-occupied Alsace, on stages to Metz in 1907–10.

The army insisted, however, on an optimum weight for the bike of 10.5kg; this was, at the time, beyond reach. The average for a racing machine at the time was 13kg.

The bicycle wasn't universally popular. Combining practical usefulness with the benefit of exercise, it drove many gymnasiums, riding schools and swimming-pools into bankruptcy. Sales of bikes soared and the publicity campaigns to sell them often featured sportsmen – track-racers, male and female, and long-distance men. Popular sport was comparatively recent, anyway, and a proletarian sports machine was a wonder. Athletic prowess, sporting celebrity and commercial sponsorship joined hands vigorously, as manufacturers scrambled for a share of the exploding bicycle market. Many factories which had already converted from rifle and pistol manufacture to the production of sewing-machines (the light-engineering plant being fairly adaptable to components for both – swords into ploughshares, indeed) were soon turning out bicycles, too. This survived many years in the famous BSA acronym, originally the Birmingham Small Arms company.

One of the biggest nineteenth-century French industrialists with diverse interests, besides his bike factory, was Comte Dion. His main outlet for advertising was in the pages of *Le Vélo*, a sports journal owned by Pierre Giffard. In 1899 an event occurred which made them implacable enemies and gave birth to the Tour de France.

Five years earlier, an officer in the French army, Alfred Dreyfus, an Alsatian Jew from the vexed territory conterminous with Germany, had been found guilty of passing military secrets to the German attaché in Paris and sentenced to life imprisonment in the Devil's Island penal colony off the coast of French Guyana. The process of the trial had been far from regular; the outcry against the transparent injustice of the verdict was vociferous and a powerful lobby of liberal intellectual opinion demanded his release and the exposure of his false accusers. This was as much an exercise in radical politics as in libertarian support for (it must be said) a singularly uninspiring scapegoat: Dreyfus himself was entirely unlikeable. But the Dreyfus Affair split France: socialist, pro-republican, anti-clerical Dreyfusards, among them Pierre Giffard, versus Catholic, imperialist, anti-semitic, pro-establishment anti-Dreyfusards, including Comte Dion.

Zola's famous diatribe, *J'Accuse*, rang with indignation, fired up

the opposition and the campaign of protest succeeded, to a degree
– in 1899 Dreyfus was retried and, though once again found guilty,
his sentence was reduced to ten years. However, the second trial, as
summary and flawed as the first, provoked a violent outcry which
exploded into civil strife. The Third Republic was tottering and it
seemed in grave danger of collapse, and so the President stepped in
to calm matters with an offer of clemency, which Dreyfus accepted.
(He wasn't legally exonerated until 1906, after a third trial.)

On 3 June 1899, on Auteuil race-course a hostile mob of anti-
Dreyfusards, mingling with the punters, greeted the President of
the Republic, Emile Loubet, with chants of 'Resign. Long live the
Army'. A bunch of them scrambled up on to the President's tribunal
and one, a baron, clumped Loubet with his cane. Comte Dion
was among those arrested and taken to the Sainté prison. Giffard
visited him in gaol and the two of them quarrelled. Giffard, never
shy of mixing sport with politics, had run a fervent, pugnaciously
moralistic account of the anti-Dreyfusard demonstration in the
green pages of Le Vélo.

Dion took exception to Giffard's partisan encomium and
(versions differ), Dion either withdrew or Giffard refused to
accept any more advertising for the Dion products. So, needing
a new source of publicity, Dion gathered a syndicate of other
manufacturers – including Adolphe Clément and Edouard
Michelin – and set up and financed a rival journal, L'Auto Vélo,
to be printed on *yellow* paper under the editorship of one Henri
Desgrange, former holder of the world hour bicycle record. The
circulation war was on. At the time Le Vélo sold 80,000 issues
daily; it had no rival and its network of contacts with bike clubs
and commercial interests was very wide, its influence on popular
opinion immense. 'The bicycle,' said Giffard, in a statement of
policy, 'is more than a sport and a means of transport, it is a social
benefit.' He had, though, fatefully antagonised his new rival editor.
When Desgrange created the Parc des Princes velodrome 'the green
paper' hardly commented, save to say that it was 'too big, too far .
. .' – from the centre of Paris, that is.

Giffard demanded that Dion drop Vélo from his title; Dion
refused; Giffard took him to court and, in 1902, the new journal
became L'Auto, reporting on cycle and automobile sport, fencing,

gymnastics, alpinism, weight-lifting, horse-racing, athletics and ballooning.

While the principal source of interest in cycle-sport was the track – the famous Parisian velodromes d'Hiver, de L'Est, de Clignancourt, Parc des Princes – which provided an avid public with a continuous spectacle, road-races had begun to establish themselves. Their drama unfolded more slowly, but they were a gift to journalists with flair for telling a good adventure story *and* to rival manufacturers eager to vaunt the reliability and speediness of their bikes. (In one poster, a park-keeper nabs a pair of trespassing lovers who'd outridden him before: 'Ha, now *I* have a Gladiator bike, too: you couldn't get away *this* time.')

Long-distance races gained popularity and caught the imagination of the legions of bike fans. *Le Vélo* had sponsored a race from Bordeaux to Paris in 1891, the Paris–Roubaix (263km), doyenne of the classic marathon races, in 1896 and, in 1901 as a publicity stunt to boost sales, a second edition of a race from Paris to Brest and back. The possibility of extending sales across the whole of France was irresistible; it matched precisely the trend for commercial backing of professional riders attempting new endurance records. In 1891, Charles Terront (sponsored by Giffard, then of *Le Petit Journal*) covered the 1,185km of Paris–Brest–Paris in 71 hours on a one-brake Humber weighing 21kg. His pneumatic tyres – a novelty – punctured five times. In 1901, Maurice Garin bettered Terront's time by 19 hours, riding a La Française machine, brand name 'Diamond'. Other races proliferated, most of them centring on the main hub: Paris – to Tours, Clermont-Ferrand, Nantes, Brussels, Ostend, St Petersburg via Vienna – as well as to Paris from Marseille, Liège and back, Lyon and back, Rome . . . Stéphane completed the 572km from Bordeaux on a Clément bike in 25 hours and 37 minutes, and in 1895, Terront, by now a celebrity, proposed to ride all the way around France on a motorbike. His arch-rival (another eternal second) Corre went one better: he'd do it on a pushbike, but was pipped by Théophile Joyeux who, in May of that year, covered 4,429km in 19 days at an average of 235km per day. The first *boucle* (loop) around the six sides of France had been forged. In September, Corre took 25 days to ride his solo journey of 5,012km, and an idea for a race had been germinated.

Mooting ways and means to publicise *L'Auto*, and thereby shut Giffard up, Desgrange's assistant, the 26-year-old Géo Lefèvre, remarked: 'What about a race around France?' Except that for the first time he uttered the magic words: Tour de France. (There had already been such an event for automobiles.)

Being a good Frenchman, Desgrange proposed that they eat and drink on it.

Desgrange discussed Lefèvre's idea of a big new race with him over lunch at the Paris office of *L'Auto* at 10 Faubourg, Montmartre. Desgrange needed some persuading. His first objection was to the vast distance that the riders would have to cover over chancy roads in extremes of weather.

'You want to kill them?' he said.

'It's okay. We'll split it into *étapes* (stages).'

'You know how much it would cost? What's Goddet going to say?'

Victor Goddet, father of the future Tour director, Jacques, was the financial administrator of *L'Auto*; he kept the keys to the safe.

However, as an undoubtedly bibulous lunch progressed, Desgrange got fired up with Lefèvre's crazy wheeze. 'The more I thought about it the more I thought we could do it.' The French say that red wine cures almost everything; it's certainly a potent remedy for natural scepticism and a replete Desgrange agreed to approach Goddet.

Goddet listened, cheerfully threw open the door of his safe and said: 'Help yourself. This Tour of yours will buy me a bigger safe.'

Desgrange's sterner motive must have been to outdo his rival Giffard: 'He'll go as green as his paper.' But he was a man of quixotic idealism and remarkable vision; unabashed romantic and steely ascetic in one. Writing his last article before he died in 1940, he described the day, 11 May 1893, when he took the world hour record on the open track of the Buffalo Vélodrome in Paris, built to his specification with funds from the Folies-Bergères:

> Under a blue sky, I mounted a bicycle weighing a good 25kg with tyres an outrageous 500mm in diameter ['balloons'], a multiplication of 4.70m [the distance covered at each full revolution of the cranks] . . . As a measure of prudence, I slung

a bottle of milk from my handlebars, in case of bonk.*

When I got off the machine at the end of the 60 minutes, I wasn't only the world recordman for the hour on a bicycle, I was an object of horror to the people who took care of me after my 35,325km. I was filthy, streaked with oil and snot, covered with dust; in short, nobody would touch me with a pair of tongs. My director bought me lunch at La Porte Maillot, a sumptuous meal, 2.50 francs a head; he also offered me several bank notes which I could cash for gold louis; because of my amateur status I refused instantly. But my God! How happy I was.

The rage to be a track-racer never left him; he transmuted it into championing cycle-sport.

This Tour would become, for him and all France, '*la grande croisade morale du sport cycliste*' – the great moral crusade of cycle-sport. But not yet.

In January 1903 *L'Auto* announced: A cycle race to cover 2,428km in six stages, between 31 May and 5 July. No trainers or physios for the first five stages so that all riders will compete on equal terms.

('Equal terms' refers both to a distinction between professional team riders with commercial sponsorship and freelance solitaries riding for prizes and, more significantly, to the fact that most back-up men were emphatically *not* Corinthian in spirit, but hard-nosed cynics, ready to do anything to ensure victory and its profits: any sharp practice or skullduggery for their men; barefaced mischief and finagling to obstruct their rivals.)

A week before the closing date, only 15 riders had signed on: the conditions were too severe. Press reaction to the proposed race explains why: 'A monster' one paper called it; 'colossal . . . grandiose . . . gigantic . . . an enormity' chimed in the others. Desgrange softened his stipulations: the race to be staged between

*(Bonk is cyclist's slang for ravenous hunger, total depletion of blood sugar.)

1 and 19 July; entry fee reduced from 20 to ten francs; five francs-per-day expenses to be paid to the first 50 finishers, provided that they had won no more than 200 francs in prizes; total prize money on offer – 20,000 francs.

(Yearly subscription for the daily *L'Auto* in 1903 was 20 francs, while five cents bought a postage stamp or also the eight-page weekly *National Illustrated*. A new Clément bike sold for 450 francs.)

At 3.16 p.m. on 1 July, 21 sponsored men – plus 39 others – rode away from the Réveil Matin ('Morning Call') inn at Villeneuve-St Georges, a suburb 18km south of Paris, headed for Lyon, 467km distant. Desgrange stayed in Paris; Lefèvre accompanied the race – intermittently on his bike – along with other controllers to clock riders through checkpoints and curb cheating; some were at secret locations, some driving the route. The French stars, Maurice Garin, aged 32 – 'The Little Chimney-sweep', Edmond 'Pioupiou' Jacquelin – the demon sprinter whose star was waning; Léon 'the Brute' Georget – who stoked himself with gargantuan quantities of strawberries, rough red wine (*brutal* in French) and biscuits; René Pottier, the taciturn unknown, riding for Garin; and Hippolyte Acouturier (one of several riders who openly admitted he was competing only for stage wins, an oddity of the first Tours: each day's stage being a discrete entity). They were racing against provincial French as well as Swiss, Belgian and German riders.

Garin won the first stage in 17 hours 45 minutes 13.2 seconds (Desgrange was nothing if not a stickler for detail) on a La Française bike and wore the first yellow armband as stage victor, also the first green *brassard* as leader of the overall classification. Acouturier, riding a Crescent, took Lyon to Marseille, 374km in 14 hours 28 minutes 53.2 seconds and Marseille to Toulouse, 423km in 17 hours 55 minutes 4.6 seconds; the Swiss, Laeser, another stage-victory man, won Toulouse to Bordeaux on a La Française, 268km in 8 hours 46 minutes 0.8 seconds; the fifth went to Garin, Bordeaux to Nantes, 425km in 16 hours 26 minutes 31 seconds and, on 19 July he headed the leading group of 21 race survivors (the last man two days behind) along roads lined with what the German champion described as 'a hedge of fans opening out in front of us' – 100,000 according to estimates – and through Ville d'Avray, by Versailles, and at last on to the 666m of new concrete cycle track at the Parc des Princes in Paris where a crowd of 20,000 spectators was waiting to cheer them in. Seven minutes after the *Arrivée*, a special edition of *L'Auto*, 130,000 copies, went to press.

The impact of the race on popular attention was nothing short of phenomenal; everywhere it went it enjoyed a veritable *succès fou*. Casual cyclists even joined the race for the last few kilometres into Bordeaux. Most important for Desgrange, sales of his paper rocketed and the interest in the commercial backing of cycle manufacturers' for the enterprise was thoroughly whetted.

The first laureate, Garin, weighing 64kg as he had at the start, rode a machine of just under 20kg at an average speed of 26.450kph, pocketed 6,125 gold louis and landed a substantial fee for promoting a weekly magazine *The Fresh Air Life*. He led home 20 survivors from the original field. Crowds had lined sleepy roads in the backwaters of France – even at 2 a.m. – to see the Little Sweep's ghost-white face go by, caught in the glow of the officials' green car's headlights. The same officials were regularly passing food out to Garin and the other La Française team men; but when Pottier gave up his bike to Garin there was no spare for him on hand. Even so, he eventually came in second, with a deficit of nearly three hours. Further on in the race, Garin gave a spectator 100 francs not to lend his bike to a rival, Augureau, who had just punctured. Cyclotourists, seeing these men ride past pushing a gear, six-metres multiplication, said: 'They're bulls, not men.' They had endured a torrid 30°C in the Marseille shade; pelting rain that turned the roads into slurries of mud; shivering-cold night departures, 'dark as an oven'; riders pitching off as wheels caught in tramlines; Fischer and Samson, 80km from the arrival in Nantes, rode into a scree of broken glass – bottles discarded purposely by the leaders – and punctured five and six times; on the first stage Acouturier, going well, took a drink from a bystander – 'lemonade made from sulphuric acid' he said – which turned his legs and arms to jelly; he had to abandon the stage. He recovered, rejoined next day to win that and the third stage. Georget fell out with his La Française boss during the race and refused to rejoin the team, even after the chief mechanic decked him. No penalty, no disqualification, followed: Desgrange needed the high-profile, strong La Française team with its champion Garin; he needed publicity for *L'Auto*. He turned a blind eye. During the Tour, circulation of *L'Auto* rose from 20–30,000 to 65,000 daily and *Le Vélo* did not survive. Desgrange wrote that this race provided the 'best way of exciting wonder among the people of France, of encouraging emulation, energy, willpower on a wide scale' – he linked this Tour of his to national morale, no less – and concluded his report: 'We are satisfied, for this year we have given cycle-sport its finest, its greatest competitive event at a time when know-alls were saying it was impossible to better what was already on offer.' After the 1904 race he was saying: 'The Tour is finished and I am very afraid that its second edition will be its last. It will have been killed by its own success, driven out of control by blind passion, by violence and filthy suspicions worthy only of ignorant and dishonourable men.'

The second Tour was marred by blatant sabotage of the meanest kind: powdered emery and itching dust in riders' shorts; fouled drinks, spiked drinks; a bike frame filed through which collapsed and pitched off its rider in a heavy fall; obstacles flung into the road; composite nails like anti-cavalry coltrops which always point upwards; there seemed no end to the thuggery of envious rivals trying to dish each other and fanatical supporters ('fans') getting out of hand.

At Nemours, local gendarmes, instructed to keep the crowds in order, planted themselves across the road on horseback: the *peloton* swept round the corner straight into them and there was a huge pile-up. (Some 90 years later, a lone policeman stepped out in front of the bunch sprinting for the line at a stage finish to take a picture on his instant camera with similar disastrous effect. In 1958, Darrigade was brought down in the Parc des Princes by a race marshall who leaned out too far at the edge of the track. Darrigade was carried off on a stretcher; the official died.)

Acouturier and Samson took tows by way of a string attached to a cork which each gripped in his teeth. On stage two, the leaders Garin and Pottier – now christened 'the fierce butcher of Sens' – found themselves flanked by an open car full of men in goggles, telling the two La Française men to give their man, Faure, the stage victory. La Française was having it too easy. Harrassed, the leaders were caught by Faure. Past St Etienne, Faure's home town, on the col de la République, (1,161m) at three in the morning, the riders were confronted by a large mob, some hundred-strong, brandishing cudgels. They let Faure through then blocked Garin and his four teammates and set about them. Géo Lefèvre drove up firing a revolver into the air to disperse the mob. Garin and others were bruised but carried on; the Italian, Gerbi, had to retire hurt. Even so, Faure didn't win and was disqualified in Marseille. The next stage, riding into the control at Nîmes, the local man, Payan, was disqualified for taking shelter behind a car. There was a riot: 2,000 locals versus police, officials and riders. Payan was not reinstated. His supporters took silent revenge by strewing the road with nails and broken glass: the riders punctured in droves. Lefèvre did all he could to avoid trouble: altered the route, set new start times, called in more police; to no avail. Malcontents blocked the road into Paris with logs and farm wagons. Eventually Garin got through, the *de facto* leader but, inevitably, a furore ensued.

Three months later an official enquiry under the aegis of the *Union Vélocipédique de France* found Garin guilty of various 'irregularities' (taking car rides, for instance, had been a staple method of cheating in long-distance races). He was banned for life and his win annulled, along with Pottier, second, César Garin (Maurice's brother), third, and Acouturier, fourth. The fifth man, Cornet, nicknamed 'Rigolo' (which means, appropriately enough, 'joker' or 'revolver') found himself the winner, the youngest ever, at 20 years old. He rode seven more Tours. Garin, who belonged to the old century more than the new, protested his innocence till he died aged 86 in 1957, and it's by no means sure that he was guilty of any misdemeanour; he probably had no need to cheat. However, the Tour was already bigger than the men who rode it. Garin did return to bike racing in 1911, aged 40, to come tenth in the third Paris–Brest–Paris race, beating his 1901 victory time by six hours. It was a riposte of sorts, if too late.

The disqualifications purged Desgrange of his pessimism; and, it must be said, scandal sold newspapers. He had, for the moment at least, won the circulation war. Giffard was declared bankrupt and his *Vélo* left the stands. Desgrange generously hired him as a reporter for *L'Auto* and wasted little time in announcing a third even tougher course for his nascent Tour, and this time the mountains were in, 11 stages including the Vosges, côte de Laffrey, col Bayard and the famous Ballon d'Alsace, some 10km of climbing to 1,247m at the summit, whence could be seen magnificent vistas across the Vosges, the Jura and the Black Forest. The classification for overall victory was changed to a points system to obviate cheating on times. This applied for the next seven editions.

On the first stage between Paris and Nancy there were nails strewed across the road. Puncturing right, left and centre, the field of 60 dwindled to a mere 15, the last man arrived five and a half hours after the stage winner, Trousselier. The organisers, outraged, cancelled the race then relented and reinstated all those riders who'd managed to reach Nancy, whether by bike or train. Over the Ballon d'Alsace, Pottier in his trademark linen cap changed bikes and rode up at 20kph. The mountains were an instant hit and Pottier was dubbed 'first king of the climbers'.

Trousselier, on leave from the family flowershop in Paris, won overall, though pipped of a fifth stage win, he broke the inkstands at one checkpoint so that his pursuers couldn't sign on and after the race he stomped off back to his sprays and bouquets.

Desgrange had his dander up now; if the public wanted tough he could be tough. For 1906 he proposed 13 stages, 4,637km, and when a friend of his, Alphonse Steinès, suggested taking the Tour across the Pyrenees, he said: 'Fine. Go and scout them out.'

Steinès drove his car to within 4km of the Tourmalet in worsening conditions till snow forced him to abandon his car and make for safety on foot. He slogged some 12km down the exposed southern slopes through the night, frozen, feverish and scared and stumbled into the gendarme post in Barèges. From there he sent a telegraph to Desgrange:

HAVE CROSSED THE TOURMALET ON FOOT BY NIGHT.
ROAD PASSABLE FOR VEHICLES. NO SNOW.

From 1906 the high mountains were in, though not till 1910 the Pyrenees and the Tourmalet, their loftiest peak at 2,114m, a monster, the original *juge de paix*. (The Tour has crossed it 76 times, a record.) 'The mountain is the legend of the Tour.'

Firstly the 11, and now 13, stages made the Tour resemble more closely the hexagon that is France. It crossed the great Alpine massif of la Grande Chartreuse in 1907 and established the big climbs as a feature of the race: the desolate wastes of the mountain tops, the wilderness where the first Carthusian monks built their austere monastery, the forbidding landscape of rock swathed in mist or blizzard. In what locals called the 'Circle of Death' in the Pyrenees, bears roamed and some riders, finding themselves alone in the remote high places, stopped, fearing attack from the wild creatures.

Alert to the cheating of riders whose first loyalty was to their sponsors – the bike manufacturers – not the purist Henri Desgrange (HD) who made the vaunted English insistence on fair play sound rather mealy-mouthed, Desgrange imposed new, more stringent rules. Each rider's bike was taken, in secret, to the offices of *L'Auto* where officials hallmarked the crankshafts and the head of the forks with a stamp. And, to be doubly sure that the rider rode in on the same machine as he'd ridden at the start, they planted a secret cipher somewhere else on the bike.

The 1907 winner, Lucien Mazan, known as 'Petit-Breton', also took the first double, in 1908, and circulation of *L'Auto* nearly doubled, too: 140,000 to 250,000. The Luxemburgeois François Faber rode through snow, gales and rain, over roads prickling with flints and scored with ruts, to a final victory in 1909; between Roubaix and Nice he won all five stages on the trot, and when his chain broke in Lyon he shouldered his bike and ran to the line.

In 1910, the race produced a ding-dong battle between Faber and Octave Lapize. Desgrange watched his circulation soar as 300,000 readers read the epic tale of Lapize and Faber racing, elbow-to-elbow, as the French say, on the tenth stage over the stupendous Pyrenean chains, Peyresourde, Aspin, Tourmalet, Aubisque, all in one stage. Garrigou was the first man ever to cross the Tourmalet for a handsome prize; Lapize, tiring, was down on the regional rider Lafourcade over the Aubisque and very nearly abandoned from exhaustion – this was the year the broom wagon made its début, sweeping up riders who'd had enough – but he hung on and retained his four-points margin over Faber into Paris.

Apparently mountains didn't kill cyclists and the 1911 Tour (won by Garrigou), the longest so far, 5,344km, crossed the monsters of the Alps, including the Galibier of which, in an Act of Adoration the Father of the Tour wrote: 'In the history of human affairs, does not this ascent of the Galibier on bicycles constitute the first triumph of mortal intelligence over the laws of gravity? Before this giant one cannot but doff one's cap and bow very low.' Never short of purple ink, HD.

For the 1912 Tour, no fewer than 131 riders started the race. The Belgian competitors formed a coalition which demoralised Lapize and even the danger man, Christophe, could not dent their power. Odile Defraye won overall and they placed six others of their men in the first ten. In 1913, classification on points having proved unjust, Desgrange restored the fairer system of time difference and, for the first time, sent the Tour around France in an anticlockwise direction. (Since then, tradition sends it vice-versa in alternate years. Tradition has been flouted, notably in 1998, and is no longer a regular pattern.)

Petit-Breton was well-placed behind Thys but fell, broke his kneecap and had to withdraw on the last-but-one stage. Then Thys fell, yet managed to stagger in to take the win.

On 28 June 1914, at 3 a.m, the Tour set out. Later that same day the Archduke Franz Ferdinand of Austria was assassinated in Sarajevo; the Tour finished nearly a month later, shortly before the Austro–Hungarian Empire declared war on Serbia on 28 July. Five days later France was at war and these very Alps became a front-line war zone with mountain regiments from Italy and Austria entrenched across the valley chasms.

JERSEYS OF THE
TOUR DE FRANCE

Yellow jersey (*maillot jaune*).

Maillot: a theatre costume designer's original *maillot* was a skin-tight dancer's outfit.

The *maillot jaune* is worn by the rider with the shortest accumulated time overall. Nowadays, the opening stages of the race, usually over flat terrain, carry time bonuses at the finish as well as at the intermediate Hot Spot sprints en route. This stimulates competition among the leading sprinters, who have little to look forward to in the mountains and therefore make the best of the first week, going for stage wins and a good haul in the points competition.

The yellow jersey is worth a daily €350. The final yellow earns its wearer €450,000, a sum which, traditionally, he shares out among the members of his team who have cooperated to work for his victory. A leader comfortably made up for that formal generosity with add-on earnings in the year following his win. In the past, riders had to supplement their basic earnings in round-season prize races and a Tour win made a huge difference to their pay. Nowadays, the contractual earnings of a rider like Armstrong, indeed of even the lesser riders, render such a protocol immaterial.

Second place overall is worth €200,000; third €100,000; fourth €70,000; and so on in decreasing amounts to €400 for every other rider who finishes the Tour.

Polka-dot jersey (*maillot blanc à pois rouges*). The King of the Mountains jersey was introduced in 1975, although the prize was awarded from 1933 on. First winner, Vicente Trueba.

Points are awarded to the first 10 men over the above-category climbs, 20 down to 5; 15 points down to 5 for the first eight over the first-category climbs; 10 down to 5 for the first six over the second category; 4 down to 1 for the first four over the third category; and 3, 2, 1 for the first three over the fourth category. In addition, every major col carries a *prime* – a cash prize for the first man to cross – *hors-catégorie* climbs yield €800, €450 and €300 for first, second and third; fourth category, €200 only to the first man over. Every day in the polka dots, from the second to the twentieth stages only, earns €300 and eventual victory in the competition €25,000.

The rules for assigning categories are arcane, depending on altitude, steepness of gradient, quality of road surface – the Pyrenean climbs tend to be less well paved than those in the Alps – and the position of the climb in the day's racing (nearer the end an otherwise second category might be designated a first, and l'Alpe d'Huez, though relatively low for a *hors catégorie*, but steep for an Alpine ascent – nine degrees average – being a cul-de-sac, always features at the end of the stage.)

You may see, painted on the road up to a col: GPM 10km. This means *Grand Prix de Montagnes 10km ahead.*

Green jersey (*maillot vert*) introduced in 1953. The points prize.

Points are awarded for the first finishers on every stage; more points for the flat stages – to encourage the sprinters – so that the eventual winner will be the rider who has been most consistent over the whole Tour. The 2011 race brought in significant changes in the regulations for the points classification. Instead of the traditional two or three intermediate sprints per stage where points have, in the past, been awarded to the first three riders over the line, there is now only one sprint per stage, and the allocation goes down to the 15th rider. Hitherto, 6, 4 and 2 points were awarded, now first takes 20, 17 for second, 15 for third . . . etc. and prize money of €1,500, €1,000 and €500 for the first three. There is also a new allotment for the finish of each stage depending on the category: high mountain, undulating, flat or time-trial. Flat stages:

first place takes 45 points, then 35, 30, 26, 22 . . . 2. Medium mountains (undulating): first place takes 30 points, then 25, 22, 19 . . . 1. High Mountains and Time-Trials: first place takes 20, then 17, 15, 13 . . . 1. Further, no time bonuses will be awarded for intermediate sprints or stage finishes. Stage finishes in 2011: €8,000 for a stage winner and a sliding scale down to €200 for 16th to 20th. A day in green earns €300 and the overall points competition is worth €25,000 to the winner, €15,000 to second, €10,000 to third, €2,000 to eighth.

CHAPTER ONE

L'ALPE D'HUEZ

Fear, Moral Strength and Eddy Merckx

Monday.

We ride 32km east from our overnight stop in Vizille, most of the way in placid sun, along the Gorges de la Romanche which sidle up a mild gradient from about 250m to 750m, a gentle loosener, no great strain; vista of skyscraper mountains all round. They call it the Valley of the Dead because the mountains crowd in so close very little sun gets in. And a signpost right indicates the ominously named village La Morte ('the Dead Woman'), as if we need any warning. We're heading for l'Alpe d'Huez, which has a reputation as daunting as its own gigantic bulk. It *looks* horrible on the map: like a squat concertina of diseased yellow worm. The raw statistics aren't sociable, either: a climb of 1,000m in 14km, corkscrewing round 21 snap-comb hairpin bends. It *sounds* gruesome: it must *be* gruesome. I'm thinking: 'L'Alpe d'Huez, today we cycle l'Alpe d'Huez,' as if jingling the name alone can make the prospect somehow less unhomely, more my size.

★

The climb was introduced to the Tour de France in 1952, when many of the remoter Alpine roads were still little more than minimally improved cart-tracks: rough, narrow, littered with scree, split, potholed and rutted from arctic cold in winter and the oven heat of summer, titubating up and down the mountains in what looks, from old photos, like a trance of fatigue and asthma. Or traversing perilously narrow corniche paths no better than rude shelves cut in to the rock, the precipice edges bare and unprotected: one lapse of concentration and you're over. And at night?

In those early days, the Huez road extended to 1,495m, stopping short at the village which christens the Alp. It was eventually driven on to the deep snow line at 1,860m, giving cul-de-sac access to the modern ski station, and has been a near fixture of the Tour ever since; dreaded by many riders. A mountain-top finish is especially punishing after two or three major climbs already the same day: nearly an hour for many of them, racing the steep flights of the road against a merciless clock and dwindling strength and stamina, gasping at thinning air in thick July heat. Mountains are classified, by length and gradient, in five categories, the monsters are *hors catégorie*. They epitomise the stark challenge of the Tour; on them it is so often won or lost, even today when a multiplicity of gears equalises the riders in a way that the pre-*dérailleur* machines could not. In those days, the chasm between the best climbers and the worst yawned wide. One thing hasn't changed: the awe that the high mountains inspire. When the Englishman Bill Nickson, winner of the Milk Race, riding for the Raleigh team, first saw l'Alpe d'Huez from this same valley approach he voiced what many riders think: as knackered as he then was, he simply couldn't believe he'd ever get up the mountain; it would have to be an act of faith heavily larded with luck. Freddy Maertens, the Belgian speed-merchant, *flahute* in the slang, chose this very alp on which to quell his dread of the mountains. He fancied his chances in the Tour overall, a class sprinter keenly aware that he faced possible disaster on the high climbs. Sean Kelly, the great Irish rider who held the record of wins in the points competition – four green jerseys in Paris – until Zabel (six consecutively by 2001), was known to dismount and rest on the climbs. The pace up these ascents is ferocious, the toll severe.

No rider, not even the strongest, can match the natural fluency of the gifted climbers. When the pace accelerates on to the mountain and the high-flyers mount like weightless creatures and leave the rest of the field trailing with shaky legs and bursting lungs, the men with any ambition have to hang on by raw power and unshakeable self-belief; or lose. Winning the Tour generally demands a complete rider, one who can contend sprints, climbs, time-trials with the best, but with a consistency that outstrips them all. Few pure climbers have taken overall victory. Federico Bahamontes, the Eagle of Toledo, won the mountains prize six times between 1954 and 1964, the Tour only once, so, too, Van Impe, though not in 1976, the year he won overall. Bahamontes won the prize and overall in 1959.

As to the biochemistry of fear; it is as fundamental as the instinct for survival and the competitive spirit, both of which it fuels *and* thrives on. Fear originally meant 'ambush, a sudden fright or threat'; and there is no shame in being startled. The compelling lure of sport is to observe contestants face their fear and conquer it: as in the boxing ring, the 'four corners of truth', so on the pitiless roads of the Tour de France. We are witness to a supreme test of nerve; an inspiration to face challenge. We all nurse fear inside us. Fear is one of those sewer beasts in the mind's bilge that has to be ruthlessly cleaned out, time after time. Fear lives on indecision, self-doubt, prevarication: go in hard, ride it into the ground. If you see the mountain and say 'No way' and ditch the bike, you'll never know if you would have made it, if you had it in you; and your demons will multiply. Demons are the killer dogs prowling the grounds of self-knowledge. To face them is to follow aspiration.

In the 1976 Tour, Maertens wore the leader's yellow jersey for nine days and eventually took the green points jersey in Paris by a distance. He also won eight stages overall, a record shared by Charles Pélissier (1930) and Merckx (1970 and 1974), then crowned a glorious season by winning the World Road Race Championship. The December before, Maertens, a redoubtable sprinter with no stomach for mountains, came to l'Alpe d'Huez with his friend and teammate, Michel Pollentier, to steel himself for the ordeal ahead, by wrestling with and taming this savage climb that rears up zigzag, zigzag, like the ramps flanking a sacrificial Inca ziggurat. All mountains are gruelling; what makes this climb so hard – at an average nine degrees, unduly steep for an alp – is the absence of natural flow, a disregard for contour; it is a road hacked out of the bare rock without finesse, like a firebreak. Many Alpine cols, even first category, run smoothly over good surface, dawdling bends and steady gradient.

The two Belgians rode up and down l'Alpe d'Huez, over and over again, till Maertens had quelled his panic, even if he hadn't beaten the jinx. On the ninth stage of the Tour, 4 July, he set off for l'Alpe d'Huez in yellow, with two minutes and four seconds advantage over his lieutenant Pollentier. At the end of that day, he had dropped to third overall, with a deficit of 54 seconds on the eventual winner, the diminutive Belgian climber, Van Impe. Who can say where he'd have been without that winter's psychological toughening? He finished the Tour in eighth, 16 minutes down. Poulidor, over 40 by now, came third. Incidentally, Maertens, in his autobiography, claims that the Belgian public never supported him because he was born in proletarian Ostend, whereas the great and favoured Merckx – who, he swears, cynically dished him in the Worlds to secure the title for Gimondi – came from posh Brussels. (The reason? Gimondi and Merckx had a contract deal with Campagnolo.)

Maertens also says that often, during the final kilometres of a long race, he had his team car pass him a bottle containing champagne: a booster shot for the sprint. It's not unknown.

His friend Pollentier was a considerable rider. In the 1974 Tour he beat Merckx in a time-trial – almost unheard of – and in 1978 took the yellow jersey when he trounced Hinault on the stage to l'Alpe d'Huez; only to be disqualified for supplying a false urine sample.

★

As we near l'Alpe d'Huez, the temptation is to wonder: 'What's it like? Will I be all right?' Comparisons won't work; seductive, but no more than a way of dodging the issue. Like self-help manuals: largely useless, unless you're prepared to undergo the same trials that went into compiling them; these High Alps have to be taken as they come; each has to be ridden into temporary submission; each presides over its own judgement and nothing you have ever done before matches up to the first encounter.

The summer's daydream poring over maps is about to meet solid reality. We are no better acquainted with the solid reality of l'Alpe d'Huez than with television miniatures of it, ten-minute cameos from successive Tours: vivid images of Sermon on the Mount-size crowds; shimmering heat haze thickened by exhaust fumes; coruscant spokes; *perpetuum mobile* of bicycles; riders on form, riders flagging, riders dropped, sweat-drenched, emptying water bottles over their heads; ardent fans running alongside their heroes and dowsing them, even if their heroes don't always want to be. Torrid heat going up the mountain; fierce cold going down: watch the riders take newspapers from fans on the cols to stuff up their vests against the wind on the descent. (Anquetil took an unsolicited soaking in 1966, caught a chill at the top of the next col, the Great St Bernard, and abandoned next day.) The riders plough on through a cacophony of klaxons yodelling like a jamboree of deranged Tyroleans, exhaust pipes snort plumes of carbon monoxide, the whole circus parade of team cars, service cars, official race cars, motorbikes with and without cameramen perched on the pillion seat, broom waggon snaking up the mountain – as fast as the leader at the front, as slow as the stragglers at the tail – through a jungle of spectators crammed so deep by the road's edge they leave no more than a single file path down their middle and then bulge shut again over the riders as they pass, like a python consuming its lunch. The July sun blazing on full joules, the Alpe d'Huez stage drama played out metre by metre on the one in six . . . vital minutes lost, saved, gained. But television has virtually no real emotional power; it's a peepshow. The closeups from the motorbike cameras are as close as most people get; better than nothing but they are only a cartoon of the enormous strain involved: the habitual pain-streaked rictus of some riders, the impassive introspection – or icy control – of others; the blank, frayed, drained mask of the men whose will and physical resource has been pared down to the quick but won't give in; the hunched, bobbing, shoulders, pushing their bit of extra weight to the tired legs, the pistons driving the pedals; the extremes of physical and mental stress written in a sort of enigma: the restless twist of fingers round the handlebars . . .

★

SNAPSHOT: The Spanish ace Ocaña, dead to the world, on his way to a high col, index finger of his right hand extended to touch the brake cable, as if it were his pulse, telling him he's still functioning, earthing the whole force of his concentration through that single contact.

The slack gape of the mouth, the dip and lift of the chest pumping the lungs to capacity, the sea-deck swaying gait of a rider dropped by the leaders, heaving his own leaden frame out of the saddle to flog the bike frame that gets heavier than Christ on St Christopher's shoulders, through oxygen-depleted air and the deadening drag of gravity, dredging up scraps of acceleration, a semblance of fluency, more *rhythm*, to catch the leaders again. He can still see them a hundred metres ahead, still within reach, tied on by the unravelling thread of possibility which links him to them, *don't give up*, dig, dig into the reserves, if there are any in such extremes, to keep the pursuit alive until the incomparable relief or despair of the *Arrivée* line shuts pursuit off.

★

We are soon to adjudge the inadequacy of television to tell the truth about the gradient. Any frailties will be routinely exposed, though failure, it goes without saying, is unthinkable; maybe succeeding isn't possible, either. I am riding incautiously big gears, and recall the remark made by Bernard 'Nanard' Thévenet, shrinking at the size of the gear Merckx was pushing round in the Alps: '*un méchant braquet pour les montagnes*'; (*méchant*, of a dog: 'it bites', a vicious gear for the mountains.)

We ride the last bit of level road to the bend that broaches the climb, wheel 45 degrees and nose on to the first ramp. It's horrible: a long, wide section of road as steep as Highgate West Hill, which I climb every day. No, it looks steeper in this ungiving prospect, us at the bottom of an ugly concrete slab of wicked uphill. I think: 'This is going to be a bastard.' Two days earlier I had ridden Highgate West Hill, the same kit loaded as I carried now, in a sly drizzle, not warmed up and tired, but I struggled and, as I struggled, I said to myself, 'And you're going to ride in the Alps?'

And now my heart taps out messages far too urgent, quite at odds with the even tempo I should be aiming for. Pulse and nerves are performing a double act of frantic percussion. A sudden fragility. 14km? 1,000m? Yet if pro riders dread the mountains, no matter how often they climb them, at the foot of l'Alpe d'Huez I have a macabre advantage over them: I don't know what's coming. I push the forebodings aside. Patience. And forget the pros: they do nothing all year but ride a bike, and get paid for it, they're decades younger. Besides, they have a less flexible incentive – their *directeur sportif* barking at them from the team car and the need to put on enough show to win a contract for the following year; all that plus the ticking of the clock and the threat of elimination on time.

The 21 hairpins are numbered from 20 in descending order as you climb. Number 21, the first, isn't marked for some reason. I was relieved that they count down as you go up. Somehow, piling the total up would make the ride psychologically harder. A new assistant in the Moscow department store Gum was set to work on the dry goods counter. Several customers complained that she was giving short measure of sugar and rice which were weighed and sold loose. The girl protested innocence; a supervisor observed her at work. The measures were exact; but instead of putting too little into the pan to start with and *adding* more to make up the weight, she was pouring in too much and *subtracting* the surplus. The customers felt cheated; she was robbing them before their eyes. I was glad to see the hairpin numbers getting slowly lighter in weight.

Small comfort: the hairpins on l'Alpe d'Huez are unlike any others. They come every 700m or so, ugly as sin, hoisting you roughly 50m nearer the top. Every inch of the way there is no escaping a sense of the mountain's massive, intimidating bulk.

And here you are, playing at it. What keeps you going? Mostly the fact that you set out to do the climb and, barring accident or misadventure, bodily or mechanical, climb it you will and must. *So far so good.*

★

Boardman has admitted that he doesn't really enjoy the business – it's dangerous, painful and exhausting – but he does derive huge satisfaction from it, and the satisfaction is what we can all indulge in, and be grateful we don't have to race up this rotten steep seemingly endless road.

The early Tour traversed the mountains by way of tracks familiar to mules and smugglers but only recently made passable to cars. The second ever Pyrenean stage quit Luchon for Bayonne at 3.30 a.m. and when Lapize, near-spent, struggled to the top of the Tourmalet, he rounded on two of the race marshalls posted on the col to check the riders through and screamed: '*Vous êtes tous des assassins* !' – You're all murderers. Sure, he went on to win, but the vehemence of his reaction gives the lie to any cosy dilettante idea that the Tour was some kind of play up, play up, play the game, all good chaps, taking part's the thing. These were hard men in a hard *métier*, unromanced by fey illusions about what they were being asked to endure or notably reluctant to voice protest. One of them, Emile Georget, the very first Tour rider to vanquish the Galibier, 10 July 1911, arrived in a filthy state; his moustache clogged with bits of snot and food from the last control point, his jersey filthy with mud, soaking wet from the last stream he'd pitched in to. He vaulted off his bike – he must have been an absolute fright to look at – gathered up some dignity and said to the official observers: '*Ça vous met un coin dans la bouche.*' (That's given you something to think about.) Then rode on.

Those early *coureurs* crossed the high mountains in conditions unthinkable to the riders of today, and even with the material support they enjoy, it's never anything but a hard, hard ride. The Dog Days heat they face is the same, the bitter cold, the rain, the fog. The overwhelming physical fatigue and mental strain. And the persistent danger. Boardman, riding down the first category col du Soulor through dense fog in 1997 told how he followed another rider who shot off, apparently well acquainted with the descent. Suddenly the road turned green and they were riding up an embankment. Boardman nearly held on but couldn't, and fell heavily, damaging vertebrae in his back and neck. He rode on, even managed another cruel day in the Pyrenees and a 55km mountain time-trial, but the pain became so intense that he was forced to abandon on the Alpe d'Huez stage.

The pioneers had to carry their own food, repair kit, spare tyres, water, extra clothing, lamps, and could only call on two gears. No wonder they became heroes to sports fans eager to own the brand of bike ridden by a Tour rider. They were demigods, muscles of steel, apparently indomitable, survivors of the amazing adventures described in *L'Auto*. For strength, physical and mental, willpower and apparent immunity to the combined onslaught of natural obstacles and human malevolence, they matched the great heroes of antiquity, pound for pound, exploit for exploit.

The epic has changed as little in essence since its inauguration as the basic road-racing bike: two wheels, chain, a frame. Technical innovation has crucially reduced the weight of materials and increased mechanical efficiency (even gear-changing is automatic these days – another manual skill lost, when riders would jump an attack on hearing a rival's clumsy shift of gears). Modern cyclists are mollycoddled by comparison with the *forçats de la route* (the convict labourers) of the early Tours, but the *Grande Boucle* – the Big Loop – of France (with occasional excursions into bordering countries) was, and remains, bike and rider against himself, the road, the other riders. It is the most uncompromising test of stamina, willpower and athletic prowess for any pro cyclist, perhaps any sportsman. They climb l'Alpe d'Huez after a hundred miles or more of mountain roads; they race up its exposed flanks knowing that if they crack, or even look like cracking, their rivals will pounce on the weakness ruthlessly. Seconds lost, minutes lost and tomorrow's mountain will seem twice as steep, twice as long, twice as back-breaking, twice as disheartening. They get paid, the rivalry spurs them, but that doesn't level the mountain, and they're as prone to fear of it as any of us who ride a bike: the greater the talent, the greater the dread and the penalty of falling short.

Lance Armstrong, the strong man, on his début Tour won a flat stage – joy – then came to the Alps (cols du Glandon and Galibier in one day) and barely had the strength to finish; he collapsed in his hotel room, wanting only to abandon. His team persuaded him to start next day, helped him all they could, but he was empty and quit that night. Such wretched depths is the spirit forced to.

Learning to cope with the misery and the elation is at the root of all challenge.

★

And now, at hairpin 15, six to go, the road glares at me like the Gorgon. Age pants at my heels and they are no longer what could be called in athletic terms a clean pair. Nonetheless, I *am* grinding on and the kilometres recede beneath my tyres.

The nearer you get to the top, the tougher the mental battle gets. Behind the fences of your self-control lurks a greyhound of impatience, straining to cut loose, make a dash, get it over, sprint up there and across the line whatever the cost. The cost will be spontaneous combustion of lungs, a flood of lactic acid into the muscles and you gasping at the side of the road like a beached fish. Rhythm and a clear head, self-belief and arithmetic, these are reliable. Undue haste is a plausible liar. Impatience reminds me that, on the Tour, the run-in to the *Arrivée* is flat if not marginally downhill. Well, praise be.

At last, the hairpin is the precious *numéro un*: gate to the city. My spirits lift. Any minute now the steep up will tilt forward in my favour like a seesaw as my weight crosses the fulcrum. But it doesn't. Never rely. Anything not the top is not the top. You can't argue with fact. Fact is the old pro with all the tricks up his sleeve. The Tour actually takes a fork to the right, skirting the steep bluff below the ski station centre. I ride straight on, up the bluff, the last snarling ramp of this 14km to cap the climb. I sprint it in a real *haka* of defiance, wringing out the last ounces. I'd ridden l'Alpe d'Huez in one and a quarter hours.

As destinations go it has all the innate charm of a ski resort out of season: none. A hotchpotch of purpose-built hotels, souvenir shops, bars and restaurants designed by a stripped-pine vulgarian certificated in architectural tat. As a totem of cycling achievement, however, it's pretty fair wampum.

A placard informs me that the *Maire* will gladly sign a diploma officialising my ascent of the mountain after his siesta at 2.30 p.m. It's barely 2 p.m. and I don't need proof or ratification. I drink from the water fountain; a couple of English cyclists rest in the shade. We exchange laconic greetings. The view from the top is all the better for the sight of those tortuous snake-and-ladder hairpins, silver as snail trails in the sun. The valley is a long way off, the girdling mountains, too; but retracing the hard path at downhill speed makes a splendid feast of self-indulgence.

★

'Who would you like to be?' a friend asked me at home before I set out. I demurred: I couldn't *be* any of them, so I didn't want to be – the great *géants de la route* ('giants of the road') were far beyond me. This is why I came: to prise open my imagination, to get closer, to root round in my fascination. 'But which of them do you most admire?' she said.

No hesitation: Eddy Merckx. In 1964 he won the world road-race championship for amateurs, having been first refused permission to ride by the Belgian Federation's doctor because 'his heart was too small'. His own doctor went crazy and scotched that. Contracted to an Italian team, he scored his first major win in the 1966 Milan–San Remo: *La Primavera* ('the race of springtime'). Next year a second *Primavera,* plus a hatful of classics and the second of his four world road-race titles. He won the 1968 Giro d'Italia and was strongly placed to win the 1969 edition when a random dope test eliminated him. Two flasks of his urine sample had gone missing from the mini laboratory set up in a following car and the doctor told him, sorrowfully:

'I know you're innocent, but the test was positive.' Years later a rumour circulated that he had been offered a considerable bribe to hand the race to Gimondi. Unthinkable.

The rigged disqualification – a Belgian winning the great Italian stage race *again* – might have dealt a devastating blow to his morale. Instead, he came to his first Tour a month or so later, smarting and parched for revenge and did what no rider has ever done before or since: he won all three prizes – leader's yellow, mountains, points. On one stage, over the Aubisque, he attacked on the summit of the Tourmalet, and continued over the

Aubisque in a breathtaking solo break of 130km. He pulverised the opposition and won the Tour by 17 minutes 54 seconds, a margin that hasn't been approached in recent years. At Luchon, a journalist sighed: 'My friend, you're squeezing the race to death; it's not funny.' Another wrote: 'Merckx was like a gaoler with absolute power, each day ragging his prisoners in the *peloton* with another rough joke.' He went on to win the next three Tours and was victorious in five altogether, in succession to Anquetil; add to that five Giro d'Italia, Vuelta a España, four road-race titles, some 50 one-day classics, countless other victories, world hour record . . . On 13 July 1975, the 15th stage Tour de France, Nice–Pra-Loup, wearing yellow, he appeared to be on the verge of an unprecedented sixth victory.

After a rest day, at the beginning of this tough stage – 216km in all, across five cols and a withering 7.2km climb to the finish – Merckx led the Frenchman Thévenet by a minute and 58 seconds. However, Thévenet had looked strong in the Pyrenees and, more worryingly, imperturbable. Like Poulidor and many outstanding French cyclists, he'd been a farmboy; his muscles and sinews toughened by gruelling labour on the land; his mind inured to the grind of long days in the saddle. He attacked on the col des Champs, 1,000m in 16km of climbing, his teammate, Delisle, supporting him. It was his first show of open challenge. Merckx, flanked or paced by his men Janssen and de Schoenmaecker (ready to ride themselves to a standstill for their boss), stayed in touch and, 72km from the finish, went out on his own, as it was always his style to do. He headed the leading group over the col d'Allos, class riders every one, no wheel-suckers keeping the shade of the men doing the work. 'Never gets a tan', they say of the slipstreamers. Thévenet said: 'Merckx went so fast to take the col, he had 50 or 60m on me before I realised I was at the back of the group.' He simply could not match the pace.

From the tiny perch of the summit at 2,095m, Merckx attacked again; rocketed at breakneck speed down a tortuous descent no more than three metres wide, slippery with melting ice, into Colmar, 740m below. He was a famously audacious descender and Thévenet notably cautious: it's not only climbs where minutes can be gained. 'You have to switch your brain off and let it roll,' one gravity-surfer replied after a particularly hair-raising descent at speed, trying to explain what can't be explained. Merckx may have been no great stylist, all bunched strength, but going downhill he embodied panache. Tomba on a bicycle. Behind him, Thévenet and the Italian ace, Moser, had punctured; a hurried wheel change and a frantic pursuit for them to regain the leading group. Merckx was riding with the uncalculating fury of a man betting every scraping of his reserves on the attack. Some way down, he nearly careered into a group of press cars. The press usually ride way ahead of the race, gleaning material for their columns from Tour radio; they rarely *see* any of the action live, save start and arrival. This day, they had the scent of a bitter, perhaps decisive, duel being fought; an elbow-to-elbow between the two men going for yellow. They wanted to catch some of the bloodletting live and stopped to watch the race, their cars parked loosely off the verges. Merckx shot down nearly straight into them, just managed to swerve past, screaming blue murder. He'd lost time, precious seconds, momentum and cool. He was never a man to show excessive emotion, never winced in defeat or glowed overmuch in victory – beyond the ecstatic grin all winners crack wide when they cross the line and there's no more stupid bike for a while.

As he flew on, the Italian Gimondi's Bianchi team car swerved at the same obstacle, but too late, and went over the edge; driver and manager spilled out, slid 40 feet, clutched hold of the undergrowth and watched their vehicle somersault down the mountainside, bouncing off the spare bikes on the roof-rack.

Merckx hurtled on, hotly pursued by Gimondi, at 80kph. Behind them, Zoetemelk, Van Impe and Thévenet squeezed the brakes more circumspectly. From Colmars in the valley, 24km to the col d'Allos, 2,240m, Merckx head down, all out, never frugal with his effort. With only 24km, plus the short finishing climb to Pra-Loup, the stage and the race overall seemed to be his.

But, 20km from home, he lost everything, his power went, he cracked. Two days before, in the closing metres of the climb to the Puy de Dôme, a crazed French fan had leapt out of the crowd and punched him heavily in the kidneys. He held on to his bike and came in third behind Van Impe and Thévenet. (Months later the miscreant was fined a hefty sum of which Merckx claimed a token one franc in damages.) The medication he'd been given almost certainly upset his system. It is scarcely conceivable for a man of his class not to have eaten enough and got hit by the bonk, the wolfish hunger that afflicts cyclists. Perhaps there was even some jealous dragon of Destiny guarding the unprecedented sixth victory. Whatever happened he went to pieces. He struggled on, driven by what tatters of willpower he had left.

Gimondi (winner 1965) caught him, offered Merckx his wheel, but Merckx was in a wretched state and couldn't raise himself. Gimondi, riding for a rival team, had to press on.

Thévenet caught Merckx, by now almost delirious, 3km from the finish, and rode by. The pictures show Merckx's face torn with anguish, eyes hollow, body slumped, arms locked shut on the bars, shoulders a clenched ridge of exertion and distress. Thévenet, mouth gaping to gulp more oxygen, looks pretty well at the limit, too, but his effort is gaining; he's out of the saddle, eyes fixed on the road. He said he could see that one side of the road had turned to liquid tar in the baking heat and Merckx was tyre-deep in it. Behind Thévenet came the Dutchman Zoetemelk (winner 1980) and Van Impe (winner 1976). Both overtook Merckx.

Thévenet surged on, caught Gimondi, sat on his wheel a while to recoup, changed gear and rode on to the stage victory. When Merckx eventually crawled in, he trailed Thévenet by a minute and 56 seconds; he had ceded nearly four minutes on the day. Thévenet was in yellow.

The following day, Bernard 'Nanard' Thévenet suffused with a new confidence, stormed away from Merckx on the infamous col d'Izoard, a brilliant solo exploit, to win, alone, at Serre Chevalier, valuable minutes added to his lead. 'Ah . . . the last 3km,' he said, 'cutting through the crowd, pressing right on my front wheel, even though there was a motorbike *gendarme* escorting me. They were going crazy.' Bastille Day ended sweetly in France.

Next morning, in the neutralised zone which precedes the start of the racing proper, Merckx touched wheels with the Danish champion Olé Ritter and came off; his face hit the road and he was stunned. The doctor diagnosed a broken maxilla and perforated sinus bone and advised him to abandon. Merckx was in considerable pain, his jaw wired so he could take only liquid or liquidised nourishment, but he wouldn't give up the race into Paris, five days away. The doctor disowned responsibility. Merckx even regained some time from Thévenet in a mountain time-trial.

The race finished on the Champs-Elysées for the first time. 'Nanarchy' reigned in France, and by mounting the podium next to the first man to beat him in the Tour, Merckx afforded him unimpeachable triumph. As the old pro used to ask when a rider bragged of winning a race: 'Who came second?' Merckx came second . . . hell of a victory. Anquetil, when asked how he felt about Poulidor, his arch rival, winning the Tour, replied: 'Of course I'd like him to win it, in my absence. His victory would only enhance my reputation.'

Merckx's all-out gesture was heroic, generous, typical of a peerless champion; even if he later called it an unthinking mistake. Also, had he not finished in Paris his team would have been denied substantial prize money. The fact is, if Merckx was still in the saddle he could never be discounted. In 1971, for instance.

★

The following is partly based on Merckx's own account.

The winter before the Tour, there had been a mounting hate campaign levelled at Merckx in the French press. His domination of 'their' Tour had become repugnant. He chewed up all the French riders and spat out the pieces. The man wouldn't even smile. *Paris-Match* put it bluntly: 'Is Merckx going to kill the Tour de France?' Of course the organisers of the Tour knew that Merckx was vital to the race: he was, without question, the man to beat.

The classy Spanish champion Ocaña assembled a strong team round him – including the Dane Mortensen – and came to the Tour in cracking form. Merckx had missed the Giro because of a bad knee, his preparation had been nowhere near as thorough as usual and Ocaña fancied his chances. Anquetil advised him: 'Keep your nerve, wait for the mountains and when you strike, make it count.' This he did. On the descent of the col du Cucheron, 30km from the finish in Grenoble, the col de Porte still to climb, Merckx, riding with a lead group which included Ocaña, punctured. His director, Driessens, in the team car, was giving help to Wagtmans and doling out *bidons* (water bottles) to Van Springel. Merckx, fuming, lost 40 seconds waiting for a bike change, and then had to mount a team machine not set up to his own exacting size specifications. Hurtling down the descent in pursuit of the leaders, one tyre rolled off the rim and, unable to control the bike, Merckx ricocheted some way along the roadside safety rail before managing to stop. Another repair, another delay: the Driessens Peugeot 404 was having trouble keeping pace with their man on the bike.

Merckx shrugged off the trauma of the crash and flew on to the bottom of the col de Porte where he launched into nearly 500m of ascent to 1,326m in 8.5km. The climb seemed interminable; he could find no rhythm, the effect, surely, of that punishing chase on an unfamiliar bike. When he was 300m from the summit, he caught Aghostino and three Spanish riders behind a procession of cars following the break ahead. In the race director's words, Merckx made a 'ferocious effort' to get through the jam of vehicles to his own car at the front of the cavalcade. Here he came level with Ocaña's team rider, Mortensen. Tour rules permitted a rider who was behind because of accident or mechanical failure to ride past the leading team cars. A rider who had simply been dropped, however, was required to let the cars through to catch up with the leaders. Mortensen had, very conveniently, slipped off the back of the leading group when word came that Merckx was on them; the cars were overtaking him even as Merckx was chasing up on to his wheel and, 80m from the summit, the organiser Goddet, reluctantly enforced the barrier. The drama heightened: '80 derisory metres,' said Goddet, which 'the man who dominated modern cycling, probably the greatest rider of all time' could not, for the moment, ride across. When he eventually emerged on to clear road, Merckx fought and fought, livid with fury, but for a long time could make no inroad into the two-minute advance the leaders – working together at maximum effort – had over him. The effort left him breathless. A frenzied descent recouped a few seconds and in Grenoble he was a minute and 38 seconds down.

After a fitful night's sleep 'hatched like a zebra's skin' – waking, sleeping, waking, sleeping – Merckx came to the start next morning. A few miles out, on the col du Laffrey, Ocaña, gambling on Merckx being weary and heavy-legged from the previous day's exertions, launched an all-out attack. This was bold: the stage had 177km to run. At the top of the col, Merckx was already two minutes down on Ocaña, Zoetemelk, Aghostino and Van Impe, pedigree climbers each one. Supported only by Wagtmans and Huysmans, Merckx had to pursue virtually alone, neither of his *domestiques* (the servants, water-carriers, of the *peloton*) being equal to the fierce pace he set. He rode the whole distance to the finish in Orcières-Merlette with a hostile *peloton* champing at his heels; a bitter struggle, flogging himself 'like a madman'. The temptation to abandon was strong; he very nearly capitulated but tottered in at last, eight minutes and four seconds down. He said: 'My morale was crushed.'

He had been jeered at and insulted by French crowds over the preceding days; the hated Mossieu Merckx, finally getting a taste of his own medicine. 'Mossieu' the contemptuous form of Monsieur. But now the French press, shamed by his enormous courage, rallied to him:

> In defeat, the Belgian champion has revealed an unknown and admirable side of his character. He showed himself to be a man of iron through a long, terrible and, yes, in the greater context, catastrophic day. A day which bankrupted him . . . For four hours, the former wearer of the yellow jersey expended superhuman energy, demonstrating how justly he merited the glory his victories have brought him, a glory that is untarnished. As for those who whistled at and booed him, their only excuse is ignorance of his real worth and the blindness of chauvinism. In truth, Merckx's behaviour in defeat offers us an exalted, a solemn, lesson in the conduct of sport as well as in dignity.

Merckx offered his own tribute to the hammer blow Ocaña had delivered: the Spaniard had despatched the rest of them as the great matador Cordobès dealing with a bull.

In the modern Tour, such a huge deficit as Ocaña had imposed on Merckx is nearly impossible to make up but Merckx set out to do it. A criticism levelled at him constantly was that he did too much, overstretched himself, expended energy unnecessarily in the drive to stamp his authority on the racing field. When other riders were sheltering from arctic conditions in the 1968 Giro, Merckx rode on, apparently impervious. Sure, he felt the cold: he just didn't let it get to him. They kept telling him to ease up; the words weren't in his vocabulary. He was the sort of rider who'd read a SLOW sign as an insult, a speed limit as a challenge.

The day after his trouncing, he went off from the start in sweltering heat on an extremely hilly course, with Wagtmans, Huysman and others, 14 in all, and, as they peeled off, with four survivors, rode himself and the rest of his team into the ground all day. A break of 250km, average an amazing 45.351kph, for the paltry lead over an increasingly frantic *peloton* of never more than two minutes ten seconds.* They reached the finish in Marseille so far ahead of race schedule no one was around: it was siesta time. Merckx had clawed back a mere one minute 56 seconds on Ocaña.

This riposte was characteristic, though it made neither sound tactical or common sense; as a psychological blow it can have had very limited impact on the man who had more or less crushed him the day before. It stemmed, finally, from pride and phenomenal moral strength. Merckx, forced into a hopeless position, fought back with everything he'd got. They all say that of him: he'd never give up, even when he was off-form and riding for someone else. A *jusqu'auboutiste* (whole hogger), winning from the front, not the shelter of the bunch.

Two days after Marseille, 12 July, a cold, drenched ride towards St Béat descending the col de Menté in the Pyrenees – torrential rain, night in day, thunder tearing the sky in ruins – a small group, Merckx at the front, Ocaña sticking as close as he dared, led the race. Suddenly Merckx aquaplaned and careered into a parapet; Ocaña tried to avoid him, slid and crashed. He got up, tried to remount but Zoetemelk coming behind ran into him and then Aghostino. Ocaña was out, his legs and shoulder badly wrenched

*Other sources record a lead of one minute and 56 seconds at the finish, the advance never exceeding two minutes ten seconds.

and contused. On arrival at Bagnères de Luchon, Merckx refused the yellow jersey as reinstated race leader – he hadn't earned it nor would he wear it till he'd done so at the end of the following stage. Four days later, he found time at the end of the day's racing to visit Ocaña at home, laid up in bed. A visit of friendship. (Ocaña eventually won the Tour, in Merckx's absence, 1973.)

The day after Ocaña's crash, Thévenet also fell, this time on a treacherously wet descent on the Aubisque, in the Pyrenees. He did what most pro riders do instinctively, remounted and set off. His *directeur sportif* drove up alongside him to check that he was all right and Thévenet said: '*Où sommes nous? Qu'est-ce que je fais ici?*' 'Where are we? What am I doing here?')

Merckx said that the only time he experienced any real physical pleasure in a race was when he passed the finishing line. That momentary joy over, he could start worrying about whether someone was going to damage his bike or else clap him on the back and exacerbate the constant pain he endured after a heavy fall on the track one autumn that nearly wrecked his career. Riding on the velodrome in Blois, a race paced by Derny motorbikes, Merckx fell and was badly hurt. He didn't race for three months and suffered extreme depression. His pelvis had been displaced and he never recovered his true efficiency in the mountains; moreover, he was never free of pain in his back. That he achieved all he did following that misadventure is astonishing.

★

I join John and Angela, my cycling companions, at Huez. We cycle off around the back of the mountain to find our lunch spot on a patch of grass whence we gaze out across a chasm to the mighty, folded flanks of the Châine de Belledonne, where the Romans mined copper and lead, their workings still in evidence near the Lac Blanc. There were anthracite mines, too, till the pits were swamped by avalanche in 1952.

From the map, the col du Glandon presents little problem: 10km down into the valley, then a 29km ride from 720m to 1,924m, with a couple of steep sections marked. If not easy then manageable, and from the col a 22km glide all the way downhill to La Chambre, an apt place for an overnight stop. So much for maps. Clouds begin to accumulate in the sky ahead and the air grows damp while the breeze becomes cold. Here's Virgil on the brewing of storms which portend trouble:

> *interea magno misceri murmure caelum*
> *incipit; insequitur commixta grandine nimbus*

> The sky rumbled, deep, thundrous borborygmus, and clouds rolled in, loaded with hail.

A portent of just how ugly the mountains can be.

We set out at 4 p.m. and scooted down to the valley floor, in freshening temperatures, on past a village called Oz, blithely unaware.

CHAPTER TWO

COL DU GLANDON

Hinault and Fighting Spirit

Bernard Hinault, nickname *le Blaireau* (the Badger), five-time winner of the Tour and now part of the organisation, has complained in recent years that salaries are too high and riders have lost what ought to be central to their trade: fighting instinct. It's the kind of complaint that the old pro might be expected to unleash on the new bunch, the men who have no idea how hard things used to be. The Indurain stranglehold had its effect, too. The simple countryboy Spaniard with the freakish lung capacity and a heart-rate so low even some doctors disbelieve it, commanded such baffled awe yet such affection, too – no one can find a hard word to say of him as a man – that his invincibility was underwritten by even those riders with the talent to stretch him. They shied away from attacking him as if he were just too nice to be given a hard time. But, as Merckx said once: 'You can't *like* a rival.' Not when he's on the bike, at least. And the fact is, Indurain rarely had to drive himself hard against real threat.

Pantani made him suffer one memorable day in the Pyrenees on the 1995 Tour, leaving Big Mig and the rest trailing in his wake when he launched a scorching solo attack, dancing over the col d'Agnès to 1,527m and on up the slopes of Guzet Neige at unremitting pace. Indurain, in yellow, had to heave himself out of the saddle again and again just to survive, and came in over three minutes down on the Italian climber. But, such challenges were rare and Pantani had not the reserves to convert one day's gains into a longer siege. The rest of the would-be heirs to victory behaved as if it were a kind of *lèse-majesté*, treason, to call out the amiable, slow-witted Spaniard's lingering superiority.

I believe the Badger has a point. He was a formidably aggressive attacker; a man who'd announce to his teammates that he was going to win that day and win he would. If he got beaten one day – as Hinault was, against all prediction in the time-trial up the Puy de Dôme on the 1978 Tour – he went out and crushed the rest the following day, which he did in the sprint into St Etienne. He'd ignore the day's predetermined team plan if he thought it propitious to do so, observing what his rivals were doing, and seizing on the mistakes and frailties of the moment rather than following a tactical blueprint. That ability to adapt, to change rhythm, to ditch the agreed tactics and ride as circumstances, or instinct, or just plain fire in the belly, dictate, is what all the great champions possess.

On the 1979 Tour of Lombardy, for instance, the Italian stars, Moser amongst them, were sitting on Hinault's teammates, so Hinault went off on his own, with 150km still to ride. Cyrille Guimard drove up in the team car. 'You must be mad,' he said, 'you'll crack way before the finish.'

Hinault replied: 'Give it a rest.' Held out and won.

Like the badger, most dangerous when cornered, Hinault, with Coppi and Anquetil and Merckx, possessed what the French call *le coup de maître*, the master-stroke, which combines supreme physical strength and durability, moral power and a need to win that nobody can match. That need the French call *rage*, also their word for rabies. One of Merckx's ploys was to spring repeated flat-out sprints to pulp the rest of the field into submission. He used it to effect in the Milan–San Remo one-day classic, which he won an unequalled seven times. Nearing the finish, he'd fly off the front and take a hundred metres; the pack clawed their way back up to him; then he went again and again until they were spent. Anquetil they nicknamed *Maître* (more usually the title of a lawyer). An example of his audacity on 29 May 1965. At 5.12 p.m. in Avignon he received the winner's bouquet after the Critérium du Dauphiné Libéré. At 6.52 p.m. he boarded a Mystère jet in Nîmes and flew to Bordeaux for the start of the Bordeaux–Paris race (572km) at 1.30 a.m. next morning. At 5.33 p.m, in the Parc des Princes, he rode in first. In that race he fought a titanic duel with the great English rider Tom Simpson, the 1963 winner, who came in third.

In 1979, his second Tour, Hinault won the yellow and the green jersey plus seven stage victories. (Aside from Merckx, three other riders won overall and mountains in one Tour: Coppi, 1949, 1952; Gino Bartali 1938, 1948; Sylvère Maes 1939). In 1980, tendonitis had forced him to abandon the Tour – a very public humiliation – leaving the field clear to the Dutchman Joop Zoetemelk, a specialist climber who had not, till then, made a strong run for overall victory.

Zoetemelk, admittedly a rather uninspiring rider, was much disparaged for 'wheel-sucking' – notably by Merckx – that is sitting on the wheel of more energetic, more ambitious men and getting a free ride to his own advantage. (A rider in the slipstream of another bike has to do up to a third less work for the same speed because of reduced wind resistance.) This is a little unkind, maybe, because Zoetemelk certainly did not lack class. Moreover, a horrific head-on collision with a car whilst out training in 1974, left him in a coma with a fractured skull, close to death. Lesser men would have thrown in the towel but Zoetemelk recovered and in his first stage race after the accident, the 1975 Paris–Nice, he beat Merckx into second place by a thumping one and a half minutes. Like many Tour winners, the one field of combat Zoetemelk never joined was the massed sprint finishes of the flat stages – far too dangerous: why risk broken limbs for a few seconds' bonus? That madness is for the men built like wrestlers with more nerve than sense, many would say; chancy, twitch-nerve men like Abdoujaparov, the Tashkent Express who, in 1991, head down in the mad drive for the line, collided with the crash barriers on the Champs-Elysées and had to stagger the last metres with a broken collarbone to claim final ownership of the green jersey. The last few years have seen a rash of desperate pile-ups on the flat stages and wiser men stay clear. Merckx and Hinault never avoided the sprint if it was on offer. That willingness to mix it with all and sundry shows in the impressively long lists of their stage victories: Merckx 35 (a record), Hinault 28. Hinault returned to win in 1981 and 1982.

In 1983, he was forced to withdraw from the Tour before it even started; this led to a souring of relations with his manager and mentor at Renault, the exceptional Cyrille Guimard. (Guimard rode five Tours, 1970–74; in '72 he gave Merckx a pasting, only to be forced into the broom wagon with a knee injury, and from there watch the great Belgian take his fourth victory. He met the Tour finish in Paris where Merckx, in sympathy at his enforced retirement from the race, made him a present of his green points jersey.)

The argument began in a restaurant: Hinault wanted another glass of wine, Guimard refused to permit him one; the row thickened and widened. Hinault, a pugnacious Breton, like Astérix, and not famously diplomatic, told the Renault bosses they'd have to choose between him and Guimard. The bosses stonewalled and Hinault stormed off to join La Vie Claire. In his absence, the 1983 Tour was won by his former teammate Laurent Fignon – the ex-dental student whose fiery temperament and Parisian cynicism disinclined him to think well of his former *patron*, or journalists, or press photographers or, it seemed on occasion, anyone in the immediate vicinity. He was always a contender, often winner, of the unofficial Prix Citron awarded by the French press to the sourest, least helpful rider in the *peloton*. Fignon was, by the way, just short of 23, a good age for winning a first Tour – Anquetil, Merckx, Hinault, Ullrich . . .

Hinault returned for the 1984 Tour and the former champion took on the usurper; had Fignon's victory been a fluke? Hinault didn't shirk the duel; he went for Fignon hard, but Fignon was out to prove he was no lucky profiteer of Hinault's absence. Hinault, a long-distance time-trial specialist, most unusually, won the short Prologue time-trial, riding at 49kph, but he lost time to both Sean Kelly and Fignon in the first major race against the clock. In the Pyrenees, Fignon began to flex his muscles and to ride with mature confidence and assurance, demonstrating class and bravura. In the Alps, wearing the yellow jersey, he caught the Swiss rider Jean-Mary Grezet 12km from the top of the day's final climb, went past and rode on alone to the mountain-top finish at La Plagne. That day Fignon showed himself to be a true champion.

Admittedly, Hinault's team was weak; he was having to do most of the work more or less unaided; Fignon's Renault team was supreme. Yet, Hinault showed enormous courage in taking on the rampant Fignon when none of the other grand men of the *peloton* would challenge the ex-dental student. His efforts were exhausting, however: dropped on the climbs – the Galibier seemed to take personal revenge by deriding his former superiority – he rode manically along the flat to catch the leaders and, without pause for breath, attacked instantly. This sapped his energy drastically and left him suffering, once more, on the climb. Merckx concluded that his attacks were more 'panicked than calculating'. But at least he was going for it.

Fignon countered his erstwhile leader's assault in the valley of the Oisans with obvious ease and taunted his rival scornfully at the finish on l'Alpe d'Huez: 'I don't know what the effort cost him; personally, I thought it was comical.' Fignon went on to win in Paris. Hinault, smarting from the reverse, shook himself down and, later that summer, took victory in the Grand Prix des Nations (an annual time-trial which saw Anquetil's début pro win, aged 19, the first of nine victories in the event); the Tour of Lombardy, 'the race of the falling leaves'; the Barrachi Trophy, a two-up against the clock, (what's called 'the race of truth') paired with the Italian ace, Francesco Moser. Some pride was salvaged.

In the 1985 Tour, Hinault crashed heavily head first in the dying metres of the bunch sprint stage into St Etienne, broke his nose and crossed the line, blood pouring. He'd been controlling the chase to allow his young teammate, Greg Lemond, to lead home a break some distance ahead. The wound was patched up and, despite severe breathing difficulties from a bent septum, Hinault refused to quit the Tour and, in Paris, led Lemond, the American pretender, by a minute and 42 seconds. It was his fifth victory. He had already said he would retire on his 32nd birthday, a year hence, and declared that in the 1986 Tour he would work for Lemond. The king would sacrifice his efforts for the dauphin.

Within months he seemed to have changed his mind, though with typically Gallic enigma. He repeated his intention to retire in mid-November 1986, but added: 'Why give up the chance of another Tour victory or a world championship title?' He added: 'I said I'd help Lemond win the Tour but he's got to earn it; he's got to be worthy of the yellow jersey.'

As soon as the Tour reached the mountains, it became plain

that Hinault had no intention of simply handing victory to Lemond. Over the first 11 stages he attacked relentlessly and with characteristic passion, forcing Lemond to keep up or shut up. This tactic, though confusing to the American, was old hat to the wily Frenchman. He had been wearing the climbers down. 'By the time they reached the Pyrenees the climbers had nothing left, no reserves of strength. You've got to attack them until they can't recover. That's not hard to do.' The querulous Lemond wasn't impressed. He complained to reporters that Hinault was stiffing him.

Between Bayonne and Pau, over the col de Marie Blanque (a killer in disguise) and the first Pyrenean giants, Hinault once more attacked, in company with the Spaniard Delgado, to come in four minutes and 37 seconds ahead of the American. Lemond, for sure, never understood the arcane workings of the continental *peloton*, the intricate alliances and almost feudal sense of hierarchy and pecking order, the imperious requirement of wholesale, un- questioning loyalty. He was impervious to irony; neither, it seemed, could he distinguish between patronage and patronising. An intelligent, articulate and garrulous man, Lemond was a gift to journalists: he gave them reams of clean copy off the cuff which they could transfer direct down a phone line. But his amiability was a thin carapace for an aloof personality: he notoriously preferred to eat alone – ice cream and Mexican – with his family, lawyer– negotiator father included, rather than with the team in the hotel. He would even play truant from eve-of-Tour team receptions.

Nonetheless, Hinault's blatant flinging down of the gauntlet on the excuse of team ethics might seem a bit rich from the former boss who had promised him a lieutenant's support. 'I gave Lemond the chance to sit on my wheel today and relax.' Hinault explained. 'He knows we have to attack to make the opposition work, to tire them out.' Besides, who told Lemond not to keep up with Hinault? The fact is, Hinault made Lemond realise the brutal truth that victory would cost him, *must* cost him, dear; and what would victory be worth if Hinault merely stepped aside handed it over? To win the Tour is something; to beat Hinault in doing so, that's another thing.

Goaded, Lemond, as fine a rider as he is strident a whinger, did rise to the challenge. He took a stage victory – one of very few over his career – in the Pyrenees, and erased Hinault's lead. Moreover, time was catching up on the Badger. So too were the High Alps. On the approach to l'Alpe d'Huez, Herrera and the Swiss rider Guido Winterberg, a Vie Claire teammate of Hinault and Lemond, were first over the Galibier, while Hinault was leading the chase in company with Bauer, a teammate, Zimmerman, Pello and Ruiz-Cabestany, all rivals. Lemond had been dropped. On the descent, taken at a furious speed, the group reformed and Lemond, in yellow, caught up. Along the valley, on to the Télégraphe, Hinault drove the pace like a fury. Herrera was the first to go off the back, then Winterberg. On the descent, Hinault and Lemond went clear and stayed clear for the final 70km, Hinault punishing them both without respite towards the foot of the col de la Croix de Fer. From the valley they climbed 32km and some 1,500m in altitude to the pass; thence another 30km sweep down the col du Glandon and so to the foot of the last climb of the day: l'Alpe d'Huez. They rode it together, Hinault in front, as he had been all day.

At the finish, Lemond came up alongside him and they rode into the mountain station side by side, hands clasped. It was the moment of transition, all smiles, the old wolf yielding leadership of the pack to the young challenger . . . as if Hinault would have surrendered. It wasn't in him.

'I've really thrown everything at Greg in the last 48 hours. I've pushed him as hard as I can, sparing him nothing to put him under maximum pressure. If he doesn't buckle, that means he's a champion and deserves to win the race. Next year maybe he'll have to fight off another opponent who'll make life difficult for him and he'll know how to fight back.'

Lemond, inevitably somehow, cast a very different interpretation on the psychological games and harsh treatment meted out by this devious Frenchman; in fact, he more or less discounted Hinault's share in his victory, a singular lack of generosity given the essentially corporate nature of *any* victory in the Tour. Hinault remarked: 'It wasn't my fault he didn't understand how to lead a race . . . I spent all my time wearing out his opponents. Throughout my career I worked hard for other riders without having the kind of problems I had with him.'

In the 1985 Coors Classic in USA, for instance, Lemond did what was unthinkable in a continental pro racer, he attacked his teammate Hinault in tandem with members of rival teams. Loyalty wins loyalty. On the climb of the Stelvio in the 1980 Giro d'Italia, Hinault and Jean-René Bernaudeau were alone in the lead, Hinault waved his ally through for stage victory, to thank him for his help; in the 1968 Blois to Chaville, Merckx pulled aside to give Guido Reybrouck victory as a reward for selfless help earlier in the season. Merckx never won the race; Reybrouck counted three wins in his *palmarès* – honours list – 1964, 1966, 1968.

A racing team of cyclists must function somewhat like a racing eight of oarsmen, the obvious difference being that the crew of a boat is always in the same place at the same time. However, merely because they are all in the same boat does not mean that they all work in perfect accord and synchronised effort; that harmony has to be worked for and achieved by total commitment to the united aim: to make the boat go faster than any other. With racing cyclists the united aim is to produce an overall winner, if there is a man capable of complete victory; if there is not, then daily stage victories. To those ends every member of an effective team must be devoted, sometimes – mostly – at cost of his own ambitions. A good team is a coherent unit, smoothly organised, each individual performing a task he is best suited for; those tasks differ with each individual. But even the most lowly, the most obscure contributions can often be the most efficacious for the team's greatest potential. Some riders are even rebuked for lack of personal ambition, in that they subordinate all their own effort to that of a markedly superior teammate. Zoetemelk was one, till the absence of Hinault provided the spur to overcome self-doubt. Some men do not, apparently, suffer from such inner frailty: they ride at bust-a-gut limit for themselves or for others if they're having a bad day. But, *par excellence*, the Tour de France, much as the Bourbon kings of France, imposes a demand of total fealty from riders; in reward, the accolade of victory – be it the race or a stage – and recognition of the unstinting combined effort to win it. No more, no less.

This renders some of the tactics witnessed on the television coverage perplexing to the uninitiated: two riders well clear of the *peloton* (the same word in French as platoon, incidentally) will generally work together to get to the finish where they can duel for the stage win. Sometimes, however, they jealously refuse to work with each other and the pack, like a speeding whale, swallows up the pair of minnows and their chance for individual glory is blown. Or else that day, their team managers decide that the sprinters need a showing; a bigger splash in place of a small flourish. So, orders go down the line, once via the team car, now through earpieces. (The cat-and-mouse tactics do draw scorn from many riders and race organisers: the patent lack of real desire to go for a win even at the risk of defeat on the line.)

The basis of team tactics is to protect the leader, or a member of the team who attacks. When one of their men goes off the front, the best riders, those of the *grand métier*, know how to worm their way to the front of the *peloton* and disrupt any other team trying to wind up the chase. They will sit in, let one of the chasing team get a metre or so clear and block any attempt to link with him from the riders behind; what they call a *cassure* or fracture. This slows the whole *peloton* by damaging jolts to the even rhythm of the pursuit.

Or, a break of several riders goes comfortably clear, none of them a great threat to the general classification. However, one of the race leaders sends one of his team men to sit in on the escape and do no work. This tactical 'wheel-sucker' is there to get an easy tow to the finish where, fresher than the rest, he may save his strength and thus have a better chance to slip through for a win; or, should the escape prove half-hearted, his failure to help it along will see it founder sooner, rather than later, and thus allow his own team men to race back into contention for the final sprint. Often, two escapees jockey endlessly with each other as the finish line heaves into view, one, a better sprinter than the other and anxious to choose the exact right moment for his jump – not too far out, not too close – only to miss out because his rival, no speed-man, suddenly determines it's all or nothing, do or die, and lets rip, hangs on by his nerve ends and imaginary strength to take the stage. This isn't tactics: it's opportunism winning over stupidity.

Most significant, though, is the surrender, the literal surrender, of time by a lesser man to his leader. The examples of it are legion and they belong to the peculiar masonry of this unique sport, a tradition positively seigneurial, where princes really do have to win their spurs on the battlefield to earn the right of their noble calling and the plaudits of their older peers, by perceived courage, by show of nerve under extreme duress.

Hence Hinault's passionate, unequivocal rebuke of what he called the gutless slipstreamers who formed the procession behind Big Mig – a supreme athlete without a spark of panache or wit in him; a man marginally less interesting than his bike, tallying an unprecedented five consecutive victories of bromide regularity and hypnotic boredom built on classic time-trialling superiority, the slavish efforts of a devoted and characterless team, limiting losses in the mountains by picky calculations of seconds rather than from any discernible *rage* to win. This metronomic accumulation of wins had been obediently abetted by the docility of the men who might have whipped up some opposition, or at least have exposed what the thoroughly likeable Basque had in his head when push came to shove and he had to get out of the saddle to fight a bit. Not much, it turned out. Rijs' taming of the rider that nobody thought could possibly fail to record a legendary sixth victory proved Hinault right: if you want to win you have to attack, to the point of exhaustion and a long way beyond it, on strength, nerve and mad confidence, the full monte. Until Rijs took the Spanish robot on, the Spanish robot was, apparently, ready to grind the rest into mincemeat as per usual. *Coup de maître*. There were excuses: Indurain didn't like the rain and cold, he forgot to eat enough, and so on. But no pro at that level and with that experience, forgets, like a rookie, to stuff in the daily quota of 8,000 calories. And cold and wet? *Please*. The fact was, he'd been hit hard, gone down and couldn't get up. The will simply evaporated. Desgrange always said it: to win the Tour you need your head as well as your legs.

Rijs' tactics that day on the climb to Hautacam, July 1996, when Indurain bowed to mortality, caused a few raised eyebrows, not least because of the prodigal expenditure of energy it took. This, ironically, was the ground Indurain had picked for his Tour-winning attack – he very rarely attacked – in 1995. He had reconnoitred two stages: the individual time-trial and this stage up to the mountain near Lourdes. Clearly he was nervous: he needed some security early in the race, a step-up to his fifth victory. When he jumped on the climb the rest of the pack were so completely mesmerised – Indurain going out alone? Must have sunstroke – that they lamely watched him go until it was too late; he gained a couple of minutes, ample cushion for a time-trial specialist and another win was shuffled into his hand almost without murmur.

In 1996, Rijs launched his assault on this very slope – unjustly, perhaps, one wouldn't naturally impute such wit to Danes. He flew away from a small group of leading riders, including Indurain and his own lieutenant Ullrich, Virenque and other danger men. Hammering at them, like Merckx, he sped off a hundred metres; then, inexplicably even to our own Channel 4 commentators, he sat up and waited for the others to haul themselves level, glancing over his shoulder at them as they approached. Then he soared off again. It was, I must say, obvious to me at the time what he was doing. Whereas the admirable Phil Liggett deplored this tactic as the act of a madman, what he ought to be doing was keep pace with the others waiting to see who would crack – a very English timidity, that seems – it was quite apparent that Rijs was testing them, flaunting his own strength and challenging them, old-style, to the duel. None answered. Rijs went away a couple of times more and then for good and he was uncatchable. What must Indurain have thought when he saw him disappear around the far hairpin? Only what he must have been thinking for several days already: that his meeting with the sad destiny had arrived.

Of course, questions were asked about Rijs' startling form, his unsappable energy and, later that year, he and Ullrich, both members of the Deutsche Telekom team tested positive in a pre-Olympics dope sample and were refused entry in their national teams. The communist bloc Eastern Germans didn't invent drug-enhanced sports performance but they certainly developed it into expert science and some habits have persisted. There is the alchemy of head and legs and the pharmacopoeia of who knows what else?

Indurain recently criticised Pantani and Virenque, both explosive climbers who have stood on the podium in Paris, for not riding more intelligently. 'They attack absolutely anywhere, even when they have no chance of succeeding, and these attacks cost them a lot of energy. To win a Tour you must concentrate on one consolidated strike and make sure it's a knock-out blow.' That *may* win a Tour; it wins no place in my roster of real champions. Jalabert, censured for wasteful solo efforts, retorted that he might as well attack as get dropped.

If I have been harsh on Indurain it is not through lack of consideration for his talent – no one wins a single Tour, let alone five in a row, unless he is a remarkable sportsman – but rather from disappointment in his disposal of it. For example, by stage seven of the 1995 Tour, Indurain's fifth victory in store, Rijs had already emerged as a, or perhaps the, danger man. The route, from Charleroi, led the race into Liège and the Belgians would certainly be on the alert for a possible win in front of their home crowd. Towards the end of the stage, a group went clear and Indurain, acting on orders from his *directeur sportif*, joined. Here was a chance to put some time into the impatient Viking from Telekom. When they were 15km from the finish, the group confronted the fourth category Les Forges climb, one of the sudden sharp inclines for which Wallonia is noted; Indurain surged up it, offered only perfunctory support by the Walloon Bruyneel and the Canadian Boyer. They went clear of the other chasers, including Armstrong, usually a man for exactly this kind of break, but not lively enough this day. Boyer fell away, too – doomed, like the rest, to be swept up by the following *peloton* which was still moving quite sluggishly – neither Berzin nor Rominger, named threats to the big Spaniard, seeming much bothered that he was robbing them of precious seconds a long way before the mountains.

Over the top of the climb, Indurain and Bruyneel were in tandem now, Indurain beckoned the Belgian through to help in the pacing. Bruyneel, presumably acting on orders, refused. Either the break would succeed, in which case he'd be fresh for the final dash to the line, or it would fail and Indurain would have used up energy for nothing and a Belgian sprinter could crash out of the pack for the day's honours. Indurain shrugged his shoulders and got stuck in. On the 50kph descent of Les Forges, into the outskirts of Liège, he took every risk imaginable, on tricky corners and a chancy surface – one of the riders in the pursuing pack misjudged and flew into a shop window – and built a 50-second lead, Bruyneel clinging to his wheel. Behind them Rijs and the Belgian ace Museeuw were, at last, cranking up the chase.

Into Liège, Indurain was plainly in some distress, elbow wobbling, head tilted to one side, mouth sagging, but he was generating phenomenal speed. Flat out for the line, inevitably he had no change of gear left in him and Bruyneel came past, a smug grin on his face, to acknowledge the cheers of the locals as he swiped the stage win and with it the yellow jersey from the man who had towed him to the line. 'It was like riding behind a Derny motorbike pacer,' he said afterwards.

And Indurain? 'My legs were hurting.' But he'd gained 50 seconds on Rijs and next day in the 54km time-trial he added a further 50. Rominger lost 58 seconds and Berzin a massive minute and 38 seconds. With that power in his frame, what adventure Indurain might have put into his riding, instead of sheltering in the bunch. Lovely man; no brain.

Hinault, most assuredly, had a head on his shoulders. An interesting insight into his psychological toughening was that when he started work as a 16-year-old, he cycled daily from his home village, Yffiniac, by bike. Outside the village is a 2 to 3km long, steepish hill, where he would wait for an approaching lorry. He'd start riding towards the slope and, dicing with the possibility of misjudgement, latch on to its slipstream to ride close behind it at 50kph. To stay with the fast-moving vehicle became a matter of pride. On the way home at night, he'd try to match cars for speed going *down* the same hill. This, he said, developed both his muscles *and* his will to win, as well as the challenge of keeping a good rhythm.

These competitive rides entailed pedalling as fast as he could, but this isn't where he found his strength as a rider; that strength was innate and the fast pedalling on low gears would eventually lead to rapid turning of the cranks on the big gears, eating ground at ten metres a revolution. No, I'd say the principal benefit of those daily lorry-chasing rides was psychological; Hinault got used to racing flat out beyond what he might imagine to be his normal limit. There is, in many of us, a fear of succeeding far more crippling than any fear of failure, which is, by comparison, fairly routine. In his boyish refusal to give in to those lorries, Hinault was doing himself the precious service of eradicating from his spirit any dread of one day riding everybody else off his wheel. He is, too, a Breton, heir to the legacy of two of the finest Tour riders, rivals in their day: Bobet and Robic.

★

This goes through my head as I grind up the col du Glandon. It is a pig. I have no stomach for it and, bad sign, I am complaining. Complaining about the gradient, the scenery, the wet, the fact that there is a bloody mountain in the way of my basking in the earlier triumph of the day. How dare this ugly, endless, unforgiving col du Glandon muscle in on the glory of my l'Alpe d'Huez climb?

★

Hinault himself wasn't shy of bitching about excessive physical demands: for instance, he denounced the Paris–Roubaix – the Queen of Classics, part of which traverses the Hell of the North, the wicked *pavé* (cobbles) of the old wagon roads – and called it 'this stupid race' after winning it in 1980, 25 years to the day after Louison Bobet's victory, the last by a Frenchman in the rainbow jersey of the world champion, too, as had Bobet. 'It's a circus,' he said. 'Why risk a fall that would mean missing the Tour?' A resolutely professional attitude. Riding a bike was a job; the old 'giants of the road' stuff was romantic myth, though he did describe his victory in the 1977 Liège–Bastogne–Liège as a 'beautiful thing'. (A few days earlier he had won another Belgian one-day classic, the Ghent–Wevelgem; a double achieved only by one other man – Merckx.) Yet, when Hinault deplored a time-trial stage of 140km as 'inhuman', Marcel Bidot scoffed. In the 1927 and 1928 Tours they rode 200km *contre la montre,* against the clock, every day, except in the mountains. And the 1973 Tour, the stage from Bourg-Madame to Luchon, in the Pyrenees, was to include the col de Péguère, three and a half kilometres of horrible gradient, the early part one in five and scarcely more forgiving after that. I've ridden it thrice: it's a brute. The day before, a rest day, when France was commemorating the fall of the Bastille, the national radio news reported that: 'The Tour organisers have just announced that two of their technical experts have been inspecting part of the itinerary for tomorrow's stage and, as a result, the col de Péguère has been eliminated from the route. The descent is considered too dangerous.' Local reaction was contemptuous: the riders had complained the climb was too steep and chickened out. The big names did not want to be caught getting off their bikes and walking – modern Tour riders didn't know how to suffer.

In 1978 Hinault was asked to lead a protest by the *peloton* against late arrival times, early-morning starts, enforced transfers by train or air – no fewer than five that year – which was all the fault of a system which allowed commercial interests to supersede those of the riders and the sport. The result: an inhuman race. When they were 50m from the finish in Valence d'Agen, the *peloton* dismounted and walked in; the stage was declared null. Jacques Goddet responded: an inhuman element was integral to the very nature of the Tour; excessive demands lay at the heart of its mystique, its ageless success. He claimed that the proper course of preparatory training for any rider should be two years, 80,000km of road-riding and a hundred post-Tour criteriums – one-day races – in towns dotted round the hexagon of France.

And yet, however pampered a rider is in the form of material and psychological support, there remains the equation on which all calculus of *who has it toughest* is based, and that is: man/woman + bike + mountain = hard work. There is a corollary to that unforgiving solution which is that proving yourself against mountains and achieving the top is extremely satisfying, even if it doesn't feel much like pleasure.

☆

This rotten col du Glandon certainly doesn't feel like pleasure. At the risk of hearing the ghost of Marcel Bidot scoff me off the road, I was bitching.

Unhappily, now I'm not sure how I feel about complaining. The fact is, I'm up against it, face to face with heroic sentimentality, picking a heavy plastering of romantic fiction off Pandora's sealed box containing truth. I want to ride the mountains and I am, so far. But can it really be as hard as this? I have no option but to confront my own weakness and sort out romance from reality. (Getting off and walking isn't an option. I'm a cyclist.) At least this climb is forcing me to a new discovery, a peep into the darker places of my psyche; because I do want the whole story, complaints and all. I want to observe my reactions closely and here I am, head down into the handlebars, observing my reactions.

The impression is that I am riding naked, on nothing more substantial than willpower; when the willpower runs out, that's it, *finito*. I have a sudden recollection of Boardman's face in the Alps, 1996, 'the worst day I've ever spent on a bike,' he said. He had nothing left but the tenacity to hold on till the end of that awful day and a wild hope there'd be enough left to get him through tomorrow. The image of his pain and distress was as eloquent as any anguish panted into a microphone. Fatigue may be only skin deep, as a nutcase sculling champion once remarked, but fatigue does exist and it can't always be held off: even heroes crack. But that's when the tougher heads get belligerent; the struggle to get back into the action when you've been dropped takes even more juice than the effort to hang on, and pugnacity is no more than hardboiled complaint. What you don't want is raw complaint: like spilt milk it goes all over the place.

Cursing a headwind or a broken engine, ranting at lost keys to come out of hiding, pleading with a bus stop to send a bus may kill time but, as Thoreau said, 'As if you could kill time without injuring eternity.' We occupy the time we are in, its now, its past and future. I'm dicing with a kind of cosmic suicide here.

Of course I am not racing. The Tour, amongst a whole battery of inflexible rules, imposes a strict time limit based on a ratio of the daily winner's time – a rider who comes in too late to duck under the barrier is eliminated. In the mountains, the anti-gravity men – sprinters, *domestiques* – form what's called 'the bus' (latterly, *grupetto*, the termed coined by Eros Poli) for mutual help, aiming to scrape in inside the limit. They also bargain on the race officials waiving the rules if too many riders miss out. Not to deplete the field drastically, the Tour finds some arcane reason which permits *ad hoc* bending of the inflexible rules and reinstatement.

A few hundred metres outside the village of le Rivier d'Allemond, the road ahead begins to dip and blow kisses at the high ground; not a slight downhill, a headlong black run; bad news, very bad news. I go on, but I begin skidding down a glacier of suspicion.

The road twines like a rubbish chute to the bottom of a gorge being speed-cleaned by the Eau d'Olle in spate. Beyond stretches a dismal valley, the Défile de Maupas, a sombre cleft between the towering Grandes Rousses to the east, le Massif d'Allevard to the west. Défile . . . Grandes . . . Massif . . . they make me feel very puny all of a sudden. The uphill looks villainous too, even as I freewheel into the trough of the descent, and villainous it proves. I pedal at it furiously. Momentum shoots me no further than 20m up the slope and peters out. I am numb, reduced to a gasping crawl, nearly forced into the zigzag routine back and forth across the hill to soften the gradient. A brief spell of utter dejection: I am simply *not* going to make it; I'll teeter to a halt and have to get off and *walk*.

I recollect a weekend training run before a school continental cycle tour: we tackled a steepish hill near Ivinghoe. One boy got off to walk. When one of the others ribbed him, he patted his bike and said, laconically: 'Metal fatigue.' (Not so fatuous, actually: the severe torque of wrenching at a bike can twist the frame out of track. From what I remember of him, though, wrenching anything, apart from himself away from work, wasn't his style.)

Getting off to walk is utterly against my instincts and I've rarely been compelled to; but even pros walk. The Koppenberg, 1km-long cobbled acclivity – one in four at its worst – like the outside wall of a pyramid on the Tour des Flandres (one of the Belgian one-day classic races at Easter) has them dismounting their over-geared machines in droves. The whole race is peppered with similar obstacles, why bother to slog up slower than you can walk? Well, I didn't come to the Alps not to bother. Pride is the spur and pride dug its big-rowelled spurs in.

Hinault fell on the descent of the col de Porte and tumbled into a ravine, Critérium Dauphiné Liberé, 4 June 1977. The motorbike television camera zooms in and France watches as Guimard pulls him up on to the road. A momentary grimace of sheer dismay on Hinault's face as he clocks what might have happened. Then he is taking his bike from the mechanic and riding on. He wins the race over Thévenet (a few weeks away from his second Tour victory) and a true champion is born. Victories alone don't make champions so much as victories fashioned out of defeat.

Knowing when to get your arse out of the saddle is how Marcel Bidot put the difference between a champion and an also-ran: a mixture of not being too proud to work like a commoner and being too proud to allow a commoner to beat you.

✶

The Tour passed this way in July 1995 heading for the Madeleine and beyond. My tyres cross names daubed in white on the road; the usual smattering – local heroes, national heroes, foreign heroes – but a lot here for the Italian trio of Chiapucci, Bugno and one Bourgni, except that he's no rider I know of. I conclude that Bourgni is *tifosi* slang for 'dig in', an alternative to the more common *Forza!*

Italian cycling fans – *tifosi* – are notoriously partisan, deeming it a time-honoured part of their national duty to spit at, abuse and jostle foreign riders invading the home turf. (*Tifoso* properly means 'typhus patient'. Typhus, also known as pestilential, putrid or gaol fever, produces severe nervous symptoms.)

Nicholas Freeling recounts how he saw Anquetil, the hated Frenchman, riding up a *passo* in the 1960 Giro d'Italia, jeered and spat at by the *tifosi*. He took it all, impassive, aloof, and made the best riposte by winning the Giro, the first Frenchman ever to do so.

In 1987, Stephen Roche famously took back the leader's pink jersey in the Giro from his co-leader of the Carrera team, Roberto Visentini: the Italian had reneged on their mutual agreement that whoever proved stronger should go for victory. 'Let the road decide,' they say; so Roche attacked. His team did not want to chase, Visentini was screaming blue murder at them, other teams refused to co-operate – they weren't offered enough money. The Carrera manager, Davide Boifara, bowed to partisan claims and drove up alongside Roche to tell him the team were in pursuit.

Roche said: 'Well, Davide, you tell them to keep something under their saddle because they'll need it later.'

He was caught but had enough left to stay with the lead; Visentini, meantime, had cracked and was blown off the back. Roche actually punctured 10km from the finish, but no one told Visentini, a selfish rider and extremely unpopular. Next day, though, the *tifosi* were baying for Roche's blood, lining the roads, some of them waving chunks of raw meat: very Mafia. Roche rode flanked by Eddy Schepers, his teammate, and his fellow Celt Robert Millar, on a rival team, for protection.

Forza Bugno! Forza il Diablo! the nickname they gave ·the unpredictable Chiapucci, hot as devilled sauce who attacked when he felt like attacking, even when it made no tactical sense, just for the sheer hell of it, because he had a worm in his head telling him to give it a try and because even out of form he was a menace – mountains prize in 1991 and 1992, hero of a prodigious, all-day solo ride across the Alps into Italy that year – always ready to ginger up the action to see if anyone would respond.

✷

I stare at the *Forza!* It's like a V-sign in my face.

I so badly want to come and ride these Alps with flair but that's pure fantasy. Chris Boardman, speaking of a race early in his pro career, recalls how he was riding in the bunch – some 100 riders – at full stretch, when they hit a hill and the front riders simply changed a gear and flew off at such a pace he watched them go and thought: 'No way. If this is pro racing, I'm not going to make it.' Holder, since 1996, of the world hour record and the world pursuit record, he is one of the great speed-merchants of all time, but this road-race business was an entirely new reality. Such revelations of how we match or do not match up to unfamiliar demands are a shock, and few riders who enter the Tour for the first time can have any conception of the extreme demands it makes, even if, on the flat stages, the real action tends not to pick up until the final hour or so.

More of my own fictions are being deflated by the shock of a new reality. On this tiresome alp, imagining myself up with the rest, steaming up l'Alpe d'Huez at 32kph, tyres drawing a long cancel line through the tarmac autograph book – Yates, Kelly,

Breukink, Roche, de las Cuevas, Indurain el Grande, even Merckx, still lionised, I'm pleased to see. But even as my efforts sag, I gain insight into 'attacking spirit'.

In 1997 Pantani, *Il Pirata*, from the gold earring he wears, raced up l'Alpe d'Huez – that implacable arbiter of uphill speed – in 37m 35s, beating his own record. He arrived at the foot of the climb with Ullrich, Rijs, Virenque and Casagrande. One hairpin was enough for him to settle in and he was gone, a spurt of pace which left Rijs and Casagrande for dead. The others tried to match him but 3km from the top he was 25 seconds ahead of Ullrich and at the *Arrivée* the deficits ranged from Ullrich at 47 seconds to Rijs at two minutes and 28 seconds. Customarily, it is the Dutch fans who monopolise the slopes of this climb; this day the *tifosi* crowded them off the verges to cheer their man who was making his comeback after a bad crash a year before.

Pantani celebrated stage victory; Ullrich moved forcibly into the limelight; Rijs, who had been repeating his view that Ullrich was too young to carry the day-to-day pressure and burden of leading the race, had to accede to the old adage 'If you're good enough, you're old enough' and found himself nine minutes 42 seconds in arrears on his erstwhile lieutenant. However, the emerging dominance of the most consistent *grimpeur*, climber, around – Virenque – in the Alps and Pyrenees was, I believe, the crucial factor in the 1997 Tour. He set out to win if not the Tour then decidedly the mountains prize, and did so for the fourth time in a row, but his attacking spirit animated the field in a way which made this race one of the most exciting in recent history. In the mountains, his Festina team were at the front constantly, forcing a relentless pace. Rijs announced that Ullrich had him to thank for his second place in 1996 and that he was coming to the 1997 Tour as the man to beat. For a while, team tactics dictated that Ullrich accept his incumbent role as second. So, the big challenge to Rijs in 1997 came initially from the uncompromising aggressive effort of Virenque at the head of the pack, launching into the mountains with ferocious intent. Pantani fuelled the drive to win summit finishes, but even he nearly caved in, victim of the unpredictable Italian temperament (typified by the arch drama queen Cipollini, a rider with legs and vanity in roaring health and the moral power of a spoilt brat. Showman, show-off, he is, of course, a publicist's dream and a sporting director's headache). After the Alpe d'Huez ride Pantani complained of a sore throat and wanted to abandon. His team manager talked to him (gave him a bollocking) and two days later he took a second mountain stage and, eventually, third place in Paris. So much for waking up with a bit of a cold and wanting to skive off work.

Virenque's impetus never flagged, however. His capacity to chase a break on the punishing climbs has never been in doubt, but his combativity at the front of every mountain stage in 1997 undeniably broke Rijs and allowed Ullrich – quite clearly an exceptional talent on whose backing Rijs took victory in 1996 – to emerge as an indisputable champion, a leader in his own right. Whatever Virenque and Pantani did, he followed with the sort of implacable inner resolve that is intimidating to lesser men. Rijs, who had claimed to be even stronger than in the year of his victory, had no answer; he was dynamited out of the race for final honours, though, to his lasting credit as a sportsman, he worked tirelessly for the man who had replaced him as leader. The plaudits – 'Yes, Jan is stronger, he deserves his win' – are expected, which doesn't make them insincere; the actions, though, cannot be anything but genuine support, the leader being the leader in fact, not theory. Emerging from the Alps, Rijs succumbed to a bad stomach bug and, with the Tour lost, might have quit; he didn't. The year before, on the stage into Pamplona, patently marked out as a victory parade for the local man Indurain who was on his way, or so everybody had predicted, to a sixth successive win, Rijs lost the stage win by a whisker and Indurain trailed in already minutes down, his Tour lost. Rijs, however, beckoned him on to the podium and gave him the leader's bouquet. It was a magnanimous gesture.

Stage 14 of the 1997 Tour began with the col du Glandon. Several heroes of the previous day's charge to l'Alpe d'Huez were blown out before the finish at Courchevel, 2,004m, via the 2,000m of the mighty col de la Madeleine. Rijs lost a minute and 24 seconds on the day, Pantani three minutes 26 seconds, Casagrande three minutes 38 seconds. The winner, Virenque, pushed the race ahead from the start and arrived in imperial fashion, with Ullrich two bike lengths behind.

✯

Approaching the Barrage de Grande Maison, I see ahead what had every chance of being another excruciatingly steep bit of misery. My heart sinks. I ride up to it and, in some remove of delirium, up it. Can't be so far now. Some way on I find out how far: a whole lot.

Once again, the road gets altitude sickness and dives for low cover. It is almost too much to bear. I charge at it manically and console myself with pondering the treat I have promised myself when I eventually reach this col du Glandon, wherever it is located in the stratosphere beyond silver linings and rainbow crocks of gold. Just below the summit of the col du Glandon, the road forks: left to the col, right to another pass, the col de la Croix de Fer, an extra 2.5 km and 159m to 2,067m. I tell myself, kid myself, that this could be no longer or tougher than Highgate West Hill and worth the detour. Down in the valley, far from queasy air and solitude, the plan had seemed reasonable. From the moment this same road went AWOL down the slide, I reserve judgement on the idea. And the way things are going, reserves, whether of judgement, energy or any humour better than fractious, might very soon run out. Nor am I going to bother about the col de la Croix de Fer. Nor am I going to bother that I am not going to bother.

✯

In the 1956 Tour, ten years after I was born, the col de la Croix de Fer was the scene of a famous break by Roger Walkowiak, an unlikely-sounding Frenchman, who, like Cornet in 1904 and Lambot in 1922, did not win a single stage *en route* to victory. (Firmin Lambot, first man to win in the yellow jersey in 1919, was down by 48 minutes quite early in the 1922 Tour; the Belgians seemed to have the race sewn up but Heusghem was docked an hour penalty and Lambot took the final yellow jersey.) 'Walko', who must have had *some* Polish impetuosity in his make-up, was noted for his willingness to tag on to what the bosses of the *peloton*, the *patrons*, team leaders, called *échapées bidon*, attacks doomed to failure incurring a waste, perhaps irreclaimable waste, of effort. To their cost, on this occasion. The regional team man Walko went off with some small fry, and the big fry – including Bidot's French national team – left it too late to reel him in; the gains he made held until Paris and he took the overall victory without winning a single stage. It didn't endear him to the French public or the press, who called him 'wet' for his lack of enterprise, strolling into yellow with neither merit nor panache. After ten years of pro bike riding he went back to working in a factory.

An attack off the front is always a test of nerves: whether to follow or at least send a team member, if there's one strong enough, to join and hamper it by sitting on the tail doing no work. If the attack succeeds, it means you're fresher than the rest and better poised for a stage victory; if it fails then your own team leader is in at the finish. Nobody ever knows it's too late till it's too late.

In the 1955 Tour, the leading riders reached Bédoin at the foot of Mont Ventoux. Among them, in the rainbow jersey of the world champion, was Louison Bobet. Five days before, Charly Gaul had beaten him by 14 minutes over the Galibier in foul weather; but Gaul hated heat and that day the Provence skies hung over them like hot lead. At the start of the climb – 22km to 1,583m on slopes between 4 and 14 degrees – Bobet allowed the Swiss Ferdi Kubler, and his own French teammate Geminiani, 'the Big Shot', to go ahead. Keeping his nerve, riding his own race, his own rhythm, his own speed, he watched as they surged away and went out of sight. Bobet came on, steady as a metronome. Halfway up the climb he'd cut the gap to a minute and a half. Then, 10km from the top, Kubler, as was his custom, launched a crazy attack. He'd never ridden the mountain before and Gem called after him:

'Careful Ferdi, Ventoux is no ordinary col.'

'Nor is Ferdi an ordinary rider' cried Kubler, accelerating away. Higher up the climb he cracked; Bobet came on, passed both men and reached the summit alone, in the lead by 50 seconds, and then began the descent. By the time he reached the town at the foot – Malaucène – 60km from the finish in Avignon, the advance was one minute. His attack was looking shaky; it had stemmed more from the default of the others than from his own aggression. Nonetheless, he was ahead and over the next 23km he increased the margin to two minutes and 20 seconds but then punctured and lost a minute changing the wheel. The chase was bearing down fast. Rattled by the enforced stop, jarred out of his rhythm, Bobet had grave misgivings about the wisdom of this *échapée bidon*. His team director, Marcel Bidot, drove up alongside to urge him on. Bobet asked how much lead he had. Bidot prevaricated: there was sufficient advance to see him home. Bobet wouldn't be put off. 'I want to know exactly; if it's less than a minute, I'm sitting up [giving up].'

Bidot checked: the lead was 55 seconds and they were 16km from home into a headwind. Bobet grew impatient.

'Come on. How much?

'A minute and 10 seconds.'

For 20 minutes Bobet put his nose in the handlebars, as they say, and took the stage by 50 seconds. Bidot, who records the story in his excellent *L'Epopée du Tour de France* (The Epic of the Tour de France), said it was an appallingly long 20 minutes, sweating on whether he had obeyed a good instinct or blown the gamble. Bobet was a brilliant rider but very suggestible; his morale could be brittle as an eggshell.

Kubler crawled over the Ventoux eventually. As the British rider Brian Robinson went past, Kubler croaked, '*Pushez*, Ferdi.' Robinson's reply was terse. When Kubler reached Avignon, he was finished; eyes rolling, raving to other riders: 'Go on. Ferdi's gone crazy.' Behind him on the mountain, Jean Malléjac fell to the ground in a delirium, the bike on top of him, his free leg pedalling like an automaton. Unconscious for 15 minutes, he was revived with an injection of the decongestant solucamphre and oxygen. That evening, Kubler lay on his bed muttering: 'The Tour is finished for me. Ferdi's too old, too sick. Ferdi committed suicide on Ventoux.' Words that would resound with appalling truth 12 years later.

★

There will be no one waiting on the col de la Croix de Fer for me to shout *Ça vous en bouche un coin* at and by now, frankly, I couldn't care less. The *croix de fer* must be one of those ornate, wrought-iron filigree items set by the side of the road to mark the old pilgrim routes; my own pilgrimage was well beyond such pieties.

Another clutch of tight hairpins and a steep gradient bring me back to the level I'd had to wave goodbye to a mile back. I cycle on towards Le Rocher Blanc, a giant bluff projecting from the side of the Massif. Cloud pours over its rim, as it were from a hidden chimney serving the troll furnaces in the mountain's heart. Billows of smoke as white as steam, enough to herald a whole consistory full of new Popes. A diabolic machine stoking up ready for the engorging of the lone, the *intrepid,* Knight of the Campagnolo Gears advancing to meet the Dragon of the Mount Vicious in its swirls of inspissated mist.

With the mist comes a thin drizzle, a damp lining to the veil of fog. The sky moans like a turbine starting up and is soon whining a gale and discharging its ballast of rain, the full-weight article from pewter-grey clouds in a lead-grey sky on to my battle-grey spirits; everything is sinking, sinking, sinking. The road is one long dipsy-doodle. I'll be cycling off on to the grassland soon, convinced I'm a sheep, baaing at clouds which bark back at me like collies.

Suddenly, out of this unremitting slog, there looms up through the opacities a signpost which indicates the col at 0.5km. I grit my teeth. You do grit your teeth, it's a way of showing off about the effort you're putting in. Sleet mixes in with the rain. More cold mixes in with the existing cold.

One switchback turn past a hostelry. It's closed, deserted, dark. 'There is nothing,' said Dr Johnson, 'which has yet been invented by man by which so much happiness is produced as by a good tavern or inn.' Nor anything, perhaps, more depressing than a shut pub when you need an open one. A short drag upwards, another turn and there it is, unmarked, a hump in the road and flat ground: the col du Glandon in all its nondescript bleakness.

As I draw near, I sense a brackish jubilation rising in my chest, something akin to that stupendous relief (it's wonderful) and discomfort (it hurts) when you get to the WC at last and pee out from a bursting bladder. I round the final bend, hit the last slope and am at the top, where, to a bemused audience of sodden, bedraggled sheep rambling about aimlessly, like commuters waiting for a cancelled train, I yell: 'FUCK! FUCK! FUCK!' at the top of my voice. My treat.

I roll down once more, over a road that has recently done duty as a river bed, but down, and in the direction of the evening's comforts.

Gloves soaked through, my hands stiffen with the cold and from pulling the brakes near full on. The worst drawback of descending is that the legs don't turn, the heart engine slips into neutral, burns no fuel and stokes no heat.

A signboard for a hotel at 10km. My knuckles and wrists are aching horribly with the strain of braking. I can't see far enough ahead to risk any speed and the road is slick and skiddable. I am lucky. On such a night in 1919, Léon Scieur (winner, 1921) rode the Le Havre–Cherbourg stage carrying four spare tyres wrapped round his shoulders; in short succession he got punctures in all four. He spent what money he had left from food and drink on two new spares and, for security, decided to mend the others. This required unpicking the outer easing of the 'balloon' tyre, sealing the hole of the puncture, then resewing the case. There was a bitter wind blowing. Scieur took shelter in a house doorway and, by dim lamplight, set about his repair work under the watchful eye of two witnesses: the old lady who lived in the house and one Lucien Cazalis, Desgrange's right-hand man, a race commissaire, on duty to check that the rider didn't cheat by asking the old woman to thread the needle for him because his hands were too numb to do it. If she did . . . penalty.

At 10.5km there is a sign for St Colomban des Villards. A second sign: *Centre*. Ahead there looms a deserted village street, flanked by houses, one street lamp valiantly aglow like a good deed of 'welcome' in this naughty world of 'piss off'; one side of the road beside it is a covered market place, and, opposite, a bar with a lit doorway, and therein food, drink and a bed for the night and no commissaires to penalise me for begging help or stealing comfort.

CHAPTER THREE

COL DU TÉLÉGRAPHE

Tours of the 1920s

Front-runner for the title 'Most Unlucky' of Tour riders must surely be Eugène Christophe; motto: 'He does his duty who does what he can.' In 1921, Cri-Cri lost the Tour yet again when his front forks broke for the *third* time and he had to descend the Galibier on foot in search of a blacksmith's forge. Three times . . . you begin to suspect that it might even have been a protracted publicity stunt, *grâce à* Desgrange, sponsored by a rival tube manufacturer.

The first, and most celebrated, fracturing of the forks occurred in 1913 on the descent of the Tourmalet, the highest modern main-road pass in the Pyrenees, at that time a goat track. A car swerved into him and knocked him over – his forks sheared at the crown. It was a calamity, but this was no time for tears and tantrums. Christophe held the overall lead by 20 minutes. He simply shouldered the broken bike, trotted 14km – two hours – to the nearest village, Ste Marie de Campan, and rooted out a blacksmith's shop. He begged a length of metal, softened it in the fire, shaped it into an 18mm pipe to match the broken fork, punched a hole in the end to receive the axle and set to to weld it in place. This took another two hours. Tour officials stood by in relays to ensure fair play – HD himself, then two others – and observed as Christophe made the mistake of asking the smithy's boy to pump the forge bellows for him. Restricted to just the two hands, he couldn't manage the job without a third. Now, he clearly wasn't a man to cadge assistance on a whim, but such mortal frailties as not being possessed of three hands or prehensile toes cut little ice with a tartar such as Desgrange. The man was another Draco, a Bligh. (When told of Lapize's choked cry '*Assassins*' he took it as proof that the race was as tough as he intended it to be.)

The commissaire hovering in the doorway of the forge docked Cri-Cri ten minutes for accepting help. That the breakdown had already cost him four hours was of no account. The rule was the rule. After two hours, one of the commissaires felt peckish and asked Desgrange permission to go to the restaurant next door for a sandwich. 'If you're hungry,' growled Cri-Cri, 'eat some coal. You're holding me prisoner: you stay on guard.' Christophe reassembled his bike, remounted and rode on, any chance of final victory gone but determined to finish. He came seventh, 14 hours and 41 minutes behind Philippe Thys, who sacrificed his celebrated walrus moustaches that year to cut down wind resistance. The French Cycling Federation put a plaque on the wall of the old forge where Christophe mended his bike to commemorate the Homeric gallop down the mountain. It concludes:

'Eugène Christophe did not abandon the race which he might have won. An example of wonderful determination.' Hear hear.

(The plaque records that he covered 'many kilometres on foot'. The figures I give are those of Christophe himself, aged 74, in an interview with the late Jock Wadley, cyclist extraordinaire – Paris–Brest–Paris, etc. – and for many years correspondent at the *Daily Telegraph*. His ashes are scattered on the road through the Défile de Maupas.)

At Valenciennes, on the Metz–Dunkerque stage in 1919 (468km), having caught an escape by Firmin Lambot over the infamous monster cart-track cobbles of the Hell of the North, Christophe's forks started to shudder and then snapped. He avoided a fall but, as he climbed off, a voice from the *peloton* shouted: 'The old man's dropped: let's go.' Firmin Lambot, 28 minutes down reached the finish and took the lead; Christophe had lost 70 minutes finding replacement forks in a small bike factory. When the race reached the Alps, Christophe was clawing some time back, but Thys got away over the Vars and Izoard cols – the first crossing by the Tour – pursued by Lambot, and the attack effectively gave Lambot the final victory. However, the readers of Desgrange's *L'Auto* were so impressed with Christophe's fortitude that, although he arrived in Paris in third place, he was awarded the same prize money as the winner.

Incidentally, he wasn't the only man to shoulder a broken bike and continue the race. One year, Alavoine's bike broke under him 10km from the finish in the Parc des Princes, Paris. He picked up the bits and ran in. A nice irony for the man who never got off and walked in the mountains. These precautionary tales had a lasting effect on Firmin Lambot. He never set out without 500 or 600 francs in his pocket, in order to buy a replacement bike if his broke. The 'touch wood' precaution paid off: in 1922 he won the race aged 36, a record.

Christophe was a meticulous man, analysing gear sizes, careful what food he ate to provide high energy – rice cakes, bananas, ham sandwiches, chocolate – but such ill fortune he suffered; they said he was a victim of the 'witch with green teeth', the rustic bugaboo who scatters bad luck on the mountain winds. He never did win the Tour, *le vieux Gaulois*, though he surely deserved to. He was second in 1912, in spite of having a faster overall time than the winner, the Belgian Odile Defraye, but victory was awarded on points for positions on stages at the time. This was clearly unjust; even Desgrange could see that and the system reverted to classification on time the following year and forever after.

Christophe holds a unique record appropriate to the galvanised-iron breed of man he was. He rode his first Tour in 1906, his eighth and last in 1925, aged 40. *Chapeau*! Well done! (He sold millions of toe clips with his own brand name on them; my own toe straps put money into the Christophe estate.)

On the subject of accumulated masochism, Zoetemelk started and finished 16 Tours, George Hincapie has started 16 and finished 15, Van Impe, Guy Nulens, and Vjatceslav Ekimov started and finished 15, Darrigade 14 and finished 13, Poulidor and Sean Kelly 14 (12) and the British riders Hoban and Sean Yates both 12 (9).

✳

The second night I can't sleep a wink: too tired to rest, too tired to read, tossing and turning as if round an endless gyration of hairpins. Half-dreams come and go on the small screen of my feverishly active mind: riderless bikes cast in goblin silver . . . a scraggy Bo-Peep in hobnailed boots slumps drunkenly on a boulder, torn skirt, lips stained with blackberry juice and hair like seaweed . . . a gauntlet of dwarf shepherds in soiled wool capes brandish blackthorn cudgels at me as I hobble past in cycling shoes with pedal plates stuck to the soles like squashed tar-pats, scribbling frantically in a tiny notebook with the stump of a blunt pencil – the writing smears like mascara in the driving rain . . . a donkey tramples my bike and brays derision at me . . .

What makes tiredness unmanageable is having to be around while it's happening to you, to have to prowl around in its locked waiting-room till it decides to let you out. In the old days we'd already be on our way.

★

The 1920s were the epoch of the original *touristes-routiers*, freelance professionals independent of the trade teams. They provided everything for themselves, even to booking their hotel rooms each night. No *soigneur*, no *directeur sportif* dictating tactics. They fended for themselves completely – like the Parisian Robert Jacquinot, six Tours (1919–24) photographed with spare tyres looped round his shoulders, his legs caked with mud, at a table in a small *estaminet* gulping down a bowl of soup, glass of wine and hunk of bread to hand, precious bike propped against the table. And the Belgian Brackeveld sprawling in thick grass in a field at the side of the road eating sandwiches, two tin bottles of drink in the rack on his handlebars to wash them down. They all had to do their own repairs – a buckled wheel tied on to your back to carry to the next blacksmith's shop, maybe – but at least with a team the loss of time from running repairs, or accidents, could be limited.

Departure time: midnight. Setting off to work like miners down the long, unlit tunnels of the night. Hubert Opperman, the great endurance cyclist – who won the Paris–Brest–Paris in 1931, some 50 hours non-stop – says he rode up alongside another cyclist in the dark on one Tour stage and addressed him in French. '*Comment ça va?*' The other man didn't respond. Oppy repeated the question.

No reply. He got angry and swore at him, in native Australian, whereat the other guy swore back, in native Australian.

Emerging from the night into day, it's cold, unfriendly and still two thirds of the stage to ride. No ready-made energising drinks in bottles passed up by race cars. Food bought from villages *en route*; eating as they climbed the mountains – chickens, bananas, fruit tarts, biscuits, toast, bolting the food like Pantagruel. No spare wheels, tyres, parts or clothing on tap; what they needed they had to carry, weighed down like a First World War *poilu*. No doctor in the caravan, no masseur waiting in the hotel room. Moreover, the draconian rules Desgrange imposed seem eccentric if not insane. For instance: no item of equipment was to be discarded; what you were carrying at the start of a stage you had to carry in at the end. No help was to be offered or received from fellow riders; any rider *not* pursuing victory *or* sacrificing his own chance of victory in favour of a teammate would be eliminated; any rider sticking to another rider's wheel would be instantly disqualified. Not only were there fixed controls, but secret checkpoints where the commissaire would spring out to stamp an inky time and date on the riders' wrists.

In 1920, having won the stages into Brest and Sables d'Olonne, Henri Pélissier quit the race when a commissaire penalised him for throwing one of his spare tyres away. Desgrange, who had a Luddite aversion to new-fangled technical advances and a slave-driver's distaste for anything contrived to make life easier for the men who rode his Tour, remarked of Pélissier's defection: 'This Pélissier does not know how to suffer; he'll never win the Tour.'

He was wrong. Henri, perhaps the most able of three Pélissier brothers, had his victory in 1923, when two-minute bonuses for stage winners were introduced to liven up the racing. Speaking for the three brothers, Henri told journalists: 'We're out to win, to prove to Desgrange we're not clowns.' He made big gains crossing the Allos and Izoard cols, followed by the Galibier and the Aravis, enough to put him out of reach. In the first half of the Tour, Henri had been badly adrift. Robert Jacquinot trounced him one day in the Pyrenees, crossing first the Aubisque (1,709m) then the mighty Tourmalet (2,115m) riding over it as did the great Merckx in his first Tour, 1969, *comme un bolide* 'like a meteor', wrote one journalist. Except that poor Jacquinot had shot his bolt. A kilometre from the summit of the third climb, the Peyresourde (1,569m) a relatively undemanding ascent from the west these days, he cracked with fatigue and fell off his bike into the ditch to recover. Watching Jean Alavoine surge past at a brisk pace, he croaked: *'Je te salue, gars Jean.'* I salute you, young Jean.' Chivalrous gesture.

Jacquinot's early flourish seemed to have cut him to size; on the other hand, Henri Pélissier was nowhere. Desgrange must have shrugged: Pélissier *was* feeble, a loser. And, a couple of stages later, he trailed into Nice a full hour down on the leaders. That seemed to have written him out. What happened overnight? Did he say, like the Civil War General Ulysses Grant assessing the day's defeat: 'Give 'em a hell of a licking tomorrow,' and go to sleep? Or did he lie awake and turn his miserable insomnia into creative rage like Dickens stomping 15 and 20 miles around the London streets during the nights when he was working on *A Tale of Two Cities*? Whatever, he made up his mind all right, and tore off next morning as if his life depended on it.

Pélissier gained a quarter of an hour on his pursuers, but they got the wind up and clawed back. He had it all to do again if he was going to do it at all, and surely they wouldn't let him give them the slip a second time? But he did go again, took one minute, two minutes, ten and, by the time the Tour left the Alps he was in yellow. Desgrange recounted the story himself in glowing terms, eight years later in the journal, *Match*. Time hadn't mellowed him, it never would, but he'd changed his mind about Pélissier's exceptional talent; indeed I suspect he always liked to believe that he had invented his winners. Needless to say, victory was Pélissier's way of sticking it to the old bastard, and the old bastard loved his winners, especially if they were French, just as he reviled his losers, especially if they were French. He knew how hard victory came; he made extra sure it came as hard as it could be made.

Vapouring about that 1923 Tour, Desgrange compared Henri to Debussy and Monet: sheer artistry on a bike. 'His victory has the beautiful order, the classicism of Racine's works . . . the mountains seemed to sink lower, shrunk by the victorious thrust of his muscle. More than a score of times on the most vicious gradients, hands on the top of the bars, he looked down at the valley bottoms, hairpins twisting endlessly out of sight, like an eagle staring at its prey.' HD was a journalist first and foremost, after all, lavish with vitriol and saccharine in promiscuous quantity, inspired by his own publicity, convinced that his opinion moulded the champions who came into their own in his great bike race. That wasn't so far from the truth.

Riding for Pélissier's trade team, Automoto, was a young Italian, Ottavio Bottechia. The French fans were sceptical about the recruitment of this ex-bricklayer and horse-coper from the wrong side of the Alps, ignoring the fact that he was a fervent racer and a brilliant climber. Perhaps his own glacial attitude to cycle racing – 'You don't need to be any good at this job' – got up their noses; the fact is, he'd won his first races by such huge margins that he hadn't yet grown conscious of his class. He won the second stage of the Tour, Le Havre–Cherbourg, autographed his yellow jersey and made a present of it to his team leader Henri Pélissier whom he eventually followed into Paris. Little 'Toto' Grassin broke his forks on the Le Havre stage, did a Cri-Cri and rode the rest of the 300km on his own.

Pélissier was generous about the country bumpkin with the style and grace of a fluent athlete, his legs in perpetual motion. Desgrange, too, was full of praise: the Italian had stormed over the Galibier and consolidated his second place; he was in the hunt every day; he may have fouled up on the Izoard – forever stopping for drinks – but when courage was needed, Bottechia was always at the forefront of the action. He didn't even speak French – can you *imagine*? – but here he was teaching some of France's homegrown champions how to ride in the Tour de France.

Bottechia was the revelation of the '23 Tour, and in 1924 he became the first Italian ever to win. Remarkably he wore the yellow jersey from start to finish. He crossed the Aubisque (east to west) in a record time – 37 minutes and 40 seconds – into the bargain.

But the big news was made by the Pélissier brothers, Francis and Henri, who quit the race at Coutances. They had been penalised for '*abandon de matériel*', namely ditching one of the jerseys they had started out with. Desgrange counted the articles of clothing out and he counted them back in. Outraged that instead of a bike race they found themselves participating in a sort of militaristic fashion show, the Pélissiers packed, pulled up outside a bar and ordered coffee. The journalists flocked in. One of them quizzed Henri: had they abandoned on impulse?

> No impulse; only we're not dogs. This morning in Cherbourg, the race commissaire came up to me, pulled up my jersey, didn't say a word. It was bitterly cold so I was wearing two jerseys. Later he stopped me and did the same thing; the sun was burning hot by then and I'd ditched one jersey. What would you say? I won't take behaviour like that.
>
> Two jerseys, three, it might have been 15: we have to arrive carrying the same number we set out with. We not only have to ride like animals, they want us either to freeze to death or suffocate. Seems it's all part of the 'sport'. I went off to find Desgrange and asked him why I couldn't discard my jersey by the roadside. He said: 'You're not allowed to throw away anything belonging to the organisation.' I told him it didn't belong to the organisation, it was mine. He said he wasn't going to discuss it in the road and I told him if he wasn't prepared to discuss it in the road I was back off to bed, and got on the bike. 'We'll sort it out in Brest' he said and I told him that *everything* would be sorted out in Brest because we're packing it in, and we have.

One of the scribes listening, Albert Londres following the Tour for the *Petit Parisien*, wrote up the débâcle and entitled his article: *Les Forçats de la Route*. The phrase seems to have been coined in 1913 in *L'Auto*, Desgrange's own paper, and he was characteristically exasperated at the plagiarism: he had meant it as a compliment; Londres had used the term pejoratively. *Forçat* means galley slave or chain-gang convict. Worse, Londres wasn't even a cycling journo. In 1923 he had published an exposé of the penal colonies, the *bagne* in French Guyana, 'the dry guillotine' in *Le Petit Parisien*. The brutal Napoleonic penitentiary code was still despatching men to prison colonies and Devil's Island, where Dreyfus found himself. The Pélissier story caught Londres's investigator's attention and, working the parallels for all he was worth, he painted a grim picture, as he saw it, of Desgrange's martinet mentality in a series of reports later published as *Tour de France: Tour de Souffrance*. Desgrange riposted: these Pélissiers, so-called stonebreakers, were in fact millionaires, fractious, dimwitted, myopic; they hadn't prepared themselves physically and had just given up, beaten, without a fight. One wonders how badly podgy little HD was bullied when *he* was in short trousers.

✶

An unsolved mystery surrounds the death of Bottechia, who took a second victory the following year; and Henri Pélissier made a curiously ominous remark after the 1924 win. Bottechia – a strikingly handsome man, darling of the Italian papers, a sporting hero – had been pursued by an obsessive woman fan plainly suffering from amorous fixation. Bottechia had been flattered, tempted to put ego before domestic peace. Pélissier voiced the fear that Bottechia's wife, a volatile woman herself and volubly jealous, might easily flip and blow Bottechia away with the family shotgun – a traditional Italian vendetta. (In 1935, Henri Pélissier was shot dead by his lover.) The circumstances of his death were quite as strange.

On 14 June 1927, he was found unconscious at the side of a country road in Italy, his head and body broken and drenched in blood, his bike, undamaged, leaning against a tree. He was murmuring *Malore, malore* . . . it hurts. He can't have fallen: the bike proved that. Had he been attacked by peasants, enraged that he was stealing grapes? Yet in June grapes are sour. Rumours, even, of a Fascist killing – Bottechia made no secret of his socialist leanings – yet his status as sporting hero leant weight to a pro-Fascist national subscription to raise money for Mussolini. An anti-Fascist plot, then? Or, wait a minute, a Fascist conspiracy, after all, to eradicate a man whose popularity threatened to eclipse that of their Duce?

In the mid-'30s, an Italian immigrant, dying from stab wounds on the New York waterfront, confessed that he had murdered Bottechia. He had lain in wait for him when he was out on a training ride; a contract killing, ordered by a man called Berto Olinas. He died before he could enlarge on the story and no Berto Olinas was ever traced.

In 1973, the Italian priest who had administered the last rites to Bottechia in a back room at his church, to which a group of men carried his body after his 'fall', corroborated the version that it had been Fascists, livid about his massive popular acclaim, who had zotzed him. Perhaps it's not so unlikely. On the '24 Tour he came down on several mornings to find his tyres flat; one night in Toulon, he received an anonymous note in his hotel: 'Anti-Fascist: you'll get what's coming to you.' Whether the reasons for his death were political, vengeful or accidental, his loss was a tragedy for cycling.

Desgrange had taken umbrage when Bottechia swapped his own purple jersey for the leader's yellow because he wanted to go unrecognised by crazy Italian fans.

The *maillot jaune* was introduced in 1919, halfway round the Tour at Grenoble, a publicity gimmick, advertising Desgrange's paper which was printed on yellow paper. Eugène Christophe was the first to wear it, a slight but worthy recompense to a fine rider. For years, it bore no markings at all; then, after Desgranges died, his initials, HD, were embroidered on the right breast; subsequently, a strip showing the team name of the rider was fixed across the chest. These days, like all the rest of the jerseys, it serves as yet another portable advertising placard.

There is, though, some doubt about the first appearance of the yellow jersey. In the July 1953 edition of the Belgian magazine *Champions et Vedettes*, Phillipe Thys – then 67 and in lively good health – said: 'In 1913, I was leader on general classification and one night HD came to me with the idea of a coloured jersey: would I wear it? I refused – it would make me a target for everyone else. He pressed me but I was adamant. HD wouldn't give up and persuaded my boss, the unforgettable Baugé, to advise me to give in as the jersey would be great publicity for our Peugeot team. We went to the shops and bought a yellow jersey, more or less my size, but the neck was so narrow I had to enlarge it, and rode several stages, *décolleté*, like a society woman.'

Only three men apart from Bottechia have worn it from the first day to the last. In 1928, the Luxembourger Nicolas Frantz, wearing yellow as the '27 winner, won the first stage into Caen and is the only man to have worn it literally 'end to end', including victory on the final stage.

In 1935, on the first stage from Paris to Lille, the 22-year-old Belgian, Romain Maes, not reckoned to be a contender for victory, but clinging to a slender lead with the *peloton* breathing down his neck, rode through a level crossing at Haubourdin, a few miles from the finish, just before the barriers came down on the rest of the bunch. While the train roared past and the bunch cursed, Maes went lickety-split for home, took the yellow jersey by two minutes and never relinquished it. Also on that same Tour, on 11 July, the diminutive Spanish climber, Francesco Cepeda, fell during the descent of the Galibier, fractured his skull and, three days later, Bastille Day, he died: the Tour's first fatality.

In 1961, André Darrigade won the opening half-day stage, Rouen–Versailles; Anquetil took the afternoon time-trial and wore yellow from then on.

The yellow jersey probably only made sporadic appearances, a passing gimmick, in the 1913 and 1914 Tours. By 1915, the armies were entrenched along the Marne, Luxembourg's first winner François Faber (1909) had died at the Front and not till after the War did the jersey establish itself.

They called the 1926 edition 'The Tour of Suffering', the longest of the 20 so far: 5,795km (the modern race rarely exceeds 4,000km – 4,231km in 1987), 17 stages averaging 340km, the last three stages alone totalling 1,000km. From Metz to Dunkirk, 435km, over the wicked cobbled cart-tracks of old France; a marathon from Cherbourg at the tip of the Cotentin peninsula to Brest in Brittany, thence all the way down the Atlantic coast to Sables-d'Olonne, the longest stage ever, 480km.

Between Mulhouse and Metz, the shank of Marcel Bidot's pedal snapped and he was left pedalling one-footed. A hasty repair, improvising with a strap from the toe-clip, jammed the pedal in position for a while but it soon failed again. The chief commissaire allowed Bidot, riding his first Tour, to borrow a bike from a local man who was following the race, on condition that he swap its wheels for his own. This done he remounted; the bike was entirely the wrong size for him and he finished the day in a state of collapse braced for the next instalment of misery.

The race moved south. Midnight. Bayonne in the torrential rain, 76 riders set off into the Pyrenees. Some 300km on, the road up the Tourmalet was awash with mud; a cyclocross course; wheels slithering about till there was no ploughing through it and the only option was to get off and plod up. Even Lucien Buysse, a dromedary of a man, more nervous, they said, about his gears than anything human, like thirst, was forced to walk. Bystanders were kept busy heaving the following cars out of the sticky mud drifts.

The descent off the Tourmalet plunged into a dense icy fog which so frequently sinks out of leaden Pyrenean skies. At this point, Bidot's 24-tooth freewheel broke. In those days, the back wheel carried a freewheel sprocket either side of the hub; a larger size for the mountains, smaller for the flat and downhill. Later they carried two either side; a gear change was effected by turning the wheel round. The breakage of Bidot's larger sprocket meant he had to ride up the Aspin on the downhill sprockets, 43 x 22, a strenuous development of 4.10m. The deluge got worse: cold rain obscured vision, eating into flesh and bone, its carrying wind lunging at the frail machines. Snug inns nestled temptingly by the way; oh to stop for a bowl of hot soup . . . no, no, *retro me Satane* . . . once you stop you'll never get back on.

Buysse took this hellish mountains stage 387km, crossing the Osquich and then a quartet of massive climbs, Aubisque, Tourmalet, Aspin, Peyresourde and took the yellow jersey by 25 minutes. At midnight, only 47 riders had clocked in; a dozen of them called quits on their torment and scrambled into the commissariat cars, pardoned for this licence 'in view of the sky's anger'. Others never made it home: lost on the dark mountain slopes, they had to be sought out and rescued in charabancs. Bidot trailed in an hour and a half down on Buysse. Desgrange scolded: 'Bidot doesn't know how to suffer. He won't finish the Tour.' Buysse later became proprietor of a hotel and named it 'L'Aubisque', one of the Pyrenean giants, in memory of his epic ride.

A rest day followed and the next midnight they set off for Perpignan over another beastly mogul of mountains: cols des Ares, Portet d'Aspet, Port, Puymorens, Rigat and de la Perche; three spare tyres looped around the shoulders, pockets crammed with food, spoke key, spare toe-clip, extra spokes strapped to the bike frame to restore the almost inevitable buckled wheels, they had 18 hours in the saddle ahead of them. Lucien Buysse won again, and led home his brother Jules by seven minutes.

Between Perpignan and the Alps, Bidot incurred further wrath from Desgrange who blasted him in a newspaper article, accusing him of controlling all the escapes, sitting at the front of the *peloton*, managing the pace. In other words, doing his job, a determined, professional job, for the Alcyon team and its leader Nicolas Frantz, a potential winner. 'As for me,' wrote HD, 'Bidot can ride any race he chooses next year between 19 June and 19 July *except* the Tour de France.'

Frantz agreed to reward Bidot's service with the stage win into Nice, then outsprinted him along the Promenade des Anglais; the instinct to win couldn't be kept down and loyalty to underlings came cheap. The team manager tore strips off Frantz at dinner that night.

Into the Alps and Bidot punctured twice *en route* to the col d'Izoard but caught the Buysse brothers on the lower slopes; Lucien attacked and went clear; Jules followed. At the foot of the climb proper, Bidot rejoined and passed them when they stopped to change their wheels around on to the climbing gear. Bidot went by as Lucien shouted 'Change your bracket.' He demurred, feeling good, surged ahead and then, disaster: a third puncture. Hands so cold he couldn't peel the tyre off the rim, he tried to pick it off with his teeth. Impossible. Minutes passed; the Alcyon car drew up and the driver tossed out a knife. The commissaire – they seemed to have been, like vultures, ever-present at calamity – strode up: 'I forbid you to pick up that knife.' Bidot unscrewed a butterfly wing nut from one wheel and used that to prise off the holed tyre, just as the Buysse brothers rode past; but he repaired the tyre, caught them and was third into Briançon.

Desgrange wrote: 'I fancy Bidot has a somewhat sluggish temperament, he lacks drive, a bit lazy, not much of a head on him; he could have won that stage, I believe. However, he's strong, in good shape, solid; he climbs well, descends adroitly and he doesn't stop at water fountains. Such a début in the Tour de France suggests he is a man of courage.'

Never pulled his punches, HD.

For 1927, all the flat stages were team time-trials: this guaranteed fierce racing, since the whole team of 12 had to stick together as long as it could. The tendency to conserve energy in a muted approach to what they all knew was the real proving ground in the mountains had become ingrained. The drama of the Tour went limp and journalists could not be inspired, or inspire their readers, with a saga of monotony. On the first stage, the Alcyon team sustained a total of 20 punctures but the least known of the Pélissier brothers, Francis, had his moment of family glory and put on the yellow jersey. On the second stage, Bidot was left behind when near Cherbourg both wheels punctured simultaneously.

He slogged on through Brittany, thoroughly demoralised, and eventually abandoned. His teammate Frantz fulfilled promise and won. Amongst the riders that year were two destined to join the all-time greats: André Leducq and Antonin Magne.

Another innovation in 1928: Desgrange ruled that the nine regional teams, including the Australians, which had replaced the trade teams, would be allowed to call on substitute riders during the race. Bizarre. On one stage in the Pyrenees, Francis Bouillet and Arsène Alancourt were dropped and cadged a lift in a small lorry. The lorry slid off the road into a ravine – those mountains have witnessed many such incidents in this race – but luckily they all climbed out uninjured. More luck: a taxi drove up; Alancourt and Bouillet piled in and rode the rest of the stage in some ease. The *directeur sportif* coughed up for the fare and, three days later, in Marseille, draughted Bouillet back into the team after one of his riders, Gallotini, abandoned. Frantz took a second overall victory in a Tour which, perversely tame, eschewed the Aspin, Peyresourde, Vars and Izoard.

That year, the flat-stage team time-trials were axed because the teams could too easily conspire to control the pace; better, after all, to let individual ambitions have play. Bidot had a shot at the yellow jersey: he was on the same time as three Belgians, behind them only because he had not won a stage. A unique event in Tour history, this: the three leaders, Fontan, Frantz and Dewaele, each wore yellow at the end of the stage into Bordeaux. A few days later, the trio still in yellow, the race was heading out of Bayonne for the Pyrenees and a good ride would put Bidot himself in yellow. As he set out, a woman stepped into the road in front of him; he went over the handlebars. Badly bruised, one wheel rim in pieces, he eventually reached the finish in disarray. But, he took the stage into Nice on Bastille Day and continued to help his teammate, the Belgian Maurice Dewaele, to final victory. Dewaele had fallen ill and was on the verge of packing in the Alps but courage, sheer talent and the transcendant magic of the yellow jersey got him through his Calvary. The efforts of his team also helped. They nursed him steadfastly after a sleepless night of malady and a fainting fit and rode shoulder to shoulder across the road out of Grenoble and prevented any other riders getting through.

At Luchon, in the Pyrenees, Fontan was clear; an exceptional climber, 37 years old but still in hot contention. Some 10km from the start, in pitch-black night, his bike collapsed under him, the front wheel ruinously buckled in a pothole. He lost 45 minutes and, despite valiant efforts to regain the time on the climb of Portet d'Aspet, abandoned after the descent.

A journalist, Louis Delblat, wrote angrily in *L'Echo des Sports*: 'How can a man lose the Tour de France because of an accident to his bike? I simply do not understand. The rules should allow a rider with no hope of winning to surrender his machine to his leader or provide for a back-up vehicle with spare bikes on board. You lose the Tour to a better rider; you should not lose it because of a stupid accident to your bike.'

It took a long, long time for those eminently sane suggestions to be adopted. Desgrange remained implacable. He was not impressed by Dewaele's win, either: 'How can such a soft touch retain the yellow jersey? Why didn't his rivals attack him more resolutely? What can one make of their tactics and the real worth of the winner?' Meantime, other complaints were being levelled.

Delblat moaned: 'What's wrong with the Tour? No French winner for six years and the public at large aren't interested in it.'

Henri Poulain lamented: 'What can be done to haul cycle-racing out of its rut of tedium? New ideas. Bold initiative.'

Bold initiative was on the way: what amounted to a veritable palace revolution.

Professional cyclists were earning a good living, even if much of their work might justly be compared – as it was at the time – to life in a penal colony. In addition to a monthly contract of 1,500 francs, Bidot's purse for the 1928 Tour was around 10,000 francs. To give some idea of relative values, at the time a suit would set you back 300 francs, you could dine handsomely on 20 francs and a newspaper cost 25 cents (a quarter of a franc). That money was generated by commercial interest: the race itself had been inaugurated to sell more papers and it sold more papers; bicycle manufacturers sponsored teams because success in the Tour de France sold more of their machines. But, commercial interest then, as today (like the Grand Prix organisation *vis-à-vis* tobacco advertising) has, like the great champions, a ruthless *rage à vaincre*. Desgrange fumed about it, and he was not one to fume in vain. 'The constructors,' he fulminated, 'want to see their rider win, even if he isn't the strongest in the field. The organiser wants to see the best man win.'

Victory had to be deserved – hence his disparagement of Dewaele, in his view unworthy – and the noble cause to be served above grubby, meretricious bargaining or worse. Desgrange set out to reform radically the Tour's creaking state.

All machines would be of the same make, supplied by the Tour and painted yellow; national teams of eight riders apiece; only five jerseys from the countries of the competing riders: France, Italy, Germany, Spain, Belgium; 60 *touriste-routiers* to be selected by HD and his organisation; an International Challenge prize, for the best showing of participating nationals; a publicity caravan of trade vehicles selling to roadside crowds, separate from the riders, but stimulating the very necessary commercial interest attached – but now controlled – to the Tour, and a source of new funding; prizes to be given in kind. Finally, for the first time, national radio and local stations in Paris, Lyon, Bordeaux, Toulouse would broadcast reports of the Tour's progress.

Of these changes a journalist wrote: 'The Father of the Tour has underlined his hardihood; he has erased the past. Commercial interests were, he was convinced, fatally prejudicial to the health of his cherished child. He has made bicycle manufacturers, sporting directors and managers subject to one licence: that of the Tour.'

L'Action Française, capitalising on the new multinational flavour of the Tour, published special profiles of the French and Italian team captains, Fontan and the *campionissimo*, Binda. (*Campionissimo*, 'champion of champions' was coined for Constante Girardengo, Italian road-race champion, 1913–25.)

The French team were riding a superior freewheel which gave them a higher development, useful in the mountain descents; nevertheless, Alfredo Binda arrived as favourite. Winner of the first World Championship Road Race at the Nurnburgring motor-racing circuit in 1927, his *palmarès* also included the Milan–San Remo, Tour of Lombardy and 10km, 20km and 50km world records. A fine climber and a formidable sprinter, he had taken the 1929 Giro d'Italia by such a devastating show of superiority – nine stage victories in all, eight of them (second to ninth) consecutive – that the organisers paid him a rumoured 22,000 lire not to enter in 1930. With Binda around there would be no race. He did return to win the 1933 Giro and held the record of 41 Giro stage victories until Cipollini took his 42nd in 2003. However, in 1930 he lined up for the traditional opening stage of the Tour de France: Paris–Caen.

Charles 'Charlot' Pélissier – probably the strongest finisher in the *peloton* but no climber– made a break 20km from the line. Binda chased, caught up but could not outsprint him on the Venoix track. Pélissier took the first of what was a record number of eight victories in a single Tour (matched, since, by Merckx and Maertens) and pulled on his first golden fleece.

The French were up against it when another Italian leapt out of the pack: Learco Guerra. Outside Dinan, the Frenchman Mauclair jumped and took 300m before anyone reacted. Guerra flew off, caught Mauclair and sped past without a sideways glance. The French team rejoined Mauclair and gave him a mouthful: 'Listen, egotist, you make a break you make it work or else you *don't* make a break; you're with us, we're not with you . . .' And the whole team set out – time-trial fashion – to reel in Guerra, but he held them off took the stage by a minute and a half and with it the yellow jersey. He merited his sobriquet '*la Locomotiva di Mantova*' – 'the Mantuan Locomotive'. After Guerra's win, the Italians began to show their strength, albeit Binda, having arrived as the great champion, now hit a run of bad luck.

A few days later, he threw down the gauntlet again and the Italians shot off. The French team, habituated to rough-riding over cobbles, launched a ferocious chase across the *pavé* in Labouheyre, an old market town in the flatlands some 70km south of Bordeaux. Then disaster – a touch of wheels and the bunch went down in a heap. They rallied, caught the Italians and the sprint was on with 60 riders haring for the line. Leducq led out Pélissier, who chose his moment and flew past Binda and the Belgian speed-merchant Aerts – a classic victory. Binda recorded his version for the Italian press: '120m from the line, I attacked, Pélissier grabbed my jersey and then catapulted himself off my shoulder. If this is French bike racing, I'm quitting.' Desgrange relegated Pélissier, gave Aerts the win and persuaded Binda to reconsider.

Next day, Guerra came back at the French on his own but Binda had fallen and was in trouble. Even so, the team placed six men in the first eight home into Hendaye behind the French winner, Merveil. Alas for their captain, Binda, *he* finally trailed in an hour and ten minutes down and was now 50th overall. The journalists swarmed like sharks to a pall of blood: Binda wouldn't start next day; he was finished . . . abandon imminent.

Binda refused. He knew what he was worth and he'd lost the Tour because of an accident; he owed himself a lap of honour. He took the next two Pyrenean mountain stages – into Pau, where he outsprinted Pélissier, and Luchon, where he won ahead of the two French aces Pierre Magne and André Leducq, sole suvivors of a long break. Then, on the road from Luchon to Perpignan, the bolt securing the pillar of his saddle snapped. A botched repair took 15 minutes, but he chased and caught a small group containing the yellow jersey Leducq on the climb of the Portet d'Aspet. On the long descent, the saddle pillar's holding-bolt gave way again and he packed, deaf to the entreaties of his team. 'I have my reasons,' he said mysteriously.

On to the Alps. Guerra took the first stage into Grenoble. Next day, in yellow still, Leducq flanked by Pierre Magne (Tonin's brother), reached the top of the Galibier, two minutes behind a leading group comprising the Italian, Guerra – whom Leducq led overall by 17 minutes; the French *touriste-routier* Benoît Faure – a tiny man, prodigious climber, nickname The Mighty Mouse; another lightweight, the Spanish Flea, Vicente Trueba; and the

Belgian Jeff Demuysère (second in 1929). The two Frenchmen hurtled off on the descent at 80kph; Leducq lost control of his bike – probably hit a stone – overshot a bend, somersaulted off the bike and was knocked unconscious. He came to, badly bruised, his knee cut and pouring blood, shorts ripped open to his right hip to reveal a deep graze, the fingers on both hands lacerated. In addition, one pedal on the bike was bent out of true. His Tour seemed to be over; he slumped at the side of the road in terrible distress. Marcel Bidot, a short way behind, rode up, saw Pierre Magne standing at the side of the road, assumed he'd punctured then learnt the truth. He and Magne talked Leducq back onto his feet, Magne bent the pedal back into shape and they remounted. A hundred metres on, Leducq's brake failed; another repair stop. Leducq was in poor straits.

'They had to work very hard simply to get me back into the saddle again.' The trio set off downhill, but painfully slowly; 19kph reckoned Leducq, his hands hurting so cruelly he could hardly pull on the brake. They staggered into Valloire on the valley floor and on to the first slopes of the col du Télégraphe. Leducq, too shattered for any vocal complaint, was struggling to find any speed or rhythm and, no more than half a mile up, out of the saddle, desperate to keep going, his right foot shot off – the damaged pedal had snapped. It looked like curtains; Guerra must be building an unassailable lead. But Magne and Bidot refused to give up. Bidot even offered Leducq his own bike – strictly forbidden in those days.

However, the bad luck was running out and a spectator cyclist offered them a pedal; a car belonging to the newspaper *L'Ami du Peuple* provided an adjustable spanner and, like the US Cavalry, up rode three more members of the French team: Charles Pélissier, Merviel and Magne's brother, Antonin. The timing was perfect: the rules forbade any more than two riders attending any rider who had fallen or needed repairs. Another man arrived, the *touriste-routier* Guiramand, who undoubtedly pocketed some money for his assistance in the chase. They calculated that they must be some 20 minutes behind the Italian and his breakaway, which made Guerra leader on the road by three minutes.

'I was totally dispirited,' said Leducq. 'The winding descent of the Télégraphe passed safely but we took it very easy. At the bottom we joined the fast valley road of the Arc and heard that Guerra's lead was now only 14 minutes. I felt my courage restored, gradually my muscles warmed up and soon the whole team was riding at 40kph, working flat out, all of us, in pursuit of the group ahead. My pals swapped turns at the front and rode with their noses in the handlebars.'

(The modern English slang is 'eyeballs out' or 'on the rivet' – i.e. the brass rivet at the front of the old-style leather saddle.)

They rode the 40 miles along the valley in two hours. Merviel stopped to switch his back wheel round – to change the freewheel – and was dropped; they didn't dare wait for him; he came in alone. By Albertville, the lead had been cut to one minute, and shortly afterwards, they caught Guerra and the others. There were still over 140km to ride to Evian but, within sight of the finish, the entire French team launched Leducq out in the sprint and he won the stage; Pélissier came second. That day, starting from Grenoble, they had covered 331km through the mountains in 13h 39m 22s. Leducq tottered off to the hotel to be patched up by a nurse.

André Leducq won to be sure (Guerra was second at 14 minutes and 19 seconds), the first French winner since 1923, and confirmed the promise he had shown on his début three years earlier. Desgrange wrote an encomium. 'André Leducq is a pure child of France. He will tell you that life is good not only in the flush of victory but equally good through the most strenuous efforts and moments of anguish.' We don't have Leducq's version, but that victory in the 1930 Tour was, emphatically, built on the celebrated pursuit of Guerra, an epic of individual grit and team cooperation. The French team won the International Challenge prize.

Binda explained the faint mystery of his abandon 50 years later. He'd had no thought of riding the Tour because he wanted to concentrate on the world road race – he'd won the 1927 inaugural race but been dispossessed twice by the Belgian Ronsse. HD had bribed him to ride the Tour: the same fee for every stage as he'd earn for a race on the track.

And Faure? In his version, he admits his mistake in not helping the breakaway. He'd towed Guerra and the others to the top of the Galibier and sat on their wheel on the flat. He thought he'd be able to jump them, tired out by their efforts, and win the stage and the prize money. The freelance instinct; it didn't pay off. Had he worked with them, whoever took the stage, Guerra, not Leducq would have won the Tour and Faure would have come fifth not eighth. As for Bidot and Magne, they helped Leducq because he was their man, their potential winner; self-interest and selfless hard work need not cancel each other out.

The following year, 1931, having become a team man, Benoît Faure was still getting it wrong: he found it hard to know when to help or block an attack because, he said, he couldn't remember what jersey he had on and therefore where his affiliation lay. With his team leader, Tonin Magne, up on the Italian, Pesenti, by ten minutes, it was Faure's job to shadow Pesenti and keep tabs on any attack. However, as they approached the lead-in to a 2,000 franc *prime*, the old instinct surfaced. These prizes were offered as bait to ginger up the action, to guard against the whole race being stifled by team tactics. Extra cash on offer, Faure jumped; the Italians, Pesenti included, leapt on to his wheel and they all flew off ahead of the main pack. Pesenti eventually took the stage and gained five and a half minutes on Magne, who subsequently had to work like a horse to keep the yellow jersey. Magne was furious with Faure, the whole team was furious with him but angriest of all was Desgrange. Faure just blundered along on his legs; where was his *brain*? What offended him most was the vulgarity. Desgrange was a notorious stickler for rules and regulations but he was an unapologetic romantic, too. Riders must ride hard but, above all, they must respect the concept, the high idealism of his, Desgrange's, Tour. The team cooperation – augmented by some ready cash for extra help – was, by and large denied to the *touriste-routier* whose only obligation was to their earnings from various prizes and one-off pay to help other riders; they were mercenaries, pure and simple. The origin of the word 'freelance' was just that: a knight with no fealties other than to his pocket.

The man Jacquinot saluted on the Peyresourde, Alavoine, never won, but he was a great stayer, always difficult to shake off. Second twice, third twice, he was one of those men who scorned walking, too. When others got off, which they frequently did to tramp the mountain passes on foot, he ground on. He probably weighed up the economies on blisters and shoe leather. They said he could look at a map and point to the exact spot where he would have to change his rear wheel round. Incidentally, the *dérailleur* gear had been long since invented, but the tyrant Desgrange derided it as an unnatural gadget and forbade its use; he didn't lift his embargo until 1937. (His resistance lay partly in his belief – correct – that they weren't reliable and would cause endless mechanical problems to impede the race; also that a larger number of gears would make the mountains too easy to climb and diminish the incentive to ride hard.)

Professional cyclists were never averse to the darker skills and the changing of the back wheel offered the opportunity for 'professional' skulduggery. A man who knew the road ahead might leap off his machine at the top of a climb, pretend to change his wheel to engage the higher gear and remount. The other riders who didn't know the road would follow suit, only to find that after a short descent there came another big climb and have to change *again* while the local man flew off, turning the lower gear he never actually shifted.

*

Tuesday. St Columban-des-Villards.
A slow start. The clothes all just about dry, except for the gloves which we put back into the oven to bake. We slouch down for breakfast at 9 a.m. and don't wheel out the bikes until past 11 a.m. in warm sunshine. Roads, houses, roofs, trees freshly rinsed. We oil the chains and gears, turned orange and squeaky with rust from yesterday's rain. The *femme de maison* waves us off. Halfway down the long, steep descent into La Chambre, not the best way to put heat into stiff legs, we pass a lone cyclist toiling up the climb on a mountain bike loaded, back and front, like a pack mule: panniers, top bags, bar bags, tent roll, bag roll, pockets bulging and a crammed rucksack hitched to his back. Poor creature probably thought that by schlepping it himself he was saving his bike the weight. He keeps pace with the grass growing in the verges. Forgetting my

misery of the day before, I wonder what could be the pleasure in it; total independence for 5kph and 48km a day. Not for me to say. It was his choice to sleep in a tent and rejoice in nature at ground level. He doesn't even glance up as we pass: locked in his thoughts and the long struggle; we know how far he has to go and he knows we know.

I check on the local saintly *patron*, Columban. He pitched up in this village in AD612, an Irish monk, a whole-hog killjoy with uncompromising sentiments on moral fibre and penitential toil, ancestor of the notorious Maynooth hellfire and damnation wallahs. He'd been sent to put some bogside backbone into the continental brothers – lacing their soup with gravel, ensuring that bare knees were on cold granite during prayers . . . that kind of thing. Plainly the sort of hairy ascetic Desgrange might have pledged to dig some true grit out of the *Frères* Pélissier. He quarrelled with almost everybody, including the neighbouring royalty – accused them of slacking – and the incumbent Pope, a ne'er-do-well. The similarities between him and HD fall smartly into place the more you ponder them. His emblem is a bear – with a sore head presumably.

The Glandon valley is ripe green, lush and chilly from the previous day's downpour. Ahead lies the col du Télégraphe; beyond it, depending on the time, the Galibier – two climbs traditionally linked on the Tour. It doesn't seem likely we *will* make them both today; we have set out too late. After some discussion last night, we have shelved our original plan to move north from la Chambre to cross the col de la Madeleine (2,000m) and ride the big loop round to the col de l'Iseran, (2,772m). The Iseran will have to wait for another trip.

✫

On his last Tour in 1959, the triple winner (1953–55), Louison Bobet, abandoned on the descent of the Iseran. He'd been suffering and clearly was not going to make it to Paris; for two days he had been riding on reputation, glued to his bike by willpower. When he finally packed, he was asked why he'd persisted so long in a lost cause. He made the astonishing reply, the simple answer of a true lover of the bike: 'I'd never climbed the col de l'Iseran. It's the highest road in Europe. I wanted to ride up there.' It's probably the loneliest moment a rider ever encounters, the moment of abandon. Bobet is done with the 1959 Tour, with the Tour for good; someone from the team car brings a fawn gaberdine raincoat to put over his shoulders against the cold; Bobet's face is drained, his eyes shut, the humiliation of the defeat on that high road palpable; to one side stands the former Italian ace, Bartali, Coppi's great rival – sad, contemplative – holding Bobet's bike.

There is, perhaps, sometimes more than a dash of sentiment in this love of the bike and it was probably sentiment alone that kept Poulidor, a decent man, if unimaginative, from the winner's podium. He won plenty of other races but never the Tour, though he came close several times. He never even wore the yellow jersey. But his sunny disposition fended off the demons which drove Anquetil and they speak of Poulidor's love of the bike, of Anquetil's pride. Anquetil, who spared no feelings, least of all his own, in his incessant ambition to win, informed by Bidot, then French team manager, that Poulidor had promised to ride for him in the world road race instead of for himself, said bluntly: '*Il est plus con que je croyais.*' He's more stupid than I thought. Bidot walked out and slammed the door. Anquetil didn't win, never did win a world title but that reply was lack of sentiment in spades. How did he sum up his glittering career: five Tours, two Giro, one Vuelta, two hour records, five Paris–Nice, nine Grands Prix des Nations, a hatful of other races? Prosaically, almost dismissive: 'I earned a living by countless millions of turns of the pedals,' and, unsentimentally about the bike: 'No miner *loves* his pick.'

After he retired, Anquetil never rode a bike, though he did command great respect as an intelligent, shrewd commentator on the sport in general, the Tour above all. Poulidor, however, evinces, still, something of the poor farm boy from Limousin given his first bicycle, a blue racer, by a local bike-shop owner when he was 14; till then he had been riding, and winning, races on his mother's old sit-up-and-beg rattletrap. He never really escaped that upbringing; you might say that he couldn't really believe how big his talent was. He assessed his life as a pro with the ingenuous: 'Even a hard day's racing never lasts as long as a working day in harvest.' (It is appropriate then that the first bikes were advertised as 'The horse which does not need hay.')

Yet, it's difficult not to see in that first vault to liberty on to the blue racer – all cyclists make it, one way or another – the laying of hands on the bike, a near-consecrated taking up of a long destiny. Anyone who remembers the exact thrill, the magic of that moment when you ride a bicycle free for the first time must recognise that. In my case, I was six when Christopher Thompson, whose bike it was, a powder-blue-framed item with solid rubber wheels, took his hand away from the saddle and left me to my own flight in balance on a machine which, since its invention and popular acceptance has symbolised, embodied, independence. Anquetil, son of a Norman strawberry grower and never as poor as Raymond, Poupou, borrowed a friend's bike and discovered a mysterious affinity. Or, could one detect in that act of borrowing, the inherent disdain which was central to Anquetil's character, the need not to be owned by anything, anyone, any outside claim. Exceptional, focused rider he was, but he never allowed his *bon viveur* tastes to be hampered by the strict calls of pro racing. He drank champagne late into the night; ate amply and with gusto. During a rest day in Andorra on the 1964 Tour he was invited to a social bash, he wolfed down a hearty meal of barbecued lamb with sangria. The other riders were out for a rest-day ride and Henri Anglade remarked of Anquetil's gourmandising: 'Does he take us for idiots?' Antonin Magne, now a team director, turned to Poulidor and said: 'Okay Raymond, this is where you make your play.'

Next morning, on the big Envalira climb Anquetil felt sick and heavy, his sunken face showing all the signs that he was in a bad way. Poulidor, in company with Esteban, Bahamontes, Julio Jimenez, Manzanèque, all class riders, attacked. Anquetil showed no sign of being prepared to counter. One Vuelta he'd actually vomited, still on his bike, trying to make sure that no one saw him. This was different: his will seemed to have evaporated. The escape was well established when Geminiani, a veteran rider now director of Anquetil's team, drove up and, passing his man a *bidon* full of champagne, rounded on him. 'Jacques,' he said, 'you're five minutes and forty seconds down on Poulidor so if you feel like dying please wait till the broom wagon goes through,' then handed him the bidon of champagne (at risk of a fine). 'Either that finishes him off,' he said, 'or kick starts him.' Anquetil bestirred himself, his team rallied and they made hot pursuit with Anquetil belching a nauseous aftertaste of roast lamb. At the foot of the climb he caught a small chasing group, among them Anglade, who asked: 'Are you riding with us, Jacques?'

'I'll tell you in 10km' he replied. His legs were still leaden; but 10km on he was flying.

The accompanying team car speedo read 50kph and the Poulidor–Bahamontes break, at one time four minutes up, was doomed. In Paris he took his last victory; the luckless Poulidor once more second.

★

In truth, after l'Alpe d'Huez, the Télégraphe – in clear warm sunshine – is not hard; after the Glandon it's a positive treat, and I am beginning to find the new steadier rhythm – physical and mental – you need for the long hauls. Any activity that stretches you to the limit physically trims unwelcome flab off the morale. My heart sings.

> I count life just a stuff
> To try the soul's strength on.
> Robert Browning, *In a Balcony*

It is a pleasurable climb; hard in places – as is inevitable when the hairpins are kinked like nipped wire – but a steady ascent into the heady aerial company of the Dôme de l'Arpont, Chasseforêt and the Aigle de Péclet, crowned with glaciers, dwarfing the Télégraphe (1,566m) from the ethereal vaults above 3,600m. Amply rewarded, too, with the sight of St Michel de Maurienne in the valley, where Leducq and the others got their time check; there it is dwindling through the trees, snapshots of Lilliput as the hairpins wind us up, up, up. And I am there.

CHAPTER FOUR

COL DU GALIBIER

The 1930s

The sun on the Télégraphe is warm. I park the bike, unpack a sweater to insulate me as the sweat cools and go into the café on the mound. I calculate that the others will be about half an hour behind me and by the time they come it will certainly be too late to press on towards the Galibier. That, and the next leg into Briançon, will take at least four hours, maybe five. I order a beer and scan the racks for postcards.

My bicycle postcard collection numbers way over 3,000 to date – modern, reproduction and original – some of which date from the 1860s. Here's a gem: family of four picnicking by a roadside, salute the Tour de France *peloton*. Father waves a plastic sauce bottle, mother makes conductor's left-hand *fortissimo* gesture, the elder child, about eight years old, sitting on the grass behind the table, scans a map, while at the table the toddler turns to watch in wonder. This is St Veraud, 1954. You can tell it *is* the Tour from the numbers on the bikes; spare tyres looped round the shoulders. They set out from Amsterdam that year; Bobet took his second victory and either the 'witch with green teeth' or her demon sidekick *Hammerman* pushed the great Swiss champion Koblet over the edge on a climb in the Pyrenees. The man on his wheel, Robic, swerved and rode straight into a photographer. Koblet, 'the pedaller of charm', survived. An exceptional rider, he won on his first attempt in 1951. He underlined his superiority – as all great champions do, some time or other – with a stunning solo break of 135km between Brive and Agen. He told his team director Alex Burtin he'd had enough, he couldn't go on just 12km from the *Arrivée*. Burtin dissuaded him. As he rode up to the line, he nonchalantly sat up in the saddle, took a comb from his pocket and combed his hair. He never went anywhere without a flea-rake; best-groomed rider on the Tour. The Frenchman Mahé, halfway up a very steep climb on the 1951 Tour of Switzerland, gasping on, empty with the effort, was flabbergasted to see another rider come up alongside him, take his hands off the bars and proceed to comb his hair. Koblet psyching the rest of them out. It was effective: Mahé climbed off. (The story got out that he'd been suffering badly from piles and kept it quiet in case the others attacked him.) Next day, the sun so hot the tar was melting, he went again, 140km, the rest of them – Bartali, Bobet, Robic, Ockers, Geminiani, Coppi (still in mourning for his brother and way below his best) – toiling in his wake. He just sat rock steady and rode them off his wheel.

After Koblet's victory in that Tour, Jacques Goddet described him as the 'perfect specimen for demonstrating the miraculous power of the human race'. Goddet's purple prose notwithstanding, Koblet was never the same rider again and his life ended tragically when his sports car hit a tree in 1964.

Robic 'Biquet', The Kid, five-foot nothing, was so light in weight, he ballasted his water bottles with lead to increase his momentum on the downhills. This was illegal. At the top, his mechanic handed him the weighted bottles and, at the bottom, retrieved them. Tiny guy, blond curls crimped under a string-of-sausages racing helmet – another nickname 'Leatherhead' – gnarled face and Mr Punch hooked chin and nose, he could sprint, climb and roll on the flat with the best. He won the first post-war Tour in 1947 and was still giving his fellow Breton, Bobet, a ride in 1954. He wore a ring inscribed *kenbeo kenmaro*, 'to life, to death' in Breton.

Jacques Goddet, who took over from Desgrange after his death in 1940, called the first edition of the Tour after the Second World War 'an act of faith'. The occupying Germans had pressed him to run the Tour during the War to demonstrate that life in France was good, that the country was *en fête*. 'Out of the question,' he said. In 1947 he wrote in *L'Equipe*:

'This Tour de France sends a message of joy and of confidence . . . because it spreads a frieze across all the radiant landscape of our country, a moving, inspiring, astounding frieze of a heroic adventure from which hatred is absent.'

(There might be no room for sentiment in cycle racing itself; in the journalism, particularly the French journalism, the scope and appetite for it was always, and remains, bottomless.)

The departure was uncertain, right to the last minute. Post-war stringencies bit deep. The Government intervened. The President of the Council called for widespread economies *except on the Tour*. Potential entrants were asked to confirm their ride by telegram (the French Post Office was on strike) and to validate their passports for Belgium and Luxembourg. Rationing was severe; the organisers rustled up a ton of meat, 800kg of sugar and the same of bananas to provision the Tour.

On 25 June the field of 100 riders – 90 newcomers, 10 *brisquards* ('old soldiers, veterans') – rode out. The hot favourite was René Vietto. In 1934 young René had made all France ache with compassion at the picture of him sitting forlornly by the side of the road on the descent of the Puymorens in tears, alongside his bike, minus its front wheel. 'The living image of despair.' Having given up the wheel to his team leader, Antonin Magne, whose rim had snapped, he sat and waited and waited and waited for the service lorry which followed the last man on the road. By the time it came, his high overall placing was lost. The next day, another sacrifice. On the descent of the Portet d'Aspet, Magne's chain broke and Vietto rode back up the mountain to surrender his bike. Nonetheless an amazing talent, a thoroughbred cyclist, had burst on to the scene. Only 20 years old, the man from Cannes took the King of the Mountains title and was, surely, due his own victory eventually. In 1939 he wore the yellow jersey for 11 days. When Sylvère Maes failed to shake him off on the Izoard, Vietto offered him half a peach. He paid for the generosity: Maes raced over the mighty Iseran at an average of over 16kph.

On the opening stages of the 1947 Tour, Vietto was riding well. He took the yellow jersey with a solo escape of 130km into Brussels; lost it at Grenoble, in the Alps. Over the Galibier, Robic began to show his hand and would have taken the lead had he not punctured and lost a lot of time. He clawed it back little by little and positively flew over a four-col stage in the Pyrenees, where

Vietto reclaimed his yellow jersey, at Digne. One reason given for Robic's growing threat was his access to plentiful food. Wearing the white jersey of the Western France team, he and his fellow Bretons had bypassed post-war stringencies and were tucking into 2kg of butter, three baskets of fresh eggs and ten dozen oysters daily, all supplied by regionals keen to see their men prosper. However, three stages from Paris, Vietto appeared to have his first Tour victory within grasp. But in the time-trial in Brittanny, 139km from Vannes to St Brieuc, he cracked and lost nearly 15 minutes to a recently married Robic, cheered by a parcel of 72 letters from his family, friends and acquaintances. Robic had told his bride: 'I have no dowry, but I'll give you the Tour.'

She wrote to him: 'Show them you're the strongest.'

Had Vietto succumbed to the ill-effects of a bottle of iced cider? Had the obsession with a Tour win broken his nerve? Whether the collapse was moral, or physiological, or both, he slumped to third place by five minutes on the Italian, Brambilla, in yellow; Robic was second, nearly three minutes behind. On the final stage, Caen to Paris, the race crossed the côte de Bonsecours; 140km from the finish seven riders were in the lead but none of them of any threat to the leaders. The heat was intense. Robic records:

'Ahead of me I could see everybody out of the saddle, a mass of heads bobbing about. I spotted Brambilla, surrounded by his guys. Instinct kicked in. The *pavé* was smooth as mosaic. I took 50m out of Brambilla. He closed on me; I went again, he came again. He thought I'd shot my bolt but he was as exhausted as I was; spent. I got going again and took 50m. He came back at me. It was agony; we were both near asphyxiated, cooked. And at that point my generous-hearted friend, Brambilla, a man of superhuman energy, cracked, he was completely shattered.'

That didn't finish it, however. One of the French team men, Fachleitner, six minutes and 56 seconds down on the overall in fourth place, saw that Robic hadn't much left and offered him a deal: 50,000 francs and he'd ride for Robic. (That was the equivalent of two post-Tour one-day contracts – from which most of the Tour men used to make the bulk of their money.) In Robic's words, he needed to drop some ballast; he agreed and they rode on. Shortly after, Fachleitner upped the ante to 100,000. Robic coughed up.

The point was that if they co-operated, Robic stood a chance of winning the Tour and Fachleitner of coming second; if they didn't there was a chance that Brambilla would recover and the bigger prize money would have been lost. In the event, Robic did win by three minutes and 58 seconds – Brambilla at ten minutes and seven seconds – having never worn the coveted yellow jersey once the entire Tour. Brambilla took the mountains prize.

Besides Robic, another man won the Tour without ever wearing the yellow jersey; that is, he never led the race until he crossed the line in Paris. In 1968, the Belgian, Herman Van Springel, led the race by 16 seconds to the last stage, a 55km time-trial from Melun to Vincennes, to the east of Paris. But he lost the Tour by 38 seconds – till then the narrowest winning margin – to the Dutch rider Jan Janssen, already three times winner of the green points jersey. The first Dutchman to win the Tour, Janssen, like Robic in 1947, hadn't worn the yellow jersey once. Janssen was actually more of an all-rounder, boasting a lively mix of one-day and stage races in his *palmarès*.

Another sad end for Poulidor that year: forced out when he crashed near Albi.

A curious symmetry was at work here. Robic's last-minute victory in 1947; 21 years later Janssen scraped home; 21 years after him, in 1989, Lemond won by the smallest margin ever, eight seconds, having started the final time-trial on to the Champs-Elysées 50 seconds down on Fignon.

∗

In pleasant warmth and the satisfaction of a day well cycled, I ponder the Galibier.

One card in my collection is of a view north of the Galibier taken from Le Roc Noir, above the Briançon road, showing the approaches to the switchback climb up the southern slopes from the col du Lautaret as well as the peak of the Grand Galibier itself; at 2,704m it is nearly 60m higher than the col. The card is dated 6 April 1908 and the enigmatic message reads: *162 demain matin! Franck.*

No bike to be seen, but one of the most famous climbs in the Tour. You can visualise the phantom machines picked out like microdots in the grainy sepia, the road traced like a thin trickle of quicksilver down a jumpy circuit board.

☆

The audacious changes Desgrange instituted in 1930 had worked. Influential journalists had inveighed against the risk but the risk had paid off. Desgrange reaped a handsome profit: daily circulation of *L'Auto* rose from 500,000 to 750,000. Commercialism might be deemed bad for the riders but it was good for newspaper business . . . which helped to sell the Tour, and so on and so on. But, instead of a Tour providing a field of combat for industrial tycoons promoting their bike-manufacturing business, the race had been restored to the men who rode them. The Tour de France was proving itself adaptable; it could change, and with change grow even more popular, and become even more taxing proof of heroism. Unquestionably it helped having a French winner, and a personable, likeable one at that. More, the French team scooped 51,900 francs in prize money and counted four riders behind Leducq in the first nine. Of him, a journalist rhapsodised: '*Dédé, geule d'amour, muscle d'acier*' (Dédé, matinée idol looks, muscles of steel.) His time had come. He became *de facto* leader of the French team. Fontan ceded place. Pélissier, the strong man, won eight of the 21 stages, the last four consecutively, and came in the first three no fewer than 18 times; though in the course of three mountain stages he lost over an hour in time. However, a cyclist of great style and poise, he was, too, immensely popular. He landed a richer posse of post-Tour contracts than anyone else, Leducq included. Among the other French successes were the Magne brothers, Pierre and Antonin, 'Tonin', a man whose destiny had arrived.

Born in 1904, 12 days before Leducq, Magne, third in 1930, was a quiet, even introspective man. Each morning he went to the bottom of his garden, hefted a massive chunk of stone into his arms, staggered a few feet and put it in a new position. This exercise he dedicated to the hardening of his will. Every May he went into pre-Tour retreat in the Pyrenees, there to reconnoitre the cols, acquaint himself with the climatic vicissitudes, steel himself for the battle, toughen his physique on the big climbs. No detail of preparation was too small to overlook. Years later, as Poulidor's *directeur sportif,* he told Poupou that the work of the Tour de France is as complex and intricate as a spider's web and reproached him for his lack of method.

They talk of training for the great race as a bit like entering the monastery. Desgrange yielded to the call of natural impulses but said that once the racing season was on, women were in the same category as a pair of socks. Merckx described entering the Tour and penetrating its strange world as a quasi-religious experience: 'The paradox of the test condemns the champion, by definition a public figure, to the life of a recluse for 20 days.' (This reclusion is complicated by the daily obligation of press conferences – an added 45 minutes or more to the already gruelling demands of the ride.) On and off the road, he might have said. Yet, why else is sport inspirational, if not in the magnified example it sets for life, a life in or out of the limelight? Achievement and the manner of achievement in any pursuit of goals beyond easy reach is governed by similar tolls. The Tour de France as *Odyssey?* Certainly. Odysseus the lone wanderer overcoming vicissitudes and disaster. And that side of sport, the reclusive nature of being number one, your entire existence embattled in continuous rivalry is little appreciated by the public who thrill to the exploits. Anquetil put his view of it bluntly: 'Follow a career in sport and it must be like passing through a jungle: you beat your own path, you fight on your own.'

In contrast to the ascetic Tonin Magne, Leducq seemed to need no extravagance of effort: he enjoyed robust health, had natural class, unshakeable morale and sweet temper but was passionate to boot. Like Anquetil, a *bon vivant,* he would declare that he owed his victories to good humour. Magne said he imputed his to sleep. It was he who said: 'Wearing the yellow jersey doubles your strength.' And, in proof of the old adage that if you believe in yourself you can make your own luck, Magne's second victory came partly thanks to an ex-hotel pageboy who gave him a bike to replace his own broken machine. Leducq won the 1930 and 1932 Tours, Magne the 1931 and 1934. (Georges Speicher kept the tricolour flying in 1933 when Guerra came second for a second time.)

In 1932, Desgrange endeavoured to swing an advantage behind

Charles Pélissier, a rider whom he favoured and, perhaps, felt had been unlucky not to win at least one Tour. Poor climbing had reduced his chances, so Desgrange inaugurated time bonuses. Pélissier, a consistent stage victor would profit. First home: bonus of four minutes; second, three minutes; third, one minute. In the 1930 Tour this would have shortened Pélissier's time by 56 minutes, nearly enough to give him victory. However, Pélissier withdrew from the field, Leducq took yellow on day three in Bordeaux and kept it. He also won six stages, one of them over the Galibier in a snowstorm.

The intense Leducq v. Magne rivalry was gentlemanly, however; there was never the bitterness which marked the Poulidor–Anquetil duel, for instance. On their last Tour in 1938 the two of them rode into the Parc des Princes five minutes ahead of the *peloton* and acknowledged the plaudits of the French crowd by linking arms across their shoulders. It was a mutual gesture of respect, affection, shared privilege in the talent they had so generously deployed. Hinault and Lemond may have done the same on l'Alpe d'Huez, but the motives were very different.

★

We book into a hotel in Valloire – the town where Merckx had his neutral zone fall in 1975 – bathe, wash clothes, hang them in Widow Twanky garlands on the balcony to dry in warm evening sunshine. I go off to explore the town and recce options for dinner; trawl in a few cards, several pictures of the Galibier, the Desgrange monument on the south side and La Louison Bobet, a *touriste-routier* event.

It is a pleasure, dawdling along that tangle of quiet streets in the late-afternoon sun, sniffing at the aromas issuing from fruit shops, bars, restaurants with dinner and wine in store. I stroll back to the hotel and instal myself with Virgil and a bock in the bar. The others join me after their perambulations and we agree on the restaurant, local cuisine just round the corner: *tartiflette*, a Hell-of-the-North-sized cobble of melted cheese, potato and onion, speciality of Savoie; Savoy sausage, creamed potatoes and sauce, in a dining-room plainly decorated for the après ski, pitch-pine panelling festooned with old wooden tools and implements, cooking utensils, copper pots and pans.

I sleep ill, wake far too early and hear the rain start. By 6.30 a.m. it is teeming, the sort of rain which, if it had a sense of humour, would be pleased with itself; except that it has the monotonous insistence of a Scottish presbyterian minister. Dawn rises with all the enthusiasm of a late-night drinker evilly hung over. We're in for a soaking. I pray there isn't wind.

★

Galibier. Giant of the Alps. Desgrange's favourite (introduced in 1911). Next to the Galibier, he declared, the Tourmalet, the Bayard, the Laffrey cols are like 'colourless, common-or-garden gnat's piss'. The Galibier is *grand cru*. On its south side they built a memorial to him, *father of the Tour*. Born 1865, died 1940. International tensions had kept the Germans, Spanish and Italians out of the 1939 Tour, but on 14 April 1940, Desgrange contumaciously announced the 33rd Tour, albeit over a reduced itinerary. Paris fell undefended to the invading Germans on 14 June. Admitting that little hope for the Tour remained but clinging to it anyway, Desgrange, HD, Le Patron, died aged 75 on 16 August. 'A will of pure steel, tempered without finesse, a blade levelled at *action* . . . Born for sport, it is as a sportsman that HD dies.' (R. Coolus, *L'Auto* 18 August 1940). On the rest day of the last Tour he directed, in Perpignan, he'd gone for his traditional 12km run. He returned to Paris before the finish to be there at the Parc des Princes, in his suit, to welcome his family, the giants of the road. An amiable Spartan, someone called him and let this – his own words – be an epitaph:

Le Tour idéal serait un tour où un seul coureur réussirait à terminer l'épreuve. (The ideal Tour would be a Tour in which only one rider would come through the test.)

There was something decidedly Knights of the Round Table about Desgrange; he knew what evil demons inhabited the high passes and what terrors they awoke in the cyclists he sent up there. And a touch nostalgic of this latterday French *petit général* to refer to the Laffrey, 900m, a col of no great height or difficulty nowadays, but cited because it was one of the first included in the Tour, in 1905. At Laffrey, *en route* from exile on Elba to Paris, Napoleon and his ever-growing army were intercepted by a battalion sent out by the military Governor of Grenoble. Napoleon marched up, alone, confronted them, opened his coat to reveal the Légion d'honneur on his chest and invited the troops, many of them veterans of his European campaigns, to shoot. To a man they broke ranks and swore fresh allegiance to him on 7 March 1815. He marched directly to and into Grenoble, boasting that he had only to 'knock at the gates with his snuff box to gain admittance'. Curiously, there is a French slang expression *faire à quelqu'un une conduite de Grenoble* which means 'to run someone out of town' but that must refer to the 'day of tiles', 7 June 1788, in the run-up to full-scale Revolution, when the independent-minded Grenoblois bombarded the royalist forces from the city rooftops and forced them to capitulate.

✶

From Valloire (1,430m) to the col (2,646m) is 17km, via Plan Lachat, (1,961m) about halfway, at which point, as we can see from the map, the climb begins to get up on its hind legs: double chevron denoting severe gradient. We load the bikes and wheel out into the downpour. Rain slanting into us, we fill water bottles at the town fountain and set out. John and Angela in full waterproof togs, as suits their more laden pace, me in shorts. Legs take a while to warm up and I've left my gloves off – better to keep them dry in reserve for the downhill. Somewhere up beyond those cloud-swathed ramparts at the head of the long valley rears the Galibier.

✶

The King of the Mountains competition was instituted in 1933: The first winner, the diminutive Vicente Trueba, known as the Torrelavega Flea, a featherweight with no claim on the overall classification or stage wins. Points are awarded to the first men across

113

cols which are classified in categories: fourth (100–300m), third (300–600m), second (600–1,100m), first (1,100–1,500m) and *hors catégorie* – super category – (1,500m-plus). Classification is based on a fairly arcane system which takes into account quality of road surface and steepness. The paving of some of the remoter Pyrenean climbs is very poor and they are rated higher in consequence; and because the Pyrenees were less frequented by cars in the early days, the gradients tend to be sharper than those of the Alpine cols, an exception being the Alpe d'Huez ascent, super category because of its steepness and the fact that it always comes at the conclusion of a stage. Ratings are not consistent, moreover: the col de la Madeleine, which has a mile downhill section on the northern ascent – enough for a short breather – is either first or super, even though it tends to be in mid-stage, depending on whether it's approached from north or south. The ability to climb – like perfect pitch – is innate; it's a misconception that you have to be born in the mountains to be a climber: many of the best climbers come from the flat lowlands. In 1997 Paul Sherwen, commentating on television, expressed surprise that Laurent Brochard, a teammate of Virenque's should have held the lead in the mountains competition 'because he was from the north of France, which is very flat'. Northern France isn't very flat, actually, and plenty of the finest climbers have come from Holland. Lung power is what counts; a light body frame is a bonus. All the other attributes – stamina, fitness, morale – are essential to any Tour rider, whatever his speciality. Boardman, a natural speed-merchant, made, I believe, the costly error of purposely reducing his body weight in his Tour preparation to adapt himself to the demands of riding the mountains. The assumption is that a reduction in body weight and the resulting loss of a few metres of speed over time-trials – his speciality – will be more than recompensed by greater efficiency on the climbs. This has, on the evidence, drastically cut into his natural strength. In 1997, shattered by a heavy fall and four days of riding in intense pain through the Pyrenees and a long mountain time-trial – 'I've never been forced to ride so far below my full power,' he said – he looked horribly gaunt when, finally, he had to retire on the Alpe d'Huez stage. The confidence he expressed in 1994, that in three years he would be physically capable of winning the Tour was, I fear, too much based on laboratory calculations.

A computer can tell you many things: it can't tell you to forget about monitoring effort. After his magnificent attacking victory in the 1998 Giro, Pantani – 56kg of heart, say the *tifosi* – disparaged the gadgetry of modern bike racing. Riding out of his skin in the final time-trial to defend his narrow lead he actually beat Tonkov, a time-trial specialist. The pink jersey lifted him into another level of effort and he's no stranger to that. But he had his head buried in the handlebars not a cardiometer. 'That instrument,' he said, 'has detracted from the nobility of cycle-racing.' A view confirmed by Roche when he observed that young riders, festooned with computers and gauges, would do well to remember that riders rode hard long before the invention of the heart-rate pulsometer.

The Tour is a race like no other; the devastating changes of rhythm and physical stress it unleashes are vicious, abnormal; simply finishing it cannot be subjected to analysis in the same way that track racing – Boardman's great arena before he turned pro – can be. Refining technique and patterns of lung litrage, heart rate and watt output may work to brilliant success in a pursuit race; the Tour imposes its own reality and, like humour, it can't be explained logically. The Tour's learning curve is as steep as the mountains themselves; the psychological strain is enormous, the physical toll crushing. Merely seeing those bloody great cols from the valley floor can reduce the finest athlete's ability to perform at his best.

Boardman has, though, worn the yellow jersey longer than any other Briton – Tommy Simpson and Sean Yates each held it for a day, David Millar for three days – by winning two Prologues. The first in 1994 saw him in yellow for three days; the second in 1997 and in yellow for one day. I don't believe he had the capacity – mental, physical, moral – to win the Tour; there is a fine element of steel in his moral power, something so candid and nerveless in the courage of his ambitions; but he probably needed to follow something like the Tonin régime to achieve them. As Tonin said: 'To shine in the Tour, you have to learn staying power, to be as effective at the end as at the beginning.' *And* you must train on the battlefield itself.

French riders top the list of mountains prize-winners with 18; Spanish 14, Italian 12, Belgian 11. The Belgian, Lucien Van Impe, equalled the six-times record of Federigo Bahamontes but shied away from bettering the great Spaniard's supremacy. The Frenchman Virenque suffered no such qualms. In 2004, his final year in the Tour, he took his seventh polka-dot jersey. Neither of his illustrious predecessors was impressed. Virenque, they said, and with some justification, was an opportunist, a snaffler of easy points, not a real climber, a man who could dominate in the mountains day after day. Bahamontes, 'the Eagle of Toledo', once flew up a Pyrenean col and sat at the top eating ice cream waiting for the rest to catch up. Whence the legend of his insouciance. The truth is more prosaic. 'A spoke snapped halfway up the climb,' he explained, 'so I attacked to win time for the team car to catch up and replace the wheel. But it got stuck behind the main bunch. I had to wait, so I bought an ice cream to pass the time.' Unusually for an anti-gravity man, however, he hated descending and preferred to have a wheel to follow. He also took the mountains prize when he won overall, in 1959; this Van Impe did not do when he won overall in 1976. 1959 marked the last year of national teams and the French were top-heavy: Anquetil, Bobet, Rivière. Their internal rivalries, compounded by the moral blow of losing Bobet in the Alps, allowed Bahamontes a freer rein and he became the first Spaniard to win the Tour.

★

I ride on and muse about punctures: none so far but it would be a drag in this weather on the exposed lower approaches to the Galibier, on this rainswept, down-in-the-mouth day. Lower down the valley, clumps of farm buildings, which high summer could hardly make handsome, crouch dishevelled, sodden and morose in muddy yards. Shuttered chalets. Bleak moorland. The waters of the Valloirette river course unseen. Water everywhere. To the west, a massive wall of mountain, the Aigles d'Arve; to the east La Sétaz Vieille. It's an impressive show of mountain force. Ahead looms the col overshadowed by two mighty steeples of rock at the end of these opposing ridges – the Grand Galibier and the Pic des Trois Evêchés.

★

In 1967 a puncture committed Poulidor to defeat once more. He came to the race as the odds-on favourite: his team was strong, he was at the height of his powers, Anquetil had retired. Misfortune struck again, almost inevitably. Had he but been blessed with luck . . . it was the quality Napoleon most prized in his generals – luck, above all luck at two in the morning (or in the high mountains) when moral power is at its lowest ebb. Approaching the Ballon d'Alsace, Poulidor fell and was given a replacement bike not his size. It was a pain to ride. Then he bonked – the musettes had been packed for 160km whereas the stage was 215km long. On the big climb he lost 12 minutes. His own chance of victory gone, he decided to work for the Frenchman Roger 'Pinpin' Pingeon against their main threat, Gimondi, winner in 1965. Gimondi was a better climber than Pingeon and Poulidor's sumptuous riding over the Galibier in tandem with Pinpin effectively snuffed out the Italian's challenge and launched the Frenchman to final victory which he ensured with a solo escape between Roubaix and Jambes. Poulidor, one of nature's gentlemen, was, as ever, gracious in defeat. This is not to detract from his class – no stranger to heady success he was no willing loser, either. Or his wise good humour. He once said: 'My big luck was to meet plenty of bad luck.'

Say what you like, some of these Tour riders have a queer way with aphorism.

★

Plan Lachat heaves into view, a huddle of ugly, wooden ski chalets in a crook of the ranges. The meandering road swings a sharp corner to the right and steeply up; the first of the ramps. I have been in my lowest gear since we started; the only shot left in the locker is out of the saddle.

★

Asked for his opinion on the best rider of all, Bidot replied: '*Merckx.*

Faut voir son palmarès. Il savait lever le cul de la selle, pas comme certains champions très médiatiques mais peu entreprenants.' (Merckx. You have only to look at the list of his victories. He knew how to lift his backside out of the saddle, not like some champions who are very conscious of their media image but not very daring.)

An indication: taking one point for a win in the Tour, Giro, Vuelta, Paris–Nice, Tour of Switzerland, world road race, nine major classic one-day races, Merckx scores 46, ahead of Anquetil 24, Hinault 23, Kelly 21, Coppi 20, Indurain ten, Bobet nine, Lemond five.

Hardly a controversial claim, therefore, choosing Merckx, who dominated pro cycling during the '70s, although the reasoning might seem eccentric. Anquetil, who dominated the '60s, was famous for rarely getting out of the saddle, but *in extremis* he would be dancing a fast treadmill jig on his pedals squeezing more speed out of the machine, like a jockey urging the last gasp out of his mount.

Bidot's summation of Merckx does not neglect to say that if he had spared himself more, he would have won even more victories; but caution was alien to the man and he saw it as part of his talent, part of his calling, an essential part of his professional requirement, too, to ride and ride and ride, wherever the calendar offered races. In December 1994, to mark the retirement of Sean Kelly, the great Irish rider – a record four green jerseys, bronze in the 1982 world road race, Vuelta a España and a long list of classics – his home town in Ireland, Carrick on Suir, organised an open invitation race: pros, current and retired, amateurs. They all came, including Fignon, Roche, de Vlaeminck and Merckx. 'I am very busy,' he said, 'but I had to come. Sean is such a great champion.'

Kelly said: 'The people have done me a great honour turning up in such numbers [1,200] and that riders such as Merckx have spared the time makes me even prouder.'

That's cyclists for you.

During his first Tour in 1969, the veteran English sprinter Barry Hoban put this joke round the *peloton*.

'Did you hear? Poulidor and Gimondi have been fined 50 francs. They took a tow from a lorry all the way up the Tourmalet, didn't turn a pedal.'

'What about Merckx?'

'Oh, he got done 50 francs too: he was towing the lorry.'

Merckx has said, and repeated, that that first victory meant more to him than the other four put together. The accident on the track later that same year not only meant that from then on he was never completely free of pain in his lower back when riding; it jangled his nerves, too, made him extremely pernickety about the setting of his bike. He'd get up in the middle of the night to make minor changes of adjustment. And, during races, the team car frequently came up alongside to lower his saddle a fraction to reduce the centre of gravity going into the mountain, then raise it for greater leverage on the flat. His resistance to the incessant physical discomfort was remarkable; he owed his unequalled success as much to durability and stubbornness as to sheer class.

A revealing story about Kelly and the physical demands on class riders appears in Paul Kimmage's book *A Rough Ride*. Not so much a book as a protracted sermon of self-pity. Kimmage, a first-class amateur, never settled in the pro ranks and moans incessantly about how hard his chosen career turned out to be. Of course it's hard. That's what makes it special. He was *surprised*? He also, as they say, 'spits in the soup', breaking the fraternal code of the pro racers by sneaking on the practice of dope taking. At the end of the book, he recalls how he and Kelly went for a sauna one time and Kimmage tottered out, drained by the heat. 'I've never felt so knackered.' he said. Kelly, the consummate pro replied: 'I feel like this all the time.'

In praise of Kelly, Merckx said: 'Kelly [then aged 30] has an exceptional professional awareness. That is his only secret. Like me, he loves competition and never thinks of taking part as an also-ran. For Kelly, only winning counts and you will see him fighting like a demon in the Basque Tour in April, a few days before the Paris–Roubaix (48 hours after the finish) as if the hell awaiting him further north didn't exist.'

Asked if he didn't look out of the window on some grim winter days and wonder how cold and wet it was and if he'd go training after all, Kelly said: 'You never know how cold and wet it is till you get out there; so you get out there.'

Hoban's joke reminds me of a story Merckx tells of a prank his teammate, the Dutchman Wagtmans, pulled that same Tour. The *peloton* lined up for the start of the stage from Clermont-Ferrand but, before the gun heralding the off, Wagtmans jumped and disappeared from sight. Immediately the gun went, the *peloton* streaked after the cheeky fugitive. He, meanwhile, had nipped down a side alley and dismounted. Hidden, he watched the bunch roar by, slipped out to pick up a tow from one of the support vehicles and surreptitiously rejoined the bunch. They were going crazy, a mad speed, when Lucien Aimar launched a sudden attack off the front, in pursuit of the man who was actually bringing up the rear.

✫

The Galibier is very exposed; the road up it breaks every vertebra in its back over bare rock. No trees obscure the way forward. I can see the next hairpin on the climb swinging past me overhead, as the hairpin I'm on bends open from the tight turn. Progress is slow. Suddenly it's very daunting: this is a massive alp with a deserved fearsome reputation. I feel as if I'm gatecrashing the giants' committee. Occasionally, I stand up on the pedals to relieve the ache in the small of my back, 50 yards or so, and then settle back again. I am reminded of Charly Gaul of Luxembourg sitting near motionless in the saddle, turning his low gears, lower than anyone else's, soaring up this mountain on his way to a stage victory in the 1955 Tour. They called him 'Angels of the Mountain'. He shaped overall victory in 1958 with a heroic escape in the Alps – cols de Porte, Cucheron and Granier – through torrential rain and won by 15 minutes, over a field including Bobet, Geminiani and Anquetil who had dysentery and was spitting blood and vomiting by the finish. In the mountains – the Massif of the Chartreuse, near Grenoble, and Ventoux – he was untouchable that year. There was little love lost between him and Bobet – Bobet had attacked him one day in the Giro d'Italia while the Luxembourger was taking a pee – so the Tour victory was sweet. Gaul himself ended sadly at first: a virtual recluse, dishevelled and run to fat, after a failed comeback in 1964. He retrieved himself and died in 2005.

Something is bugging me: the matter of stage wins and the relation to overall victory. The record of stage wins recorded by winners is instructive. Head of the list is Merckx with 35, Hinault 28, Leducq 25, Darrigade and Armstrong 22, Frantz and Cavendish 20, Faber 19, Anquetil 16, Indurain ten, Coppi eight (five in the '52 Tour) and Lemond five. Out of interest, in the Giro after Cipo's 42 and Binda's 41 stage wins, Girardengo won 30 (two overall wins), Merckx 25 (five overall) Coppi 23 (five overall). No victor in the Tour deserves less than frank admiration but there are wins and wins. And as to the manner of victory, nothing testifies to fighting spirit more conclusively than the strength and swagger it requires to challenge the rest of the field to take your slipstream. 'If that's all they're prepared – or able – to do,' Eddy told his son Axel, a pro himself, 'then let them.' Axel did exactly this in a fine stage win, Dauphiné Libéré, 2005.

This Galibier is packed with history. Where exactly did Leducq fall on this descent that I am ascending? Not far from the top, I catch sight of a huge gully to my right, a funnel between two massive pillars of rock, a chasm plunging over a precipice, swirling with spectral white flurries of snow in spirals of wind. The ventilating chimney of an erl-king's refrigerator. Winter doing the dance of its ice veils. Awesome portico of monsters. I am riding into the lost regions where frost makes rainbows and the witch with green teeth trails nets of crystal snow for unwary summer, and unwary summer is caught fast, like the fish in the frozen lake. This is the realm of Ice-Blink and I am riding a glacial brook not a road.

I get nearer and the realisation begins to break, although I don't tempt the moment by cheering it too soon. Then I see the snow-plough, beyond the cars, facing me, beside a large buttress of rock above the left-hand verge. I ride up and say to one of a large group of spectators staring languorously into space, all togged up in mufflers and warm coats:

'*C'est le col?*'

'*Oui.*'

No ceremony. This is it. What? I get off the bike and lean it against a low wall of this mountain's fundamental stone and attack the saddle-bag containing my fleecy-lined top and gloves. The gloves are a saviour. I hadn't packed them originally, and put them in only at the last minute. Suddenly I feel the cold intensely, my fingers unlocked from the handlebars. I can only fumble woodenly at the bag straps. It's painful and clumsy. I'm just peeling my waterproof *off* so I can get the jacket *on*, when the driver of the snowplough, cigarette drooping from pursed lips, catches my eye and shouts. '*Vous nous assistez avec cette voiture glissée au défaut du bord.*' (Come and help us with this car, it's slipped over the edge.) More of a statement than a request. I stare impassively back at him.

'*Je viens de grimper le Galibier au vélo et vous me demandez assistance avec une voiture, merde.*' (I've just cycled up the Galibier and you want me to help you with a *car*?) More of a statement than an answer.

He stares impassively back at me, unimpressed. '*Oui.*'

I suppose the fact is that these mountain johnnies can't properly relate to any silly bugger trooping up their locale at any time of the year, and as for mad foreigners doing it by bike, *unpaid*, well, *c'est faire le con, quoi*? . . . that's just plain stupid.

I pull on my warm clothes, hobble over on the tip-up sole plates to join the snowplough driver and his mate by the car which had slipped off the road a yard or two down the slope. Danish, from the number plate; the driver, also Danish, from the passing resemblance he bears to an iced pastry, stands by with his hands in his pockets. I know he is the driver: he gets straight in without a word of thanks or apology the minute his motor is back on the road.

The three of us artisans clap on; I'm braced at a wheel arch. Monsieur Chasse-Neige chants: *Un, deux, trois*: we heave. *Un, deux, trois*: we heave. Inch by inch we swing the rear end into a position where a tow rope from the snowplough's winch can be attached; they hook on and safely up comes the motor, only after one violent twang, a broken line and a rehitch.

Monsieur Chasse-Neige makes no comment, simply coils up the rope and looks vacant, all in a day's work. No one else says anything. I hobble back to my bike, remount and head off for the first sign of hot drinks. The descent looks treacherous. As I tip over the flat of the col into the fall of the south side, a woman standing under a chandelier of icicles says: '*Chapeau bas.*' ('Hats off'.)

A surge of elation and wonderment flows through me. The Galibier. Wow.

A short way from the summit stands the monument *A la Gloire de Henri Desgrange, Créateur du Tour de France Cycliste*, a stumpy obelisk thrusting up out of the snow like a petrified tarboosh.

In Briançon we settle the price at the hotel with the woman owner and, pointing to the open garage adjacent to the building, ask if we might leave the bikes there, under cover. She quivers in protest. She flaps her hands and arms, eyes glaring, head shaking – charading *Non, non, NON!* We've overstepped our welcome; but no. She explains that she wouldn't dream of letting us expose the precious machines to villainy, for villainy there was all around, a wicked lawless contagion and endemic thieving, everything down to humble rivets going missing. Apparently, a team of club cyclists had stayed in the hotel the night before a race, parked their racing machines in the garage, come down for breakfast at 5.30 a.m. and found the cupboard bare, every bike nicked.

She insisted that we bring our bikes into the hotel and park them at the far end of the restaurant. We drip through and park the bikes against tables. She looks relieved; we feel awkward. I express our gratitude. We go off for hot water and clothes-drying.

★

The yellow bike with which Desgrange furnished the riders in the Tours of the 1930s was an all-steel affair – frame, wheels, handlebars; total weight around 12kg. (The French army's target of 10.5kg had to wait till the '50s, though they did deploy units of bicycle-mounted soldiers in WWI.) It carried two brakes, of the caliper variety, shoes clamping either side of the rim, which hasn't much changed since. The single 'bean' brake had been a rectangle of rubber fastened to a metal pad which a rod and lever simply pushed down onto the front tyre: inefficient and dangerous. The dropped handlebars were mostly of the ram's horn shape, though Nicolas Frantz favoured a distinctive curving top bar and a shallower drop, a sort of eyebrow in outline. Hooked over each tyre, affixed to the frame behind front stem and seat stays, was a flint-scraper, a simple half hoop of thick wire which rubbed the tyre and, with luck, dislodged inhering pointed stones before they got driven into the inner tube. Nicolas Frantz placed little trust in them, preferring to scan the road ahead of his tyres constantly and thus avoid the sharp stuff. It worked. He rarely punctured.

The back wheel sported up to three sizes of freewheel on either side. Gear changes were still effected by switching the wheel round, and butterfly nuts made that operation swifter. (A sensible rider carried spare wing nuts: easy to lose one in the fumbling to mend a puncture or change gearing in the darkness of night.)

Desgrange still held out against the *dérailleur*, but the influence of *dérailleur*-using cycle tourists on the refinement of the bicycle and its equipment was decisive. The Tour riders might have to conform to puritanical edicts against an easier ride; Joe Public did not and Joe Public was stimulating the quest for lighter metals with high resistance to stress, such as duralumin, an alloy developed at the instigation of a cycle club called the Parisian Mountaineers.

The single chainwheel usually varied in size – between 46 and 48 teeth; the freewheels round 16/18 for the flats and 22/25 for the climbs. (Benoît Faure, recalling the Leducq-Guerra pursuit, said that they rode 46 x 22 on the climbs then switched to 16. For a flat stage they'd ride on a 48 chainwheel. Riding such big gears almost always necessitated tackling the climbs *en danseuse*, the modern preference tends to be towards a fast-whirring smaller gear, such as Charly Gaul favoured, though specialist climbers like Virenque (retired) and Pantani (dead) always got out of the saddle as soon as the gradient steepened and swung into a remorseless hip-rolling rhythm which called the full body power into play.)

✷

'A bicycle is a work of art which you take up to the bedroom every night. Anybody who doesn't is not a real cyclist.' René Vietto.

I attempted to follow Vietto's advice in a small hotel by Lago di Como, *en route* home from the Dolomites: the proprietor thought I was joking. In Barcelona, asking where I might park my bike, the reception clerk simply assured me that the room was plenty capacious enough to accommodate me and my bike comfortably.

René Vietto was not preaching bike-fetishism or sentimental attachment. Care and scrutiny of the bike was a wise precaution against more than coincidental breakdown. During the Boule d'Or, a 24-hour track race in Paris, Hubert Opperman's chain broke and he lost several laps before he could get back into the race – which he won. His rivals had sawn partway through the chain to eliminate him. By the closing laps, and a long way in the lead, he was also on schedule for the 1,000km record. He wouldn't hear of it and climbed off. His pal Bruce Small shouted across: 'They'll never forget you in France if you do it. 'He rose to the task, rode on for another hour and 19 minutes, the crowd yelling 'Oppy! Oppy!' and took the record. He said he hardly felt that extra hour and a bit. A seemingly tireless long-distance cyclist, Opperman arrived with two fellow riders from Australia to ride in the 1928 Paris–Brussels race, 361km; he came third. They raced in the Tour that year, when every stage, except those in the mountains, was contested as a team time-trial. Given that the major teams put ten men into the race, Opperman's 18th position is astonishing. One rider who rode the 1931 Paris–Brest–Paris, 1,200km, said he'd ride into the checkpoint towns and ask if they'd seen Oppy. Yes. Where did he stop? He didn't. He died aged 91, pedalling his exercise bike.

Gustave Garrigou (first 1911, second 1909 and 1913, third 1910 and 1912) took his bike up to his bedroom every night. The commercial rivalry of the bike manufacturers was bitter and unprincipled. Garrigou won his early fame as the first man ever to cross the Tourmalet on a bike – 1910, the year of the great duel between Faber and Octave Lapize, a head to head which increased the daily sales of *L'Auto* massively. Halfway through the Tour he went to bed, took his bike with him but forgot to bolt the door. Shortly after the start of the next stage, 3 a.m., crossing the Lunel, near Montpellier, his front wheel began to buckle. Ballbearings spilled out over the road. The opposition had sawn through the ball-race. The repair cost him an hour and a half – he probably performed the celebrated trick of bashing the wheel rim into somewhere near round, then standing on it to make it true enough to go through the forks and rode on – he finished third. Garrigou formed part of the Alcyon team which dominated the Tour 1909– 12. Alcyon sales rocketed: everyone wanted to own the bike that had won the Tour. Another Alcyon man, Duboc, was leading the 1911 race, sauntered up the Tourmalet with insolent ease but, at the control in Argelès grabbed a *bidon* from a spectator. Ascending the Aubisque he drank the contents and almost immediately pitched off the bike with violent stomach cramps. Since he was in the lead the intention seemed blatant: to impede if not actually to poison him. He lost an hour and Garrigou assumed the lead. A rider of few words, minimal gesture and a studiously economical style of riding, he unexpectedly beat the more flamboyant Luxembourger, Faber (winner in 1909). Duboc recovered to win two stages and finish second overall, but after the race he returned to his carpenter's shop in Rouen and never mounted a bike again.

To conclude with the story of another drama played out on the Galibier.

It is 1966 and the riders are 70km into the stage from Bourg d'Oisans to Briançon, Tom Simpson of Britain in the rainbow jersey of the world road-race champion breaks clear; 10km on he's built a small lead and begins the climb of the Télégraphe with one and a half minutes' advance on the *peloton*. It's an ambitious move: 60km still to ride and the Giant of the Alps to cross. One minute and 20 seconds after him, the eventual mountains winner for the second year in succession, Julio Jimenez, riding for Anquetil's team, appears, clear of the bunch. By the time he was 5km up the 12km climb, the lead over Jimenez has fallen to 20 seconds; the chasing group of 20 men, including several Spanish riders as well as Anquetil and Poulidor, is at one minute and 30 seconds. Simpson's solo effort was all but over; the Spaniard catches him, sits on his wheel briefly and then sprints past. Now begins Simpson's long torment of trying to hang on, fighting against oxygen debt, sagging morale, sapped strength. He launched the break too early. He tries desperately to match Jimenez's pace; it's beyond him and Jimenez dumps him, rubbing the desolation in with every turn of the pedals. All Simpson can do is grit his teeth and wait to see who comes up in his slipstream next along the valley towards the monster at the head of it. The following group has split; Poulidor and Anquetil are on their own having dropped the other survivor, Huysmans. Anquetil has won five times; he's written off a sixth victory this year. He has one ambition only: to stall Poulidor's chances. Being a teammate of Jimenez, he could legitimately sit on Poulidor's wheel and let Poupou do all the work. He had too much pride to do that and on to the first steep ramps of the Galibier they ride side by side, reeling in Simpson. There he is; Anquetil out of the saddle, Poulidor, that awkward swaying leaning gait of his on the climbs, but firmly seated, go past the ailing Briton. It's always a melancholy moment for most riders, to drop another fine rider who will have to slog on alone on an empty tank.

But here comes the Belgian, Huysmans; Simpson takes his wheel for a short distance, the Galibier's one in seven gradient exacting a fearsome toll; he has paid a heavy price for going early and trying to outdistance a man of Jimenez' ability. Huysmans allowed Anquetil and Poulidor to go and has reserves of energy as a result. He'll reach the col in better shape and has the long swift descent to come. Simpson will be in a sorry state by then.

At the col, Jimenez has already taken the *prime* (£140) but Anquetil goes flat out for the second prize (£70) to show the Poulidor fans gathered at the summit that he is still the boss. Then the descent begins. Back down the road, Huysmans is two minutes and 30 seconds adrift, Simpson at four minutes and 30 seconds in company with a small group of chasers, including the man on his way to winning the Tour, Lucien Aimar.

Anquetil lets Poulidor go ahead – no fans here to boo him – and he can't risk helping Poulidor catch Jimenez. His own man, Aimar, is well placed to win a second time. Huysmans, a strong decender, is breathing down their necks and Aimar is taking all kinds of risks behind him, flinging himself and his bike into the hairpins at an outrageous speed. Simpson has taken a boost from the arrival of the others and is redressing his losses.

When they are 20km from the arrival in Briançon, Jimenez is in no danger; he leads Anquetil and Poulidor by two minutes and 30 seconds; Huysmans at three minutes; the group with Aimar three minutes 45 seconds. Suddenly, a motorcyclist carrying a TV cameraman skids on some loose gravel and brings Simpson down. Blood streaming on to his rainbow jersey, he remounts and rides into the finish in severe pain. Next day's stage begins with the second category climb of the Montgenèvre, 9km and 524m. Simpson's right arm is virtually useless and, 15km on, he abandons. The customary ritual of removing the numbers from bike and jersey – so reminiscent of the breaking of Dreyfus: badges of rank torn from his uniform – and another Tour is over for Simpson; another lucrative post-Tour circuit of one-day events vanished.

Why did he attack? He explained that he expected Anquetil to control the race behind him, that the climbers wouldn't bother to go until the last kilometres of the Galibier and that he'd made the fateful error of trying to stay with Jimenez and blew up.

CHAPTER FIVE

COL D'IZOARD

Coppi and the Modern Era

Briançon, *petite ville et grand renom* ('small town of great renown') held out for three months against a besieging Austrian army with a garrison of 300 in 1815. Vauban's fortifications, built after the sacking of the city by Sardinians in 1692, perch on a high prominence way above the new suburbs, an untidy conglomeration of faded grand mansions – some Italianate – and ghastly concrete modernity. The usual civic architecture on ugly, self-satisfied authoritarian scale: massive school, barracks of an Alpine regiment, administrative offices, hospital . . . it's not easy or rewarding to distinguish which is which as you stroll by.

We walk up the steep hill towards the old city in the shadow of the church of Notre Dame, another of Vauban's bastions; this one, cordoned with cypresses and dedicated to God rather than gun-powder, though carefully sited to double as a defensive salient if need be.

In a small bar, cosy, coffee-warm, redolent of black tobacco and anis, we talked ourselves back up the Galibier and down; and panegyrics of the bicycle. Angela sums it up:

'I feel really sorry for people who have never discovered the fun of a bike.'

★

Perhaps one doesn't associate Tour riders with the fun of a bike. The melancholy tale of the 1906 Tour winner, René Pottier – first home of a mere 14 survivors from the field of 75 – who, on 25 January 1907, after a broken love affair, hanged himself from the garage hook from which he suspended his bike. Not so much fun, more an obsession.

'*Le problème avec Eddy c'est qu'il a été vacciné avec un rayon de bicyclette. Une semaine sans courir et rien ne va plus.*' – Claudine Merckx, his wife. (The trouble with Eddy is that he's been vaccinated with a bicycle spoke. A week away from racing and nothing works.)

We have been vaccinated with a bicycle spoke, too, though we share more with the old *touriste-routiers* than with the champions like Merckx – save in the deep fascination with and love of the bike. Bidot summed up why Desgrange – an unapologetic admirer of the 'Aces' or 'first violins' as opposed to the mere trombones, the drudges created the freelance *touriste-routier* category:

'He particularly liked them because they stirred things up, turned the race into total disorder. He sent them off at different times which was a nightmare for us. If they rode in a bunch, they could block the entire road all day long.'

There was, too, the innate antagonism between team men, riding to tactical order, and the freelances, ready to go for any prize on offer, not giving a pint of stale air for anyone else. There was big money to be won and the independents chased after it, mindful of no team responsibility, no larger tactical scheme which, so often, can throttle brisker competition in every Tour.

The earning life of a racing cyclist is, generally, short. Anquetil, who put all his money into property and land, also pointed out that as freelances, the riders made their money 'under the constant surveillance of the tax inspector. Lucky amateurs, not to have that.'

Taxmen see sportsmen as fair game: bungs and backhanders are as old as sport itself, especially among the ancient Greek chariot-racers. Olympian–Corinthian amateur idealism is a modern invention. In 1951, Hugo Koblet, the pomaded *pédaleur de charme*, was arguing about tax returns with the Swiss revenue men. They demanded more tax; he ducked and dived. One day the inspector returned to Koblet's house with photographs of two famous Swiss bike riders of an older vintage, now dead, and asked if he recognised them.

'Of course.'

'And you know very well they won a lot of races, as you have. And they wound up destitute, dependent on public funds to live. They owed the daily bread of their old age to public charity. So, since you're going to end up the same way, don't bitch about paying taxes – you're contributing to the fund you'll have to draw on one day.' Bleak prospect.

Poulidor, who perhaps epitomises the fairly uncommon combination of the race-hardened pro who still loves riding the bike (most of them do), retired a wealthy man. How much would he sacrifice to have won the Tour, to have worn the yellow jersey? He won almost everything else: burst on to the scene in the 1961 Milan–San Remo (the 'spring' race) and beat Anquetil's lieutenant, Stablinski, to become Champion of France later that year; but the self-doubt set in.

He was giving Anquetil enormous trouble in the 1964 Tour but, on the stage into Toulouse lost time after a stupid fall. Next day he mustered a near-decisive punch over the Pyrenean cols and won, on his own, at Luchon. Interest in the Tour revived but he lost, just as he missed out in that year's Worlds at Sallanches – the bronze when he was ideally placed for the gold. He often beat Anquetil and was far more popular with the public – he still is. But, his destiny was, it seems, less for his own success than to force even sterner efforts out of his formidable rival. Anquetil admitted it: 'There were times when he crushed me, this Poulidor.' But this was the man who swore fealty to the old cliché that winning isn't the most important thing it's the *only* thing. Poulidor never could evince that merciless attitude to racing, what amounts to a bloodlust. Yet the love affair with the bike survived. Robert Millar now loves the motorbike the same way he loved the bike in the beginning, before it became a machine he earned his living on. In retirement, Poulidor still went for bike rides. The days of 250km races were over; now he could ride 60km without any thought of performance and declare that he'd keep going till he was 65, then he'd see.

★

And tomorrow the Izoard. I've seen pictures of it. The famous, the clichéd 'lunar' landscape of the Casse Déserte: huge rock stooks amid boulder rubble, like windworn columns of a collapsed arcade. The camera surveys the desolation of scree, the tiny road cleared by dwarvish pickaxes and a lone rider ascending, bike and man, wayfarer braving the ambush of sun, thirst, exhaustion, puncture, even the circling buzzard. The archetypal rock and hard place in one. Arid. Totally exposed. Fearsome heat in summer, reflecting off the bleached stone. A meteorite artillery range. A foundry for Titans' stone slingshot. This is the Tour mountain terrain *par excellence*, the traditional *High Noon* battleground of the Alpine stages.

✶

On the Izoard, Sylvère Maes delivered his *coup de grâce* to beat Vietto in 1939. He'd nearly lost the yellow jersey in the Pyrenees – a teammate launched a withering attack and Maes chased with Vietto glued to his wheel. In the Casse Déserte, Thévenet sealed his victory over Merckx in 1975. Here, in 1972, Merckx had left the rest toiling behind him to take his fourth victory, the 60th edition of the Tour. He capped that by taking the hour record. Across this wilderness Coppi and Bobet in their time launched what the French call the solo exploit. It's the heroism at the core of this race. Later, Bobet told Thévenet that the real mark of a champion was to cross the Izoard in yellow, alone. Thévenet duly obliged in 1975.

Ill-named Fausto (Italian for 'Lucky') Coppi died aged only 40; cursed with fragile bones, he missed years through injury and the War. Born in 1919, he turned professional in 1937 and, aged 20, won his first Giro in 1940. Drafted into the Italian army, his unit was captured by the British 8th Army in Tunisia and he spent two years as a PoW.

Coppi ushered in the modern era: the first complete bike rider, inspiration of Bobet's early career, Anquetil's ambition, Merckx's childhood. Won the Tour de France twice, five Giro d'Italia, five Tour of Lombardy, Paris–Roubaix, Milan–San Remo, world hour record, world pursuit champion twice. First man to use a double clanger (two chainwheels) . . . even Desgrange's actuarial supervision did not extend beyond the grave. But he had known, as Coppi knew: winning depended on the intelligence as well as the physique and an event as brutal and demanding as the Tour de France took more than exceptional talent and the strength of a packhorse. Coppi said: 'The mistake made by young cyclists is that they are over-eager, too impatient to be world champions. They must look after themselves physically, they must learn the fibres of muscles and body, they must learn tactics, they must live, eat and dream road-race.'

Put another way: it's no earthly good being capable of winning unless you know how to. Winning, succeeding as a professional in whatever sphere, it amounts to the same. To be the best, you compete not with the opposition but against yourself. They don't call the time-trial the 'race of truth' for nothing.

The journalist Pierre Chany called Coppi 'the heron': 5'10", ten and a half stones, long spindly legs, hunched, scrawny shoulders, disproportionately small torso, handsome aquiline features with long beak of a nose and high cheekbones, he seemed an ungainly man off the bike, yet:

> Dans un ensemble paradoxalement harmonieux, ce héron . . . haut perché sur une selle invisible . . . ne connaissait pas la hantise du poids morts et des muscles inutiles que certains hissent tels des mulets jusqu'à la cîme des montagnes.

> (His overall physique was, paradoxically, harmonious . . . this heron perched high on an invisible saddle knew nothing of the shame of dead weight and non-functioning muscles which certain riders, like mules, drag to the mountain tops.)

Heron is an apt image: observe the ungainly bird stalking its prey at the edge of the water, stiff and awkward in its movements, then lumber into flight and once aloft float effortlessly on the breezes, its thin legs atrail the powerful wings.

Gino 'the Pious' Bartali was already established – winner of the 1938 Tour – when Coppi arrived on the scene in 1939, but the ignition of the great rivalry came in 1946, Milan–San Remo, when Coppi went clear for 147km, and led the second man Tessière by 15 minutes while Bartali and Ricci slugged it out for third place along the Via Roma ten minutes after him. When Bartali found out who'd won, he knew he had a fight on his hands.

The Coppi v. Bartali duel animated cycling, particularly in their native Italy, during the late '40s and early '50s. Coppi, the radical thinker who revolutionised methods of training and racing, versus the Tuscan Bartali of peasant stock; atheist ranged against devout Catholic. Culzio Malaperte said of them: 'Bartali is for the orthodox, his talent is spiritual, the saints look after him; Coppi has no protection up there. Bartali has blood in his veins, Coppi has petrol.' Bartali had such a slow heart rate that his doctor insisted he smoke three cigarettes per day: one in the morning, one after a race, the third in the evening before bed. If he won a race he smoked a fourth to celebrate. Coppi's attention to diet was fastidious, and he fortified his strict régime with vitamins. It was no secret; though Bartali occasionally searched his hotel room for secret potions, the wonder dope that the lanky wonder from Piedmont must be taking. On one occasion, the story goes, he retraced the route of a race to hunt for a bottle he'd seen Coppi discard. He found it and had the traces examined: it was bicarbonate of soda in water.

In 1948, at 34 years of age, Bartali took his second Tour; a ten year gap which remains a record. He slumped early on – 21 minutes down on the newcomer Bobet – and was written off. But he surged back in the Pyrenees – a stupendous victory into Lourdes, which must have pleased his Catholic heart and confirmed divine blessing – by the time they reached the Alps he really had sprouted wings and took three stages in succession, one of them over the Izoard . . .. through hail and snow on the Croix de Fer and Glandon (touché) and pelting rain over the Chartreuse massif. An emphatic demonstration of his class. He took the mountains prize and won overall by a massive 26 minutes and 16 seconds.

In 1949, spindleshanks Coppi trounced Bartali in the Giro, came to the Tour – a year before he'd planned to ride it – and left his indelible mark on it: yellow jersey, mountains prize and

Bartali beaten into second place by ten minutes 55 seconds. Coppi bided his time while the tiny Parisian rider Jacques 'the Parakeet' Marinelli held the yellow jersey for the first 17 days – surviving a bad fall on stage five – and then struck.

He didn't so much climb the mountains, they wrote, as levitate: cols de Vars, Izoard, Galibier where he rode past the newly installed monument to Desgrange, wearing the first yellow jersey to be embroidered with the initials HD. One day, when the race crossed the massive Alpine cols, Coppi dropped Bartali at the foot of the Izoard and won the stage alone by over 20 minutes; an awesome show of power. Contributing an article on his reflections on the world and sundry matters he entitled the piece 'We all have two legs.' It was something of an understatement.

He missed the 1950 Tour having broken his pelvis in the Giro; in 1951, his morale badly shaken by the recent death of his brother from a heavy fall after the Tour of Piemont, he lost 33 minutes on the stage into Montpellier under the furnace heat of the Languedoc. He must have felt as if he were cycling through a still photograph. But he came back and so dominated the 1952 Tour that no one could live with him – in the mountains he simply vanished into the distance. In Paris he led by 28 minutes 17 seconds. Every day he made detailed notes about the course of the stage and the gear developments of the Italian team:

> Bagnères–Pau km 148
> Coppi 45–50 14 16 20 23 24
> Bartali 46–50
> Abagni 46–50 etc
> col du Tourmalet 1st category
> col d'Aubisque etc
> Limoges–Clermont-Ferrand km 246
> Coppi 45–50 14 17 20 22 25
> Bartali 46–50 etc
> Puy de Dôme 1st etc

In 1960 the cycling world mourned his premature death. The power of his inspiration and his influence on professional racing methods were incalculable.

Louison Bobet, who idolised him, won three Tours in succession 1953–55, the first man to do so. He did ride against Coppi, in the 1951 Giro. Penalised five minutes for changing a wheel, the Frenchman wanted to abandon. His *directeur sportif* dissuaded him but, at dinner, Bobet was still brooding. Then, his inner turmoil wonderfully cleared, he said, in level tones: 'I'm not only going to start tomorrow but I shall wear my French champion's jersey and take them on. It may finish me but I'll show them I'm a Bobet.'

He rode over the mountains in imperious fashion, Coppi on his wheel, the rest of the bunch weaving up the slopes behind in disorder. Bobet finally rode Coppi off his wheel in the sprint, and eventually finished 7th overall.

★

1953. The Izoard stage.

From the small village of Arvieux on the southern approaches to the summit of the col via the Casse Déserte is 10km along a road which was still a rustic track, corrugated with ruts, scattered with flints and loose stones, swathed in plumes of dust. Since the crossing of the col de Vars, Bobet had found la bonne carburation (writes Bidot, then manager of the French team): his engine working well, fire in his spirit, legs going like pistons, perfect efficiency, balance and rhythm.

> Not far from the col itself, on the left side of the road, I saw, amongst the spectators, Fausto Coppi, in shorts, a camera slung across his chest. As Louison [Bobet] went past, in the lead, Coppi gave him a friendly wave and said to me: 'He looks good.'
>
> The Italian champion clicked his stopwatch. Eight minutes later, he clicked it again when Bartali rode by. Coppi, on the look out on the slopes of the Izoard . . . it was a bit like the artist contemplating his work.

(This was Bartali's last Tour, ending a career that spanned an exceptional 26 years.)

That same year, Jacques Anquetil, aged 19, rode his first season as a professional cyclist. After the Tour he won the prestigious Grand Prix des Nations – the only classic-rated individual time-trial – and immediately added the Grand Prix de Lugano. On 30 October he arrived at Coppi's villa in Novi Ligure, unannounced, hoping 'to see face to face the only man still ahead of him, the one man he dreamed of dethroning'.

Coppi had been out training; his *soigneur*, Cavanna, was massaging him. The message came through – a young man wanted to see the maestro. Anquetil was called in; Coppi asked him why he'd come, quizzed him – ambitions? training methods? diet? And so on. But what was all this about? To Coppi, another young admirer, self-possessed and evidently showing huge promise; but . . . a long way to go. And for Anquetil? Entering the presence. Measuring himself against his hero. Even the most prodigiously talented do not spring fully-formed out of callow ambition; rivalry, emulation, is the stuff of our first striving, till we learn to improve ourself, not our own necessarily inadequate version of someone else.

> Coppi stayed silent a long time and for that moment, those minutes when I had only the sense of a strange complicity between us, I would have gone round the earth. (Jacques Anquetil, *Je suis comme ça.*)

In fact, Anquetil accompanied Coppi on his last ride – an appearance race in Ouagadougou in the French West African territory of Upper Volta, now Burkino Faso, on 13 December 1959 – along with other stars: Geminiani, Rivière. It was there that Coppi caught the malaria that killed him but 20 days later.

Anquetil was known for an ice-cool temperament. Nothing unnerved or unsettled him. His focus was as concentrated as a laser. Bobet was altogether different. He could be as jumpy as a cat, as temperamental as a racehorse. A grease mark on his front tyre which he couldn't take his eyes off . . . the wrapping of his spare tyre in a colour he found disagreeable . . . such irritations could ruffle his nerves and send him into a decline, drain him of fight for the day's racing . . . a badly written letter could stop him sleeping. (Ah, insomnia: I'm suffering from a touch of the Bobet's . . . if only.) On one occasion, he despatched a *domestique* into a café to get some mineral water. *Domestiques* (second-string support riders) are often called 'water-carriers' and in the days before the team cars supplied everything – taking no risk of spiked bottles – they would often hustle drinks wherever they could, without payment if possible. However, this *patron* insisted on cash. The *domestique* pleaded: it was for his boss. The *patron* wouldn't budge; certainly he was a sports fan but he was running a café not a cyclist's charity.

'But it's for Monsieur Louison!'

'So Monsieur Louison pays.'

(He may have been an anti-Bobetiste. France was split into rival camps: Bobetiste and anti-Bobetiste.)

The *gregario* argued but to no avail; he stumped up for the bottle, rushed out, leapt back on his bike. The *peloton* was by this time eight minutes ahead: a lot of chasing. Still, he was no mean *coureur* and in 13 minutes of hard riding he caught the bunch. Very proud of his solo chase, he rolled up alongside Bobet and handed him the bottle – thoughtfully unstoppered so the great man could drink it straight off. Bobet glanced at the bottle, grimaced in disgust and spat: 'You know very well I don't like that brand of water.'

A lot of riders try to make do with the bare minimum of water intake, imitating, presumably, the camel. Besides, cold water tipped into an overheated stomach can cause severe cramps. It is recorded of Pierre Brambilla (who tracked Robic over the Izoard in 1947 and came third to him in Paris) that he was powerfully resistant to thirst, although he fought some chronic battles with the demon *Soif* . . . verbal duels with his own faltering will. His dessicated body weakening, he'd cry out in a parched voice like St Antony in the desert, wrestling with temptation: *Tu vas avancer, vieille carcasse. Ah, tu ne veux pas. Eh bien, tu ne boiras pas.* 'Get going, you bag of bones. You don't want to? All right, no drink for you.'

One day in the Canicule, the torrid Dog Days of July, dry as a water biscuit, Brambilla cracked. Spotting a roadside fountain, he drank his fill in great gulps, then topped up his water bottles and remounted. He abandoned 10km further on. He never raced again and, to avoid any temptation to revoke the decision, he buried his bike in his garden. He did come back, though. When Jock Wadley rode the bi-annual Brevet des Randonneurs des Alpes time-trial in 1973 (from Grenoble over the Glandon, Croix de Fer, Télégraphe, Galibier and back to Grenoble, 245km and 4,500m of climbing) Brambilla was also entered. They were old buddies from Wadley's Tour reporting and met in Grenoble the day before the start. The race began at 2 a.m.; Brambilla caught Wadley on the approach to the Galibier. Wadley thought the Italian veteran (now 53 years old) would have been miles ahead, but he'd overslept and set out an hour late. He offered to give Wadley a tow up the Galibier; Wadley declined and Brambilla sped off. Wadley remembered the buried bicycle story and called out, but too late . . . the chance to confirm or scotch missed.

Jacques Anquetil once said: 'Driest is fastest,' and, like T.E. Lawrence, trained himself to survive on small intakes of water. He was frequently beaten on open stages; in five Tour victories he won only 15 stages. His abiding principle was to conserve every scrap of energy until he needed to make an emphatic push. The pictures of him out of the saddle show eyes glinting, body arched with effort, as if all the hounds of hell are chasing him. But he was a supreme strategist. Had victory in the Tour been more dependant on climbing than his speciality, the individual time-trial, experts agree that Anquetil would have made himself a climber.

He wasn't above professional cunning, either. Two seconds down on a Bahamontes in roaring form in the mountains during the '63 Tour, Anquetil's team manager, Geminiani, told him to ride one stage on a lighter bike than usual with lower gears. The race crossed the col de la Forclaz that day, close to the finish in Chamonix – a perfect launch pad for the Eagle of Toledo's *coup de maître*. However, since the descent was narrow and steep, Anquetil would have to change back to the heavier, more rigid bike for safety.

'But changing bikes is forbidden.'

'Leave that to me,' said Gem.

They rode to the foot of the Forclaz into rain and a headwind. Poulidor, who didn't know the climb, launched another furious attack but he blew and was soon zigzagging over the road. Anquetil stuck to Bahamontes, who varied his rhythm constantly to disrupt the Frenchman: dancing on the pedals, a cruel surge of speed, back in the saddle for a steady drive . . . he was giving Anquetil a real pasting.

At the summit, Anquetil glanced at Gem in the team car. Prearranged: he stopped riding, got off the bike and called out: 'My *dérailleur*'s gone.'

Out leapt the team mechanic with the replacement bike, Gem signalled to the commissaire to verify the mechanical failure. Meantime, Anquetil was off down the mountain in pursuit. The commissaire checked the bike: the cable was indeed broken . . . snipped through, actually, by the mechanic. The trick was obvious but there was no proof. The following year a new rule came in: bike changes were permissible.

Anquetil had weaknesses, all riders do, but he never gave in. A day lost was never the campaign lost. His constant rival Poulidor, the gadfly who never metamorphosed into the stinging *maillot jaune* bee, famously beat him in a *coude à coude* duel up the Puy de Dôme on 13 July 1964. (A blunt tooth of volcanic rock, 1,465m high, 5km of 1 in 14 gradient, a level stretch and the last 5km of one in eight; the road ends at the top.)

'Elbow to elbow' it was too. The pugnacity, the hostility starkly evident in the photograph. Locked in a bitter contest, shoulders bumping as if each was trying to knock the other sprawling, bikes flung sideways, front wheels all but touching at the base and tipped sideways in a vee, like two haunches of a log split by an axe. Both of them in the saddle, at the limit, Anquetil in yellow, his cheeks sucked in, gasping for air, Poulidor holding the brakehoods as if they were the traces of Pluto's chariot, a flotilla of motorbikes and cars in attendance.

'France holds its breath,' said the radio commentator.

Anquetil yielded first, and at that level a jingle of the chain on a less than smooth gear change can turn the affair – momentary lapse of concentration, your opponent pounces, a gap opens, precious advantage. Poulidor went clear and won by 42 seconds. Anquetil held his overall lead by a slim 14 seconds – 'Thirteen more than I need,' he said. He'd already won four Tours; no one had ever won five. Next day, Bastille Day, final stage into Paris:

the time-trial. The *maillot jaune* always sets off last.

Anquetil, crouched over the bike, the best possible position for streamlining, total absorption in the task: the beating of Poulidor and finish the job . . . dispatch the victim. A bird of prey, they called him. Worth remembering that the raptors eat their prey alive, tear them to bits still breathing; there's no merciful stunning and oblivion before the talons go in. Anquetil, riding the race he excelled in and relished because it released his killer instinct, that capacity to drive himself way beyond ordinary limits, a combination of impregnable self-belief and indifference to physical distress heightened by the fact that it was Poupou just ahead of him. Anquetil tore 41 more seconds out of Poulidor – at that level a cruel margin, especially given Poulidor's undeniable class, except that his effort seemed hampered by that crucial inability to exceed his natural limits. A failure, if failure it was, in imagination.

He did beat Anquetil in the individual time-trial in 1966; but Anquetil turned a deaf ear, as they say, to defeat. He set up his young lieutenant, Lucien Aimar, for victory in Paris. Everything – anything – to beat Poulidor.

In one one-day classic, the English rider Brian Robinson, teammate of Anquetil's, rode up alongside Jacques and told his boss: '[Tommy] Simpson is looking good today. I know him. All you need to do is follow him and you'll have nothing to worry about.'

Anquetil replied: 'Forget Simpson: keep your eyes on Poulidor.'

It is my belief that Anquetil, knowing full well that Poulidor possessed a killer punch, despised him, as a rider at least, for lacking the moral capacity, the chilly-hearted ruthlessness, to deliver it at will. Despising him as a rival, he revealed just how much he feared him; perhaps the only rider he truly feared because defeat cost him so dear, and at the hands of Poulidor it was insupportable.

★

We roll out at about 9.30 a.m. and do a mini sightseeing tour of the suburbs in quest of the route to the col. The air is damp and chilly, as in a coalhouse. I am, this dank morning, about as yeasty as a matzo, musing Izoard . . . Izoard . . . eez so ard . . . bloody hell, and feeling hopelessly of another race entirely from the various aerial wizards who've soared up this one.

The Breton Jean-Marie Goasmat, '*Farfadet*', 'Goblin', in his element here . . . Charly Gaul the Angel cruising up the slopes, whistling happily like a thrush . . . Federico Bahamontes the Eagle of Toledo dancing on his pedals as if they were springs . . . Coppi the heron . . . Van Impe the canary.

★

I saw Van Impe once, at the Worlds in Belgium, 1975. The race went to Hennie Kuiper who broke from the pack two or three laps from the end and profited from the hesitations of the big men who'd rather let a small rival win than risk towing one of the *peloton* grandees to the line for an easy sprint. As we straggled across the dusty road after the race, Van Impe and Merckx rode by, Van Impe impassive, Merckx a wry expression on his face – *not our day*. Their faces brown with filthy spindrift off the circuit, tired, off for a bath, work done. Next year Merckx missed the Tour, but Van Impe came determined to swap the polka dots he'd won three times ('71, '72, '75) for the yellow. It was a big leap of imagination for the diminutive Belgian climber but Guimard, his manager, was convinced he could do it and had persuaded him to up his ambitions. (See my *Inside the Peloton*.) So was Mme Van Impe. According to Geoffrey Nicholson in his book *The Great Bike Race*, when Van Impe's teammate Tierlinck beat him to become Belgian champion in 1976, Mme Van Impe said: 'Lucien, I'm not having that: you'll have to win the Tour.' He took the yellow jersey from Maertens on l'Alpe d'Huez, lost it to the 33-year-old Delisle in the Pyrenees three days later and set out from St Gaudens two minutes 41 seconds in arrears and leading the mountains prize by a whisker.

It was 139km to Saint Lary-Soulan over two second-category climbs and two first. Over the col de Menté, Van Impe took the *prime*, but in the valley towards Bosost across the Spanish border a break went clear, none of the riders in contention for anything beyond a stage win; Ocaña chases for the honour of Spain and takes four men with him, including Maertens the sprinter who has swapped the yellow for the green of the points leader. At Bosost, the escape of 16 men leads the *peloton* by two minutes and 40 seconds. Van Impe has been acting up, pretending he's going badly and wanting more support from his team. He's got the idea that it would be best to wait for the last climb of the day, up Pla d'Adet to the finish. Zoetemelk and Poulidor, riding for the Gan-Mercier team, spotted his indecision and decided they could hot things up. One of Van Impe's teammates got wind of this and told Van Impe to be on the alert. Van Impe wanted his rivals to burn themselves up with some aggressive riding: all he would have to do was sit in and pick up a tally of seconds, even a minute, at the end when he was still fresh. Guimard had other plans. He wanted a grand gesture, minutes in the bag not paltry scrapings from what other riders left him. He sent a message via one of the *domestiques,* telling Van Impe to have a crack now. Van Impe wasn't impressed; if Guimard wanted him to attack he could deliver his own messages. Ocaña flew off ahead; Van Impe paid no heed. Guimard raced up the *peloton* in the team car, klaxon blaring, alongside Van Impe and told him to go. Go now, you win the Tour, and if not *not.*

Out of Bosost, on to the col du Portillon, a long wind up through pine woods to the French border along the ridge, Van Impe attacked. He might have been reluctant to accept the command but there is no questioning his will to make the effort succeed, and this was his terrain, after all. Up ahead, Ocaña topped the climb with Van Impe four minutes and 20 seconds down and the *peloton* – Poulidor and Zoetemelk for the GAN team, Delisle and his team leader Thévenet among them – at five minutes 50 seconds. The Portillon drops down the helter-skelter into Bagnères de Luchon, a beautiful old spa town, the thermal baths still in working order, a low-roofed, arcaded building in a leafy square of gracious tree-lined walks. The col de Peyresourde leads straight out on the west side, climbing from 630m to 1,569m in 14km.

At the col, Van Impe had caught Ocaña and Riccomi and the trio led the race; the escape group had fragmented, riders scattered down the slopes behind them; the first, Talbourdet and Menendez at 55 seconds.

Zoetemelk, meanwhile, having been told by his manager to

attack near Bosost, refused; a defining moment. On the Peyre-sourde he mastered his caution and, finally, got moving. He was a rider of undoubted talent but never a great shaker of events, what the French call a man who never catches the sun because he's riding in other men's shadows. He produced a bold ride up the col and crossed two minutes and 25 seconds down on Ocaña and Van Impe, but the day was lost. Van Impe made the attack he planned all along and streaked into Pla d'Adet on his own. The seconds, the minutes ticked by, Delisle's lead evaporated, Van Impe pulled on yellow and, three minutes and 12 seconds after he did, Zoetemelk appeared. He had lost this Tour. His victory came in 1980, at his tenth attempt, aged 33. French commentators were disparaging. *Le Blaireau* wasn't riding; Zoetemelk's win was no more than a bit of insulation between the solid walls of Hinault's supremacy.

Over the following 46 minutes and 23 seconds, the rest of the field limped in: Poulidor in fifth overall now and by over 11 minutes, Thévenet at 13 minutes 15 seconds, but his strength was waning – he was ill with a liver infection – and he abandoned five days later after a disastrous time-trial. He had been riding on his strength alone for some time and there was not much left.

Van Impe held his lead and took the yellow jersey home to Mme Van Impe in Belgium. It was Poulidor's last Tour. Aged 40 he came third, once more the best-placed Frenchman. He'd come back from 19th in the '75 edition, his worst-ever placing.

At the conclusion of this Tour, Poulidor had a road named after him in Sauviat-sur-Vige, near his birthplace, where M. Marquet who owned the local bike shop gave the poor farmboy his first racing bicycle to replace his mother's old sit-up-and-beg which he'd been making do with, and ferried him to his first races in his car. He always acknowledged the genius of Anquetil but the telling factor between them was perhaps that Anquetil could support any suffering on a bike to stay number one. Anquetil said: 'Together we could have produced some incredible results but it wasn't possible: our interests were opposed and the public wouldn't have understood.' A plan to unite them in the Gan-Mercier team for Anquetil's last season, 1969, fell through. Anquetil became a television commentator. One day, his five-year-old daughter asked to go to a race with him so that she could meet her favourite rider.

'Which?' said Jacques. 'Poulidor, of course. He's the best.'

The year following Anquetil's last Tour, 1967, the Norman said to Poulidor: 'You know, Raymond, it would give me pleasure to see you win the Tour. To make sure of it, you mustn't let them take more than four minutes in the Pyrenees.' Sadly, the early fall in Alsace meant that by the time the Tour arrived in the Pyrenees, Poulidor's race was devoted to Roger Pingeon. But Poulidor had lost his old verve; resigned to yet another defeat for himself and, worn down by his stupendous riding in the Alps, he seemed incapable of any more and hesitant to boot. Pingeon left him to it; on the descent from Portet d'Aspet, Poulidor crashed into a police motorbike and fell badly. He rode out the stage but he was too badly injured, his nose was broken, and he retired declaring that without him the Tour would go on.

Something of an eccentric, Pingeon. He rarely declined an interview but insisted on being in the bath when he gave it, so as not to waste time, and occluded every single source of daylight in his hotel room and slept in a blindfold to ensure that no daylight disturbed his sleep. He reckoned that an extra half an hour each night gave him three night's extra sleep over the duration of the Tour. In the 1974 Tour he was leading the pack together with Ronald de Witte. Nearing Dieppe, de Witte decided the break was doomed and sat up. Pingeon flipped, got off his bike, kicked it and walked out of the Tour. (That year saw the Tour come to Britain for the first time – a stage near Plymouth sponsored by local asparagus growers.)

Thévenet came back for the '77 Tour in much better shape, drove himself into the ground to limit stage winner Hennie Kuiper's gains up l'Alpe d'Huez and got a tremendous ovation at the finish. He went on to his second victory, by 48 seconds, over Kuiper. He said that two moments stood out in his career: that welcome on l'Alpe d'Huez and finishing at the summit of the Izoard on his own, in the yellow jersey, especially the last 3km when he was riding through a dense crowd of spectators.

★

I am already pulling ahead up the first slopes of the long haul to the

Izoard when John pulls up alongside. I am ready to say 'Listen, you know very well I simply can't hack that brand of mineral water,' when he says: 'Nearest place for a drink?'

I say 'Fine' and he drops back to rejoin Angela, her aching knee strapped up with a woollen scarf. I turn, wave, and push on, wheezing as if my lungs were stuffed full of Copydex glue.

It continues to be damp, threatening rain. This southern approach imposes some 22km climbing from 1,321m to 2,360m. Ostensibly, a steady climb, but we know better now. The Glandon factor. Northward along the ridges, along which the grey clouds roll like vapourised cannonballs, looms the Sommet des Anges, among them Charly Gaul, no doubt. There is a Musée de Vélo at the summit. Postcards.

About halfway, the hamlet of Cervières with its fifteenth-century church dedicated to St Michel all that survived the destruction of the old village in 1944. The Germans moved several divisions into the Dauphiné to stamp out resistance, a ruthless campaign prosecuted until just before the end of the war. Centuries before Hitler's Germans came, their ancestors, the Teutons, were slaughtered by the world's first professional army: the Roman legions led by Marius. *Plus ça change* . . . Napoleon . . .

At Cervières, the road doubles back on itself, a real French pleat. And the rain starts, borne on a flukey wind. Only one hard spat of gradient so far; the worst to come, doubtless. Into an open stretch of country, the forest barricades pushed back across empty grassland. Headwind; 200m bent over the front stem and I am into the tree cover again. Two more steep sections which I take in my stride. Le Laus, a handful of houses about 16km away; well over halfway on the map. From the road I'd hardly guess it. The kilometre stones pass in ultra-slow motion in my imaginary record of the long grind to the top; the film where nothing much happens. Me thinking: oh for an hour to ride like Merckx, even 20 minutes, just to feel what it's like. But, I know from my imagination: the same effort, the same grisly sick feeling; the only difference, I'd be moving a whole lot faster.

It's not only talent, either, but mileage. The year he won the Worlds, Freddy Maertens habitually cycled up to a hundred miles to a day race, then raced – 96km or so, and not infrequently rode part of the way back. At the time, an insular rump of the English professionals was grumbling that they stood no chance in the Worlds because they didn't get enough racing mileage.

I think of my younger self; that day we cycled through the Ardennes (I was 14) over what the masters told us was the highest climb in the chain. I had an old Coventry Eagle, passed on to me by a distant relation who hadn't ridden it for years. He told me it was the lightest bike you could buy. It was not, however, the lightest bike you could palm off on a gullible kid, short of a loaded butcher's bike. It took me some years to grow into it, and by the time I could ride it, the Coventry Eagle was an extinct species. Most of the others in the party owned sleek machines from a new generation; one in particular, Perkins, two years older than the rest of us, was a pretty sharp Club cyclist, handbuilt frame, alloy everything; lugs.

I found myself in the lead on the big climb and reached the top, none of the others in sight. I sat down contentedly under a tree to wait. Twenty minutes later, the first of the following group hove into view – the two masters with them – on foot. The dribs and drabs straggled in. When Perkins found out I'd ridden the whole climb, he was furious. He unstrapped his saddle bag and, while the others flopped on the grass in a boiled pink state of sweat and despondency, cycled back halfway down the climb and rode up it without dismounting.

The closest I ever got, I think, to where the dream is stitched into reality.

The rain becomes snow. The climb gets harder. I've got to get this mountain out of my head. *Rien n'est extrême qui a son pareil,* as Montaigne put it, in the era AV, *Avant Vélo* . . . 'Nothing is extreme which has its equal.' It is finally a matter of perspective out of experience; and patience. If I push myself too far, I'll be the first to know.

A sign nailed to a post: Réfuge de Napoléon; one of the Alpine hostels set up by the emperor Napoléon III and confirmed in state ownership by decree in the 1860s. I know it to be just below the col. Another bend, and another bend and there's the building set back from the road. Hard to say whether it's open or not. The road swings by it and up, nothing visible but banks of squalid salt-white mountain emitting dry ice. I set my teeth and forge on. I want this whole climb in one.

Another kilometre, another stone and still no col. The gradient nearly defeats me, steep as a ladder it feels. I stay in the saddle, saving the last resort till I have no choice. My eyes ache with the strain; but at last I make it to the midget plateau which is the summit of the Izoard.

Half a blizzard, sky merging with mountain in a spectrum of frost. The Museum, a square shack has windows boarded up, probably shut since the end of summer. Opposite stands a large stone obelisk, a monument to a Tour which hardly needs one, but here is as good a place as any.

We meet up in the Refuge, crowded with walkers in a fug of damp clothing, heat and cooking, and an hour after omelettes, apple pie, hot chocolate and coffee are on our way down to the Casse Déserte. If there are ghosts anywhere on the Tour de France's tangled ley lines, they certainly hold their sabbaths in the Casse Déserte, lit by red Jack o'Lanterns. (The red lamp, *lanterne rouge*, is fixed to the seat pillar of the last rider in the race.) It's an eerie sight, an apparition to set the nape hairs tingling, as the prospective opens out below the falling road. Across birdless chasms, a massive rampart of rock leaning like a seawall, its slopes thick with scree. Midway down it, the road is scored across like a white Schläger scar. Below the road tower the weird rock stacks, a petrified dental template – gaunt worn molars moored in crumbling gums. On these gigantic stalagmites you imagine eagles perch or vultures or the phantoms of Desgrange's commissaires, keeping watch for the dying things crawling away from the merciless sun's glare . . . the puncture victims making illicit use of the clasp knife . . . the standing stones of the Casse Déserte make an awesome sight. The panorama that suddenly opens out as you round the bend on the descent quite moved and bewitched me.

It is hostile; there is danger in it; the immanent menace of a mountain waiting to unleash its worst temper. A dragon asleep, they'd have said once. It exemplifies the unique challenge of the mountains to the riders who compete in this great race. (Women, too: the Tour de France Féminin was inaugurated in 1984.) No matter what physical preparation they undertake, the awesome scale

of the high cols interposes a huge psychological barrier for which
no preparation is of any use, other than the experience itself. Riding
up these ascents cannot be contained by statistics. Boardman,
under the direction of his technical advisor, tried it: training on the
treadmill, an hour of one in eight on a calculated gear development
and at so many revolutions per minute. Better than nothing, but the
mountains have a way of dealing with that. They instil an elemental
fear, in torrid heat or biting cold and the Izoard, weird and remote,
embodies that fear totally.

Even as we cycle down through that bizarre rockscape in freezing
vapours, I sense that the Alp was shifting into its murky winter
cruelties of which the precocious snow and mist we had ridden
through were no more than a flurry. I say precocious though in the
1995 Tour, the stage over the Galibier had to be shortened because
the col was snowed in, impassable, in July.

At the side of the road, not far from where Coppi watched Bobet
ride past, stands a tiny belvedere and a monument to both of them.
We stop for a photograph more in homage than wannabe.

Comparisons are impossible. I'm sure the ghosts compare times
and squabble about how hard it was in their day, but even Merckx
smiles after the last competition number is peeled off. Of Rominger's
shattering of the hour record, he said with fulsome generosity: 'Seeing
Tony today, I suddenly felt that I was a very, very minor rider. To
achieve such a mark at sea level . . . I take my hat off to him.' *Chapeau.*
Merckx achieved his own hour record on a conventional track bike,
titanium frame, tyres inflated with helium, in Mexico City, 1972.
Sixty minutes, as he described it, of 'continuous battle with pain' for
49.431km. He said afterwards: 'That's not the sort of thing anyone
does twice.' In October 1994, in a warm-up ride on an ordinary bike,
Rominger covered 53.832km; two weeks later on a special bike he
rode 55.291km. In some ways it was a surprise. Rominger's *palmarès*
include the Giro and the Vuelta and he was a noted time-trialler, but
this world record seemed to come more as an afterthought to his
career than its ultimate goal; even as a counterbalance to the major
disappointment, that of not winning the Tour de France. His threat
to Indurain in the Tour was probably the most serious on at least
one occasion; it never materialised; perhaps through an uncertainty
of morale. Indurain who had beaten him in four Tours de France,

pushed the hour distance to 55.040km. Rominger's reply was decisive, at last.

In 1996, Boardman, erstwhile holder of the record, set an astonishing new mark of 56.375km to regain it. The week before, he'd beaten the world record for the 5km Individual Pursuit. This egregious double was totally ignored by most English newspapers.

Occasionally I glance behind me; we are going down what the Tour most usually comes up. Impossible to gauge its difficulty against the way we have ridden. It's hard work, the road is slippery, I'm frozen and wet, the brakes are on non-stop.

Guillestre: one of the stations where English prisoners of the Napoleonic wars were interned. Hot baths, full laundry session, a walk round the town; the church with a sundial on its exterior wall (the local vogue) . . . *Tempus fugit – Horas non numero nisi serenas* ('Time flies, I count the hours only when life is sweet'); a back garden where vegetables are interspersed with flowers to ward off pestiferous insects reminds me of Monet's garden in Giverny where the flowers grow in strips like vegetables.

John and Angela have set their sights on Corsica: a week in the sun to restore. Over the col de la Bonnette, 2,802m, and a delicious long descent into Nice to catch the ferry.

'Bit hilly,' says Angela.

'You'll hardly notice after this lot. Piece of cake.'

'No cols.'

'Sadly, no.'

'You concerned about your reputation, John?'

'No, just looking for a bit of excitement.'

'You can always get lost up a goat track at night and wait for Corsican bandits.'

'Don't encourage him, he *will*.'

As it turned out, the Bonnette was closed and they didn't make it to Corsica. They were lucky. I heard from friends who happened to be on the island that week that the weather was unspeakable.

CHAPTER SIX

COL DE VARS

Drugs in the Sport

> If you didn't actually see it you'd never believe the
> amazing courage of these young men who ride
> 1,500km in four stages through mud, completely
> drenched with rain from the sky and puddles in the
> road. Wind, storm, hail, snow, biting cold cannot
> stop them. They wear bits of sacking or canvas in a
> vain attempt to keep the wet off. Whenever they get
> off their bikes, in next to no time their feet turn into
> lumps of murky yellow mud, treacherous mud that
> seeps in everywhere, even through the most resistant
> shorts, and scrapes the skin like emery paper.

So wrote Marcel Violette in 1909.

We're having it easy in comparison. Nor are we experiencing the
depth of oxygen debt that racing exacts on the high climbs, the
speeding heart rate, 180 to 200 beats per minute – Stephen Roche
at the limit on the climb to La Plagne in 1987, to stay in touch
with Pedro Delgado; not only hung on, he very nearly caught him,
but the strain of the chase meant they had to haul him straight off
the bike to give him oxygen.

As I gaze out of the window, first thing, the sky shows a band of
swimming-pool blue above the mountains to the south, which, in
topologies of piety, is the side of the *spirits made just*. Northwards
dwell the faithless, barbarian no-hopers, Teuton scallywags,
Tungrian bugaboos. Above the blue streamers of hope in a bright

day hangs a dismal pall of gunpowder-black cloud: smoke from the Devil's chimneys. Even as I watch, the satanic cloud sinks; the blue droops and is squeezed out. Rain it will be. Odin's dog pack gathering for the hunt through the stormfields and cloudbrakes. What comfort? Remember Elihu the Buzite endeavouring to cheer up Job. 'Look unto the heavens and see; and behold the clouds which are higher than thou.' (Job xxxv; 5)

And Job saying: 'So?'

Today we part company and do so, inauspiciously somehow, outside the bank. John's front brake cable shears on the way there from the hotel and I emerge to find him rooting out a replacement from his repair kit. Maybe this is the moment to go; no ceremony.

'You won't have to wait for us at the top of the cols any more,' says Angela.

'Ah, but I'll miss your company.'

I give her a hug. John switches the spare cable into his left hand and we shake hands.

'Enjoy Corsica,' I said.

At the bar in Valloire, Angela had suggested I write something for the wind quintet she plays in. I store the idea, uncertain about it one way or another; but of course I will have to come up with something. Such ideas, like mountains, do not go away.

Angela's slightly bandy-legged riding style reminds me of Greg Lemond, another knees-out cyclist. Fine rider, triple Tour winner, twice world road-race champion, he made no secret of being intent only on victory in the Tour de France; lesser races didn't interest him, hardly even the classics which are the salients of the continental racing season. He started a trend which has changed the sport irrevocably. There are now two divisions of cycle racing: the men who concentrate on the Tour and little else and those who honour the richer tradition of the sport. Thus Jean-Marie Leblanc, one of the Tour organisers, expressed the opinion that on the eve of the 1998 Tour, Ullrich could hardly be considered the favourite to repeat his 1997 victory. Ullrich's total failure to respect the dictates of his professional duty – putting on some eight kilos over the winter to reappear for spring training bloated and utterly out of athletic shape – was a disgrace. His early-season record was miserable; the example he set tawdry. In the not-so-distant past, racing cyclists felt an obligation to take the whole calendar of races seriously. It is partly the fault of the sponsors who encourage their big stars to expend energy only on the main chance and to use many other races as training rides, pulling out after a few stages if that suits them.

Indeed, Merckx criticised Lemond on this very point: for lack of generosity with his exceptional talent. Lemond, answering back, slights Merckx for being envious of him because his brand of bikes sells better than Merckx's. Hoo ha. Of course the Continentals did not understand the totally self-absorbed American who appeared to find his teammates a nuisance and retired to his camper van every night to be with his wife, whereas the orthodox rule is for a celibate Tour . . . *sexe coupe les jambes*. Kelly said he abstained for some six weeks before the Tour. (Semen is a valuable repository of vitamins.) Desgrange's credo was simple: total commitment to the bike during the season; and, since men needed sex, self-denial of sex was the truest test of supreme willpower.

Lemond was, moreover, on record as saying that the *peloton* these days is full of riders as good as Merckx and, as if that weren't preposterous enough, claimed that the only reason why Merckx had the success he enjoyed was because he spent the entire pre-season period in preparation. Well, now. Lemond always did talk a good race, before and after the event.

That Merckx was prodigiously generous with his talent cannot be refuted. His record of seven wins in the spring classic, Milan–San Remo, is unique anyway, but the very fact that Merckx was winning at the start of the year with a gruelling calendar of races ahead is astounding. That and a punishing round of winter track meetings . . .

But Lemond suffered a lonely and ignominious end. The acknowledged leader of the GAN team at the beginning of the 1994 Tour, he was soon in trouble and clearly not going to make Paris. A team leader has always been allowed the singular privilege of abandoning into the team car, rather than the broom wagon – it used to have a besom tied to the back – which sweeps up the lesser riders. When Lemond's Tour seized, he underwent the indignity of being placed in the wagon; the team had a new leader, it seemed (Boardman), and not sufficient loyalty left over to accommodate the old one at his demise. He didn't deserve that.

153

Lemond had made an astonishing return to pro racing after a gun-shot accident in 1987 which very nearly finished his life, let alone his career. It was a painful, slow, morally punishing, often debilitating return to fitness and the form and ability to contend with the best. By 1989, he was showing some sign of his original class, but in the Giro that year – always Merckx's preferred ride to prepare for the Tour – he was dropped on the relatively simple climb to Mount Etna and lost eight minutes. He was going badly; he seemed to be out of the hunt. However, in the time-trial – always his speciality – he came second and, he said, it marked the turning point.

A month or so later, he lay second in the Tour and set off on the final time-trial into Paris; speeding down the ramp, he passed Fignon, in yellow by 50 seconds, warming up on the road, waiting his turn. The 24.5km from Versailles to the Champs-Elysées offered no better than an extreme outside chance of making up the deficit. A Frenchman would, it seemed, win the Tour in this year of years: bicentenary of the fall of the Bastille, prologue to the French Revolution. Fignon, riding with a callous next to his urethra, could hardly bear to sit down. (To ease the excruciating discomfort of saddle boils, Zoetemelk put raw steak inside his shorts.) But, the man with the reputation for foul temper nobly advanced none of the excuses he might have made. One can barely surmise the anguish which afflicted him when he came to stand on the podium alongside Lemond, having conceded victory by the narrowest margin ever: eight measly seconds. The tri-bars he used in the time-trial (strictly against the rules) almost certainly won him the Tour and were allowed on a mere technicality. As for Lemond, he added gold in Chambéry that autumn in the Worlds. It was, truly, a stupendous return. Had he matched his outstanding athletic prowess and hardness of ambition with anything approaching a grace of disposition, I'd think better of him.

✶

'Strange people, bike riders,' said Anquetil. 'They imagine a racing bike is made for going quickly. They're wrong: a racing bike is made solely for winning races.'

At the very start of his career, and no more than a highly promising beginner, he was given this advice by the veteran journalist Alex Virot: 'Young man, listen: if you concentrate on making money you'll lose races; if you concentrate on winning races you'll make money.'

Good counsel for much else besides bike racing. Alas, Virot didn't live to witness the accuracy of his wisdom. On Anquetil's first Tour, 1957, Virot and his motorbike driver René Wagner plunged off the road on a Pyrenean descent and were killed.

The Dog Day sun blazed infernally that summer and the tar melted on the roads. Bobet wasn't there and the 23-year-old Anquetil had to overcome a bout of dysentery and the shattering challenge in the mountains of the powerhouse Gastone Nencini to win in Paris.

It was 1957 that saw the Tour riders wearing jerseys plastered in commercial advertising. Teams had hitherto been sponsored exclusively by cycle manufacturers but that support had dwindled and more or less petered out. A new injection of finance was needed and Raphaël Geminiani, who'd come second to Koblet by 22 minutes in 1951, convinced advertisers from a variety of other trading marques that the Tour offered a fantastic marketing opportunity; the *peloton* might be a travelling billboard covering 4,000km of French roads, observed, what is more, (since 1952) on daily televised reports of race action. They bought it. On their team jersey, Gem and Anquetil sported an affiche for the aperitif St-Raphaël, the aperitif of France (plus quinine), whose faded mural adverts still cling to many a French roadside building in faded flaking paint. The range of advertisers was wide: food stores (Potin), ice-cream makers (Miko), brewers (Kas, Pelforth, Stella), insurance brokers (GAN), coffee-machine manufacturers (Faema), *charcutiers* (Molteni), car factories (Peugeot, Ford), tyre manufacturers (Hutchinson), as well as a rump of bike firms who saw a new boost in the Tour commercial (Bianchi, Campagnolo, Flandria, Gitane) . . . Many other sponsors followed.

In 1958, Anquetil abandoned with severe stomach cramps – intestinal infarction. The remaining French leaders were beyond their peak: neither Bobet nor Gem had the legs any longer and Charly Gaul left them gasping, his supple turning of the cranks like a *perpetuum mobile*. His majestic conquest of Mont Ventoux was televised live; the storms raged over the Chartreuse Massif but nothing could stop him.

In 1960, the Frenchman Roger Rivière, aged 24, came to the Tour as double world pursuit champion and holder of the hour record. In 1956, Anquetil had set 46.159km; three months later, Ercole Baldini topped that by 234m. A year later, the 21-year-old Rivière stepped on to the track, mounted his bike and set off, turning the classic 52 x 15 gearing deployed by Coppi in 1942 when he extended the Frenchman Archambaud's 1937 mark of 45.840km by 31m.

At the side of the track stood Coppi himself, the maestro encouraging the young pretender. Rivière scorched off at a perilously fast pace: the first 5km in six minutes and 15 seconds, nearly 50kph. He held the speed, flagging briefly – 40km at an average of 47kph – to finish at 46.923km, a staggering improvement of 530m. A year on, he pushed that record to a mammoth 47.346km. Now, bagful of promise, he began his first, and last, Tour.

Leader of the French team, he took the first time-trial stage in Brussels, the flat stage into Lorient and opened his account in the Pyrenees with a win at Pau. Healthily placed, a minute and 38 seconds behind Nencini, he was descending the col du Perjuret, crashed, fell 20m into a ravine and broke his back. He was crippled and died 16 years later. It was an apalling tragedy; what dark sadness overhung Nencini's only victory.

The Pyrenees claimed another victim in the 1995 Tour: the young Italian Olympic gold medallist of 1992, Fabio Casartelli. Virenque, horribly unaware of what had happened, was already way out ahead, riding to an audacious all-day solo win. Next day, in muted tribute, the entire *peloton* rode the stage in a bunch, at a pedestrian crawl, a tortured ride in torrid heat – many riders abandoned – and, at the finish, Casartelli's Motorola team led in the cortège. The riders donated all the *primes* for the stage to Casartelli's widow; the Tour officials matched the total from their own coffers. In what other sport . . . ? It was a moving testimony to this extraordinary fraternity of cycling, even in the ranks of the race-hardened professionals. Save that Rijs called the truce on racing an absurd and inappropriate memorial, if that's what it was, to a man who had dedicated his short life to racing. He added that it gave Indurain time to recover and without that respite he'd have lost the Tour that year, to Rijs.

It was rumoured that Casartelli had pitched headlong into a wickedly sharp-edged granite bollard marking the open verge. The stone, like the blade of an axe, had apparently split open his skull. But, no blood was found on the stone. He seems, rather, to have hit the hard road headfirst and lay there, curled as if in sleep, the dark stain of his blood barely visible in the sun's glare. The frail mortal frame of the human body mounted on a flimsy racing bike rides a precipice of danger in head-over-heels descents at breakneck speeds on surfaces often skiddy with stones, a slick of wet, the camber uneven and treacherous – and the Portet d'Aspet's descent is particularly steep and tortuous – always with the hurricane of competition blowing from behind.

Simpson crashed once, tumbled down an embankment and crawled back up to find his bike, apparently undamaged, lodged in a tree. He pulled it out of the branches, remounted and set off down the descent only to find that the crash had, in fact, compacted the front forks so that the bike was now too small and a brute to control.

The Tour officials tried to impose the obligatory wearing of helmets some years ago. The riders protested. In the mountains, especially under a baking sun, even crash-hats of the latest aerated designs were intolerably uncomfortable. Fines were imposed. The riders held out. The helmet law was repealed. It was reinstated in 2003.

An early proponent of helmets was Jean Robic, the 1947 winner whom the Italian *tifosi* nicknamed 'Glass Head'. He was endlessly prone to falls, predecessor of the vulnerable Alex Zülle, whose new Festina boss reckoned that it was his posture on an ill-fitting bike which made him come off it so easily. Robic turned up for the 1953 Tour with a white rubber helmet, a sophisticated version of the string-of-sausages hat he'd previously worn. This occasioned much hilarity and mirth, to Robic's extreme irritation. Furious, he proffered François Mahé a screwdriver and said: 'Go on, whack me on the head with the handle. Give it everything you've got.'

Mahé needed no persuasion and gave Robic a sound thump. Robic swayed around a bit and said: 'See? Completely resistant.'

And walked off with a trickle of blood running down his nose from a split in his head.

On that Tour, Koblet fell on the col du Soulor in the Pyrenees, Robic went down in the Fauremont and the race was left to the other Bretons. Mahé passed the yellow jersey to Mallejac who gave it up to Bobet after his solo exploit through the Casse Déserte.

'This is a tough profession,' said Anquetil, 'and we're not in it for pleasure; it is hard and dangerous; we risk our health for many reasons. I consider myself a professional: I do my job, just like anyone going to an office or a factory.' His career spanned 16 years and his great successes came in the big Tours: first Frenchman to win the Giro d'Italia, 1960; five Tours de France and the Giro–Tour double, 1964; Spanish Vuelta, 1963; five Paris–Nice, first stage race of the season, the 'race to the sun'. His great expertise was in the time-trial and he won the only classic race against the clock, the Grand Prix des Nations, a record nine times. From the other one-day classics, he stayed clear; he called them lotteries, not races. It was a judgement tailored by defeat. He trained hard for the 1958 Paris–Roubaix, punctured 12km from the finish and never bothered again, though he won the Ghent–Wevelgem in 1964 and, in 1966, the Liège–Bastogne–Liège by a hefty five minutes. He held the hour record twice.

Rivière had beaten his first mark by some 1.2km and it was Geminiani, now his sporting director, who persuaded him back onto the track in 1967. (Gem it was who had prompted the 'stupid bet' on the Bordeaux–Paris immediately after the Critérium Dauphiné Libéré.) Anquetil was reluctant. Gem knew his man, however. 'Your name is Jacques Anquetil,' he said, goading that prickly Norman pride and, 11 years after the first record, Anquetil, now 33 years old, turning a massive 52 x 13, rode 47.493km, almost 347m further than Rivière. He presented the record-breaking bike to Jeanine, wife of his doctor and his own – as they say – 'constant companion'. She eventually left her husband for Jacques.

After the record ride, Anquetil failed to turn up for the routine dope test within five hours – stipulated by the sport's ruling body – and instead went home. He eventually pitched up to a local doctor in Normandy some two days later. His record was, therefore, not ratified, although his supporters claimed that, since he'd ridden under the same lax conditions as Rivière, the time should be allowed to stand. Compromises were proposed – records with and without drugs control – all to little avail in Anquetil's case. Ferdinand Bracke beat his record a month later *and* produced his bottle of urine on time.

Anquetil's last Tour – 1966 – ended in retirement on the côte de Serrière in the Ardeche; once more a stomach infection. Beaten by Poulidor in the time-trial at Vals les Bains, Anquetil knew he was done but held on and abandoned only when he had ensured the victory of his protégé Lucien Aimar over the old foe, Raymond. Three years later, Eddy Merckx burst on to the scene, beat Poulidor into second place *again* – a new *bête noire* dogging the luckless Poupou – and Anquetil into third on the Paris–Nice. True, the *maître* did beat Merckx in a post-Tour track omnium, but it was over. Anquetil quit racing altogether, saying that he'd rather give up before the strain of combining an indulgent life style *and* racing killed him. The cycling must never be allowed to inhibit his gourmanderie. Just after he turned pro, he polished off a whole lobster in white wine as a pre-race snack, a flourish of bravado. The veteran Lazaridès, he who feared the Izoard bears, remarked: 'He may be starting as a bike racer but he's not going to last long.' How wrong he was.

Just over 20 years after his retirement, Anquetil died of cancer of the stomach. Doctors had removed his stomach and put him on a minimalist diet. The *bon viveur* went home and carried on as he always had: champagne and caviare. He and Poulidor had become friends at last: the rivalry was buried, irrelevant now. But, in the hospital, saying goodbye, Anquetil turned to Poulidor and said: 'Sorry, Raymond, you'll come second again.' He died next day, 18 November 1987.

He was never popular with the French public, who found him too distant: he seemed simply not to need their good opinion. Goddet called him 'yellow dwarf', refusing him the accolade 'giant of the road' that his feats ought to have accorded him. Yet time has mellowed remembrance of this great rider. His outright genius can, finally, stand clear of the brooding complexities of his character, the chilly hauteur, the steely scorn of his tongue. When Rouen, in his native Normandy, hosted the Prologue of the 1997 Tour, a dockside

road by the Seine which cuts through the town was named Quai
Jacques Anquetil. For the civic-minded French this represents true
acceptance. Anquetil won his first Tour stage in Rouen in 1957. It
marked, too, the tenth anniversary of the master's death and on the
morning of the Prologue, Merckx, Hinault and Indurain, the other
quintuple winners, laid flowers in the cemetery in Anquetil's home
town, Quincampoix, where the first Hot Spot sprint of the Tour was
to be contested next day. The Tour pays its respects and due heed to
history. This Tour also marked the 50th anniversary of the first post-
War Tour, in which Robic sealed his victory on the Bonsecours hill
. . . just outside Rouen.

So much has changed now that stringent controls limit the
amount of racing a pro cyclist can be required to do in any one
year. The new Pro Tour is designed to give better shape to the
season and afford more opportunity for rest. Even so, men like
Armstrong and Ullrich may race on not much more than thirty
days in one year, nineteen of them on the Tour de France. However,
until about ten years ago, the racing cyclist routinely faced a long
and arduous season beginning in late February and continuing
until early October. Added to that, some riders competed in a full
round of six-day track races in the winter off-road season. Racing
day by day, nearly all year long; then the enormous strain of the
stage races. There is virtually no let-up. The Tour de France is the
high point and the day after it finishes in Paris? Some riders plunge
immediately into the whirligig of one-day criteriums, here, there
and everywhere; operating as independents for the most part, team
obligations suspended, on direct contract – so that local races can
bill the Tour heroes – putting money straight into the bank, but
having to make their own way to events how they will or can. Pedal
all afternoon, drive through the night to the next venue, little or
no sleep and off again. After one such post-Tour appearance race,
Anquetil said to the newcomer Merckx: 'You'll see, this is no piece
of cake, this criterium riding.' (The criterium circuit is much
reduced, now.)

In such a context, the temptation to stave off the encroaching
exhaustion is probably outweighed by the sheer necessity. I make
no apology for performance-enhancing drugs; but medication to
mask or numb extreme fatigue?

Riders would arrive at the post-Tour criteriums, it was common knowledge, with two suitcases: in the smaller one, a clean change of clothes; in the larger, the pharmacy.

An eminent physician remarked to me, 'There are winners and racing cyclists.' Implying that the whole *peloton* is using medication – not all of it junk – of greater or lesser potency, of one sort or another; and young hopefuls, what the French categorise as *espoirs*, on the fringes of a pro contract, are keenly aware of the choice that will face them sooner or later: to take dope and keep up with the bunch or not to take dope and get dropped. And if all of them are taking dope are they all then guilty? One prominent athletics coach has recently voiced the opinion that the wholesale ban on drugs in sport should be revised; the interdiction is ludicrously punitive on men and women exposed to the stresses of top-level sporting competition.

The situation isn't helped by fuzzy statements from the authorities. Thus, Juan Antonio Samaranch, president of the International Olympic Committee said: 'We really must produce an exact definition of doping. The existing list of what are labelled dope products should be drastically reduced. In my view, nothing which does not impair the health of an athlete should be called dope.'

Desgrange's regulations for his Tour had been draconian from the start, but the official attitude to the use of dope has never been less than vague and equivocal. In 1975, Thévenet, *en route* to the famous defeat of Merckx, tested positive, but the President of the French Republic was waiting on the Champs-Elysées for the first time to welcome home the first French winner in eight years . . . Following his victory in 1988, Pedro Delgado tested positive for probenecid, a substance which, argued the officials in exoneration, had not yet found its way on to the banned list. Probenecid is a diuretic which Delgado said he had to take because he sweated so much on the mountains he found it difficult to micturate and thereby void the acids (lactic particularly) which build up in the urine. Probenecid dilutes the urine; this has the useful effect of masking the presence of any stronger, performance-enhancing drugs such as steroids. Delgado was, controversially, confirmed as winner. The next year, he dithered up to take his mark in the

Prologue time-trial fully two minutes late and his chances for the Tour were sunk. What the dope test made of that, we don't know.

Athletes have been using performance-enhancing herbal juices for millennia. The ancient Greeks, who invented athletic sports in devotion to a physical – masculine – ideal, also as training for war, then formalised them in sacred games as a forum of state rivalry, were no strangers to the pharmacopoeia. Their oracular prophetesses were drugged to the eyebrows in the mephitic fumes of smouldering laurel leaves; the magic herb moly (either the mandrake or a species of garlic) given to Odysseus to ward off the enchantments of the sorceress Circe, testifies to the use of pain-inhibiting herbal decoctions such as the hellebores which have strong narcotic effects. Nor were they averse to banning ingested substances. An athlete was disqualified from one of the early Olympic Games. His crime? He'd been training on a diet of dried figs. The judges ruled that an honest athlete should stick to fruits available in their season, only.

Soldiers have always had recourse to stimulants, though not so frequently in such outfits as the highly drilled professional Roman army. The barbarians who met them in battle were rarely short of fighting spirit, Welsh *hwyl*, fuelled by alcohol often as not. Henry V's army came to Agincourt field riddled with dysentery, soaked to the skin, starved and weary; but roaring drunk. Frightened men going into battle swigged lavish slugs of artificial (bottled) courage – Dutch courage was the gin originating from Holland – to steel them to face what, even in an irrational mood, is a thoroughly terrifying, awful business. Rum to fire the stomach and devil the nerve before the great gun encounters on the wooden ships or in the hellish trenches of the First World War . . . whisky to quell the overshot nerves afterwards . . . hashish to calm and embolden the Old Man of the Mountain's deadly assassins (Arabic '*hashhashin*') . . . South American coca leaves chewed to prolong intellectual concentration or for a brave high . . . the hallucinatory mushroom . . . opium, and its derivative laudanum, to deaden the agony of table-top surgery and numb the senses to life in the Dark and Middle Ages which was nasty, brutish and short . . . the list could go on.

The principal sources of drugs banned by the International Cycling Federation are ephedrins, amphetamines, anabolic steroids. A brief summary therefore.

Apothecaries were known as druggists from Shakespeare's day, but 'drugs' was the late nineteenth-century medical student slang for a pharmacist, and this points to the origin of the distinction we make today between legitimate medicine – used on prescription to remedy or ease illness or infection – and a chemically prepared substance used, *mis*used, when there is no malady to cure. The slang is 'dope', an American word (from the Dutch for 'sauce') originally for any thick fluid or semi-liquid taken as food – e.g. a gloopy milk-shake bought at the drug-store soda counter.

Ephedrins were, until the early years of this century, prepared from an evergreen shrub *Ephedra*, and in ancient times by the Chinese who macerated its leaves in alcohol and water, then blew off the liquid to leave a speedy tincture, sovereign for the stimulation of a sluggish heart. In the 1920s, pharmacologists began chemical preparation of the same substance, and chemical preparation, more and more sophisticated in the modern age, lies at the root of drug abuse.

Thus, if a patient presents with a very low blood pressure, ephedrin will counter by increasing the systolic rate. The systole is the contraction of the heart, by which oxygen-rich red arterial blood is pumped into the system. Diastole is the dilation of the heart as deoxygenated blueish blood courses back through the veins. The transfer of oxygen from the lungs into the bloodstream marks the beginning of the energising cycle; any substance which gingers up that exchange will, necessarily, enliven the system generally and, as a bonus, make the patient feel better. The moral factor is important. Ephedrins promote the release of noradrenalin, a neurotransmitter which relaxes the muscles round the airways, complements the inflation of the lungs and aids respiration; the greater the intake of oxygen, the more efficient the human motor. Blocked nasal passages dry out through the action of ephedrin. And how does a cyclist suffering congestion from overtaxed lungs and famished gulping at oxygen-thin mountain air, oppressed, what is more, by the petrol fumes of team cars, choking dust and furnace heat, cope? Many hay fever and asthma remedies contain ephedrin: the dope controls insist on those which don't.

Whereas a drug like laudanum had a dual use – social and medical – from the beginning, the ephedrins have, all along, served only in the medical context, whether unlicensed or for illicit use.

From ephedrins are derived amphetamines which stimulate the central nervous system. Alcohol is a simple amphetamine and it can promote a temporary energising stimulus. Here before me is a picture of the Swiss riders Colle and Parel, the 1921 Tour: they are sitting on steps in a doorway in some rural backwater, a baking hot day, by the light. Their bikes parked by them, a gaggle of admiring boys gawp at the supermen as they each contemplate a large stein of lager.

The effect of amphetamines is to boost the action of excitatory chemicals in the brain to render the taker more alert through speeding up the breathing and heart-rate. The problem with them – speed, bunnies, uppers – is that the body soon develops a tolerance, so that for any appreciable effect the dosage has to be steadily increased; this risks dependency. Long-term side effects are muscle damage, weight loss, constipation, all deleterious to a racing cyclist, of course.

The zingy effect of drinking strong black coffee, for instance, is to make you think you're doing better than you are; but also to inure the brain to protracted stretches of deeply boring, routine activity. Many Tour riders take belts of espresso before the start of every stage. Even smoking can be an aid to physical exertion: chewing tobacco doesn't release the nicotine very fast, but inhaling charges up the flow of adrenalin and prompts the flow of blood sugar out of the liver into the bloodstream quite rapidly. Another picture: 1920s, on the road, the *peloton*, riding four abreast, forges on; in the front row Vervaeke and Geldholf light cigarettes.

Muscle-building drugs, such as anabolic steroids, are tempting to cyclists in need of raw strength. A drug called clenbuterol was developed in East Germany for cattle: its effect is to reduce body fat and produce a leaner animal with more saleable meat on it. Body fat is one thing cyclists can well do without – useless kilos to heave up the big climbs – and it is known that wrestlers have used it. Reduce your body fat and you achieve a body more or less packed full of muscle with the added advantage that, now stronger, you are also lighter, allowing as much as 5 per cent, even 10 per cent power, to bodyweight advantage over an opponent still carrying some fat.

A drug called erythropoietin came to the fore in the early

'90s; EPO. Literally 'red-making', it increases the number of red blood cells, the oxygen carriers, in the bloodstream. That is to say it's an artificial haemoglobin, supplementing the vital work of the kidneys. In the mountains this happens anyway, so the result of taking erythropoietin is to mimic the effect of high-altitude training/riding where, granted an optimally high resource of oxygen, the athlete is less likely to enter the zone of anaerobic effort, when the build-up of lactic acid in weakening, oxygen-starved muscles begins to increase rapidly. EPO is used medicinally on anaemic patients. When injected, it is completely untraceable; only in the exaggerated performance it underpins can suspicion arise. A number of Dutch cyclists who had used this substance were riding in extreme heat; they became dehydrated; one of them, suffering from a bout of gastroenteritis occasioned by food-poisoning, vomited which exacerbated the dehydration. His blood, already thickened by the effect of the drug, was further drastically coagulated by the loss of body moisture. The dangers of drug-abuse in sport are all too apparent.

When the Pélissier brothers abandoned in 1924 – as aces they were comparatively well looked after – they said: 'We are treated like dogs.' Henri went on to describe the Tour as a road to Calvary, *un calvaire*, except that instead of 14 stations it had 15. 'And you want to know what keeps us going?' He pulled a small bottle out of a bag containing numerous other small bottles and canisters. 'Cocaine for the eyes,' he said. Another bottle. 'Chloroform for the gums.'

Maurice Ville emptied his musette. 'And this is pomade [liniment] to warm the muscles. And pills? You want to see the pills?' They each tipped out three bottles.

'In short,' said Henri, 'we keep going on dynamite. You've seen us when we come in at the end of a stage? When we've washed the mud and grime off, our flesh is as white as a winding sheet, we're empty from diarrhoea, our eyes are swimming. Every night we dance the jig like St Guy [French St Vitus] instead of sleeping . . .'

They omitted: wine laced with strychnine and ether-soaked handkerchiefs to dull the fatigue.

Rubbing chloroform into their gums was a crude method of absorbing a painkiller. Cocaine masked pain, sharpened reaction and response to stimulus and accelerated the pulse rate, and thus the oxygenation of the blood, but pump too much into the bloodstream, by intravenous injection, for instance, and it could prove lethal. I myself remember the effects of cocaine injections from the dentist's chair in the '40s and '50s. Very pleasant, given the gruesome nature of the rest of the experience.

A revolt led by Anquetil in 1966 centred on the matter of drugs. Earlier in the year, he had decided the time had come to speak out. He even roped decent old Poupou into the arena, declaring that he was on drugs too, 'Everyone's doing it, no exceptions.' A few months later, Anquetil repeated his accusations and added: 'You think you can race Bordeaux–Paris on mineral water? First you eat a sugar cube, then you take some coffee, then chocolate and from then on you go crazy, you're doped to the eyeballs.' Challenged, he replied: 'Small trees don't grow in the jungle.'

The first open drug tests were carried out on that year's Tour, under the direction of a French law passed in June – 12 months earlier – making illegal the consumption or prescription of a list of drugs with the aim of enhancing any athlete's performance. The first enforcement of the law by the Tour organisers caused uproar. Poulidor very reluctantly provided a urine sample and the next day the riders, Anquetil at their head, protested against the dope controls and the inconsiderate methods of applying them. As the French journalist Antoine Blondin wrote: 'Four men in raincoats hammer on the door of your hotel room, they barge in and demand a urine sample and your papers; then, without a by-your-leave, they rummage through your suitcase. This is more like a police raid than the Tour de France.'

When they were 5km out of Bordeaux on the stage to Bayonne, the entire *peloton* slowed down to a halt, dismounted and walked 200m en masse, chanting '*Merde*', 'Shit to you', which is what Marshal Ney shouted back at the English when they called on him to surrender at Waterloo. The *peloton* then remounted and proceeded with the race. Poulidor's urine sample was conveniently forgotten.

Geoffrey Nicholson, the distinguished cycling journalist, points to the paradox at the heart of this question by recording the remark made by a French colleague who gazed over the dinner table they'd just vacated. There had been a long day's racing, a morning stage and an afternoon stage. All the scribes had done was sit in the car, write up the race and eat and drink. The table was strewn with 'crab and oyster shells, empty wine bottles, full ashtrays'. What stimulation could they reasonably deny the riders who'd actually raced the route and faced another trial the next day? (In the old days, even journalists had it harder. Desgrange insisted they turn up to dinner in *un smoking*, dinner jacket.)

Riders are occasionally caught cheating the dope control, though given the expertise of modern team doctors they say only an imbecile gets caught these days. Yet, one rider was told that his urine sample was negative but to take special care of himself because he was pregnant. Other times it's not so funny.

On Monday, 17 July 1978, the Tour de France was riding from St Etienne to L'Alpe d'Huez. Jos Bruyère (formerly Merckx's lieutenant) was in yellow, followed by Zoetemelk at a minute and three seconds, Hinault, a minute and 50 seconds, and Michel Pollentier. On the first category col Luitel, 1,262m, Pollentier attacked and, at the summit, led a strong group containing all the main men by 22 seconds. He decided to risk the escape: 50-odd kilometres down to the valley and the final climb to the dead-end alp to conclude. His lead built to three minutes and 20 seconds but, as the chase picked up, he had only a minute and 58 seconds at the first of the 21 hairpins. No stylist on a bike, he was to elegance of pedalling what a dishcloth is to a silk scarf, but he hung on, lashing himself and his bike up the unforgiving mountain and took the stage by 37 seconds over the next man in, Kuiper (another ibex from the flatlands), and enough over the rest to put him in yellow. Bruyère trailed in eight minutes down.

The daily dope test is levied on the overall leader, the stage winner and runner-up, plus two other riders chosen at random. Pollentier had peed in his shorts on the way up the climb and had none left. He missed the dope control and cycled directly to his hotel. He had, in fact, taken a fairly innocuous adrenalin stimulant, alupin, to aid his breathing. It was a common drug, sold over the counter in Belgium but Pollentier took fright: his lead was narrow, the yellow jersey wouldn't give him immunity as it had Thévenet.

He stuffed a length of tubing and rubber bulb containing what he knew to be clean urine into his shorts and set off for the dope test. Meantime, one of the other riders, Gutteriez, was trying hard to produce a specimen. Extreme fatigue and dehydration inhibits the flow, of course, but a trickle appeared. Then the doctor spotted that the urine in the test flask wasn't coming from Gutteriez's penis but from a length of rubber tube. The doctor checked all the riders in the room; Pollentier took off his shorts and the ploy was exposed. He produced a genuine sample of his own urine and returned to the hotel.

At 8 p.m., Félix Lévitan, co-organiser of the Tour with Jacques Goddet, announced that Pollentier had been caught red-handed trying to cheat the dope control. Under International Cycling Union (UCI) rules, he was forthwith suspended for two months and fined 5,000 Swiss francs. Seven other riders, three from the Peugeot team, were also disqualified for taking over ten pushes from spectators.

Pollentier was stunned; after all, he'd eventually provided a fair urine sample and the doctors had signed him out clean. Why the protracted delay in declaring him a cheat? Moreover, he hadn't tested positive in any other race that season.

Pollentier's Flandria team, including his close friend Maertens, talked of quitting the race *en bloc*. (It had happened in 1950: the Italian team walked out in the Pyrenees. On the climb of the col d'Aspin, crowds had swarmed so close in on the riders that Robic and Bartali fell in the scrum; then the luckless Italian was set on by drunken French thugs spoiling for a fight. Bartali was kicked and punched but escaped and made it to the finish. But, even though their man Magni had the yellow jersey, the Italians quit; Kubler refused the yellow jersey next day, but took it into Paris.)

Like Kubler, Zoetemelk found himself in yellow by default and publicly castigated Pollentier for taking unfair advantage: his use of stimulants had put his pursuers on the rack; they had to fight merely to limit their losses; any thought of attacking was out of the question. This sounds overly pious.

Hinault couldn't credit that a rider of Pollentier's class should need to take drugs or make such a crass mistake as to try to cheat the control. However, the exclusion of Pollentier cleared the way for him – Zoetemelk packed a much lighter punch and the coming time-trial would probably see Hinault leap-frogging the Dutchman into yellow.

The hapless Pollentier wrote to Lévitan and Goddet. He apologised; said that he was no more guilty than the majority of other riders and asked why Gutteriez had not also been punished. (They would probably say that the wearer of the yellow jersey bears extra responsibility.) He had given a sample of his own urine and, besides, was in such a confused state after the debilitating ride up the alp that some mitigation might be in order. He pleaded for clemency and concluded: 'Believe me when I say that hardest to bear is the charge of sullying the standing of the Tour. You know how I have committed myself to the racing on the roads of the Tour. This should have been the finest day of my career. Unhappily it will be the saddest. Please accept my sincere expression of regret.'

He was, in the circumstances, dealt with harshly; another of the Tour caprices; what a miserable thing to have to live with.

★

The fingerpost indicates col de Vars 19km. On the first bend the rain starts. I decide to remove the silk long johns I'd put on to keep my legs warm. Wet, they'll be no use anyway. This change means a full strip, waist down, at the side of the road. I'm just putting my shoes back on when a police car drives by. Tour riders are fined for relieving themselves in built-up areas, but not behind trees or (to the side of the crossbar) on the move in open country or, like Pollentier, let free in full throttle.

I hated the col de Vars. It had little to commend it at the time and I can't stir much charm out of it in retrospect, either. Many Tour riders, asked what their objective is for a day in the mountains, retort: 'To survive.' Absolutely. The weather didn't help: the day had already cried itself to a standstill, given up and turned its face to the wall of the mountain. There was nothing besides wet trees, wet roadsides and wet mountain slopes to look at. The water of the River Chagne might be tumbling over itself down the gorge in a chattering giggle of foam but I can't take to cheery babbling about being cold and wet. I've got water on the soul.

✷

On 14 July, Bastille Day, 1975, Merckx, whose powers of recuperation were miraculous, put the misery of the previous stage into Pra-Loup behind him and attacked down this very climb *en route* to the Izoard, 2,361m. He was hitting back as hard as he could; Thévenet was adrift, his first day in yellow. But the long haul up to the Casse Déserte lay ahead; Thévenet kept his nerve, reeled the Cannibal in and left him to ride alone through the lunar landscape past a young girl in a swimming costume with a placard which read: *Merckx, the Bastille has fallen, Thévenet has won.*

Thévenet hadn't sprung out of the *peloton* overnight. Débutant in 1970, he came fourth in 1971, winning that telling stage into Grenoble ahead of Ocaña's group, and second overall in 1973. His victory initiated a renewed French domination of victories. Merckx's own first win put an end to a Belgian drought which had lasted from Sylvère Maes's win in 1939.

✷

The town of Vars itself, a ski station flung together out of quick-drying concrete, may be a jolly place on a sunny winter day when the snow is crisp; in rainswept September, draped in a fog that leans like a morning drunk against a side wall, Vars is as unattractive as a waste bin. And it seems to go on for miles. There's Vars this and that de Vars and Vars the other. Home, what's more, to no fewer than three saints: Marcellin, Marie and Catherine. Says a lot about the place that it needs such heavy canonised insurance.

The guidebook says that the time to come to Vars is in June when the flowers are out in gaudy profusion. And when the Tour comes through, in a profusion of lycra.

Placards as big and flimsy as Hollywood film-set façades exhort me to sample the delights of cross-country skiing, bobsleighing, snow-biking. The cash kiosks stand empty. The ski lifts creak, gaunt and immobile, like pit-head winding gear all across England now. The boutiques sulkily *fermé* for business. The restaurant menu boards hang out like self-conscious schoolkids, full of chips and 'look-at-me' self-advertisement.

At the far side of Ste Marie de Vars, halfway through the Vars holy triple jump, at 1,658m, from the 1,000m at Guillestre, the road suddenly springs up in my face. I groan, snarl and get stuck in. The Vars conurbations behind me, the rain changes to snow.

★

The col de Vars, 2,110m, was first included, as was the Izoard, in the 1922 Tour, and ever since generally put in tandem with it. The road is vastly superior to what they climbed then, but it is still a rough gutter for debris off the mountain, its wrinkled surface littered with stones. Belgians had won every Tour since 1912, and now Lambot, the winner in 1919, lined up again to challenge for a second victory. His relegation at Le Havre seemed to turn the tide, but everything changed on the Nice–Briançon stage, over the Vars and Izoard in quick succession.

A formidable group of Belgian riders led the way: Philippe Thys, first triple Tour winner 1913–14, 1920, tracked by the only Frenchman who could stay the pace, the great climber Alavoine; then Lambot and Heusghem. Alavoine cracked; Lambot and Heusghem moved up and caught Thys. Heusghem seemed to be the strongest and was heading for yellow which he must then surely keep till Paris – he'd come second in '20 and '21. But he committed some minor infraction of the rules, was docked an hour and Lambot took yellow.

In 1933, the Frenchman Georges Speicher rode down the Vars heading for eventual victory in Paris with the aid of a new secret technological advance: a rear brake whose stirrups were fixed inside the rear stays instead of on the outside. This avoided snatching and delivered a smoother application of the blocks.

The first crude braking system – augmented by applying foot to wheel – often caused the bike to rear up if applied too abruptly which added to the perils of descending. This harked back to the penny farthing or 'ordinary' and many riders came a purler over the front wheel. Technical innovations were advertised by Tour riders, of course.

Watching the 1935 Tour *peloton* containing Speicher, Leducq and Vietto as it passed through his home town St-Méen-le-Grand was an apprentice baker, named Louison Bobet. Three years later, Speicher came to an ignoble end: eliminated for taking a ride up one of the Pyrenean cols, hanging on to a car door. It was Bartali's Tour, his bike fitted with the *dérailleur* whose use Desgrange had finally permitted; the Archbishop of Reims sent Bartali a photograph dedicated: To a champion of the Catholic faith and of the pedal.

I feel as the specialist sprinters must feel when they are on the mountains, except that I can't join their *autobus*. On Van Impe's triumphant day into Pla d'Adet in 1976, the time limit for the stage was set at 10 per cent of his winning time. Only 52 riders made the cut – approximately 28 minutes deficit; the remainder, 43 members of the *autobus*, faced disqualification, thus reducing the Tour to a pitifully small field. The officials decided to relax the rules and allow the men who came in under 40 minutes to stay in; the remaining nine riders, down to 46 minutes, would be eliminated. Five of them belonged to the Raleigh team who had dropped temporarily out of the race to nurse their leader Kuiper after a fall. He was too badly hurt to continue, and so he abandoned – by which time the loyal *domestiques* were miles behind the race. In fact, only one member of the Raleigh team – Pronk – had beaten the guillotine and the manager threatened to withdraw him if the others weren't reinstated, especially since they lost so much time waiting for Kuiper, as it was their professional duty to do. After a heated argument, the officials relented. The spirit of Desgrange the pragmatist lives on.

✵

By the time I reach the top my hands are frozen. I had hardly noticed while I was riding; I arrive without any sense of jubilation; dismount without fuss and at once feel the extreme pain throbbing in my hands.

★

Benoît Faure described how on a 200-mile stage in the 1926 Tour, across the Tourmalet and Aubisque, riders were sobbing because of the cold: fingers locked and stiff, unable to brake on the descents; spectators rubbing life back into their frozen legs and bodies, plying them with cognac. Faure swore this, his first Tour, would be his last. He was a tough farm boy, used to privation and exposure, but this was unbelievable. Worse for such as him, a *touriste-routier* – one of the *ténébreux* 'shadow men' as they were known – was that, unlike the stars, he had no hotel room booked, no back-up or team support, no comforts laid on. He vented his spleen in an article about the miseries of his Tour de France for the magazine *Match*. Torture on the roads and bedbugs in the sleazy hotels. Desgrange was not amused and fined him 4,000 francs. (First prize for a stage win in those days would be around 5,000 francs).

Iron man Eugène 'Cri-Cri' Christophe described the 1910 Milan–San Remo:

> That was a race. Mid-March. It was bitterly cold from the start and as we began the climb of the Turchino pass [532m in the maritime alps above Genoa] we ran into snow. I was leading but I was shaking with cold and the road was so rough I could hardly control the bike. I fell into a ditch. Some bystanders carried me into a cottage, gave me hot drinks and rubbed me all over to restore my circulation. They gave me a pair of long trousers to wear over my shorts and I pressed on. Meanwhile I'd been overtaken, but with about 130km to ride, I chased and caught the leaders and finished the race alone.

Some understatment. He beat Ganna by 20 minutes but Ganna had taken a tow from a car and was disqualified. Next man home, Cocchi, was an hour and ten minutes down on the Frenchman. Even Christophe's abnormally robust constitution took a beating from that race: he was so weak he could barely walk, had to spend a month in hospital and lost the rest of that season and much of the following one.

Imagine puncturing in such circumstances – at night, in the snow, trying to peel the tyre off with fingers frozen numb. Poor Léon Scieur on that day of eight punctures: one minute and 30 seconds to repair each one, then stitch up the regulation tyre and off again, pulling on the bulging mica eyeglass goggles the Belgians favoured, which gave them the look of frogs. And victory in Paris.

✶

The snow is driving in at 45 degrees. I park the bike against a noticeboard and fumble at the fastenings on my saddle bag, fingers like vulcanised rubber, hands pulsating with cold. I windmill my arms to try to restore the circulation and resume the fumbling. The café across the road does not tempt me in the slightest. The col de Vars has drawn the fight out of me and I am not ready to let the fight slip back inside. Sitting in artificial heat and having to step back out into the cold is no pleasurable prospect. My every instinct is to press on and work up my own heat.

✶

It was on the col de Vars, the day before their great duo ride to l'Alpe d'Huez, that Hinault came very close to breaking. He was in fearful pain from a pulled muscle in the knee. It was, he said, the only time he ever wept on a bike. Urs Zimmerman and Lemond were ahead, Lemond heading for yellow, when Hinault, in awful trouble, heard a moto-cameraman say to his driver who was setting off to follow the rest: 'Stay with *him*, he's going to abandon.' It was every cliché you like to deploy; start with a sting of the whip. Hinault reacted with pride; there was little else left, but those words rang in his ears like the final voice of shame on doomsday when there's no redress. He fought back, so far beyond any present thought of pain and discomfort that he limited the day's losses to four minutes on Lemond, who took over his yellow jersey. He started the next day

174

still in considerable pain, but if pride is no great cure it's a powerful anaesthetic. The pain eventually left on the Croix de Fer and a Calvary had been endured.

On his first ever climb of that col de la Croix de Fer, during the 1977 Dauphiné Libéré, his assistant manager handed him a bottle filled with champagne which he guzzled to the dregs and finished the highest pass he'd ever ridden 'half blotto' he said. That same race, when he'd been dropped by Thévenet, Van Impe, Zoetemelk and Martin, it was Merckx who urged the struggling newcomer on. 'Come on, stick at it, go on, you're still winning, don't give in.'

Such banalities the words may frame on paper, but when uttered by an established rider of such class to a new man of obvious talent, the banality achieves the simple moral direction of the epitaph, the crack regiment's motto, the family blazon. And that is what it comes to: the moral imperative. As Hinault said: 'No technology can increase the energy or the willpower of the rider, nor can it lessen the doubts which sometimes overwhelm him.'

Anquetil said of the 1986 Tour won by Lemond that it was fantastic and, 'We owe it all to Hinault. Even if he didn't win, it was his Tour.' He took the mountains prize and, as the French journos say, he *dynamited* the race. Testimony to that comes from Robert Millar, too: 'This was my fourth Tour and by far the hardest. I don't think we ever climbed the mountains so fast.' This from a specialist climber is praise indeed.

That moto-journalist may have been instrumental in the Hinault fightback; it's impossible to say. But journalists, even highly experienced ones, certainly get things wrong. The truth can be so swayed by subjective interpretation. What seems, on the face of it, a dull, uneventful stage may have been seething with tactical jiggery-pokery inside the *peloton*. On the '74 Tour, a television crew set out to station themselves at Besançon to catch the demise of Poulidor, now 38, and matched, after Anquetil, with Merckx. Nobody gave him a chance once the mountains had dug their teeth into his legs. The cameramen got there in time to see Poulidor dump Merckx on the climb of the Relais du Chat. Merckx caught and passed him on the descent and took the stage win. Next day, the buzz amongst the journos was still that maybe this was Poupou's year at last. And from Monsieur Eddy, too. Alas, on the Galibier, Poulidor caved in, the pressmen started scribbling about irreparable losses, luck running out, once more defeat only to watch, amazed, as the veteran trounced Merckx over the Ventoux and led him a dance in the Pyrenees.

The one thing you do learn if you ride the mountains is that nothing is ever certain. Often a rider with no obvious pretensions at even a stage victory will overturn expectation. On stage five of the '97 Tour, Cédric Vasseur, not a fancied rider, made a brave solo attack of 147.5km to take yellow. Four days later, he was still in the lead but none of the pundits gave him any prayer of holding it that day, over the col du Soulor, first category; Tourmalet, super category; Aspin, second; Azet, first. He surprised them all with a wonderfully gritty ride and held on to yellow, even if he ceded it next day.

A team rider will sometimes perform extraordinary feats in the service of his leader, though never able, seemingly, or inclined, to put such audacity into riding for himself. This is part of the racing ethic: a strict pecking order of jobs and status. The *domestique* is paid to obey orders and if the orders require him to ride like a star for a day, very well. Sean Yates did it frequently. On the sixth stage time-trial on the Tour in 1988, 52km, the strong man ('Animal') from Sussex won at one hour, three minutes and 22 seconds, the fastest average speed hitherto recorded; yet, he always maintained that he'd been lucky in his career, no more. This is over-modest. He was, in many respects, the *domestique* of *domestiques*: a tireless worker, self-effacing yet unpitying with his own energy and efforts in the team's cause. He never complained and was never wanting in a ride. His *palmarès* boasts wins in several of the big-stage races and his entire professional career compels admiration. A complete sportsman, a pro to his shoe plates.

★

In Barcelonnette, I squelch into a small bar/resto in town, eat an omelette, bread, green salad with half pitcher of red wine and an espresso, and by 1.45 p.m. I am back on the drenched road, saturated from the neck up and the waist down. I ride past the turn off to Pra-

Loup; I had wanted to ride up that fateful climb where Thévenet left Merckx for dead; but in teeming rain, an added ten miles with hard climbing does not appeal. I still have 40-odd miles ahead of me to put me within strike of Ventoux. Another time.

When I returned to England, John and Angela told me that they had ridden into Barcelonnette at about 2 p.m. and called it a day. John said he'd never been so cold on a bicycle. (Merckx said that in severe weather they'd sometimes get off the bikes and run 200m or so just to get some circulation back into their legs). They discovered a fresh pasta restaurant round the corner which serves portions so big they couldn't finish them. In fact, you could have served Angela's leftovers to a party of four. Not that she is no trencherwoman. She once ate three pasta courses on the trot in a trattoria in Vietri, Italy. The *patrono* was so impressed he brought out a fourth plate, which she tucked into heartily.

I must have missed them by a whisker. 'We'd have tried to persuade you to call it a day,' they told me afterwards. But I was spurred on by the challenge of Ventoux.

'I aim to enjoy Ventoux,' I'd said.

Angela gave me a wry look and said: 'You don't really *enjoy* Ventoux', which was odd, even cautionary, coming from her who had called after me on the first ramp of l'Alpe d'Huez: 'Enjoy it.'

Mountains have their summits and there is no obligation, no exterior compulsion, other than pride, to finish the climb. We can at any moment choose not to. A good lesson, then, to stay in the moment. When you get to the col you do not cast off the frailties of halfway up, you absorb them and carry that weakness into the triumph of getting there, the triumph which owes more to patience than to effort. Statistically, the demands of the mountains can be expressed like this: riding full out on the flat, or at speed downhill, up to about 82 per cent of the resistance to forward motion comes from the air. Riding in another rider's slipstream reduces that by nearly two thirds. On a climb the air resistance falls to around 6 per cent; everything else that gets in your way is provided by gravity – about 78 per cent – and grip of tyres, tendency to roll back and so on. Applying the same effort to 30kph on the flat, a rider will make only about 10kph on a one in sixteen, and less, obviously, as the incline steepens.

Everything we do may teach us something about ourself. *We are part of all we have met.* And if we do not know ourselves how can we know others? Those who know – or admit – less about themselves have little capacity to think of anybody but themselves.

Too often our experience of the tedious routines establishes our value of life. As a result, transcendent feelings tend to become uncommon and so, untrustworthy. We cannot rely on the validity of a feeling we rarely, if ever, encounter. Life isn't like that, will go the complaint. Whatever these mountains have taught me it is that there are different strengths to uncover in our spirit, beyond the commonplace of head down and run at it. And I am very conscious that from this new encounter I have drawn a singularly limited experience; just how limited that experience was I would find out on the slopes of Ventoux. Even to label them slopes makes it sound risibly chummy and casual.

★

Merckx out on his own for 60km into a vicious headwind on the 1971 Liège–Bastogne–Liège; his sporting director Driessens told him it was pure madness. Merckx didn't even bother to look at the man. When he was 3km from the finish he was rejoined by Georges Pintens but refused any relays from him, simply hooked him on behind and took the sprint from the front. He was hardly off the bike when Driessens was all over him, hugging and kissing him, saying what a great idea he'd had to advise Merckx to attack when he did.

★

Towards evening, in drenching rain, I can't find anywhere to stay. The way I feel I could cycle another 40 miles without concern, but this is being pig-headed. Just beyond the junction with the N85, which, like Napoleon's army in 1815, forges straight along the valley of the Durance, I turn off to La Saulce on a whim and spot a signboard. I ask for a room; they have a room.

My bike is in a filthy state but there is nothing to be done except oil it next day when it is dry. Vietto would have been cleaning it and polishing it like a gold watch, shoes too. If Christophe had only checked and cleaned his bike after 17 hours in the saddle, those forks might not have snapped. But I leave my cherished Alan Shorter unwashed, untended, in the corridor and clump up to the room in shoes aslosh with rainwater.

I have a glorious warm shower, wash every stitch of my wet gear, pat and roll it dry in the spare towels (a pro's trick). There is a knock on the door: the *femme de ménage* to take away all my wet gear for drying.

Down in the bar, I drink several *demis* of light beer. The place is fuggy-warm and crowded, men stopping for a drink or two on their Friday way home from work, followed by men and women taking *apéritifs*. They shake hands as casually as we say hello. The air is loud with conversation. Four card players – two men, two women – unroll a strip of baize at the table next to mine and play a noisy rubber of piquet.

I order the set dinner – menu scrawled in chalk on a slate – for 7.30 p.m. *Hors d'oeuvre* of leeks in olive oil, *pâté en croute* and bread, red wine. Then rosé for the baked hake, baked red peppers and a mountain of rice. A board of cheese, as much as I want. Rum baba – the only disappointment: sponge the texture of wet bread and cream from a grease gun. Shop-bought. The rest of the meal is home-cooked and entirely delicious, 65 francs all in, prepared and served by the *femme de ménage*.

By 9 p.m. the café has all but emptied. Dry, glowing, nicely plump, I take a stroll through a dark maze of tiny streets – the rain has stopped – and at 9.30 p.m. go to bed. My dry clothes, the purple jersey of leader in my own tour among them, lie folded on the chair.

CHAPTER SEVEN

MONT VENTOUX

The British Riders

The col de Macuégne, scarcely more than a pimple after the high passes, 809m to 1,068m in 4km, leads me to a crossroads. I consult the map. The road to Montbrun les Bains plunges off downhill to the right in what looks like an attractive scenic ride. Above me rears the Montagne d'Albion and its pass, the col de l'Homme Mort at 1,212m. That way I have to go. This day has death brooding over it.

Albion was the ancient name for Britain before King Arthur came to Camelot, but Albion is still in the French dictionary for 'Britain', normally as 'perfidious Albion'; and the col of the Dead Man? It's not a wholly unusual name in these parts, but here is a chilly coincidence.

In 1989, I wrote a sequence of seven radio plays (and a book) about King Arthur. David Buck, who was originally commissioned to write the series, died of cancer while he was working, at desperate speed, to finish them. The illness had advanced so far that what he wrote was degenerating into distracted incoherence. The spooky thing was that as soon as I heard he was writing the plays, just before I met him – he acted in another play of mine, coming out of the hospital ward to the studio each day, ill as he was – I had a premonition that I would be doing the job, not he. Nothing I could do, however unsettled I felt. He did die and, in his memory, I started my own work from scratch. In the final play, Arthur leaves the field of the last battle to fulfil the prophesied end, by restoring the sword Excalibur to its true owner, the Lady of the Lake. Mortally wounded, imbrued with blood, I had him say to Sir Bedivere: 'Put me on my horse. Put me on my horse.' There was almost a fearful row about that on the last day of recording; the producer insisted on 'Set me on my horse'. Amenable on most changes, I refused point blank on that. At the time, I believed it was what a dying man *had actually* said, as you will see.

★

The first British riders to enter the Tour were Charley Holland and Bill Burl, in 1937, first year of the *dérailleur*: 20 stages, 4,415km, six rest days. (The *dérailleur* mechanism comprises a dolly-wheel on an articulated arm, extending below the chain-ring, through which the chain passed. Worked by a simple switch lever, it shifts another mechanism below the freewheel cogs back and forth.)

The bold duo formed a three-man team with Pierre Gachon, a French-Canadian. Gachon missed the time limit on day one, Burl crashed twice and abandoned after stage two, so Holland lined up for stage three on his own. He rode well, finished in the top 30. On the Ballon d'Alsace, 9.5km to verdant pastures at 1,247m, the officials decided that Holland had taken a tow from one of the cars and relegated him to final place. That probable injustice apart, Holland spoke of the endless drag up that climb and the choking fug of car fumes which made breathing that much harder. The Tour reached the Alps. At the start of the Galibier, Bartali attacked; Holland and the others grabbed some food bags and rode on into snow, Holland's first taste of the big mountains. On to and across the Pyrenees and the end of his Tour, on a technicality. He punctured twice on the col de Port but carried only the regulation two replacement tubulars, so had to wait for someone to come along who'd give him a third spare. A priest gave him a bottle of beer, but his sacristy did not run to bike equipment. Finally, a tourist cyclist gave Holland the wherewithal – an oversize tyre, but a tyre – and he rode on; the tyre kept slipping off the rim; he searched out another but when he reached the checkpoint, the officials had packed up and moved on. Holland had no option but

to peel off his number and retire. Some journalists told him he'd
be reinstated but he demurred.

In the Alps, Bartali seemed to have the race secured. He'd been
required by Mussolini to ride the Tour instead of the Giro and to
dominate it for Italy. Shades of Hitler's 1936 Olympics. After the
Galibier, he arrived in Grenoble with eight minutes' advance on
Maes of Belgium, 16 minutes on the French hope, Lapébie. Next day
he added to his lead over the col du Laffrey and began the descent,
guided by his teammate Rossi. But Rossi fell, Bartali hit the parapet
and hurtled off the road into the torrent below. Stunned, he was
hauled out of the icy waters by another teammate and remounted.
But the shock of the crash and the chilly drenching had bitten him
to the bone. He couldn't get warm; the cold had seized up his lungs
and muscles. Over the Izoard, Vars and Allos he lost 20 minutes.
Maes took yellow and in sunny Marseille, Bartali shook Desgrange's
hand and abandoned. He was ready to regain yellow from Lapébie
but the Italian Federation had ordered him to quit.

In the Pyrenees, the bitter rivalry between the French and Belgian
teams got nasty. Setting out from Luchon, Lapébie's handlebars
broke: they'd been sawn through. A change of bikes; no *bidons*.
Tension mounted. The Belgians accused Lapébie of taking extra –
illegal – food from his brother Guy, Olympic champion in the '36
Olympics. Dropped on the Peyresourde, Lapébie reached the foot of
the Tourmalet five minutes behind Maes. He saw, by the side of the
road, Antonin Magne watching the race. 'Tonin,' he called out, 'I'm
pooped. What do I do?' Magne didn't reply.

A bit further on, around a long bend, flagging now, Lapébie saw
Félix Lévitan, later race co-director. Their eyes met. Lévitan saw
what was what and, hidden from the other riders by the bend, gave
Lapébie a long push, two-handed. It was sufficient to launch the
revitalised Frenchman in pursuit of the Belgian 'Black Squadron',
so-called from their all-black strip.

Lévitan dutifully owned up to the push: it cost Lapébie a minute
and 30 seconds penalty. Next day, 40km from Bordeaux, Maes
lost a minute and 33 seconds with a puncture, and in the race to
get back accepted help both from his own team *and* independent
Belgian riders. He was penalised 15 seconds. Lapébie's deficit was
reduced to 25 seconds.

The Bordelais fans mobbed the Belgians, however, and threw pepper in their eyes. It was disgraceful and the Belgians decided to abandon the race in protest. Lapébie won.

The unfortunate Holland was not forgotten: he became a popular hero in France – the plucky Brit who'd ridden so well, against the odds and without any support, human or material. The partisan French may enjoy hating the English, *de rigeur*, but when it comes to riding their Tour, every rider who shows exceptional pluck is a hero deserving of respect.

One such was the Briton Brian Robinson. In 1955, he and Tony Hoar were part of a ten-strong British team which competed in the Tour. Robinson and Hoar alone finished, the first British riders to do so; Robinson 29th, Hoar as *lanterne rouge*, six hours five minutes and 37 seconds behind the winner, Bobet. In 1956, riding on Charly Gaul's team, Robinson came third on the first stage and arrived in Paris a very respectable 14th in 1956. In 1958, he won the seventh stage, into Brest: the winner Arrigo Padovan was disqualified for dangerous riding in the sprint. Alas, Robinson was forced to abandon and didn't see his leader Gaul take yellow in Paris. After an epic, and record-breaking, solo ride of 140km, Robinson took the 20th-stage victory at Chalon-sur-Saône by 20 minutes and six seconds, in 1959. Another Briton, Vic Sutton, also finished – 37th – that year. Robinson's example undoubtedly drew Tom Simpson to the continent. For any amateur with serious ambitions to make road-racing a career, there was no option but to cross the Channel. Track-racing flourished in Britain, but the legal ban on road-races continued until well after the Second World War. The racing code was rigidly amateur; illicit time-trialling took place at crack of dawn, riders wearing black alpaca tops to ensure invisibility.

During and after the War, the British League of Racing Cyclists campaigned for open road-racing in Britain, but even after the inaugural (professional) Tour of Britain, and its reincarnation as the (amateur) Milk Race in 1958, official attitudes were not malleable.

Moreover, British cyclists were, and remain, obsessed with time-trialling: one man and his bike on the dual carriageway, shaving fractions of seconds off last week's time over 25 miles, 50 miles. It is insular, introspective, self-serving and no preparation, mentally or psychologically, for road-racing. It is a useful exercise only to a very limited point; it reminds me of what Anita Roddick, of the Body Shop, said about basing commercial strategy on market research, that it's a bit like driving a car looking only into the rear-view mirror. Things are changing. British cycling is waking up.

In his début year, Simpson entered the eight-day Route de France stage race for under-25s. Here he encountered the mountains for the first time. His French was still patchy; the team mechanic was trying to tell him to ride within his capabilities, to keep something in hand. Simpson couldn't understand until the guy started making slow pedalling motions with his hands and saying 'touriste, touriste'. Simpson cottoned. He rode the approaches to the Tourmalet in the leading group and, at the start of the climb proper, changed into his lowest gear. He said: 'It was awe-inspiring going up the Tourmalet. There were great banks of snow piled at the side of the road for miles . . . I felt very small and insignificant. Still, I was learning fast, although I still had the dread inside me that I would not finish: a disgrace which I could not face.'

He managed the climb comfortably, crossed the col feeling good, not even sweating, ten minutes down on the field. He was on his way. Next year he won the Grand Prix Mont Faron, a mountain race, beating the great Charly Gaul and several other renowned *grimpeurs*, and that summer lined up for his first Tour: he finished in 29th place; his talent was solid enough, but the demands of pro racing, as of any professional activity, go way beyond mere talent. Like all foreigners seeking to break into the continental racing scene, Simpson had a hard fight on. He was nervously ambitious, driven by the need, the desperate need even, to make a mark, to make money, not to catch the ferry home with empty pockets and a broken dream behind him. The Tour de France was where a reputation could be made, and a reputation led to bigger contracts and the happy possibility of retiring with enough money to live on. In spring 1961 came his first major victory: he won the Tour des Flandres, a Belgian classic, and in the '62 Tour became the first Briton ever to wear the yellow jersey; for only a day, yet he had pulled on the golden fleece of cycle racing and his desire to do even better in the Tour tightened its grip on his senses. He came sixth that year, the highest placing ever for a British rider. Simpson was a natural one-day racer – victory in the Milan–San Remo, 1964, followed by a majestic win in the world road race of 1965 proved that – but his physique was not ideally adapted for taking a daily hammering and producing the kind of dominating performance he yearned for in the stage races. True, he won the Bordeaux–Paris, but the Tour is the Tour. (Curiously, before the inaugural Bordeaux–Paris in 1891, the great Charles Terront, winner of the Paris– Brest–Paris that year, the poor working-class boy who began his starry career on hired wooden bikes – together with all the other French riders – was refused entry by the British amateur contingent, whose federation made the rules, because they were professionals.)

On 13 July 1967, 13th stage, the Tour riders faced a ride of 136km from the overnight stop in Marseille to the town of Carpentras and a further 75km loop over Ventoux and back to Carpentras. Riding with Simpson in the British team were Barry Hoban, Vin Denson, Colin Lewis and Michael Wright. The French called Simpson 'Major', from the publicity photos of him sporting a city-slicker suit, bowler hat and umbrella, in teasing mockery of the stodgy '*rosbif*' image. He had a lively good humour, unlike most Brits whom the French found impossibly dour, never allowing any emotion to set the stiff upper lip aquiver. Simpson was also a fine racing cyclist with a touch of steely class in him: the continental fans not only liked him, they admired him, too. If Simpson could make a good showing in this Tour – he was 29 years old and not kidding himself that he had time in abundance at his disposal – a round of fatly paid post-Tour appearances might see him clear for his future. It was the basic insecurity of all professional sportsmen and women, made more acute as physical powers decline and anxiety about the future increases in proportion.

This Tour promised success. Simpson was climbing well; a brave ride on the Ballon d'Alsace lifted him to seventh overall, the position he held that morning in Marseille. He'd been sick on a hard stage in the Alps but seemed to have recovered.

Of the first time he rode Ventoux, Simpson said: 'It is like another world up there among the bare rocks and the glaring sun. The white rocks reflect the heat and the dust rises, clinging to your arms, legs and face. I rode well . . . doing about five miles to the gallon in perspiration. It was almost overwhelmingly hot up there; my pants were soaked and heavy with sweat, it was running off me in streams.'

At the start of the climb to Mont Ventoux, in Bédoin, Simpson darted into a bar with a few of the other riders and is alleged to have drunk a small cognac. (One witness says it was more like a full glass; another rider, Riotte, downed two glasses of red wine.) This practice of raiding local cafés and bars on passage, an immemorial tradition of the Tour since its inception – in the absence of organised water supplies by the organisers – is strictly forbidden nowadays.

The heat was intense: 131°F. Poulidor and Jimenez attacked, the pursuit splintered and strung out along the climb; Simpson was in the main group of chasers. Bédoin stands at 275m altitude, Ventoux's col des Tempêtes at 1,829m; the distance between them is 21km. The record stands at around 45 minutes. Simpson was going badly. The road was lined with fans cheering him on, cheering them all on, but 3km from the top, Simpson faltered to a dead stop and toppled sideways, the bike under him, pedals gripped fast to his feet by toe-plates and straps. He was by this time delirious, incoherent. (In his book *Put Me on my Bike* William Fotheringham suggests he mumbled 'on, on, on'; the more dramatic plea was invented by a journalist.) A spectator helped him remount and he wobbled up that cruel slope in furnace heat enduring who can imagine what mad torment to stay on the bike somehow and reach the top for some relief on the downhill. He faltered up another kilometre of that brutal climb; 1.5km from the summit, he slumped to the ground a second time, all but unconscious now. A spectator gave him the kiss of life; the Tour doctor Pierre Dumas arrived with oxygen, radioed for the police helicopter and tried to revive the dying man. Airlifted to Avignon hospital, Simpson was pronounced dead at 5.40 p.m. The attending doctors also announced that there would be an autopsy of his body: a clear indication that they suspected he had taken drugs. Indeed, in the team baggage van a box belonging to Simpson was found to contain various stimulants, including two kinds of methylamphetamine.

The dose of amphetamine that he had taken had not been large enough to kill him; it did, however, allow him to push his body way beyond normal endurance. His overriding concern had been to dull the pain he knew he'd go through in the supreme – the mortal – effort he needed to stay on the leader board. The night he died, Jacques Goddet said that he thought Simpson was a 'great guy who was probably scared of losing'.

Three days later, Anquetil dismissed any moralising about the dope Simpson had taken. He said that no rider could have climbed Ventoux in that asphyxiating heat without the aid of some decongestant simply to be able to breathe. The likelihood is that Simpson ignorantly used an unproved brand instead of one that any doctor would prescribe to anyone else other than a racing cyclist.

The British team was poleaxed by the news. Their manager Alec Taylor persuaded them, numb with grief and shock, to ride on in Simpson's memory. They went to the start line next day wearing black armlets; the crowd applauded. Denson, a friend of Simpson's for 14 years, was in tears, so too Hoban. A short speech, a brief silence before the race drew out on to the road; Denson was asked to go ahead and take the stage as a tribute to his friend; he couldn't do it and the doleful honour went to Hoban instead. Denson abandoned soon afterwards; the remaining three riders continued to Paris.

The following year, what they christened the Tour of Health started in the spa town Vittel, home of the mineral water. Goddet said that since doping had been forced out of the shadows it could now be controlled. The riders seemed united in their determination to purge the sport of drug abuse. 'Dear Tom Simpson,' said Goddet, 'your death in the stony desert of Ventoux will not have been in vain.' But the racing was lacklustre, the event a bore from start to finish.

Simpson had been promised a lucrative contract with one of the best Italian teams – Salvarani – riding for its leader Gimondi, if he finished the Tour. But the long stage race had never been his forte and, at this end of his career, his strength was naturally depleted. A three-week race was probably beyond him, but the twin imperatives of all riders – money and racing instinct – forced him on. He was dosing himself with extra glucose during the Tour, but the effect on his alimentary system was disastrous and he could hardly ingest more substantial food. It is almost certain that, even before Ventoux, he had already driven himself beyond the limit of physical punishment that his body could absorb. As for the amphetamines, this was nothing out of the ordinary.

US Airforce pilots took them *de rigeur* to obviate drowsiness on missions. Simpson, it can be said, broke his own heart on that mountain.

It was – still is – a tough world that all amateur English riders faced when they crossed the Channel, hoping to succeed in a harsh profession, contending against continental riders whose traditional *métier* is road-racing. The training and competition was, is, unforgivingly hard, the homesickness often worse, and until they secured any sort of reputation they remained the outsiders. Add to that the gnawing anxiety that they will have to give up and go home penniless failures. The crushing sense of waste; self-confidence chewed out: racing for a living in the one race they can't win, against time. But: 'Half the failures in life arise from pulling in one's horse as he is leaping . . .' (Julius and Augustus Hare) and Simpson wasn't one to flinch from the risk.

As Dr Johnson said of another cruel profession: 'Sir, he who would earn his bread by writing books must have the assurance of a duke, the wit of a courtier and the guts of a burglar.' I would add: 'and the staying power of a *touriste-routier*.'

Britons have made the trip across the Channel and succeeded: their tally of stage wins in the Tour gives some indication. Adding to that melancholy stage victory in Sète that day, Hoban, a rated sprinter, took seven others in 11 Tour appearances (1964–68) and was a valued *domestique* of both Poulidor and Zoetemelk. Michael Wright, born in England but brought up in Belgium, won three stages between 1964 and 1974. Robert Millar rode every Tour between 1983 and '93 and finished eight, but in 1984 achieved the highest placing yet of any Briton when he took fourth and the mountains prize. Wins at Luchon, '83, two summit wins – Guzet Neige '84 and an elbow-to-elbow with the '88 yellow jersey Pedro Delgado in 1989 – reinforce the reputation of Millar as a climber of exceptional class. A consistently fluent and strong example of that rare breed of rider who loves to see the Alps and Pyrenees ahead, he has crossed a whole clutch of cols ahead of the Tour *peloton*. In a later Tour, climbing to that same finish on Guzet Neige, Millar inexplicably took a wrong turn 2km below the summit, following the signal of a gendarme waving the cars into a car park. He missed what might have been a second victory up there. A case of bad luck, perhaps. Millar attracted bad luck.

In 1985, he was well placed to win the Spanish Vuelta but found himself racing virtually unaided against the entire *peloton*. He went into the penultimate stage with ten seconds on the Colombian Rodriguez and a hefty six minutes and 13 seconds over the Spaniard, Delgado. His Peugeot team was exhausted; a wholesale effort to protect their leader had overextended them and the manager, Berland, had, reportedly, refused an offer from Luis Ocaña, now manager of the Fagor team, to sell his men's services to protect Millar's jersey. A case of French hauteur: Peugeot, said Berland, didn't need help.

The attacks came on the first climb of the day; the Peugeots were all over the road, in the parlance, even the ultra-hard man Yates climbed off his bike. And the attacks kept coming: this was a concerted effort by the home riders to rip the Peugeot challenge apart. Millar punctured. Delgado was off the front in a breakaway group; Millar in a chasing group of 20 riders, none of whom would work with him; why should they? At 23km from the finish, Millar's original lead over the Spaniard was down to one minute and 17 seconds. Millar tried vainly to enlist support for his pursuit. 'But there was no chance,' he said. 'They all knew what was happening. They just sat there and laughed at me.'

He was 400m from the arrival line when the crowd roared: the ticking clock had swallowed up the remaining seconds of the deficit and Delgado pulled on the amarillo (yellow) leader's jersey. Millar complained about a coalition against him that day; certainly partisan feeling in both Vuelta and Giro was always very strong

Max Sciandri, another Brit with a continental education, won the flat stage into St Etienne in the '95 Tour and miffed the parochial British cycling magazine editor by conducting his post-victory press conference in Italian.

The British domestic scene is a backwater, no proving ground nor efficacious preparation for that big league. Short on money, contacts, social habituation, language and, above all, professional nous, the Brit abroad, however highly gifted, finds himself matched with comfortably paid rivals – even the amateurs – born into and shaped by a tough system. It's hard to acclimatise; the transition to pro is hard enough anyway. The problem of language, first of all. Simpson records being in a restaurant early on and the waitress asking him:

'*L'addition, monsieur?*'

Thinking she was asking him if he wanted more, he said: '*Non.*'

She asked him again; '*Non*' and so it went on. She was actually asking him if he wanted the bill. Another time, at a hotel in Pau, he asked the French riders how to ask for the toilet. They told him to say: '*Avez-vous un chiotte, s'il vous plaît?*' Do you have a shit-house, please? and stood back to watch the fun, when he strode up to the receptionist. Part and parcel of the pro job, laughing and making people laugh, the kidding and gamesmanship, an old pro told Simpson.

Unless a foreign rider can somehow make himself at home, like Sherwen who not only learned to *speak* French but, as it were, to *do* French and ditch all preconceived ideas about the way to do things, the *peloton* will give him an extremely rough ride and, like as not, he'll go under. Over there, they do things differently. A rider finds himself in a sort of feudal organisation, a tightly closed shop observing and imposing quasi-masonic rituals of duty, status, loyalty and what is and is not permissible. Riders untutored in the rigid team ethic will simply not survive. Robert Millar, who a while ago undertook an experimental role as national coach in Continental bike racing, found the home-based British riders unruly and self-centred, driven by personal ambition and to hell with anyone else. No lack of talent or basic motivation; almost complete ignorance of the need for unquestioning cooperation, the anonymity of the individual within the team set-up. A wholly insular attitude, in fact.

Simpson records an example of how the hierarchy works. He entered the 1964 Paris–Nice intending to use is solely as preparation for the Milan–San Remo, first classic of the season, the 'race of springtime'. On the last stage, Anquetil wore the leader's jersey. Simpson, sticking to his own private plan, with no interest in the race, and chuckling at the thought of stirring up the pack, attacked on the big climb of La Turbie near the start and raced off at such a speed that the *peloton* peeled off in all directions. Anquetil sent Altig after him. He caught the Briton halfway and gave him an angry scolding: this was no way to pace a stage. Simpson ignored him and attacked flat out; Altig was dropped, chased, caught up again.

Once more Simpson leapt clear and was gone, over the top and down towards Monaco, leaving the field behind him in ribbons. The Philco team abandoned *en bloc*. 'Everyone hated my guts, but I didn't give a hoot.' He stopped, and watched the *peloton* as it rode by, calling out cheerily: '*Ciao*', before riding along the coast road to Nice, having ridden only 40 of that day's 180km.

He won the Milan–San Remo and later that year was in the lead on stage two of the three-day Tour du Var. 3km from the finish, he came to the bottom of a sharp hill which he'd failed to spot on the course map and took sudden fright. Anquetil and Henri Anglade, deadly rivals in normal circumstances, launched a fierce attack in tandem. Anquetil took the leader's jersey and Simpson cursed the pair of them. Anquetil took him on one side, smiled his quiet smile and said: 'The coin has two sides you know, Tom. Good deeds are always repaid and bad ones, too.' Simpson was puzzled. Anquetil explained: 'If you hadn't made such monkeys of us on La Turbie, you'd have won this race.' Hard lessons.

Sean Yates and Paul Sherwen, for instance, both typify the solid reliability and ability, if not blue-chip, star quality of those handful of British riders who have made an indelible mark on continental bike racing. They also epitomise the willingness to embrace the continental ethos wholeheartedly. Sherwen's own record is admirable if not outstanding. Now a respected television commentator, he completed five Tours (started seven); never won a stage, but, testimony to the high regard in which he was held is the fact that when he crashed heavily on an Alpine stage in the '85 Tour and missed the time limit, he was generously reinstated on merit. The caprice of the race organisers isn't always ill-natured.

The story deserves full recall. Just 4km out from the start in Epinal, Sherwen spotted one of his La Redoute teammates heading for a collision, grabbed his jersey and held him upright; the unselfish deed cost him his own balance, though, and he slammed into a metal barrier at the side of the road. He came off, his back badly bruised and, even as the race doctor was tending to him, the Colombian team launched a ferocious attack to show Hinault that he couldn't have everything his own way. Hinault reacted angrily; his own team took up the chase and then drove the entire *peloton* at high speed before Hinault sat up, punishment-beating over.

Meanwhile, two of Sherwen's teammates, Alain Bondue and Régis Simon, had pulled back to help him rejoin. Sherwen, his back in such agony that he could hardly sit on the bike, simply could not go fast enough, even relayed by his men – the bunch was now cruising at fully 3kph faster than them.

It became obvious that Sherwen probably wasn't going to make it: he told them to leave him, not to risk elimination themselves. They were professionals; there was no refuting the imperative of duty and so, 20km into the stage, Sherwen was left to his fate, flanked by the backmarker motorbike gendarme and dogged by the sinister broom wagon, those two engines grinding in his head like a dentist's drill. 'Having that truck behind me all day actually helped,' said Sherwen. 'That would be a very undignified ending . . . going out of the world's greatest bike race by the back door.'

Three and a half hours later, 66km from the finish in Pontarlier, Pedersen launched what proved to be the winning break; Sherwen was an hour down, excruciating sharp pains shooting down his back with every turn of the cranks. When Pedersen crossed the line at 4.20 p.m., Sherwen was 40km adrift, facing a long weary climb to the finish at 1,200m. The punishment of that cruel day's pursuit, driven only by pride through pain and the yearning for it just to stop, can only be guessed at.

Sherwen reached the line 26 minutes outside the elimination time and it is a mark of the esteem in which he was held and the courage he showed that day, that in a gesture of flamboyant generosity the officials simply waived the rules and reinstated him. Never had a prize for the day's most combative rider been more richly deserved. Handing him a dry top as he sprawled, exhausted, against the team car, Sherwen's manager said, 'Paul, this is your yellow jersey.' And next morning? Back on the bike, Paul.

One British rider, Graham Jones, was, in the opinion of many, more or less crushed by the system. He showed enormous promise on his début in 1980, yet, forced into the humble role of water-carrier in a French team, he never emerged as the leader he clearly had the prowess to be. Phil Anderson, first Australian to wear the yellow jersey, was also harshly treated as a foreign rider by a chauvinistic French team. Anquetil dismissed such excuses haughtily. But he was French.

A French rider who'd made a splash in the amateur ranks was asked by a journalist why he'd achieved so little as a pro. 'I'm in Jacques Anquetil's team.'

'So?'

'Well, we all have to work exclusively for him. If only I could ride for myself.'

Anquetil read this and told the man he might ride the Dauphiné Libéré and the Grand Prix du Midi so that he could 'express himself with complete freedom' while he himself rode the Giro. Even the French phrase 'express himself' hints at the very different attitude to this whole business of bike-racing; a difference of culture, even.

Merckx sums it up: Coppi first came to the fore in the Giro, when riding in the same team with the acknowledged leader Bartali. Pingeon's victory in the Tour owed much to the support of the established leader Poulidor. 'Being in a team with an out-right *leader* (French uses the English word) limits the possibilities for an individual, it's true, but a gifted rider can always find some way of showing how good he is. I never saw a man capable of taking victories sacrificing himself all year round. On the other hand, I do know of men who get unexpected wins solely because they were riding in a champion's team and every rival in the *peloton* was concentrating on *him*.'

In the end it is a matter of *will*. As Merckx says, you can test a rider's potential approximately with morphological and physio-logical tests, but no one knows what laws govern the will, nor can the will be measured. There can be no theory as to what constitutes a racing cyclist.

★

I'm wondering when I will catch my first sight of Ventoux. The fascination of its coming epiphany in the distance works on me. I know of its distinctive barrow-like shape by reputation. Its other characteristic reputation, too – '*Le Mont Ventoux ne tolère pas le surrégime* (Mont Ventoux takes orders from no one),' wrote Marcel Bidot, who died on 26 January 1995, at the venerable age of 92. Can a mountain have a personality? Believe it.

My nerves are beginning to flutter, there's no denying, and on the 10km downhill into Ferrassières, a narrow road which eats too much ground, grows a big gut and opens out into the width of a boulevard, the wind starts to rip into me with dire force out of the north west, an onslaught so violent that it buffets me sideways now and then, like a lorry's slipstream. Manageable if you know it's coming, but dangerous in ambush. This was the Mistral, one of the scourges of Provence. I nearly lose the front wheel a couple of times. And, suddenly, there, in what seems like another world, miles away, rises up a preposterously large mountain into a torn blue sky. Incalculably vast and aloof, a naked summit, white as monumental alabaster, the bloodless white of death, topped by a radio mast, like a steeple. So remote is it that I imagine any roads going up there must belong to different scales of tick-tock and map measurement, with time locks between them and the road I am riding. A real ogre with winter in its hair, a gale screaming out of its throat and an extremely uncomfortable way of staring at a body. I didn't want to believe this was Ventoux. I couldn't believe it wasn't Ventoux. It was Ventoux, all right.

At the bottom of the valley, in Sault, the wind is headed off round hidden breaks and I ride into the lull gratefully. A lovely peace, all at once. It was siesta time in the town; baking sunshine, and I'm as warm as a pie. Here I have the option to stay, that choice like a newly minted fifty pound banknote tucked in my wallet. A trio stroll by; almost certainly on their way back from a long lunch. I slow without stopping and ask the time. Quarter past three.

In fine weather, feeling strong, in all practicality and honour I couldn't not go on.

From Sault, at 735m, to the top (at 1,829m) I face 26km to add to the 96km I have already done.

Overhead, the wind moaned like a bittern in mourning, a constant whine that occasionally altered pitch to a grumble or a howl.

The road emerges from the trees. Effulgent sun glares off the white shale of *lauzes*, chalk lozenges that litter the bald eminence of Ventoux and, like Mount Fuji, give an effect, from a distance, of snow. And towering aloft, 200m up into the sky, 6km away, the crest and the radio mast. And the wind, my God, the wind.

This is Mont Ventoux and in a stark fury, too. Briefly, its summit looks undreamable, beyond me. Only briefly; I can't admit such doubts. I know that this is going to be hard and steep. Not only is the mountain bare, the road has become no better than a nasty metalled causeway: broad, exposed, ugly, its ramps piled up like zigzags on an Inca pyramid and raked by a raging gale force wind.

Those meagre 6km make a horrible, unremitting, gut-wrenching, demoralising slog. I hate it; it nearly finishes me; it is cruel to a power beyond rational grasp. I cling on, literally cling on.

And here was what I knew I'd see: a granite stele on which is cut a polished intaglio of Simpson, hunched over the bike, riding at speed.

À LA MEMOIRE
DE TOM SIMPSON
MEDAILLE OLYMPIQUE, CHAMPION DU MONDE,
AMBASSADEUR SPORTIF BRITANNIQUE,
DÉCÉDÉ LE 13 JUILLET TOUR DE FRANCE 1967
SES AMIS ET CYCLISTES DE GRANDE BRETAGNE

Scattered in front of it lies a wrack of dry flowers and old tubular tyres like exotic seaweed from a flood tide. I have not a scruple of energy to pay for a stop, nor even to contemplate.

★

Merckx had ridden with Simpson in the Peugeot team at the start of his career. On his second Tour he crossed Ventoux in the yellow jersey and, as he passed the spot where his old *patron* had fallen, he removed his cap and clutched it over his heart, in silent tribute. Jacques Goddet lay flowers on the memorial stone as he rode by.

Merckx was one of the few continental riders who attended Simpson's funeral. Years later, he paid him generous compliment: 'It's unjust that his name should forever be so indelibly linked with drugs. The controls in those days weren't systematic and I don't pretend that Simpson didn't use a prohibited substance; he was far from being alone. He was a great rider who boosted me from the benefit of his own experience in training methods, dietary regimes, racing nous and the study of race routes. Not all old pros would do that with younger riders; especially with a rider they could see posed a serious threat to them. Simpson was warm-hearted and open-handed. Nor was he the dope-head some people paint him as. On the slopes of Ventoux his ambition killed him. His pride had no limits. He never relinquished the belief that he could win the Tour de France. If he'd had the support of a sporting director in a commercial team, he'd never have been put back on his bike when he was so groggy. Nor was he a drinker, but on very hot days it's not unusual for a rider to take a glass of cold white wine or a beer offered by a spectator. That day was so hot: ten people died from the heat in Brussels.'

An example of Simpson's education of the young Merckx in racing nous. The 1967 Paris–Nice. Merckx had already won a stage and was wearing the leader's white jersey. On the stage over the col de la République Simpson attacked and wrested the *maillot* from him, reasserting his position as team leader. Two days later, the irrepressible Merckx was once again leading the race on the climb of Mont Faron, alongside the '66 Tour winner, Aimar, with Guyot and Simpson in pursuit. Gaston Plaud, the Peugeot sporting director, drove up and told Merckx to wait for Simpson. He did so and relayed him 25km to the stage finish and overall victory in Nice.

This submissive loyalty, a sort of vassalage, is hard for the uninitiated to understand. It is taken to extreme lengths in Italy where if the *campionissimo* decides he wants an easy day the entire *peloton* conforms and any hothead who launches an unauthorised attack gets a roasting. Hinault was a known *patron* who could put the damper on a day of the Tour; but that must be seen in the context of the peculiar nature of the stage race, where, for the most part, the serious business of the day is concentrated in the final hour and the acceleration and jockeying for pole position in the sprint home. If the Tour takes in a rider's home town or, more poignantly, his village, he will be allowed to go ahead and lead the race through – on the proviso that he doesn't use the temporary release as the basis for an escape. Sean Yates had this honour in Forest Row, Sussex, when the Tour came to England in 1994.

The subservience of the young rider to the senior is no more than an apprenticeship; the newcomer has to earn his spurs, pay his dues and assimilate the rules which apply to team racing: that the individual ambition can only operate within the demands of overall victory and the success of the designated leader. This may lead to a clash of interest. In the 1997 Tour, the manager of the German Telekom team, Walter Godefroot, a great sprinter in his day, one of Merckx's most energetic rivals – a wonderful solo ride to beat the Cannibal in the 1969 Paris–Roubaix, for example – was diplomatic about his co-leaders: whichever of Rijs and Ullrich proved stronger would be *de facto* leader; time would tell. The road would tell.

On the first day in the Pyrenees, stage nine, over the Aubisque, the Tourmalet, the Aspin and the Azet cols, Ullrich played the obedient second and Rijs struggled. Godefroot praised Ullrich's power but made no statement about the leadership. Next day, whatever decisions had been made in private, the event proved the fact: Rijs was weak – he always had a bad day on the first mountain stages, he said – and Ullrich showed his hand to the climbers, Virenque and Pantani. They held on but the young German took the stage, the yellow jersey and the leadership of his team. Rijs slipped back into the ranks.

Merckx's assessment of what makes a good team rider is revealing: he was careful to choose men to whom not even a suspicion of drug-taking was attached; they had to have an instinctive feel for a race, knowing when to control an attack without having to be told. 'I hate having to give orders.' However diverse their individual talents they were alike in one trait: total devotion to their leader, a loyalty which he repaid handsomely by converting their selfless support for him into victory after victory, the financial rewards of which they shared in. And their victories, too – Merckx sat up at the end of one race to let his faithful lieutenant Jos Bruyère ride through for the win. Merckx could afford it, but champions aren't notably free with their victories and the gesture carried weight.

The Italians used to carry the hierarchical system to extreme lengths: the offer of lump sums in cash to a rival to throw a race. Very often this arose from bitter memory of a harsh childhood, as in the case of Gianni Motta who came from extreme poverty to the ranks of pro bike-racing. He left Simpson panting on a climb in the 1964 Tour of Lombardy and won on his own; on the descent of the Vars, next year, he tried to 'persuade' Poulidor to ride with him – if they reached the bottom of the Izoard in tandem, nobody would catch them and one of them would win the Tour. Poulidor refused.

★

I can see the radio mast and station overhead; only three bends and three ramps left. I turn into the first of the ramps, straight into the teeth of the Mistral roaring at me with appalling ferocity. I weave 30m, the handlebars twisting as the wind tries to take the wheels from under me, and come to a dead stop. I hastily kick one foot out of the pedal footplate – I might simply have toppled sideways like a tipsy Centaur passing out – and rest for a bit astride the bike, staring up this shortish climb, in what passes for the lee of the mountain; 200m to a bend, another similar ramp and the last bend at the top.

A lull in the wind; I try to ride on; 30m and I am blown to a standstill once more. This is a gale out of the invention of primal wind, an elemental fury. Aeolus or the god Vin Tur have unleashed the entire sackful of the hurricanes that howl through Chaos over this terrible rock. Impossible to ride in this. I clamber off the bike to walk and can hardly even do that. My shoes slide on a rink of wind, the bike leaps and bucks like a loose toe of canvas in a storm. Yes, time dies in my shoes. It isn't that I am out of strength; I have never had strength sufficient to cope with that wind's force.

On the 1969 Tour, the Mistral hit the *peloton* at 70kph throughout the stage in the Camargue. Goddet and Lévitan, the race directors, took pity and allowed the riders to tuck in behind the support vehicles for the last 50km. As Poulidor described it: 'An authorised en masse doping.' Little comfort to me.

I struggle to the dog-leg turn at the top and find a bit of shelter. The wind shrieks over the parapet embankment. I remount and cycle the last few hundred metres.

My senses have been turned inside out like a skinned rabbit.

I have no room for elation, no room for joy, no mental energy to give it standing room in the foyers of my imagination. Nor is there any obvious sympathy with this demonstration of Nature's power, either. Nature has subjected me to an alarming spell in the rough house and I can't see this mountain in any but the terms of a screeching gale and a wild, steep place.

One thing remains to do: I pick up a stone from the scree near the radio mast, an unlovely iron tower set in soda-white concrete, and stuff it in a side pocket of my saddle bag – for my friend Ronnie's cairn. Cyclist, poet and piper, he'd died before his time of a brain tumour the year before. There is a lot of death brooding on this mountain.

Shuddering with rage, relief and jangled nerves, I struggle to the very top, the absolute summit, where nothing can be higher, and recoil with dismay. The road simply snaps in two and disappears over a precipice: no parapet wall, no safety barriers, like a fledgling's plunge from a nest into fresh air boiling with Mistral. I have to go over that?

For the moment I retreat back down from the summit to a café, a dodgy enough descent, all of 200m. The view which stretches beyond, in a gaseous haze south, across the sprawling Plateau de Vaucluse towards the Lubéron catches my eye, but only for a few seconds: I have to concentrate on getting safely into the shelter of the café wall. I drink hot coffee and steeped sugar lumps. I ponder Simpson's passing and my passing of his memorial stone, and Yeats' epitaphic poem:

> Cast a cold eye
> On life, on death.
> Horseman, pass by.

The 48km from Sault to Malaucène over Ventoux is the more ecstatic, paradoxically, because even as I fly into town on the last wingbeats of that fantastic swoop off the mountain's summit, I am promising myself *Never, never, never will I ride up that mountain again, never, never.* (Five years later, I did.)

It springs from an indescribable cloudburst in my head of joy, relief and thanks due to whatever spirits guard us through adversity and when we are close to breakdown. In ancient times, stranded up on that inhuman pinnacle, I would have vowed my *own* votary cairn to Fortune who protected me and the god of the mountain who spared me.

I find a hotel in the main street, secure my bike in a sort of lock-up store room with a higgledy-piggledy collection of discarded furniture, electrical apparatus, boxes of newspapers, and go up for the shower of showers. My walking-out clothes on, and across the street for my reward: several beers and dinner in the same bar/restaurant. A bottle of Côtes de Ventoux, of course. I keep the bill for my scrapbook. I brim over with contentment; 140km and Mont Ventoux.

They called my hero Merckx, *Le Cannibale*, but the word was, it seems, first used in cyclist journalism of Poulidor in a stage of the 1965 Tour – another second place, to Gimondi by two minutes and 40 seconds. The writer said he swallowed the Mont Ventoux climb '*avec la voracité d'un cannibale engloutissant le mollet d'un archevêque . . .*' (with the voracity of a cannibal wolfing down the leg of an archbishop.)

About a week after my return to England, I was going smoothly at a fair pace to the top of Highgate West Hill, that evil little pimple whose gradient sprang to mind on the first ramp of l'Alpe d'Huez, when a paunchy, oldish man on the far pavement yells: 'Push harder on the pedals.' No hint of a smile or cheer of encouragement.

In France they shout – pedestrians or cyclists, it makes no difference – *Allez! Courage!*

A month after the return, I did climb Mont Ventoux again, in a manner of speaking. The piece for the wind quintet, *Mountain for Wind*, arrived.

CHAPTER EIGHT

TOUR '98

The Tour is Dead, Long Live the Tour

At 5.30 a.m. on the morning of Wednesday, 8 July 1998, three days before the Tour de France Prologue, French Customs officials in the town of Neuville en Ferrain, just inside the Franco–Belgian border, made a routine search of a Fiat car driven by Willy Voet, *soigneur* to the Festina team. In the Fiat, part of the official Tour fleet, were packed over 400 phials of human growth hormones and testosterone-based steroids, boxes of EPO, masking products, anti-hepatitis vaccines and quantities of syringes. Voet was taken to Lille police HQ for interview and later that same day a squad of French judiciary (criminal investigation) police searched the Festina base in Lyon and impounded more drugs. Bruno Roussel, the Festina *directeur sportif*, haughtily dismissed these events as a sick joke.

The following Monday, as the Tour rode out of Dublin, Willy Voet admitted that this was not the first time he'd ferried such a haul of performance-enhancing dope to big races, generally, as on this occasion, under orders from the Festina team bosses. Two days later, the 'sick joke' blew up in Roussel's face: after the stage finish in Cholet, he was taken in for police questioning, the Festina riders' hotel rooms were searched and the team doctor, Eric Rijckaert, joined Roussel in the local jail. Next day, the Tour de France organisers announced that Roussel had been banned, while the riders of the Festina team would be allowed to ride on.

Next day Roussel's lawyers issued a statement: the Festina manager had informed the police that within the Festina team controlled doping had been introduced to safeguard the riders' health and wellbeing. Rather than leave the matter of drug-taking to chance, team, policy was to monitor the riders' intake of chemical substances under strict medical supervision. The subtext of this was, naturally: we know all (or even most) professional riders take dope; we can't put our men at a disadvantage; it's our concern, our professional, *responsible* concern, to make sure they take safe dope in safe quantities.

The can of worms was open.

At 10.50 p.m. on the evening of Friday, 17 July, the eve of the individual time-trial, Tour officials announced that the Festina team would, after all, be expelled from the race. The French judiciary police had charged Roussel and Dr Rijckaert with importing and circulating illegal substances. Ironically, the other teams would ride the race of truth against Festina chronometers but not the Festina riders. At a private meeting, Richard Virenque begged Jean-Marie Blanc, the Tour director, to reconsider the decision but emerged, in tears, to inform a press conference that Festina were out of the Tour.

In the Mosaic ritual for the Jewish Day of Atonement, two goats were chosen, one of which – the scapegoat ('escape' goat) was sent out alive into the wilderness, the sins of all the people having been symbolically laid on it. The other goat was appointed to be sacrificed. Festina had been cast out into the wilderness; the sacrifices were to come.

Virenque, protesting that he had never in his life taken drugs – abjuring declared team policy thereby – called for the Tour organisers to investigate all 22 sporting directors: 'then we'll see what conclusions to draw'. His lawyer declared that Virenque and the rest were being victimised. It is fairly clear that at this point the *peloton* wanted to quit the race en masse.

News leaked that as early as the previous March a TVM team lorry had been stopped by customs in Reims and quantities of EPO impounded. The Tour rapidly spiralled into near chaos: police rough handling, fresh revelation, dismissal and strike.

Festina riders' medical dossiers were seized; the riders were detained for questioning in Lyon. Virenque and Pascal Hervé protested their innocence of drug-taking 'with or without our knowledge'; for the time being, the others kept quiet. The TVM riders were hauled out of their hotel after the stage finish on 23 July and detained, without substantial refreshment, until midnight. Their hotel rooms contained cortico-steroids and masking agents. Next day, shocked by the ruthlessness of the police intervention and the ill-treatment meted out to the TVM men, the entire *peloton* sat by their bikes on the road at the start in Tarascon and, for two hours, the Tour de France ceased to be. One Italian rider, Gian Luigi Stanga of the Polti team, remarked that the Gestapo couldn't have done better than the French police, but hysteria of this sort was becoming a commonplace.

The riders eventually set out; Jalabert and two others launched an attack but, having 'made his point' he sat up on a big lead 60km from the finish. No one was interested in racing. The day's stage went for nothing. Interestingly, the Deutsche Telekom team (Ullrich, Rijs, Zabel *et al*) had been ill-disposed to the strike and joined only reluctantly.

Before the next day's stage, Saturday, 25 July, spokesmen from the *peloton* met the UCI president, Daniel Baal, to air grievances about the mishandling of the drugs affair. It has always been the case that the riders bear the brunt of any organisational foul-ups. In the summer of 1998 they were landed with the hardest consequences of the tussle between Tour organisers, UCI and French judiciary police. Some reacted petulantly, but when the so-called authorities were swaying and dipping in whatever breeze of controversy happened to be blowing, the riders, at least, showed a solidarity lacking elsewhere.

If the authorities knew about drug-taking, and when the leading team in the *peloton* had a policy of controlled doping it is inconceivable that they did *not* know, their failure to act is culpable, reprehensible. End of story. As someone said at the time: 'Intellectual honesty and solidarity have been rare commodities these past few days.' Except, I would add, amongst the riders; *de facto* guilty, most of them, but at least prepared to declare common cause.

Next day, three Festina riders – Armin Meier, Laurent Dufaux and Alex Zülle – came clean; they *had* taken EPO and so, too, had most of the other riders they raced against. Zülle, recruited from the powerful Spanish ONCE team at the beginning of the season as co-leader with Richard Virenque, the mountains ace, expatiated on his confession.

> Everybody knew that the whole *peloton* was taking drugs and
> I had a choice. Either I buckle and go with the trend or I pack
> it in and go back to my old job as a painter. I regret lying but
> I couldn't do otherwise. I had to think about my sponsors and
> people with family responsibilities who worked for Festina. I had
> no wish to be a traitor. It was my free decision to take EPO and I
> did so under the supervision of the Festina doctor.

It later emerged that every Festina rider was required – *required*
– to pay a yearly subscription into a slush fund to finance the
purchase of performance-enhancing drugs for the whole team. It
may well be true, as Zülle said in mitigation, that EPO does not
turn a donkey into a racehorse, but that is not the point. EPO
may well turn an inevitable runner-up into a winner: and that *is*
the point.

Zülle's confession is, in some aspects, touching. Arrested by the
police in Lyon, he was strip-searched, his spectacles and watch
confiscated, and held in a cell for 24 hours, given no sustenance
but one glass of water. He was, he said, treated like an animal. He
had been so keen to win the Tour that year that he'd been prepared
to take a banned substance; to cheat. It's a horrible admission
and one wonders how he will live with it. And how Virenque will
reconcile in his mind the repeated disavowals he had made against
the appearance of his name on the Festina doctor's list of the riders
who have had EPO administered to them.

After the Tour, the directors of Festina announced: 'The Tour
de France was sensational for our image and reputation.' A claim
which the sporting paper, *L'Equipe*, described as '*ubuesque*',
anarchic. In this business, cynicism comes dirt cheap.

Even the Canadian doctor who had devised tests for tracing
EPO claimed that the UCI was simply not interested. He'd met
officials from both the UCI and the IOC but they showed no
enthusiasm for establishing tests – using antibodies – which could
have proved the use of EPO. Their stated reason was that no such
test would bear legal scrutiny. Of this professed nervousness about
litigation, Dr Brisson said:

> It was too easy for them to say that, because then nobody can

be accused of taking EPO. The arguments they used made it clear that they didn't want to catch athletes. That's always the situation when your responsibility is to promote a sport . . . The solution cannot come from the IOC. I'm sure that they will only act if they are forced to do so . . . But they have to test. Users will change their approach, the trafficking will become more subtle; but now everybody knows the problem is there.

The gradual unravelling of the scandal continued. Blood and hair samples were taken from the TVM team; a BigMat-Auber team lorry was searched and medicines taken away for analysis and the *peloton* reacted again. On Wednesday, 29 July, 32km from the start of stage 17, the *peloton* dismounted and sat in the road. Thence began to-and-fro diplomacy between them and the race organisers. When the riders eventually remounted, Pantani tore off his race number and the rest of the bunch followed suit. There ensued a protracted discussion *en route* between Leblanc and Bjarne Rijs speaking for all the riders. Rijs delivered an ultimatum: no more persecution from the police or we quit. Leblanc replied; Rijs returned to the ranks and the entire *peloton* dismounted a second time. More negotiations, a second restart, followed almost immediately by the abandon of the ONCE, Banesto and Riso Scotti teams. Laurent Jalabert, the ONCE leader, climbed off his bike and said he was finished with the Tour. Hard-nosed commentators said this wasn't moral outrage; Jalabert was going badly, now he was off the hook; but that's an indicator of what miserable depths current opinion was plumbing. The race rolled into Aix-les-Bains at walking pace and another big story broke. The police searched the ONCE team rooms and interviewed Jalabert; the Française des Jeux rooms and interviewed the manager Marc Madiot; and, as Virenque was once more reiterating his denials on French television, police emerged from a search of the Casino team rooms having detained one of their men, current leader in the mountains prize, Rodolfo Massi. (The new mountains leader, Christophe Rinero, refused to wear the polka-dot jersey until he had won it on the next stage.)

Two days later, Massi was charged with selling banned drugs. The Tour de France had spewed out its first drug peddler. A suitcase full of corticoids, growth hormones, steroids, plus a large sum of cash were discovered in his room. He explained, somewhat lamely, that he needed the drugs for his asthma. The man who informed on him, Gilles Bouvard, formerly of Festina and now a teammate in Casino, had fallen out with Massi earlier in the season. Not only were banned substances going down the pan, so too was loyalty. The ONCE team doctor, Nicolas Terrados joined Massi in custody (both were released on bail) two days before the Tour arrived on the Champs-Elysées where Pantani took victory, the first Italian since Gimondi in 1965 to do so and only the second Italian, after Coppi, to win the Tour and Giro double.

Public reaction to the scandal as it unfolded and as the Tour proceeded was generally in support of the riders. The tarmac bulletins, usually daubed with riders' names, carried: *Le Tour est mort. Vive le Tour.* The Tour is dead. Long live the Tour. And: *Le Tour est innocent. Faut pas toucher au Tour.* The Tour is innocent. Hands off the Tour. But there was this, too: *Ne vous dopez-pas. Faites-nous rêver.* Don't take dope. Allow us our dreams. And wherever blame might be apportioned, one message to the riders, the officials, all of them, individually, was clear: *Il y a de soi – c'est évident.* It's up to you – wake up.

Someone wrote: 'There's something rotten in this sport – the Festina affair is proof enough. But that does not stop one admiring the cyclists.' The magnificent, shattering solo ride of Pantani's up to Les Deux Alpes, in atrocious weather, wind, rain, fog, to trounce Ullrich by over seven minutes and effectively seal his final victory, was awe-inspiring and Ullrich's audacious attack the following day on the Madeleine, some 54km from home, a heroic strike to salvage pride worthy of the great champions. Only Pantani could hold his wheel and, at the finish, the two of them drove themselves over the line, exhausted, like two prize-fighters who'd slugged each other to a standstill. It was legendary stuff and put the whole dismal drugs brouhaha into a very squalid perspective. These were men still capable of riding into extremes of suffering. Ullrich's bravery gave Pantani a triumph worthy of the little Italian's own great courage. In such actions are the real champions revealed.

Even as Pantani and Ullrich were demonstrating that the basic instinct to attack at all costs and damn the consequences was still alive in some riders, the reputation of those who quit the race was sullied; not so much because they seemed to be dodging the issue of culpability on the drugs charges, but because to abandon is, without pressing cause, at very best undignified. When Bobet pulled out in 1959, he climbed into the car of *Le Parisien* and asked one of the journalists to lend him a hat so he could disguise himself. 'I'm ashamed to abandon,' he said.

Censure of the 1998 escapees was robust: 'Every rider who abandons is blameworthy because in that act they are destroying what earned them their glory.' (The glory of riding in the Tour, that is.)

Luc Leblanc commented: 'Jalabert should have stayed out of respect for the Tour, that is what one would have expected of a French champion.' (Jalabert was wearing the tricolour jersey as national road-race champion.)

A rider who abandons snaps something essential in his own spirit; he abandons an ideal. Lofty sentiments which had to be retrieved from the sordid detritus of post-Tour revelations and deal-mongering. Grubbiest of all came the announcement by the Festina sponsors that as a result of the scandal Festina had sold far more watches than any of their market forecasts predicted. Here is the real source of the evil: greed.

The Tour organisers handle an annual budget of 25 million pounds: 15 million pounds from the various corporate-backed sponsors, eight million pounds from television rights, two million pounds from the *villes d'étape*. Cycling teams dispose of between two million pounds and four million pounds per annum, and commercial imperatives drive the whole shebang. The ruthless profiteering of international pharmaceutical corporate firms is notorious; the financial rewards for highest-level success in cycling sport are exorbitant; the venality equally so. *Le Parisien* commented: 'We are all accomplices in this grotesque hypocrisy because we all know that drug-taking is prevalent in the Tour de France. Taking into account the fact that the race is dependent on high financial stakes, you realise it couldn't be otherwise. When you are in a team and have to earn a living you have no choice. For this reason, it is inconceivable that the Festina team is the only guilty party.'

Festina had the ill luck to be caught first. The UCI even

considered forbidding the Spanish-sponsored Festina team from the national tour, the Vuelta a España but, in the upshot, took no action for fear of litigation from the Festina lawyers or individual riders seeking damages for loss of earnings. The Vuelta organisers, like those of the Tour, invite whatever teams they choose. Thus, the UCI has no legitimated power to exclude riders from a large proportion of the yearly racing calendar; much of what they do is no more conclusive than posturing and bold talk. However, pronouncements on the subject were sufficient to provoke a feud between the Spanish and French cycling federations. The route of the Vuelta was altered to remove a couple of stages which had been planned to cross the Pyrenees into France.

Nearly two weeks after the Tour, the UCI promulgated a list of measures designed to combat the use of drugs in cycling:

1. There would be no change in existing dope controls – classic blood and urine tests to be used.
2. From 1 January 1999, there are to be four annual checks on riders' health (both physiology and hormone levels), this to be the responsibility of national federations and conducted by an independent medical inspectorate appointed by the UCI.

   These checks will go much further than in the present checks on red corpuscle levels and produce a more general profile of the athletes' physical condition 'to verify that an athlete's organism is functioning well and to avoid accidents from the misuse of drugs'.
3. Responsibility is enjoined on team doctors:
   – to maintain regulations
   – to uphold ethics
   – to protect health and advise cyclists (who, if left to their own devices, face too many risks).
4. An anti-EPO programme, centred on laboratories in Lausanne and Cologne.

The issue of racing fatigue is addressed by ordinances which:

1. Limit the length of the racing season, whereby each rider

might be confined to racing on between 90 and 120 days only. (This was put up for discussion.)
2. Reform the system of selecting teams for the major events. The present system is based on team rankings; but classification is derived from an assessment of performance in every single race in the calendar, so as to avoid losing the top teams and their star riders in the lesser races.

From 1999, there will be fewer qualifying events (two of the three big Tours, every World Cup race plus a few other senior events, such as the Dauphiné Libéré).

Thus there will be a qualitative not a quantitative assessment 'to encourage the top teams to compete less often but harder.'

On the face of it, a genuine attempt to address the symptoms of the disease, at least. Except that less than two months later, on Monday, 5 October, the UCI issued a statement: The original eight-month ban levied on the three Festina Tour riders implicated in the drugs scandal (Meier, Zülle and Dufaux) had been reduced by one month, to allow them to ride in next year's Tour. The fines imposed – a paltry £1,346 apiece – stood. So much for the authorities.

It is the opinion of many – amateurs and professionals – that the penalty for taking drugs should be an immediate, unequivocal ban from the sport for life. It is a view implicitly supported by Bertrand de Gallé, for instance, the president of La Française des Jeux: a clause in his team contracts warns any rider caught taking banned substances of instant dismissal from the team.

There have been noises lately from riders about a new 'clean' *peloton*. In October 1998, the Festina sponsors vowed to take a lead in fighting the use of drugs and pledged a fund of $725,000 to wage war on dope-taking. They've even nominated a French doctor, Gerard Dine, to work as scientific consultant in analysing and monitoring the effects of industrially produced substances on cyclists. There may well be a huge collective relief attendant on this. However many pro cyclists take drugs, it is undoubtedly the case that many do so reluctantly, only because they know that if they don't they risk being consistently beaten by lesser talents. Commentators have adjudged Boardman's career in the pro ranks to have been so hampered; the promise he showed on the track having faltered, somewhat, in the long stage races. As the French paper *L'Equipe* put it: 'It depends, above all, on the determination expressed by the riders to show a genuine will to escape from a system of which, ultimately, they are victims . . . and then, finally, *happily* [my italics] there are the police . . .'

That great opponent of drug-testing, Jacques Anquetil, always backed the police as the only neutral authority whom he could trust. The calamitous events of 1998 rather endorse this view. Perhaps the very professional meticulousness of the French judiciary police, experienced as brutal and ruthless by the riders, delivered the harsh visitation of some kind of truth-telling – at last – without which the drug-taking would, once more, have simply been ignored by authorities whose attitude to positive dope tests was wholly in line with their own lack of positive action.

CHAPTER NINE

1999

The Tour of Renewal

With an irony even the French could not have foreseen, the organisers of the Tour de France chose to launch the last race of the millennium from Madman's Bluff – Le Puy du Fou – in the Vendée. The Festina affair had all but scuppered the '98 edition: it seemed to many cynics and ill-informed, sniping commentators an act of pure folly to run the race at all, mired as it had become in the drugs scandal. Examining magistrates in France had spent the winter trawling through grisly evidence of systematic doping in the professional *peloton*; riders who had owned up to the practice served their suspension; others kept quiet. Richard Virenque continued to protest his total innocence under judicial oath and in May, Willy Voet, the ex-*soigneur* from Festina, now out of a job, blew the whole gaffe with a book packed with 'revelations of 30 years of cheating'.

Massacre à la Chaîne ('Serial Murder' or 'Murder as a job requirement') is a shocking book, its gruesome candour fuelled by a distinct – and understandable – bitterness that its author has been made to carry the can for a whole phalanx of parties as guilty as him. Voet reproduces extracts from his notebooks recording the dosage of EPO and growth hormones dispensed to the Festina riders over a number of years. Names, dates, quantities. He talks of pills doled out like sweets, dope controls tricked by means of a urine-filled condom attached to a length of rubber tubing – 'a pipe up the arse' – of injections administered to riders on the move, once driving the needle in through a rider's shorts, a boost to carry him to the finish; of intravenous drips rigged in hotel rooms; and of one scene of grotesque farce when a visitor blundered into the Festina dope lounges and Virenque and another rider had to scoot into the bathroom, hauling the drips, still attached, with them.

Nor was it only the riders caught up in this routine drug culture. Voet kept himself going through endless car journeys and long séances of work as masseur and mobile dispensary with a heady cocktail of amphetamines, analgesics, cocaine, heroin and the occasional dash of corticoids known as *le pot Belge* – the Belgian slug, shot, pick-me-up.

Voet's confessions and the extensive testimony that the French judicial police drew out of him make depressing reading – one doctor was nicknamed 'Mabuse' (Self-abuse) from his readiness to dole the stuff out. What price enthusiasm, now? How can we not *all* be cynics in this seamy light?

So, whether or not one believes that Tour director Jean-Marie Leblanc really did not know to what extent drugs had dominated cycling, his announcement of this *Tour de Renouveau* was a brave call for a fresh start. There could be no eradication of suspicion – the scandal had been too traumatic – but in the true spirit of Desgrange, the real challenge was to demand that the Tour reinvent itself. This was, of course, greeted with derision by many. It had become horribly clear that the '98 Tour de France? Tour de Farce was too salacious a story for the muckraking journos wallowing in their own whited-sepulchre piety to pass up. No matter that the cyclists were, willy-nilly, bearing the brunt of the witch-hunt and that drug-taking was suspected in practically every other sport: if the Tour de France is not *all* cycling it is certainly cycling's enlarging mirror. If the Tour de France could not clean up its act, what chance for the sport as a whole? There was much to play for.

The Tour's renewal extended further than the elimination of drugs. Within a month or so of the Prologue, several of the main contenders were out. Jan Ullrich, the '97 winner, aggravated a knee injury in the Tour of Switzerland and withdrew. Bjarne Rijs, the '96 laureate, broke his arm in the same race and would not start. Laurent Jalabert, the world number one, who had enraged many by not only quitting the '98 Tour but persuading others to follow, had effectively exiled himself from France by going to live in Switzerland and refusing to submit to the new strict, even harsh, mandatory drug tests lately imposed by the French Cycling Federation. The 1998 yellow jersey, Marco Pantani, had been playing cat and mouse all year: he might, only might, ride the Tour. The course was too easy for a specialist climber like me, he said, but he said the same before his victory. And there is no such thing as an easy course: you just ride harder. Yet, cruising towards a second successive victory in the Giro d'Italia, a routine blood test revealed an abnormally high count of red corpuscles in his bloodstream, and he was eliminated 'for health reasons'. The implication – without incontrovertible proof – was that he had taken EPO; this he strenuously denied, but the UCI had set an upper limit of 50 per cent and Pantani showed 53 per cent.

This was bold of the Giro directors: to ban Italy's sporting hero, darling of the *tifosi*, on the eve of another triumph took considerable nerve. Whatever credit it did them, it inevitably complicated things across the Alps. Double Tour and Giro winner in 1998, the famously incendiary attacker Pantani was suspect of doping. Well, he wouldn't be riding the Tour: the field was being cleared of compromise.

At a press conference in Paris on 16 June, Leblanc (who rode the Tour in 1968 and 1970) posted warning that the new stringency would apply to everyone, no favours. Philippe Gaumont and Laurent Roux, who had both tested positive earlier in the season, were banned; Serguei Gonchar had been kicked off the Tour of Switzerland for a high haematocrit test (registering the proportion of red blood cells) and he and his Vini Caldirola team were expelled from the Tour. So too was Manolo Saiz, team doctor of Jalabert's ONCE team, for persistently making defamatory remarks about the Tour in the wake of the drugs scandal. The TVM team, who had mounted a very public protest after being rough-handled during the '98 Tour and then quit *en bloc*, were refused entry to the race because they had discredited it.

Controversially, Richard Virenque, darling of the French public, four-times winner of the mountains prize, baby-faced pin-up the women swoon over, star of *Virenboum*, Virenque mania, made the start. Booted off the 1998 race, still protesting his innocence of any doping and due for trial, he was allowed to ride.

That, sadly, wasn't the end of it. The UCI intervened, presumably having been leant on by Virenque's Italian team Polti (by racing in Italy he too avoided the draconian French régime), insisting that the Tour de France organisers had not given Virenque sufficient notice of disqualification. Virenque squeezed back in, ill-prepared, maybe, but ready to cut the rug in his chosen show.

The UCI, often in the person of its president, Hein Verbruggen, has been much criticised for playing the ostrich, and for its indecision, lack of clear leadership and equivocation, but this latest fudge and jobsworth primping of strict rule and regulation was disgraceful. A shameful rebuke of an organisation trying hard to wipe the slate clean.

And so to Madman's Bluff.

Some pundits opined that, without many of the big names, this would be a Tour lacking in quality. Such opinions get in the way of renewal. The American, Bobby Julich, who unexpectedly took third in '98, started an obvious favourite. Zülle, restored after suspension and – surely – clean had come second to Indurain in '95 and boasts two Vuelta victories in his *palmarès*, '96 and '97. Here, too, are Abraham Olano, a master of the time-trial but yet to prove himself in the mountains; Pavel Tonkov, Giro winner; Ivan Gotti, Giro winner; Rinero, mountains prize and fourth overall in '98; Michael Boogerd, the Dutch champion; and Lance Armstrong. The big man from Texas became world road-race champion in 1993 and two years later was diagnosed with testicular cancer which had spread to his lungs and brain. His being here at all, let alone at the highest level of bike-racing, he freely admits is a miracle. He has prepared for the Tour as 'Tonin' Magne always prepared: 12 days' seclusion riding the mountain stages.

Armstrong took the 6.8km Prologue by seven seconds over Zülle with a matchless display of speed and technical control. Boardman, the speed merchant fancied to take a fourth Prologue victory, was beaten into fifth place, by 16 seconds. This opening ride is no great indicator as to the shape of the race: the time bonuses on offer for sprint prizes and stage wins during the first week of racing tend to make tenure of the first yellow jersey brief, but there is no doubt that Armstrong's win was testimony of two things: his racing form and the intensity of his focus. His eyes are hardly blinking.

For the first six days the sprinters rule. Towards the end of each stage, the Telekoms drive for the line to bring up their man Zabel, aiming for a fourth green points jersey (to equal Kelly's record); Rabobank wind it up hoping to launch their man McEwen to a win; the Red Train, the scarlet-shirted Saeco riders, Camesso, the young champion of Italy in the tricolour jersey at their head, blast through to shoot Big Mario Cipollini out of the maelstrom of the sprint. Except that Mario, the Lion King, is subdued this year. Saeco think he has had his day and aren't offering to renew his contract. 'They think I am a clapped-out banger,' he says, plaintively, 'and they want to send me to the breaker's yard. A group of friends is splitting up as well. I thought Saeco cared for me more.' The group of friends is the team devoted to getting Cipo onto the podium, and he is out to show his sponsors that his engine is still the fastest in the bunch. But not yet: the 'win merchant' from Estonia, Jaan Kirsipuu, takes the first stage. A historic day for his small country, as he puts it.

Riders take all kind of crazy risks to land a win so the sprint finishes, and the hectic run-up to them often provokes crashes. Recent Tours have been marred by some dreadful pile-ups: riders miscalculating the angle of bend and hurtling into the barriers . . . a touch of wheels in the close press of the accelerating bunch . . . narrow town streets, speed calmers, roundabouts . . . one rider down and the whole troupe behind him. Chris Boardman in '98 had a terrible fall which, had he not been wearing a helmet, would surely have killed him.

And in '99, before stage two, Boardman said: 'Today will be the worst day of the week. There's that causeway halfway through the stage and the race will split there for sure. It's so exposed . . . the race will fall to bits.' *That causeway*, the Passage du Gois, joins the Ile de Noirmoutier to the Vendée mainland; 5km long and no more than two cars wide, it disappears under every tide. Riding onto it, Boardman's front wheel skidded on some seaweed; he pulled over and counted to ten. Then, as another rider described it: 'A gust of wind suddenly went across the road; one rider fell and the rest began to go down like dominoes.' The narrowness, the treacherous surface, made recovery very difficult. Ahead of the crash, a 75-strong group, half the field, containing Armstrong, Tonkov, Julich and Virenque, were clear and whipping up the pace towards the finish. Behind it, Zülle, Gotti, Rinero and Boogerd eventually mounted a chase which trailed in over six minutes down. The crash had effectively denied them any realistic chance of winning the race, barring another accident. The demoralising impact of such a heavy loss so early on is cruel. It adds immeasurably to the threat of the mountains. One of Boogerd's team men, Marc Vauters, ended up in hospital, as did Armstrong's henchman, Jonathan Vaughters.

Cipo made history that week. His mood lightened and, whereas his racing had begun to look tentative, even nervous, he began to expand into his hallmark ostentatious flourish of power-sprinting. The Red Train came out of the siding of failed confidence as sleek as ever, threw the points and, on stage four, Cipo scorched in comfortably ahead of Zabel: a wondrous turn of speed, on Fagnini's wheel till it's the moment to say the word, Fagnini pulls aside and the man goes. Fagnini has agreed a contract with another team for the end of the season; that must have a lot to do with the glitch. But, four times in a row they worked the old one-two this year. Last man to do that was the specialist stage winner Charles Pélissier in 1930 (eight stages all told) and, before him, René Pottier in 1906 (five overall).

The day before, Cipo was beaten to the line by Tom Steels, the short-tempered Belgian rider disqualified two years before for flinging a bidon at another rider in the closing metres of a sprint. But, locking onto Cipo's wheel, Steels had shouldered the Czech strongman, Jan Svorada, into the barrier before jumping past the Italian. Had Svorada gone down there would have been carnage, and Steels was rightly relegated to the back of the field. He complained of injustice but had no claim and Cipo equalled the record held by his compatriot Gino 'the Pious' Bartali since 1948 when he achieved his three in a row across the mountains (seven stages all told and overall yellow). Cipo modestly discounted his effort in comparison to that of the great Bartali and then paid heartfelt and uncharacteristically self-effacing tribute to his team. His victory next day, in pure grace of speed, majestic style – invincible – catapulted him deeper into the record books. I warmed to him at last.

Back down the road, the luckless Zabel – no stage wins but already in green – crashed and rode on with a bloody chin, lacerated knee and thigh and badly bruised testicles (run-of-the-mill stuff for these bruisers) slipstreamed to the finish by his team, among them Guerini, Ullrich's nominated mountain tow man, now promoted to team leader.

In the first major test of individual strength, 56.5km against the clock in Metz, Armstrong produced what he called one of his greatest ever victories, adding, 'I have never felt so tired, though.' He overtook Olano, who started ahead of him by two minutes, added nearly a minute to his lead over Zülle, and pulled on the yellow jersey. (Boardman went down by three and a half minutes.) It was a superlative show of time-trialling class: speed, will, concentration, deployment of power, control of the bike. Seconds can be lost on sloppy cornering, misjudged gear changes or ill-gauged expenditure of effort. Sadly, Bobby Julich crashed when his back wheel collapsed on a tight bend; he was taken to hospital.

Stage nine. The Alps. 213.5km.
A couple of small climbs early on, one third, one second category, before the main agenda: col du Télégraphe, the monster Galibier, and Montgenèvre on the way to a sapping 12km climb to the mountain-top finish at the Italian ski resort of Sestriere, where Claudio 'the Devil' Chiapucci left the rest for dead and rode to a glorious solo victory in front of his home crowd in 1992.

The day began cold and wet, mountain fogs, thoroughly miserable: many riders hate these conditions, the chill gets into their bones, the roads are slick and difficult to negotiate. Armstrong actually enjoys them, or perhaps has learned to relish them, knowing that to do so gives him a physical and moral advantage over the others.

Armstrong and a small élite breakaway group – Zülle, the Spanish climbers Escartin and Beltrán, Gotti, Virenque – led the race onto the final climb and, some 8km from the finish, under no pressure to make any time gains (indeed, more prudently advised to caution this early in the mountains), Armstrong attacked. Pedalling with superb fluency of rhythm at unfluctuating speed, he simply rode away and could not be caught. He went too soon, he admitted as much, and the last 2km were murder, but such spontaneity is innate in him. He felt good, so he went. 'Headstrong' they sometimes called him at the start of his career, but this was champion's style. Impetuosity is the kernel of what Merckx called 'the religion of attack', *le punch*, and though Armstrong didn't make huge gains in time (31 seconds on Zülle, 1m 26s on Escartin and so on down the field), the psychological blow was heavy if not mortal. Far from limiting his losses, that small-business principle upon which so many winners have based victory, he carried the fight to his rivals, to the specialist climbers on their ground. True, he might have a bad day and there were more Alps and even more Pyrenees to cross, but his audacity had secured him priceless advantage for the time being at least. Up to the rest to respond in kind, or not.

There were enough specialist climbers around still to make him suffer, but he had shown such impregnable confidence that it would take a bad day indeed to cause him serious grief. Nevertheless, the Tour is the Tour: in 1998, Ullrich had suffered as never before, his face ravaged with the pain of a crucifying effort, when Pantani danced off through the damp chilly mists of Les Deux Alpes. He lost over seven minutes and the Tour.

Armstrong paid for his extravagant ride to Sestriere: on the ascent of l'Alpe d'Huez he left Zülle and Virenque floundering, only to be reeled in. They had kept their nerve and plugged away. Two brave escapees, Bourguignon and Heulot, had spent 150 of the day's 220km in the lead; Heulot went ahead at last but, 3km from the finish, exhausted, he watched Guerini and then Tonkov rob him of glory. His, and all France's, dream of stage victory crumbled and so, too, very nearly, did Guerini. He went clear with just 2km to go and Tonkov couldn't match him, but, on the flat run-in to the *Arrivée*, a spectator planted himself in the middle of the road, bang in front of Guerini, with a camera, then blundered into the rider as he tried to avoid him. Guerini fell; he might easily have broken a collarbone, been winded, lost the stage. Luckily, there was no injury and the adrenalin was coursing so fiercely that he scrambled back onto the bike, took a push from the imbecile who had felled him, and scampered for the line in a frenzy. He made it, lifted both arms to the sky and rolled across the line, stage winner, Tour de France. Bliss.

On the climb to l'Alpe d'Huez, Virenque took the familiar polka-dot jersey. Ostracised by some in the *peloton* and vilified by many who felt that his protestations of innocence in the Festina affair were cowardly, that he funked the issue at the start and dug himself further into a hole of defiance from which he cannot extricate himself, he retained huge loyalty from the French public. *L'Alpe d'Huez needs Virenque. Fight for your fans. We will always support you* joined the banners on the big climb. Other fans, incensed at his sneaking back into the race, daubed the route of the Prologue with his name below the needle of a huge syringe filled with EPO. He brazened it out; Leblanc finally shook his hand and, by the end of the Tour, his postbag in the count of riders' fan-mail outweighed the rest amply. His riding in the mountains in 1999 was notably less fiery than before, but he was clearing the cols with regular determination and, after the Alps, led the competition comfortably. Guerini was followed in by Armstrong's group, only 25 seconds back.

At the side of the road on the climb to l'Alpe d'Huez, an enterprising drinks vendor, advertising his al fresco bar further up the road, had posted a sign reading: *EPO 100 metres.* That is *eau, pastis* and *orgeat* (barley syrup flavoured with sweet and bitter almonds) mixed into a cocktail known as *mauresque*, a 'Moorish'. The Tour was probably too raw for such wisecracks.

There were already rumblings in the French press about the so-called clean race, the 'race of fresh water'. Disgruntled French riders were bitching about a two-speed *peloton – aux deux vitesses –* and one told an interviewer that he had been struggling to turn his lowest gear on one of the climbs whilst alongside him two riders (not French) were chatting casually as they twiddled the big chain-ring as if there were no gradient to speak of. The French fans have had to get used to foreign winners of their Tour since Hinault's fifth victory in 1985, but in the jaundiced climate of suspicion, the niggling bad temper hanging over from the mess in which the Tour and the sport has found itself toiling these past 12 months, the French are clearly feeling hard done by. The regulations on blood tests and dope controls imposed by their Federation are assuredly draconian. Whether these methods are more efficient is another matter, but given the marked inferiority of the French contingent in general, the unworthy sense is that there indeed *are* two gears available: with and without dope. The resentment was particularly fierce against the Spanish teams, regulated by a federation known for its lax attitude to controls.

This general resentment was talked up by the gutter press desperate for a story, eager to reopen the drugs scandal. Knowing nothing about bike racing, many of them, their *raison d'être* is to find and tip out any worms they can rake up. They turned on Armstrong. His strength was, by comparison with the rest, superhuman and therefore, almost by definition, drug-assisted. He was, one writer said, a Martian. (Thirty years ago, another French journalist spoke in awed terms of *la planète Merckx* and *Merckxissimo* when the Belgian crushed the Frenchman Roger Pingeon, winner in 1967, by 17m 54s in his first Tour. Such generosity is not in large supply these days.)

The best-placed French rider in the *peloton* halfway through the race was Laurent Brochard, world champion in 1997 and already an hour lag of Armstrong. How could this be? Yet, when he won the rainbow jersey, Brochard was riding for Festina, pop-full of EPO, and actually tested positive after the Worlds. Maybe he isn't that good after all when, finally, he is riding at his natural speed.

And the speed that so many of them were riding at: it's unnaturally high, whined the journos in the non-specialist French papers. Not true, in fact. Certainly the average speed of the '99 Tour did turn out to be the highest ever – over 40kph – but one entire stage had been raced with a strong assisting wind, and Pantani's overall time was very nearly 40kph over another relatively flat course. These accusations were pretty thin straws to be clutching at. And what of the performance of their darling, the professed innocent, Virenque?

One French doctor said that there was no known case of a sportsman surviving cancer and being stronger for it. Medically this may well be true, but so what? The exception neither proves the rule nor limits the possibility of exception. And, I should say, that anyone with a grain of insight into the psyche of a top-level athlete who has picked himself up off his death-bed, fought back to fitness and then into the highest level of competition of a sport which he loves and once excelled in, would not find the new intensification in will, commitment or even resistance to physical suffering at all astonishing. Statistics cannot disprove what is self-evident. It is a truism that the difference between amateurs and professionals is in preparation; and between the very best pros and the also-rans even more preparation. Champions win because they work harder, all the time.

The press had an ally. A young pro, Christophe Bassons, formerly a junior rider with Festina and now riding his first Tour with the French team sponsored by their lottery, La Française des Jeux, was trumpeting himself as Mr Clean in a *peloton* composed largely of dope-heads. This was not helpful. In articles about his experience of the Tour commissioned by *Le Parisien*, Bassons was blowing the whistle on the hypocrisy, cheating and double standards of the sport. He openly attacked his fellow riders, in swingeing language, for keeping their traps shut, not owning up to the fact that no one, *no one*, could win a Tour stage just by turning the pedals. This last charge he made even before the Tour started. He had, he said, always refused drugs and been mocked and reviled by the other riders for his purist stand. The *peloton* put up with him for a while but finally had enough and he became a leper in the ranks. He finally quit because he was mentally – not physically – drained. Armstrong himself had ridden up alongside him to advise him that his sermonising had no place in the Tour; that it was unprofessional to bleat about what he imagined to be going on in the pro ranks he had only just joined and that if he wouldn't stop the rant he ought to leave. Bernard Hinault commented that it was the duty of a rider to ride the Tour not to moonlight as a journalist and, besides, for all his holier-than-thou opinionation, Bassons habitually slept in a hypobaric tent to boost the count of red cells in his blood. He was overdosing on oxygen.

The press seized on the story, naturally: the yellow jersey putting the frighteners on the young small fry as proof of a general complicity amongst the members of the *peloton* to maintain *omertá* – the vow of silence.

To cap it, in the last week of the race, the French heavyweight journal *Le Monde* broke the story that traces of corticoids had been found in Armstrong's urine after a dope test on 4 July, Independence Day; how they love a bit of synchronicity. Corticoids are cortisone derivatives which hasten relief from swelling and skin ailments, notably, but which can also aid recovery from fatigue.

The article in *Le Monde* followed a denial by Armstrong at a special press conference, that he had taken any corticoids which, in this immediate post-EPO era, are the most topical doping agencies. It was nauseatingly apparent that some pompous asses of the non-sporting press were desperate to gather themselves up in their prophetic mantle and scream *J'accuse!*

Armstrong was an enigma, said *Le Monde*, not so much because he had survived one of the most virulent forms of cancer (neglecting to add that if caught early it is also one of the cancers more amenable to cure) but because he had achieved the remarkable feat of producing traces in his urine of a banned substance which he claimed never to have taken. The French National Laboratory for the Fight Against Doping states: either the body contains banned substances or it does not; that is the sole question to answer. In Armstrong's case the test showed a level of 0.2; normal levels, without doping, lie between 1 and 6. However, *Armstrong had without shadow of doubt taken corticoids.*

This kind of rationale is veering towards the kind of nasty legalistic petty-fogging on which Robespierre and company based their Revolutionary law – you are either for the Republic or against it; neutrality is a crime – and McCarthy his disgusting witch-hunt of communists, party members or sympathisers.

In answer to the question put in French by the *Le Monde* journalist 'have you taken corticoids?', Armstrong said he had not *taken* corticoids, thinking that *taken* must refer either to pills or injections. In fact he had used a cream commonly used by bike riders to ease a saddle sore; the cream contained tiny amounts of corticoid and some of this must have seeped into his system. The attacks took some time to peter out. Armstrong, with admirable composure, remarked that one thing he would certainly advise any cancer sufferer not to do would be to wear the yellow jersey in the Tour de France, stress being a prime factor in susceptibility to the disease. Eddy Merckx, surely mindful of the agonies he endured after being banished from the Giro in 1969, visited him to give him encouragement at this difficult time. It is worth pointing out that Armstrong lives in France, races in France and is subject, therefore, to the same constraints imposed on all French riders. If he does go on to sue *Le Monde*, the action may compel a more measured approach to fact and unsubstantiated and irrelevant information among journalists. For all their harrying of medication in cycling, they would do well to examine their own addiction to sensational gossip as the unvarnished truth. But, ignorance has become a stock-in-trade. One British writer, the France correspondent for a broadsheet, indeed, said that of course the modern Tour is much tougher than the pre-war Tour which was a leisurely affair, averaging around 25kph . . . blah blah blah. Twenty-five kilometres per hour on those roads up those mountains? That is *fast*. And on what did he base this absurd statement? A photograph of the 1920 *peloton* dawdling along at the beginning of another 300-plus kilometres of riding on dirt tracks, as two riders light up cigarettes (see p. 164).

In the Pyrenees, Armstrong's fellow US Postal riders – Tyler Hamilton and Kevin Livingston in particular – gave a sterling display of team riding. They rode themselves into the ground over Peyresourde, Aspin, Portillon, Tourmalet, Soulor and Aubisque to protect their leader; no effort was spared to keep the speed high at the front of the leading group until, spent, they could peel off and leave the day to Armstrong himself. This was classic Tour sacrifice of the lesser ambition to the greater, achieving precious advantage by total dedication to final victory rather than intermediate gains. Armstrong himself had worked as *domestique* for Jonathan Vaughters in the Dauphiné Libéré earlier in the season, driving the race up Mont Ventoux with his teammate on his wheel. The loss of Vaughters in the pile-up on the Passage du Gois was a heavy one; but Livingston and Hamilton earned their share of the prize money by some magnificent support riding. This always puzzles those uninitiated in the protocols of bike-racing, but the work of the *domestique*, who is not capable of winning the race, in devotion to the cause of a leader who *is*, can be simply explained. They are doing for him what the pacemaker is employed to do for the record-breaking track athlete. Bike racing demands many varied strengths and talents; the best riders must have a broad talent but even they cannot do everything, and every Tour victory is a combined effort to which every contribution, however humble, is vital.

The drug hounds did make one paltry scoop: the Belgian Ludo Dierckxsens, breakaway winner of the 11th stage into the hotbed of

French cycling, St Etienne, reported to the dope control and handed over a doctor's prescription for a banned corticoid – Synacthen – which he'd used to cure tendinitis in his knee. Unhappily, though he tested negative, he had not informed his team doctor about the medication. The doctor said he almost certainly would not have prescribed the drug, and, applying the strictest rules of team ethics, the manager sent Dierckxsens, 'honest but a bit silly', home.

The flat stages between the mountain ranges and after them towards Paris are traditionally where lesser riders can sometimes steal a victory; it takes cheek and a willingness to bury yourself in the handlebars, hoping that the rest of the bunch will be happy enough to let other idiots cane themselves through the heat and exhaustion of the latter part of the race. Dierckxsens had his day, briefly; so, too, Comasso, the Italian champion riding for Saeco, a sweet reward for all the selfless work he had done for Cipollini (out after a crash in the first mountain stage).

Tom Steels clocked his third victory, in the sprinters' home-from-home, Bordeaux, two days before the final time-trial, but a few riders at the back of the bunch had the grim experience of riding into a cloud of tear gas (or mace?) sprayed on them by a delinquent who darted out of the crowd with a canister and let rip. Laurent Madouas spoke for them: 'Coming off a bend, I saw a man in the crowd holding a spray can; he squirted it over us: I thought it was water. But quite soon I felt my eyes burning . . . it was terrible. I called out for the doctor; I thought I was going to fall off. For ten seconds I couldn't breathe. What if it had been poisonous?' Even after the race they were all feeling groggy, with irritation in their eyes, throat and lungs.

Time-trial. Stage 19. 57km, Paris Futuroscope.
This science-fiction business park south-west of Paris hosted the Départ of the 1990 Tour and a stage finish in 1994, when the victor, Jan Svorada, was in his pomp. Armstrong won it, to be sure, but only by nine seconds from Zülle and, for all the talk of the American's massive superiority, it must be recalled that, discounting the calamitous loss he suffered on stage two, Zülle was second by only one minute 24 seconds. That Zülle rode on after the disaster on stage two and raced with such tenacity and class

was the mark of a true professional; effacing the miseries of the past year, he showed great courage. By winning all the Tour's time-trials on his way to overall victory, Armstrong joined an élite trio: Merckx, Hinault, Indurain.

Champs-Elysées, 25 July.

The crowds gather early; the sun is broiling; the big screens show pallid images of the progress of the race, 143.5km from Arpajon up through the outlying suburbs of the city. They are due to erupt onto the grand avenue at around half past three in the afternoon but they are late. Policemen patrol the piste beyond the double line of barriers, one per ten metres or so. More people arrive and swell the numbers close to the smooth *pavé* of the road. Up to the left, caught in the haze above the avenue of trees, we see the Arc de Triomphe, the route either side hung with pendant flags: French tricolour and the red and blue of the city of Paris. The mood is good-humoured; this is the city *en fête populaire*. Earlier that morning I had done some shopping and the man in the wine shop, down from Les Arts et Métiers where I am staying, voiced his opinion about the Tour de France: 'They should have two Tours: one with drugs and one without. Then you could choose which one to ride in.' He said it with a smile but the scepticism was weary. Nice man, intelligent, good on wine, but, evidently, no bike fan. The race – oh, just a bike race, for heavens' sake – didn't excite him, and the drugs scandal sickened him. Not sport. Unworthy of the French people. Fair enough. I didn't argue the case: he may be right. I feel differently and want to believe in the renewal; without trust and a determined attempt to remove suspicion, what chance have the cyclists, ever, of riding on fresh water?

At last we can see from snatched glimpses of the big screen – some Swiss patriot is waving his flag across the line of vision, damn – the city outskirts. And soon they will see what every Tour rider who has completed the race has seen: the Eiffel Tower. How wonderful it will look to Boardman, no pretensions this year other than to grab a stage win at the outside, if he could, but above all to finish the ride, only his second finish in six starts.

Our view of the road is piecemeal, too many heads in front of us, but when the procession does come in, heralded by the publicity caravan, on a spree of driving, blonde girls hanging out of cars, and the crumpled race organisers slumped in overheated saloons making the final lap, motorbike police outriders, suddenly, there is the long line of gaudy lycra, polished enamel and the bronzed legs and arms of the riders, the men going for home. A shiver of speed, muscular grace, choreographed it looks, says my companion, a dancer, beautiful, rhythmic, supple, *exciting*. And, for the flash of time's open eye as they shoot by on the far side of the carriageway from us, it is *exciting* and the crowd cheers and whistles and settles, nerves akimbo, into the short wait, two minutes or so, for them to round the U-turn at the top of the avenue by the Place de l'Etoile and so back down past us, in a whirr of spokes and alloy mechs. And out of sight to make the laps, ten of them.

Next time round, a stab at a break, but it's quickly swallowed up by the bunch, which seems to be generating a sort of combined speed, like a multi-celled dynamo. Another circuit and another break goes further ahead; two men gain a minute, but it's not long before that advance is being chewed away like a leaf in a locust's jaw: not so much because the bunch is exerting itself as that the two escapees have had it, done what they could, a bit of viewing time, publicity for the French lottery and then it's gone, the day we rode the Champs-Elysées at the head of the Tour de France.

The Telekom team had this last chance to get Zabel onto the winner's podium. He has the green points jersey secure enough, but no stage victory. In truth, though, however consistent he has been at the finishes and in the intermediate sprints – where guile is quite as important as raw speed – he hasn't looked the sharp sprinter he was; a few metres lacking in pace, a hint of caution in his handling of the hurly-burly, maybe. He misses out again, and the Australian McEwen rides into his own page of history with a dazzling rush to the front past the big hitters. Joy.

And as we go, we hear the strains of the Star-Spangled Banner drifting across the road. Armstrong: the greatest comeback of the century, *L'Equipe* called it. *Chapeau bas*.

CHAPTER TEN

2000

Answering the Cynics

Some French fans have grown cynical about the Tour de France. *Les Bleus* have carried off football's World Cup and Euro 2000. Mary Pierce has won the French Open tennis. Their rugby team reached the final of the World Cup. But the French cyclists? *Rien.* Altogether fishy.

When the American Lance Armstrong sealed his 1999 win with an emphatic ride in the final time-trial into the Futuroscope theme park in the Vienne region, large sections of the French press were incredulous. Armstrong was from another planet: so utterly superior to the other riders. What was he taking? Were the French riders really so markedly inferior? Impossible. Virtual reality had taken over and, as if in wry amusement at the notion or else determined to scotch it, the Tour organisers announced the opening of the 2000 Tour back in this centre of the world of virtual reality: a first stage time-trial over 16.5km back into Futuroscope. Perhaps the hope was that the symbolism of quitting fantasy land for the hard roads of truth would signal a return to a clean Tour, an honest race, a genuine contest.

Armstrong faced much tougher opposition than in 1999. The German Ullrich started in the rainbow jersey of reigning world time-trial champion, but, if the pressure on him to repeat his '97 victory was intense, the same could not be said of his preparation for the race. Overweight during the winter months, he had renounced or abandoned a clutch of early season races through illness or lack of training. The Tour is not a race in which a rider can improvise: lack of racing miles cannot be hidden and it says a lot for the patience of the Telekom management that they are prepared to keep faith with a rider who has, so far, delivered much less than his talent promises.

The Italian Pantani, booted out of the 1999 Giro d'Italia, came to the Tour after a miserable year. He had done very little racing and a deep crisis of confidence and chronic depression had reduced an explosive attacking spirit to extreme diffidence, muddled up with vague talk of return or retirement. No one knew what he was going to do; least, perhaps, Il Pirata himself. However, with a week of flat stages to ride himself in, Pantani might well be a real threat.

Of the other major contenders, none, in my view, had a genuine chance of overall victory. Despite his class and early promise – yellow jersey in his first Tour – Zülle never really looked like a Tour winner. The Frenchman Laurent Jalabert affronted home opinion when he climbed off his bike and quit the race in '98 in protest against the rough-handling of riders by police investigating the Festina affair (see chapter 8). He refused to ride in France for two years and his motivations were suspect. His Spanish ONCE team is not subject to the Draconian anti-doping routines of the French federation and he was accused of dodging the crack-down that, so many domestic riders claimed, had unfairly crippled French cycling.

French riders aren't winning the one-day Belgian and Italian classic races, say the home riders. But, says Jalabert, they never have. There is no cause to question his motives on this. Without question the most complete pro cyclist in the *peloton*, he sacrificed his place as number one in the world rankings by not riding several rated races to concentrate on preparing for his return to the Tour – almost certainly his last – with a view to a podium place.

The darling of the French fans, the ace climber Richard Virenque, five times winner of the King of the Mountains prize, is always touted – not least by himself – as a potential winner of the Tour. Very few specialist climbers have won the Tour but, when they do, they transcend themselves. Virenque is a commanding man in the mountains; elsewhere, he is ordinary.

Mario Cipollini crashed while training in Tuscany a few weeks before the Tour, broke two ribs and was out. In the past few years, the 'red train' of the Saeco team, driving the chase of escapees or winding up the speed for the final sprint, had controlled the *peloton* with imperious power: all to get Cipo into the frame for the last 100 metres to the *Arrivée*. His absence from the Tour meant that, for the first time in a few years, the role of chief pursuit was open to takers. In the event, no team consistently took it on.

Almost inevitably, the doping scandal hung round the Tour before the off like an old has-been. Routine blood tests eliminated three riders – Rossano Brasi, Andrej Hauptman and the Russian champion, Serguei Ivanov – from the Tour for high haemocrit levels of over 50 (i.e. the proportion of red oxygen-carrying cells in the blood). Ivanov was sacked by his Dutch Farm Frites team a few days later and Brasi – labelled a 'moron' by his Polti manager – was immediately suspended by his team until he could explain himself. The Tour director, Jean-Marie Leblanc, said that 'this shows that the Tour de France is not prepared to tolerate cheats.'

Lance Armstrong has always declared forthrightly against drugs; his fight-back from cancer is, he says, proof enough that the very idea that he is taking dope to enhance his performance is absurd. Asked what he is on he replies: 'I am on my bike.'

The Prologue featured a slight climb around halfway, a minor ascent to 109m, which the Tour organisers had given a fourth category ranking in the mountains prize. On it, the German sprinter Marcel Wüst, stole a media coup for his Festina team. Wüst mounted a light road-racing bike, rather than a slightly heavier time-trialling machine, rode steadily to the foot of the one km climb, then gave it all he had. This won him the polka-dot jersey of the King of the Mountains prize and four subsequent appearances on the winner's podium.

The stage was won by the only Briton riding: David Millar, at 23 of the age that many of the greats have actually won the race – Anquetil, Fignon, Ullrich – but nurtured over four seasons of professional cycle racing to enter the race, not as a contender but a future prospect. He took the time-trial by two seconds from the reigning champion, 14 seconds over Ullrich, 15 seconds over Jalabert. It was a superlative performance: into yellow on his first day in the Tour. It might prove to be a shirt of fire. This was only the beginning of a three-week ordeal. Nothing can detract from the glory of that moment; but the Tour exacts a far higher price than any other race.

Millar was, from the very start, up against things which would either harden his resolve or, possibly, reduce him from a potential winner to a catch-up man, and there are plenty of those around. That night he could not sleep, wondering if it was a dream. *Golden fleece? Me?*

The Belgian fast man Tom Steels won stage two and brief ownership of the green points jersey after the Dutchman Erik Dekker, silver medallist in the '94 Olympics, launched an early attack and was joined by the renowned *baroudeur* – the man who will attack for honour's sake alone – Jacky Durand. This was to become the pattern of the race: with the big men slogging it out for the high placings, the rest were animating the day's action, day after day, in the only way open to them: attack. And here, the pathos inherent in bike racing, where the men who have been out on their own, up to 250km in the attempt to take a stage win, are caught within metres of the finish by a pack driven to crazy speeds to overhaul them. At the moment of junction, there is not even a sideways glance: there is no mercy, whatever sympathy the individuals in that great train of overtakers may harbour. That is the race. No room for sentiment. Dekker paid heavily for his failed bid: he came in with two other riders nearly 15 minutes down.

Here is an interesting insight into team tactics, however. When the *peloton* split in the run-in, with Laurent Jalabert in the front group, his fellow ONCE rider, the Spaniard Abraham Olano, fourth in 1997 and a noted time-trialler, headed the chasing bunch. Olano could see no yellow jersey, nor Lance Armstrong in the lead group and, knowing that the time gap between the front group and his chasing group – which must, therefore, include Armstrong and Millar – would be that which elapsed from the time the winner crossed the line to when the chasing leader crossed, he slowed the pursuit. Although the distance between the two bunches at the finish was only a few metres, the time gap was nine seconds, which moved his leader Jalabert into third place – a mere six seconds down on the yellow jersey.

Steels also took stage three after Jens Voigt of Germany and the

Dane Michael Blaudzun broke clear for 124km. Since Voigt had a deficit of only 46 seconds on Millar, the Briton's Cofidis team felt obliged to lead the chase: always a gruelling expense of effort, since the other teams are content to sit back and slipstream the pursuit. In the final kilometre and a half of the run-in, Millar rode into a pile-up when Jean-Patrick Nazon – of whom more later – and Markus Zberg crashed and Millar, some way back, swerved adroitly past the heap of bodies and bikes and somersaulted over the barriers of straw bales. In the tumble his chain went adrift and he had trouble relocating it. But, the sole team rider who was there pushed him back to speed and Millar saved the yellow jersey by seconds. 'It scared me,' he said 'but I'm not hurt.' Whatever volcanic emotions they feel, these guys have an entirely charming way with understatement.

Millar lost the golden fleece two days later in what many regard as a grossly unfair element of racing: the team time-trial, where the talent of the individual is squashed into the best that the weakest member of a team can do. It is the severest test of any team's strength, cohesion, organisation and collective will; it exposes any frailty. It's unrelenting; quite horrible, even if you're strong. The time is registered on that of the fifth man over the line.

Jalabert's ONCE outfit took the stage by 46 seconds over Armstrong's US Postal team, despite the attempt of a disgruntled night-club owner – anti-Jaja – to sabotage their ride by lobbing five straw bales into the road near the start. Armstrong made a tactical error on the final climb, across the bridge over the Loire into St-Nazaire, 3.3km long, 60m high and buffeted by fierce winds off the Atlantic, by forcing the pace too hard and dropping the rest of his team. Nervy moments – time lost regrouping. However Ullrich's Telekom team lost one minute 26 seconds on the day, Pantani's Mercatone Uno three minutes 34 seconds, Zülle's Banestos four minutes 23 seconds. Zülle was furious with his team: he said he had to do so much work on his own to keep the momentum going that, finally, he was exhausted and got dropped. They had to wait for him. A bad case of disarray.

The ONCE victory was significant in time gains and psychological dominance. Millar's French Cofidis team lost nearly three minutes on the day and Jalabert, on this American Independence Day, took the yellow jersey for the first time since 1995. It was, he said, a symbol of his comeback, heralding, he hoped, a new start.

The fifth stage witnessed another cruel act of highway robbery: Jens Voigt and Sebastian Demarbaix shaped what turned into a long breakaway and were joined by five others, including the restless Dekker. Twenty km from the finish, Voigt and Dekker jumped from the rest of the escapers to try for the win. The *peloton* had timed their effort to perfection, alas: Dekker and Voigt were engulfed by the chasing pack a tantalising 400m from the line. King of the Mountains, sprinter Marcel Wüst took the stage edging out his fellow German on a rival team, Zabel, who had not won a stage since 1997.

Generally riders accord the yellow jersey a certain respect, until the racing gets serious. However when Jalabert stopped at the side of the road for a pee a few miles from the Départ in Vitré on stage six, the French firebrand Jacky Durand – last year's *lanterne rouge* and winner of the combativity prize – launched an attack. He almost certainly hadn't seen Jaja by the side of the road, but the *maillot jaune* was furious: this was a mild form of treason. 'Next time, I'll piss in the hotel,' he said.

Durand was joined by Zabel's 36-year-old Italian team mate Alberto Elli and 10 other riders; the attack succeeded, by seven minutes 49 seconds over the bunch. The Dutch champion Leon Van Bon took the sprint and Elli, who had been only two minutes 15 seconds down on Jalabert, took yellow. Jalabert's ambitions were higher than interim possession of the jersey, but he was understandably miffed at the shabby way in which he had lost it. As to why his ONCE team did not organise a chase, he offered the excuse of tired legs; also, that since there were 12 men in the break working well together, the eight men plus one leader of any other team would be hard put to match the effort.

Durand is a famous stirrer. Himself a former yellow jersey, after winning the '95 Prologue, and French National Champion ('94), his swashbuckling attitude may be unsettling – '*doucement, Jacky,* steady on,' ran the cartoons – but it makes for lively action. He doesn't often win, but he is always ready to deliver some punch. He was last year's *lanterne rouge* – traditionally the last man in the race – and winner of the overall combativity prize (points are awarded daily for the attacking spirit) and Durand typifies the breed who win it. Better, too, the *lanterne rouge* than the anonymity of a place in the middle order.

The *lanterne rouge* that day, Jean-Patrick Nazon, in his first Tour, typifies another breed of rider. The Australian sprinter Stuart O'Grady was brought down by another rider 80km from the finish in Tours. He was badly hurt – X-rays later revealed that his shoulder had been broken in three places – but he rode on. The hope always persists that there is nothing but heavy bruising; few of them quit the Tour without the most pressing cause. O'Grady draped the useless arm over the handlebars and caught three riders, including the man who had crashed into him. On every small climb he faltered; as he faltered, Nazon, honouring the code of mutual help in distress, came behind to push him. Meanwhile, the man who'd crashed into him was griping that O'Grady wasn't doing any work to help the *grupetto*, the last men on the road, escape elimination on time. O'Grady, of course, had to abandon that evening. And Nazon went later, completely exhausted in the mountains.

France won not a single stage in the '99 Tour so, when the unlikely sounding Frenchman Christophe Agnolutto hoisted the tricolour again after a lone break of 79 miles on stage seven, France rejoiced. Agnolutto held off the chasing bunch which timed its effort poorly and Wüst spoiled Zabel's charge for second place. It was Zabel's birthday but there were no presents on offer.

Next day, Erik Dekker, riding his seventh Tour without a win, timed his effort more sagely and went with a mere 30km to go. Victory at last. There followed the last flat stage before the climbing, final chance for a while for the opportunists. This time Paolo Bettini outsprinted his fellow escapee, the Belgian Geert Verheyen, after 180km miles away to add a Tour win to his victory in the Belgian classic Liège–Bastogne–Liège. But the race was about to explode.

Stage ten ran 205km over three severe climbs – one first category, two *hors catégorie* – to the mountain top finish at Lourdes Hautacam.

Monday 10 July. Dax. Heavy rain; driving wind; cold. The conditions were appalling: as if the Pyrenees were unleashing a foul bout of bad temper because the Tour had spared them but one measly day this year. Lance Armstrong, who likes the bad weather as much as the rest loathe it, was in chipper mood.

A few abortive attacks after the start, but, at 33km, the irrepressible Durand went and was joined by the Belgian Nico Mattan and the Basque Javier Otxoa. The trio cut loose. Durand was dropped on the first category col de Marie Blanque, a nasty 10km climb. Over the top, the *peloton* behind by 15 minutes, Otxoa and Mattan pounded on down into the valley towards the col d'Aubisque, a steadier ascent than the Marie Blanque but much longer. When the main pack reached the foot of the mountain, the attacks began and the field split. Armstrong's team went hell for leather trying to contain the action but, one by one, fell off the pace and Armstrong found himself unsupported, in company with his main rivals, Ullrich and Pantani. Virenque attacked and crossed the summit one minute ahead of them; two class climbers – Jose Maria Jimenez and Fernando Escartin – at 35 seconds.

Jalabert, like many of the others, was suffering and way back: the cold and wet had eaten into his bones, his muscles were inert, he could not, as he put it, get into the red, i.e. push himself over the limit of comfort. This is the harsh reality of the mountains: riders crack or lose all force. They hear voices in the crowd, some urging them on – *Tiens bon! Courage!* Hold on, courage – others, probably drunken and big-bellied, taunting them: 'You're 10 minutes down. Weakling. Washed up.' Is it surprising they lose heart? Even the best find themselves demented with fatigue, reduced to the *grupetto*, which normally contains the sprinters, struggling to scramble in under the guillotine. This is the Calvary: the high road to suffering and mere survival.

Armstrong rode onto the final 13km climb with Pantani, Ullrich, Zülle, 10 minutes 30 seconds behind a group containing Virenque, Escartin and Jimenez. One kilometre in, Pantani attacked and was instantly checked by Armstrong and Zülle. Ullrich couldn't answer. The pace was ferocious; Zülle fell away, Pantani held for a while but Armstrong, who had come to the Pyrenees and ridden this particularly hard ascent several times, was pedalling with the rapid fluency of a born climber and aggressive sustained power. His acceleration took him up to and past Virenque. Only Jimenez could hold his wheel. Five kilometres from the summit, Otxoa's lead had shrunk to four minutes 58 seconds. In 8km the American had gained over five minutes on the lone escapee. At 3km Jimenez was done for and Armstrong, out of the saddle still, was hunting down Otxoa, by now clinging onto his lead by willpower and the hectic dream of victory. He made it, by a mere 42 seconds, and Armstrong took yellow. He had distanced Ullrich, now in second place, by four minutes one second, and Pantani, hitherto the best climber in the *peloton*, by almost six minutes. The Frenchman Christophe Moreau, riding for the reborn Festina team, claimed third position at five minutes 10 seconds. Armstrong's resistance to cold and wet, coupled with an exceptional focus, an instinct for the kill that marks out all the best, had simply stunned them all. Pantani confessed that, whatever hopes he'd cherished of an early resurgence, reality had hit him on that climb.

On the relative flat next day, Dekker took his second win; in 10 days of the Tour he had spent no fewer than 592km off the front in breakaways.

After a rest day, the riders set out for Mont Ventoux, the first time in 13 years the Tour had finished at the col. It was Thursday 13 July, 23 years to the day after Tommy Simpson's death on the mountain. The Mistral was in full career; temperatures on top of the bald mountain were not much above freezing. David Millar's ambition to win the white jersey, for best young rider, had died in the wind and rain up to Hautacam when he conceded nearly seven minutes to the Spaniard Francisco Mancebo. Now his aim was limited to reaching Paris. Shortly after the start for Ventoux in Carpentras, he got caught in a pile-up; contused ribs and a bad tyre burn (from a spinning rear wheel) made riding very uncomfortable but he bravely continued.

Pantani and Armstrong fought the victory on the mountain to the last. Pantani, who had ridden himself into something approaching his true explosive form, unleashed the kind of attack on the bare slopes for which he is celebrated. Armstrong was dropped and, for a while, made no move to follow; however, he rejoined and rode elbow to elbow with the Pirate up the last cruel three kilometres. It was clear that the American had the legs of the Italian but, in a gesture as gauche and naive as it was intended to be generous, he allowed Pantani to cross the line ahead. The misunderstanding which sprang from this clumsy attempt to reward Pantani's courage in his comeback led to an undignified spat. Pantani interpreted the gift as patronising. Armstrong insinuated a lack of gratitude; the strongest should win on Ventoux and everyone knew who was the strongest. In which case, why did the American yield to a sentimental whimsy and not show himself superior?

The American showed a distinct lack of grace, referring to Pantani as Elefantino, Dumbo (his old nickname), as having shown his true colours. Ullrich was a gentleman – and the most talented of them all, Pantani behaved without honour. While the Italian said he was not insulted by the use of the nickname, Armstrong plainly meant the gibe. The gathering spat, conducted through press conferences, was unseemly; Pantani's reaction – on the road – was to prove far more eloquent. If Armstrong thought the Tour was finished, he was wrong: there was, said Pantani, still Pantani to deal with.

Ullrich lost a further 29 seconds on Ventoux; Moreau one minute 31 seconds and his third place to the young Spanish climber Joseba Beloki who could, it is said, hardly believe he was in the Tour, let alone riding third overall. After the stage, David Millar, in an interview, summed up his feelings about being in the race and surviving the mountain despite excruciating pain: 'I've always thought of cycling as having an epic, romantic scale. It's a beautiful sport, a great sport. I've always like the epic nature of all that suffering. That appeals to me a lot.' Two days later, having traversed three mighty Alps over 2,000m, and 249km, he was saying: 'That's ridiculous. Eight and a half hours on the bike. That's not sport. That's sado-masochism on a major scale. It's ridiculous.' But, he added: 'You have to hang on and never give up.' Plainly he does not lack courage.

The stage went to the Colombian climber of the Kelme team, Santiago Botero, who wrested the King of the Mountains jersey from his team mate Otxoa. Pantani, at two minutes 46 seconds, just spurted clear of Armstrong to take third place and no favours.

In the second Alpine stage the day after – Galibier 2,645m, Madeleine 2,000m, mountain top finish at Courchevel 2,004m, 63.6km of climbing all told – Pantani applied real pressure in something like his old style. Armstrong began to look vulnerable; so, too, Ullrich, who had neither the legs nor the will to take advantage. Fifteen kilometres from the finish, Pantani attacked. Armstrong's team mate, the climber Kevin Livingston, relayed his leader painfully back to the Italian but then faded. Pantani spotted this and surged again, Armstrong had no answer. Pantani was flying. Up ahead Jimenez was clinging to the possibility of a lone victory, but he was out of luck. Pantani caught him and, riding into and out of a tunnel in the closing kilometre, emerged in bright sunshine to take a stupendous victory. Armstrong limited his loss to 50 seconds; Ullrich went down by 3 minutes 21 seconds, but Pantani had, most brilliantly, announced himself back. The American, lacking humour as well as *politesse*, said that, after the gift of the Ventoux stage, for Pantani to attack on Courchevel was ungentlemanly. A charmless comment which betrays his ignorance of the *mœurs* of continental bike racing.

If, barring accident, overall victory did seem decided, the game was not yet played. After a second rest day, the race took in a dreadful 196km across four more Alpine monsters with virtually no valley links between for recuperation. The climbing started at 67km, on the col de Saisies, and Pantani attacked, a move calculated to hurt Armstrong. The American's team had no option but to chase; the effort wore them thin and left the *maillot jaune* badly exposed. Pantani persisted and opened a clear gap, in wary company with three others: Virenque's team mate Pascal Hervé and two men from the Kelme team – Fernando Escartin and Pascual Llorente. Over the second climb, the second category Aravis, Llorente lost contact. Armstrong, in a group of some 30 riders, was containing the deficit to around a minute as the leaders crossed the third climb of the day, the col de la Colombière. On the descent, Virenque counter-attacked with Moreau, Botero of Kelme, the current King of the Mountains, and his teammate Otxoa; they rejoined Pantani. The yellow jersey group came up to them shortly after; with the lead group reassembled, it was all left to do.

Pantani, though, was spent. He had been suffering bad stomach cramps and had received no help from his fellow escapers, but he had blown the race to bits.

Moreau fell away, the Spanish climber Roberto Heras attacked and was quickly joined by Virenque. Ullrich found his legs and began to test Armstrong who was having a desperate time. He had made the elementary – amateurish – mistake of not eating properly and became a victim of *une fringale*: the bonk, hypoglaecemia, radical loss of energy. Riders with the *fringale* can black out. It was, he said afterwards, the worst day he had ever spent on a bike. He felt light-headed, he ached with hunger, was scared that he was going to lose the Tour. (He might have done, had Ullrich been in riper condition, and primed for the kill. Pantani lost 13 minutes 44 seconds on the day.)

Virenque and Heras hurtled into Morzine in tandem; the unfortunate Spaniard overshot a bend, crashed into the barriers and trashed his front wheel. The four-times winner of the mountains prize Virenque, due to face criminal trial on charges of drug-taking in November, took his first win since 1997. It was the most beautiful of his career, he said – revenge for the exclusion in 1998. Ullrich took second and two minutes out of Armstrong, who showed enormous fortitude and courage in battling through the horrors of that calvaire on the mountain.

But, his reaction to Pantani's audacious riding was telling. 'It was,' he said 'a waste of time and energy. I provoked him and Il Pirata walked the plank and I almost lost the Tour.' But that is exactly the point, and Armstrong missed it, spectacularly.

His strategy for the Tour had been, quite clearly, decided in advance: to paralyse the opposition early on Hautacam and then sit on the lead. Like many riders, he wears a two-way radio and is in constant communication with his *directeur sportif* in the following car. Pantani, by contrast, does not wear an earphone. He rides on his own gut feelings. Armstrong, once nicknamed headstrong, *had* a similar wilful quality, if less astutely deployed. Now he is almost *too* controlled by the voice from the team car. His victories, accordingly, have a rather clinical look. Pantani, having shelled himself out, succumbed, that night, to a bout of dysentery and abandoned.

The race was, effectively, over. Armstrong had been forced to hang onto his lead with every ounce of strength he had left. Ullrich was paying for yet another cavalier winter off and on the bike. Pantani had returned to the highest level, but too late. Who knows what an epic there may be should both those former winners come to next year's Tour, fully prepared.

Armstrong had, nonetheless, shown himself worthy; just. He is the ultimate professional. He prepares harder and with greater industry than anyone else – he shrugs off extremes of weather, and, as he puts it, nothing the road throws at him by way of suffering gets close by comparison to the miseries of chemotherapy. Surviving what might have been a mortal cancer has imbued him with a supernatural capacity to absorb punishment and this saved his Tour. But, he built this win, as his first, on a single killer strike and, for all his perceived superiority in this Tour, his win owed as much to the default of Pantani and Ullrich as to his own enforcement throughout.

In the final time-trial, however, 58.5km from the German town of Fribourg-en-Brisgau to Mulhouse in Alsace, he achieved the stage victory which gave gloss to the overall win. Only four riders since the war – Walkowiak 1956, Nencini 1960, Aimar 1966 and Lemond 1990 – have taken overall victory without winning a single stage. Armstrong salvaged that honour by beating Ullrich by 25 seconds. This was, in moral terms, a decisive margin.

The interest of this Tour lies both in what it promised for the next race and in the intrinsic merits of the victory that crowned it; memorable more for what might have happened. The first week was certainly the best of the flat stage openers for years: the absence of the Saeco 'red train' encouraged a flurry of quixotic attacks. Erik Dekker's three stage wins born of lone enterprise marked a welcome return to a buccaneering spirit amongst the lesser lights of the *peloton*. Zabel took a record fifth green points jersey. No fewer than nine team leaders did not finish, including poor Zülle, second in 1999.

The young Basque Joseba Beloki held onto the third place he took on the stage to Ventoux and joined Ullrich – second for a second time – on the podium. Beloki and his teammate Moreau – fourth and first Frenchman respectively – restored the image of the Festina team so besmirched in the doping scandal of 1998. Happily, the drugs controversy hardly resurfaced. Cycle sport has taken the issue on in a way that no other sport has. There is no room for complacency: the problem had been radical and endemic.

However, a bold start has been made; except that Giorgio Squinzi, the boss of the Italian Mapei team, (which had a bad Tour), said that it was simply not possible for any cyclist to lead a race like the Tour de France without the use of a performance-enhancing drug. There may be proof, or rebuttal of this claim in the offing. The Tour organisers have kept riders' urine specimens to be submitted to a test for EPO as soon as it is approved as scientifically accurate.

The Tour was scarred by a tragedy. A 12-year-old boy was hit by one of the following cars as it overtook down the line of the caravan and later died of his injuries. Before the start out of Morzine, the riders observed a minute's silence in his memory, a silence shamefully broken by a hovering television helicopter. The Tour de France stopped out of respect for an innocent casualty of its remorseless progress. Whatever cynics say about the race, it is as true now as it ever was that it is prepared to stop, look hard at itself and renew. There is an extraordinary humanity at its heart, a humanity forged in what may seem like a strange crucible – of suffering and overcoming self-imposed pain – but one that is probably unique in sport.

CHAPTER ELEVEN

2001

Armstrong v. Ullrich

Rules for selection of teams for the Tour de France, based on Union de Cyclisme Internationale (UCI) rankings and Tour organisation conventions, seemed clear enough: the top 12, plus the reigning champion's team and any French teams within the top 20. However, in January 2001 the Tour director, Jean-Marie Leblanc, changed the rules with apparent caprice. He picked the top ten, added one Belgian and five French (including two Second Division) and reserved four wild-card entries to be named later. This provoked dismay. Wild-card entries are almost always suspect: grace and favour above true worth, although when Greg Lemond won the Tour in 1989, it was as the leader of a wild-card team. He was now spokesman of the American Mercury-Viatel team who, by results, certainly merited selection for the Tour. They, like several highly rated Italian teams, had to sweat out a long wait.

The professional cycling world and the Tour de France – its great showcase – in particular, has been under enormous pressure since the Festina affair in 1998. The willingness of the Tour organisers to enforce draconian measures to eliminate the scourge of drugs has been energetic and laudable. Yet, international cooperation has not been solid; the French Cycling Federation, following the lead of the Minister of Youth and Sports, Madame Buffet, has imposed fierce discipline; other authorities have been less prompt. Leblanc not only wants the Tour to be rid of the suspicions which cling to the race, to all cycling – and what other sport has been so vigorous in its efforts to purge itself of doping? – he is adamant that the new strictures which apply to French riders must and should apply to all foreign riders who enter the Tour, whatever less stringent rules apply to them on their home turf. This is controversial and, when the four wild-card entries were announced, the controversy looked wilful. No Mercury, no Mercatone Uno – led by Marco Pantani, the 1998 winner – no Saeco, home of the flamboyant sprinter Mario Cipollini. Instead, a ragbag of three more Second Division French teams and one obscure Basque outfit.

Leblanc might well plead that Pantani was not welcome because he still faces criminal charges of drug-taking, yet a French judge is pursuing a judicial inquiry into Lance Armstrong's US Postal team on similar suspicion, after bags containing unspecified medical supplies were dumped in litter bins in the autumn of 2000. Leblanc told *Le Figaro*: 'The sword of Damocles that hangs over riders who dope is heavier than ever. We wanted to turn the page and put our trust in the younger generation of riders.' Fair enough. But if Pantani and the Italians were being snubbed because of suspicion what of the wild-card French CSC-Tiscali team, one of whose riders tested positive in the Giro d'Italia? This was chauvinism, surely, and blatant favouritism; the greatest bike race in the world sadly reduced for partisan reasons. French cyclists – acknowledged by Laurent Fignon, winner of the Tour in 1983–84, to be second-rate – were being given an undeserved leg-up. But Fignon, at the time director of the first major stage race of the season, the Paris–Nice, had included several Second Division French teams to expose them to top-flight competition: sink or swim.

Leblanc shrugged off the outcry. The race would make its own decisions, just as the road decides the winner. As to the favourites, the exclusion of Pantani – a fiery climber of real threat in the mountains – effectively meant that the Tour would be a duel between Armstrong and his runner-up in 2000, winner in 1997, Jan Ullrich. He had been ill-prepared in 2000 but seemed to have concentrated harder, physically and mentally, before the 2001 race. He chose to ride the Giro d'Italia, always Eddy Merckx's favoured preparation for the Tour, whereas the Texan Armstrong chose to ride – and win – the lesser Tour de Suisse (which included a mountain time-trial). Hounded by the smart French press who have always doubted his honesty, he had renounced all racing in France before the start of the season and was even quoted in an American paper as regretting the fact that the greatest bike race in the world had to be in France. Texans are notoriously insular, even within the USA. His prickly attitude came over as arrogance; his brashness as Francophobia; his exaggerated smarting at criticism, direct and implied, as guilty protest. However, he softened; diplomacy both ways. He added a French stage race to his calendar – the Circuit de la Sarthe. It was a welcome gesture, a signal that he was prepared to understand and manage French reactions to him rather than bite back and, like Achilles, sulk in his tent. Yet, just before the Tour, it transpired that he had been working since 1995 with the infamous Italian doctor Michele Ferrari, who is now under investigation for drug abuse. Rather naively and with belligerent unconcern for perception, valid or not, Armstrong said he couldn't see what the fuss was about; Ferrari was an essential part of his team, they'd been concentrating on altitude training and, until proved guilty, the man was innocent, wasn't he? Armstrong said: 'My personal experience leads me to say that I have never had to question his ethics or standards of care.' His personal manager added: 'Ferrari is a brilliant scientist and physiologist with a chequered past but he's an essential part of Lance's support team,' which seemed to beg more questions than it answered.

One of the men who had given him trouble in the 2000 Tour, the Colombian climber Roberto Heras, had been neutralised: made an offer he could not refuse, he had joined Armstrong's team, to help the Texan in the mountains, in return for support in the Vuelta a España. One of Armstrong's closest allies, his boyhood friend Kevin Livingston, had left the team to ride for Ullrich, a move which Armstrong likened to high treason. This gives some measure of his egotism. The Frenchman, Christophe Moreau, was the only local man likely to have any impact, but whatever encouragement his victory in another Tour warm-up race, the Dauphiné Libéré, might hint at, the hope far outweighed the possibility.

The Circuit de la Sarthe was won by David Millar, who came to the Tour burdened with a huge weight of expectation, expectation not much justified by miserable early season results. Could he repeat his victory in the 2000 Tour first stage and win the yellow jersey?

He'd talked a lot since, but hadn't done much. The pressure on him – internal and external – was intense.

★

Prologue. Dunkerque. 7 July.
Not since the summer of 1940 can have there been so many British crowded into the nondescript Channel Port. Millar defined the 8.2km Prologue as 'one of my biggest objectives of the season' although surviving the whole Tour 'and learning a lot more' was far more important. He is realistic; at 24, he is three years off the age when most riders think seriously about doing well in the Tour. US Postal have approached him, but he remains faithful – for the moment – to the French Cofidis team who have nurtured him for nearly four years. 'When I was suffering early this spring, they would tell me just not to worry. I really appreciate that.' Agreeable modesty on the eve of the Tour. Then he distributed invitations to his post-Tour party, an act of hubris if ever there was one. About 1km from the finish, he went into a tight bend too fast and tried to correct his line, the back wheel locked and he went down heavily on his left side. The friction of the crash burst his back tyre and he lost nearly a minute on the bike change; he struggled in with a badly bruised kneecap and a lacerated thigh and arm.

Moreau, of the formerly disgraced Festinas, won the Prologue and gave France the first yellow jersey of the Tour. On stage one, two other French riders set out as if to prove that if overall honours were beyond them, individual panache was not. Two Second Division riders, Christophe Oriol and the irrepressible Jacky Durand – who once won the Tour's combativity prize as well as holding the *lanterne rouge* (for last man in the race) into Paris – attacked after about 56km and built a lead of 8 minutes, only to be held up by a level-crossing barrier. (In 1935, the unknown Romain Maes ducked under such a barrier and sped into Lille minutes ahead of the fretting *peloton*, a lead he held all the way back to Paris.) Durand and Oriol whiled away the wait jocularly signing autographs for a crowd of bystanders until Leblanc pulled up and ruled this undignified. When the goods train finally rumbled through, the escapees had lost 3 minutes

20 seconds of their lead and though race regulations should have detained the *peloton* for a similar time, they were reined in for only two minutes. Durand and Oriol were caught 14km from the finish. Erik Zabel, chasing a record sixth green jersey, took the stage but he was riding the Tour without a lead-out man. The team managers had opted to back Ullrich for overall victory; there'd been no room for a man to serve Zabel and as he crossed the line he eschewed the traditional raised arms salute in mute protest. For Millar 'this was the worst day of all – I've been bleeding down my leg all day'. Yo-yoing off the back all day, he came in 5 minutes 45 seconds down and though he was facing the task bravely – 'if I got through today I can get to Paris' – the humped uphills on the cliff-top road to Cap Gris Nez over which he'd just struggled, are nothing by comparison with the massive climbs of the Alps and Pyrenees which lay ahead.

Racing into Antwerp on stage two, a break of 16 riders went clear, including 4 from Stuart O'Grady's Credit Agricole team. The plan was to get him into yellow but Marc Wauters, watched by the Belgian royal family, did his patriotic duty, jumped clear across the line, took the 20-second time bonus and became the first Belgian to wear the yellow jersey since Johan Bruyneel (now *directeur sportif* of Discovery Channel) in 1995. However, O'Grady's points gains boosted his longer objective of the green jersey. For Millar there was another session of torture, another pile-up at the back of the main field near the finish. 'I've never been in so much pain in my life. God knows how I'll get through the next few days.'

Stage three finished at a hectic speed over the flatlands of Flanders, home territory of the beefy Belgian sprinters, the *flahutes*, 'flat-outs', brought up on local *kermesses*, mill-race round-the-town wallops that breed three essentials for close-quarter bunch breaks: bike-handling, nerve and feverish out-of-the-saddle dives for the line. Zabel can mix it with the best and keep a cool head; he took the sprint out of the stampede. Marc Wauters was nowhere. O'Grady put on yellow. Millar reported some improvement: he'd managed to sleep better and even suggested that 'later I could even make a show on a stage'. If this sounded more like self-convincing than a genuine possibility, it is a tribute to the depths of mental toughness and physical resilience that these bike-racers have to take for granted.

Next day the race went back into France. Laurent Jalabert, 'Jaja', the former world number one, back in a fairly new team (Danish-sponsored CSC-Tiscali) after falling out with the Spanish ONCEs for whom he'd ridden for many years, has been out of favour with the French public since he retired from the 1998 Tour in protest. He went into exile in Geneva and rode no French races. In February, he fell off a ladder doing some DIY, fractured three vertebrae and might well have missed the Tour. On stage four the ONCE-Eroski team made a concerted attack at a feed station, in flagrant violation of the Tour's code of ethics. The US Postals reacted swiftly and chased furiously for around 80km to reel them in, the pace so hot that the *peloton* split into five bunches. Jalabert, like many others, was caught napping and missed the first split. Furious that he had been dropped, *and* by the ONCE team he'd quit in some dudgeon, he and two others immediately counter-attacked, as soon as the leaders were caught. They came in just clear of the chase and wily 32-year-old Jalabert, who hadn't won a race since the previous June but was now revitalised and keen to make a point, matched Belgian Ludo Dierckxsens' surge to take his third Tour stage win. Any disaffection the French public had felt towards the absentee Jalabert vanished. He was winning for them again. They smiled with him. French riders were, it seems, determined to repay local support. Leblanc's controversial selections may have been shrewd after all. Signs near the *Arrivée* underlined the riders' half of the bargain: '*Dôpage . . . Dégage*' (Dope . . . Nope).

The well-drilled ONCEs, even without their ace time-trialler Abraham Olano, started as favourites for the stage five team time-trial; they had won in 2000 when the event was reintroduced for the first time since 1996 and may even have used the compact team attack on stage four as a warm-up. Continental racing calls the time-trial 'the race of truth' but regards it as a minor delicacy in the larger feast. Not all riders can be bothered to devote extra training to solo clock-beating: it can be soul-destroying. From that perspective, the team time-trial counts for absolute self-destruction; the slowest men stretched on the rack of the fastest. Time for the stage is taken on the fifth rider across the line. Cohesion is vital. Losing weaker men intensifies the strain on those left in the hunt. O'Grady's Crédit Agricoles had dropped two of their nine men long before the finish of the 67km course and the survivors were looking ragged. However, the *directeur sportif* Roger Legeay (who rode seven Tours), a man deeply imbued with *fougue*, fire in the belly, drove up alongside in the team car and gave them the sort of rousing talk – a mélange of bollocking and *'die for the country'* – which Napoleon appreciated in his generals. They rallied, took the fastest time in the intermediate time check and were inspired to an unexpected show of aggressive team spirit. They won the stage and O'Grady kept the yellow jersey.

Armstrong's US Postal team suffered. He, a time-trial specialist, bore much of the hard work at the front. Normally, the teams ride in two parallel lines: one line brings men up to the front; as each successive man reaches the head of the first line he usually relays for only as long as it takes him to peel off and onto the front of the second line. Meanwhile, the rider at the back of this line will be swinging onto the back of the other line, thus making his way back up to the front. Armstrong was holding the front far longer than the rest – relays lasting up to a minute, sheltering the weaker men in his slipstream but distancing them with sudden accelerations. Suddenly, around the 45km mark, Christian Vande Velde skidded on the central white line, which was wet with rain, and went down, taking Heras with him. Vande Velde wounded his arm; Heras was unhurt. Armstrong generously (or prudently?) pulled up and waited and the team lost about 45 seconds, the margin by which the ONCEs, with one of his rivals, Joseba Beloki (3rd overall in 2000) beat them. The Deutsche Telekoms split to pieces; Ullrich and four others came in alone, 24 seconds down on US Postal. Ullrich was now 30 seconds down on Armstrong overall. Even such small cracks have to be plugged later.

Stages six and seven took the riders down through the Vosges mountains into Alsace-Lorraine – Jan Kirsipuu won the bunch sprint into Strasbourg – and on through the Doubs where, on Bastille Day, with the timing of a magician, the resurgent Jalabert took his second victory of the Tour. Suddenly, euphoria turned to shock when a deranged man drove a maroon Renault 21 headlong at the finish line. He'd heard voices telling him to go and embrace France's rehabilitated hero but been turned away from the finish enclosure because he had no pass. He was stopped only when someone smashed his windscreen. A middle-aged woman standing by the barrier was flung into the air and taken to hospital with serious injuries to her head and legs.

Jens Voigt, O'Grady's teammate, took yellow. Millar was slogging on, his directeur talking about 'character being forged by suffering', but the rider admitted that he hadn't been able to hold on even over the small climbs. 'Any other time I would have packed it in. I honestly thought I was out of it. If I hadn't had another rider – Bart Leysen – with me, I would have been eliminated.' Vande Velde was forced out when he crashed into a metal stanchion on the descent of the col de Fouchy mountains and aggravated his arm injury.

On Sunday 15 July, a 14-man break made Tour history. Led by Erik Dekker, the Dutchman who took three flat stages in breakaway attacks in 2000, the group were away for some 209 kilometres in miserable conditions – low cloud, 10°C, rain. The main *peloton* left the pursuit largely to the US Postals who eventually gave up interest. The lead group contained O'Grady but no one of real threat for the overall victory, save for two who might just give the main contenders trouble in the mountains: Kivilev and Aitor Gonzalez.

The break eventually began to split; Dekker attacked with the Paris–Roubaix winner Servais Knaven some 25 kilometres from the finish; they were joined by Dekker's teammate Wauters and Aitor Gonzalez and in Pontarlier, Wauters led out for Dekker to sweep in, clear. The main *peloton* came in 35 minutes 54 seconds down on his time, the largest gap in post-war Tours and one which put 161 riders well outside the time guillotine – fixed at 10 per cent of Dekker's time. Strict ruling would have reduced the field to the 14 of the break. Exceptional cases allow exceptional decisions and strict regulations were waived.

At the finish, Dekker was trembling with cold but as he pointed out, at least they'd endured the foul weather half an hour less than the rest. Kivilev, a rated climber, had gained 13 minutes on the day. O'Grady profited: he took back yellow and green.

In 1998, the Russian Serguei Ivanov led a go-slow ride into Aix-les-Bains, at the foot of the Alps, in protest at the rough treatment meted out to his TVM team during the drugs scandal. Three years on, he attacked on his own 9km from the finish and crossed the line as victor of the ninth stage, to the annoyance of Tour officials, who are very sensitive to symbolic coincidence. (That same day, a court in Reims handed his ex-manager Cees Priem a suspended 18-month prison sentence, plus a fine of £7,420 for illegal distribution of drugs.) And a Spanish rider, Txema del Olmo, was expelled by his team, the Basque newcomers Euskaltel-Euskadi, for testing positive for EPO. Leblanc commented: 'This proves that the EPO test works perfectly. I am pleased about this but it confirms that we have no reason to relax vigilance: obviously some riders are incorrigible.'

It is riders who make a course hard and there is no such thing as an easy Tour de France. Race routes differ but so, too, do difficulties. The first two weeks of the 2001 Tour were ridden at fierce pace; relentless attacks tore holes in the *peloton*; the early taste of climbing sowed further fatigue. The lesser teams seemed to be set on damaging the US Postals before the real challenge of the mountains. The fighting spirit of the perennial *baroudeurs*, men like Durand and Dekker, had flared like a contagion, to the delight of the public, at least. On the eve of stage ten, first of the Alpine forays, the mood was unduly sombre. Tomorrow, for most of them, there would be little breath left nor much inclination for talking. There was 209km to go. A few minor ascents leading to three *hors* category climbs: col de la Madeleine, 2000m; col du Glandon, 1,924m, finishing atop the dreaded mountain cul de sac l'Alpe d'Huez, 1,850m. Total climbing, 60.7km. O'Grady, who admitted that the day before he had been in terrible straits and only wearing the yellow jersey had kept him up with the race, knew that he would surely lose the golden fleece this day, probably to second-placed François Simon whose brother, Pascal, lost it on the stage to l'Alpe d'Huez in 1983.

Nasty as the Huez stage would be, it was but the first of a block of mountain stages.

Stage 11.
32km individual time-trial, the final 18.7km an average 8 per cent climb to the mountain-top finish in Camrousse. (This was the first mountain time-trial to be included since 1996, when Evgeni Berzin won in the yellow jersey.)

Rest day. Transfer by plane to Perpignan.

Stage 12. Pyrenees. Perpignan–Ax-les-Thermes.

Distance: 166.5km. Total climbing: 53.1km. Col de Jau 1,506m, col de Coudons 883m, col des Sept-Frères 1,253m, col du Chioula 1,431m, Ax 1,375m.

Stage 13.* Foix–St-Lary-Soulan.
Distance: 194km. Total climbing: 68.4km. Col de Portet d'Aspet 1,069m, col de Menté 1,349m, col du Portillon 1,320m, col de Peyresourde 1,569m, col de Val-Louron-Aspet 1,580m (St-Lary), Pla d'Adet 1,680m.

   * The stage was originally scheduled to cross the col de Port (1,249m) too but a local speculator, a politician, *persuaded* the Tour organisation to re-route the race past his new golfing and leisure complex.

Stage 14. Tarbes–Luz-Ardiden.
Distance: 144km Total climbing 47.1km. Col du Haut de la Côte 645m, col de Mauvezin 520m, col d'Aspin 1,489m, col du Tourmalet 2,115m, Luz-Ardiden 1,715m.
   Rest day.

Statistics are of limited value. Selective facts and figures tell only the story you choose to tell. The statistics quoted here tell only one story and are stark enough to dispense with superlatives – no extremely, no very, no anything, just five *hors catégorie* hard days.

   And a word about rest days. All riders hate transfers by plane. Their work is rooted in rhythm and anything that disrupts that rhythm is stressful. The break from racing may be welcome, but that rhythm has to be sustained: an hour and a half ride to keep the muscles loose and to bypass the body's immediate impulse to begin to wind down. A tricky balance between relaxation and routine stress.

On the first major climb of stage ten, the col de la Madeleine, Millar knew he was finished. The appalling physical effort merely to hang on at the back like a tin can tied to a car bumper, the wasting effect of scratching up the strength and willpower to stay in the race had drained his morale dry with the force of a turkey-farm eviscerating suction pump. But, with enormous courage, he made the col – nothing, he said, would have induced him to abandon on the climb, the shame of it – and cruised to a stop on the descent. The dread of giving up was at last overwhelmed by the terrible certainty of not being able to go on any longer.

The col du Glandon is reckoned one of the worst climbs in the Alps by many, including Bernard Thévenet who virtually wasted himself towing a chase group up it in 1977, the year of his second victory. He was riding to save his yellow jersey. The others had their own agenda and left him to the work. Dead in the saddle at the summit of l'Alpe d'Huez, unable to walk or eat, he had nonetheless held onto his lead over the day's winner, Hennie Kuiper, by 55 seconds. It seemed quite possible that Armstrong was in similar straits this year. Ullrich's Telekoms were driving a fierce pace and Armstrong's team had fallen away, save his climbers, Heras and Jose-Luis Ribiera. Armstrong appeared to be suffering – roiling at the back, eyes sunk. The Basque climber from the wild-card Euskaltel team, Roberto Laiseka, 32 years old in his first Tour, even reached out at one point to pat him on the back in encouragement, so grim did he look. Perhaps he would crack – he nearly had in the Alps the previous year. Ullrich piled on the pressure down the long valley descent and out onto the approach road to the final beastly 14km up l'Alpe d'Huez. Ahead of them, Laurent Roux, who had escaped with two others at 6km and went clear solo on the Glandon, was tantalisingly close to a miraculous victory.

A right-hand bend and there it is, the first slab of the massive wall, a horror. The Armstrong/Ullrich group contained a clutch of ace climbers. This was their terrain, but suddenly, the hitherto resolute line of Telekoms wavered, as if they were unsure whose turn it was at the front. Ribiera and Heras charged through and, fast as you like in their slipstream, Armstrong. He sped past and, with one withering look at Ullrich as if to say: ' Here's my hand. Time to see you,' he was out of the saddle, accelerating on low gears; 39 x 21, 3.95m for every full turn of the pedals and turning those pedals at around 85/90 rpm. It was breathtaking; a show of irresistible force. No one could follow.

Some 4km up he had established a gap of 2 minutes; at around 7km he went past the luckless Roux with nary a glance. The speed of his pedalling – chainwheel a blur like a *moulinette*, a child's hand-held windmill – has drawn comparison with legendary pure climbers such as Charly Gaul, Federico Bahamontes, Lucien Van Impe. Gaul notably first adopted low-gear 'twiddling' though he stayed in the saddle. Others preferred the dancing style, out of the saddle, which requires huge stamina and lung-power. In the rarefied thin air of the mountains, most big men prefer higher gears which take more strength to turn but less toll on breathing. Ullrich has tried to adapt to faster pedalling but admits it simply doesn't suit him. Armstrong has, from the first, pedalled at high revs; having lost some 5 kilos of body weight in his fight against cancer, he now has a leaner frame which responds to specialist preparation for tremendous accelerations on the climbs.

At the finish, there was no evident jubilation. Armstrong gritted his teeth and jabbed the air; a gesture of spite, it seemed, an *I told you so . . . get off my back*. Perhaps he felt overjoyed; the perception at the time was different. Later he confessed that he might have expended too much energy; he had ridden himself to the limit and though Ullrich, grinding away, had lost 1 minute 59 seconds, there was still a long way to go. Incidentally, he pulled out his earpiece at about halfway: no advice he was being given could possibly help. He rode the climb at 21kph (Armstrong at 22kph) more than 1 minute slower than when he took overall victory in 1997.

Armstrong had become only the second American to win on the alp – after Andy Hampsten in 1992. Lemond, the eventual victor, and Bernard Hinault crossed the line together in 1986, though the Frenchman is credited (in French records) with the win. That case apart, only Fausto Coppi had won on the alp (the first time it featured in the Tour, 1952) and in Paris. Armstrong was clearly moved and had, at last, begun to reveal some sense of the history of this race; that it is not simply the greatest bike race in the world, but possessed of a legendary status, a mythology which sets it apart as a sporting event. You don't just turn up, win and go home. The reach of merely riding it is far longer and deserves a greater respect than he has demonstrated, being too preoccupied with his own concerns. This apparent indifference to the unquantifiable mystique of the Tour de France has alienated Armstrong. He has, if tardily, begun to evince a welcome sensitivity to the peculiar hold the race has on the French. It is rooted in their national tradition. Armstrong, surely prompted by his Frenchwoman PR advisor, has softened and begun to open up to the impact of his deeds, *and* to talk in less hesitant French: 'L'Alpe d'Huez is a classic climb, a very special stage and it means a lot to everyone in cycling. It's probably the most famous climb in the sport and that motivated me today. I wanted to win on the Alpe and it's not something that many people have done, so it's an honour to win the stage. [Earlier on] I continued to 'suffer' a little, I played poker, because I assumed that if I bluffed then they would ride harder.' His time for the ascent, 38 minutes, was only just slower than Pantani's 1997 record of 37 minutes 35 seconds.

(A 60-year old cyclist, attempting the ride before the race collapsed with a heart attack and died.)

François Simon took yellow – his brother Pascal had phoned him to tell him to get the jersey for the family – but he had no illusions about his 20-minute lead over Armstrong who, if he had overcooked it showed no sign next day to Chamrousse. During the winter, he had come down to train on these Alpine stages and, when the big cols were closed by snow, he rode the mountain time-trial several times. That is where his Tours are won: in the freezing cold of February, Bruyneel videoing him as he rides, producing a monitored profile of how to ride each and every climb. Work, work, work; you prepare best for something by doing it. He took the stage – the route forms part of the col de Luitel, scene of one of Gaul's epic stage wins in 1958 – having led at every time check, by 1 minute over Ullrich whom he now led by over 3 minutes. Kivilev lost over 6 minutes: his potential threat had had no real substance.

It was the first time anyone had taken consecutive Alpine stages since Pyotr Ugrumov (another of Dr Ferrari's consultees) in 1994. The last defending Tour winner to do so had been Merckx in 1972.

Two kilometres from the finish on the climb up to Plateau de Bonsacre above Ax-les-Thermes, Armstrong once more turned coolly to stare into the grimacing face of Ullrich, his mouth agape with punishing effort, before racing away; never was the phrase 'putting down the hammer' more expressive. Ullrich had led all the way, punishing himself to tire the American, but Armstrong showed no fatigue, even seemed to be smiling before he overtook the German champion. The Colombian Felix Cardenas beat his fellow breakaway Laiseka by 13 seconds, and Armstrong by 15 seconds.

Stage 14.

The 1971 Tour crossed the same climbs they face today. The ridges are steeped in history – Allied airmen and soldiers escaped from Occupied France into neutral Spain guided by local mountain men, at considerable risk to themselves; many of them were smugglers well-used to dodging the revenue patrols on the cols. In the Middle Ages, Jews fled the Spanish *pogroms* over the same passes, and when Franco's Falangists took Barcelona, the roads filled with Republicans straggling into exile, many of them with no more than a suitcase. One such refugee traipsed over the col du Portillon and 35 years later his son, Luis Oçana, racing towards that same mountain, crashed out of the Tour. In 1995, Fabio Casartelli died on the Portet d'Aspet and the day before at the signing on in Perpignan, Lance Armstrong was presented with a small replica of the memorial to his friend. We could only guess at how he would feel, how they would all feel, when they rode past. Nearing the end of the stage, the race would pass through a village called Garin, the name of the winner of the first Tour de France. History was crowding in on us that day.

I rode up to the col to wait for the race across a graffito scrawled on the tarmac: *Dieu Armstrong . . . Jaja dans le Baba* (marginally less crude than 'up your arse'). 'God Armstrong . . . Jaja's kidding himself.' Back down to my station at a hairpin.

The break went through and, five minutes later, the main bunch. The overriding impression, especially if you've recently crawled up the climb, is of the sheer force, the power, the ruthless focus; this drive is already wilting in two guys off the back – Steffen Wesemann and *lanterne rouge* Bart Leysen, caught up in the following traffic of cars and petrol fumes, haggard, suffering, both due to abandon later that day, cast adrift like the empty *bidons*, food bags and wrappers that litter the route. Spectators are asked to chuck their refuse in official Tour de France waste bags attached to small wooden stakes.

The buccaneering Durand got a big cheer – 'Ja-cky! Ja-cky!' Armstrong, a few riders off the front, looked impassive, though arriving at the Casartelli monument in training not long before he had wept like a child; this is the hidden face of these men. All the suffering in training, the cold dark days of winter etch the pain; once the race is on, they wear the mask of apparent indifference.

The rest of the escapees wilted, Jalabert rode himself into a lone lead, 162km out in front, over five of the six cols and took the mountains jersey from Roux. The chase behind him crossed the Peyresourde and down. Ullrich, never a very handy descender, carried the fight on, risk be damned. He took one corner too sharply, shot off the road, only just short of a metal barrier – which might well have crippled him – turned a somersault over the bike and disappeared from view. A few seconds later, he scrambled out of the undergrowth, passed up his undamaged bike and remounted. Armstrong had waited. The respect for his rival was plain.

Jalabert was eventually caught on the last climb of the day, his legs gone, by Armstrong, riding with magnificent ease. Armstrong actually offered Jalabert his wheel but, as the Frenchman said, he'd have needed a motorbike to stay with him. But what a marvellous show of professional dedication that day out in the blistering Pyrenean sun had been. '*Allez Jaja!*' they cried. Leblanc called it '*grandiose*'. Jaja had reclaimed French hearts, as well as the mountains jersey *and* overall in the combativity prize. This had not been the only day he'd shown aggression and tenacity.

Armstrong had sworn this victory for his dead friend Casartelli and, mirroring that day in Limoges in 1995 when he had dedicated the stage win to him, he crossed the line at the Pla d'Adet with both arms pointing to the heavens. He really had opened his heart to the race and those who honour it. Confidence had allowed him more generosity.

Jalabert took no mountain points but retained his polka-dot jersey and would hold it to Paris, thus becoming the only man apart from Hinault to win both green and mountains jersey outright. (Merckx won the mountains competition in 1969, but the *maillot à pois* – a copy of one of the famous jerseys worn at the popular night racing in the Vélodrome d'Hiver from the 1930s to '50s – was inaugurated in 1975 at the insistence of Félix Lévitan.) Kivilev was now second overall; Simon had ceded yellow to the American and Oscar Sevilla of the Kelme team, who were well ahead in the team competition, had established an unassailable lead in the young riders' (under-24, white jersey) competition. (Young rider? He looks about 15 years old.)

Ullrich had not given up. Next day he fought hard over the Aspin and the monster Tourmalet but could not shake Armstrong off. 'I tried hard to put him in trouble. I have never been so strong but there was nothing more I could do.' Laiseka rode to a glorious solo win that afternoon at Luz-Ardiden. One minute eight seconds behind him, Armstrong and Ullrich rode in together and as they crossed the line, Ullrich, just ahead, gallantly put out his right hand, conceding victory. Armstrong clasped it. Nothing symbolises this Tour better: the frayed nerves, suspicion, discourtesies and bickering of the previous year gone; a compelling rider who had matured into a great champion, with a rival of exceptional tenacity. There was unmistakable respect between them. A race worthy of the Tour's legend. Asked when he knew he could not win the Tour, Ullrich replied: 'On Luz-Ardiden.'

Armstrong even addressed his unpopularity. Speaking of the *prix citron*, the mock prize journalists award to the least cooperative rider, he said: 'I don't like small talk or posing for photos doing stupid pointless things. I give them intensity in the race and I'll go on doing so; isn't that enough?' He had a point and speaking candidly about it was immeasurably more convincing than the bristling of previous years. Another regular *prix citron*, double winner Laurent Fignon supported him. Some people find Armstrong cold but that is nothing to reproach him for. Maybe when so many people want a piece of you there is no other way to be. On the other hand, Armstrong had hired a bodyguard. He had, he admitted, been very nervous at the start of the Tour. Fignon with a hint of irony remarked: 'Maybe that's a sign of the times.' Nonetheless, at a press conference he himself called in Pau on the rest day, Armstrong appeared relaxed, ready to field questions with genuine concern, to help and inform. In the bilious climate of relations a year ago this would have seemed ingratiating, sheer politicking. Now, it had the feel of a rider who had overcome a number of personal gripes and emerged into a clearer frame of mind.

There were other, less seemly events to report. Italian riders complained that the *lanterne rouge*, Jimmy Casper (more French panache, if at the back of the race) had been shamelessly taking tows up the mountains, a practice well-established in Italy, but then as shamelessly popping up at the front of the race to contest the intermediate sprints next day. This was not fair play. On the second rest day someone stole the Départ bell and Leblanc had to borrow one from the director of the Dauphiné Libéré. Jonathan Vaughters was stung by a wasp; his right eye puffed up so badly that he was compelled to take anti-inflammatory corticoids (a banned substance), which meant that he had to withdraw from the race early in the next stage. The French Minister, who followed the race that day, agreed that there are occasions when medical treatment ought to be permissible, clear of any charge of doping. And as Ullrich decelerated across the line on stage 16, a spectator made a grab for his hat and nearly decked him. The yellow jersey decided, there remained the duel for the green jersey between O'Grady and Zabel.

Stage 16 was won by Jens Voigt from the Australian Bradley McGee, two survivors of a long break. McGee was so exhausted that he could do nothing at the finish. Descending into Tulle, a bunch of 30 riders took a left-hand bend too fast and piled up. Five riders were evacuated to hospital, their season finished, with three broken collarbones, one fractured wrist and a serious facial wound amongst their injuries.

Next day, Voigt punctured 5km from the line and rode like the devil to get back into the bunch to help his team mate O'Grady contest the sprint with Zabel, but the lead was shrinking.

The 18th stage, a 61km individual flat time-trial, was won by Armstrong in matchless style. So laid back on the starting platform as to be signing an autograph – he had done his warm-up in the company of his wife and son, a domestic intrusion of the kind once distinctly alien to the Tour's ambiance – he took 1 minute 24 seconds out of Gonzalez de Galdeano, one of the ONCE *domestiques*, and 1 minute 39 seconds from Ullrich. The big gain of the day was the 2 minute 8 second margin Beloki got over Kivilev, which hoisted him into third overall, so that the order at the head of the leader board stood exactly as it had a year before.

In the tussle for the green points jersey, Zabel was reeling O'Grady in: another win on the penultimate stage 19 and 45 more points amassed brought him to within two points of the Australian's total. On the final run-in to Paris, the Telekoms – organised by their *directeur*, former fast-man Walter Godefroot – backed Zabel with impressive efficiency and cropped all the intermediate sprint bonuses on offer; the Crédit Agricoles, unable to revive the cohesion they had displayed in winning the team time-trial, seemed to have given up. Zabel took the lead by four points, his lieutenant, Alexandr Vinokourov, who had already worked so tirelessly for Ullrich in the mountains, sprang his lead-out efforts with faultless timing and still had energy for a solo break on the last lap of the Champs-Elysées. He very nearly made it; what a reward that would have been for surely the most industrious *domestique* of the Tour. But the pack was on him, the Czech sprinter Jan Svorada led in, with Zabel and O'Grady on his shoulder.

Armstrong, Ullrich, Beloki: the same three on the podium as in 2000, but what a change in the shape of the Tour, in the atmosphere. There is an enduring image of Zabel and O'Grady smiling together after the race, arms about each other's shoulders, the accord of friendship after a tough duel clean fought. The hitherto taut American confessed '*C'est le Tour où j'ai pris le plus de plaisir*': it is the Tour that has given him most *pleasure*. Leblanc suggested that there was indeed a fresh optimism abroad. 'I have the feeling that most of the riders have turned the page. It has been a good Tour. We have regained vigour, oxygen, we have put the smile back.' Such a smile as Rik Verbrugghe's when he was heading for the line on stage 15, Marco Pinolti on his wheel; he even had time to adjust his glasses as they plopped off his nose *twice*. What's he *doing*? we thought. On a stage victory and he's worried about his bins? He made it.

It was undoubtedly an unusually taxing race. The Banesto doctor, Jesús Hoyo, said that of all the five Tours he had followed, it was by far the hardest on the riders' powers of recovery. But, despite the domination of Armstrong, it was no procession. The attacking spirit animated it from start to finish and, as Fignon said, 'either at the side of the road or in front of the television, people want to see riders at their limit, some going well, others not so well. The Tour resembles life: there are heroes and there are losers. I think this time, the public has been well served'.

CHAPTER TWELVE

2002

Armstrong's Four-Square Triumph

The shape of the 2002 race had a decidedly lopsided look: ten flat stages, a week's worth of mountains – twenty-one in a lump interspersed by one flattish stage and a rest day – leaving a bare three-day run-in to Paris. Lance Armstrong, going for a fourth consecutive win, predicted that this would be his hardest Tour yet, but that was no more than self insurance against what he calls the suicide of projecting victory. However, although the opposition was talked up, there was nobody of real challenge to the reigning champion who makes no secret of his obsession with the yellow jersey. 'When I stop riding the Tour de France, I stop riding.' He can afford to. There is no commercial pressure on him to race elsewhere. His sponsors – the US Postal Service – have no particular interest in anything other than the most prestigious victory and if Armstrong and the team delivers that, the rest of the racing calendar is of very limited publicity appeal. It's an emphatically self-serving attitude with which those more deeply imbued with the traditions of cycle sport do not have much sympathy. But, while Armstrong's passion drives him, there is unlikely to be a halt in his wins.

It was Greg Lemond who began this trend of concentrating solely on the Tour win, although Lucien Van Impe, in his day, framed his entire season round the hunt for the mountains prize.

The biggest threat, Jan Ullrich, was out with a damaged knee. The Italian opposition was depleted and in disgrace: Marco Pantani was under investigation for doping, but, after a dreadful ride in the Giro d'Italia, his career is almost certainly finished; Gilberto Simoni, winner of the 2001 Giro, had been bragging that he could give the Americans trouble, but tested positive for cocaine after a short Italian stage race and he and his Saeco team were banned; Stefano Garzelli received a fine of £45,000 – 100,000 Swiss francs – and a nine-month suspension for the use of probenecid, a masking agent, during the Tour; and Dario Frigo had only just returned after his suspension. The police raid on the Giro d'Italia, 6 June 2002, caught him in possession of pots of dope which, he protested, he had no intention of using, they were 'for inspiration' . . . by some mystic purpose, presumably. (Bought through the Internet, delivered at Milan Linate airport on the hush hush, one bottle, which cost him £500, turned out to contain salt water. If it had contained Hemassist, he'd have had to keep it at -6°. Dope? Dupe.) Of other riders in the race, only two looked close to being dangerous: the Spaniard Joseba Beloki, third in 2001 and the Columbian Santiago Botero, an all-rounder – King of the Mountains in 2000 – who can race against the clock. Botero had even had the effrontery to beat the specialist Armstrong in a time-trial in a warm-up race before the Tour. The French clung forlornly to their only overall contender, Christophe Moreau, whose win in the 2001 Prologue was as close as he had come, and would be likely to come, to any challenge. But, as Armstrong never tires of saying, the Tour is unlike any other race: a bad day in the mountains, such as he suffered in 2000, can wreak havoc. Luckily for him both Pantani and Ullrich failed to capitalise on that occasion, but there is no such thing as a safe margin. In 1972, Eddy Merckx, riding for his fourth victory, lost ten minutes to Luis Ocaña and only took the race back after the Spaniard had to abandon after a dreadful crash. But, Ocaña was a potent rival: Armstrong has none.

That said, this year's Tour was full of wonderful racing and quite a few upsets and surprises which make it the great event it is. Jacky Durand, the man who loves to go out alone, darling of the combativity competition, was booted out for a silly infraction. The Norwegian Thor Hushovd, was nearly eliminated by missing the time barrier on stage two, but stuck to his job and took the win on stage 18. David Millar was blown out of contention for best young rider – his stated aim for the race – after the very first mountain stage but, two days later, managed to win a stage. As to the battle for the green jersey, Erik Zabel aiming for a seventh win in a row, it became the story of the Tour: settled with a majestic flourish on the Champs-Elysées.

The Tour began in Luxembourg. The last time it had started here, in 1989, Pedro Delgado, the reigning champion, got lost in town on a warm-up ride and missed his Prologue start by over two minutes. This year, the US Postal's local man, Joachim Benoît, the only Luxemburger in the race, gave his team an in-depth guided tour of the route – 7km of fast descents, sharp corners, cobbles and a wicked uphill drag – only to fall off on his own ride the next day. Armstrong, riding in team colours – he said he needed the motivation, the incentive, of chasing yellow – won by two seconds from the amazing, evergreen Laurent Jalabert, a former world time-trial champion. Millar, who admits that his concentration on training in the mountains had cost him some speed, nonetheless came fifth and was full of ambition. He had been making all the sacrifices essential to a good ride. He was, it seemed, beginning to let the bike do the talking for him.

The race spent two days in the tiny Duchy which has produced three Tour winners and four victories: François Faber, 1909; Nicolas Frantz, 1927 and 1928; and Charly Gaul, 1958. On the first stage, the young Swiss rider Rubens Bertogliati made a do-or-die break on the last climb to take the win and, by virtue of a time bonus, the yellow jersey – the first Swiss to take a stage since Alex Zülle in 1996. Robbie McEwen, one of three Australian fast men in the race nurtured on track racing – with Bradley McGee and Stuart O'Grady – was riding in some pain from a pinched nerve, but made no secret of his intention to battle with Zabel for green. Back in Germany, Zabel's teammate Ullrich, who two months earlier had been booked for drink-driving, had now been caught taking amphetamines in a disco at three in the morning. His manager, Walter Godefroot, close to exasperation with the froward rider of more promise than returns, said he didn't know whether Ullrich would have the willpower, now, to return at this level: 'He's been saying all the right things but he hasn't backed that up with actions. We need to know what he's going to do. Maybe he'll just go and live off his money,' he said wearily, 'he's got enough of it.'

(The six months suspension imposed on him subsequently means that he won't be able to race until March 2003.)

The last rider to win a Tour stage wearing the rainbow jersey of world champion was Bernard Hinault who took three in his third overall victory in 1981. The Spaniard Oscar Freire, the current rainbow jersey, has twice jumped the pack to win the world road race, and did the same on stage two, pipping Zabel and revenging his loss to the German in his home-town, Torrelavega, during the 2001 Vuelta a España. Hushovd limped in 19m 22s later weaving unsteadily through crowds who thought all the riders had already finished. Stricken with severe cramp, he had struggled on and was applauded for his heroic effort at the line by the Tour organiser, Jean-Marie Leblanc. In view of his courage, the time rule was waived and he stayed in the race.

Next day, it was McEwen who relegated Zabel with an irresistible turn of speed down the barriers, though Zabel's time bonus put him into yellow as well as green. The Australian said afterwards that no sprinter can claim to be the best in the world, only to be the best on the day. As to the reason for his startling speed – specific muscle-toughening and high-rev pedalling developed through track racing – he said, of himself and the other Ozzies, with professional bluntness: 'We try harder.' Example? O'Grady, who had taken up the fight with Zabel in 2001, suffered a bout of tachycardia during the stage: his heart-rate went up to 225, way beyond his racing maximum of 184. He received medical attention in the saddle, and not only recovered, but even raced up to the front to contest the sprint.

The team time-trial, won by Beloki's Spanish ONCEs, caused ructions in Jalabert's Danish CSC Tiscali team, managed by the 1996 winner Bjarne Rijs. The stated plan before the ride was to dump any rider who punctured apart from Jalabert, Tyler Hamilton and Carlos Sastre. With 20km to the finish, the Danish champion Michael Sandstöd punctured. Rijs said wait, the radio in the mechanics' car wasn't working – they drove on. Rijs dithered, then ordered them to get going, but in the muddle they had lost 53 seconds and Jalabert an almost certain yellow jersey. A terrible disappointment but, as he put it when tempers had cooled, no cause for bad feeling; the Tour goes on, so must they.

Two days later, Jalabert, 'Jaja', was signing autographs when a bell rang but locals assured him it was for Mass. It *was* in fact, for the start of the stage. Somewhat stressed, he chased on, reflecting that he had good legs and . . . maybe a chance of doing something. The ONCE rider Gonzalez de Galdeano took over the lead and became the first Spaniard to wear the yellow jersey since quintuple winner Miguel Indurain.

Idle in Italy, the great speed merchant Mario Cipollini, whose new team Acqua e Sapone were not ranked high enough to ride the Tour, announced his retirement. 'I feel bitter at not being able to ride the Tour and have a chance to win a stage. The sponsors do not recognise my value.' He's said as much before. Another fit of petulance? Italian cycling being under such a cloud of suspicion, it badly needs Cipo's crowd-pleasing, dope-free image and, given that this autumn's world road race over a flat course should be ideal for him, he soon reversed his decision.

Back in the Tour, Christophe Moreau, riding with a fractured vertebra, was having a wretched time, heading straight for every crash going, it seemed, and there were plenty – Millar was caught up in several but, luckily, shrugged off the bruises. However, crashes put paid to Tom Steels, Freire and, in a 70kph pile-up, Marco Pinotti (nose split open) and Rik Verbrugghe (broken collarbone), although the Belgian somehow made it to the stage finish, one handed. On the same day, the Estonian sprinter and former yellow jersey Jan Kirsipuu took the honours riding for the second-division French Ag2R team, in the Tour as the last wild card selection in May. 'We ought to congratulate the Tour for letting us ride,' he said, with a dig at the often arcane selection criteria applied by the organisation.

Zabel got his win on stage six. Dutchman Karsten Kroon, a Tour rookie, grabbed the win of his life on Bastille Day, having only one previous victory in an obscure Swiss one-day race – in his palmarès. However, the big news at the start of the second week was Botero's victory in the individual 52km time-trial in Brittany. It was the first time in four years that Armstrong had lost such a stage and suddenly there was talk of a loss of form, a vulnerability, a chance that he might wilt under attack. He admitted that he hadn't felt good and was expecting to come 22nd not 2nd. Claiming not to be making excuses, he said: 'When you start at different times, the conditions can change and in the last 5km I was suffering.' Conditions can change, for sure, to help or hinder – Merckx himself lost a couple of races of truth in the Tour – but really, the loss of 11 seconds was not going to worry Armstrong, even if Botero's *directeur sportif* was saying: 'So Armstrong is human, after all.' Later, US Postal directeur Johan Bruyneel let slip that they had chosen the wrong gearing and deprived the American of the necessary power – a curiously elementary mistake, given their scrupulous attention to every last detail. However, Armstrong positively welcomed the bullish commentary. 'It's attack until they crack, or I do', which is about as succinct a definition of the will to win as you could get. He was, though, still sounding off like the po-faced Yank he is, and made an unworthy side-swipe at the ONCE boss: 'I think Manolo [Saíz] has a problem with the fact that one of his ex-riders [the then US Postal director Johan Bruyneel] has been far more successful as a manager in this race than he has.'

Millar, who had had to 'hang on for grim death at the end' pulled on the white jersey of best young rider and professed himself happy: he didn't even feel on his best form and yet there he was, close to the top guys. Alas, not for long.

On the rest day before the Pyrenees, Jaja announced that he would be retiring at the end of the season, but this old-school rider, complete professional, competitive at all times and in all disciplines, had more surprises to pull yet. After 14 years it would be time to end 'the story of a young kid who rode bikes with his friends and dreamt of becoming a professional rider and riding the Tour de France'.

Close to the village of Poteaux, 26km into stage ten, a seven-year-old boy, Melvin Pompele, who may have had the same dream, ran across the road to rejoin his grandparents, straight into the path of one of the publicity caravan Land-Rovers and died instantly. It is a mark of the mannerly police handling of the bystanders out in the country that the roadside atmosphere is relaxed and good-humoured. One can only hope that such a tragedy – the second in three years – will stiffen vigilance rather than crowd control.

Col d'Aubisque, stage 11 (the last Pyrenean col traversed by the Tour in 1910) continues to the climb that concludes the day, the

Tourmalet, but only to 6km below the summit at the ugly ski-station, La Mongie. The US Postals had a simple plan: to ride for the win and race as if they already had yellow. The heat was intense, the expected attacks on the Aubisque did not come, the lead group arrived at the foot of the last 14km climb intact and the Postals opened up. First George Hincapie blasted off the front at a cruel pace, José Luis Rubiera relayed and then the specialist climber, Roberto Heras went to the front, Armstrong on his wheel, and suddenly upped the pace so high that only Beloki stayed with them over the last 5km. Even Armstrong was at his limit, telling Heras to slow down; he could barely keep the pace, no thought of attacking and, though it would have been seemly to allow Heras the stage win, Beloki was close, they could take no risks. There were time bonuses on offer – 20, 12 and 8 seconds. This might suggest a lapse of moral strength. Armstrong could surely afford a handful of seconds? More likely, he and Heras were required to abide by team orders – as Rubens Barricchello, bidden cede victory to Michael Schumacher in the Austrian Grand Prix. The sponsors make a huge financial investment: minor details of sportsmanship, moral power versus naked force, cut no ice with them. The man they have enriched by hiring them has the no-frills responsibility to win the big race for them. End of story.

Some metres from the line, Armstrong dropped behind the Basque rider, then, to the dismay of the crowds of Basques cheering their man on, jumped past both him and his teammate to pocket the 20 seconds time bonus on offer; his weary wave did for a victory salute. At the close, he was once more in yellow with Beloki at 1 minute 12 seconds, Botero at 4 minutes 13 seconds and Millar, perhaps reassessing his 'curiosity about the mountains' for which he had prepared hard, losing 7 minutes 23 seconds to the lead and any realistic hope of the white jersey in Paris. Jalabert, plainly driven by tireless professional enthusiasm, had spent 120km out on his own in a bid for the stage win and accumulating points in the mountains competition, which he'd won in 2001, entirely against expectation and by similar opportunistic forays. Three kilometres from the line, riding on empty, he watched the leaders flash by. Only 4 minutes down overall, he had known they would have to chase him. Armstrong, he said, bestowed a wry look of sympathy.

There was no sympathy next day on the hard road to Plateau de Beille, crossing the col de Menté where Ocaña crashed out of the 1972 Tour, the col de Portet d'Aspet, where, in 1995, Armstrong's teammate and friend Fabio Casertelli crashed and died, the col de la Core and the col de Port, whereon a series of punctures drove Charlie Holland, the first Briton to compete, out of the 1937 race.

Jalabert attacked early once more, amassing points in the mountains *and* the combativity prize – worth 200,000 francs in Paris – awarded daily to the rider who shows most aggression. Past signs pleading 'Don't go Jaja' and 'Jaja in peas' (i.e. the red polka dots of the mountains jersey) he rode another 143km in a breakaway, expressly to get ahead in the mountains competition, but after a while, as he said, beginning to enjoy himself. The former specialist sprinter (green jersey 1992 and '95) wanted to finish his last Tour on a high. The Plateau de Beille proved just too high: 16.5km of 8 per cent average gradient to a summit at 1,780 metres. Once again, Rubiera then Heras led the onslaught and the rest, save Beloki, dropped away. Nine kilometres from the top, Jalabert, unheeded, watched them go. He ended the day 11 minutes 36 seconds down but in the peas . . . the jersey of *panache*, he calls it. Another 5km and Armstrong struck for home, up the climb he had trained on in May, using his familiar high-revving style, out of the saddle. This sudden burst of his strength may be unanswerable; so far, for sure, it remains unanswered. That dizzy whirring of the pedals, devouring a kilometre virtually every two minutes of uphill, is the hallmark of his superiority, and it derives from the exhaustive training methods and analysis which he and his support team apply to winning this race.

He experimented at two different rates: 75rpm and 100rpm. Both produced similar power output, heart-rate and speed – around 30kph on the climbs – however, the faster rate on a lower-gear ratio is ultimately less taxing on the muscles if more demanding of the lungs and so that is what they plumped for. In winter, accompanied by Bruyneel in the car, he comes to the Alps to ride and *learn* the climbs. At the end of one 8-hour session, to the top of la Plagne, back down, up again – all this come rain or snow – he was actually turned back by a heavy fall of snow which made the col unpassable. The American Jonathan Vaughters, former medical student riding for the Crédit Agricole team, has drawn sharp contrast between what he terms Armstrong's modern scientific preparation and the old-school methods. Armstrong leaves nothing to chance, to the extent of doing special work on his middle body to sustain the heavy strain of holding an extreme crouch position in time-trials. He weighs pasta and checks what difference the greater or lesser intake produces on the bike. He scouts the ground, he rides it at race speed: there is no terrain for which he has not readied himself psychologically and that is where he gains so much over his rivals. The deliberate absence from the extended demands of racing which most teams feel obliged to answer, leaves him mentally fresh anyway; the specific reconnaissance means that he has all but eliminated the chance of being surprised at any part of the route. Such meticulous provision added to a natural athleticism which he has honed to supreme physical efficiency is at the root of his supremacy . . . in this race. True, he won both the Midi Libre and the Dauphiné Libéré, two of the shorter mountainous-stage races, traditional leg-stretchers for the Tour, (as did Merckx in 1971 and Indurain in 1995), but he rarely makes much of a showing anywhere else. It is a moot point, of course, but many argue that Armstrong gave more to professional cycling before he became obsessed with the Tour de France. Until another rider of equal talent, mind and body, adopts similar demonic methods to winning one race per year, Armstrong is likely to stay 'up there' as Gonzalez de Galdeano (yellow jersey for 7 days) put it, gesticulating at the sky. He is not a great climber, he does not stun the field with massive gains; his victories are built on accumulated small gains and his own impregnability to attack.

The French call his swift cadence 'the coffee grinder'; it might more aptly be called the mincer through which he shreds the hopes, and strength, of anyone who tries to stay with him.

Looking back for Heras on the climb to Plateau de Beille, he was clearly ready to hand over the win if he could, due reward for his Spaniard lieutenant's sterling work, but Heras had not the legs and came in 1 minute 4 seconds adrift, just ahead of Beloki. Like all the other climbers, Beloki can maintain a steady pace – he never lost much more than a minute on the climbs; it is the abrupt surge of speed which he cannot counter. To put some perspective on the impact of his crushing attacks, Rubiera, having mounted the first assault with frantic acceleration, fell away when his turn was done and finished nowhere. That is the cost. Armstrong holds the wheel and saves energy but, on a mountain, not nearly so much as on the flat. Thus, from nearly the same effort as his front man, he then turns on the irresistible force and they all fall away behind him. One who had crumpled the day before was poor Vaughters; things had not been going well. The Crédit Agricoles, prime players in recent Tours, were having a dreadful time of it and Vaughters having climbed off after a crash – the fourth year in succession he has had to abandon – declared that he had done with the race and the sport altogether. He was in profound distress and may change his mind.

The stage did for Durand, too. The inveterate chancer of the solo break chanced the beady eye of the race commissaries, hitched a tow from his second team car, was spotted and, after he trailed into the finish 40 minutes down, protesting innocence, was kicked off the race, the car too. Sad end.

Routinely, Armstrong batted away any hint at complacency – he had no great time advantage yet, there was still a long way to go, anything could happen. Truth was, he had built an unassailable lead. What's more, his team, a very shaky outfit during his inaugural win in 1999, has become a well-drilled, solid, immensely strong unit dedicated absolutely to their leader's victory. And, not even Merckx ever won the first two mountain stages of a Tour back to back two years running as Armstrong has now done.

Millar trailed in over 50 minutes down which bodes ill for any notions about one day going for the overall victory. The bout of glandular fever early in the season which allowed him to come fresher to the race than might otherwise have been possible, may have tapped deeper into his physical resources than he'd thought. And yet, the white jersey already forfeited and his ribs bruised after a tumble in Alençon, he'd saved energy on the Plateau de Beille and took to the road next day determined to win. He felt good all day and 'it's easy to be cunning when you feel good'. He had written a note: *Today I win*, which is almost formulaic in French cycling parlance, a favourite dictum of the great Hinault, and 8km from the start in Lavelanet, he joined a break on the first climb in company with his idol, Laurent Jalabert, patiently consolidating his rather cheeky lead in the mountains competition, and two others. Another seven riders jumped across the gap to them and when Jaja botched an attack some 18km from the finish in Béziers, Millar and four others, including the notably fast men – David Extebarria, Laurent Brochard, Michael Boogerd – went clear. The last kilometres were hard on the nerves and the legs but Millar outwitted and outsprinted the rest with a fine show of *attitude* as much as anything. It was, he said, 'a sublime race today' and declared that professionally, it was his best moment. The last Briton to win a Tour road stage had been Max Sciandri into St Etienne, in 1995. Millar's winning streaks are certainly bold; for the time being they are short-lived. Jalabert had now ridden 429km in breakaways over three days.

All the riders dread Mont Ventoux: the bald mountain thrusting up like a gazebo of the gods to survey the distant encirclement of Alpine chains and Cévennes catches every caprice of wind and weather, and the final 6km of road up to its summit is as ugly a stretch of metalled concrete as can be found. In 2000 Armstrong made the crass error of gifting the win to his rival Pantani: he was surely bent on making that good this 14th stage, the second longest of the 2002 race, 220km from the old cloth-working town of Lodéve and source of most of France's uranium to the col at 1,912m, the forbidding high place which the novelist Antoine Blondin christened 'the despot of cyclists'. Blondin lived in the St Germain quarter of Paris, neighbour to Jean-Paul Sartre and the rest, and refused to stray beyond its pavements except once a year for the Tour de France, which he followed 28 times. This does not explain the grip the race continues to hold on the French, but it does give some hint at the potency of the dream which stirred the young Jalabert and countless others.

Ten escapees, including the five-times King of the Mountains Richard Virenque, left the main *peloton* early, stayed ahead and reached the lower slopes of the Domaine of the Angels with 21km to ride in 35°C heat, some 10 minutes up on the chasing yellow jersey group. Virenque, suspended for eight months after finally admitting to taking EPO as a member of the disgraced Festina squad and shunned by all the French teams, had taken a lowly-paid contract with the Belgian Domo-Farm Frites team. He announced his comeback with a bold 242km break to win the sprinters' classic Paris–Tours, by *two seconds* over the chasing bunch – a race not even Merckx won. (One Belgian rider quipped: 'Merckx and I won everything between us: I won Paris–Tours and he won everything else.') Reviled by some, yet still the darling of many, Virenque, a slave to camera lens and column inches, looked dead in the saddle as the first steepness began to bite. He said later that some of the breakaways had done no work; perhaps his fatigue was an act; what followed was certainly an amazing performance. One by one the others fell away and he was alone, in the lead. Behind him, Armstrong was isolated in company with Beloki and his teammate Mikel Pradera. Heras was having a miserable time this day; as Armstrong put it, in defence of his champion *domestique*, Ventoux does strange things to people. Botero slumped by over 15 minutes, Millar by 18 and the oven-baked slopes were littered with stragglers of considerable class.

Some 6.5km from the top, with Virenque hanging onto a four-minute lead, Beloki attacked, if you can call it that. It took Armstrong no more than a second or two to catch his wheel and go past at such velocity that the impression was of royalty spurning the vulgar. Within 3km, the American had opened a three-minute gap but he had let slip the chance to catch Virenque. Had he gone no more than a kilometre earlier, he would probably have nobbled him; as it was he was 2 minutes 20 seconds behind, but another 1 minute 45 seconds up on Beloki who consigned any hope of overtaking Armstrong to dust: 'We've been on the moon today and we've seen what the astronaut is capable of.' Armstrong, whose time to the col, 58 minutes, beat Pantani's 2000 record by 53 seconds, was stung by the chants and boos of a small number of beer-swillers at the roadside: 'Dopé Dopé' which is not French for one of the Seven Dwarfs, but nor is it anything other than the tattle of a moronic few more interested in ring-pulls than bike-racing. The American ignores the vast number of genuine fans cheering him on and instead he pillories the abusive idiots who shout louder. It's a pity, but rage is one of his prime motivators, apparently. Even in speaking of popularity he reveals how thin his crust of self-belief is: 'It's sometimes frustrating. You see the guys they [the fans] accept and cherish and really love and cuddle and it's the guys that in the group you say "I don't *ever* want to be like that guy". I want to be the guy that keeps his mouth shut...' Pardon? Dwelling on the matter of popularity in his book, *It's Not About the Bike*, he says that he is indifferent to being liked in general because 'my wife likes me, my son *will like me*' – my italics, but a telling point. No one could possibly doubt Armstrong's passion; but it is, in many ways, very two-dimensional.

The French have never warmed to the hauteur of winners; there is something inhuman about the aloofness of the men apart and the one aspect of the Tour de France which is possibly unique in all sport is the very stark human dimension of the race between man on his bike and the hard road, the rivals, the weather, the crushing psychological combat. Any rider who appears impervious to all that becomes something of an ogre. It was not until Merckx had been trounced in 1972 and then fought back with such patent courage that his true stature was recognised by the French public, and not till their man Thévenet beat him in 1975 that they *liked* him. He emerged as a man who could live past frailty and sublimate the effect of harsh adversity by sheer character and determination. Armstrong has not yet had to show such qualities, save in the loneliness of the cancer ward.

As for Virenque, who lives nearby Ventoux, it was a gallant victory, a real gain for his morale and, be it said, his image. It also confirms how much he owed to the performance-enhancing power of EPO: evidently he can still climb a mountain with panache, but not day after day as hitherto. He cannot challenge for the overall mountains prize now that he rides on his own legs.

Hushovd had put the agony of the cramps behind him and won the last sprint of the day at Châteauneuf-du-Pape – prize, a hundred bottles of the vintage.

The 30-year-old Lithuanian Raimondas Rumsas, riding in his first Tour for the Italian Lamprei-Daikin team, had been plugging away and now moved up to third overall.

The emergence of one rider who dominates the Tour, even for a number of years – and several have – does not reduce the race. The tussle for overall victory may be decided long before the arrival in Paris, but that does not stifle the competitive spirit in genuine men of the Tour, the riders devoted to the nobility of their profession as well as the routine obligations. When it becomes pointless even to imagine a rider like Armstrong having a bad day – 'a day without' as the French put it graphically – there are yet still laurels to be won and on stage 15, Botero seized his chance. With a rest day in which to reflect, he turned the calvary of Ventoux into a Sacred Way of victory on the longest haul of the race – 226.5km over seven climbs to the first category finishing ascent to Les Deux Alpes.

He'd decided to forget about the overall classification after the Pyrenean ordeal. Although a former mountains prize-winner, he is not a natural climber, more dependent on raw strength and, as the final kilometres to the day's win showed, of pretty uncooked style, too. Leading a break containing six others, he reached the foot of the last climb with 9½ minutes on the chasers. Mario Aerts was the first to stick his neck out, Botero ground after him, Axel Merckx countered, but steadily Botero pulled himself clear, clamped awkwardly to the bike, shoulders rolling with the strain, head lolling, mouth agape, a picture of desperate, in extremis, effort, but strong enough to hold clear by 1 minute 51 seconds on Aerts. The yellow jersey stuck close to Beloki and gave away nearly 7 minutes from an ample chest of spare time.

On the last climb, Beloki actually attacked and, though Armstrong was on his wheel at the time he didn't react for some time. When he did go, it took some ten seconds or so – uncharacteristically long – to put the dampeners on the insolent Basque. In an interview later he explained that he *hadn't known Beloki was attacking*. Since these riders can detect trouble at the hiss of an opponents accelerating tyre, this is very odd; except that, of course, he was, mechanically, awaiting orders from the earpiece. In another interview Botero was saying that a stage win was more important than coming fourth or fifth on general classification, that he'd had one day and come back and 'like the rest, I'm a human being, not a machine'.

On the day when Moreau finally had had enough – another crash and a badly cut lip – and climbed off, Botero, joining Luis Herrera as only the second Colombian to win two stages in the Tour, had hoisted himself back to 7th from 18th, taken a glorious stage win and shown that any serious rider can – and should – take his chance.

Next day it was Michael Boogerd who showed the requisite audacity, and, after a 127km solo break, became the first Dutchman to win atop a mountain in the Tour since Gert-Jan Theunisse won on the 'Dutch' mountain (because always crowded with Dutch fans) l'Alpe d'Huez in 1989. Boogerd's only other stage win had been at Aix-les-Bains on a cold wet July day in 1996, at the end of which Armstrong, riding his fourth Tour, abandoned, feeling 'blocked'. Three months later, he was diagnosed as having testicular cancer. To complete the vignette, Armstrong has twice narrowly lost the Amstel Gold Dutch classic one-day race, once to Boogerd in a two-up sprint.

Boogerd mounted his attack at crazy speed on the twisting descent of the Galibier – Giant of the Alps, first included in 1911 and, at 2645m, the roof of this Tour – and shook off his pursuers at the foot of the climb to the col de la Madeleine. From there, the plunge into the valley and finally up to la Plagne, where in 1987 Stephen Roche rode himself into oxygen debt to claw back time on the yellow jersey Pedro Delgado, an act of sheer will unconnected to heart-rate monitors which brought him overall victory.

At 3km to go, Armstrong launched his attack, without response from any of those on his shoulder. Once again, he, or rather Bruyneel in the team car at the other end of the radio to Armstrong's earpiece, mistimed his move – half a kilometre earlier would have sufficed to take the stage victory – and, whereas two years back Armstrong was rather naively dismissing the idea of potting stage victories as beneath the dignity and professional status of a Tour winner, he has since matured. Stage victories, especially on the open road, whether on mountains or flat, are the stamp of enduring class. His Prologue win gave him 12 such – level with Zabel and Cipollini – and he added three more to put him level with Freddie Maertens, one behind Jacques Anquetil (5 times overall winner), René le Grèves and Charles Pélissier, neither of whom won the race. Merckx has the record with 34; Hinault 27.

Both the Frenchman Laurent Dufaux and the Spaniard Oscar Sevilla, best young rider and 7th overall in 2001, abandoned with stomach upsets. Jalabert stretched his lead in the mountains prize over Botero and saw Virenque buckle on the climb to the Galibier. Perhaps he was working the extraordinary magic of his number in the race: the 51 that Merckx carried on his first ride and victory and Ocaña in his 1973 win, that Thévenet was given in 1975 when he beat Merckx, that Hinault bore to victory in his first ride, 1978.

Boogerd, 'Boogie' to his flatland friends, relied for his luck on a necklace medallion containing his first tooth, his girlfriend's first tooth and a four-leaf clover he'd been carrying that day in Aix. Such jewellery is not always a good idea. Towards the end of one stage, O'Grady's neck chain got caught in the computer attached to his handlebars; he had to break the chain to rip it free and found the bits tangled up in his jersey later.

Frigo escaped on the final long downhill of the Tour, third day in the Alps, a tricky descent from the col de la Colombière with his fellow Italian Giuseppe Guerini and the Belgian Aerts. They had held off a chasing group of 13, animated by Jalabert, grabbing mountains points with relish, and on the sprint into Cluses, home of a National School of Watchmaking, Frigo timed his jump perfectly and saved Italy from a second barren year in the Tour. Reflecting on the more disagreeable events of the recent past, Frigo said: 'I prefer to think of beautiful moments like today; what's happened before is forgotten', although the point about the drive to eradicate doping from the sport is that it must *not* be forgotten.

Next day gave any small fry, keen to work, their last chance for a win before Saturday's individual time-trial and the procession into Paris. There were still mountain points on offer so Jaja had a full day's employment ahead of him and the battle for the green jersey points was hot. McEwen and Zabel had been swapping the lead during this final week, but were now level, McEwen wearing the jersey because of higher placings overall. McEwen suspected the US Postals of an agreement to help Zabel; he had some cause. Eighteen months before, at a small early season race, he'd launched an attack, unaware that Armstrong was taking a pee. There is an unspoken rule of gallantry in the *peloton* about such calls of nature – witness Jalabert's rage in the 2000 Tour (see p. 232). Armstrong raced to rejoin McEwen and gave him such an earful that the redoubtable Ozzie, who might have been inclined to apologise, was riled and told him to let it drop. Armstrong, not one to let things go on past showing, had been taunting McEwen sarcastically with that one lapse of manners from halfway through the Tour. Finally, McEwen had exploded and spat back (the French verb is 'lancer' . . . touché): 'Shut it or I'll stick my fist in your mouth.'

On this stage 18, McEwen took the lead by one point and, there being no points awarded in the time-trial, there would be a showdown on the Champs-Elysées for the second year running. Introduced in 1953 to give the riders with no hope of winning overall another competition to ride for, the green jersey had been won by many illustrious Tour men, but never by an Australian. McEwen was in bullish mood. If Zabel wanted to send his men up ahead to collar the hot-spot sprints, that was fine by him – he was denying himself as well as McEwen and the Australian had shown himself to be faster than the German. Besides, he knew what it was to win on the Champs – in 1999 – which Zabel, four times second there, did not.

The last Norwegian to win a stage had been Dag Otto Lauritzen in the Pyrenees, 1987. Today, Hushovd, the former under-23 world time-trial champion, now 24, theoretically eliminated on day two, beat two fellow escapees, although the former Danish champion Jakob Piil had the misfortune to pull his foot out of the pedal in the final metres and, even worse, to land full crutch on the crossbar as Hushovd snatched the win by a tyre.

Zabel's Telekoms, this year devoted to his cause in the absence of Ullrich, cannot have been cheered when news broke that the former Tour winner had been suspended without pay but not – yet – sacked from the team.

On the first occasion that Macon hosted a time-trial, in 1991, Indurain beat Gianni Bugno by 27 seconds over 57km. Armstrong, launching into the leg-sapping roller-coaster 50km with the zeal of a man determined to show why he was wearing the yellow jersey, delivered the coup de grâce. Rumsas, runner-up, conceded 52 seconds and Beloki, 9th, lost a further 2 minutes 11 seconds. Millar rode superbly to take 4th place at 1 minute 14 seconds.

The Australians had had a great Tour. Baden Cooke and O'Grady – disappointed of the green jersey but still full of fight – were rarely far from the action in the sprints, McGee had taken a stage win and so too McEwen, who now had the chance of the big prize. There were two intermediate sprints on offer in the final stage: McEwen, bursting with confidence, took the first at a gallop, charging past the group of pink-jerseyed Telekoms trying to squeeze him out, and put himself a further three points ahead of Zabel. The second Hot Spot disappeared under a small swarm of blue-jerseyed US Postals. Conspiracy theory proven. In fact McEwen says he overheard Armstrong in conversation with Zabel: that in Zabel's place he wouldn't contest the sprint because if he lost it he'd be handing a big advantage to McEwen. A very negative attitude.

And so onto the final circuits of the Champs-Elysées, paradise fields indeed for the 153 weary survivors of the original band of 189.

The usual flurry of attacks went off and were trawled back, Rumsas, in the thick of the forlorn attempts to deny the sprinters their last flourish on the uphill of the famous paved avenue to glory and blessed relief of no more bike for a few hours.

The field came together and McEwen and Zabel's Telekoms started the run-in.

On the final corner, Zabel missed his line, took it too fast, checked and lost precious ground. By the kind of sharklike killer instinct that marks out the best fast men, McEwen virtually sniffed the mistake and went pell mell for the line, thrusting off the challenge of his fellow countryman Cooke to cross the line, second-stage win, this the more illustrious, and crowned with the marvellous prize of winner: points competition, green jersey on the podium, where Armstrong shook him by the hand and said: 'Nice work'.

This victory McEwen dedicated to his baby boy. The first win on the Champs he'd given to a close boyhood friend, a fellow racer, killed by a truck whilst out training after the Olympic Games in Barcelona. That is another very particular aspect of cyclists: the passion of their friendships.

It was the first time since 1996, their third contention of the Tour, when Rijs took the overall win and Zabel his first points prize, that Telekom had no man on the finishing podium, but Zabel was already saying that he could not quit the race with this bitter taste of defeat and that he would be back.

Jalabert, by contrast, made a sweet farewell to the race he has ridden with such ardour: King of the Mountains and the combativity prize, both by emphatic margins and the deserved applause of a benevolent crowd as he rode the final stage on a specialised polka-dot bike given to him by the manufacturers, the legend 'Thank you Jaja' on the down tube.

Armstrong, having nearly lost his life to cancer has dedicated the win to the Tour. Giancarlo Ferretti, manager of the Fassa Bortolo team whose Ivan Basso won the white jersey as best young rider, does not approve of this narrow focus. He raced with Anquetil at the end of his career and Merckx at the start of his, and says: 'In 10 or 15 years time, Armstrong will be remembered only as a rider who won the Tour de France. Merckx and Hinault won everything – one-day classics and other Tours and Indurain won the Giro and Tour double, twice. Armstrong's focus is bad for cycling in general – it distorts the calendar but he has no commercial need to ride in other races.' There's the rub: the *commercial* need. The world has changed and the big corporations control the race, not the ambitions of individuals riding it. Ferretti has a point, but to an extent, Armstrong is in hock to his employers and there can be no denying that, paid to do a job – win the Tour – he does it with professional, with ruthless efficiency and he is, simply, without peer. In the Tour de France. He will not stifle interest in the race. Anquetil didn't. Merckx didn't. Not even the metronomic Indurain could do that. The race is and will always be larger than the life of all those who ride it and so long as the dream is vivid, so the race will endure.

Miguel Martinez told a reporter in the French press: 'I come out of my first Tour with immense souvenirs. I crossed the Galibier in the lead group as my father did when he won that stage [Mariano, 17th stage 1980]. I lived something huge that day and I am already impatient for next year.' The baton handed on, the tradition maintained, the continuum of the Tour.

Next year, the centenary race will start with a Prologue time-trial round the Stade de France and depart next day from outside the Café de Reveil in Montgeron, from where the first riders set out on the début *Grande Boucle*.

NOTE: Driving away from Chamonix in the French Alps on the last day of the Tour, Rumsas' wife was stopped by French police. Her car was loaded with testosterone, corticoids, EPO, growth hormones and anabolic steroids, enough to supply the entire team for the length of the Tour. Whether the fact that she was still ferrying them about suggests none was used remains to be seen. She was immediately incarcerated in a Lyon gaol; Rumsas himself missed the plane back to Italy and, at the time of writing, the case is still *sub judice*. Doubts had been expressed about Rumsas and, though riders *do* occasionally come from nowhere, they rarely can do so nowadays without incurring suspicion. Jean-Marie Leblanc confessed himself mightily surprised at Rumsas' third place on the podium but, in the light of the sorry mess in which Italian cycle racing finds itself – riddled with dark secrets, it seems, if not entirely manned by dope fiends – the cause of the Italian Lamprei-Daikin team, who dumped Rumsas instanter, is nevertheless in some peril.

CHAPTER THIRTEEN

THE CENTENARY

In planning the route of the centenary race, the organisers took full account of the Tour's great history and the epic nature of its enduring appeal. Stage one of the 1963 race began in Paris (the last time) but there had never been a Prologue in Paris. The riders launched down a ramp in the loom of the famous landmark that greets their arrival back in the capital, the Eiffel Tower; official start of the first stage, next day, after a neutralised parade through the eastern arrondissements, the heart of revolutionary Paris, past the place de la Bastille, out to the Café Reveil (now a Tex-Mex bar/ restaurant) where the first race had begun. The six finish towns of the inaugural Tour – Lyon, Marseille, Toulouse, Bordeaux, Nantes and back to Paris – were on the itinerary, for sure, and a special competition for the rider with the accumulated lowest finishing position into each. To emphasise the heroic stature of the great race since its inception, the core of its appeal, the beauty, the folly, three days in the Alps, followed by a couple of flattish stages, an individual time-trial and, without pause, a gruelling three days in the Pyrenees; three mountain top finishes all-told, before a second rest day and one final ordeal of climbing.

With Armstrong bidding for a record-equalling five straight wins, his opponents were eager for their own bit of history and staking verbal claim, at least. Gilberto Simoni, recent winner of the Giro d'Italia, who missed much of last year under suspension for doping and hadn't ridden the Tour for six years, said he was ready to take on the American without being frightened of him: 'I don't think he has ever confronted an adversary like me in the mountains.' The Basque leader of the ONCE team, Joseba Beloki, three times on the podium in Paris, second in 2002, promised a more aggressive ride than in previous years when, to the dismay of many, he appeared content to lurk in Armstrong's shadow but could mount little more than token attacks which were ferociously quashed by the American. Another Basque climber, Iban Mayo, came second to Armstrong in the Dauphiné Libéré and gave him a hard time in the Alpine stages. He was eager to stir things up in the mountains, especially the Pyrenees, where the home support would be fanatical. Santiago Botero, now riding as leader of the Telekom team, winner of the mountains prize in 2002 and current world time-trial champion, had matured into a more balanced rider but, on his own admission, was prone to at least one off-day in the mountains: not a good basis for other than an intermittent challenge. His teammate, the Kazakh Alexandr Vinokourov, was enjoying a record season: winner (for the second year running) of the early season stage race Paris–Nice and the Amstel Gold classic, he had been hard hit by the death, in a crash, of his great boyhood friend Andrei Kivilev. Those victories he said he owed to Kivilev whose strength he felt riding in him.

Of the other heavyweights in the *peloton*, Jan Ullrich was the rider whom Armstrong admitted he feared most. However, after 14 months out of competition because of injury and a ban for (recreational) drug-taking, it seemed unlikely that his form would be sufficiently strong to realise any potent threat. Team Coast, for which he had signed after leaving Telekom, had folded for lack of funds only months before the Tour and Ullrich was rescued only by the return to sponsorship of a classic marque: Bianchi, the legendary Italian bike manufacturers whose sky blue colours were most famously worn by the great Fausto Coppi and Felice Gimondi. On the Friday before the race, Gimondi, winner of the 1965 Tour, appeared at the presentation of Team Bianchi to the press and made Ullrich a gift of one of his jerseys from the 1960s. A poignant historic moment entirely apt in the context of this centenary. Ullrich was, nonetheless, diffident about his chances of doing much more than, maybe, taking a stage victory. To pose Armstrong any real problems was, he suggested, beyond his slowly recuperating powers and morale.

Marco Pantani, depressed and distrait, languished in a

rehabilitation clinic, but perhaps the most colourful, if not, in terms of long-term ambition, the most notable, absentee from the line up was Mario Cippolini, the world road-race champion. How could the Tour de France not invite the fastest man on two wheels, resplendent in his rainbow jersey? Jean-Marie Leblanc was adamant: the Lion King roared a good race in the first week but where would he be when the gradients began to bite? He'd been excluded from the 2002 edition and, after the unveiling of the 2003 race route, Cipo said, rashly: 'If invited, I will race there for the first week as far as the Alps.' Leblanc took him at his word and, against considerable opposition and the decided opinion of many, including some of Cipo's sprinter rivals and a lobby of French journalists, said bluntly: 'We weren't convinced he deserved our total confidence. The Tour de France is a competition, not a show.' To Cipo's further chagrin, the wild card he felt due to his team was awarded to the relatively humble French outfit, Jean Delatour, a very obvious chauvinism, in the view of the volatile Italian who manages to crawl over the mountains in his own national tour but has never shown the same commitment – or regard for its tradition – in the older race.

A similar failure of respect – whether real or perceived – had, hitherto, alienated Armstrong from the French press and it seemed that his ignorance of, or disregard for, Tour custom would, once again, raise their hackles and his bile. The centenary yellow jersey reverted to a tradition which blanket logo advertising snuffed out in the mid-'80s: it would bear the initials HD, commemorating the father of the Tour, Desgrange. Armstrong, as reigning victor, ought to wear the jersey in the Prologue. At first, he demurred; he 'preferred to earn the right to wear it'. This apparently trivial insensitivity to time-honoured protocols actually amounted to a weighty failure to observe Tour tradition and Leblanc prevailed upon him to bow to it.

Suffering from a stomach bug – a bad reaction to antibiotics – may have contributed to a departure from his habitual custom: he did not reconnoitre the Prologue route, a 6.5km loop from the Eiffel Tower, across the river and back to the south end of the park at whose head the Tower stands.

David Millar had ridden a strong Dauphiné Libéré and gave signs of hardening into a fully committed professional. He had firm ambitions: to win the Prologue and 'have a crack at the overall if I'm well-placed after the Alps'. He admitted that turning pro so young and staying with the same team had rather cocooned him. He'd at last realised that serious preparation for the Tour cost rather more than he had hitherto been willing to pay; that riding up a mountain once wasn't enough. To be ready for what a climb was going to do to him on race day he needed to ride it once, twice, three times in succession to inure himself to the frailties that always emerge under extreme duresse. For years, he said, it was as if he'd been asleep: it was time to wake up and stretch himself to the limit.

Fully awake, then, and riding out of his skin, Millar sprinted out of the penultimate corner of the short Prologue a meaty five seconds ahead of the field, when, jarred by the cobbled surface, his chain jumped on the freewheel and then unshipped from the chain ring. He was forced to slow and lean down in the saddle to replace it. Four other members of the team had had the same problem – mechanics usually fit a double ring whose changer acts as a guard against losing the chain. Millar raced back to speed with venom but the advantage had gone and he lost the first yellow jersey to the Australian sprinter, Bradley McGee, by 0.08 of a second. No words can or should intrude on disappointment of that order.

Having thrown his bike at the mechanic's feet in an access of fury, Millar rounded on the Cofidis team boss. He demanded, and got, the demotion of Alain Bondue, with whom he has long had a testy relationship, from head honcho to domestic organiser and declared himself not only ready to lead the team from the front but, more pertinently, determined to match words with actions.

Stage one into Meaux ended in a catastrophic pile-up. In the final 400 metres the *peloton* en masse, sprinters like barracudas scenting blood, charged into a sharp right hand bend at about 75kph, José Enrique Gutteriez, perhaps shunted out of what may have been an uncertain line by another rider, lost balance, one foot sprang out of the pedal and he went down and took many others with him including Armstrong, who rode over the line on a replacement machine. Samuel Sánchez bunny-hopped over two stricken riders but Tyler Hamilton, a strong contender for the podium, rode into a sprawling Jimmy Casper and sustained two hairline fractures in his collarbone; Casper had to be helped away wearing a neck brace and Levi Leipheimer, the American who, as a rookie, came eighth in 2002, fractured his pelvis. Amazingly, only Leipheimer and a teammate Marc Lotz, did not make the start next day. The stage was taken by the Italian Alessandro Petacchi, winner of six stages in the Giro: he's quick, clever, nerveless and certainly aware of home expectations that he would fill in for Cipollini and fill in with style.

Robbie McEwen, overall winner of the green jersey in 2002, pulled it on again; the points competition was going to be a fierce tussle – a quartet of feisty Australians, among a record seven riding the Tour, McEwen, McGee, Stuart O'Grady and Baden Cooke, prominent among the contenders.

Hamilton's decision to ride on – 'I'm not doing this for the team, I'm doing it for me,' he said – is typical of the man who learnt how to suffer when, as a young downhill skier, he bore up through long freezing stretches on ski lifts. During the 2002 Giro, he somersaulted into a tree at 60kph and broke a bone in his left shoulder. However, he kept quiet about the injury, rode on for another 16 days, 3 of them over the Dolomites, and finished 2nd in Milan, having ground the enamel off 12 of his teeth because of the pain. His CSC team osteopath, a charismatic Dane, Ole Kaare, is something of a wizard: he works on not just the injury but the response, mental and physical, of the patient to the trauma. He was sanguine about Hamilton's capacity to survive, his shoulder firmly bandaged to reduce jarring, so long as he could make it through the first 20km of the next stage. The team mechanic bound his handlebars with three rolls of tape, further padded with strips of gel, and raised them to make braking and changing gear easier, as well as lowering the pressure in his tyres. He finished stage two 'as white as linen' having got through five hours of excruciating pain partly by going through every song he could think of in his head. Casper also suffered horribly but brushed aside the misery: 'That's cycling for you . . . you block out the pain.'

(On the ninth stage of the 1920 race, Honoré Barthélémy crashed, broke a bone in his shoulder, one wrist and lost an eye, but battled on through six more stages to come 8th in Paris.)

An audacious 197km break by the young Frenchman, Frédéric Finot, was ridden down in a searing attack by David Millar but the *peloton* mowed them both down just before the finish in the old fortress town of Sedan where Cooke beat Jean-Patrick Nazon, Jaan Kirsipuu and Erik Zabel, celebrating his 33rd birthday. Now three Australians commanded the race: McGee in the yellow jersey, McEwen in green and Cooke in the white of best young rider. Next day, Nazon, from the Delatour outsiders, missed out again but having moved up the order thanks to the 12-second time bonus for second place in Sedan, garnered enough intermediate sprint points to become the first Frenchman to pull on the leader's jersey since François Simon in 2001. Born in Epinal he had the added prestige – perhaps inexplicable to anyone who does not appreciate how passionately the French feel about the Tour – of winning yellow as a boy of the region, a local hero. Petacchi, whom the French press had dubbed 'the gentleman sprinter', took the stage, and wrested the green jersey from Cooke, despite narrowly missing the Austrian Rene Haselbacher who lost control of his bike some 200 metres from the line. Haselbacher wobbled, leaned on McEwen who leaned on Cooke who stayed upright and leaned back and Haselbacher careered into the barriers. Petacchi swerved, stamped on the pedals and made a long run for the finish. Earlier he had been saying that his form wasn't good enough to get him through the Tour but this win, he thought, at the end of a stage ridden at a average speed of over 48kph, had boosted his confidence for the long haul. Four days and two more stage wins later he rode 52km of stage seven onto the second category col de Porte, first uphill of the Tour, and climbed off 'having run out of energy'. He had not only emulated Cipo's speed during the first week of the Tour but his predictable rapidity of departure at the end of it. (Another of his teammates also abandoned and, the following day, four more which reduced the team to three riders, one of them Ivan Basso, best young rider in 2002.)

The 69km team time-trial into Saint-Dizier, 'a flourishing industrial centre better by-passed,' says the *Blue Guide*, won by Armstrong's US Postal put his teammate Victor Hugo Peña into yellow – by one second – the first Colombian rider ever to wear it. Peña started his athletic career as a swimmer but, inspired by radio reports of the exploits of Luis Herrera, winner of the Alpe d'Huez stage in 1984, saved his earnings from giving swimming lessons to buy his first bike. Uncharacteristic of most of the cyclists who have come from the high Andes to dominate in the European mountains, particularly Herrera and Fabio Parra (3rd overall in 1988), whose brother Ivan was riding the Tour with the Kelme team, Peña is no climber, but the taking of yellow was a huge personal honour and an affirmation of the team's overall strength. Top riders in weaker (poorer) teams suffered – unfairly, it may be argued. Beloki and Ullrich lost over half a minute to Armstrong, Botero and Vinokourov 1 minute 31 seconds, and Mayo a demoralising 3 minutes 33 seconds. Given Armstrong's strength in the mountains, such a deficit effectively put Mayo out of serious contention. The team time-trial is spectacular and it exposes those teams – Millar's Cofidis, for instance – who are not well organised, but I am not convinced that it has a true place in this race. The winner owes much to his team; the victory is never his alone, but the proof of a team's strength in depth is, perhaps, better left to the vicissitudes of battle on the open road.

Peña's temporary status as race leader was not allowed to hamper his role as *domestique* for Armstrong: how often do we see the yellow jersey going back to the team car to load up with water for his boss up the road with the *peloton*?

From Lyon, the race headed for the Alps: a couple of introductory climbs before the first category col de la Ramaz, 1,000m of height gained in 15km before the rundown into Morzine. Two riders attacked from the start; two more, including one of Virenque's team men, Paolo Bettini, joined them and, at one point, had a lead of over seven minutes on the main bunch. At the foot of the col de Porte, Virenque set off in pursuit. 138km from the finish, he caught the escapees and rode up the slopes of the col de la Ramaz on his own. A similar lone attack had carried him to victory in Morzine in 2000. He was also aiming to match the six-times mountains prize-winners, Bahamontes and Van Impe. From the summit, 22km, a short third-category climb, a jubilant descent to his sixth Tour stage victory and, 11 years after he first wore the yellow jersey, in his début Tour (after a break of 235km), he pulled it on again. Laurent Jalabert, now riding motorbike pillion as a television commentator, praised Virenque's audacity. 'Too many cyclists weigh what they might lose before considering any possible gain. Virenque doesn't bother to ask that kind of question. He attacks to win, he is not afraid of blowing up. If that happens, so be it, at least he's tried.' The yellow jersey was certainly on loan but he had also won the polka dots.

They say that a rider can lose the race in the mountains but cannot win it there. On this day, when Armstrong and most of the main contenders rode in together, Simoni and Botero were fried, 6 minutes 15 seconds down; not so much an off day as a long weekend.

Leading Armstrong by 2 minutes 37 seconds, Virenque must have believed he could stay in yellow until Bastille Day but the long solo ride had taken its toll. Fortified with EPO he could sustain prolonged effort day after day. Now, in the savage long haul over the Galibier and on to l'Alpe d'Huez, his bruised frame wilted and he trailed in 9 minutes 29 seconds down.

Armstrong set up his 2001 win with a scorching attack on the first ramp of the Alpe. Nothing like that, this day. At the base of the climb, two escapees, Mikel Astarloza and the French champion, Didier Rous, held a lead of 2 minutes 10 seconds. Manuel Beltrán and José Luis Rubiera of US Postal upped the tempo so high that it blew the chase group to bits. Virenque was dropped, so, too, Ullrich. Armstrong looked as if he was doing no more than hang on; he admitted as much later – Beltrán, a newcomer to the team, had revved too quickly, from lack of experience. 'A fast tempo is good but this was supersonic . . . not good.' Ullrich fought his way back but when Beloki attacked, 10.5km from the summit, no one answered. He passed Rous and Astarloza but was himself reeled in after 3km. Mayo broke clear 500 metres on, followed by Hamilton and Beloki. This time Armstrong countered but, 4.5km from the summit, the astonishing Hamilton, scarce able to get out of the saddle because of his injury – every time he did he lost 50 per cent of his power and 'it hurt like hell' – launched another attack. Beloki, with the fortitude of a rider intent on burying his reputation as a wheel-sucker, also went again. They could not get clear, but Beloki's assaults on Armstrong, six in all, (Hamilton tried five times) were evidence of a welcome new vigour and spirit. Vinokourov did get clear and clawed back 39 seconds of his deficit on Armstrong – 27 seconds on the road plus 12 seconds bonus for second place behind Mayo who took the stage and a gain of 2 minutes 32 seconds. Millar faltered but, driven on by pride, limited his losses to 4m on Armstrong. For Simoni, who arrived in a state of near collapse, nearly 13 minutes down on Mayo, and Botero, a massive 42 minutes 19 seconds, it was a humiliating end to their pretensions. Botero, who'd ridden only the Tour de

Catalonia and Germany in preparation for the Tour, attributed his lame showing to 'lack of vice, the spirit of competition'. Other Colombians came to racing hungry – he had grown up with food in his belly. As for Simoni, his powers of recuperation had gone. Armstrong, now in yellow, was harsh: 'It's easy to talk before the battle and Simoni is a big mouth. He underestimated the Tour de France – it's not the Giro. He needs to come back to earth.'

Of his own form he was surprisingly candid: '. . . what's important are my sensations and they're not good. I'm not as strong as I have been in other years. I actually felt worse at the start of the stage and on the Alpe I was slightly better, but even so Beloki's attacks were really hard to answer.' This boded well for Beloki's promise to be on the attack in the Basque Pyrenees.

In blistering heat, on the final descent into Gap the next day, Vinokourov away on his own, Beloki led the perilous high-speed chase, Armstrong on his wheel. The tarmac had melted; wheel rims and brake blocks smouldered. Apparently Beloki felt his front wheel puncture; he applied the rear brake and the blocks seized on the carbon rim. (A risk with carbon.) The back wheel locked, flicked one way then the other, ripping the tubular tyre out of its seating and poor Beloki went down, a sickening fall onto his right side. Behind him, Armstrong steered left in a near panic, off the road, past a gendarme and into a stubble field. He kept going, cross-country, across the neck of the hairpin, dismounted, shouldered the bike over a ditch and back onto the road to rejoin the small chasing group.

In a terrible strife of pain, Beloki lay on the road, his right wrist and elbow broken, the top of his femur fractured. (A second fracture was reported some days later.) It was a sickening end to the brave race he was riding.

Vinokourov took this Bastille Day stage – the first Frenchman home was Rous in 12th spot – and a further 56 seconds on Armstrong to move into second place, 21 seconds behind the lead. He was clearly prepared to act on his promise: to isolate and disrupt Armstrong by persistent aggression.

Through temperatures of up to 52°C, the riders sweated down to Marseille where Jakob Piil took the stage in a two-up sprint with another member of a long breakaway, the first escape of the Tour to succeed in staying away. Nearing the line, Fabio Sacchi reached out to shake the Dane's hand and muttered something in Italian. 'May the best man win?' Piil took that as a good omen and, allowing the Italian to jump for the finish, coolly rounded him and took the win. It was some recompense for losing out in a similar sprint with Hushovd the year before when his shoe came adrift from the pedal metres from the line.

When the pack came in, Millar made a surprise appearance at the front to lead out his pals McGee and Cooke 'for fun'.

From there, on another broiling day of Languedoc sun, to Toulouse in readiness for the first individual time-trial, 47km from Gaillac to a new outdoor pursuits park built in a disused open-cast mine at Cap'Découverte.

It was stifling hot: 38°C in the air, 61°C on the road. We walked into Gaillac past the bike shop which the Bianchi team had rented for their warm-up – a sweet coup for a local enterprise and a smart move by the team to permit their riders to prepare in an air-conditioned interior to reduce sweat loss. Armstrong, by contrast, prepared outside the team bus, under a canopy of plane trees, for sure, but in the airless heat, earphones clamped over his head, eyes fixed on the ground, spinning the turbo trainer.

In these two vignettes the circumstances which swung the day: Ullrich came to the start cool, Armstrong hot and dehydrated.

Ullrich took the stage – 47km across the exposed rolling landscape of the Tarn flayed by the Dog Day sun – and beat Armstrong by 1 minute 36 seconds. It was a triumphant return to the top level, a resonant drubbing of the American, a time-trial specialist. Ullrich, now a mere 34 seconds off the lead, (what he'd lost in the team time-trial), was always brimful of talent but, as his former boss Walter Godefroot put it, he takes some shaking out of his torpor. 'You constantly think he's going to drown but he doesn't get moving till the water is up to his nose.'

After the rest day, David Millar had succumbed to a lung infection, could hardly breathe at night and was convulsed with coughing fits. This made his effort in the time-trial – 7th at 3 minutes 55 seconds on Ullrich – the more commendable.

Ullrich himself had only just recovered from gastritis, having to peel off the back of the *peloton* to relieve himself: taken short and given the speed at which they were riding, he had to make it short.

Stage 13. Toulouse–Ax Trois Domaines.

I rode up the grisly final 9km climb ahead of the race (though not the wicked 14km Port de Pailhères which immediately precedes it) under a torrid sun, frequently compelled to weave through the crowds lounging across the road. This reinforced the impression of just how taxing it must be for riders at the limit of endurance faced with a mêlée of fans jinking about ahead of them. It's unnerving. On the commentary box monitors I saw the bunch hit the lower slopes, the wicked gradient I had just toiled up, saw one of them take off his helmet and ditch it into the verge – a nice souvenir for one fan. Following the death of Kivilev, the UCI imposed a rule that riders must wear helmets at all times except on a mountain top finish so long as the climb is longer than 5km.

Ahead of the field, Hamilton's CSC teammate Carlos Sastre rode clear for victory from his fellow breakaways 7km from the finish. CSC, managed by former Tour winner Bjarne Rijs, assisted by Sean Yates, now led the overall team competition.

Back down the climb, Armstrong, in a small group of six riders, was suffering. Three and a half kilometres from the line, the Basque climber Haimar Zubeldia attacked, Ullrich and Vinokourov caught him but the American couldn't reply. Another kilometre and Vinokourov jumped away, Ullrich caught his wheel and the two of them accelerated, ticking off seconds, precious seconds, of their deficit on the yellow jersey.

Zubeldia recovered and overhauled them, Vinokourov faltered and could only watch as Armstrong, mustering a desperate effort, went by. I watched them cross the line, each one of them, head sunk with fatigue, drained. Ullrich was now only 15 seconds adrift.

Armstrong had so far shown no flash of the dominance of the previous four years. There were signs of hesitation, an involuntary flinching, almost, from the extremes of pain.

Jalabert commented that it was clear, now, that Armstrong was vulnerable and 'in the *peloton* any sign of weakness is public enemy number one'. However, I talked to Paul Sherwen, who knows the American well, and he said he'd never seen him so calm, so unperturbed, despite this unwonted frailty. Asked whether he was having trouble with his back after an 80kph crash in the Dauphiné Libéré, Armstrong said 'No' and smiled. A specialist osteopath had recently flown in to give him some treatment but there was no pain or incapacity. Sherwen reckoned that Armstrong would make his move on the climb to Luz-Ardiden on Monday. 'It's a climb he knows well, the last mountain-top finish and he's done it there before.'

I cycled back down the climb and was held up by a policeman to make way for a line of team cars speeding off to beat the traffic. Seconds after I meekly dismounted, a French cyclist rode up, brushed the admonishing hand of the gendarme aside brusquely and continued down the road, civil disobedience being something of a national tradition in France.

Stage 14. Saint-Girons–Loudenvielle.
Distance: 191.5km. Col de Latrape 1,110m, col de la Core 1,395m, col du Portet d'Aspet 1,069m, col de Menté 1,349m, col du Portillon 1,320m (and 10km of Spanish road to Luchon), col de Peyresourde 1,563m, followed by a nice gentle 3km cruise down into the valley.

We rode up to the Portet d'Aspet and stopped in Orgibet, a small roadside village, what must have been most of the population gathered in knots to watch the race go through. A gaggle of little girls perched on a window ledge. National policeman assigned to patrol this tiny sector of the millions-strong audience across the country reproving the kids who darted across the road, heedless of any danger. But . . . beware. The publicity caravan is on its raucous way, tearing past, filling the road, a klaxon-blowing cavalcade of motorised water bottles, coffee pots, advertising billboards, Camembert cheeses, carnival floats, hurling out sweets, yellow musettes, card games, picture magazines, baseball caps, key rings (*lots* of key rings) and so on, disco music blaring, young girls the French call '*les miss*' waving from the open-top cars, the bare-flesh glossy smiling fanfara of commerce and come-on.

An hour or so later, the race approaches. A break: 4km from the start in Saint-Girons, 17 riders, including Virenque and, keen to reahabilitate himself, Simoni, went clear and they swish past, too concentrated to be bothered with the food bags they've collected at the feed station just down the road. However, when the main field comes through, about 15 minutes later, riders are sitting up going through the musettes, flinging out stuff they don't want – energy bars, mostly – another random largesse for the straggle of spectators. And suddenly, there's Armstrong rummaging through his lunch. He tosses out a round object wrapped in silver foil more or less at the feet of one of my companions, Karen from Rhode Island. When the race has gone through and calm returned, we repair to the bar up the road for lunch. What's she going to do with what turns out to be 'Lance's muffin'? This is kinda like the Eucharist, ain't it? She reflects, decides, takes a nibble. We lean forward. So, what's it taste like?

'It's terrible,' she says.

At the foot of the Peyresourde, the breakaway group, thinned out on the Menté, held a lead of nearly 8 minutes on the yellow jersey group which contained all the favourites. Mayo and Christophe Moreau laid down the gauntlet, Vinokourov picked it up, Armstrong stuck to Ullrich and let them go.

All the way to the summit, Mayo sat on Vinokourov's wheel, doing nothing to support the attack. On the far side, down in the valley, the survivors of the escape group were battling for position and Simoni, another rider who did little but follow this day, jumped to the line just ahead of Virenque and Laurent Dufaux. Simoni had struggled the day before and been told to abandon by his director but refused. 'Fighters always overcome,' he said.

Vinokourov gained 43 seconds on Armstrong who came in with Ullrich and was now a mere 18 seconds behind him. Next morning, Simoni went to the US Postal team bus to call on a rather startled Armstrong. Given the acrimony of earlier exchanges, it was a conciliatory gesture on Simoni's part. Knowing that Simoni has a child, Armstrong made him a gift of one of his yellow jersey Crédit Lyonnais toy lions.

On the lower slopes of the Tourmalet, I passed a trio of Gallic cross-dressers – dimity frocks, splash lipstick and five o'clock shadows – sporting a banner: 'What we most admire about the bike is the pedal', *pédale* being the French for 'pansyland'. The approaches to the summit were densely packed, caravans and motor homes which had been up there for several days – picnics and parties – and the swathes of orange, the Basque colour, spread like beds of French marigolds. They say that the Basque language is so unfathomable that when the Devil tried to learn it he could master only seven words though what they were he wouldn't disclose – possibly the

Deadly Sins, in which he has a vested interest. Halfway up the climb I'd passed a bunch of grinning men sporting orange favours who'd taken prisoner the Dutch nutter who follows the bike race dressed as Beelzebub, possibly to pummel some specialist vocabulary, if not rude sense, into him. Three kilometres from the col, another party, some 30 strong, sat on one side of the road, three abreast, laughing and shouting as they rowed themselves up some imaginary stream of their own exuberance. Suddenly, I feel the bike pitched sideways and turn round to swear at the idiot who has lumbered into me, but it's a jovial bearded man in a tangerine cloak smiling at me, all teeth, as he gives me a hefty push up ten or so metres of gradient. Thanks, mate, whatever the Basque for that is. I wave, anyway, and reach the summit just as the police move across the line to close the road ahead of the publicity juggernaut.

From the hot sun at the col, back down to the cool overcast drizzly grey of a light Pyrenean mountain mist in La Mongie. Standing outside a café, the road no wider than 10 metres, we see the young Frenchman Sylvain Chavanel race past, giving his lowly Brioches-La Boulangère team spectacular air time. He broke from an early escape and has dropped Botero. Chavanel has 4km of this 2114m climb to do, a long drop to the base of the last climb of the day, 17km up to Luz Ardiden at 1,715m. It's a tall order but he looks strong. When Botero comes through, a different story: ashen, grim-visaged, he looks near cooked.

A lull, expectation hangs heavy, and suddenly in a rush of speed that makes your stomach clench, the main field is on us and past, up that unforgiving tarmac which cost our heart so dear, but each one of them looks drawn, the muscles of the face pinched as if – and it is surely true – every fibre of their frame is stretched taut with effort. The small men and the titans alike race at these climbs like demons of the chase. We learn that 4km lower down the climb, Ullrich attacked and Armstrong didn't respond. He said later: 'It was a trenchant attack but I said straight away it wasn't the time to move. The Tourmalet is a long climb and there's a long descent towards Luz-Ardiden . . . I decided to keep my rhythm and come back steadily. But Ullrich was super strong and I said to myself, "If he continues at that rhythm he's going to win the Tour".' He did reel him in. Ullrich's failed attack was censured by many – he went too soon. But, his ardour for the fight was showing and he felt good, he was doing his job.

Further up, responding to team orders, Botero waits for Vinokourov who had been dropped in the Ullrich tentative and is already five minutes off the pace. Botero began the Tour as team leader; now he is just another *domestique*. Had he managed to stay with Chavanel he might have been allowed to go for stage victory; as it is, his job reverts to that of support for the main man.

And, in the quiet after they have gone by, we observe the very wretched misery of the men who haven't been able to stay with them, who have been dropped, even by the *grupetto*, the group which sticks together in mutual self-help to beat elimination on time, isolated broken riders facing a lonely trek to almost certain disqualification but refusing to give in. Jean-Patrick Nazon, wearer of the yellow jersey for five days, had dropped out of the *grupetto*. He was afraid, he pushed on the pedals, but without force – it's like trying to walk in wet concrete – then saw the tail-enders and breathed once more: he was safe. No such luck for Axel Merckx, another victim of stomach upset, shelled out early on. He toils past us, gaunt with dismay, his body slumping, eyes hollow, eyes that will flood with tears when he trails in way past the time limit. Merckx was one of only eight Belgians riding the Tour and no Belgian rider has won a Tour stage for two years. It marks a sorry decline for a nation with such a vibrant history in the race.

At the foot of Luz-Ardiden, Chavanel had 5 minutes lead on the 18 riders of the yellow jersey group, to which Vinokourov had gutsily fought his way back. Chavanel, it appears, had cracked mentally on the morale-sapping stage to Ax Trois Domaines and nearly quit. This was his way of repaying himself for that close call.

In each of his four victories in the Tour, Armstrong had delivered one withering hammer blow on a mountain top finish to pulverise his rivals: in 1999, 6km from Sestriere, 2000, 3km from Lourdes Hautacam, 2001, 13km from l'Alpe d'Huez, 2002, 3.5km from La Mongie. It was, surely, now or never.

Ten and a half kilometres from the top Mayo attacked. Armstrong answered with Ullrich close behind. But, Armstrong, rounding a corner too close to the spectators (his own fault, he said) clipped one of them, his right brake hood caught in a musette and he fell heavily on his left side, taking Mayo with him. Ullrich swerved to avoid them. They remounted and Rubiera relayed his leader back. Suddenly, Armstrong's right shoe slipped out of the pedal (his gears, jarred in the fall, had jumped), he wobbled and fell onto the cross bar but somehow stayed upright and regained poise. An attack might have won him the tour but Ullrich very decently slowed and Hamilton curbed the rest. The lead group reined in and waited for Armstrong to rejoin.

At the 9km board, Mayo attacked again and Armstrong pounced. It was, he said, a desperate move and the very fact that he said that suggests that he was not ready to go or thinking of it, beforehand. Evidence of an unwonted shakiness of will? He said he'd had a number of problems during the Tour, even discounting the incident before the race when a pigeon had shit on Bruyneel's suit and the Czech rider Pavel Padrnos had muttered 'bad omen'. Pretty bad jitters, to be bothered about a bit of stray birdlime. After the fall he had sensed a great rush of adrenalin and said to himself: 'Lance, you want to win the Tour? OK, you attack.' Would he have gone further up? Would he have waited on Ullrich's move?

But he went; not perhaps with the fluency of previous years but with a concentrated ferocity which swallowed Mayo and spat him out, left Ullrich with the pursuers and, 4.5km from the finish, brought him alongside Chavanel, who had been out at the front for 123km. Passing the luckless winner of this year's Tour du Haut Var, he slowed to pat him on his back, a consolation much appreciated, not only because it demonstrated an overt expansiveness of spirit for which he has not been conspicuous but a due homage to the ethos of the Tour. In showing respect, this year Armstrong won it.

He crossed the line having gained, with the 20-second bonus time, 52 seconds on Ullrich. Mayo, in an obstinate show of pusillanimous self-interest, nipped past the German – who had done all the work of chasing – to snaffle the 12 seconds bonus.

Vinokourov, the big loser of the day, came in two minutes seven seconds down.

Millar was in a pitiable state. Racked with chest pains and coughing fits he had been dropped and fought his way back, without help, only to vomit violently from the strain. The prospect of a rest day comforted him but 'in view of my condition, I'm not optimistic'. His team doctor said: 'He's at the limit of what a cyclist can stand . . . in any other race I would have sent him home. The Tour is a race of excess.' Indeed, Millar had rounded on the doctor and, in his distress, shouted: 'When are you going to tell me to stop? I can't get better on this fucking bike.'

There remained one more day of climbing, in the Basque Pyrenees, but the stage finished with a long run downhill into Bayonne. Millar, who lives in adjacent Biarritz, naturally wanted to cut something of a dash on his home turf, even against the odds of his poor shape. He attacked 15km from the start in Pau, chasing a small group that had flown off at the gun. Anything, he said, not to have to crawl into his home town with the tailenders. In this last week of the Tour when the climbing is all but done, many riders are content to bowl along, stay out of trouble, getting to Paris intact their only objective. Some while ago, Millar himself was lambasting the 'idiots' who hit the front at crazy speeds when everyone was exhausted. But, this day, ill or not, he was showing a similar fiery enthusiasm for madcap and ultimately fruitless attacks.

As the escape fragmented on the first of the climbs, the first category col de Soudet 1,540m, it was the amazing Hamilton who, leading the descent to the base of the col Bagargui, a horribly steep ascent to 1,327m, attacked and passed over the col with an advance of two minutes ten seconds on the pursuit. He faced 95km of solo riding. Rijs, his manager, spoke of the exceptionally strong team spirit of CSC. 'Our strength is in our motivation. Tyler Hamilton is the proof of that.' As a result, they held an unassailable lead in the team competition which could earn them automatic selection for next year's Tour.

It was a quite remarkable ride. Hamilton held off the *peloton* with a display of sheer determination, digging for every scrap of force and energy in his body, his mind set on getting to the haven of the white line drawn across the road, alone, first. And, as he drove the excruciating weight of his bike and body, the seeming tons of it by now, towards the line he sat up, turned round and beckoned to Rijs, driving the car which had shadowed him all the way. The team cars have to turn off before the finishing strait but Hamilton wanted to thank the man, his friend, who had given him such support, not just this day, but throughout, to thank him publicly. Rijs drove up and the men shook hands.

Another story lay behind the victory. Hamilton, through lack of vigilance, had got caught at the back of the *peloton* near the start and his team had been obliged to work very hard to relay him back. It was for them, he said, that he wanted to win the stage.

Virenque was now assured of the mountains prize but the competition for the green jersey seemed likely, as last year, to be decided in Paris. Cooke led McEwen by 8 points and Zabel by 13.

Bordeaux, the cradle of French cycling, has hosted more Tour stage finishes than any other city, bar Paris – 78 in 90 editions – and, because of its position in the flat coastal plain of the Landes, it has traditionally offered a big arena for the sprinters. The great sprinter André Darrigade, born near Dax from which today's stage began, took 22 stage victories in the Tour, the last of them in Bordeaux – surprisingly the first time he had won there.

Just as the Tour evolves, so is tradition thwarted. A bunch of spoilers hit the road out of Dax. By 68km – and away to their right near Labastide d'Armagnac, a small country church dedicated to Nôtre-Dame des Cyclistes – they had built a lead of over 16 minutes. Twenty-five kilometres from the finish it was still over 10 minutes. With 18km to go, the surprise winner of the 2002 Paris–Roubaix, the Dutchman Servais Knaven, went off on his own. None of the others seemed inclined to mount a challenge and Knaven rode into the heart of Bordeaux in lone state more than eight minutes ahead of McEwen who outsprinted Cooke and Zabel at the head of the jostling pack.

There followed another flat stage, another long break and, at an intermediate sprint, Ullrich accelerated behind McEwen to take the four bonus seconds on offer ahead of Armstrong, who took two. Cooke missed out and his lapse meant that he surrendered his green jersey to McEwen. The tension between them was palpable – McEwen sitting on Cooke's wheel all day to unsettle him. The younger man was beginning to show signs of self-doubt and McEwen is a bullish individual who, having won the competition once, must have an edge in these final nervy days.

Individual time-trial, Pornic–Nantes, 49km.

It was all to play for: Ullrich a mere one minute five seconds lag of Armstrong, substantially less than he had taken on the earlier ride against the clock. In 1989, Lemond beat Fignon by 58 seconds over 24.5km to win the Tour on the last day. However, on the morning of the penultimate day of this Tour, a chilly rain swept across the Atlantic coast of the Vendée and Armstrong smiled.

He reconnoitred the course by car, knowing that the weather conditions were going to make it a highly technical ride – ultra-light bikes prey to any buffet of wind, slick tyres very prone to slip on the raised gloss paint of the white line and, the cause of his crash in the Dauphiné Libéré, metal manhole covers. Inexplicably, Ullrich did not recce the course – perhaps it's a superstition with him. More puzzling, he opted to ride a bike he had never ridden before on a five-spoked front wheel which all the experts pronounced extremely difficult to control in strong winds. He also took the considerable risk of fitting a huge gearing, 56 x 11, which would make cornering very dicey. If he could turn it with consistent rhythm, it would develop a rapacious velocity; if not . . .

In 2001, Millar lost the world time-trial championship to Ullrich, having established a faster time till near the end of Ullrich's ride. However, when the German caught the rider who started ahead of him, the man rallied and fought back. This resistance gave Ullrich the needed spur and Millar saw his winning lead eaten away. He has since re-jigged his time-trial position and technique on the Manchester velodrome.

When he woke up in Pornic his cough had gone; he felt well again, *pleasure* had come back. After a sketchy warm-up, he rode the course at an average of 54.36kph, despite a fall 6km from the end which cost him around 20 seconds. The bike was upright, the tyre simply hit a patch of oil and went from under him. Even as the mechanic fumbled to reset the chain, Millar stayed cool – it is, he says, one of his traits never to panic.

Second to last down the ramp: Ullrich. Three minutes later, Armstrong. At the 35km time check, Armstrong was only six seconds down. Then, calamity: Ullrich took a bend too sharp, fell and skittered into the barrier of hay bales. He remounted, but the Tour was gone, out of reach. Watching him on television, Millar said he knew from the chancy way he was riding that he'd fall. Bruyneel told Armstrong the news and the American at once relaxed. He could afford to ride safely and Millar took the stage (his third win level with Robert Millar and Boardman) by nine seconds over Hamilton who leap-frogged the two Basques Mayo and Zubeldia into fourth overall: what a reward for a truly heroic ride in this truly stirring Centenary race.

The last stage onto the Champs-Elysées set out from Ville d'Avray, (site of the Parc des Princes velodrome, built 1936) where earlier Tours, including the first, always finished. The US Postals turned out in an ugly battleship grey strip and were fined £3,100 for 'equipment that did not conform with the rules'. What you wear at the start you have to wear at the finish. Not quite as draconian as the early days of HD (see p. 85) but a timely reminder that his crotchety spirit lives on.

Jean-Patrick Nazon's Jean Delatour had announced that it would be withdrawing from sponsorship at the end of the season. There was no more cogent way of making fools of his bosses than to win on the Champs-Elysées and this he did, with great éclat, ahead of the two Australians battling for green. At the first intermediate sprint, Cooke beat McEwen and was level with him. At the next, McEwen regained the advantage: two points. Into the final sprint, very close, McEwen's elbows out, Cooke on his wheel, alongside, McEwen bristling, Cooke barges up, their shoulders touch, overt spoiling or routine rough-house? There was no disqualification, Cooke made it and took green by two points. (McEwen was asked by officials immediately after the finish to view a tape of the incident. He had made no objection, watched the replay for form and said nothing. Uncompromising on the course, he is honest and uncomplaining in defeat – what they call 'correct', in the best tradition of the *peloton*.) O'Grady, to his surprise, won the Centenary prize for best showing in the six original finish cities – compensation for the frustration of being caught after a long break a mere 500 metres from the line in Lyon.

L'Equipe's assessment of Tour winners as cyclists for all time, placed Armstrong seventh, behind Coppi who won only two, even though the American has now joined the élite club of quintuple winners. Well, other times, other ways of doing things. He has never been so popular in France as when he was having a hard time. (The French journalists, who award the least helpful rider their lemon prize, this year gave Armstrong an orange for his benign manner. He is not so kind to journalists whose remarks he dislikes – they are blacked from the list of members of the press to whom he is prepared to speak. He even has a journalist monitoring opinions in the Press Room.) As to his future, he faces what has so far proved to be the most intractable Tour gremlin of all: number six. This year he lacked the punch he had in the past; his power less explosive, his willingness to suffer impaired, yet, he did win. He surmounted trials and problems and, in that, took his hardest victory. It remains to be seen whether Fignon's poignant description of decline applies lastingly to Armstrong as it applies with summary force to all the other five-times men:

'You don't see it coming but there is a time when it just becomes more and more difficult to win . . . The cyclist's style grows more laboured. His attacks have less vigour about them. He controls the race a little less by waiting and thinking before reacting to something rather than responding instantly.'

Ullrich had limited ambitions for this Tour but the move to an Italian team and more flexible training methods has made him leaner, more resilient; Beloki suffered terrible luck just as he had begun to flourish; Hamilton's efforts under duresse diminished his threat. Next year? It is a juicy prospect.

★

POSTSCRIPT
News was released after the Tour that only one rider failed a drugs test: the Spaniard Javier Pascual Llorente of the Kelme-Costa Blanc team tested positive for EPO after the 12th stage.

CHAPTER FOURTEEN

2004

A Historic Sixth

Liège, hosting a Tour start for the first time, has an illustrious place in the history of continental bike racing. Victory in the Liège–Bastogne–Liège, oldest of the great one-day classic races, first contested in 1892, stands high on the palmarès of any rider. Hinault, no great fan of the roughhouse of the Belgian roads, won it twice and came second once. By choosing to launch the Tour in the heartland of Belgian cycling – Prologue and the first three stages, the organisers seemed to be making a veiled statement about the way things are going. The Tour evolves and always has; adaptability underlies its perennial appeal. But the latest evolution as a global event on which a cyclist will concentrate to the exclusion of almost the entire racing calendar deviates sharply from the spirit and long tradition of cycle sport. From being the Great Bike Race it has become, for many, the *only* bike race. Greg Lemond began the trend: as Cyrille Guimard, his early mentor, pointed out in *L'Equipe*, Lemond won only five major races as a professional but he chose them carefully. Two rainbow jerseys and three yellow. Success in what Americans have come to call 'old Europe' counts for little unless it comes with profile high enough to rank on the global scene. Tyler Hamilton, one of the men expected to give Armstrong trouble in the 2004 edition of the Tour, said tellingly in a pre-race interview: 'It's the biggest race in the world, the Superbowl of cycling.' The Superbowl? But then, he comes from the land which calls an internal nationwide baseball competition the World Series. In this new era of cycling, different imperatives apply. 'I have a feeling that we have left behind the cycling culture altogether and entered a culture of athleticism' says Guimard. 'Everything is measured, all training is quantified . . . and if you have the mental strength, it's better to train than to race.' This is exactly what Armstrong does, from the precise counting out of calories onto his plate against the calories lost on his bike to the eight-hour training stints in freezing cold. One time this winter, during a reconnaissance ride in the Pyrenees, Bruyneel asked him to get into the car – it was too cold to ride on. Armstrong refused. They struck a deal: if the temperature fell below 4°C he'd climb off. It oscillated all day between 5°C and 6°C. This solitary, monkish style doesn't suit many riders who need the impulse of racing – in the past, a minimum of 140 days per year – to push them routinely beyond their comfortable limits. Armstrong, his naturally obsessive temperament hardened by the purgatory of the cancer ward, has no such problem. He seems to be impervious to pain and a glutton for self-inflicting it, though he remains hypersensitive to critical slight. He harps enough about his indifference to popularity to suggest that being loved is the one thing he craves, that not being loved is the spiky root of his anger and anger a prime motivation, no matter against whom it is directed. This year, the journalist David Walsh obliged with the cattle prod of a book accusing the American of long-term doping, as if he needed extra stimulus, planted under his shorts, like a thistle – charges which Armstrong rebutted furiously.

Some time ahead of the race start, Brad McGee, winner of the 2003 Prologue, had said: 'If I lose, I hope it is to David Millar.' Millar, however, was out. A week before lining up, he'd admitted to using EPO on three occasions, the last prior to taking the world time-trial gold in 2003. That he had never tested positive is worrying, and further corroboration (said Walsh and many others) that abuse of drugs continues to be far more sophisticated than their detection.

In the event, the young Swiss rider Fabian Cancellara won the 6.1km flat Prologue by two seconds from Armstrong who was clearly bent on laying down the challenge for a record sixth win as early as possible. The unwonted frailty of his fifth win, when Ullrich came as close as 18 seconds to taking yellow, had spurred even closer attention to detail. Ullrich trailed him in the Prologue by 15 seconds – a massive deficit so early in the race, over such a short distance. Once more his declared belief that this would be his best chance to beat Armstrong looked shaky. His springtime preparation had lagged behind even last year's slow start and his aversion to reconnoitring the course, which in part cost him the final time-trial in 2003, was well publicised. Speaking of the third stage over the cobbles of the Hell of the North, he said: 'If Lance wants to prepare by training on them, that's his choice . . . but I won't be.' He added that he knew much of the course and the finishes from previous years – it was no longer necessary to go over the terrain and train on the route. Armstrong repeated that Ullrich was the rider he feared most. One began to wonder why. Probably the strongest man on a bike in the Tour, Ullrich nonetheless lacks tactical nous, cunning and basic dedication.

Sadly absent from the T-Mobile team, which Ullrich had rejoined after quitting Bianchi, was another lively contender, Alexandr Vinokourov, injured in the Tour of Switzerland, which Ullrich took by one second. Another potential challenger, Joseba Beloki, following his terrible crash in 2003, had joined a French team, Brioches-La Boulangère, but left when their doctors said he was not asthmatic, as he claimed, and refused to prescribe specific drugs. He was not riding.

McGee came in nine seconds down but complained of dreadful pain in his back. He'd been shifting olive trees in his garden a while before.

The course of the race had been designed to nullify what had become established as Armstrong's natural advantages: deficits sustained in the team time-trial would be capped at a maximum of three minutes and subject to a Byzantine bonus system, based on the times of the first five men across the line. Also, the mountain stages had been lumped together late in the course as an encouragement to attacking strategy. Mayo, the Basque climber, had lost a hefty 3 minutes 30 seconds in the 2003 team time-trial, which effectively neutralised him.

Lining up for the first-stage sprint into Charleroi were two Italian aces, lion king and successor: Cipollini, 37 years old, riding his first (and probably his last) Tour since 1999, and Petacchi, 29, leader of Cancellara's Fassa Bortolo team, winner of an amazing 9 stages in this year's Giro d'Italia. (Cipo holds the overall Giro record with 42.) The Fassa Bortolo team whipped up the speed for a bunch finish, both to launch Petacchi, who admits to being scared in every sprint he contests, and to preserve the yellow jersey. But, led out by Mark Scanlon, the first Irishman in the race since Roche and Kelly, and then following the wheel of the Norwegian champion, Thor Hushovd, the Estonian Jan Kirsipuu, 12 days off his 35th birthday, took victory on the line. Petacchi came 8th and Cipo, who had taken a fall, was skulking way down in the pack. For sure, the battle for the green points jersey was going to be hot – the Australians O'Grady (first Aussie to wear it), and two overall winners, McEwen (who ceded this day to Kirsipuu by less than half a wheel) and Cooke, were all in form, Hushovd was game, and the veteran Zabel, six-times winner, still quick and astute.

Day two went to McEwen, who is married to a Belgian and has spent most of his eight-year career riding for Belgian teams and therefore delivered what the partisan crowd in Namur saw as a local victory. To emphasise this loyalty, he promptly explained how he'd taken his fourth Tour-stage win in Flemish rather than the by now less familiar English – Strine – of his birth. (On one stage, a local bystander tried to grab one of McEwen's *bidons* as a souvenir as he went past. McEwen took the time to dismount and give him the full benefit of his fluency in the language.) There were only 8 Belgian riders in the race which they have won 18 times, so the brisk showing of an adopted son may be some consolation. The 12-second bonus Hushovd took for second place put him in yellow, the first Norwegian to lead the Tour. He had crashed 19km out but his Crédit Agricole team worked hard to bring him back. Cipo's lead-out man, Gian Matteo Fagnini, went down, too, and had to quit with a broken collarbone.

The French sprinter Jean-Patrick Nazon seized a fine win on stage three, surging over the line ahead of Zabel, McEwen and the stocky 23-year-old Flandrian Tom Boonen, who has been much talked of. McEwen's consistency not only kept him the green jersey, he also took the race lead, two years after wearing yellow for the first time. A temporary bonus. 'It's always hard fighting for the green in the first week' he said 'because there are lots of points on offer – to win or lose – and a crash can upset everything.'

Behind him, Mayo had once again found his race upset, probably irretrievably. As the road passed through the deep blue of chicory fields and the gold of corn, between redbrick mining villages, the big-hitters of the *peloton* geared up at 60+kph ahead of the first of two sections of *pavé* – on the cobbles, safety lies in being first – a rider next to Mayo clipped his handlebars and he went down. Hurt, shaken, he finished the day, which had begun in Waterloo, 3 minutes 53 seconds down on Armstrong. He had, he said, worked for a year preparing for the Tour and 'it has been finished by bad luck'. News of his fall had been passed up the line but Armstrong did not see fit to slacken the pace. In the light of what happened last year (see p. 294), he would pay later for this discourtesy.

The arcane rules of the team time-trial were much criticised. They penalised excellence. Lesser teams, knowing they could lose no more than a pre-capped time, would simply not bother and 'If that makes for good sport, I'd be surprised' commented Armstrong. His US Postals duly turned in an immaculate display of precision team riding. Their neophyte, Benjamin Noval, could not hold the fierce pace and fell away, but at the finish of the 64.5km course, the team had beaten the rest of the field handsomely and put the boss in yellow. It was his sixtieth day in the golden fleece and only Merckx and Hinault have worn it longer. Rounded down, the losses of Armstrong's so-called challengers meant that Hamilton now trailed by 36 seconds (though ceding 1 minute 17 seconds in real terms), Ullrich by 55 seconds (at 1 minute 19 seconds), Heras, the American's former lieutenant, by 1 minute 45 seconds and Mayo by 5 minutes 27 seconds (2 minutes 35 seconds adjusted to 1 minute 20 seconds). Hamilton, in particular, had a dreadful day on a course made perilous by driving rain and headwinds. His Phonak team punctured four times in the first 24km, two riders crashed and were abandoned, Hamilton cruised for nearly 200 metres before the rest of the team realised he was ahead and waiting for them. A muddle unthinkable with the highly-drilled Postals, even riding disc wheels which are notoriously difficult to handle on wet roads. Others crashed in the ghastly conditions: Ivan Basso, leader of CSC, Levi Leipheimer, the feisty American, and, within sight of the finish, Gilberto Simoni, twice winner of the Giro, skidded into the barriers.

French riders have not made much of a showing in the Tour for some time, but stage five between the two cathedral cities of Amiens and Chartres, and via two others, Beauvais and Mantes, gave the home fans something to cheer. The French rider Sandy Casar, who hails from Yvelines in the region, broke clear at 16km in company with Thomas Voeckler, the French champion, O'Grady, Magnus Backstedt and a man who has succeeded the indefatigable Jacky Durand as the maverick of the lone escape, Jakob Piil. (He abandoned before stage 15, having spent an accumulated 551km out in front.) The *peloton* were content to let them go and trailed in 12 minutes 33 seconds down on the day's winner, O'Grady (who rather tactlessly dedicated the win in part to his friend, the disgraced Millar) and the new wearer of yellow *and* the white of best young rider, Voeckler. Armstrong lay 9 minutes 35 seconds down. '*Y a de la joie*' in the words of the celebrated chanteur Charles Trenet. 'Joy, joy.' But not for McGee. Drained of strength and will, he climbed off.

Next day, Cipollini did not start: a fall had reopened a nasty gash in his shin inflicted by a chainring in the Giro – 40 stitches – and Petacchi also withdrew with torn shoulder ligaments. Cipo's manager said: 'I don't know if he will race again. All I know is that it was his last Tour. I wish I could have heard him say: "I've taken a stage, I'm off home."'

Stage six, 196km Bonneval to Angers, more rain, more crashes. Armstrong fell at 13km but he wasn't going fast so lost no time. The mayhem came in the last kilometre as the bunch sped at hectic pace into a barriered corridor a mere 4m wide. Just inside the red kite, there was a huge pile up. Rene Haselbacher clipped the barriers at 64kph and went down. (He later said his handlebars broke.) A small posse of 25 riders ahead of him raced in and Boonen took his fourteenth victory of the year, including the Belgian classic Ghent-Wevelgem. O'Grady in second place wrested green from McEwen. McEwen had been caught in the crash, his buttocks excoriated, his fingers badly grazed – an injury riders dread because it makes holding the bars, working brakes and gears, exceedingly painful. He walked over to Haselbacher and said: 'This was your fault, you've done it again.' (see p. 284) Since the Austrian was crumpled on the ground (with three broken ribs and injury to liver and kidneys), this appeared needlessly harsh and his Gerolsteiner team made an official complaint. But McEwen knows the routine dangers and rues the presence of those who increase them needlessly. Hamilton also went down and bruised his back severely.

The Benjamin of the race, Filippo Pozzato, 22 years old, gave his retired leader Petacchi a going-home present by winning stage seven; McEwen's Lotto-Domo teammate, Christophe Brandt, went home too, under suspicion of doping, and Gilberto Simoni nearly followed suit, his morale in his boots. The Italian who had boasted that he would give Armstrong a pasting in 2003 was already talking of hating this race and never wanting to ride it again.

McEwen regained green and Hushovd got his win on stage eight in an uphill final sprint. 'I had so much power it was really easy' he said. Armstrong, happy not to subject his team to the pressure of defending the *maillot jaune* or himself to the tiresome duty of attending the daily press conferences to talk about it, said it had been a perfect first week and that he would be attacking on the morrow. A rest day. Ha, bloody ha, the others must have thought.

Out training on the rest day, McEwen was in such pain from the tendinitis caused by the Angers crash, aggravated by the stiff muscles in his backside, that he had to stop six times. Moreover, the osteopath, having to work on raw flesh, could do little to help, yet, next day, McEwen led in a chasing group to swallow up two escapees in the last 30 metres. It was a cruel disappointment: they'd been away for 120km and McEwen felt sorry for them but said 'I timed my throw to the line perfectly.' As to his injuries: 'You don't feel the pain in the last 100m, you just throw everything you can at the finish.' The robust indifference of these riders to physical distress is truly remarkable. McEwen became the first sprinter to win two stages on the race but way down the field, Jan Kirsipuu had already called it a day.

The day after Martin Hvastija and Stefano Casagrande were ejected from the Tour for being implicated in anti-doping investigations in Italy, the US Postal rider Pavel Padrnos heard that he would have to appear before a tribunal investigating doping during the 2001 Giro, 'the San Remo blitz'. Jean-Marie Leblanc explained: 'We're taking the fight against doping to the absolute limit.' The organisers reserved the right to exclude riders or team members at any moment if they brought the reputation of the Tour into question. However, the UCI defended Padrnos – his Czech Federation had cleared him – and would not support his exclusion. Armstrong weighed in, too, a not inconsiderable advantage of sheer weight of support if not sophistication of plea: 'I know all about this affair and there is no affair.' He also lambasted Cipollini's teammate Filippo Simeoni calling him 'an absolute liar'. Simeoni had admitted taking EPO under instruction from the notorious Michele Ferrari, whose notoriety hinges on his oft-misquoted remark that EPO was 'no more dangerous than orange juice'. In fact, he said that, like orange juice, EPO was dangerous only in its abuse. He has, moreover, made a complex study of climbing techniques in the ensemble of a rider's acceleration, heart-rate and cadence, particularly the high-rate pedal-turning Armstrong has always favoured, vis à vis effort required and gradient. Armstrong had consulted Ferrari in 2001, maintaining that it was in search of just these advanced training techniques and Ferrari is certainly engaged as a consultant by the US Postal team. However, as a confessed doper, Simeoni's implication was more sinister and Greg Lemond had tried to dissuade Armstrong from resort to Ferrari, convinced that his relations with the rogue doctor were a disaster. In an interview with *Le Monde*, the French newspaper which has harried Armstrong for some time, now, Lemond said: 'Lance's problem is that you can't talk to him. For him, you're either a liar or you're trying to destroy cycling.' He pulled no punches: 'Lance is ready to do anything to keep his secret. I don't know how he can continue to convince everybody of his innocence.' Lemond's querulousness has already been directed at Merckx and conclusions about his judgement are not sanguine.

Stage nine had set off from Saint-Léonard de Noblat, birthplace and still the home of Raymond Poulidor. His Tour career began in 1962, he rode it fourteen times, took seven stage victories, was three times second, five times third. This homage to one of the greats of Tour history was cued in almost 40 years to the day after the famous duel with Anquetil on the Puy de Dôme. Interviewed by *L'Equipe*, he reflected on the label 'eternal second' which might have cast lesser spirits into a lifelong melancholy. 'The unluckier I was the more the public appreciated me and the more money I earned. Sometimes I think that winning is pointless.' Certainly Anquetil, his constant rival, was loathed by the French public for the cheerless, unfeeling nature of his domination. Victory was all and he begrudged bitterly their failure to appreciate his mastery.

Bastille Day, stage ten, started in Limoges, at 237km the longest stage, and, for the first time in Tour history, headed east into the Corrèze and beyond, over the extinct volcanoes of the Cantal. None of the climbs was particularly long or steep, but the unpitying up and down, up and down, over the first half led to a remorseless drag of some 50km to the col du Pas-de-Peyrol, followed swiftly by a sharp hoist to the Plomb du Cantal before the helter-skelter into Saint Flour.

Riders attacked almost from the start; at 29km, Richard Virenque and Axel Merckx went clear of an 18-man group and built a 10-minute lead over a *peloton* with neither need nor desire to chase. Apparently the two men agreed to work together and either sprint it out or, Virenque bagging the mountains-prize points, Merckx to be gifted the win. Virenque was aiming for a record seventh polka-dot jersey though a new regulation hampered his habitual scrumping tactics. Van Impe, six times winner, is scathing about Virenque. Not a true climber, he never crosses the big cols in the lead, just jumps out of the bunch and grabs the points. This is not wholly fair – Virenque has made some audacious long solo rides, including bold exploits to the top of Luz-Ardiden in 1994, Cauterets 1995, Ventoux 2002. A début Pyrenean break into Pau in 1992 scooped him all three jerseys – yellow, green and polka dots. However, Van Impe and Bahamontes, the other sextuple winner, pure climbers in the old style, each won the Tour overall and Virenque has never even come close to that. Besides, he took four of his titles – 1994–7 – whilst using EPO. Although he is rehabilitated and, once more, the darling of the more sentimental of the French fans, the *peloton* is more cynical. Among the many slang terms for doping – having a magic suitcase, pissing violet, messing up the soup – they have added 'dining with Virenque'.

As Merckx flagged on the Peyrol, Virenque surged ahead and over the top without waiting. He pressed on alone, battling with cramp, whilst Merckx cracked and was swept up. At the finish, Virenque held a lead of 5 minutes 19 seconds and Merckx, a man of immense generosity, said: 'I continue to respect Virenque as a rider but, as a person, he disappointed me enormously today. We had made a pact, he broke it. I don't appreciate that.' Inexplicably, Hamilton came in seven seconds down on the bunch, gobbets of time he could ill afford to be scrapping for in the mountains. Voeckler's Brioches-La Boulangère team had done most of the hard work of chasing and, in truth, this was barely necessary, save for the pride of protecting their leader. Neither Merckx nor Virenque was a threat to the overall lead; Voeckler might simply have sat behind the Postals and watched Armstrong. But, over eager or not, they were showing great spunk. Voeckler's name rhymes with *eau claire*, i.e. fresh water, 'no dope', and the next stage was won by another French rider who famously rejects any kind of drug, whether legal recovery products or the shadier substances. He also refuses to wear an earpiece, preferring to attack on instinct. For a long time David Moncoutié continued to live in Paris, where he'd worked as a postman, training on the hills in the city parks, to the bemusement of his Cofidis teammates (not least the fallen idol, David Millar), who think him something of an oddball. He hails from Biars, not far north of the finish town, Figeac, thus is not only a local to the area but also of the département. Wins by local riders are uncommon in the Tour, departmental wins extremely rare – last time Francis Campaner into Bordeaux, 30 years since. Moncoutié went away with two Spaniards, Juan Antonio Flecha (Fassa Bortolo) and Egoi Martinez (Euskaltel Euskadi) at 48km. Nine kilometres from the finish, Flecha jumped, was swiftly reeled in and, as swiftly, Moncoutié ran free down the roads he knows so well. The two Spaniards could not agree to chase and his attack succeeded sweetly, 2 minutes 15 seconds clear.

On Friday, 16 July, Voeckler, in yellow for longer than any Frenchman since Pascal Lino in 1992, faced a stern test; the first of two Pyrenean stages, ending on the climb to La Mongie, 4km below the summit of the col du Tourmalet which is too cramped to cope with a stage finish. Armstrong somewhat coyly declared: 'We have the best team in the race; the question is whether or not the leader is the best.'

I rode up to the ugly ski station in blistering heat, past a guy wearing a T-shirt with the legend 'Steep is good'. He was sprawled by a sumptuous picnic at the roadside. The *L'Equipe* cartoonist has depicted La Mongie – basque fans everywhere – as 'The Orange Planet', a strange lunatic world overpopulated with a cloned tribe of corpulent smoke-jawed men in tangerine bolero tops, bikini bottoms and frizzy wigs, some distinguished (if that's the word) by red tie-on clown's noses. The elders of the clan, possibly. The rain comes, the cold cold driving rain. The *peloton* once more doused by an unkind sky. The Basques sing and party on, alfresco. The rest of us huddle under the beer-tent canopies, watch coverage of the race through a blur of static interference and spray-shot lenses. At last the storm passes over, sun comes out, and we're at the side of the road with the countless others, waiting, waiting. Gendarmes try to stem the encroaching tide of fans, but the Basques seem to have the situation under control. This is their stretch of tarmac, don't you know, a bare 10 ft wide, and they mount guard across it jealously, joshing the police, grinning wide at the very idea of meekly doing what they're told. Suddenly, the familiar klaxons hee-haw hee-haw down the road, Jean-Marie Leblanc's red car speeds through and motorbikes and press vehicles follow, like tailor's scissors ripping cloth, and . . . and . . . it's Armstrong and Basso, at terrible velocity, faces drawn, bodies hunched and taut. In the vivid snapshot of their flying past us, inches away, I say to myself: 'Armstrong just won the Tour.'

Seconds tick away, too many seconds, before the chasers squeeze through in a burst of speed. The dense crowd opens and closes to allow them narrow passage, like a boa constrictor digesting mice. Pallid masks of pain and shock stand out in this bunch of men who've been dropped: Hamilton (ceding 3 minutes 27 seconds) Ullrich (2 minutes 30 seconds), Mayo (1 minute 3 seconds), the contenders who must even now be giving up contention. But here is the gutsy Voeckler, hanging onto yellow, he'd been weaving lower down, digging down into his entrails, as the French say . . . and, winging the last stretch by some kind of atavistic memory, the sprint specialists O'Grady and McEwen, who, even as he wheelied over the line, might have offered some ripe Aussie response to Monsieur 'Steep is good'.

The photographer Phil O'Connor, standing at the finish line, told me that he could see the haze of defeat clouding their eyes as the effort to propel the bike the last few metres across died in them, so, too, the knowledge that they had probably lost irretrievable time. Hamilton had cracked first, Ullrich and then Heras fell away as the Portuguese rider José Azevedo took over the Postals lead-out duty for Armstrong, piling on the pace to catch and pass Michael Rasmussen about 4km up the climb. When Armstrong, knowing that the opposition had collapsed, turned on the pressure, only Ivan Basso (white jersey in 2002, seventh overall 2003) stayed with him and, towards the line, surged past to take his first victory in three years. He dedicated the win to his mother who is fighting cancer. Outside racing, this has made a bond of friendship between him and Armstrong, whose commitment to the support and encouragement of cancer patients is as dedicated as that to his bike.

Voeckler saved his jersey after a heroic struggle. Five kilometres from the finish, Virenque lost contact with the leaders, watched them drawing away and, slipping off the back, the yellow jersey, plainly in distress. Virenque rode up alongside to encourage him: 'Every day in the yellow jersey is a day well earned . . . pace yourself, I know you have the legs, you can keep it another day . . . ' And so he did. If victory in the Tour has become more a matter of calculation than ever it was, the essential spirit of combat survives and Voeckler typifies the breed.

I watched him next day, too.

I rode the 13km up from Nick Flanagan's cycling lodge in Massat, to just below the Port de Lers. The view is stupendous: I look across a deep basin to the ramparts of rock towering over the col d'Agnès. Folds of mountain plummet down to the lake below the road along which the riders will first descend and then climb once more. I and a thousand other spectators, more, will see them coming, tiny figures far in the distance, plunging off their fifth col of the day, brief respite before they climb up the next one, past me, and onto the last descent and the day's grim finale: 16 withering kilometres to the Plateau de Beille. And from where I sit, a grand tableau of what makes this sporting event unique: 5km of serpentine road lined with people come to linger for hours so as to snatch a glimpse of a race that, from the very start, lit a fervour across the entire hexagon of France. The 'giants of the route' riding like mythic heroes into even the remotest regions, appearing on mountain tops and vanishing into the long perspective of the endless road. Epic stuff – always was, always will be.

People who've camped up here are well provided. I passed one family tucking contentedly into barbecued steak, green leaves, chilled rosé. Transient chancers like me liberate a banana from the back pocket and sip the last of the lukewarm water from the bidon. The *Vélo* car scorches through – a commentator tells us over the loudspeaker that the *maillot jaune* is in trouble on the vicious ascent of the Agnès. An Irish voice behind me tells a mate he's heard that Mayo climbed off on the fourth climb, got an earful from his manager and climbed back on.

A flurry of excitement ripples along the road: action in the distance – the publicity caravan approaches. The very different Tour de France surges by: motorised Aquarel bottles . . . a glum-looking bloke driving a giant Crédit Lyonnais winner's lion clamped to a pop-pop tricycle . . . a large cylindrical cheese with no visible means of locomotion . . . in quick succession a rubber duck, a garden gnome and a horribly sunburnt pink pig each mounted on what may be a stripped-down Robin Reliant. Girls with glassy smiles hurl out the free gifts and an elderly couple next to me pitch in to amass the full collection, everything from sticks of liquorice to Mickey Mouse magazines. At one point, Madame scrambles off down the precipice to retrieve what turns out to be a pair of mulberry-coloured flip-flops. Their battle for the bonbons is ferocious, though what they'll do with a pair of ill-fitting Champion polka-dot caps, who knows?

A lull. Five helicopters herald the arrival of the riders. At the foot of the climb, the little troop of boy scouts in cornflower blue shirts take up the cheering again – they cheered me as I went past, they cheered everything that moved – and two riders fly past us, Rasmussen, the bald ex-mountain biker, and Chavanel whose break will take the pressure off his team trying to defend Voeckler's lead. The rated climber Francisco Mancebo, former white-jersey winner, had attacked on the col d'Agnès but when he looked round, nobody wanted to come with him and he felt, he said, a bit dumb.

The Postals go through a couple of minutes later, a compact, ruthless hunting party, chasing down the escape. And here's Voeckler, riding with enormous pluck, only a small gap. Yo-yoing off and on the pace, he's fought his way back and continues to give fight. After him come the stragglers, heavy with fatigue. The drama at full pelt along the narrow road on whose verge we stand. It fills out what the television can never show, just as riding the mountains is the only way really to know what the effort of the Tour riders costs.

This was the killer stage: 205.5km, two minor cols as overture to the col de la Core (first category), col de Latrape (second), then, for the first time in the easterly direction, the steep col d'Agnès (first) and Port de Lers (third) towards the brutal 17km to the finish at the Plateau de Beille (far too high and nasty to categorise). The Basques were up there in force and as Armstrong and Basso, once more in command of affairs, came through, the orange men spat at the American – he'd done the dirty on their man Mayo. They crowded him, wagged stubby fingers right in his face, jeered and screamed abuse at him in their strange tongue. It was a vile display but Armstrong kept his cool; his focus didn't waver and, this day, he proved the stronger – rage the spur, perhaps – and rode past Basso to the line. Behind them trailed the elite field – Hamilton had climbed off early, his injured back robbing him of essential strength, it was, he said, like trying to drive while stuck in second gear. So, too, Haimar Zubeldia, a noted climber and Mayo's teammate. Leap-frogging Ullrich, the young champion of Germany Andreas Klöden was beginning to show the sort of form which suggested a change of leadership in the T-Mobile team. The day before, Giuseppe Guerini had done all he could to tow Ullrich (complaining of a chest cold, not helped by the cold and wet conditions) but his leader hardly spoke, so entoiled in his difficulties was he, so uncomprehending of what was happening to him. The *directeur sportif* of the team, Mario Kummer, made it plain that the loss of Vinokourov had been very damaging. 'Without Vino, we've lost our aggressive spirit.' But aggressive spirit was generally lacking among the big hitters. Young Voeckler, however, riding out of his skin up the punishing last gradients, beating down the terrible pain and fatigue with indomitable spirit, held on to his yellow jersey by 22 seconds. Hats off, indeed.

Of Ullrich, his former teammate, now *directeur sportif* of the CSC team, Bjarne Rijs (winner 1996), is impatient: 'Why isn't Jan in shape in the spring? Why, except for the last week of the Tour, is he constantly above his ideal weight? It's beyond me . . . He rides gears that are too big and suffocates on the accelerations and he's too heavy to keep the right tempo.'

The 14th stage from Carcassonne across the Languedoc plain offered some relief to the flatlanders, but a chance, too, for anyone with the energy to profit from the temporary armistice. For two hours and nearly 100km, escape after escape went away, despite a headwind, the *peloton* strung out behind, cursing the workload, down the long avenues of plane trees through vineyards and olive groves. Finally, a ten-man group got clear, among them Aitor Gonzalez, winner of the Vuelta a España in 2002, who had once boasted that he would 'crush Armstrong like a toad in the road'. That was when they were calling him Aitorminator. He'd done little to merit it since. 'I was hired to win big tours and I didn't so it's normal that they should be angry with me. I was angry with myself, too.' *They* was his boss Giancarlo Ferretti, who criticised the haughty Spaniard for lack of professionalism – he went to this year's Giro overweight and came 19th. Today he sought to make some amends and, 8km from the finish in Nîmes, went off on his own to take the stage. A victory in the Tour counts high, a blue bargaining chip in the matter of contract renewal. As ever, Brioches-La Boulangère led the chase to preserve the yellow jersey and the nine days of such punishing effort they had expended so far was almost bound to cost Voeckler the white jersey which he also held. Normally, he said, he would have been in the *grupetto* on the climbs but the yellow jersey obliged him to be at the front, to scrap it out. 'For me, the fear of being a disappointment is heavy.'

The caustic Ferretti had sacked Basso from his Fassa Bortolo team saying that he would not 'pay big money to a rider who doesn't win', but the move to CSC had proved beneficial. (He had turned down an offer from US Postal three years ago.) Rijs had spent time with him, coaching him, talking with him so that he might *believe in* himself . . . emphasising, once more, old Henri Desgrange's simple formula: 'To win the Tour takes head and legs.' Klöden, for example, reacts badly when demands are made of him, according to Walter Godefroot his team manager. 'He's a fragile boy but he's drawing mental strength and confidence from his perfect physical condition at the moment.' Godefroot doesn't have a particularly good record in motivation of riders, it must be said. Under his tutelage, Ullrich has largely squandered his talent. Although he and Rijs didn't get along well, I do believe Ullrich would have done better to join CSC when Rijs approached him early in 2003. His agent asked too much. Now the German press likened him to a big diesel engine in need of an oil change.

The rest day brought news of a full confession, in court, by David Millar. He had, he said, been trapped by his own mental state, by fear of failure, 'by glory and by money'. The confession, taken as tantamount to a positive doping test, cost him his place at Cofidis and (some time later) the world title he won in 2003.

On the morning of the first Alpine stage, Mayo came down to breakfast and announced that he had no strength left and was quitting. The stage covered three big climbs and Ullrich, who had done some extra training on the rest day – really, what does the man have between his ears? – went away on the second of them, the col de l'Echarasson, and quickly gained a minute. Armstrong was not bothered: he knew the course well – it had been part of the Dauphiné Libéré – and Ullrich had little chance of getting away with a substantial lead. The Postals and the CSC formed a temporary agreement to work together. Mancebo had been dropped and it was in the CSC interests to extend Basso's lead over him. Such a pact between teams of leading contenders was odd. Ullrich's mentor, Rudy Pévenage, called it 'unsporting'. Ullrich rode through an earlier escape which included Jens Voigt of CSC, who was immediately ordered back by Rijs to help tow the Armstrong/Basso group. This he and his teammate Sastre did with that unstinting devotion so difficult to explain to those unfamiliar with the internal workings of the professional *peloton*. Azevedo, riding for Armstrong, is a potential man for the podium, in the view of Bruyneel, the Postals' directeur, but he has elected to serve the lesser rôle of sacrificing his exertions to help his leader. It is a further mark of the Postals' tactics that team men are given specific tasks in advance of each stage. Commenting on the win at the Plateau de Beille, Armstrong said that everyone had done his job during the approaches to the climbs, up the climbs, regrouping for the descents, showing total obedience to the game plan to leave him to finish off the day. In hotels where other teams are staying, they even eat in a separate area screened off from prying eyes and the presence of bodyguards has become a feature of their entourage.

On the short climb up to the finish in Villard-de-Lans, a quartet of strong men, Armstrong, Ullrich, Basso and Klöden, shelled out the rest and shaped up for what the French call 'a royal sprint' of the best in the pack. Bruyneel was screaming into Armstrong's earpiece, quoting the title of the American's second autobiography: 'You have to win, *every second counts*.' This he did, sprinting fiercely for the line to snatch the 20-second bonus; only Basso could hold his wheel and Ullrich and Klöden came in 3 and 6 seconds adrift. Voeckler, who had spent 10 days in yellow – the longest holding by a Frenchman since Hinault in 1985, lost 9 minutes 30 seconds on the day and reverted to the white jersey.

Spectators had been arriving on l'Alpe d'Huez for the individual time-trial for over a week. By 4 p.m. the day before the race, there was a 10-mile queue of cars backed up from Bourg d'Oisans at the foot of the climb; many were still there late into the night.

The decision of the organisers not to barrier the entire length of the course, for whatever reason, was, I believe, a grave error. Thus, the riders had to ride the first 5km of the 13.8km ascent through the dense press of crowds, unprotected. Leblanc saw two moronic German fans spitting at Armstrong and the American later said that the ordeal on the Plateau de Beille had been scarier, but lasted only one kilometre. Jens Voigt was abused as a Judas for helping Basso against Ullrich. McEwen had been terrified and, having seen how close the unruly sots come to the riders, and the imbeciles who run ahead or alongside them, one sympathises. (I've ridden through the crowds in very different circumstances and it can be deeply unsettling.) José Luis Rubiera, riding for the Postals, said of the abuse heaped on the team that he had never witnessed anything like it.

Each of the 21 hairpins of the climb carries the name of a winner on the Alpe – the Dutchmen Kuiper and Winnen lend their names to two, as do the Italians Bugno and Pantani. Earlier in the year, Pantani died a lonely death in the hotel room in which he had shut himself away for a week. Hounded by police and press he had, it seemed, no will to continue. Life off the bike treated him cruelly. His record for the ascent of l'Alpe d'Huez still stands and the stage was dedicated to his memory.

During a fifteen-day Alpine training excursion, Armstrong had ridden the Alpe ten times – three times one day – in anonymous black, but the spectators spilling onto the road made it impossible to pick out the reference points he had so studiously conned and forced all the riders to take what was often the steeper line of the bends. All he recognised were the hairpin numbers, the changes in gradient he knew they signalled. Ullrich, unprepared, came second at 1 minute 1 second, Klöden third at 1 minute 41 seconds and, emphasising his class, Azevedo fourth, trailing his leader by 1 minute 45 seconds. Virenque, thinking of the next day's haul of mountains points, on his own indiscreet confession, made the stage a rest day. Armstrong's passionate dedication to victory was apparent every metre of the way. He rode with a concentrated fury for speed and not a single ounce of effort wasted. Around 3km from the top, he caught sight of Basso, who had set off 2 minutes ahead of him. It was the perfect motivation. Without a sideways glance, he moved past and on to the 19th Tour-stage win of his career.

Having been especially motivated by this time-trial, Heras nonetheless withdrew from the race the following morning. Whilst he rode for Armstrong, he seemed to some (not me) to be a potential Tour victor. He joined the Postal team on the understanding that Armstrong would ride for him in the Vuelta. This didn't happen and I believe that the years of riding as a lead-out effectively blunted his attacking spirit and nullified his threat. Expectation can quench the vital spirit.

The scenery of the next 204.5km is richly varied: exposed rock and scree of the col du Glandon (first category), gentian, orchids, clover and sorrel spangling the slopes of the Madeleine (beyond category), hay fields and apple orchards flanking the Forclaz (first) and pinewoods shading the final climb up the Croix Fry (first). Simoni, sick to death of the whole bangshoot of Tour and organisers out to make things hard for him, attacked on the first climb, but it was more out of petulance than with any serious intent. The day – 79.8km of climbing – was too long, too hard for such foolhardiness. Virenque set out on his mission to collar as many points as he could and, knowing that he had amassed all he needed on the summit of the Croix Fry, he punched the air and sat back. He has indeed left his mark on the Tour but not everyone would agree as to its exact quality.

Floyd Landis, another rider greatly esteemed by Bruyneel, did the last work up the Croix de Fry, towing Armstrong and with him, the hungry limpets, Ullrich, Basso, Klöden. Breasting the col, Armstrong asked his Myrmidon how badly he wanted to win a Tour stage (dumb question) and Myrmidon replied: 'Real bad.' Having ascertained that Landis could descend 'really quick', he said: 'Run like you stole something, then. Allez allez.' There were 13km of downhill to the finish. Landis was already tired from riding tempo unaided up the climb and Armstrong must have known that he would not be allowed to escape. Sure enough, Landis went off at breakneck speed, pursued by Ullrich and the others soon rejoined. Landis was, once more, the luckless hare pacing the much fresher greyhounds. At the bottom he was, quite evidently, spent and the hounds were ranging for the kill. Under the red kite, Klöden attacked, Landis had no answer. Armstrong, whose wheel might have given Landis the tow he needed for victory 13km earlier, or, better, in the final kilometre, took up the chase and, Basso and Ullrich left trailing, sprinted past the German champion on the line. It was Armstrong's fourth successive mountain-stage victory, a feat never before accomplished. A while past he had been saying it was not his job to bag stage wins; now he was fighting for them like a man uncertain of contract renewal.

The following day produced what the French riders are pleased to call 'an image of the Tour'. On the first kilometres out of Annemasse, heading for the Jura mountains, a number of riders broke clear only to be given short shrift, until, at 11km, 8 riders managed to establish a lead of around 40 seconds. Two of them, Nicolas Jalabert and Ronny Scholz, punctured and were dropped, but on the minor uphill of the côte de Collonges at 34km, when the gap was down to 25 seconds, Simeoni attacked and was followed by Armstrong. This was bizarre. Not only did the pair join the escape but Armstrong actually worked on the front several times. By 40km, the gap had lengthened to 1 minute 50 seconds and Ullrich's T-Mobiles were stirring up the chase. With the yellow jersey in train, the escape was doomed; Armstrong and Simeoni dropped out and were caught by the *peloton* at 46km. To give an idea of how frenetic the activity was that morning, the race covered 47.8km in the first hour.

The story emerged later: when Simeoni attacked, Armstrong followed to tell him there was no way he would be allowed to join an escape with any chance of a victory. Simeoni is not popular in the *peloton* because of his bad-mouthing of fellow riders along with his own admitted miscreance. However, this peremptory dressing down by 'the boss', described as 'absurdly comical' (Jean-Marie Leblanc), 'lowering' by the chief referee Mirco Monti and 'miserly' by others, was another show of the Texan's gaucherie. When he rejoined the bunch, he says, the others applauded his action, but it seemed entirely beneath the dignity of the leader of the Tour de France, indeed, of any champion. Bollocking small fry in public, on the bike, is simply *infra dig*. and, if Armstrong complains that the truth is different, he should accept that perception – of the public as well as of expert commentators – counts high, whatever the circumstances of the case.

His determination to stamp his authority found a better province in the final individual time-trial, a 55km round Besançon, which he rode at 49.4km. Ullrich lost a further 1 minute 1 second, Basso 2 minutes 50 seconds and ceded second place to Klöden. Armstrong had never taken more than four stage victories in one Tour. Now he had won six, including the team time-trial. The shape of his overall victory was different, too: none of the lone attacks which had become so much a trademark. He always finished in company and only Basso had been consistently able to hold his wheel. However, this victory seemed by far the least arduous. His team, drilled, trained, prepared for one sole objective, winning the Tour – a 365-day-a-year commitment as Bruyneel puts it – make a huge difference. They have ridden the mountain stages in advance, they know exactly what is expected of them and they know, too, that whatever exhausting effort their leader demands of them (and he never stops talking to them, cajoling, persuading, chivvying) he is prepared to match them. This training together, suffering together, has imbued in them what Hinault described in himself as a 'morale terrible', a fearsome will. Brioches-La Boulangère made them a surprise gift, too: by taking and defending the yellow jersey so fiercely, they took a week's worth of pressure off the Postals and Armstrong, sparing him the nightly media scrum meted out on the Tour leader. Their dominance in the mountain stages, their vigilance in the flat stages, all testified to a strategy eliminating risk. Above all their breadth of experience. Several of the Postals would be leaders in other teams – Azevedo, Landis, Hincapie (who alone has accompanied all six of Armstrong's

Tour wins). A perfectly disciplined team honed to computerised victory, maybe, and while Armstrong says he loves his job, it is rather the crushing of the opposition – another self-confessed passion – which drives him. Was he as strong this year or was it simply that the expected rivals simply fell away? Of the apparent challengers only Ullrich, fourth overall, his worst placing, actually made it to Paris and of the general challenge little was seen and then when it was too late.

The battle for the green jersey was still tight on the last stage into Paris. McEwen led the competition by 11 points over Hushovd, 17 over Zabel, 23 on O'Grady. Two intermediate sprints offered 6 points, 4 and 2 for 1st, 2nd and 3rd, the winner on the Champs-Elysées took 35 and so on down the order of finishers. It was still mathematically possible for McEwen to be beaten and, when the rest of the *peloton* rolled out across the start line that Sunday afternoon, only the sprinters looked drawn and stressed. Having slogged their way miserably over the mountains – McEwen organising the *grupetto* – they now faced yet another nervy day. McEwen, canny professional, sat on Hushovd's wheel all the way, piling on the physical and psychological pressure. A win on the Champs (which he achieved in 1999) was immaterial and, pipped on the line by the young Fleming, Boonen, he won the points competition handsomely. A fine second-stage win by Boonen, at 23 showing great maturity as well as daring and speed.

It later came out that McEwen had been riding for nearly two weeks with a broken back – in the crash in Angers the wings of two of the vertebrae in his spine had snapped. That he finished at all is remarkable and, without that painful disabling, he must surely have won the green jersey by a huge margin. Certainly he has never been in better form and his courage goes along with Voeckler's (who lost his white jersey to the Russian Vladimir Karpets) in making this Tour memorable. Their fighting spirit, their refusal to give in, relentless effort at whatever cost . . . these are the true hallmarks of the race and the triumph of the spirit it evokes.

A sign by the side of the road into Paris read: 'Tour de France – in American ownership since 1999.' So little they know and so little search to comprehend of the world beyond their provincial ambit. Armstrong loves France, he says, second only to America,

Two jokers in the 1920s toting a sort of Chinese lantern, or collecting box, *lanterne rouge*. (courtesy of the author)

Original controls, as here on the col de Peyresourde in 1926, set up in secret, checked riders through (to rule out the taking of short cuts) as well as bikes and equipment. Of medication (see pp. 165–6), in those days long before the advent of performance-enhancing drugs, nothing was said. (courtesy of the author)

Pyrenees, 1969. Merckx, wearing the yellow jersey, Felice Gimondi (winner in '65) close on his wheel, and behind Gimondi, Raymond Poulidor. The 1967 winner, Roger Pingeon, in the white and chequered jersey, is to the right. It was the Belgian's first Tour. He took the race, the points jersey and the mountains prize. (© Topfoto)

1985. Bernard Hinault, in commanding form, strings out the bunch on a flowing descent; Sean Kelly, in green, on his wheel. It was the Frenchman's last win and Kelly's second points jersey. Note Hinault's shoes – he was one of the first to adopt the clip-on pedals, and Kelly one of the last. (© Topfoto)

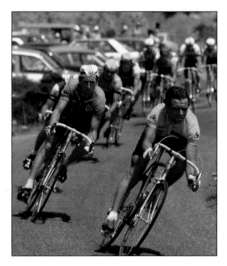

Eddy Merckx out on his own in the Casse Déserte, heading for the col d'Izoard, 1972. He won seven stages (including a team time-trial), the points jersey and the fourth straight win of his eventual five victories. (© *L'Equipe*)

Bernard Hinault drives the pace up l'Alpe d'Huez to the high summit of victory, in a public show of support for teammate Greg Lemond, the first American winner of the Tour. 1986. (© Phil O'Connor)

Stage 16, 1990. Pyrenees. Miguel Indurain, tenth that year, began his reign the following year, displacing Greg Lemond, the 1990 victor. (© Topfoto)

Men of the Tour, 2011: Contador leads Andy Schleck, Evans (obscured) and Voeckler on the climb to Luz-Ardiden, stage 12. Contador was later disqualified for doping and Schleck was awarded victory. (© Graham Watson)

Tour 2012. Michael Rogers, in front, leads his Team Sky leader Bradley Wiggins nearing the summit of the col du Tourmalet. Vincenzo Nibali clings onto the yellow jersey's wheel. (© Gerard Brown)

Left: Stage 15, 2013. Froome on the slopes of Mont Ventoux, in scorching heat, two kilometres from the top. **Right**: Tour 2014, Stage 13. Vincenzo Nibali, eventual winner, takes solo victory on Chamrousse. (© Graham Watson)

Left: 2014: Stage 1. Mark Cavendish. Broken collarbone. Out of the Tour. **Centre**: Stage 4. Chris Froome's perdition begins. **Right**: Stage 10. Alberto Contador, minutes away from having to abandon. (© Graham Watson)

Above: Tour 2015: Champs Elysées. André Greipel takes his fourth stage win of the Tour. (© Graham Watson)

Above: 2015: Stage 12. Plateau de Beille. With two kilometres to go, Chris Froome is back in control ahead of Nairo Quintana. (© Graham Watson)

Left: Stage 20. 2015. L'Alpe d'Huez. Chris Froome and Alejandro Valverde cross the line together, Valverde securing third place overall, Froome riding into history as the first Briton to win two Tours de France. (© Graham Watson)

but lives in Spain and imports Hollywood to the VIP tribunal in Paris. He has won and merited huge respect. Of sympathy, fellow feeling, he commands far less but maybe that is the price of being such a champion. If only he would seek to understand those whom he simply dismisses for their lack of understanding of him, nor speak of being humbled by victory in the greatest race in the world. Whatever else he does so imperiously and tenaciously on the bike, he most certainly does not do humbled. Let him be, simply, the great, peerless Tour de France rider he is and leave excuse-making to the rest.

CHAPTER FIFTEEN

2005

Seventh Heaven: Armstrong's Last Tour

In late spring 2005, Lance Armstrong announced that the coming Tour would be his last race as a professional cyclist. Of Jan Ullrich, the man he has always considered his main rival, he said, 'He doesn't keep me awake at night, but he does get me up early every morning.' It has always been Armstrong's tactic to flatter a rider who has only once come anywhere close to beating him – in 2003. Praise can unsettle confidence where contempt or dismissal will spark a fight. And, for all Ullrich's defiant response – 'I cannot conceive of victory except at the expense of one of the best cyclists in the history of our sport' – there was little to inspire belief that he would, at last, match performance to words. The tired excuse, that he needs a week to ride himself into the Tour and always comes good in the mountains, is piffle. No one wins the Tour de France on a strategy of catch-up. Significantly, when Ullrich nearly toppled Armstrong in 2003, he rode for Bianchi, a new (and now defunct) team whose shambolic organisation seems actually to have given him the spur his seemingly sluggish psyche needs to perform well. The year away from the Telekom, now T-Mobile, team for whom he had always ridden and to which he returned woke him up. But he threw away possible victory by amateurish aberrations in professional discipline – he didn't recce the final time-trial course *and*, in wet conditions, rode on wheels he had never tried out. Almost inevitably he crashed and handed Armstrong a secure ride instead of pushing him to the very limit in defence of what was a very slender lead.

Back in the T-Mobile comfort zone, Ullrich could rely (supposedly) on the support of two riders whose own individual threat to the six-times winner Armstrong was being much talked up: Andreas Klöden, second overall in 2004, and Vinokourov, third overall in 2003. Also in contention was Ivan Basso, third overall in 2004, riding for the CSC team. The brilliant young Italian, Damian Cunego, winner of the 2004 Giro d'Italia and former number one in UCI world rankings, had intended to ride but was recovering from a serious blood disorder. The young Spaniard, Alejandro Valverde ('*Il Imbatido*', The Unbeatable), his teammate Francisco Mancebo and the 2004 best young rider, Vladimir Karpets, each showed considerable class and were an outside bet for a challenge. However, all talk of unseating Armstrong carried with it an air of unreality, of wool-gathering.

Of T-Mobile's top men, Walter Godefroot, *directeur sportif* for the last time, trotted out the standard vagary: the road would decide. But, three potential winners-cum-devoted-lieutenants? 'Three stags in the same enclosure is two too many,' said that most knowing of Tour gurus, Cyrille Guimard. Godefroot has never got on with or got the best from Ullrich, who defers to his own private *directeur*, Rudy Pévenage. As if to underline the muddled tactical thinking in the German team, Erik Zabel, a rider of singular professional integrity and consistency – a record of six green points jerseys – was not selected to ride the Tour. (He has since left the team, as eloquent a statement of its curious approach to management as any.) This was, surely, bad for team morale if nothing else. And morale was what Armstrong undermined on the very first day in the Vendée.

The race began with a 19km individual time-trial – a gift to Armstrong, who is always at racing peak on day one. This would also deny the sprinters their usual chance of a yellow jersey in the first week. (A new ruling, aimed at reducing the incidence of crashes in the overcrowded sprint finishes, allotted to anyone falling in the final 3km, rather than the last kilometre, the same time as the group in which he was riding.)

On the eve of the Grand Départ, Ullrich, out on a training ride 'to accumulate some kilometres' as he put it, (a bit late, surely?) rode into the back of his team car at 60kph and the back window exploded. He sustained cuts in his neck but reported fit. Armstrong, meanwhile, was required to give a blood sample for a random dope control ordered by the French Ministry of Youth and Sport – his third in three days. He saw this as needless provocation, but, to a man of his temperament, it was an absolute bonus. He rides well on anger. Three kilometres from the finish, he overtook Ullrich, who'd set out a minute ahead of him. This was a real psychological haymaker. Ullrich began the second day of the Tour with a weighty deficit of 1m 6s. Vinokourov ceded 51s, Basso 1m 24s, Klöden 1m 59s. The road had already delivered several hefty, perhaps crucial, decisions. Surprise winner – by two seconds – of the first yellow jersey coveted by Armstrong, was his fellow-American, the Tour neophyte, David Zabriskie, a time-trial specialist formerly with US Postal and now riding for CSC at a new record average speed of 54.676kph. (This first day was classified as stage one; a Prologue is limited to a maximum of 8km.)

Ullrich had pushed an enormous gear – 55 x 11 – and never looked at ease. He says he has tried a fast cadence on smaller developments and that it doesn't work for him, so he persists with a weight of gears more suited to track racing. Even Pévenage questioned the wisdom of sacrificing fluency of pedal stroke to the massive physical strain of big ring power, especially when choice of gearing was left to the riders.

On stage two, Thomas Voeckler, the young Frenchman who held onto the yellow jersey for ten consecutive days in 2004, snapped an opportunist attack over a fourth-category climb on roads he knows well (he lives nearby) to take the first polka-dot jersey of the Tour and an appearance on the podium that night. It was a clever move as the escape he was in neared the finish, a small burst of publicity for his team. The pack scorched up and engulfed the fugitives. Robbie McEwen attacked for the line from too far out and the 24-year-old Belgian Tom Boonen – winner of two legendary classics earlier in the year, Paris–Roubaix and Tour des Flandres – added another Tour stage victory to the two he'd taken in 2004. He put on the green jersey. His principle opponents for the points prize were, undoubtedly, the Australians McEwen, Stuart O'Grady and Baden Cooke and the Norwegian Thor Hushovd. The flamboyant 'Lion King' of sprinters, Mario Cipollini, had retired and the other Italian speed merchant, Alessandro Petacchi, was not riding.

Boonen also took stage three. Close behind him, a contretemps between McEwen and O'Grady resulted in McEwen's relegation to last place, thus almost certainly ending his campaign to win the points competition for a third time. McEwen claimed that O'Grady came past him, stuck out his elbow and locked his arm: 'The only way I could prevent myself from falling was to lean into him.' O'Grady counter-claimed that McEwen head-butted him. Eddy Merckx and Sean Kelly, both adepts in the push and shove of massed sprinting, repudiated the judges' decision as nonsensical, but McEwen's appeal was rejected.

The 67.5km team time-trial, Tours-Blois, might well have gone to CSC had not their rhythm been upset, close to the finish, when Zabriskie crashed (and nearly took out Basso) at 64kph on the last corner, within sight of the red kite marking the final kilometre. Had he crashed beyond the kite, his time would have been reckoned as that of the team. As it was, he trailed in 1m 28s down, the yellow jersey lost, his chest, left arm and leg badly grazed and bruised. It seems that he clipped a wheel. (Being relatively unschooled in the rough pell-mell of the *peloton* and the close order of in-file time-trialling, his bike-handling appears to be less assured than it might be.) Armstrong took the yellow jersey, and his Discovery Channel team took the stage, by two seconds, the third year in a row that his team had won in this discipline.

Following a Tour tradition, Armstrong refused to wear the yellow jersey at the start of stage five out of respect for the luckless Zabriskie – just as Merckx had done after the crash which put Luis Ocaña out of the 1971 Tour, Joop Zoetemelk in 1980 after Bernard Hinault abandoned, and Greg Lemond after Rolf Sörensen packed in 1991. However, he was ordered to put it on at the end of the neutral sector of the stage in obedience to UCI rules; either that or he would not ride at all. The Texan has been slow to embrace the peculiar ethos of the Tour; perhaps he may be forgiven for believing some of its more arcane mysteries impenetrable.

Into Montargis, capital of that quintessential French delicacy, the praline, McEwen took sweet revenge for his disqualification with a superbly taken win, a maverick swoop through a slender gap, quick as a squirrel, and across the line ahead of Boonen, (in green) Hushovd and O'Grady.

Stage six into Nancy covered 199km of leg-sapping undulations, what riders call 'French flat'. It rained, too, and as an escape of five riders hit the final short uphill some 13.5km from the finish, Christophe Mengin, the local boy, attacked, went clear but was caught with only a kilometre to go, by Vinokourov and Lorenzo Bernucci, just clear of a ravening bunch. In the frantic pump of dying strength, Mengin took too tight a line on the final bend, a corner he knew well, skidded and went down. Vinokourov just avoided him but had to ground one foot to steady himself, and the Italian Bernucci was clear to the line, his first professional victory. A few seconds later, the main bunch roared in, one rider wrenched at his brakes, locked up and went down, taking twenty others with him, including McEwen and Boonen. Certainly Vinokourov was showing laudable aggression and spunk even before the mountains, but this attack, a large expenditure of energy for a mere 12 seconds of bonus, was scrapping for crumbs. (Unhappily, Mengin was too badly hurt to continue.)

McEwen was in splendid form: he took a second stage victory when the Tour crossed into Germany, his main rivals handsomely beaten. Next day the race hit the first real test, in the Vosges mountains. Approaching the second-category col de la Schlucht, first crossed by the 1931 Tour, its summit at 1,139m some 15km from the finish, Armstrong was alone, his team inexplicably scattered and well down on the pace. The T-Mobile trio, Ullrich, Klöden and Vinokourov, hovered. Their oft-repeated plan – to isolate Armstrong and attack, attack, attack – was in place.

Vinokourov duly attacked, several times, but Armstrong, unsupported, was neither fazed nor in trouble. Did he even need a team? There seemed to be no cohesion in the attempts to drop him. Vinokourov did not seem to be going all out – a single burst of acceleration and then he sat up when he was caught; Ullrich did nothing; and Klöden, eventually taking advantage of the fact that the others seemed rather to have given up on the idea of a concerted onslaught, skulked off on the descent into the picturesque Valley of the Lakes to chase down the lone escaper Pieter Weening. Weening, who had been away on his own for some time, deservedly pipped the late German arrival by half a tyre width in Gérardmer, noted for its Géromés cheeses.

Whatever was said in the Discovery hotel that night about the team's dereliction, the following day the boys in blue were back on song, all eight closely ranged around the yellow jersey at the head of the *peloton*. Armstrong claimed not to have put any pressure on them, only that he 'asked them some questions and gave them some words of support'. If that's not a euphemism, I'd like to know what is. Indeed, as I watched the latter part of the stage, I suspected that Armstrong's isolation was a ploy, a bluff to see what T-Mobile and the rest had to throw at him. The climb wasn't hard, the col not far from the finish. Whatever attacks went, he had only to stay on their wheel. He had time to spare, and, as a way of testing the T-Mobile unity of purpose at minimal risk, it reaped huge dividends. (He admitted to such a feint on the way to l'Alpe d'Huez in 2001 (see p. 251) and, for all his dismissal of being the firm favourite to win the Tour, which is sensible, his confidence in his superiority this year was palpable.) I put this interpretation to two highly regarded commentators, each of them close to Armstrong – Phil Liggett and Paul Sherwen – a week later. They confirmed that the Discovery team had been in disarray, the whole lot of them. I remain sceptical.

On the descent of the col de Grosse Pierre, a few kilometres from the start, Ullrich somersaulted into a ditch below the right-hand verge and bruised his back. He was fortunate: to the left, the road fell away into a ravine, 13 metres deep. (X-rays taken on the rest day showed no damage, but it was another telltale sign of Ullrich's ill-preparedness that he should tumble on a straightforward descent, when the riders were merely settling in before any hard racing.)

On stage nine, the Danish rider Michael 'Chicken Legs' Rasmussen, former world mountain bike champion (1999) attacked from 4km out with the express attention of taking as many mountain points as he could on this first day of real climbing – six categorised cols. He led the way over them all, including the first-category Le Grand Ballon and the first-category Ballon d'Alsace, the first major climb ever included in the Tour, 1905. (Ballon is the local name for 'mountain'.) An orientation table on the Ballon d'Alsace identifies the stupendous views over most of the Vosges range and valleys, the Belfort Gap and the Alps, and the broad acres of the summit are home to a repository of memorials. A local farmer, Joseph Grisward, was lost in a snowstorm when, in response to an ardent prayer and devotional vow, the lights of his farm suddenly twinkled through the blizzard. He set up the promised statue to Our Virgin Lady of the Ballon in 1860. A large sculpture commemorates all those Frenchmen who died clearing landmines after the Second World War. A statue of St Joan of Arc confirms France's attachment to the territory of Alsace and an oblong stele honours René Pottier, first conqueror of the Ballon, in 1905 and 1906, when he won the Tour. (See pp. 26 and 130.)

After his lone break of 167km, Rasmussen took the stage and the polka-dot jersey of the mountains prize. Some three minutes behind him and three minutes ahead of the *peloton*, Jens Voigt and Christophe Moreau, formerly teammates with Crédit Agricole, came in together and Voigt, an inveterate *baroudeur*, 'scrapper', took the yellow jersey. He had won the golden fleece once before, in 2001, also in Alsace: then, as now, his ownership lasted but a day.

After a transfer and rest day, the Tour went into the Alps: 192.5km over the first-category Cormet de Roselend and a 22km ascent to the finish at the altiport atop Courchevel. Voigt's distress – he is no climber and staggered in 29m 23s down on the winner – mirrored that of several other riders whose climbing prowess ought to have served them better. Of the so-called main contenders, Ullrich and Klöden lost 2m 14s, Vinokourov a crippling 5m 18s. Iban Mayo, the Basque specialist climber, slumped on the Cormet and finished over 21m down. Roberto Heras, once Armstrong's trusted front-man in the mountains, lost 9m 49s.

As for Armstrong himself, he mounted a formidable display of cool and strength. On the lower slopes of Courchevel, the five Discovery Channel men still with him began to exert enormous pressure on the rest of the field, winding up to a cruel speed. (Word in the Press Room was that, after their poor showing, they had had an oil change on the rest day.) As their stint of high-pace drafting at the front wasted them, they fell away – Paolo Savoldelli, José Luis Rubiera, José Azevedo, George Hincapie (who had accompanied all six of Armstrong's Tour victories) – till only the young Ukrainian Yaroslav Popovych was left. (He had fallen earlier.) The team's belligerence had been efficient: 16km from the top, Heras dropped away; 2km on, Santiago Botero went; and 11km from the top, Armstrong drew alongside Popovych and told him this was *Go* time. Popovych hit the front like a berserker and the field shredded – Vinokourov, then Ullrich, then Klöden, then Floyd Landis, who had ridden for US Postal in 2004, each and severally liquidated. Only Rasmussen, the Spaniards Valverde and his teammate Francisco Mancebo, and Basso stayed with Armstrong and Popovych, whose final exertion did not – could not – last long. He ran out of juice; so, too, Basso. And, at this fierce tempo, Armstrong nonchalantly sat back in his saddle and did stretching exercises, twisting his lower trunk left and right, as if limbering up in a gym. It was reminiscent of Koblet combing his hair as he rode past other riders toiling up a climb.

Racing over the line, Valverde beat Armstrong by a metre; Rasmussen and Mancebo followed at nine seconds. In the past six years, Armstrong has opened decisive gaps with a series of crushing lone attacks in the mountains. That he chose not to break clear for a stage victory on Courchevel but was content simply to evict all his main rivals from the lead group was evidence of his supreme poise and confidence. Back down the slope, Klöden waited for Ullrich to tow him in: it was a dismal spectacle. Here in the Alps they had promised to make life hard for Armstrong, whereas he was doling out measures of 'hard' that they couldn't get close to.

Vinokourov's challenge for a top overall placing was probably over, but he had not given up on his reputation as a high roller. Next day, on the huge climb of the col de la Madeleine (25.4km long to 1,993m, over 1,500m of height gained) he joined an attack launched by Oscar Pereiro, in company with Botero and Mancebo, then Egoi Martinez. This move, 140km from the finish, rash as it may have seemed, had a sound rationale. Vinokourov knew that Discovery Channel would lay down such a fierce pace on the Galibier, 2,645m, that it would be impossible for anyone to ride away. Besides, he'd been exposed as no real threat, Armstrong could well afford to let him go.

Martinez lost contact on the col du Télégraphe, 1,566m, Pereiro in the next valley. On the Galibier, 'Giant of the Alps', the Alpine col most visited by the race and, as this year, so often 'the Tour's rooftop', Vinokourov dropped Botero. Botero rejoined on the 40km descent into Briançon, where Vinokourov took the stage and salvaged some honour, at least. 'You don't win the Tour de France by sitting on someone else's wheel,' he said. 'You have to have it in you to take risks to regain time.' Bold words and, if the victory did indeed give back some morale to the team, the time he regained was paltry – 1m 15s. He remained nearly five minutes adrift. Voigt arrived 46m 43s after the Kazakh rider, 41 seconds outside the time limit, and was eliminated.

✬

Bastille Day.
On the final climb of the day, the col du Corobin, David Moncoutié attacked from a breakaway group and raced into Digne-les-Bains, through the lavender fields for which it is famous, with a 57-second advantage. For a Frenchman to win on 14 July, when the Tour raced along part of the Route Napoléon, followed by Napoleon Bonaparte between Antibes and Grenoble after he escaped from Elba in 1815, was glorious. Moncoutié, in the French tricolour red, white and blue colours of Cofidis, became the 25th French rider to win a stage on the national day. He attacked on the Corobin because he knew that it was his last chance for a win – he is no sprinter and 'if I had come in with six others, I'd have finished seventh,' he said. The day before, the Italian rider Dario Frigo had been expelled from the race for possession of illegal substances – his wife had a thermos flask containing a dozen ampoules packed in ice in the boot of her car; she claimed it was Botox. Moncoutié, who refuses to take most medication other than homoeopathic remedies, said, 'There's no proof. This is a delicate subject and I don't want to launch any polemics, but there is a lot of disappointment among the French riders at the moment. The speed of the race is extremely high and you can draw your own conclusions.' He added that, in the high mountains, the French simply could not compete.

Boonen, who had crashed three times in six days, did not start

330

the day – his knee was too painful. Hushovd took over the green jersey and Armstrong lost a teammate, Manuel Beltrán, to a heavy fall.

In the brief respite of a flat stage into Montpellier, Valverde abandoned in tears – he'd struck his leg on the handlebars during the team time-trial and the pain had become too much. McEwen outsprinted two luckless French riders after his Lotto team had reeled in the escape. 'People say I can slip into mouseholes,' he said, 'but I think what makes me different is that I react very quickly. I'm hard to beat because I always do something different.' This mercurial quality serves him well in the absence of a team of dedicated pilot-fish lead-out men such as Boonen relies on. The three stage victories on this Tour took McEwen's total to eight, since 1999 when he won on the Champs-Elysées. The green jersey was almost certainly beyond his reach, but emphatic shows of speed and aggression were not.

On the 14th stage, 220.5km with two horrible climbs in close order at the finish, what Tour riders called 'the queen (i.e. decisive) stage', the T-Mobile combine finally delivered some punitive speed and aggression, too. They led towards the foot of the Port de Pailhères in Indian file for several kilometres at mounting pace, so as to hit the slopes fast, keep going fast and force Armstrong to take them on. Giuseppe Guerini accelerated early and everyone winced. Armstrong said this was a critical moment: crack then and you are done for. A bit further on, Vinokourov added his weight to the assault on the American, who was now shorn of support. Then it was Ullrich's turn, relayed by Basso, but Armstrong neither lost his nerve nor tried to stay on their wheel. He said afterwards that he was never in danger – the attacks lasted no more than a kilometre on a swine of a climb which goes to 2,001m in a little over 11km, much of the way at ten per cent gradient. Armstrong knew he needed neither to counter nor match the attacks, only to contain them. His rivals had no prize on offer other than a better placing in the overall order. He might say, day after day, that the Tour was not over till they rode into Paris, but his entire demeanour and comportment were those of a man who knew he had it in him to resist anything anyone else threw at him. Every attempt to break him had petered out. He was unbreakable. Basso, in particular, kept trying but shrivelled. Recovery, in 30°+ heat, was difficult anyway. Worse, from the top of the Pailhères a rapid 20km descent into Ax-les-Thermes led straight to the foot of the Ax Trois Domaines, a sunbaked 9.1km to 1,372m with sections of over 11 per cent.

I had cycled it myself that airless afternoon, the heat sucking out every drop of spare moisture I drank or sweated, the charmless road battering all fidelity to 'the beautiful machine' out of my heart and mind. For a brief interlude before the start of the climb, I even cherished the simple-minded delusion that it might not be as bad as when I did it in 2003 (see p. 289 f.). In some ways it was worse, merely because it quickly dawned on me that I knew, more or less, exactly what lay in store. As the climb went on, so did the blistering reality of it unfold ahead: the long straights, the lack of shade, the tight, steep bends, the lash of the gradient. I rode through the zone wherein there is nor can be no rational response to questions of how and why. Later, I stood by the barriers alongside where the day's winner, Georg Totschnig, collapsed. (A bloody woman lit a cigarette.) I had, by then, recovered and having grovelled up what the Austrian rider had just ridden at an extreme of physical durance, felt mildly sick to witness his distress. Totschnig was the lone survivor of a group of escapees and it was Armstrong who came in 56 seconds after him. Basso and Ullrich lost a clutch of seconds, but Klöden ceded 2m 6s and Vinokourov 3m 6s. So far, Armstrong had won no stages, but he didn't need to. The increments of seconds on his overall lead, the metronomic steadiness of his riding, the imperturbable rhythm ensured the one thing that mattered: retention of the yellow jersey. As the other contenders faltered and then intermittently turned on the heat, Armstrong's graph of effort remained constant. It wasn't that the rest were making tactical errors: they simply did not have the strength and stamina to unsettle the impregnable American.

The second day in the Pyrenees was a humdinger: one second-category climb, four first and a mountain-top finish on the beyond-category Pla d'Adet. Michael Boogerd, one of the Rabobank warriors, launched an attack 27.5km from the start and, a kilometre up the road, was joined by 13 others, including Axel Merckx, Sandy Casar and Laurent Brochard, two French hopefuls, Ullrich's teammate Oscar Sevilla, who still looks far too young to be earning a living as a pro rider, and George Hincapie, Armstrong's faithful henchman. Just after the *peloton* had emerged from the big tunnel (420m long) through the limestone ridge near the bastide town of Mas d'Azil, two friends of mine, Britt and her father Richard, saw Armstrong and Hincapie deep in conversation at the head of the bunch. Shortly afterwards, Hincapie shot off to join the escape. They must have decided that, were the escape to fail, Hincapie would be in position (having done no work to assist it) to support his leader at the end of the stage. Were it to stay clear, he'd have a chance of stage victory.

It stayed clear. At the top of the Peyresourde (1,569m) some 40km from home, there were six riders ahead of the *peloton* by 11m 20s: Boogerd, Brochard, Pereiro, Hincapie, Sevilla and Pietro Caucchioli. On the lower slopes of the final climb, the steep, 11km haul to the winter sports station at 1,680m, Sevilla made the first move and Brochard and Caucchioli were dropped. Pereiro accelerated and, Sevilla's legs gone to rubber, only Hincapie and Boogerd stayed with him. Caucchioli recovered, came back and went past. Four and a half kilometres from the line, with around thirteen minutes of riding left, Pereiro surged ahead once more, followed by Hincapie. Pereiro later claimed moral victory and said that Hincapie had reneged on an agreement to share the work on the last climb, but Hincapie had no compunction – he had been given a job and he did it. Two hundred and fifty metres from the line, he opened the sprint. Pereiro was cooked and lost by six seconds.

It is not least of the astonishing aspects of Armstrong's meticulous and all-consuming team preparation, the year-round indoctrination of Tour, Tour, Tour, into every member of his support group, that a known *rouleur* like Hincapie, a one-day classic races specialist, can be so consistently strong in the mountains on the Tour de France, as support rider, *and* win not just any mountain stage but one of the toughest on the route ending on such an extreme climb. It is baffling.

Behind the stage leaders, Vinokourov hammered away at the yellow jersey on the penultimate climb to the col d'Azet, only to see off Ullrich, while Armstrong and Basso (whose resilience hoisted him to second place overall) refused to be shaken. Basso surged, Armstrong took his wheel, then rode alongside him as if to ram home the point that he didn't need the tow.

The tar was melting on the descent into the valley towards the Pla d'Adet. In the dying kilometres of the day, Vinokourov faded and lost a further 2m 29s to Armstrong. Ullrich, for whom Sevilla, his own chances blown, had waited, lost 1m 24s. In fact, 4km from home, the German had suffered from a *fringale*, 'bonk', an alimentary problem, and was trembling with that dreadful mix of fatigue and loss of blood sugar.

Rasmussen, with a substantial lead over Pereiro in the mountains competition, still held on to third place overall, over two minutes up on Ullrich. Afterwards, Basso said, 'I tried on the climbs today, I gave it everything, but Armstrong is too strong, he never weakens.'

★

Tuesday, 19 July.

I'd agreed to help my friend Britt's non-cycling father, Richard, (73 years old) see the Tour if at all possible and, after reflection, decided that the best way was to chance the backstairs bucolic route linking the main road from Argelès-Gazost to the Soulor descent. I've ridden some of it, couldn't imagine why it would be blocked: with luck, only cyclists would know about it. Worth the risk. The valley road west from Argelès affords one of the finest views in the Pyrenees, towards the range of massive peaks of which the Aubisque forms part; the panorama from the top of the remote col de Couraduque is breathtaking and the dizzy perspective from the even remoter col de Spandelles is a wonder.

So we drove, up and over the narrow, partly unpaved, twisty, rustic road to the junction with the D126 of the Soulor descent and lo, we had the liberty of the Tour route with a straggle of other spectators. (It's not often you can outsmart the Tour route in a car and, the day I write this, a blast from the past – riders ducking under the closing bar of a level crossing and over the lines while following team cars backed up waiting for the train to pass.)

We strolled 300m down the road to *Le Moulin* restaurant and sat by the cool of the mill-race with a beer. Perfection. And suddenly, a shocking intrusion of noise – klaxons, blaring music, Tannoys . . . bloody Tour de France. What? We've stopped by for a nice quiet lunch (*salade verte, poulet à la Basquaise, pommes frites, fromage de brebis, vin rouge*) in a quiet backwater of rural France and, startled, glance up from our table to see an oversized, motorised garden gnome flying past, followed hotly by the Champion lorry, albeit the man with the microphone saw us and generously called out, '*Bon appetit, messieurs, 'dames.*' The yellow-jersey pompom girls flounced past on the back of their lorry, and a blizzard of packets of pretzels and coffee sachets, baby sausages and Bouygues lanyards landed on the patio.

The Aquarel guy hosed us down.

There follows a lull, the curious bating of breath that tracks the caravan ahead of *Le Tour*.

All at once, the leaders hurtle down, heralded by two advance guard police *motards*, blue lights flashing – four riders, on the money, they'll make it. A bit later, a lone escapee, then another. A further pause and it's the yellow-jersey group, compact, intense. Suddenly, a whole rout of riders, weaving in and out of jostling team cars like penguins slicing underwater; one guy, rocketing towards the bend, hands off the bars, stuffing a drink down the back of his jersey, others, with bottles between their teeth, *glissando* into invisible gaps, and when they are past, it's rush hour choking the col du Soulor – cars, motorbikes, vans in a jam, horns honking, mad to get through. One rider, all but decked by the Assistance Médicale van (there's irony – nearly trashed by the guy who will scrape you off the road), hammers on its side window in a fury.

Finally, another lull, foreboding this time, because it counts in minutes the pain and toil of what has happened on the mountains behind, the last summits of the Tour. And a melancholy moment: here comes Beloki, solitary, bemused, way down on time, a leader *manqué*. Four years ago, when the Tour last came this way, he arrived in Paris third on General Classifcation. Now? Nowhere. But that's the race, just another particle of the 100 years' history.

Behind him came the *grupetto* or *autobus*, the bunch of riders at the back of the field who dread the climbs and negotiate them at a manageable pace calculated to beat the day's time limit, based on a percentage of the winner's time. (The percentages are published in the Tour regulations.) In the past, the swashbuckling Jacky Durand led the *autobus*. Each morning, he worked out the time delay on the predicted average speed of the stage: if the average went up or down during the day, he adjusted accordingly. The idea is to make up time on the valley roads between climbs, riding them as fast as possible before the steadier tempo of the next ascent, to accommodate the weaker riders. They shout '*piano, piano*' (slow down, 'softer, softer'), if the pace gets too high, or, if it starts to flag, the cry goes up '*hop, hop*' ('come on'). Sticking together in a bunch is essential. Any rider left on his own faces a hard slog to stay in contact. There can even be two or three *grupetti*, fast, medium and slow, but they all run on mutual help, team tactics aside, to bring as many riders home under the guillotine as possible.

Pereiro got his stage win at last, in Pau, from a day-long escape which dwindled to a handful. Robbed (he complained) of victory on Sunday, he had extra fire in his belly today. Among the lead group was the Australian Cadel Evans, riding his first Tour and lying seventh overall at 9m 29s. A superb performance. He and the other Australians wore a black armband: the day before, their compatriot Amy Gillett, out for a training ride with five other Australian internationals in Germany, preparing for the Tour of Thuringia, had been killed by a car swerving across the road, over the central white line, straight into her. The driver, an 18-year-old woman, had passed her test only four weeks earlier and, travelling at speed, lost control of the vehicle. The other riders were gravely injured and in hospital. Evans voiced the grief and anger of us all: 'I don't know how many people are going to have to be killed before society wakes up to the fact that cars are a threat to cyclists.'

The 17th, and longest, stage of the race, 239.5km across the undulating valleys of the Languedoc south of Toulouse, was ideal for any riders still game for action and ready to seize their chance. (Klöden, who broke a scaphoid in his right wrist in a crash the day before, abandoned.) The big-hitters wouldn't bother to chase. Of the 17 riders forming the breakaway at 38km, the best-placed was the seemingly indefatigable Sevilla at 38m 51s overall. There was no danger here to top placings. The Discovery team had two representatives in the break: Paolo Savoldelli, 'The Falcon' (winner of the Giro d'Italia, 2002 and 2005) and Rubiera. At

185km, the advance over the *peloton* reached 24 minutes, a record for this Tour. When Sébastian Hinault attacked, 9km from Revel, on the 2.7km climb of the côte de Saint-Ferréol, Savoldelli was on him 'like a meteor' – a phrase much-beloved of French journalists. Savoldelli had played steadfast *domestique* to his team leader so far and was, by his own admission, very tired, but now he showed what he could do when released from diurnal duties. He squeezed out his effort with perfect timing to win. Armstrong might not have been taking stages himself but his men were; moreover, Popovych was in white as best young rider, and the team had temporarily displaced T-Mobile in the overall team competition.

Honouring Laurent Jalabert's victory in Mende (near his home) on 14 July 1995, the final climb of stage 18, the côte de la Croix-Neuve, an evil 3.1km of 10 per cent, had been renamed 'the Laurent Jalabert Climb'. A small leading group approached the hill, way ahead of the bunch, among them Axel Merckx, keen to take a win on Belgium's national day. (On 21 July 1831, Léopold of Saxe-Coburg Gotha was elected king of the newly formed independent state of Belgium.) Thomas Voeckler attacked early but exploded. Merckx fell away briefly but fought back to the leaders, Cédric Vasseur and Marcos Serrano. In a flash, 1km from the summit, Serrano was gone. It was a big gamble, a severe test of legs, lungs and resolve, but he held on, topped the col and pounded the remaining 1.6km downhill with the breeze of victory at his back. Vasseur stuck to Merckx's wheel and jumped past to take second place. Merckx was not impressed. He'd lacked a moiety of strength in the final kilometre and Serrano had patently been the stronger of the three, but at least he had been riding to win, Vasseur only for second place.

Another French rider, commenting bitterly on the final big detour round the Lac de Ferréol: 'The lake was beautiful, but aren't we tired enough already?' The unspoken charge being that the speed of the race is artificially high and they are racing at a disadvantage. Armstrong says of the Tour that it is 'a problem in arithmetic, biology, chemistry and nutrition'. The widespread belief among his detractors, Greg Lemond and many of the French riders among them, is that his private definition of *la chimie* is somewhat wayward and reprehensible. They point to the fact, for instance, that in 2001 he mounted l'Alpe d'Huez fully ten minutes faster than the Hinault–Lemond tandem in 1986. They also resent what they see as his overweening power, even off the bike, through a battery of personal lawyers and behind-the-scenes men. The acerbity and vindictiveness of his character – as he himself puts it, 'storing slights on the hard drive' – does not endear him, either. One French journalist, asked what he considered to be Armstrong's greatest quality as a rider, replied, 'His cruelty.'

Nonetheless, he seemed more relaxed, more at ease with himself on his last Tour. My friend Nick Flanagan and his 11-year-old son Dominic watched the *peloton* racing through the tiny village of Moulis, en route to the Portet d'Aspet. They picked their vantage spot well – above a small roundabout which slowed the bunch considerably. Armstrong came through, unflanked by riders, and, when Dominic said excitedly, 'Dad, Dad, look, there's Lance,' Armstrong turned and beamed a big, warm smile at the lad.

✶

Two Frenchmen – Sylvain Chavanel and Sandy Casar – were in with a last chance for a stage win on the eve of the individual time-trial in St Etienne but, in the irresolute jockeying of the final kilometre, they let the opportunity slip. In company with Pereiro, Franco Pellizotti and Giuseppe Guerini, they headed for the red kite. Guerini, who memorably won on l'Alpe d'Huez in 1999, despite being knocked off his bike by an amateur photographer, (see p. 218) knew that he had no hope of contesting a sprint. One and a half thousand metres out, he attacked, blue streak. The others dithered fatally. Guerini held on and won, from Casar, by ten seconds. Casar wept and moaned, 'I didn't see him go and when I *did* see it was too late.'

I watched the television coverage. It seemed to me that Casar *had* seen Guerini jump but was too slow to react; he was already dicing in the loser's mindset, reluctant to follow and thereby frazzle his own strength whilst towing another rider to the line. Guerini went for bust; Casar declared himself bust. It was noticeable, too, that when riders like Christophe Moreau and Casar were buttonholed immediately after a stage, they talked volubly, articulately. On one occasion, I watched Vinokourov in front of the microphone and the man could hardly speak, so exhausted was he. Casar's 'I did everything I could' neither sounded enough nor, indeed, was enough.

The last overall winner of the Tour not to record a single stage victory was Greg Lemond in 1990 and, although Armstrong made Ullrich his favourite to take the 55.5km individual time-trial round St Etienne, this was mere kidology. His consuming desire to prove one last time, as in the past, that the yellow jersey was the strongest rider in the race put him psychologically ahead, even of a rider who was riding to save honour. In the event, Ullrich was behind the American at each of the intermediate time checks and Armstrong won the stage by 23 seconds, not a huge margin, but healthy, given that Ullrich's motivation had been rampant. Further evidence of his meticulous planning: the route undulated and a number of bends and roundabouts made it technically tricky. Armstrong alone fitted a more suitable tri-spoke back wheel where the others used the more rigid discs.

Alas for Rasmussen, one of the rear disc men, King of the Mountains and in third position overall, defending a lead of 2m 12s over Ullrich, he had a wretched time. His antics were unprofessional and bizarre, seemingly a sign of total collapse of nerves. At 3km, racing towards a roundabout which, when he reconnoitred the course, he took on the right, he inexplicably followed a motorcycle outrider to the left, missed his line and crashed. He remounted, rode on, stopped and flicked the rear wheel out, without dismounting (cardinal mistake – a rider should always stand clear of the machine to allow the mechanic free rein), rode on, stopped again for further adjustment, rode on, stopped again for a change of bike, was overtaken by Basso, (originally three minutes behind him) stopped yet again for yet another change of bike and, on the one true descent on the course, swerved off the road and fell in a ditch. He remounted, made for the only real climb, the col de la Gachet, a relatively mild 5.7km, and watched miserably as Armstrong, who had set off six minutes after him, rode by. He lost 7m 47s all told and slumped to seventh overall. It was a sorry and very public humiliation, a top-flight rider succumbing to such a pitiable loss of self-control.

Armstrong's 22nd Tour stage victory – his 11th in a time-trial – put him on a par with André Darrigade but significantly behind Bernard Hinault (28) and Eddy Merckx (34). In seven Tours, he spent eighty-one days in yellow, three more than Hinault, fifteen fewer than Merckx.

On the eve of the run-in to Paris, McEwen stated frankly that he had no thoughts of taking the green jersey – the disqualification in Tours and the crash in Nancy where Hushovd took maximum points (35) and he took none had ruled him out. O'Grady, who has bags of experience but not the same turn of speed, was fifteen points adrift of the Norwegian, had an outside chance, but there remained only two intermediate sprints – a maximum of twelve points – and the final sprint on the Champs-Elysées.

The *peloton* set off from Corbeil-Essonnes, 84km from the Seine, in a light drizzle. Through Issy-les-Moulineaux, where the Tour de France organisation has its offices, on the descent towards the riverbanks, Philippe Gilbert skidded on the glistening paint of a white line – always treacherous in the wet – and took down Hincapie and his teammates Popovych and Pavel Padrnos. Ensconced on their wheels, Armstrong had the time to avoid trouble. He put one foot to the ground, glanced behind him to check that no one was going to collide with him and remounted. Basso, meanwhile, was giving Gilbert an earful for intemperately accelerating on a slippery descent. In view of the dangerous conditions, the jury of commissaires ruled that the final time for the stage would be adjudged on the arrival at the start of the circuit in Paris, albeit every rider must cross the finish line to be classified.

The Tour finished on the Champs-Elysées for the first time in 1975, the year of Bernard Thévenet's first victory and his momentous defeat of Merckx. (He stood on the podium again this year, as a mark of that great triumph.) In a sudden deluge of rain, that day, Thévenet, Merckx and others fell heavily on the slick cobbles of the Champs. Thévenet told the then Mayor of Paris, Jacques Chirac, that they'd been riding in constant fear of crashing. Chirac, whose capacity for tact has not deepened over the intervening 30 years, laughed and said that the rain was good for drama – a few spills made good spectacle. Thévenet remarked, drily, 'He can't have cycled much in the rain.'

Interviewed on Scottish radio during the Tour, I was asked a final question: 'Come on, now, admit it, you'll be hoping for crashes, big pile-ups.' To float such an asinine proposition to anyone of sense is absurd; to put it to a cyclist is crass indeed.

The eight circuits of western Paris – Pont de Grenelle, rue de Rivoli, Place de la Concorde, Arc de Triomphe – saw a number of crashes but, luckily, no bad injury. There were drier stretches of the circuit and the attacks, as ever, shot off the front and were reeled back in. The race for the green jersey had been rather snuffed out. Vinokourov, still rustling the bits and pieces of bonus that were on offer, took the first bonus sprint, six points and six seconds. Nearing the final kilometre, he attacked again and went clear with Yuriy Krivtsov, the Ukrainian, who may well have foreseen a Baltic one–two on the horizon, and the Australian, Bradley McGee, ready to spoil their party for one of his own. McGee jumped at the red kite, Vinokourov caught and passed him and, with extraordinary grit and panache, held on to take the victory with the entire *peloton* hot on his wheel. The whole field rushed through *en bloc*. That close.

Armstrong mounted the podium for the seventh and last time. Joining him were an Italian, Basso, second overall, a German, Ullrich, third, and his T-Mobile team for the overall team prize, a Norwegian, Hushovd, in the green points jersey, a Dane, Rasmussen, in the mountain polka dots, a Kazakh, Vinokourov, final stage winner, a Ukrainian, Popovych, best young rider, and a Spaniard, Pereiro, for the combativity prize. The best-placed Frenchman was Moreau, 11th overall, and it is now 20 years since a Frenchman – Bernard Hinault – won the national Tour. There is no successor, even apparent. This may in part be due to the fact that the traditional view of professional cycle racing still obtains widely in France. Voeckler, the young rider who so delighted the home nation in 2004 with his plucky defence of the yellow jersey against all expectation, honouring, he said, the great responsibility that the golden fleece brings with it, was interviewed by readers of *Vélo* before the Tour. (The celebrity he won in 2004 has not been matched by any results since.) One reader put it to him that Armstrong races very little, never more than 50 days in a year and generally far fewer, whereas Voeckler races at least twice that number of days 'and we like you very much for that'. Voeckler was modest in his reply but made the point that if he were as talented a rider as the American, 'I would take advantage of that and ride all sorts of races, not just the Tour.' He also made the point which Guimard has made, that very few riders can substitute racing for training. It is perhaps Armstrong's greatest asset that, even in solo training rides, he can replicate the extremes of duress most usually thrown up only during a race, when the adrenalin of competition drives a rider hardest and he will unconsciously dig deeper into his reserves than normal – often so deep that he explodes (as did Voeckler on the Montée Jalabert). Ullrich, who rides as few races as Armstrong does, plainly can't achieve this intensity of effort on his own. And what of an entire season skewed to the Tour, then to lose it?

And so the Armstrong domination is over and he will stand apart, perhaps forever, as the rider with seven Tour victories. His place in the annals of the Tour is assured, but not, maybe, in its mythology. Both Merckx and Hinault raced with bravura against evidently stiffer competition than Armstrong has faced, and Hinault was beaten, yet came back to win. They fought for their wins in the cauldron of the Tour itself. Armstrong has done so on the lonely roads of training. He has removed the drama of the race itself to the calculations of his training rides and the laboratory. His last two victories have been untroubled, yet each one has been the result of a punishing year-round training schedule, exclusively for the Tour. It was no pleasure to watch him ride like a second-, even third-rate rider in the 2005 Paris–Nice, where he produced 'the worst time-trial of my life' and later abandoned. For all his talk about always entering races to win, it seems to me that this is simply not the case and is to the detriment of the sport. 'July is when it counts,' he says.

Cycle racing is more than the Tour de France, albeit the wider American public who watch only the Tour believe this is not so. It will be interesting to see what interest they take next year when Armstrong is not riding. At least Discovery Channel, unlike US Postal, have significant commercial interests in Europe. This makes their sponsorship promising. Savoldelli's Giro win must have encouraged them, and this is all to the broader good of the sport.

When Armstrong was roundly beaten by Ullrich in the individual time-trial out of Gaillac in 2003, his confidence was badly shaken. The defeat hurt him badly, not least because he made the fundamental error of not hydrating sufficiently during the warm-up on a day of blistering heat. Such mistakes – the bonk he suffered in a Pyrenean stage in 2000 – are wholly uncharacteristic of a man whose attention to detail is stupefying. He weighs his food to replace the exact number of calories that he has expended. He uses an old-fashioned chainwheel changer on the down tube of his climbing bike to save weight. But, of that fifth victory in 2003, Hincapie said it was the most hard-won because his infectious self-assurance was missing. Accordingly, the team, as ruthlessly disciplined in his cause as he himself is, wavered, and Armstrong himself had to battle with and overcome a very tenacious demon of self-doubt. There is, for sure, no doubting the steel of his will, the freakish physical strength and the mesmeric domination of the pretenders to his lordship of the Tour.

An illustrious but, in historical terms, at least, lopsided, career comes to an end. Asked his opinion, Bernard Hinault praised the seven-times Tour winner highly and then, with Gallic sting, said that had Eddy Merckx concentrated on the Tour as Armstrong had done, instead of riding, and winning, bumper-loads of classics (nearly fifty victories), the Giro d'Italia (five wins), the Vuelta a España (one win) and a host of smaller races, he would have won the Tour 'ten or fifteen times'. The truth is, he did the equivalent.

To Armstrong, then, *ave atque vale*.

✭

POSTSCRIPT
I write this as a postscript in the mood triggered by melancholy news. It has no place in an account of the race itself.

On Tuesday, 23 August, a month after the 2005 Tour finished, *L'Equipe* published a damning indictment of the American under a banner headline: 'The Armstrong Lie'. It printed the results of scientific analysis supplied by the national anti-doping laboratory in Châtenay-Malabry together with a number of official documents. An exclusive investigation by the sports paper 'showed that Armstrong used EPO when he took his first victory in the Tour in 1999, contrary to what he has always claimed'. Six samples taken from him in that race tested positive.

A reliable test (developed by French medical chemists) for the presence of EPO in blood or urine was first used – under UCI auspices – in the spring of 2001. Hitherto, no such test existed; conclusive proof that an athlete had artificially boosted his capacity to absorb oxygen was, therefore, wanting. Negative testing at dope controls meant nothing, in part because natural levels of the concentration of blood corpuscles do vary from individual to individual. Before the advent of the new test, the setting of a permissible maximum by the authorities could only ever be arbitrary.

Suspicion will probably dog Armstrong forever. He has even threatened – and the word is bitterly apt – to renege on retirement and come back to win an eighth Tour, just to rub the noses of the French in their nasty muckraking.

A Tour rider once said to me, with a bleak look in his eyes, 'Armstrong is very powerful.' He hedges himself round with lawyers; he is deeply embroiled in litigation against a number of people who have impugned his honesty; apparently he binds his entourage to oaths of silence; his greatest spur seems to be rancour. It amounts to a sorry intrusion of what, for many reasons – not all Armstrong's doing – smacks of personal vendetta and it does the great sport of cycle racing no good at all.

CHAPTER SIXTEEN

2006

The Crazy 'Bottle of Ink' Tour

I drove down to Alsace with Phil Liggett on the Wednesday before the Prologue in the all-singing, all-dancing OLN hire car. The one thing its satellite-relayed wizardry couldn't – or, skittishly, wouldn't – tell us was the time the restaurant in the motorway services stopped serving. We had to slum it in the cafeteria. Even as we tucked into coq au vin and crême caramel, Alexandr Vinokourov (fifth overall and two stage wins in 2005) and his new Astana-Würth team were disembarking in Strasbourg from the Madrid flight. However, there was no certainty that they would be riding the Tour. Their former *directeur sportif*, Manolo Saíz, was implicated in the infamous Operación Puerto instigated by the Guardia Civil. The police had searched the clinic of one doctor Eufemiano Fuentes in Madrid and unearthed a pharmacopoeia bulging with enough medication – including testosterone patches, EPO and growth hormone – to turn the entire population of the city into pituitary giants with the stamina of cruising sharks, as well as a number of blood samples marked with pseudonyms, plus oral and visual evidence – from telephone conversations and surveillance cameras – as to the identity of Fuentes's clientele. A list of riders fingered by this albeit so far no more than circumstantial evidence had not yet been published, but it was strongly rumoured to include two of the pre-race hot favourites, Jan Ullrich, third in the 2005 Tour (together with his teammate Oscar Sevilla), and Ivan Basso, second in the 2005 Tour and winner of this year's Giro, as well as another contender, Francisco Mancebo, fourth in the

2005 Tour, and one of Vinokourov's teammates, a former podium-place, Joseba Beloki. Fuentes was talking the talk, had spent some time in jail and was insinuating that, accusations of doping aside, he was Mr Big, one way or another, and not just in the cycling world, either.

The riders protested innocence and pooh-poohed the many coincidental matches, promulgated by journalists, between the codenames on dossiers and various suspect riders; for instance, that one such alias, 'Birillo', was alleged to be the name of Basso's dog. But, given that Eufemiano is Spanish for 'sweet-talker' and 'pseud' needs no elaboration, routine professions of innocuous visits to the clinic had the same old tinny sound. The Tribunal Arbitral du Sport in Lausanne, which deals with cases of incrimination against athletes, was reviewing the Astana-Würth dossier as Vinokourov was checking into the magnificent Château d'Ostwald hotel, hopeful that he would be riding the Tour.

I was staying in Ostwald, too, though not at the magnificent château. In fact, when Liggett dropped me off at what looked like a three-storey lock-up on the industrial estate – my hotel – he had that distinct pitying look of the professional mechanic watching an amateur trying to change a tube. 'I've stayed in a few of these,' he said and drove away. I checked in and checked the locale. It didn't take long. There was nothing to be bought within a broad radius of this makeshift dormitory except building materials, although on one stretch of open ground there was, incongruously, a chain steakhouse. Accordingly, my bedroom being impossible to reach by tram and bus after 8.30 p.m., on pain of the 45 minute walk I did one night from the tram stop, on three evenings I supped at – I trust not *on* – Hippopotamus.

On Thursday morning, the Lausanne court delivered its verdict: Vinokourov was in the clear and, therefore, in the Tour. Publication of the list of other riders *sub judice* was promised shortly. The UCI were insisting that the Tour organisation require a declaration from all the riders registered for the Tour that they were racing clean, but this seemed rather to be passing the buck. All teams require such declarations of their riders anyway, and the Tour organisation, at odds with the UCI to begin with and adamant about its own autonomy, could have little sympathy with such redundant pontification and attempted meddling.

The plight of the other big names remained in the balance. On Friday afternoon, as I strolled round the cobbled streets of Petite-France, the old quarter of Strasbourg, past a patisserie where most of the Saunier-Duval team, back from a ride, were sprawled in chairs outside in the sun regaling themselves on coffee and cakes, then along the frontage of the hotel being used by Telekom, on across a humpback bridge over the meandering waterway, Liggett rang me to say that the ordure had just hit the whirling blades of the ventilating equipment with projectile force. The list of implicated riders had been published to a meeting of various team managers and the consequences were dire indeed. Bjarne Rijs returned to his CSC team hotel and told Basso that he was going home. Ullrich, his personal coach Rudy Pévenage and Sevilla of Telekom were named and excluded, so too Mancebo, leader of the French Ag2R team, and five members of Vinokourov's Astana-Würth team, including Beloki. Altogether, 13 riders were ejected. It transpired that the UCI had said that kicking the riders out was not their call but the sole responsibility of the teams involved. Former Tour director Jean-Marie Leblanc, following the race for the last time, rebuked this as cowardly dereliction of duty. The UCI, the sport's ruling body, should be giving a lead. The Tour organisation, for their part, had no compunction in backing the prompt action of the team managers as well as closing the door on Vinokourov. It was hard on him but Tour rules did not permit a team to start with fewer than six riders. (Vinokourov later announced that he had asked his former *directeur* at T-Mobile, Walter Godefroot, to join him at Astana.)

The French sporting paper *L'Equipe* carried two punchy headlines next day: 'The Big Wash' and 'Not a Black Day'. Once more, it seems, the Tour de France organisation had acted boldly where others pussyfooted. The teams had expelled their miscreants; the Tour could claim to be rolling out clean. The new director, Christian Prudhomme, far from regretting the expulsion of suspect riders, welcomed the fact that the 2006 race, already marking a transition into a new era after the Armstrong domination, was now, like the shops during London's Blitz, 'more open than usual'. He said the anti-doping campaign was constant, and the focus trained on the Tour by both the anti-doping authorities and the police an essential part of that campaign. 'I hope, too,' he added, 'that from tomorrow [the day of the Prologue] we will once more be talking about sport and that the magic of the Tour will come into play again. Meanwhile, for me, this 30 June is not a black day. On the contrary, it's a great day for the defence of true cycling . . . of renewed belief, renewed trust.'

Was this a dewy-eyed mantra? Fuentes, who has no shortage of ego, later bragged that if he were to hand over the names of every rider who had passed through his door in search of 'help', there'd be none left to ride the Tour de France. Was, then, this race completely clean? Impossible to say, except that it had been purged of a thick miasma of suspicion.

The Spaniard Mancebo's ejection was particularly poignant. He was riding for a French team, and the French riders have long complained that the laxity of dope controls under other federations has disadvantaged them hugely. The Ag2R manager, Vincent Lavenu, said as much: because certain performance-enhancing products were more readily and easily available in Spain, the temptation to use them was greater. In the 2005 Vuelta, 16 Spanish riders finished in the top 20. (The winner, Roberto Heras, former lieutenant of Armstrong's, had won the race and then been stripped of his title for testing positive, to the benefit of second-placed Denis Menchov, who was awarded victory.) Lavenu said that, in retrospect, he had made an error in signing Mancebo, if only because it left him open to the kind of suspicion about the Iberian riders which was rife. However, the veteran Frenchman Christophe Moreau, riding his eleventh Tour (three abandons), would take over as team leader. Several French riders said that, having been censured for not training or riding hard enough, the public would now see that they had been riding at their maximum against cheats. Now that the cheats were banned, the door was open for the home cyclists.

The field of possible winners had widened: the Portuguese José Azevedo and the redoubtable 'Big' George Hincapie of Armstrong's team (which the Texan part-owns); the Russian Denis Menchov of Rabobank; the Australian Cadel Evans of Davitamon-Lotto; Floyd Landis of Phonak; Damiano Cunego of Lampre-Fondital, who had won his native Giro in 2004; the Spaniard Alejandro Valverde of Caisse d'Epargne; Andreas Klöden, former German national champion, of T-Mobile; the American Levi Leipheimer of Gerolsteiner.

At 3.56 p.m. on Saturday, 1 July, the starter on the launch ramp counted down for David Millar. Having admitted, in June 2004, to the use of EPO, he returned to the biggest bike race in the world without a single day's racing. It was a huge gamble. His bike case arrived on the airport carousel with a big number 13 stuck to it, and when he arrived at the Château d'Ostwald he had been assigned room 101. Enough to spook most people, but, in a text message to me, he voiced a new mental toughness: 'I'm very on top of my game, would take a freight train hitting my hotel room to distract me. Even then I'd probably be fine.'

Millar came in 14 seconds adrift of the winner, Thor Hushovd, a specialist sprinter (green jersey in 2005), who had been training hard over this distance, but he was back and determined to reach Paris. 'I've made a lot of mistakes,' he said. 'I've told lies, and I have many regrets, but I have faced up to my responsibilities and that's something very important to me. With the new generation and the scandal that just broke, things are going to change. I am 100 per cent clean; I can confirm that. I want to deliver a positive message for the sport . . . For sure, I'm eager to put myself through it these next three weeks but not like the past two years . . . that's been horrible, but the descent into hell was part of the punishment.'

Hincapie missed the first yellow jersey by a tantalising 0.73 of a second and took the first green jersey as runner-up.

In 2005, Tom Boonen, 'The Tornado' to his ecstatic Belgian fans, became the first cyclist in history to win the classic Tour des Flandres, the Paris–Roubaix and the world road-race title in one season. His declared aim in the Tour was to win the green jersey, and there were few who would dispute his boast that he was the fastest and smartest sprinter in the *peloton*. One who most emphatically did refute it was the Australian Robbie McEwen, who actually lives in Belgium – Boonen has decamped to Monaco. Perhaps he'd have done better to stay in the rough-house of the Flemish kermesse scene. On stage one, a loop from and back into Strasbourg, he attacked 350m out, far too early. Looking for a wheel to follow, McEwen tried to pass between Boonen and the perennial Erik Zabel, saw an opening and spurted, but the Frenchman Jimmy Casper pipped him by a tyre. Boonen said he'd been hit on the shoulder by a spectator waving a camera over the barriers. More seriously, Hushovd had his left arm sliced open, a deep, 5cm gash, by one of the monster green plastic hands doled out by the French tote, PMU, which sponsors the green jersey. He came in looking a fright, blood pouring all down his arm and side. He got off the bike and lay on the tarmac – his heart rate, from the tension of the sprint, so high he was exsanguinating fast. But, he got stitched up and was back next day, having lost the green jersey to Casper and the yellow to Hincapie, who'd snapped up a two-point bonus in an intermediate sprint.

Hushovd went hunting for seconds from intermediate sprints, grabbed four and took the yellow back on stage two into Luxembourg, a 228km haul through temperatures in the mid-30s. In the final 100m, he might well have ended up on the deck again. His front wheel clipped McEwen's. He bounced off, but one shoe pinged out of its pedal cleat and he finished with one foot trailing. McEwen stayed upright, too, and took the win. Hushovd crossed the line in a fury but calmed down and shook hands with the Australian. Such incidents are the common tack of the sprinter's light-blue-touchpaper existence. 'It was a bit dodgy,' McEwen admitted, ever phlegmatic.

Extreme heat always adds to the fatigue, not least in that the water-carriers, the *domestiques*, have to go back to the team car every ten minutes or so to collect water bottles for the rest of the team. Nine 250ml bottles at a time, stuffed in pockets, up the jersey, down the back, down the front, and rejoin the bunch to hand them round. Average consumption: five litres a day. Average number of bottle trips per *domestique*: 18–20.

Forty kilometres from the finish in Valkenburg on stage three, Erik Dekker, 35 years old, riding his last Tour, hit a hole in the road, went down and was taken to hospital. Fifteen kilometres on, as the bunch squeezed down a gauntlet of narrow, twisting roads, Valverde crashed and broke his collarbone. 'Bala Verde', 'the Green Bullet', as he is called, is a rider of singular class: in April, he won the Ardennes double of Flèche Wallonne and Liège-Bastogne-

Liège. The Tour has handed him evil luck, however. Tipped as a possible winner, he has started twice and twice abandoned. Klöden went down in the same pile-up but was not badly hurt. His teammate Matthias Kessler jumped clear of the bunch and won the stage. McEwen was way down the field and Boonen, fourth, took a dollop of bonus time and the first yellow of his career. Sandy Casar collided with a spectator's mobile phone and crashed near the line. One wondered what further moronic intervention by spectators crowding the barriers would add to the perils of the frenzied charge for the line.

McEwen rode a perfectly mastered sprint to win stage four and praised his lead-out man, Gert Steegmans: 'He's a real locomotive. I'm very concentrated on the sprints, I study them in detail and I knew this stage [not far from where he lives] suited me really well.' This put him in green. Two days later, after another win into Lisieux, his eleventh in the Tour, he was calling Steegmans 'a TGV, and I'm the only one with a ticket'. There was no doubt that technically, physically and psychologically he was on top. If most people had expected Boonen to lord it over the sprints, McEwen had not. He was a pure sprinter, he said, and came to the Tour in peak condition. It wasn't any surprise to him, therefore, that Boonen, a classic one-day racer, who had flogged himself through the early season events, did not.

The first individual time-trial of the race – there was no team event this year – was a 52km route of leg-sapping corrugation, hills and false flats, which suited the strongest *rouleurs*, the men who can maintain devilish high speeds. Millar reconnoitred it in June and rode it five times. 'It's deceptively hard,' he said, '. . . a bastard time-trial.' The thirty-six-year-old Ukrainian Serhiy Honchar, of T-Mobile, won the stage to take over the yellow jersey, and three members of his team finished close behind: Michael Rogers fourth, Patrik Sinkewitz sixth and Klöden eighth. Floyd Landis punctured near the start and a botched wheel change cost him most of the minute and a second he lost on the day. His handlebars broke, too, and he very nearly crashed. Menchov trailed by 1m 44s, but Hincapie lost 2m 42s and Leipheimer a miserable 6m 06s. Bobby Julich crashed heavily into a kerb early on and was out.

The 181km between St-Méen-le-Grand, named for a healing

saint with a special interest in madness, and Lorient, one of France's main naval bases since the establishment of shipbuilding yards there by a royal patent of 1664, was sure to be tempting for the *baroudeurs* keen to outrun tired legs and minds before the rest day. Boonen, still shy of a win, had his Quick Step men working hard to reel in the second major attack of the day, which included David Zabriskie of CSC, tenth on general classification and Kessler eleventh. Landis's Phonaks joined in, too, to limit the losses. This was, perhaps, premature. The other contenders were happy to sit in the slipstream armchair and do nothing while Landis cajoled the chase.

With 30km to go, on the day when France were playing Italy in the World Cup final, Sylvain Calzati, a Frenchman of Italian descent, jumped clear of the break and came in alone. Asked (of course) for whom he would be cheering that night, he said, 'Ah, Italy.'

On the rest day in Bordeaux, an astonishing story broke: Landis divulged that he would be having a hip replacement some time after the end of the Tour. He grew up in a Mennonite community in Pennsylvania – a strict religious sect whose women must never be seen without head covering and which prohibits dancing, television and 'mingling with the unrighteous', amongst whom cyclists most assuredly were numbered. Landis bought a mountain bike when he was 15 to travel to remote fishing holes, started entering races and, aged 17, won the Junior National Mountain Bike Championship. His parents told him he was going to hell if he kept riding the bike, and his father loaded him with domestic chores to prevent him from training. Landis, who has a decidedly unorthodox way with such constraints, recently said he had spent his life doing what others told him he could not do. So, he simply finished the chores and, instead of going to bed, went out training at night. (Raymond Poulidor used to do the same after his farm work.)

Landis switched to road racing in 1999 and, three years later, was signed by the US Postal team. For two years, he rode in support of Armstrong, until Phonak offered him a lot of money to ride as leader for them. Characteristically, Armstrong saw his leaving the Postals as treachery. Zabriskie commented, 'There aren't many guys in the *peloton* who are willing to tell Lance to go screw himself. Floyd just didn't care.' It is reported that, in his final Tour, Armstrong told Landis, 'Rest easy, Floyd. I'm retiring, but my team ain't gonna let go of you.' Speaking of the way this Tour was going, Eddy Merckx remarked, 'Lance has never valued Landis, so I'm not surprised that he's trying to destabilise him by getting at his team. But Landis isn't troubled, and that will certainly motivate him.'

His unconventional attitude and individualism, not quite the sort of pious non-conformism to which the Mennonites more generally subscribe, and his work ethic, which is certainly rooted in his puritan upbringing, have combined to make him extraordinarily tough, mentally and physically. The hip bone, damaged in a crash in 2003, is crumbling with osteonecrosis, a degenerative condition caused by attenuated blood supply. This, according to his doctors, makes the bone resemble 'a chunk of rotten wood, a sunbaked dessert and a scoop of ice cream'. And he's riding the Tour de France, in constant pain. He turned up in a suit to tell the assembled journalists 'something important'. He'd kept the injury secret from all but a handful of doctors and friends. Either this was just Landis being quirky – he had told the American Daniel Coyle for an article in the *New York Times*, published that same day – or it was a psychological gamble of questionable sanity. For the moment, the outcome of the Tour was totally unpredictable . . . as the French say, 'as clear as a bottle of ink'.

On bottles of ink, the novelist Antoine Blondin, who gave his occupation as 'following the Tour de France', was a famous drinker. Asked, once, what blood group he was, he said 'Vat 69', and, waking up feeling thirsty back in the hotel room during one Tour, he reached for a bottle and took a hefty swig . . . it was ink. In a report on a stage between Dax and Bordeaux, he wrote, 'What is the difference between the crossing of the Landes [the flatlands of the Atlantic coast] and Charlemagne's sword? Answer: there is no difference . . . Into Bordeaux, we have endured a long, flat, deadly stage.'

Stage nine of the 2006 Tour covered the same route but in the opposite direction, and, after a long break had been reeled in, the day went to the master of the out-of-the-bunch jack-in-the-box act, Oscar Freire, a martyr to backache and persistent injury who, nonetheless, has won three rainbow jerseys on the road: 1999, 2002 and 2004. On this occasion, he saw his rivals swinging off to the left down the barriers some 300–400m out, so he went right. Nearing the line, McEwen found himself stuck behind Zabel, Boonen and Freire and astonishingly managed to swerve out and then through a gap. He and Freire crossed the line shoulder to shoulder. Not even sure whether the breakaways had been caught, Freire didn't know whether he'd won or not and had to ask McEwen.

Asked his opinion at this near-halfway stage in the race, Cyrille Guimard said that all bets were off. 'As it stands today, an average rider who climbs and time-trials OK and who is less than eight minutes behind could win the Tour. It's a crazy race, sheer anarchy.'

On the first stage in the Pyrenees, two lesser-known riders escaped from the glue pot of the *peloton*, survivors of an early break, to ride into Pau with a lead of seven minutes. The Frenchman Cyril Dessel, of Moreau's Ag2R team (thirty-one years old and but three victories in his entire career), and the Spaniard Juan Miguel Mercado (stage winner in 2004) were out for 160km of the 190.5km route over the cols d'Osquich, Soudet – one of the hardest climbs in these mountains – and the Marie-Blanque, a known killer. Dessel, who had driven the pace high, knowing that the mountains jersey was there for the taking, wanted the stage win badly, but Mercado outsprinted him. However, Dessel's determination to press the escape all the way not only gave him the polka dots; his time gains put him in yellow with 3m 45s on third-placed Honchar. 'To cross all the cols in the lead in front of such crowds was superb,' he said. And worrying for the main contenders? Possibly not, but who could tell? (Iban Mayo, the vaunted climber, was in such trouble that he had to join the sprinters' bus at the back of the race. He quit next day.)

Stage 11 over the Tourmalet, Aspin, Peyresourde and Portillon finished, for the first time, on one of the Vuelta's favoured mountain tops, the Pla de Beret, an ultra-chic ski station frequented by the king of Spain. For much of the past seven years, Armstrong's team has been the strongest in the race, devoted solely to his victory. This time, they were blown to pieces. Hincapie, surprise winner of the toughest mountain stage last year, lost over 20 minutes altogether.

At the foot of the Portillon in Bossost, with an early break still away, an elite group set off in pursuit, among them Landis, Leipheimer and three Rabobank riders: Menchov, Michael Boogerd and Michael Rasmussen, known climbers, all. There followed one of the most impressive examples of team support and sacrifice witnessed in a long time. Rasmussen, King of the Mountains in 2005, having ascertained that his leader, Menchov, was feeling good, went to the front of the bunch and worked . . . and worked . . . all the way to Baqueira, 28km, Boogerd on his wheel. It was quite devotedly selfless. Rasmussen, with ambitions, surely, for the polka dots, was driving himself into the ground for his team's greater ambitions.

As they swung onto the final climb, Rasmussen quite simply fell away to the side, utterly spent, and Boogerd took over the relay. The image of the ex-mountain-bike champion slumping as his teammate upped the pace once more was poignant. Boogerd did not spare himself, either: he knew he wouldn't last long, but for two kilometres of the long hairpins up to the Beret he drove the pace as high as he could, and then, in his turn, peeled off, his work done, his face puce with effort. So it was left to Menchov: he repaid them with the stage victory, and Landis, who looked very comfortable, took yellow (with 1m 1s over the Russian), but only by virtue of the 8s bonus for coming third. Without that, Dessel, fighting desperately hard, would have saved the golden fleece. It was cruel luck. He was even robbed, by David de la Fuente, of the polka-dot jersey he'd won with yellow, and never got to wear it. Close behind Landis came the Australian Cadel Evans, at 1m 17s, and Carlos Sastre, the CSC leader in Basso's stead, at 1m 52s. Back down the slopes, Klöden, despite the support of four teammates, ceded 1m 30s to Landis and was now at 2m 29s.

The Discovery team, perhaps responding to the imminent arrival of Armstrong visiting the Tour, finally cut the mustard on stage 12, won by Yaroslav Popovych, white jersey for best young rider in 2005, his first Tour, even though two of their men – Paolo Savoldelli, who lost twenty-three minutes on the Beret stage, and Benjamin Noval – did what had previously been unthinkable and abandoned early on. Meanwhile, their boss had once more demonstrated a pachydermal insensitivity. Perhaps this is unfair to the elephant and rhinoceros. At an award ceremony in America, the Texan said of the French football team which lost the World Cup: 'All their players tested positive . . . for being assholes.' French: *trouduc*, i.e. *trou du cul*. This he called a joke. Funny thing about self-regarding people severely challenged on the sense-of-humour front: they find the most insulting things funny and wonder why the subjects of the slur don't catch the note of jest when the high-profile figure labels a national football team *trouduc* . . . 'C'mon, guys, lighten up.'

Stage 13 turned everything upside down, and Landis was much criticised, notably by Bernard Hinault, for what looked like a puerile lapse of strategy. Whether he was, indeed, conserving his team's strength ahead of what might well be the carnage of the Alpine stages, or else they were simply too weary to respond to the challenge, a break of 15 riders crossed the line into Montelimar a shocking 29m 57s ahead of the main bunch. Jens Voigt, an irrepressible long-break man in the mould of the great *baroudeur* Jacky Durand, won the stage, and Oscar Pereiro, in 46th position that morning, took yellow, distancing his former teammate Landis by 1m 29s. Never considered a likely overall winner, Pereiro was, nevertheless, a rider of some class, a handy climber, to boot.

However, the Phonak manager John Lelangue, son of Robert, who had been Eddy Merckx's *directeur sportif* at Molteni in the '70s, rationalised, 'Since Valverde's crash, the Caisse d'Epargne [for whom Pereiro now rides] could not hope for victory on a mountains stage, so, we gifted them the jersey. This means they will be obliged to control affairs in the Alps, where we have interests in common.'

Merckx, like Hinault, was sceptical: 'In Landis's place, I would never have let anyone take the jersey from me.' His son, Axel Merckx, in his last Tour, rides for Phonak and is Landis's closest support. As for Landis, he remained calm. The important thing was to have yellow in Paris. Surrendering it now need not jeopardise that; he did not see it as a psychological error. Lelangue remarked on Landis's extraordinary sangfroid. In the Paris–Nice, which he won, Landis had a bit of a fright one day, on a descent. Listening to him on the intercom, Lelangue heard him say, 'Shit, I just overcooked a bend' without even raising his voice. And he remounted and rode off. On the way down from the Beret in the team car, a fan tapped on the window and asked for Landis's jersey. Landis turned to Lelangue and said, 'You want anything?' Lelangue was thirsty and said, yes, he could do with some beer. So Landis told the fan he could have the jersey in exchange for six cans of beer, and the deal was done.

From Montélimar, famous for nougat, to Gap, aptly-named locale for a rest day, the *peloton* faced a punishing 180km through the Alpine foothills, across the col de Perty, 1,303m, halfway, and a nasty second-category climb, the col de la Sentinelle, 9km 980m from the finish. It was on the 90kph descent into Gap, though from the opposite direction, that Beloki crashed so horribly in 2003.

A break of six riders was away when, on melting tar and a badly rutted stretch of road, David Canada misjudged a bend and smashed into the barriers, taking Matthias Kessler and Rik Verbrugghe with him. As he and Kessler catapulted over the barriers, Verbrugghe's bike hit Pierrick Fédrigo and sliced past his head. Canada broke his right collarbone; Verbrugghe tumbled down a bank and into a ditch and broke his leg. Kessler managed to ride on but in a state of shock and came in 12 minutes down. Meanwhile, Fédrigo and Salvatore Commesso were racing for home. Unable to drop the Italian on the final descent – and mindful of what had happened to Beloki – Fédrigo waited for Commesso to make the move, which he did, 150m from the line. 'But, I had more guile than him,' said the Frenchman. 'That's not often the case with the Italians.' His victory was the first in the Tour for his Bouygues-Telecom team, in its seven-year existence.

And so to the Alps.

Stage 15. Gap – l'Alpe d'Huez, 187km: col d'Izoard, 2,360m, hors catégorie; col du Lautaret, 2,085m, second category; l'Alpe d'Huez, 1,850m, hors catégorie. Fearsome.

The 10km between the small village of Arvieux (1,600m) at the foot of the Izoard to the summit are reckoned by many riders to be amongst the most difficult on any Tour itinerary, and it's not just the gradient: upwards of 12 per cent near the top, uneven slopes all the way, long straights lower down. The Izoard presents one of the most intimidating climbs in the mythology. The southern approach winds past the sinister orange rock stacks of the Casse Déserte towering out of a bleached lunar wasteland of stones like a petrified mudslide to either side of the exposed corniche. When the sun is full, its heat is merciless, its glare blinding. As the road twists through the parched gulch of the Broken Desert, the notch of the col cut into the bare shoulders of mountain appears impossibly far away, improbably high up. The Izoard looks hard every inch of the way. It is hard, every inch of the way. The Lautaret is not particularly grim a climb – Briançon, at the western foot of the Izoard, is, at 1,321m, the highest city in Europe, and the 764m of uphill to the Lautaret takes 28km. L'Alpe d'Huez is a brute, a dead-end which merits the double entendre.

Hincapie and de la Fuente broke early and were joined by some 25 riders, among them Axel Merckx, Fränk Schleck of Luxembourg (whose father, Johnny, rode for Ocaña) and Damian Cunego, surprise winner of the 2004 Giro d'Italia. (At the end of that season, aged 23, he was placed first in the UCI general rankings, the youngest rider ever to be so.) Merckx was there to police the move, de la Fuente to consolidate his lead in the mountains competition and Hincapie, presumably, to save face.

Although the average gradient of the whole climb of l'Alpe d'Huez hovers round 8 per cent, the first ramp is a horror, the perfect spot for hitting the opposition. With the escapees ahead of them, Klöden and Kessler did just that, taking Landis with them. Merckx waited for his leader to arrive and took on the relay. Gradually, the high pace told: Pereiro, Menchov, Evans fell away. Up the road, Cunego and Schleck pulled clear and rode in tandem to 2km from the finish, where Schleck attacked at ferocious speed. Cunego could not follow. Schleck has admitted to being 'always a bit afraid of attacking near the end. I always hesitate too much. Then I told myself that I had to try not to leave it to a sprint with Cunego.' Victory on one of the mythic climbs of the Tour was the spur. The mouse had turned. Landis came in with Garzelli and Klöden, looking unruffled. To those who lamented his lack of panache, he replied that 'this is a tactical game, and for now my tactics are working'. One French commentator mused that either he was very confident, biding his time, or else he was bluffing and not feeling as good as he affected.

Boonen was certainly not feeling good: he abandoned early on in the stage. At some point, he will have to decide where to place his ambitions for the Tour de France in the general ensemble of his career in what has become a highly specialised sport. Sean Kelly certainly compromised his own performances in the Tour by his willingness to stretch the amazing versatility of his talent to extraordinary limits.

The next day's stage might seem to have delivered a resounding answer to questions about Landis's showing. On the final climb to Toussuire, the oldest ski resort in France, he cracked. In control up to that point, of himself if not of the leading bunch, he suddenly went off the back, sweat pouring out of him, his face ashen pale, his head sunk over the bars. It was sickening to watch. The climb isn't particularly hard – from 611m to 1,705m in 19km – but it closed a wicked day of climbing: 45.5km from the start to the col du Galibier, at 2,642m so often 'the roof of the Tour' . . . some 4km from Valloire to the col du Télégraphe, 1,566m . . . 23.5km to the col de la Croix de Fer, 2,067m . . . 6km to the col du Mollard, 1,630m . . . 79km of ascent all told.

Rasmussen, released from support duty for Menchov – who, at over 7 minutes down in general classification, looked unlikely to get onto the podium in Paris – was given licence to attack. He did so before the summit of the Galibier and stayed out in front all day. It was enough to give him the polka-dot jersey. He finished looking exhausted, on the verge of collapse, in tears with the strain.

On the lower slopes of the Toussuire, the dozen men in the yellow-jersey group seemed unlikely to catch the Dane, but, when Sastre attacked, some 11km from the finish, the group disintegrated. Menchov had tried unsuccessfully several times to get away and looked awful, but he kept coming back. Klöden had the support of five teammates, but Landis was alone, Merckx having fallen away. The sight of the yellow jersey being dropped must surely pierce the hardest heart. I thought he must have got the bonk – he at first denied this, but probably in the way of not making excuses. Later, he confessed that he hadn't eaten for 20 minutes before the final climb: it was, then, surely the *fringale* that slew him. He certainly had the appearance of someone running on empty. Merckx even recovered sufficiently to ride back up to him and, doughty as ever, try to relay him back, but the American's legs had nothing. It's amazing that, at the close, he had conceded no more than 10m 4s. Lelangue spoke movingly of that 'moment of great solitude' when a rider experiences such a debilitating loss of power. 'All I could do was help him find the strength to go on to the top. I took out the earpiece, drove up alongside him to speak gently to him, looking him in the eye. Words to motivate him, just that.'

The chancy game of handing Pereiro yellow had gone badly wrong: the Spaniard, a short distance behind Sastre, regained the jersey. The amazing Dessel, sixth that morning, came in not far behind in company with his leader Moreau. The AG2R duo were really showing well, determined to prove that French riders were not second-rate.

Only 67 riders of the 147 still in the race crossed the line ahead of that day's time limit, behind Daniele Righi, at 37m 17s on the winner Rasmussen. Millar made the cut, at 25m 50s; Wiggins, at 44m 1s, did not. The jury of commissaires decided to extend the limit of 12 per cent on the winner's time to 14 per cent. Thus the men of the *grupetto* were reinstated, including the Venezuelan José Rujano, last man at 46 m 45s. He had crossed the Galibier on his own, managed to catch the survival autobus in the valley and was dropped again on the final ascent.

Landis was written off. The race must surely, now, be for Pereiro, in yellow, Sastre, at 1m 50s, or Klöden, a marginally better time-triallist than either, at 2m 29s. That said, the buoyant Dessel was now fourth, at 2m 43s. The *Equipe* cartoonist showed a mountain peak carved like an Easter Island head spitting out a single bone. Caption: 'Landis'.

Meeting the journalists that evening, Landis smiled before answering questions. And what do you say about a disappointment so profound and complete? 'A smile,' he said, 'is my weapon for making the bad things in life more manageable,' and added that, right then, all he really wanted to do was 'drink some beers'. He told *L'Equipe* later that he had felt shamed that day, 'the worst humiliation of my life'.

Overnight, something happened. Landis's parents had always

told him that all the difficulties he encountered were part of a grand plan worked out for him by God. He didn't accept that. 'I have to be in reality.' The reality was that he now trailed Pereiro by 8m 8s, and what to do about that?

The third, and final, day in the Alps crossed two first-category climbs, one second and an hors catégorie before the descent into Morzine, 200.5km away. For 130 of those kilometres, Landis was on the attack. An early break of 11 riders, launched by Patrice Halgand, eventually gained 11 minutes on a *peloton* with wiser things to do than chase a bunch of lunatics out for a dust-up with altitude. Then, on the climb of the col de Saisies, 1,650m, Landis attacked. Around 25km further down the road on the col des Aravis, 1,486m, he caught the escapees – minus Halgand, who had broken clear on his own – and, taking Sinkewitz with him, pressed on at speed. The pair caught and dropped the Frenchman. At the foot of the col de la Colombière, some 50km from where he had attacked, Landis, Sinkewitz still with him, had 8m 35s on Pereiro. At the start of the 16km climb to the col de Joux-Plane, 1,691m, the pair had a little over seven minutes. Landis, forcing the pace, went clear, stayed clear and rode down into Morzine 5m 42s ahead of Sastre and 7m 8s on Pereiro and Klöden. He had averaged 37.175kph over the day. Moreau, showing remarkable grit, came third.

It transpired that Eddy Merckx, who has been engaged as an advisor by the Phonak team – he went for a ride with them on the rest day in Gap – told Landis that his only chance was to attack early, take his rivals by surprise, make them think that he had gone far too soon. It was a tactic that Merckx himself had resorted to more than once, perhaps most famously in 1971 when the Spaniard Luis Ocaña gave him a beating (see p. 46 ff.). In any event, having lost so much, the American had nothing more to lose. Shit or bust, a new reality, confuse them . . . reckless? Reckless is when you chuck it all up in the air and don't let thought of the consequences drag you back down before your willpower has had its say. Landis himself described it as 'a hit of anger'.

'Earlier in the race, I would have liked to win it like Eddy but hadn't the means,' he said. 'After Wednesday's disaster, I had no choice but to try.' Pereiro, who insisted that he would never have attacked first the day before – Landis was a friend – said that he 'couldn't do much about Floyd today . . . he did an amazing ride, full stop, and when we needed collaboration behind to try to pull him back, we didn't get it'.

Pereiro held yellow by 12 seconds over Sastre and 30 seconds on Landis. Never in its history had a Tour been run so tight so close to the finish in Paris. The final time-trial would decide, and, on current form, Landis looked sure to take his Tour back, as the jargon puts it. His mechanical problems cost him dear in the first individual race against the clock in Rennes, but he still put 1m 40s into Pereiro and 1m 10s into Sastre.

Millar had tried a couple of times to 'nuke' the race, as he put it, and tried one last time on the stage out of Morzine. The attack didn't succeed, but his return to racing at the top level has been a remarkable show of courage and mental resolve. The extremes of effort which are routine when racing cannot easily be replicated, if at all, in training. However, the two-year ban gave him a huge jolt. Not only did it toughen his mind, it actually made him reflect more on his responsibilities as a professional. 'I never doubted I could finish this Tour,' he said. 'I never had problems, but then again I've never trained properly for a three-week race before. I once started the Vuelta without riding my bike for three weeks.' If he achieved what he did without proper training, what now? Time for another Millar.

The other Briton in the race, Bradley Wiggins, world and Olympic pursuit champion, riding his first Tour, was less sanguine. The transition from track to road is always a shock, and it has not been easy for Wiggins. I have the sense that the astonishing triumphs of his track career have actually added to the difficulty of a very different sort of graft. The psychological demands of going from zenith to nadir and starting again are daunting, indeed. His performance in the Prologue, where he was counted among the favourites, was disappointing. 'This race is so bloody hard,' he said, 'that I can't envisage doing it next year. I don't feel any excitement about it. This was my childhood dream, like being Olympic champion was, and I said after winning gold in Athens I didn't want to defend it. I'd love to win a stage in the Tour, but unless I win on the Champs-Elysées, I'd need to come back, and, at the moment, if I never ride it again, I'd be happy.' He has told the team that he will never ride again just for the sake of riding, because he needs to think about whether he can be competitive. Well, he changed his mind about Beijing; perhaps distance will lend enchantment to his view of the Tour. The last time that two Britons finished the Tour was in 1973, when Robert Millar (no relation) and Sean Yates made it to Paris.

The local prefecture issued a warning of frying temperatures on Friday's 18th stage from Morzine to Mâcon, centre of the wine trade on the south-east edge of the ancient duchy of Burgundy – 38° in the shade. There were still riders willing to kick up the pace in a last bid for a stage win, among them Leipheimer. He'd come to the race as a favourite for a top placing and, by and large, disappointed. He made a break but couldn't get away. However, one of his Gerolsteiner teammates, the Swiss Ronny Scholz, did, in company with two Italians, Matteo Tosatto and Cristian Moreni. Tossato gave Quick Step their only win of the Tour in the absence of the more likely stage winner, Boonen. The news of the day, however, was the announcement, at 4 p.m., that the T-Mobile management had sacked Ullrich. This after a judicial inquiry had opened in Bonn the day before into accusations against Ullrich, his teammate Sevilla and coach Pevenage.

The final time-trial covered a sickle-shaped course of 57km looping between Le Creusot, where the first locomotive in France was constructed, in 1838, and Montceau-les-Mines, at the heart of the industrial complex of the Dheune valley. The essential in a time-trial is rhythm, and a succession of small rises here made rhythm difficult. It was on pretty well the same course, though in the reverse direction, that Marco Pantani clinched his 1998 win.

Pereiro acknowledged that Landis was a better time-triallist than he, but promised to give his all to save the Tour, and there is no doubt that wearing the yellow jersey can lift a rider into new zones of effort. Dessel had proved it this year, just as Thomas Voeckler did in 2004.

Of the three contenders, Landis went first, chasing the best time of the day – 1h 7m 45s – posted by Serhiy Honchar, an average speed of around 50kph. The Tour first included an individual time-trial in 1934, the 90km between La Roche-sur-Yon, France's first 'new town', laid out in 1804, and Nantes. Antonin Magne, that year's winner, won it at a speed of around 36kph. Today's roads are better. The riders have more efficient, and lighter, bikes. They perfect technique and posture in wind tunnels and on the track. Most of them reconnoitre the route very carefully. Not Ullrich. Most warm up before the ramp on home trainers; a few take to the neighbouring roads.

Landis looked strong, shifting position in the saddle occasionally, but, as Sean Kelly pointed out, this is normal in a time-trial: small adjustments, a bit of a wriggle, finding the easier posture for maximal power. He did pay for the superhuman effort of Thursday's mammoth solo ride in the first few kilometres but was soon at all-out power.

Sastre and Pereiro had no choice but to hit the pace hard from the off. If either got news that Landis was up at the first time check, the drag on morale would be difficult to master. Sastre didn't hang on for long and eventually lost 3m 31s to Landis. Pereiro, however, held on doggedly. His upper body rolled – always a bad sign – he seemed to be trying to squeeze more speed out of the very handlebars, he lurched out of the saddle on the incessant undulations to counter the sapping toll they had on his legs, anything not to lose time. When he did see the lead go, there was still a podium place to ride for, and this he did with commendable tenacity. No one had placed him within minutes of standing by the winner in Paris before the race: now he was close. He made it. *Chapeau.*

Klöden came second by 41s, Landis third at 1m 11s, Pereiro a splendid fourth at 2m 40s.

The French place great store on the philosophical concept of fraternity, even if their political temperament would seem more generally at odds with the idea. Their Revolution, taking fraternity as one of its central doctrines, foundered in a rather less than brotherly suspicion. However, it was part of the zeitgeist. Schiller's 'Ode to Joy', used by Beethoven in his *Ninth Symphony*, has the line *'Alle Menschen werden Brüder'* – all men become brothers. Well, it can happen. When I talked to Chris Boardman at the Tour presentation ahead of the Grand Départ in London, 2007, he said the feeling of arriving in Paris, riding through the city and onto the

Champs-Elysées, the overwhelming feeling, after three gruelling weeks on the roads of France, was one of brotherhood with the rest of the *peloton*. The *Grande Boucle* bound them all together in an exceptional experience. A unique camaraderie.

As if to emphasise that, when the *peloton* raced along the Rue de Rivoli and across the Place de la Concorde for the first of the eight circuits up the Champs, the Russian Viatcheslav Ekimov, 40 years old, riding his 15th Tour in 15 starts, came to the front and waved at the crowd. It was his goodbye and a visible sign of the Tour brotherhood that he was allowed to go to the front on his own to make his adieux. Twice an Olympic pursuit champion, Ekimov had said he might try to equal Joop Zoetemelk's record of 16 Tours, but, after the finish, he said, 'I wish to do more, but I think it's pretty much done.'

In the final sprint, McEwen, who had made sure of the green jersey earlier in the week, went too soon, and Thor Hushovd, winner of the Prologue, completed a triumphant Tour by storming past and crossing the line several bike lengths ahead of the Australian. Landis took yellow. Pereiro was now second overall and Klöden third.

And so, once more, the Stars and Stripes rang out across Paris, and, sadly, the misfit Landis reverted to American type and did go in for the dumb-ass flag-waving bit. The French had reason to cheer, too: six stage wins, two yellow-jersey holders, two riders in the top ten.

★

POSTSCRIPT

I finished writing this chapter just before lunch on 27 July. Reports were coming through on the Internet that an unnamed rider had tested positive during the Tour de France, also that Floyd Landis had failed to turn up for a criterium in Chaam, Holland, the day before. His manager hadn't answered his phone. The organiser of the race, who'd laid out considerable sums of money, was, understandably, upset. As I went through to my kitchen, the phone rang: it was a reporter from Associated Press in Paris wanting to talk to me. I suggested that no firm conclusion could be drawn about Landis's failure to turn up for a race, although it was uncouth not to do so, not even to make an appearance, ride a couple of circuits and climb off – a small decency. (He had, after all, ridden a criterium in Denmark the day before.) True, there were signs of equivocation. He had been tight-lipped in the post-Tour press conference when asked to comment on the pre-Tour doping mess. 'I have nothing to say on the subject,' he said. 'I leave that to those who speak for the sport.' Then it was put to him that, as a winner of the world's greatest cycle race, he might give a clearer message to aspirant kids, denouncing the taking of performance-enhancing drugs. 'It's up to every child's parents to explain to them when they watch the race what the best decisions are. That's how my parents raised me, and that's the best way.' This is anodyne at best. (A day later, during an Internet press conference, he was asked, point-blank, whether he had ever taken performance-enhancing drugs and replied, 'I'll say no.')

After lunch, I went for a ride on roads not very far from where the Tour will pass next year, the leafy, unfrequented lanes of Kent where I live. But a prolonged period of months of extremely hard work at my desk had left me mentally drained. A ride which would normally buoy my spirits and clear me of fatigue became, instead, a two-hour joyless slog. The countryside is beautiful, the roads were as quiet as they ever are, the sun was shining but I was mentally inert and came back to the news that the rider had been named – Floyd Landis – and a message from the AP office in Washington, asking for a radio interview. It was all very melancholy.

Landis tested positive for an unnaturally high level of testosterone in the routine dope test of the stage winner after his lone exploit in the Alps to take back the yellow jersey. Testosterone, the principal male sex hormone, is secreted in the testes, also in the female ovaries but in a quantity 20 times smaller than in a man. The hormone has a virilising and anabolising effect, i.e. it promotes male physical characteristics and the growth of muscle mass and strength, increased bone density and the stimulation of linear growth and bone maturation. It also protects against osteoporosis, the degeneration of bone tissue. (Chris Boardman has habitually low testosterone levels, and, in forcing his body to endure the extreme regime of a professional cyclist day after day, he lost bone density at such a rate that he did eventually suffer from osteoporosis. He refused to take testosterone boosters, indeed, any drugs at all during his racing career. The likelihood is, therefore, that most professional cyclists do take doses of testosterone.) Its shadow, epitestosterone, also occurs naturally, but crucially the concentration of epitestosterone is not affected by the exogenous (i.e. artificial) administration of testosterone. The normal ratio of the two hormones is 1:1, and it can go up to 2:1. After a heavy training session, a weightlifter's testosterone level can rise significantly. The anti-doping authorities have ruled that a balance of 4:1 testosterone to epitestosterone is permissible, but that anything above 6:1 is presumed to be produced either by injection or, more commonly nowadays, by skin patches which deliver a steady absorption and eliminate the more undesirable effects of high testosterone levels, like aggression.

The dope-testing laboratory at Châtenay-Malabry pronounced the first of two urine samples – sample A – given by Landis after stage 17 to be positive. According to some sources, the ratio of testosterone to epitestosterone was 11:1, which is exorbitantly high. The clinic, the same laboratory which reported last year that early samples given by Armstrong were positive, informed the UCI, which, in confidence, then informed both rider and his team management. It was they who published Landis's name. The testing process, based on the spectometry of the density of the carbon isotope, is reckoned (not by everyone) to give indisputable proof of the presence of exogenous testosterone.

Another sample – sample B – subsequently tested positive. In accordance with their own rules, Phonak immediately sacked Landis. They claim that their anti-doping regulations are stricter than even those of the UCI.

Landis has leave to appeal and has consistently professed innocence, of course. They always do, to begin with, whatever the final outcome. In mitigation, Landis has said that not only has he had abnormally high testosterone levels since he was a kid, but he has been taking daily oral doses of the hormone – for a thyroid problem – for the past year. He also needs cortisone injections because of his damaged hip. And there is his well-known fondness for and consumption of beer. In a continuing blather of protestation, he later said that the night before his epic ride he had drunk a couple of beers and at least four glasses of Jack Daniels whisky, also that he was dehydrated, and so on. Ingesting alcohol may augment testosterone levels temporarily but only in women and then only for three or four hours. (The excuse of booze has been used before, notably by Ben Johnson and Dennis Mitchell, both banned for doping.)

Landis's responses were evasive to begin with, and they did little to allay suspicion. Now he was claiming that the level of his epitestosterone was abnormally low and this threw the ratio with his testosterone out wildly. It was certainly true that he had been presumed by the press to be guilty before due process of law, but the situation was murky. Why has not the UCI put a system in place whereby the B sample is tested by a second clinic? The extremely close links between the Châtenay-Malabry clinic and *L'Equipe* are open to some question, and mistakes have occurred. The former world champion mountain biker Paola Pezzo was cleared of a drug test in 1998, in part because of flaws in the laboratory's clinical procedures.

Interviewed on Radio 4's *Today* programme, he claimed that the UCI had behaved improperly in broadcasting his name before he had a chance to defend himself. This was plainly nonsense, and Pat McQuaid, the UCI president, rebutted it. Christian Prudhomme was already implying that Landis would not be allowed to be named winner and that, although such a form of victory could hardly be what Pereiro would seek, Landis had ridden the race and nothing could change that. As for a definitive decision, there was none. Three weeks after the arrival in Paris, no absolute decision had been taken. Prudhomme seemed to be working on the assumption that a positive test was a positive test, end of story. 'It goes without saying,' he declared, 'that, for us, Floyd Landis is no longer the winner of the 2006 Tour de France.' However, the Tour organisation are not empowered to disqualify him: it is for the UCI to name Pereiro the winner in his stead.

The Tour kicked out several favourites before the race – and in what other sport such a cull? – so it would do so unflinchingly, no matter how high the rider's status. As McQuaid replied when pressed to say that cycling has a high doping culture, yes, maybe it has, but it also has the highest culture of rooting out dope cheats of any sport. The evil is there across the board: cycling is doing most to combat it. There was but one positive test on the Tour; alas that it should be on the winner.

Meantime, Landis had engaged a Spanish doctor who has dealt with a number of cases involving positive testosterone tests, none of which have gone against the rider. (A while ago, Santiago Botero, also of Phonak, tested positive for testosterone at a time when his medical consultant was . . . Dr Fuentes of Madrid.) When Hamilton appealed against his positive test for blood doping, the case took 17 months to resolve. Stripped of his world time-trial title, he nonetheless has been allowed to retain his Olympic gold medal in the same discipline. His, and Landis's, sponsor Phonak have had enough and quit in late August. In the past three years, some nine of their riders have tested positive. Who knows how many other sponsors of the sport – like the German broadcasting network ZDF – will say that they signed up to a sports event not a publicity stunt for the pharmaceutical industry and dump it. (ZDF claim to have lost 43 per cent of their audience before the mountain stages because of the expulsions at the beginning of the Tour.) Skoda, for a long time official automobile sponsors of the race, also quit in late August.

For sure, a boost of artificial hormone overnight would not have swung Landis's performance from complete collapse to superhuman effort – exogenous testosterone works over a long period; it does not deliver a quick hit – but the question having been asked, an answer must be forthcoming. It was clear, shabbily clear, that Landis's lawyers had advised him to change tack, too: quit the equivocations; deny the charges outright. Yet, was this not the time for Landis to come clean and say that all riders, conscious of the lack of bone-strengthening inherent in cycling, as opposed to sports which stressed the bones more, take testosterone exogenously? And this in a week when the world 100-metre record holder, another American, Justin Gatlin, had also tested positive for excessive testosterone.

Each of the winners of all three major national tours in the past year – Ivan Basso, Giro d'Italia, Roberto Heras, Vuelta a España, and Floyd Landis, Tour de France – is tainted with this pestilence of doping. It is unworthy of this beautiful sport, unworthy and shaming.

The only other Tour winner to test positive was Pedro Delgado in 1988, but he was not stripped of his title, on a technicality (see p. 161). Cyrille Guimard said that after the Puerto affair he thought cycling was going in the right direction. Now? 'I hope we won't see Landis on a bike again. Let him go back to the Mennonites and carry on praying not to balls things up in the future.'

★

Two weeks after the end of the Tour, Phonak sacked Landis and his case lay before the USA Anti-Doping Agency, which would probably take at least a month to arrive at a verdict, but no guarantee of that, following which, the appeals, the re-appeals, the endless litigation. The UCI made no affirmative pronouncement, but they are notoriously slow to act. When David Millar confessed to taking EPO prior to his victory in the world time-trial championship in 2003, it took the ruling body a day short of a year to strip him of his jersey and award it to Michael Rogers, the Australian. Landis had been tested before the win at Morzine, and he was tested afterwards: why had the results not been positive then? American fans weighed in with their conspiracy theories, of course. One, who wrote anonymously to the *Herald Tribune*, describing himself as 'an avid cyclist and criminal-defense attorney', said of the French clinic at Châtenay-Malabry that it was staffed by technicians who, allegedly, were 'barely able to light a Bunsen burner'. And, 'Isn't it the same lab that tried to discredit Armstrong? Might there be animosity by [*sic*] the French against another American winner of their Tour?' He might have read the *Equipe* headline the day after Landis's 'victory', saluting him as a 'worthy winner'.

CHAPTER SEVENTEEN

2007

Sunshine in London . . . Squalls into Paris

The Greek historian Plutarch records that Julius Caesar summarily divorced his wife Pompeia on the grounds that 'his family must be above suspicion'. There was some whisper of hanky-panky and the man whom salacious Roman gossip twitted as 'every woman's husband and every man's wife' dumped her: he craved high office, she had become an embarrassment. The owners of the Tour de France (Amaury Sport Organisation, ASO) take a similar peremptory approach to any hint of pharmaceutical abuse. In the steamy heat of rumour, insinuation and febrile conjecture that is the world of sport these days, sanctimonious journalists who know little about cycling and care less take a seedy satisfaction in muck-raking. Ignorant prurience fuels their disdain. When I told people that I had embarked on my write-up of this year's race, some raised their eyebrows. In their unspoken dismay I read the question *How? Isn't the Tour finished, discredited, tarnished with scandal, a seamy bed of corruption, deceit and disavowal?* I give you no slick response. There is much to confront.

In late May, Bjarne Rijs, the first Dane to win the Tour (1996), Rolf Aldag (now a manager with T-Mobile) and Erik Zabel, winner of a record six green points jerseys (1996–2001), admitted, spontaneously, to having taken EPO when they rode for the Deutsche Telekom team – Zabel once, Rijs between 1993 and '98. Rijs – 'my yellow jersey is in a case, they can come and get it if they want' – is now *directeur sportif* of the CSC team. He sacked his big star, Ivan Basso, last year on suspicion – Basso had *let him down.* After judicial investigation into Operación Puerto (see p. 345), Basso was banned for two years, despite foreseeable protestations of innocence. (T-Mobile, Telekom's reincarnation, with new managers has initiated draconian measures against drug-taking.) Rijs was barred from the Tour and his name has been expunged from the roll of winners, as has Zabel's green-jersey win in 1996. Another former Telekom rider, Jörg Jaksche, confessed he had doped but said the directors of the team (which he joined in 1999) 'knew everything. Doping was systematic.' The managers dismissed his comments as fabrication. That Johan Bruyneel had recruited Basso for the American Discovery Channel in November 2006 was considered ethically dubious at the very least. He later sacked him.

Zabel's lachrymose confession was repeated again and again at the top of every news report on German television. Inevitably, suspicion also fingered Zabel's East German compatriot Jan Ullrich, another Telekom man, winner in 1997. Interviewed in *L'Equipe*, Ullrich, now retired, spoke of his happiness and fulfilment away from the *peloton*. The German press reacted bitterly. The sinister miasma of state-organised doping of athletes under the GDR jaundices their opinion, understandably: Ullrich had made a pile of money, squandered a unique talent and still denied taking drugs. Talking about his untroubled new life to the *French* journal which has been so strident in its denunciation of cheats was galling.

This year's hot favourite, Alexandr Vinokourov, excluded in 2006 because his team had been reduced to four, now headed the Astana team. Invited to ride on a wild-card entry, sponsored by a number of companies in his native Kazakhstan and devoted to the victory of their fiery leader, their colours salute the golden sunburst and duck-egg blue of the national flag. Smarting at the injustice of his exclusion in 2006, Vinokourov had gone off and won the Vuelta a España. However, the stink of Operación Puerto clung to him. He has also consulted the man the French press calls 'sulphurous', i.e. 'diabolical', Dr Michele Ferrari, who advised Armstrong. Vinokourov, an impulsive attacking racer, responded vehemently: 'Ferrari is the best at physical preparation. Why do you think that training means doping? It has nothing to do with what Ferrari may have done 10 years ago.' This may be true – Ferrari was absolved of sporting fraud charges on appeal in 2006 – but it is also true that he who sups with the Devil, even a supposed devil, should use a long spoon.

The Tour organisers regarded Oscar Pereiro ungainsayably as the reigning champion, but made him number 11. The absence of a number 1 pointed to the fact that the Landis case was still *sub judice*: Landis and his lawyers against the various agencies – national federation, American and international anti-doping authorities, UCI, ASO. Landis has just published an apologia (*Positively False: The Real Story of How I Won the Tour de France*). Asked to comment, a passer-by in San Francisco said Landis's win was 'an awesome achievement . . . Perhaps he did dope, but we all know what happens in cycling. He was still the best out there. You gotta respect the man for that . . .' Not a very wholesome stance. And, on a day when Gary Player was reported as saying that 'drug-taking is rife in golf', you think, *What next? Curling?*

Pereiro was now with Caisse d'Epargne though his teammate Alejandro 'El Imbatabile' Valverde had a more obvious claim to be leader. However, Valverde had been leading the Vuelta when Vinokourov made a do-or-die attack. The 'Unbeatable' dithered and . . . got beat. The Spaniard Carlos Sastre, a dependable climber but no great time-triallist, rode well for the CSC team after Basso was kicked out in 2006 but could not realistically think beyond a podium place. The Australian Cadel Evans, a good all-rounder, as any winner must be, lacks a certain enterprise but is a remarkable stayer. Andreas Klöden, another East German, second overall in 2004 and third in 2006, was clearly a potential winner, except that he was riding for Vinokourov's Astanas. Denis Menchov (Vuelta winner in 2005), of Rabobank, alongside the 2005–06 King of the Mountains Michael Rasmussen, Yaroslav Popovych, Alberto Contador (winner of the 2007 Paris–Nice) and Levi Leipheimer, teammates in Discovery Channel, each had some claim to attention in a race that was as open as the last edition.

The 24-year-old Contador had been first signed as a pro by Manolo Sáiz, one of the more elusive personages in cycling's demi-monde, and, as a member of the Astana-Würth team (managed by Sáiz), had been implicated in Operación Puerto. Later cleared, he joined the American team, part-owned by Lance Armstrong.

Attempting to obviate suspicion, the UCI produced what might be called a letter of indemnity which all Tour riders were required to sign, a promise to ride clean on forfeit of a year's salary if they were found guilty of cheating. A number of riders, mostly Spanish, refused. Rasmussen also demurred on the grounds that the document constituted invasion of privacy and was not legally tenable. Under coercion, the recalcitrants signed. The threat of financial penalty was probably a gaffe, the signature worthless in legal terms, yet crying 'invalid' showed just how mired in litigious pettifogging the sport has become. This was not an affidavit but an undertaking of honour, a solemn open declaration of good faith. The contract that no court of law would uphold is just the sort you have to keep.

At the launch of London's hosting of the Grand Départ, early in 2006, Jean-Marie Leblanc, ex-Tour rider and former director of the race, spoke with huge pleasure and pride at the twinning of two of Europe's great capitals at either end of the *Grande Boucle*. The Tour de France would race on a circuit with a backdrop of some of England's most distinctive landmarks and then sweep out of the city into the Garden of England for stage one. I know Leblanc a bit, a man of great warmth and bonhomie. That spirit infused the whole joyous, festive, ebullient day, when the Tour circus swung into action round Whitehall, Westminster, Green Park, Hyde Park and the Serpentine, to finish on The Mall.

In 2006, I'd been involved in an outdoor spectacular which covered some of that same ground, staged by the French theatre group Royale de Luxe. *The Sultan's Elephant* came to town and the people reclaimed the streets. That is what the Tour de France has been doing since its inception, an anarchic, demotic, rolling roadshow on the popular machine and Londoners and visitors showed that the stuffy English can turn out and cheer a bike race, too, for the sheer dizzy fun of it.

For six weeks it had rained and rained and rained. On Saturday, 7 July – 7 7 2007, second anniversary of the bombing atrocities – the sun blazed forth and blessed the party.

Susanne and I arrived early – I had to give an interview on

Sky News. The crowds were already massing. A temporary bridge crossed the route through Westminster Square and two-way crocodiles of spectators filed patiently over it. Whitehall was packed. Policemen were giving mannerly directions to the nearest coffee house. The mood was convivial, the excitement bubbling, the hot-dog stalls already in full swing, the front page of *L'Equipe* was in English.

There were five Britons riding, the most since the ill-fated entry of the ANC team in 1987: David Millar, Bradley Wiggins, Charly Wegelius, Mark Cavendish and the 21-year-old Geraint 'the Penguin' Thomas, benjamin of the race. Thomas won gold on the track in the Junior Worlds in 2004 as well as the junior Paris–Roubaix and is one of the first riders to progress from the British Cycling Academy into the professional *peloton*. Cavendish has shot to the front of the pack as a rated sprinter – old hands like Robbie McEwen have watched the flying Manxman go past and felt the weight of their years. Wegelius has spent his racing career in Italy and had never ridden the Tour before. (At the world road race in Madrid in 2005, he tactlessly rode for an Italian teammate, *not* the Great Britain leader, Roger Hammond.) Wiggins grew up in Maida Vale, the Prologue route along the Serpentine was his boyhood piste and at the world track championships in April he once more took gold for the pursuit. I interviewed him beside the Herne Hill track on Good Friday. Everyone wanted a piece of him – clubmen, photographers, journalists, eager kids, adoring fans – but I got my time at last. He sat on the grass next to his bike and bag, wearing the rainbow jersey, for all the world just another racer. The Prologue was his big objective, of course, merely to ride it in his native city was 'a crazy dream'. His chances were high. Millar was another favourite for the 7.9km opener. 'The London course is beautiful, a classic,' he said. 'Wide, fast roads. It will be spectacular. I'm really looking forward to it.' He added that because the route was not very technical (i.e. the corners aren't too tight) it would suit the current world time-trial champion, Fabian Cancellara, and the first yellow jersey of the 2005 Tour, David Zabriskie.

On the eve of the ride, however, Millar confessed to being 'riddled with self-doubt'. The short time-trial is, more than anything, a test of nerve and mental poise. Physical class goes to nought without settled cool. 'I have never spent so long feeling so horrible,' Millar said, after early season crashes and over-training.

In the event, neither Millar nor Wiggins came close. Cancellara rode a stunning 8 minutes 50 seconds to beat Klöden by 13 seconds and George Hincapie and Wiggins by 23 seconds. He was going so fast up Constitution Hill that he almost caught the motorbike escorts. Millar ceded 33 seconds. When I spoke to him briefly afterwards, the sickening nervous tension had gone. 'I'm just going to enjoy it, now,' he said. Stuart O'Grady crashed into the straw bales on one corner but was, fortunately, the only casualty.

Sunday, 8 July. Bidborough Ridge, Kent. 11 a.m.
The route led eastwards out of London into the Garden of England.

The ugly straight graceless steepish ramp of flint-chip concrete leading south out of Tonbridge on the A227 which we Kentish cyclists know as Quarry Hill had been rechristened the côte de Southborough, a fourth category climb counting towards the mountains prize. Our party assembled at a rendezvous on a grassy bank near the Bidborough turn-off. I'd discussed strategy with Luke and June. Luke couldn't join us: he was doing moto duty for his old friend Graham Watson whose regular driver chose not to cross the Channel twice in the weekend. 'Hey, man,' I said, 'you're going to miss lunch.' Luke shook his head dolefully. 'I'm gutted,' he said.

The advance guard set out from my house with three one-shot barbecues, locally made links (sausages), buns, bin bags, beer, red and white wine, cake and nibbles. We cheated a Road Closed sign on a narrow crinkum-crankum bucolic lane essential to the prevised plan of approach and, our hardy peradventure paying off handsomely, got the car plus heavy cargo to within yards of the route and unloaded the goodies. Always *such* a giggle to outmanoeuvre the Tour de France's stern embargo on any access by car. Naturally, I should have preferred to go by bike, but I couldn't bank on any ad hoc trawl of loaves and fishes. My powers of miraculous transformation, dormant as they are, yielded to the more solid promise of actual grub. We set up our pitch. A toddler lay on a blanket nearby under an umbrageous plane tree, having her nappy changed, wide-eyed with wonder at all that was going on round her. None of my friends had ever seen the Tour either, so newcomers of all ages were in sweet accord. June trekked up from Tonbridge with essential supplies of ketchup, mustard and plastic cups. We then greeted an intrepid posse of invitees from London bringing extra tuck – lamb chops, burgers, salads and chilled rosé. We were, all told, a splendidly cosmopolitan bunch: English, German, Polish, half Chinese, South African, French, Italian and Spanish. Why, even the publicity caravan's loud speakers greeted all Kent in Jacques Tati English: 'Wall-cum to zee Tor der Frahnce.'

Millar, angry with his performance in the Prologue, attacked early on the 203km to Canterbury. He can have had no illusions about a stage win but there was the polka-dot jersey to grab over three fourth-category climbs. Joined by four others, he took maximum points on the road near us, cheered sonorously as he went through – French motorbike gendarmes leading the way – rousing cries of 'Go David', instead of the continental 'Daveed' more familiar to his ears. Luke and Graham pulled up and we handed Luke a hot dog. Watson had already eaten and didn't take a photo of us. Can you believe that?

Pipped by Stéphane Augé on the Goudhurst climb, Millar zipped up the final lift of the day at Farthing Common and, equal on points with the Frenchman, took the jersey because he was higher placed on general classification. That put him on the podium, good news for his sponsors.

The break was swallowed up and, 25km from the finish, Cavendish collided with a spectator, fell heavily and had to wait for a bike change. He had to chase without any team support, his chance of contesting the home sprint dashed. Five kilometres on, another pile-up took out Robbie McEwen. He bruised a knee and an elbow. Ridden back up by his teammates, in a furious mood, he shot out of the hidden gap that no one else in the jostling pack ever spots and took victory 'on pure rage . . . In the final kilometre of a Tour stage, you don't feel that pain.' When he got off the bike, however, even the euphoria of victory was no anaesthetic: his wrist hurt so much he thought (wrongly) that he had broken it.

Some four million people are reckoned to have watched the Tour pass through on only its third visit to England and the reception was so enthusiastic, so buoyant, that even seasoned pros had never seen such large crowds. The organisers were rapt in praise of the colossal popular success, proof, indeed, of the seductive, perhaps inexplicable, lure of the great bike race. The taxi driver who took me to the airport some ten days' later en route to the Pyrenees told me his son had suggested going to see the race near their home in Goudhurst. 'I'd rather watch paint dry,' he said, but went anyway. 'It was three hours' magic,' he said. 'Absolutely amazing, fantastic, wouldn't have missed it.' The very sentiments of my friends, Tour virgins, on Bidborough Ridge.

Poor Cavendish got caught up in another crash 2.5km out of the finish in Ghent on stage two, suffered abrasions but no worse. (Any rider who falls in the final 3km of any stage gets the same time as the first rider to cross the line ahead of the crash.) Race leader Cancellara also went down, so, too, did Thomas but he chirpily dismissed the setback: 'I landed on some fat sprinter.' On the line, in their native Belgium, Tom 'Tornado' Boonen and his lead-out man, Geert Steegmans, crossed together. Steegmans, who recognises how stressful is the responsibility of being a leader and assuredly not for him, is nevertheless quick to dice on a win and, believing that his man was coming through, actually stole victory from Boonen by a valve-length. A neat two-step for the boys from Quick Step.

Stage three ended in Compiègne outside the imperial palace, start place of the doyen of the classic one-day races, the Paris–Roubaix. The 2006 winner, Cancellara, nickname 'Spartacus', learnt his trade from Paul Koechli, Bernard Hinault's trainer. (The induction test was to ride a kilometre flat out. 'It was the hardest kilometre I've ever ridden, and the longest and it's not finished yet.') He launched his sprint a reckless 500m from the line into Compiègne, even as the *peloton* swept past the four breakaways (two of whom had gone clear at 6km) and held on to win by three bike lengths. 'When we passed the entrance to the Arenberg Forest, the amphitheatre of the Roubaix, I got goose pimples,' he said.

The race route passed through the village of Lombardsijde,

birthplace of one of the Tour's finest ever sprinters, Freddy Maertens. He watched from the roadside and gave an illuminating interview to *L'Equipe*. He regretted the advent of earpieces, the constant intervention of *directeurs sportifs*. 'There's no room for improvisation and springing surprises. But, I'm not nostalgic . . . times change. Still, I love a guy like McEwen who doesn't need anyone, just him on his own against the big trains. [He means the long line of *domestiques* working for a sprinter, such as Mario Cipollini enjoyed.] He'd be my favourite because he's the most eccentric, the most unexpected.'

Next day, news broke that the German Matthias Kessler, of Vinokourov's Astana team, had tested positive for testosterone after the Flèche Wallonne in April.

Thor Hushovd cleared the line in Joigny to take his fifth tour stage win. Cavendish, ninth the day before, came in tenth, showing remarkable resilience after the horrors of the first two days. Boonen, who had not yet finished a Tour, pulled on the green points jersey. He'd had a poor season so far, the Belgian press had given him a roasting – not only was he failing to win what they expected him to win, notably a third Tour des Flandres in succession, but he'd decamped to a life of ease and flash cars in Monaco. If his form had slipped, the points prize might shut the moaning Flemish minnies up.

The Italian *Gazzetta dello Sport* trumpeted their man Filippo Pozzato's triumph on the next stage into Autun – 'Che gioia' – but the Kazakh press must surely have keened with wild Slavic gloom over the catastrophe of the day: Vinokourov, fall.

First, with 75km to ride, Klöden went over the handlebars trying avoid a rider in front who had just braked and copped a haematoma and a cracked coccyx. If that were not bad enough – a back injury renders climbing distinctly problematic – 25km from the finish, Vinokourov's chain jumped, he went down and sustained deep cuts in both knees and lacerations on his thigh. Six of his team men tried to relay him back to the lead group who were, by then, winding up like a turbine for the sprint. One by one the Astanas worked themselves to a standstill and, finally, it was Vinokourov alone, driving himself along over the last five or so kilometres. The commissaires forbade him to take draughting from the second team car, an unnecessarily harsh application of the rules – he was, after all, racing back after a crash. He came in 1 minute 20 seconds down on the pack and all the other favourites. He emerged from the hospital in Beaune at 23h45, fifteen stitches in each gashed knee, the surgeon having sewn them up with the limbs in the bent position so that the rotary effort of pedalling would not tear the sutures. Vinokourov was adamant that he would not abandon. 'It's maddening,' he said, 'because I very rarely fall – when I do, I do it big time. But, no surrender. I know how to suffer and I am here to win.'

Wiggins has been outspoken in his hostility to drug-takers: they are cheats who should be banned for life, without appeal. On Friday, 13 July, stage six, 199.5km across the undulating countryside of the Mâcon to the threshold of High Savoy, he made a point. It was the 40th anniversary of the death of Tom Simpson, whose ingestion of stimulants hastened the debilitation in a body pushed beyond endurance (see p. 185 ff.). Wiggins cut loose from the bunch 2km from the start and, at 75km, had built a lead of 17 minutes 20 seconds. He eventually rode 191km on his own and the television image of his recapture, a mere 3km from the line, was melancholy indeed: the leviathan of the *peloton* powering up at a speed his weary legs could never counter to swallow him whole, a red shirt lost in the variegated mass and spat out at the far end to limp home, congratulated by his *directeur* in the car, his job done, the day's combativity prize some consolation.

Boonen had issued a warning in London: 'Watch out. The Boonen who wins races that ordinary riders will lose is back' and in Bourg-en-Bresse the famine was over. He took his fifth Tour stage win and announced that he was going to study the stage profiles to check where Zabel might rob him of points in the green jersey competition.

Vinokourov made it home but his morale was low: he was hard put to accommodate excruciating pain, extreme discomfort, no recovery time. On the eve of the first Alpine stage the *Equipe* cartoon showed riders confronted by a vertical brick wall up which runs a white line: 'Now we're there.' For all his tenacity and courage, Vinokourov's chances of surviving the mountains were slim indeed. However, the doctor reported that his muscles still exhibited amazing tonicity, given his injuries, and, as the man insisted, Kazakhs are not like normal mortals.

On Bastille Day 1997, Jan Ullrich won the tenth stage of the Tour in Telekom pink on his way to overall victory. Ten years later, another young German in T-Mobile pink, Linus Gerdemann, won the seventh stage, the young riders' white jersey *and* the yellow jersey. Not looking to overall victory, Gerdemann nevertheless gave hope of a clean start to a nation traumatised by the doping scandals. There is much talk of the need for the younger generation of riders to take the lead against illicit drugs – Zabel himself made the appeal in an interview during the Bremen Six-Day race in January. Gerdemann is a rider of evident class and he stressed that his team's intolerance of any misdemeanour 'must show people that cycling can be clean. It will certainly not come through the old school.' He came to cycling after breaking a leg as a kid and spending several months on an exercise bike to rehabilitate his muscles.

Gerdemann and five others broke clear at 40km, more joined and they reached the foot of the col de la Colombière with a lead of 4 minutes 30 seconds. The 16km of climbing starts easily enough but the group disintegrated and, just over halfway to the pass, where the slopes crank up to around 10 per cent, Gerdemann attacked and went for home. It was too soon. He almost cracked in the final kilometres but topped the summit with 19 seconds on a lone pursuer, Inigo Landaluze, and 3 minutes on the group containing all the favourites. He went full out for home down the final 14.5km – Landaluze arrived at the col near spent and had little left for the chase – and rode in for a wonderful solo victory. Cancellara had enjoyed a week in yellow and would now work for Sastre and Fränk Schleck. Vinkourov, 'the hardest man in the *peloton*' in Sean Yates' view, amazingly arrived with the rest of the favourites.

Cavendish was all but finished, bowed by fatigue, at the limit of his strength.

The Sunday before the Tour sets off is traditionally reserved on the racing calendar for the various national road race championships. (The British event had to be postponed because of the flooding in Yorkshire.) Christophe Moreau has long carried French hopes of a big showing in their *Grande Boucle*. Shorter on talent and fighting spirit than flattery (or chauvinism) can inspire, he has never delivered. However, he not only won the most prestigious of the Tour's warm-up races, the Dauphiné Libéré, but the mountains prize, too and, making a bold solo attack some way off the finish of the French championship, took the tricolour jersey. Would this be Moreau's, France's, year?

On the second Alpine stage, over 77km of punishing lower hurdles into a wilderness of high rock and thin air – Cormet de Roselend 1,967m, Hauteville 1,639m and the summit finish in Tignes 2,068m – Moreau showed flair and strength, if not much nous.

The feisty Thomas Voeckler stirred the action early and was joined by a small group of chancers, including Millar. Behind them, the Rabobank team marshalled a chase and shot their ace climber Rasmussen into a lead group of six on the climb of the Roselend at 93km. They crossed the col with an advance of five minutes five seconds on the main group of favourites, among them Gerdemann, battling to save the yellow, and it was Moreau who, nearing the finish, took on the arduous task of pursuit.

Rasmussen cut free of his companions some 18km from Tignes and went on alone. Around the same point that he went clear, Moreau stirred. Iban Mayo, the temperamental Basque climber now riding with Millar in the Saunier-Duvals, counter-attacked, but the rest of the group, which included Contador and Popovych from the Discovery Channel, Evans, Valverde, Schleck and Vinokourov's lieutenant Andreï Kashechkin, sat tight. They allowed Moreau to do all the work into a fairly stiff headwind, then reeled him in as he tired and watched him go again and reeled him in again. However, Moreau had shown bravely and put a lot of time into the favourites in the chasing bunch. For a heady interval, it did seem possible – to the French press, at any rate – that he even had a chance of overall victory. A number of ex-riders – Hinault, Guimard, Poulidor et al – agreed. Only the eminently pragmatic Laurent Fignon pooh-poohed. '*A priori, non.*' On past form, no. He had made a novice's mistake in attacking so often on easy slopes into the wind and, look, when Mayo hit him the day before, he'd had no answer.

Rasmussen took the stage and yellow from Gerdemann by a

mere 23 seconds (plus the 20-second winner's bonus) and the loyal Klöden rode in with Vinokourov, 4 minutes 29 seconds down. The day had a heavier toll: on the descent of the Roselend, Michael Rogers, leader of T-Mobile, in the breakaway group, fell badly, dislocated his shoulder and had to abandon. His exhausted teammate Cavendish had already gone. Another T-Mobile, Patrick Sinkewitz, riding away from the finish, collided with an elderly spectator, put him in a coma, broke his own nose and had to withdraw.

On that same descent, O'Grady, surprise winner of that April's Paris–Roubaix, careered off the road and sustained shocking injuries: five broken ribs, a broken collarbone, severe bruising of the spine and perforation of the lung. His compatriot McEwen, in severe pain from the earlier crash, had been riding on willpower. Finally, his body gave out. He came in over 40 minutes down on the winner's time and was eliminated.

After the rest day, out of the hotels straight onto the col de l'Iseran (2,772m) on whose airy summit, in 1959, the triple-winner Louison Bobet climbed off and bid the Tour adieu. Thence, a long descent to the foot of the col du Télégraphe and, beyond it, the Giant of the Alps, Henri Desgrange's favourite instrument of suffering, the col du Galibier (2,645m).

Rasmussen, aiming now for yellow rather than polka dots, simply marked his rivals and the Colombian Mauricio Soler of the wild card entry Barloworld (the team, registered in Britain, has a South African sponsor) made the winning break on the final climb, dropped the lead group and went on alone. He fled down the descent of 44km into Briançon, nearly wilted on the nasty 1.5km uphill to the finish – one 700m section of the haul is at 13 per cent – but held on to take only the second win of his career. Not the handiest of riders, prone to falls, he thanked God for aiding his victory – there was, he said, no other explanation.

On the run-in, Marcus Burghardt rode straight into a corn-gold Labrador. *Coup de chien* . . . dust-up. His front wheel folded in two and the dog wandered off, apparently unhurt, as, luckily, was Burghardt. The dog's owner – clot – bumbled up, dozily unconcerned, and ushered the bewildered hound off the road.

Vinokourov had led the race over the Galibier in 2005. This day he toiled wretchedly and lost a further 3 minutes 24 seconds. The television camera caught him sketching a cut-throat gesture. Time and physical distress were irreducibly against him. Nevertheless, like 'the Badger' (the famously aggressive Hinault's nickname) who fights back when he is cornered, Vinokourov wasn't yet finished.

The tenth stage from Tallard into Marseille went to an all-French photo-finish: ten years after his first Tour win and the yellow jersey with it, Boonen's teammate Cédric Vasseur edged out Sandy Casar by a wine-taster's nose. This marked the 21st win for a Frenchman in the 33 times the Tour has arrived in the southern Mediterranean city anciently founded as a Greek colony.

In the first of the heavy shocks weathered by the race this year, the T-Mobile team withdrew from the race. I have no taste for the expression 'zero tolerance' as mouthed at me by a piece of lowlife heat fining me thirty-odd quid for riding up onto the pavement outside Charing Cross station forecourt to dismount, but the German team management has sworn instant dismissal of dopers. A random UCI test on Sinkewitz, taken in June, was finally declared positive, another of their riders (not in the Tour) Serhiy Honchar was also named and the team pulled out. The *Berliner Zeitung* had renounced coverage of the race, Adidas threatened to withdraw sponsorship, and two television channels, ARD (*Arbeitsgemeinschaft der öffentlich-rechtlichen Rundfunkanstalten der Bundesrepublik Deutschland* – 'Consortium of public-law broadcasting institutions of the Federal Republic of Germany', a joint organisation of Germany's regional public-service broadcasters) and ZDF (*Zweites Deutsches Fernsehen* – 'Second German Television', a public-service channel), already angered by the confessions of former Telekom riders, packed up their cameras and left for home. This entailed a huge loss of revenue to the Tour organisation.

The headline in *L'Equipe* punned on their darling's ill fortune: 'Moreau loses his footing'. On the long flat exposed stage between Marseille and Montpellier, the French champion crashed after the first Hot Spot sprint at 31.5km and, as the *peloton* raced ahead at above 50kph, he and his team men, under extreme pressure, struggled to get back on – they'd have had to be hitting around 60kph. To compound Moreau's misery, one of his shoe cleats had been damaged in the fall. Ahead of them, another break, Millar included, cut loose and the tempo stayed hot. Moreau did stop to change the shoe before the cleat gave way but the wind had got up and the bunch was split into three. Outside the feeding station in Arles, Vinokourov's Astanas moved up to the front of the chasing *peloton* and, according to one of the motorbike drivers, 'they put the hammer right down, the first time Vino was turning his legs like a trackie'. As the mistral – that ferocious blast, one of 'the scourges of Provence' – blew across the road, the Kazakh train strung out in a long arrow formation, the echelon, which gives some shelter to the riders tucked in down the line but at such velocity that anyone not hooked on is forced to the far gutter without any protection from the wind. The line in the gutter stretches and snaps as unsheltered riders weaken and lose contact. The French call this *un coup de bordure*, a gutter hit. Moreau and his men, already pooped after their chase, buckled and lost some 3 minutes 20 seconds on the day. Millar, who had bridged a long gap to join the breakaway, said that 'it took years off my life getting across to that break and Astana wrecked my plans'. Latterly, he has fallen prey to a persistent allergy to heat and had to cover his arms in long sleeves and plaster his legs (angry red with a rash) in sunscreen to block out the sultry heat from a 30° sun. He also had to go to bed wrapped in damp towels. He came close to quitting. As if riding the Tour were not enough punishment.

For the underrated Barloworld team, there was, this burning hot day, further rejoicing. One win had surely justified their budget for the year. Now the South African Robert Hunter, riding his sixth Tour and so close to a win on several occasions, outsprinted a clutch of ace fast men, including Cancellara and Pozzato.

(Responding precipitately to a furious reaction from the German viewers, ARD and ZDF resumed transmission.)

Later that evening, news broke that the Danish Cycling Union [DCU] had announced *in June* that they would not be selecting Rasmussen for either this year's Worlds or the 2008 Olympics. The UCI had been informed, the ASO had not.

Rasmussen had missed, or ignored, four routine drugs tests,

two to be administered by the DCU, two by the UCI. Normally if a rider fails to turn up for three such summonses, he is automatically deemed to be guilty of drug-taking but because they issued from different sources, 2+2 did not, on this occasion, = 3. Further, Rasmussen's Rabobank managers claimed, somewhat disingenuously, not to have known exactly where their man was in the month before the Tour – he had not supplied, nor had they asked for, his schedule of training – and therefore not to have been monitoring his form, his training, his morale. This was distinctly odd. Rasmussen's wife is Mexican, they live in Italy and his racing licence has been registered in Monaco. But he was possibly also registered in Mexico where, he insisted, he'd gone for a month's preparatory training ahead of the Tour. The DCU had declared that if he was not registered with them and thereby subject to their stringent regulations *and* had flunked two of their tests, he could not ride for them. Rasmussen said that having no computer with him in Mexico he could not receive e-mails. He had written to the UCI saying yes, he knew he'd missed *one* test, then, no, it was *two* he'd missed but that his failure to report was nothing more sinister than 'an administrative error'. His vagaries convinced no one that he was talking straight.

The antagonism between the UCI president, Pat McQuaid, and the ASO men, boss Patrice Clerc and Tour director Christian Prudhomme, inflamed a prickly situation. The Pro Tour series of races established by McQuaid's predecessor, Hein Verbruggen, does not feature a number of prestigious races (including the Tour de France) organised by the ASO. The Pro Tour, a UCI confection, has none of the standing or popular appeal of the Great Bike Race, a further irritant. McQuaid said that Rasmussen's exclusion by the DCU was an internal affair, nothing to do with the UCI, although, contradictorily, he had also expressed the strident opinion that if Vinokourov won the Tour it would not be a credible victory, so intense was the suspicion that clung to him. The UCI's anti-doping manager had spoken of 'certain riders liable to be identified during the Tour'. A veiled threat to undermine the race in progress? Why not name them outright? Clerc told *L'Equipe* that he and McQuaid had not spoken since March and that Rasmussen was not comporting himself in accordance with the Tour regulations. If he had known about his ban from the DCU, he or his team should have told the ASO before the Tour. UCI, ASO, national federations, WADA (the World Anti-Doping Agency) team managements, all professing to serve the sport, yet looking to their own interests without any sign of meaningful discussion let alone consensus. The lack of liaison is most damaging. Suspicion is allayed by hard evidence and, justly or not, fomented by silence.

In Castres, Boonen won his second stage, resplendent in the green jersey and showing some of his characteristic panache.

Albi. Saturday, 21 July.
The e-mail which swam onto my screen last autumn began 'You probably don't remember me . . .' True, the sender has a distinctive name, Nigel Dick, but I *did* recall him as a pupil who left school not long after I'd arrived as head of Classics. Then, it clicked: we'd played rock and roll guitar together in the first concert I ever put on at the place. So, here we were in Albi, Nigel, a film-maker based in Los Angeles, and I, working on a project to make a documentary about the *lanterne rouge*. The Tour de France being the only race wherein a certain kudos attaches to the man who comes in last, because simply finishing is a considerable achievement, we thought this would be a good angle with which to tempt the *you don't win you're nowhere* attitude of the Americans, if no one else. [Check it out: www.rougefilm.com.]

We parked the vehicle, cycled into town in driving rain, filmed with a small camera on the first stretch away from the start ramp – cheered Millar through – and went back for a larger camera as the rain abated. Further sessions by the Caisse d'Epargne warm-up compound, the ramp itself and then, by a quick dodge of roads and traffic, out into the country to a long straight of tarmac slicing between stubble fields, knots of spectators, picnic tables under umbrellas in the grass verges. A hot breeze had dried the road out and we saw the last riders go through. Finally, the vanguard gendarme motorbike headlamps blazing in the glow of the late afternoon sun, helicopter yak-yak-yakking overhead, team car, with its Mohican of spare bikes on the roof, following close like a mad tailgater, and the *maillot jaune* Rasmussen riding out of his skin to save the lead. Given his knockabout show of crashes, changed bikes, maladroitness and amateurish spat in the 2005 final time-trial and the fact that he had not devoted any time to specialist training in an event which does not suit him, his performance was remarkable: over the 54km, he lost only 2 minutes 55 seconds to the winner . . . Vinokourov. (Wiggins, who had to ride on wet roads and negotiated the corners of the final kilometre 'like an old woman', came fifth.) Broken and close to quitting on Tuesday in Briançon, twisted with pain, scarce able to walk because of the stitches in both knees, the Kazakh, miraculously restored both physically and mentally, now lay but 5 minutes 10 seconds behind Rasmussen and promised to stay on the offensive. 'Rasmussen's exceptional performance doesn't bother me,' he said. 'Anyone can have a bad day – it's up to us to provoke it.'

The *Equipe* headline read: 'Vino is Back'.

Alas for the French fans, Moreau 'the Big Man' was decidedly not back: he lost 9 minutes 26 seconds on the day.

Nigel and I drove home to Massat, Bas-Pyrénées, in a warm gloaming of the Languedoc July.

Sunday, 22 July. Plateau de Beille.
Grown men tremble and blench at the mention of the Plateau de Beille and, although I have written a book about the Pyrenees soon to be published, I had never ridden the monster – driven it with a photographer and not warmed to it, but the only proof is on two wheels. Bracing myself for purgatory, I left Nigel at a hairpin some 2km up the climb – the first ramps are awful, steep, beastly – and pressed on to desultory cries of 'Ah, le maillot jaune', reference my jersey. 'Long long since,' I replied. The road was about to be closed and I went to 2km from the top where the gradients slacken.

Well, ladies and gentlemen, as survivor (twice) of the evil Ax-Bonascre just up the valley and sundry other exemplars of ski-station cul de sac concrete brutality, I here report the Beille to be no big deal. So there. Not soft, not easy, no mountain is ever docile, but, in the sum of things relative to bikes vis-à-vis suffering and my unquenchable curiosity if not indecent obstinacy about both . . . no big deal.

The yellow jersey bunch went through, and a string of other riders, isolated, in pairs and threes, then Millar, on the front of the Vinokourov group, his legs leprous with white sunblock. He had just plastered the slopes of the col de Pailhères with the curses of those bitching at the wild pace, notably Evans, who called such cavalier impetuosity 'incredibly stupid. It was just too hard. We were all exhausted.' He'd been leading out Mayo for a crack at the stage win. To no avail. Mayo, as ever, unreliable. Up ahead, 3km from the top, Rasmussen had blasted away from the small group of elite climbers – Evans, Soler, Levi Leipheimer and Sastre – having danced around on his pedals for a while, eying them for signs of leakage. Only Contador – tipped by Schleck the night before on French television to win in Paris – stayed with him before countering the Dane's final acceleration to take the stage.

The GC now read: Rasmussen, Contador 2 minutes 23 seconds, Evans 3 minutes 4 seconds, Leipheimer 4 minutes 29 seconds, Klöden 4 minutes 38 seconds. Vinokourov had broken on the Pailhères, struggled to finish and lost a crippling 28 minutes 50 seconds.

Next morning, he was on the rampage again, blowing the race to bits, chivvying the pace over the first climb, the col de Port, and through Massat, right past our hotel.

Having eschewed the unseemly grappling for caravan goodies on the Plateau, I took up an isolated position away from the push and shove of the town swag junkies. (One adult lout snatched a prize right out of my friends' daughter little Janey Flanagan's hand. Brute.) By dint of winning smiles and cheery Hell-o, I garnered the full complement, including a bumper selection of Haribos for Floria, Susanne's god-daughter, in Berlin who is unalterably partial to the multicoloured French jellybean. The sachets of Grand'Mère coffee I kept – it proved to be excellent.

Outside the retirement home, an old lady in a wheelchair, nearing the term of her own life, gazed out wistfully across the road, perhaps lost in some recollection of her carefree bicycling days. Propped up in her lap, a small hand-illustrated sign read 'VIVE LE TOUR'. How many times had she seen it go down a road which, since 1910, has so often featured on the route?

The speed of the long line strung out in pursuit of the early break was thrilling, hectic, scary. They scorched down the left-hand side of the road within inches of us, and this only 40km into a real batterer: 196km, five cols, and a new entry, the Port de Balès (read about that in my *The Beautiful Machine*) from which the road spills directly onto the withering climb of the Peyresourde. A sign by the road on the leafy ascent of the narrow road to what had been a dead end until the Tour decreed 5km of new tarmac to forge a pass, read: 'Welcome to the Balès Hell'.

Apparently recovered from his pasting the day before, Vinokourov dropped his companions of the early break 15km from the finish and held on to win. Once again, Contador and Rasmussen were scrapping: four times, the Spaniard attacked on the Peyresourde but the Dane countered and they rode in together.

The *Equipe* headline ran: 'The Courage of Vino'.

The death was announced of a former world champion and quadruple French champion (a record), Jean Stablinski. Son of an immigrant Pole, he'd begun his working life as a miner in northern France. Above the galleries where he wielded his pick run stretches of the fiendish cobbled roadways incorporated in the Paris–Roubaix, Hell of the North. One such, bisecting the sinister Arenberg forest, which gave Cancellara the shivers, was first included at Stablinski's prompting.

Pau. Rest day.

Nigel and I got to the Press Hall in the Palais Beaumont just after Rasmussen and his cohort had left. The goon on the door wouldn't let us through, of course, but, as I strolled back from the loo, I noticed a side door standing ajar and strolled in. (You already know what boyish delight I take in skipping the plastic.) I had a chat with Steve Farrand of *Cycle Sport* and then Jeremy Whittle of *The Times*. Rasmussen had looked shifty, ducking questions, like a man with something to hide. A damning story had been promulgated: Whitney Richards, an American with whom he'd ridden MTB before turning to road racing, claimed that Rasmussen had asked him to bring a favourite pair of shoes across to Europe in March 2002. The box, delivered anonymously to Richards' back door, was bulky. Richards decided to unpack the shoes and carry them separately. The box actually contained eight cartons of Hemopure, a human blood substitute, a haemoglobin-based oxygen carrier comprising molecules removed from the red cells of cows' blood. On request, a doctor of physiology examined the contents and agreed that they should empty the cartons down the sink.

When Richards explained, Rasmussen's initial reaction was wheedling – 'I am not educated, if I don't win there is no other way for me' – then acrimonious: 'Have you any idea how much that shit costs?'

All circumstantial but highly suspect.

Perhaps referring to the highly publicised confessions of men like Rijs and Zabel, Rasmussen said: 'You can trust me.'

We drove on to the Predictor-Lotto team hotel outside Pau to interview the current lanterne rouge, also last year's final red light, Wim Vansevenant. We went out into the garden and set up the camera. Wim was a pleasure to talk to, bright and friendly. After he retired, a quiet life on the farm in Belgium with his wife and young family, no regrets, no bikes, no memory lane pictures on the wall. Lanterne rouge two years' running? Well, why not? A stage win would be great and he'd swap that for getting to Paris, but he had a job to do and professional obligation above personal ambition.

Back inside the hotel we tucked into the generous, complimentary buffet. An atmosphere of easy welcome. Champagne. Then, like Banquo's ghost at the feast, whisper that another rider had tested positive. Later: Vinokourov had blood doped before the time-trial in Albi. The headline summed it up next day: 'Chaos'.

Vinokourov's A sample had shown the presence of two distinct types of red blood cell. It is one of the easiest forms of doping to detect, the test is reliable. However, the rider called for a second test on the B sample, then headed off back home to Monaco mouthing the usual disclaimers: an error arising from the effects of his fall . . . he'd never doped . . . radio reports that he had transfused his father's blood were mad, had he done so he'd have controlled positive for vodka . . . his immediate departure wasn't flight: he needed to get to a leading haematologist who might clear him asap. Shortly afterwards he engaged the services of the American lawyer who is defending Floyd Landis. More litigation. More small print. More prevarication.

When Millar heard, he could not hold back tears. 'I am so shocked. Vino was one of my heroes, the way he raced, a model of willpower, class.' Wiggins had been suspicious of the man's time-trial win: knowing what power *he'd* put in and then to lose by two minutes? It wasn't credible. But, outspoken as he is, he feared what he might say in an unguarded response. Now he was unequivocal: 'For me, the true heroes are guys like Sylvain Chavanel and Thor Hushovd who're dragging their arses over the mountains, hanging on, getting dropped.' He later added Geraint Thomas of the fledgling Barloworlds: riding the Tour on bread, water and sheer guts.

The entire Astana team was booted out of the Tour.

Prudhomme accused riders trying to cheat the controls of playing Russian roulette. 'It is clear that the system is not working and it will have to be changed,' he said. 'I started this job believing that we could change things, but it's not enough. There has to be a revolution.'

That revolution has to begin with the greatest bike race in the world, precisely because it is the best known, the most widely watched, for most people the *only* bike race. This indisputable verity is the sharp bone that sticks in the craw of the UCI.

Stage 16. Orthez–col d'Aubisque. 218.5km.
Port de Larrau (*hors catégorie*) 1,573m, col de la Pierre Saint-Martin (1st) 1,760m, col de Marie Blanque (1st) 1,035m, Aubisque (HC) 1,709m.

I know them all. In one day? No thank you. To get to the race route, we cycled up the Marie Blanque from the easier eastern approach, Nigel pushing himself *and* his folding Bike Friday *and* twenty pounds weight of camera. From the summit we rolled back down to a tight hairpin, where I lay in the sun as the caravan sped by spattering me with packets of pretzels, Cochonou saucisson sec, Vache Qui Rit processed cheese, key rings, biros etc. I could scarcely be bothered to shift position to gather them up, so insouciant was my mood. I had, after all, fulfilled the vital commission of Haribos and was okay for snacks.

Apart from a split-stage in 1985, the Tour has never finished on top of the Aubisque. So, an appropriate grand mountain finale for the 2007 Tour. Rasmussen, jeered by a furious crowd when he came to sign on, as he had been escorted by police to the start in Montpellier, won the stage on his own having outraced Leipheimer, Contador, Evans, and Soler, who had made sure of the polka dot jersey – further jubilation for the Barloworld team, further jeers for Rasmussen on the podium.

Later that night, the Rabobank management, no long able to sustain the pressure of bias against their yellow jersey, the spectre of mendacity and suspicion, withdrew him (why not the entire team?) from the race. A statement read: 'Several times he said where he was and it proved to be wrong.' An Italian journalist had reported seeing Rasmussen and talking to him in the Dolomites when he had claimed to be in Mexico. It was enough. In the light of all that had happened, the unexplained absences, the denials and accusations, the fact (as he admitted) that he had not taken a random doping test in two and a half years, the Tour organisation insisted that they could not support the idea of his wearing yellow into Paris. The rift with the UCI widened. Why had McQuaid, aware of the DCU's sanction of Rasmussen and having written to the rider about the irregularities on 29 June, a week before the Tour, not enforced an article in its own codex which forbids a rider who has missed a control in a period of 45 days before a major tour to compete in it? McQuaid equivocated. That sanction was too severe, he said, disproportionate to the fault. Moreover, the UCI committee would certainly abrogate it. How could he anticipate the decision of independent members of his advisory body? What measure, in a pitiless drive to eradicate doping, is *too severe* against any rider who cheats, lies and infringes regulations? 'The cycling family must unite and work together to fight against doping,' says McQuaid. Well, that's a bonny notion.

At 23h10, Rasmussen left his hotel and was on his way home to Italy. As he did, the Cofidis rider Cristian Moreni was under police interrogation – he'd tested positive for synthetic testosterone after stage 11 and gendarmes were ransacking the team's hotel rooms. Moreni made no denial nor did he ask for a second test. (His career was over, but life would go on – he later said that he had applied a muscle-relaxing cream, bought over the Internet. The label was in German, he didn't know that the substance was forbidden, he didn't inform the team doctor, he was devastated . . .) His team, including Wiggins, understandably bitter about the opprobrium with which the race had been pelted and glad to be out of it, was withdrawn.

The following morning, five French teams – Crédit Agricole, Agritubel, Française des Jeux, Bouygues Télécom, Ag2R – and two German – T-Mobile and Gerolsteiner – calling themselves the Movement for Credibility in Cycling, staged a brief sit-down protest. Sébastian Hinault voiced their disquiet: 'We are fed up and have been for some time. We want to race cleanly but are not supported by certain teams and certain riders.'

Riders get the heaviest punishment. Clearly, the move to revolution depends largely on those who refuse to take dope. They need the backing of the entire hierarchy, managers and authorities, but from them the initiative must, and surely will, come. Millar and Wiggins had stayed with Thomas over that final gruelling mountain stage and finished on the Aubisque together. *That's* the kind of united will professional cycling needs.

Unity and combined force is essential but some impediments might seem intractable. Jaksche, having 'spat in the soup' as, tellingly, they call breaking the silence, expresses the crux thus: 'In cycling, you inhabit a parallel world where no conscience about what's off-limits exists. No one forced me. Certain team managers took advantage of me in making sure we took illegal products and what I find scandalous is that they did so to make the public believe that cycling was still a clean sport.'

For only the fourth time in its history, the yellow jersey was absent for a stage – Contador wore the white jersey of best young rider. A reduced Rabobank team, including Michael Boogerd, riding his twelfth and final Tour, bid farewell to Denis Menchov: he had not the will to continue and pulled out.

Certain opinion was jaded. This race had no real chance of avoiding recrimination. Many called for it to be annulled. A fresh start for the 2008 Tour required more than a freshly drawn leader board 48 hours from Paris.

The last stage open to riders ready to chance their luck ahead of a weary *peloton* went to Sandy Casar (his first Tour win). Twenty-seven kilometres from the start, he collided with a dog and went down.

He showed *un peu de chien*, 'real guts', not only to continue but to attack 3km from the finish, hold off Boogerd and Axel Merckx, both riding their last Tour, then launch a sprint from 200m.

Leipheimer won the final time-trial from Evans, Contador lost only 27 seconds to the Australian and held onto yellow and the new GC showed the podium men within 31 seconds of the lead.

The race was barely over before Clerc, Prudhomme and the French Minister for Sport, Roselyne Bachelot, were discussing how to 'lay the foundations of a Tour de France 2008, renewed and clean'. The ASO also accused McQuaid and the UCI of 'a lack of clarity, competence and, above all, professionalism', called for McQuaid's resignation and denounced the UCI for seeking to destroy the Tour. Astana sacked Vinokourov and yet more seamy revelations were squeezing into the pipeline: Kashechkin tested positive, like him, for blood doping . . . the Tour of Germany closed the door on the Astanas (although not on Cofidis and T-Mobile), whereas the Vuelta welcomed them . . . Mayo, guilty of taking EPO (UCI control on the rest day in Pau) . . . his Saunier-Duval co-rider Millar 'disgusted' and no longer wanting to be a part of the team (he has signed for a new outfit, Slipstream, set up by Jonathan Vaughters) . . . Discovery Channel pulling out of sponsorship altogether, as predicted, despite winning eight of the last nine Tours . . . the German daily newspaper *Die Welt* writing: 'The Tour has the winner it deserves, a Spanish racer suspected of doping. The Tour is finished' . . .

In a second interview for Sky News, conducted in Luke and June's back garden, I was asked if the Tour is too hard. The Tour is *designed* to be hard – only two teams, Gerolsteiner and Quick Step got to Paris with a full complement this year – and most riders do finish it without doping. A completely clean race may be slower but it will never be less than fiercely fought. These are men who can, and always will, push themselves way beyond what even they, off the bike, would call sensible limits.

✯

POSTSCRIPT

On 20 September, the American Arbitration Association rejected Floyd Landis's appeal to overturn the sanction from the United States Anti-Drugs Agency (USADA) for his positive drug test on the 2006 Tour de France and he has been banned from competition for two years. He may still make a final appeal to the Court of Arbitration for Sport in Switzerland.

CHAPTER EIGHTEEN

2008

A Clean Start?

The dispute between the UCI (the International Cycling Union) and the ASO (Amaury Sport Organisation), organisers of the Tour de France, had grown so bitter that the 2008 Tour was run independently of the UCI under the aegis of the Fédération Française du Cyclisme, the home federation. The UCI had insisted that the ASO invite all Pro Tour teams to the Tour automatically; the ASO refused. The UCI responded by suspending from its accreditation all the commissaires for the course, so the French anti-doping agency, the Agence Française de Lutte contre le Dopage (AFLD), carried out the doping controls. For the first time, the Tour de France would be testing for growth hormone, as well as the rest of the banned apothecary, and it had a *chaperon* system: every rider called for testing would be escorted direct from the finish line to the mobile anti-doping laboratory. The AFLD were also empowered to visit any rider in his hotel before 9 p.m. to conduct blood and urine tests. The taking or injection of any illicit substances being regarded as criminal on French sovereign territory, the French police would monitor any infractions of the law. Christian Prudhomme, director of the Tour, spoke boldly at the onset of the race – 'Everything will go well' – as if glad to be rid of the interventions of the UCI.

Since the beginning of the year, riders had been required, by the UCI, to provide biological passports, i.e. a profile of their physical make-up, which introduction of any illicit substance must distort. Opinion is divided as to the efficacy of this measure, and, so far, there's been no obvious sign that it's working as hoped.

The Astana team was not invited to ride the Tour, even though the current champion, Alberto Contador, who won this year's Giro d'Italia, was now riding for them. Having kicked Astana out of the 2007 edition after their leader Alexandr Vinokourov tested positive (see p. 394), the ASO deemed them *personae non gratae*. Since Cofidis had also quit the Tour after their man Cristian Moreni tested positive but *were* riding, so, too, Rabobank, although Michael Rasmussen had been booted out whilst he was leading the race, Johan Bruyneel, the Astana *directeur sportif*, and Lance Armstrong, who part-owns the team, called foul. The argument that any winner should be allowed to defend his title is powerful and the ASO might be deemed to be acting capriciously, but they shoulder the responsibility for organising a clean race and, on the tenth anniversary of the Festina affair (see p. 201 ff.), sensitivities prickled. The Belgian sprinter and current holder of the green points jersey Tom Boonen, caught for recreational use of cocaine, had been refused entry to the Tour. His sponsors pleaded extenuating reasons for reversing the ban – a series of publicity programmes featuring Boonen destined for French television channels during the Tour . . . ASO were neither impressed nor dissuaded. (McQuaid opined that Boonen ought to have been permitted to ride.)

Two of the teams riding had taken a very public stance against doping: Garmin-Chipotle (launched the previous year as Slipstream) and Columbia (which originally rose from the ashes of T-Mobile as High Road: that is, the main road of their aim, to combat drug-taking, from which they will not deviate).

David Millar, who quit Saunier-Duval after his teammate Iban Mayo tested positive for EPO in the 2007 Tour, then joined the newly formed Slipstream team and has a strong rapport with the *directeur sportif*, Jonathan Vaughters. Early in 2007, Vaughters promoted the idea of an independent Agency for Cycling Ethics, 'a means of ensuring that riders perform to the maximum of their genetic ability, and if that means eighth or thirty-fourth, so be it'. The principle is, I believe, right: an open declaration of responsibility, shared by riders and team management, to eradicate doping. The misery of recent years, the unwillingness to speak publicly and the fact that only riders, in general, have been punished, have left too many anomalies. (Floyd Landis' attempt to overturn his conviction, which annulled his Tour win, was dismissed just before this year's race began. Rasmussen was banned for two years by the Monaco federation, which held his licence, although he successfully sued his Rabobank team for wrongful dismissal.)

In June, the French Parlement passed a law (but not unanimously) beefing up already strict penalties for any athlete in possession of doping products. In the view of the opponents, led by Marie-George Buffet (former Minister for Youth and Sport, whose drugs tsar I interviewed in 2001), this misses the central point: that it is the system that must be addressed. Mme Buffet speaks of the pressures applied to young riders joining a team – for which there is ample evidence from the riders themselves – to use dope. She says the net must be drawn wider than the riders themselves to attack the dealers and the management of teams, including the doctors. It is, one might say, an ethical as well as a judicial approach, and one with which I heartily agree. If riders *are* riding clean, any failure to perform to full capacity can have no excuse.

Millar was forthright: 'Cycling has finally woken up to the fact that it can't afford another farce . . . like last year . . . Being clean has to be an integral part of our sport. Anyone who hasn't realised that yet has got his head in the clouds.'

The only other Briton in this year's Tour, Mark Cavendish, rides for Columbia, who already led the tally of victories recorded by any team for 2008. Cavendish had supplied seven, including two stage wins in the Giro d'Italia. A disputed photo finish might have given him three, and he gifted another to a teammate, André Greipel, as payback for his help. Bob Stapleton, Columbia's manager, had been brought in by T-Mobile with a brief to eradicate the culture of doping in the team, members of which were evicted from the 2006 Tour on suspicion of systematic abuse (see p. 347). When news broke, during the 2007 race, that a test on one of his riders, Patrik Sinkewitz, taken in June, had proved positive, Stapleton was mortified. Soon after the race, all his German backers pulled out of sponsorship. But Stapleton refused to give up, and the great triumph of his faith was not only the very existence of Columbia but its top ranking in the *peloton* at the start of the Tour.

The Tour had a new logo, a heart shape formed from the words

Le Tour Toujours (The Tour Forever). There are many cynics who might bark the opposite. Well, if there was something rotten in the state – and the previous year part of it was from if not in Denmark – the determination to extirpate it was intelligent, rigorous and uncompromising, and long may it continue.

The only previous winner of the Tour riding the race this year was Oscar Pereiro – who took victory after Landis's disqualification – but he had no illusions: his job was to support Alejandro Valverde. Cadel Evans, the Australian, second in '07, was a hot favourite. (Taking time bonuses into account, he'd lost to Contador by only three seconds.) Dependable in the mountains and against the clock but often rebuked for his lack of punch, Evans seemed to have found a new confidence after his showing last year and his Silence-Lotto team said they would work for him. However, they were not, on paper, very strong.

The Russian Denis Menchov, now 30, winner of last year's Vuelta, was embarking on what must surely be his last chance of victory, but whether his Rabobank team had the necessary staying power was uncertain. Fränk Schleck, current champion of Luxembourg, was much talked of, and his CSC team packed a lot of aggressive strength: notably Fabian Cancellara, reigning world time-trial champion, Carlos Sastre, an opportunist attacker, Jens Voigt, who seems to be able to ride at full pace all day when required to, the veteran Australian Stuart O'Grady and Schleck's brother, Andy, second in last year's Giro d'Italia.

The Tour showed big changes. For the first time since its introduction in 1970, there would be no Prologue, nor any team time-trial. The 2005 Tour began with a 19km individual time-trial, strictly not a Prologue (which is limited to 8km) but a stage. However, the 2008 edition began with a 197.5km stage from Brest to Plumelec, in Brittany, finishing on a hilltop. Thus, in this home region of three illustrious men of the Tour who, collectively, accumulated nine victories – Bernard Hinault, Louison Bobet, Jean Robic – the prize this first day would be a stage win plus the yellow and green jerseys. The polka dots were also on offer.

Prudhomme described the route as being 'a test for tactical intelligence and opportunism, not just brute force'. Time bonuses for stage wins were abolished, there was an individual time-trial four days in and, three days after a mountain-top finish at Superbesse in the Massif Central on day six, the race went into the Pyrenees. This marked revision of the normal format would, the organisers hoped, reduce the frantic nerviness of the first week, when time bonuses and small gaps in GC drive the sprinters to take all manner of risks in pursuit of both stage wins *and* the yellow jersey. It would also open the race, as Prudhomme put it, to any rider who might say, 'Today I want the win.' And it worked.

Another innovation: in order to encourage early breaks in any stage and to limit the role of earpieces, the organisers decreed that Radio Tour (the organisation's official line of communication to all team cars) would not report on gaps of less than 30 seconds between a break and the main bunch – neither the time gain nor the identity of riders in the break.

Valverde had ridden in three Tours, abandoned twice and, the previous year, come sixth. He won 2008's Dauphiné Libéré, often seen as a warm-up race for the Tour, and also won the early Belgian hilly classic the Liège–Bastogne–Liège, a course for the real hard men, his second victory there. The 1.7km steep climb to the finish in Plumelec suited his strength, aggression and speed to a tee. Indeed, Prudhomme said he modelled the first week of the Tour on the sort of racing for which the Ardennes is famous. Several riders tried their luck, but when Valverde exploded out of the jostling pack, some 300m from the line, he shot past the man in front, Kim Kirchen, who had already overtaken Stephan Schumacher with what looked like insolent ease.

The Norwegian Thor Hushovd, winner of the green jersey in 2005 and '08, added a seventh stage win to his Tour tally on the second stage – one of only two in the race without a categorised climb. The finish ended up a bit of a slope, which suits Hushovd, who is not a pure sprinter. Nor did he mind the cold, wet, windy conditions; they reminded him of home. The day established what became a leitmotif: French riders on the attack. The first stage offered four fourth-category climbs that counted towards the polka-dot jersey. A break of four French riders – inevitably dubbed by commentators 'The Four Musketeers' – were away nearly all day and Thomas Voeckler, who led the Tour for ten days in 2004, came away with the first mountains jersey.

Next day, the American William Frischkorn (Millar's teammate) initiated the break right from the start. The Frenchman Romain Feillu responded instantly and was followed by his compatriot Samuel Dumoulin and the Italian Paolo Longo Borghini, known as 'The Caterpillar' because of his capacity to devour flat kilometres. The peloton never organised a concerted chase and, 10km from the finish in Nantes, the escapees had an advantage of 3m 10s. The four scrapped it out over the final 1.5km, Dumoulin took the stage and Feillu, winner of last year's Tour of Britain and already in the best young rider's white jersey, took the yellow jersey.

This was justification indeed for the organisers' radical changes. The small rider (actually, at 1.58m, Dumoulin is called the Tom Thumb of the Cofidis team) going for and getting the win. In the French television commentary box, Laurent Fignon and Laurent Jalabert were beside themselves with excitement. French cycling had needed some show of force and courage of late, and here they were showing, *baroudeurs* in the tradition of Jacky Durand, the swashbuckling escape artist himself.

Individual time-trial, Cholet–Cholet, 29.5km.
On 17 October 1793, the Vendéen army was bloodily defeated at Cholet by the Republican forces, and the revolt of the Vendée against what they saw as the criminal and irreligious excesses of the revolutionary government in Paris was effectively over.

Another, less bloody catastrophe took place in Cholet in 1998, when the Festina affair blew up. Given the Tour's long-ingrained reaching out for symbolism, certain tinges of romantic fervour and a nice regard for its own history, the reappearance of Cholet on the itinerary – it had featured only once earlier, in 1936 – was certainly earnest of a wholesale new departure on many fronts.

The hot favourite for the race against the clock was Cancellara, permitted, as world champion, to don his rainbow jersey for the event.

The stage and yellow jersey was won by Stefan Schumacher, 33 seconds ahead of Cancellara. Winner of the bronze medal in last year's world road race and the 2007 Amstel Gold, Schumacher had also had a couple of run-ins with the police – in 2005 and earlier in 2008 – for amphetamines. Given the swingeing attitude of the Tour organisation to any hint of miscreancy, there were some who questioned his very presence on the Tour.

Feillu's tenure of the Golden Fleece did not survive this first outing, though he did get a hectare of land in his home village, promised him by the mayor if he took yellow. Watching him struggle to the finish, Fignon, the 1983 and '84 Tour winner, went to the heart of this cruelly punishing all-out race against the clock: 'Its terrible,' he said, 'terrible.'

Cavendish's expression as he crossed the line in Chateauroux for his first stage victory in the Tour – at 23 the youngest Briton ever to take a stage – was ecstatic. He came to the race saying he was the fastest in the world – a declared goal when he was but 16 years old – and the speed at which he shot past some of the grandees of the front-line sprinters, including the arch-opportunist Oscar Freire, confirmed the boast. Allan Peiper, his *directeur sportif*, says that 'he can *smell* the line'. He needed this one, though, because 'unless you've won a Tour stage, you can't count yourself a great sprinter'. (The last Briton to take a bunch sprint win was Barry Hoban in 1975, the last of his total of eight stage wins.)

So intense was the team's support that, separated by a crash from the bunch, 20km from finish, Hincapie worked flat out to get back so that he could help with the lead-out. And if Cavendish was inclined to read the runes, the identical stage, from Cholet, in 1998 was won by the prolific Lion King himself, Mario Cipollini.

The day had marked yet another French buccaneering venture: Lilian Jégou, Nicolas Vogondy (the current French champion) and Florent Brard broke free 1km from the start and had sight of the line even as the *peloton*, which had judged its chase well this time, roared up behind them. Vogondy jumped for the finish but was swallowed up in the onrush a measly 30m from victory. It was a brave effort, for which he won the day's combativity prize, a competition inaugurated in 1952 to reward just this kind of aggressive enterprise. Mauricio Soler, the 2007 mountains prize-winner, abandoned following a bad crash two days earlier.

On the second-category mountain top at Superbesse next day, Kirchen took over the points jersey from Hushovd and the lead from Schumacher. The German touched the Luxembourger's back wheel as the lead group started to wind up for the final 300m. He went down; Kirchen rode on and became the first man from Luxembourg to wear yellow since Charly Gaul, on his way to overall victory, in 1958. The Italian Riccardo Riccò outsprinted Evans and Valverde, and Schumacher reached the line 32 seconds down. (Valverde had fallen badly the day before and his right leg and arm were heavily bandaged.) On flat stages, any rider who crashes within 3km of the finish is awarded the same time as that of the group in which he was riding when he fell. On mountain stages this rule does not apply. Behind the lead group, the *peloton* had been blown out all over the place, the early French attacks having petered out. Voeckler again, snapping up mountains points, looked fried on the final climb. Sylvain Chavanel, who was also vying for 'the peas' (polka dots), wilted. Chavanel, reputedly the highest-paid French rider, still moans about there being two speeds in the *peloton*. One might say that there are indeed two speeds: top and second.

Manuel Beltrán tested positive for EPO. (A sample had been taken after the first stage; the police detained him in Plumelec as he was riding away from the finish and took him, unannounced, to the doping control.) Nicknamed 'Triki' (after a Spanish cartoon character), he was arrested by French police and led away in handcuffs.

An agreement between the teams and ASO means that no team need now quit if one of its riders is evicted for testing positive.

On stage eight, from Figeac – birthplace of Champollion, the first man to decipher Ancient Egyptian hieroglyphics – to Toulouse, 'the pink city', it rained and rained and rained. Even the moto cops were whining about the miserable weather before the race began. As the bunch approached the finish down the long avenues of poplars, soaked through and, despite a relatively warm temperature of 60°F, cold and miserable, there was a lot of chivvying, bickering, shouting, reproving and urging in the fretful jostle of riders geeing up for the finish. Cavendish's posture when he once more shot off the front across the line was quite different from that of his first win: he sat back in his saddle, arms aloft, a look of broad satisfaction on his face, the winner, the man who knows he has won because, given the chance to unleash his speed, no one else comes close. Rejoicing in his second win (matching Hoban in 1969 and 1973), he insisted that he was also determined to try to make it to Paris, despite the fact that he was due to head out to the Olympics immediately afterwards to ride the Madison with Bradley Wiggins (they were reigning world champions).

There was a similar self-assurance in the victory salute of another double winner next day, the first major mountain stage: 224km over the minor cols de Buret and des Ares, then the mighty Peyresourde and Aspin (60th and 68th inclusion, respectively). Riding with the lead group, containing all the main contenders, Riccò sped away off the front 4km from the col d'Aspin. No one could or wanted to follow, and, hitting the descent, Riccò let rip all the long way down to the finish. The rest made no serious attempt to reel him in and he crossed the line with an advantage of 1m 17s over the leaders. Among them, Evans was in some distress. Around 114km into the stage, he overcooked a bend at 40kph on the approach to the Peyresourde, went down heavily and grazed his back, left shoulder, side and leg. Since Riccò did not pose an immediate threat for the overall classification – at the close of the day he was still 2m 35s adrift of Kirchen's yellow jersey – Evans' team did not bother to wind up a chase and Valverde's team controlled the chase at no frantic speed. There would surely be more urgent need to pounce on maverick escapees in the days to come.

Riccò insisted that he was not here to win the Tour but for experience and, of this, his second stage win, that he 'had a rage to win because people are trying to ruin my image': that is, calling him a cheat. His haemocrit level is naturally above 50 per cent, the allowed maximum, and he holds a UCI certificate recording the anomaly, but, of course, this is dangerous ground and he had been tested – surely targeted – five times since the start of the race.

Stage ten, Pau to Hautacam, 156km . . . over the giant col du Tourmalet at 105.5km and the finish on the big summit whose name, High Field, doesn't come close to encapsulating its nastiness. The Tourmalet is part of the infamous Circle of Death, the Hautacam lies just south of the cure centre for eternal hopefuls, Lourdes. Ask any *étape* rider what it was like. Ask me: I've done them. I can put those two and two together. Then, if you still don't get the picture, use some imagination: it's [bleep] hard.

The Frenchman Rémy di Gregorio struck out early, over the Tourmalet and down into the valley, smack into a headwind that pretty well drained him. At the foot of the Hautacam, his lead was reduced to 43 seconds, and the rider who is reckoned by some to be the new star in waiting was cooked. Cancellara and Voigt backed by the Schleck brothers gave a sort of team presentation – CSC as Club Super Class – on the mountain whose name means 'bad detour', motoring up it with that kind of aggressive strength which is a fusion of willpower, indifference to suffering and physical power of the order of the average draught horse. Sean Yates had it, Voigt has it, Cancellara calls it up when required to lay aside the greater finesse of time-trialling. For there is no technique in what these riders do when driving it hard at the front: it is pure force. Fränk Schleck, challenging now for GC, and Sastre, their nominated climber, were the beneficiaries, as well as any other riders who had the legs to stay with them. Valverde wasn't equal to it and reached the foot of the last climb, 13km from the finish, 3 minutes adrift, Cunego, Vande Velde, Kirchen (in yellow) and others with him. To compound Valverde's discomfiture, his chain slipped off and he was helped back into action by a spectator.

Up the slopes, the two Saunier-Duval riders Leonardo Piepoli and Juan José Cobo finally broke clear with Fränk Schleck. Cancellara and Voigt had peeled off; Evans couldn't follow. Piepoli took the stage as Cobo pulled aside, and Fränk Schleck followed them in. Schleck watched the clock to see if he would take over the yellow from Kirchen. He missed out to Evans by one second. 'I should have done a sprint,' he said, ruefully. (His brother Andy bonked and lost nearly nine minutes.) Evans said that he had been in considerable pain on the descents: 'Every swollen and sore bit of my body was hurting . . . I felt better climbing.' Denis Menchov was scathing, however. He had no patience with Evans' passivity, and he had a point. Any pretender to the overall win needs to stamp some kind of authority on the race, and sitting on wheels won't answer. Menchov also reckoned that Valverde's win in the Dauphiné Libéré had cost him too much and that his challenge would fade in the Pyrenees.

Pau. Rest day.

Last year's repose in Pau delivered momentous, miserable news (see p. 391 f.). This year, 17 teams riding the Tour announced that they were pulling out of the Pro Tour. Eric Boyer, the *directeur sportif* of Cofidis and president of AIGCP (Association International des Groupes Cyclistes Professionels) said that after four years the Pro Tour had divided cycling. What cycling needed was to be united with one programme. The Pro Tour imposed too many obligations, gave no leeway. Boyer denied the existence of a putsch; this was no power struggle, he said, there were no winners or losers, only cycling wins. (This was somewhat disingenuous. Boyer is French and one may suppose a desire to reestablish the more familiar, old-style shape of the Continental racing season, firmly based in Europe. The UCI, by contrast, seems bent on making cycling a global sport. Boyer tossed in the offer to hold out a hand always to the UCI with the promise of cooperation, of course.)

McQuaid said that these teams would 'be dealt with according to the regulations', which meant they would 'face exclusion from the international federation'. He added later: 'This breach of contract causes enormous material and moral damage to the UCI.'

Stage 11 brought disaster for the Barloworld team, compounding the loss of their 2007 polka-dot winner, Soler. Moisés Dueñas, whose test after the time-trial proved positive, was kicked out. Police searched his room and found banned substances, which the team insisted 'were absolutely not supplied or prescribed by the team doctor'. He was arrested and held for 'use and possession of plants and poisonous substances'. Under the new French law, use carries a sentence of two years, possession a further three. Two other members of his team were out, too, after a crash – Paolo Longo Borghini (broken collarbone) and Félix Cárdenas (bad bruising).

Silence-Lotto deployed a tactic to circumvent the new rule on early radio contact: when the day's attacks ramped up early in Wednesday's stage, their veteran sprinter Robbie McEwen stayed near the front to monitor any attack and relay news of riders who were dangerous to Evans. 'Thanks to a quick-thinking McEwen, it was a pretty stress-free day,' Evans said. 'He's our lieutenant on the road.'

Kurt Asle Arvesen of CSC took the win from Fabian Wegman

by less than a tyre width. The Norwegian champion attacked from a break of twelve that included Filippo Pozzato and Alessandro Ballan, two Italian classics specialists who might have been expected to fight rather harder on the run-in.

At 12.20 p.m. before the start of stage 12, Riccò was handed a letter from the AFLD. He had tested positive after the time-trial for CERA (continuous erythropoeisis receptor activator), a delayed-action third-generation EPO, with a different molecular mass from that of EPO Mk 1, a test for which had been recently developed. Riccò, confronted by his *directeur sportif*, Mauro Gianetti, at the beginning of the season, had 'sworn on his mother's head' that he was racing clean. He left the team bus to jeers and whistles from a very angry crowd. The entire Saunier-Duval team rode back to the bus and quit the race. (Later, Riccò and Piepoli were sacked for 'a violation of the team's ethical code'.)

Prudhomme said: 'I was pretty disturbed when I saw the superiority of two riders from the same team on the stage to Hautacam, as the rest of you were, I'm sure.'

On stage 12, the race crossed the Languedoc and twined through the craggy limestone gorges of the Berre valley, through the Corbières region (*cor*, a pre-Celtic word meaning 'rock' and '*berre*' from the river) into Narbonne. Cavendish (who was clocked at 74kph) took his third win. He held up three fingers as he crossed the line and later denounced the latest doping scandal: 'I'm in the sport I love, which I don't want to tarnish. Cycling is not just a job for me, it's a passion, and maybe the people who resort to doping don't have the same passion as me.'

Next day, around 8.5km from the finish in Nîmes, Sven Krauss, unsighted in the bunch, went straight into a sign in the middle of the road. His bike split in two pieces and he cartwheeled onto the ground but, unhurt and mystified, got up and stared about him as the *peloton* raced on by and a mechanic retrieved his broken machine. Columbia had led from some way out, but, at 200m to go, Cavendish was on his own and boxed in. With astonishing poise and speed, he ducked out and shot down the left side of the bunch, past McEwen, who was well placed, and won by two bike lengths. That morning, he'd said he was tired and in some pain from the crash wounds, and he called this – a record for a Briton –

his hardest win yet. Petacchi won four in 2003 and Cipollini four on consecutive days in 1999 but Cavendish, at twenty-three, was the youngest of them. Since there had been only four bunch sprint finishes so far, his achievement was stupendous.

On the first day in the Pyrenees, the *Equipe* cartoonist sketched a mountain smiling with pleasure as cyclists and vehicles swarm over its sides: 'At last, my nice yearly massage.' The three days in the Alps over five *hors catégorie* climbs looked more like a pugilistic pummelling: the Tour's first crossing of the col d'Agnel (2,744m, HC) into Italy and the mountain-top finish on Prato Nevoso ('Snowfield', also known as 'the big one') . . . rest day . . . another first crossing, the col de la Lombarde (2,351m, HC), Cime de la Bonnette (2,802m, HC), only thrice crossed . . . col du Galibier (2,645m, HC), col de la Croix de Fer (2,067m, HC), l'Alpe d'Huez (1,850m, HC).

On the advice of his *directeur sportif*, Cavendish, who was by now very tired, pulled out just before the first Alpine stage. There had been no pressure from British Cycling to quit the Tour because of his commitment to the Olympics.

The leader board stood thus: Evans in yellow with 1 second over Fränk Schleck, 38 seconds over the Garmin-Chipotle rider Christian Vande Velde, who had jumped out of the pack rather in this his sixth Tour. At 32, he had found renewed optimism and drive in the team directed by Jonathan Vaughters. Another new man, the Austrian Bernhard Kohl, who in June had come, at his own expense, to recce the mountains, lay fourth at 46 seconds, clearly bent on taking the polka dots from his teammate Sebastian Lang, who led him by a mere point. Menchov was at 57 seconds and still dangerous, the unassuming Sastre, a climber of considerable class, at 1m 28s. Valverde, at over 4 minutes, was still talking tough; Cunego, at 5m 37s, looked out of it.

With two men in overall contention, the CSC team mounted an exemplary show of united force to bring the race to a decision. Their locomotive, Jens Voigt, a man to whom fatigue is a stranger and weakening never an option, abetted by one of the hardest *rouleurs* in the *peloton*, Stuart O'Grady (winner of the 2007 Paris–Roubaix), and by 'Spartacus' Cancellara, with timely interventions from Arvesen, Sastre and the Schlecks, hammered at Evans unrelentingly. Some pundits, remarking on the absence of Evans' team from the fray, said that CSC were simply doing what the Silence-Lotto outfit should be doing. Where were they? The sponsor, Silence, manufactures an anti-snoring preparation.

Evans seemed equal to keeping pace but there was no sign of attack in him, no willingness to take the fight to anyone, to show any response other than dogged wheel-sucking. On the first Alpine stage, he lost yellow to Fränk Schleck and 47 seconds to Sastre. Kohl, who rode in with Sastre, took the polka dots and the first six men on general classification were all within a minute of the leader. Menchov fell when his tyre slipped on a graffito on a bend, and he struggled to get back to the main group. Vande Velde's teammate Danny Pate advanced the cause for clean riding by coming third on the stage.

On the high-speed descent of the Agnel, Pereiro took a frightening tumble. Coming into a hairpin, his tyres slid on the wet road and he went over the edge, a five-metre drop onto the road below the bend. Valverde and other teammates, terrified, stopped to attend to him, and Valverde said he had never seen such a dramatic fall. Pereiro broke his arm but not, as was first reported, his femur.

After the second rest day, CSC opened up again. Their *directeur sportif*, Bjarne Rijs, permitted to attend as, in 2007, he had been barred (see p. 374), dead-batted the question as to who the leader of the team was, whether the designated leader Sastre or the actual leader Fränk Schleck, neither particularly strong in the time-trial. The road would decide.

There was no great change and all the contenders, real and supposed, came in together behind the Frenchman Cyril Dessel into the tiny town of Jausiers (population *c*.1,000), one of nine towns hosting the Tour for the first time, and the smallest. Andy Schleck pulled on the white jersey of best young rider.

Fittingly, therefore, the stage finishing on l'Alpe d'Huez after crossing the Giant of the Alps, the Galibier, would be the last chance for an attack on the road likely to prove decisive. Clearly, the CSC climbers, Fränk Schleck and Sastre, were best placed, and Evans, Menchov and now Kohl must know that the Tour might be won or lost here.

At the foot of the Alpe, on the first ramp, the lead group all together, Sastre attacked. That his teammate Fränk Schleck was in yellow shows just how committed the CSCs were to final victory without regard to individual ambition. 'The strongest must win' is a truism at best, but in the hard causalities of pro racing, it is as good a rebuff to sentiment as any. Yellow jersey? Earn it, defend it, lose it only when you are spent.

Sastre said later: 'I knew I had to go early to make any difference.' Only Menchov tried to stay with him but soon fell away. Evans was left to it. The rest were certainly not going to help him. Kohl had limited interest – in securing the polka dots – and Fränk Schleck, under orders not to, did not chase and thereby give the Australian a tow. Even so, Evans didn't look capable of any upping of the pace. Surely over-geared, he strained and grunted, out of the saddle, looking anything but a Tour winner. He looked, rather, like a man struggling just to hang on. Limiting his losses? Biding his time? Banking on his superiority in the final time-trial? When Poulidor and Anquetil rode elbow to elbow up the Puy de Dôme in 1964, the famous *coude à coude* (see p. 140), Anquetil rode himself to exhaustion. Evans, by contrast, rode like a man who does not know the meaning of *attack*. It became apparent, in the course of those merciless 14km and 21 hairpins, that the CSC tactic all along had been to batter Evans mentally as much as physically. His legs held up, just; his mind caved in. Four kilometres from the summit, he finally stirred and took the others with him. He ceded 2m 15s to the magnificent stage-winner Sastre, now in yellow with 1m 24s on Fränk Schleck, 1m 33s on Kohl and 1m 34s on Evans. Since Rijs had said openly that Sastre (for example) needed to go into the 53km time-trial with over 2m on the Australian, who had already beaten him by over a minute in the much shorter distance, the race was far from over. But what a *directeur sportif* says and what he really believes do not readily concur. What counts is what he says to his rider wearing yellow, on the verge of riding out of his skin to confound all the pundits and take overall victory in that part of the race in which he is no specialist. Kohl secured the mountains prize.

Sastre said that before the start of the final time-trial he was 'serene, quiet, preparing for serious matters. Above all, I really didn't want to let such an opportunity slip.' One may be sure that the feeling if not the mental state was shared by Evans. The difference was that Sastre, informed en route only of the split times of his teammate Cancellara so that he had no idea what his immediate rival was doing, rode in a concentration of effort so complete, so regular, so unexpected that when he crossed the line he had ceded only 29 of the 94 seconds he held over Evans. Schumacher won the race against the clock for the second time, Millar came a very respectable fifth and his teammate Vande Velde, fourth, moved into fifth place overall: a triumph for the new Garmin-Chipotle outfit, whose ambition had been to see him in the top ten. Kohl, ninth on the stage behind Evans (seventh), jumped past Fränk Schleck onto the podium. Oscar Freire made sure of the green jersey.

The image which, somehow, epitomises the combat on what Laurent Fignon called a 'transition Tour', with no man standing clear of the pack, was of Evans on the podium, the Arc de Triomphe in the background, waving a stuffed toy kangaroo. It was pathetic, a gesture of foppish sentimentality; as has been said, there is no room for sentiment in this sport. The CSCs, winners overall, individual and team, Andy Schleck taking best young rider, showed total absence of sentiment. They were there to ride and win, and that is precisely what they did, all feelings, save those of total devotion to the cause, aside.

The French riders had some success – three stage wins and a day in yellow with two men in the top fifteen – but their great triumph had been their animation, their willingness to attack. In the accumulation of kilometres spent out ahead of the *peloton*, the escapees were predominantly French and the ace chancer Sylvain Chavanel was named 'super combative', with 417km at the head of the race, only 9km ahead of his compatriot Lilian Jégou.

A clean Tour? Four riders evicted – more than the previous year – and declared clean riders showing extremely well . . . nothing is certain. However, buttonholed by an American film crew for a brief interview in Cérilly, I was asked if this was the sport's last chance. I pointed to the milling crowds and said, 'Ask them.'

★

POSTSCRIPT

The Belgian rider Wim Vansevenant, of the Silence-Lotto team, set a curious record: he became the first man to finish as *lanterne rouge* in three successive Tours.

And, in mid-August, tentative moves were made towards rapprochement between the UCI and the ASO, and a common understanding apropos of the international racing calendar.

On 10 September 2008, Lance Armstrong announced his return to professional cycling in 2009. He said that he would give full details of the campaign in New York on 24 September.

CHAPTER NINETEEN

2009

The Comeback Tour

Amaury Sport Organisation (ASO), the organisers of the Tour, are, in line with their predecessors, conscious of the tug of history and the choice of Monaco for the Grand Départ honoured that tradition. The Principality welcomed the Tour for the first time in 1939 – the start and finish of the 13th stage, a circuit through the Maritime Alps, and the start of stage 14 – but since then has featured only six times on the route, most recently in 1964. Apt, then, that this reappearance of Monaco on the itinerary should coincide with another comeback: that of Lance Armstrong, at the time two months away from his 37th birthday. The oldest man to win the Tour was 36 – Firmin Lambot, the Belgian, in 1922. Three victors have been 34: Lucien Buysse (also of Belgium) in 1926, the Italian Gino Bartali in 1948 and Armstrong himself in 2005, when he announced his retirement. As soon as he told the press, in September 2008, that he was going to start racing again and that the Giro d'Italia would certainly be on his programme, there was, inevitably, intense speculation as to whether he would also compete in the Tour de France. Indeed, it was his reaction to Carlos Sastre's victory in 2008 – he called the previous year's race 'a bit of a joke' – which seems to have been the immediate stimulus to his return. He later dismissed his wounding denigration of Sastre's win as no more than a pleasantry, but his so-called pleasantries have often been in dubious taste, heavy-handed and, in sum, humourless. During the Tour, however, he apologised to Sastre in the press and in person.

Armstrong had kept in good shape and said that he still felt strong on the bike. He clearly missed the challenge of racing at the highest level. Although he refused to be drawn into stating publicly whether he'd ride the Tour or not, I had no doubt that he would and, gradually, the hints became plainer. His declared primary motive was to promote his Foundation, whose mission – the Livestrong message – is 'to inspire and empower' cancer sufferers and their families, under the motto *unity is strength, knowledge is power and attitude is everything*. This was perhaps somewhat disingenuous: he did not need to ride the Tour de France to achieve greater international prominence and publicity than he already commands. However, he stressed that he would not be drawing any salary from the team and that, having nothing more to prove, he was riding only because he wanted to. The team he joined, Astana, which had recently appointed as manager Johan Bruyneel, the man who had overseen his Tour victories, had been excluded from the 2008 Tour. The organisation ruled it a pariah after Alexandr Vinokourov's suspension for doping in the 2007 race. Consequently, the winner of that edition, Alberto Contador, then riding for Armstrong's former team, Discovery Channel, who'd joined Astana in 2008, had been unable to defend his title. His presence in the Astana team posed a ticklish question: if Armstrong *did* ride the Tour, who would be leader? And, if Contador were leader, would Armstrong ride for him, as a *super-domestique*? From the outset, the American's long partnership with Bruyneel appeared to set up considerable if not insoluble problems of loyalty and team balance despite all the usual disclaimers along the lines of 'wait and see . . . the road will decide . . . whoever goes stronger is the leader'. Armstrong began the season at the Tour Down Under in Australia, entered the Vuelta a Castilla y León in March but crashed on the first stage and broke his collarbone. It was the first serious injury he had ever sustained in his career. There was, unsurprisingly, a certain nervousness in his riding. 'Once,' he said, 'I was always the last to apply the brakes, now I'm the first.' His participation in the Giro looked to be compromised. However, he is a man of incorrigible will and, the broken bone stiffened with metal plates, he resumed training and rode the Italian tour, his aim, boldly declared now, being to ride the *Grande Boucle*. The Giro certainly honed both his racing sharpness and physical condition – he arrived in Monaco looking fit and lean, weighing 73kg, whereas his Tour racing weight had always been around 74 to 74.5kg. Of riding alongside Contador he said: 'The real problem for Contador would be if I were in another team.' An ominous equivocation. The Astana outfit looked formidable and half the riders were obvious allies of Armstrong: Andreas Klöden might have been a leader in any other team, though he is not a natural attacker, Levi Leipheimer has often been spoken of as a contender but has not, in my view, the requisite physical and mental toughness, and Yaroslay Popovych had ridden for Armstrong in Discovery Channel. Contador, by contrast, had only one clear confrère, the Portugese Sérgio Paulinho, possibly abetted by the Kazakh Dmitriy Muravyev. Bruyneel refused his request that his friend Benjamin Noval be selected for the Tour.

Cadel Evans, second in 2007 and 2008, reported himself stronger than he had ever been, but his failure to carry the fight to Sastre in 2008 merely underlined a consistent lack of enterprise and audacity. Sastre himself, although he, too, claimed to be in top form, cannot have had any real illusions as to his chances of a second victory. (The Tour organisers, for whatever dark reason, exacerbated his inner misgivings, voiced during the race, by not allowing him to wear the yellow jersey as defending champion on the opening stage. This break with tradition was boorish.) The Schleck brothers, Fränk – winner on l'Alpe d'Huez in 2006 – and Andy, who won best young rider on his début Tour in 2008, were likely to make life difficult for everyone in the mountains and Andy was tipped as a podium finisher, if not contender for overall victory, with good cause. He is a rider of very high class with one signal weakness: he cannot time-trial. Contador himself is a rider of all-round ability, a climber of exceptional power who has now made himself a top-flight time-trialler – he is current Spanish champion in the discipline. He is also one of few men to have won all three major Tours: he took the Giro and the Vuelta in 2008 and was unquestionably the hot favourite to add a second win in the Tour de France. Denis Menchov, having won the recent Giro d'Italia in some style, was also fancied, and the time-trial ace Fabian Cancellara, recent winner of his home Tour de Suisse, said that it was a dream to win the French tour. One pundit, to my own surprise, even tipped him this year. His manager at Saxo Bank (the Schlecks' team), Bjarne Rijs, was sensibly cautious: 'When he's strong he's *strong* but, hold on, this isn't Switzerland,' he said.

Against the clock, however, Cancellara is a decided master and he won the opening stage, a 15.5km loop up from near the waterside in Monaco, five metres above sea level, by 18 seconds from Contador. The first 7.5km consisted of a long drag of a climb up to the côte de Beausoleil, no great height at 205m, but there was scant relief in that sapping uphill. Contador had the fastest time to the summit, which was categorised in the King of the Mountains competition, and thus pulled on the first polka-dot jersey. Bradley Wiggins, another of the four Britons riding, came third at 19 seconds from Cancellara. As winner, Cancellara took both the yellow and the green jersey. Thus Wiggins wore the green for a day – the points competition being junior of the three main prizes. Double Olympic, triple Worlds individual pursuit champion, Wiggins, nicknamed 'The Metronome' for his dominant track racing, had joined David Millar in the Garmin-Slipstream team at the end of the 2008 season. (Garmin's Chipotle sponsors having pulled out, it revived the original Slipstream name.) Armstrong finished at 40 seconds and Bernard Hinault adjudged the fact that he lost most of his time on the opening climb to be a sign of his diminished power. The Belgian road champion Tom Boonen was not the force he'd been, either, but that was the result of a nasty stomach bug which had left him badly weakened. He was lucky to be riding at all. The ASO had refused him entry to the race because he'd tested positive for recreational use of cocaine earlier in the season. However, the Chambre Arbitrale du Sport in Paris – a sort of appeal court – had reversed the ASO's decision and, at the very last minute, he was given permission to ride. Charly Wegelius, who has dual English-Finnish nationality, also had a late entry. His teammate Thomas Dekker was excluded for a positive dope test and Wegelius was called up on the Wednesday to replace him. The fourth member of the British quartet, Mark Cavendish, came to the Tour as leader of his Columbia team, 13 victories already taken since the beginning of the year, with the declared ambition of reaching Paris and winning on the Champs-Elysées. He also reckoned that the green jersey was a possibility but not a priority.

The next five stages took the race along the southern littoral of France past the Camargue and round into Spain, with sorties into the immediate, hilly hinterland and a detour inland to Montpellier for the team time-trial. The coastline is prey to winds of a contrary nature: the sirocco blowing off the northern shores of Africa; the mistral, one of the three curses of Provence; the tramontana, a cold north wind from across the Alps. Joined by the routine commonalty of breezes off the sea, this blustery nuisance was bound to cause the riders problems along the exposed coast roads.

Stage two, described as flat, cut into the Maritime Alps over some lumpy terrain which the pros pooh-pooh as 'big-ring' hills. Cavendish had won three stages in the Giro and might have won more had he twigged something which Erik Zabel, now a consultant with Columbia, pointed out in analysing his performances. Most sprinters will not break clear of the pack from further out than 50 or so metres. Cavendish, however, is strong enough to launch his attack from much further out and Zabel pressed him to have confidence in that superiority. On the run-in to Brignoles, the Columbia eight-man train pulled Cavendish to the front, like an archer drawing the longbow to its full cloth yard to release the arrow. And, 200 metres from the line, Cavendish flew through the jostling bunch on his own. The Garmin sprinter Tyler Farrar – one of the few men to have beaten him this year (during the Tirreno-Adriatico in March) – was hot on his wheel but could make no impression on the velocity generated by the 24-year-old Manxman. Manx cats are celebrated for having no tail. Cavendish scorches off any planted on him. The win also brought him the green jersey, but he said that to win the final green in Paris would come through winning stages – he had no intention of contesting the intermediate Hot Spot sprints which garner six, four and two points in the competition. The flattish stage from Marseille to La Grande Motte, a holiday complex characterised by ziggurat apartment blocks, clearly suited the Cav-Columbia outfit to a tee and so it was. Behind him, drama. The buffeting winds along the coast split the peloton in what the French call *une bordure*, which is slang for no-go or, of a doctor, being struck off. A gap opened, the leading group, containing Armstrong, split off from the following bunch, containing Contador and the other favourites. Reports are inconclusive, but some riders say that

Armstrong signalled the Astanas with him to group and ride with the break which was now being driven hard by the Columbias, among them Armstrong's great friend and former lieutenant George Hincapie. In the event, Contador and the rest lost 41 seconds, which put Armstrong ahead of his notional leader by 19 seconds. Of the Spaniard's relegation, the American said that it was a basic principle of racing and it 'doesn't take a rocket scientist to figure out' that if there was a wind you made sure to be up at the front. Cavendish was blunter: if you ride like a junior, you get a junior's results. Whatever the truth, Contador's loss of 41 seconds was less significant in itself than obvious proof that he was isolated within the Astana team, moreover that he could not rely on team backing.

The team time-trial, a relatively short, twisty and narrow, highly technical, quite lumpy circuit out of Montpellier and back, was the first in the Tour since 2005, when Armstrong's Discovery Channel rode the 67.5km at an astonishing average of 57.32kph. The Astanas could not match that, but they beat the much-fancied Garmins, with three front-rank time-triallists in Millar, Wiggins and David Zabriskie, by 18 seconds. (The Garmins rode most of the way with only five riders, the minimum required to qualify. A new rule, to counter dawdling, clocked in any rider shed off the pace to the actual time of his arrival. In the past, riders who were dropped could pedal in as and when they chose, to conserve energy.) More significantly, Cancellara's Saxo Bank team lost 40 seconds, which put him and Armstrong level. The Swiss held onto the yellow jersey, thanks to the fractional split in the time by which he beat the American in the opening stage . . . 0.138, a tantalising fifth of a second. For Sastre (down by 1m 37s), Menchov (2m 20s) and Evans (2m 35s), the losses probably meant that they were out of contention. Top riders let down by a weak ensemble: it's the core of the argument against the team time-trial.

Five years after his heroic defence of the yellow jersey in the Pyrenees, the arch-chancer Thomas Voeckler broke clear of his fellow escapees five kilometres from the line to win in Perpignan, his first Tour victory. One of his companions in the break, Jussi Veikkanen, who had been snapping up polka dot points on the low-lying hills, became the first Finn to wear a Tour prize jersey.

Millar and several of his Garmin teammates live in Girona (first time in the Tour, start town for stage six), north of Barcelona (third time on the route, as a finish town). It was, therefore, home territory. After an early flurry of attempts to break clear, Millar finally got a gap at 46km and, joined by two other riders, established a lead of 3m 45s. Since Millar was tenth overall at 1m 7s that could not be allowed to widen and the chasing bunch gradually gnawed it away to 1m 50s. Twenty-five kilometres from the finish, Millar broke free on his own and, 10km out, still had a one-minute lead. At the foot of the slope up Montjuic ('Hill of the Jews' in old Catalan), overlooking the harbour to the south-east of Barcelona, Millar clung to a ten-second advantage, but the slope had no bends, the bunch could see him and, just before the red kite marking the final kilometre, they crushed him. Thor Hushovd, a *rouleur* rather than an outright sprinter, devoured the gradient – mild in essence but, at the end of a long stage, punishing – and took the win. He was now one point behind Cavendish in the points competition.

Stage seven, the longest day, 224km from Barcelona to Andorra-Arcalis, the first of only three mountain-top finishes. Time for the climbers to show their hand? An early showdown? An end to the phoney war between Contador and the old boss? Andy Schleck made an unguarded comment about Contador's vaunted climbing abilities. 'I've never seen him mastering other riders, maybe once, it's true . . . in the Tour du Pays Basque.' The French say of someone who mangles their language 'you speak French like a Basque cow'. Schleck's put-down had a similar acid tone. It also revealed how confident, even bumptious, he felt about his chances in the mountains.

'His attack went against the team plan, but I didn't suppose he'd respect it so there was no surprise,' said Armstrong of Contador's sudden acceleration less than two kilometres from the ski station of Arcalis. None of his rivals could – or chose to – follow. He took twenty-one seconds on all his main rivals and was now second overall – two seconds in front of Armstrong and six seconds behind Rinaldo Nocentini, one of eight men who had broken clear, and the new yellow jersey. The winner was a new man to the Tour, the Frenchman Brice Feillu, younger brother of Romain, stage winner in 2008. He and another Frenchman, Christophe Kern, forced the pace and dropped the rest of the breakaway. Contador had his own assessment of his action: talk about the hierarchy in the Astana set-up wearied him. He thought only of taking time out of his rivals, the pace had gone stale, no one was reacting so he went. That he had not taken the yellow jersey was a good thing – it meant that the team needn't think of having to defend it.

Armstrong was clearly riled and Contador's initiative showed something of his frustration and lack of assurance. Had he helped the American into yellow, and that was certainly on offer, he would have won an ally. Instead, he isolated himself definitively, albeit merely underlining the status quo. As for Bruyneel, he said 'my riders improvised'. He couldn't regulate their attacks because 'we had no television reception in the car'. The only team car to be without coverage. Further insight into just how closely the *directeurs* monitor and control their riders, these days.

Evans did make a bid to win time early on the climb – 10.6km at an average of just over 7 per cent – into a strong headwind, but the effort died. 'I had to do something,' he said, 'but this was a climb for a strong team.' Why, then, the futile attempt, the misplaced audacity?

Most significant was the fact that Wiggins finished up with the favourites. No one could doubt the man's athleticism, but since his preferred milieu had long been the track, dazzling speed and power over four kilometres his forte, that he was now showing himself capable of riding mountains at so high a tempo was unexpected. It was too early to make any predictions, but his declared target was to finish in the top 20 and, although it is quite possible to make accurate prognosis of performance in a velodrome, Wiggins is not a man to publicise rash ambitions in any other forum. This latest show of talent was, therefore, startling. The fact is, having been a fine climber as an amateur, he'd decided he should put more effort into road-racing, after all the success on the track. 'It's about time I got my arse in gear,' he said. At the Beijing Olympics, he'd weighed 82kg and he came to the Tour at 71.5kg, the loss mostly from the upper body, where strength is needed for pursuiting.

Cancellara, on the other hand, lost over nine minutes on the day, which put paid to any pretensions at a high placing he may have had.

The following stage crossed three major climbs: the Port d'Envalira out of Andorra, and the cols de Port and d'Agnès in the Ariège before a 45km descent into Saint-Girons. Evans attacked right from the gun, to general surprise. What on earth did he hope to achieve? Cyrille Guimard called it the last cigarette of the condemned man. 'He allowed himself to be ruled by anger and that's not a wise counsellor in matters of strategy.' Luis Léon Sánchez, winner of the Paris–Nice, from Contador, took the day but his teammate Oscar Pereiro, one of four previous Tour winners in the field, abandoned. Cavendish, riding in the *grupetto* at the back of the field, was criticised by disgruntled fellow riders for not doing any work in the general call of mutual self-help. Cavendish denied the charge and probably imputed it to envy of his stage wins.

Day three in the Pyrenees took the riders over two of the iconic climbs in what is called the Circle of Death – the col d'Aspin, 1,490m, and the col du Tourmalet, 2,115m. Once again, however, there was little chance of a major change in placings: the finish in Tarbes came over 70km from the Tourmalet's summit. A day for the mavericks, therefore, and it was a third Frenchman, a teammate of Voeckler's, who seized the chance. Contador complained that team tactics had hampered him – he'd felt the climb over the Tourmalet was too leisurely, whereas he was ready to pile on the pressure. Armstrong, for his part, said that the Spaniard's attack on Arcalis was impressive and he could probably have followed but it took him by surprise. Nevertheless, there were six hard days ahead in the Alps and 'my plan is to lift my game in the third week and we'll see who's stronger'. French journalists were ratcheting up the odds, of course, keen to accentuate this internecine rivalry at the heart of a team which professed unity. A bitter duel, such as that between Anquetil and Poulidor, sells papers. 'Has Contador signed his death warrant by attacking Armstrong on Arcalis?' wrote one. The signs were of continuing discord: Contador alone at a press conference on the rest day, Bruyneel inexplicably absent . . . a Spanish rider letting slip that Contador had told him how taxing was the psychological pressure that Armstrong was applying to him . . . and so on. It may be that the American had no conception of what effect he was having on Contador because psyching out rivals is as natural to him as making excessive physical demands on himself.

Cavendish took his third stage win in Issoudun and now lay but six points adrift of Hushovd, in green. He added a fourth and the green jersey the following day. The Columbia tactic was irresistible.

Organising their train towards the stage finish, they rack up the speed to some 50kph around 5km out, Cavendish nicely tucked in for shelter. From 5km, Michael Rogers, Kim Kirchen and Maxime Montfort force the acceleration up another 10kph and, as they pass under the red kite, Tony Martin, Hincapie and Mark Renshaw take up the lead to around 70kph. One by one they peel off and, unleashed 200m from the line, Cavendish delivers the *coup de grâce*.

On the approach to Issoudun, one of the chronometers which automatically register a gap of more than a second between riders in the final three kilometres got stuck when number 53, Simon Spilak, went past so that the bunch immediately behind him was timed separately, although they were actually part of the main field. Because their leading man was timed across the line at 15 seconds behind Cavendish, they were all docked 15 seconds. Wiggins, accordingly, slipped to seventh overall at 1m 1s. Luckily, the organisers redressed this manifest injustice overnight after the following stage and Wiggins was reinstated in fifth position overall.

The tenth stage was notable for an experiment ordained by the UCI and implemented by the ASO: the riders had to ditch their earpieces for the day, at risk of a fine of between 100 and 10,000 Swiss francs and even eviction from the race. The *L'Equipe* cartoonist depicted the riders as muzzled lapdogs on a lead held by a giant *directeur sportif*. Certain riders – Millar vociferously so – enjoyed the peace and quiet, it changed little, they said, and it was better for spectators at the side of the road to see the *peloton* go by at 40kph instead of the habitual blurred flash of 60kph, even if television viewers might find the slump in speed annoying. In fact, the public didn't know what was going on and the riders themselves weren't told about the trial – aimed at making them less nervous, more attentive – until that morning's briefing. Critics of earpieces say that because of the constant stream of information flooding through them, riders have lost all sense of immediacy and spontaneous action. They are, indeed, programmed – to details of the day's route, to what and what not to do, to all instruction emanating from their *directeur*'s car. Bruyneel was hot against the ban. If the idea was to generate a more attractive day's racing, he said, it failed. Christian Prudhomme, director of the race since 2005, expressed his disappointment – opposition to the ban and general reluctance to honour the reason for it had nullified the attempt from the start. Thanks, then, to the three men who stirred up the race in a long break, caught a mere 1.9km from the line. More voluble, Marc Madiot, twice winner of the Paris–Roubaix and now *directeur* of the Françaises des Jeux team, is an adamant opponent of earpieces, but the shambles of the day (as he saw it) made him feel ashamed. It was an insult to cycle sport. 'They have spoiled 14 July [France's national Bastille Day].' One of his riders, present in the escape, agreed. 'It was pitiable. They have no respect for the Tour de France,' and it must be said that to make trial of so exceptional a change in racing *moeurs* in the biggest event on the calendar was risky at best.

In the past, before the omnipresence of radio through the *peloton*, riders would pass messages orally – the composition of an escape, the time gains, instructions from the *directeur* – and there were men in every team who could read a race better than the others and organise reaction from the saddle. Whistles, hand signals, shouted word, all still operative, for sure, but less routinely, now. The job of relaying messages most often fell to the humble water-carriers who loaded up with *bidons* at the team car for distribution to the rest of the team. That still goes on, of course, and Nigel Dick, a friend who was travelling with the Garmin team, gives a vivid portrait of what it is like for those men trawling back and forth up and down the line of the *peloton* with *bidons* stuffed in back pockets, in the neck of their jersey, lord knows where else:

> Ever fancy the idea of riding the Tour even as a humble *domestique*?
>
> You have no idea how fast these guys ride until you sit in a team car and follow the riders on a flat stage across France. For six hours the cars rev and pant and squeal round corners just to keep up.
>
> So you're riding upfront when your team-leader gets thirsty and sends you back to the Team car for supplies.
>
> Imagine riding your bike at 40/50kph. Then imagine doing it without your hands on the handlebars. Now imagine the road you're on is strange to you, dips and curves, is narrow and lined with thousands of people

yelling and screaming at you.

Sounds insane? We're not done yet.

Now add 40 team cars, 40 other cars, 40 motorcycle riders and other vehicles in a constantly shifting ballet of steel and diesel that is just happening inches or rather millimeters from your very naked elbows and knees.

Don't relax . . . you're doing 48kph, remember?

OK, now keep up with the car beside you and start taking bottles from the driver who is driving one handed, in a car with a stick shift, also at 30 mph, and he's no more familiar with the roads than you are.

Woops . . . crap . . . here's a roundabout or a bottle lying in the road dropped by the car in front. Avoid it, keep pedalling, and take more bottles till you have 8 bottles of fluids jammed down the back of your shirt.

OK, now grab a fistful of energy bars and push yourself away from the mother-ship and you're free to go.

Well, not exactly.

While you've been dicing with death or a skin-full of road-rash some cheeky rider has decided to attack off the front of the peloton which is now strung-out a quarter of a mile up the road and trying to chase him down.

And here you are back amongst the team cars with almost 2 US gallons of water down the back of your shirt and you're supposed to catch up with the guys who are chasing down the breakaway!

I saw it all happen last week and it took the *domestique/* the water carrier/the unsung hero 15 minutes to catch up and deliver his load.

Stage 12 began in Tonnerre, birthplace of the transvestite Chevalier d'Eon (1728–1810), who, posing as Mlle Lia de Beaumont, spied for France through its various political incarnations – monarchy, republic, First Empire – in Russia and London, where he died. It finished in Vittel, a prominent spa whose waters have been gushing salubriously to the public since 1845.

The Dane Nicki Sorensen raced clear of a break which included Franco Pellizotti and Egoi Martinez, each aiming for the mountains prize. There was a handful of points on offer over a series of low category climbs – the Italian took 15 of them, Martinez 12. Certain commentators huffed and hawed about this middle week of the Tour, complaining that it lacked action and was boring. Not so. The race has always been an amalgam of individual duels for the lesser as well as the greater honours: stage wins . . . the working of a team to get their man to the front to contest the sprints . . . the *sauve qui peut* cooperation of the *grupetto* . . . and this day, the absorbing contest for the green jersey. Cavendish once more beat Hushovd over the line behind the breakaways, who had taken the first seven places and their bounty of points, to extend his lead by three over the Norwegian.

Leipheimer, who crashed and broke a bone in his wrist, had to abandon.

The Vosges mountains form part of France's natural ramparts to the east and stage 13 crossed two of their higher bastions, the cols de la Schlucht, 1,139m (first entry in 1931, last visited in 2005), and du Platzerwasel, 1,193m (only once on the route, in 1967). The stage finished in Colmar, administrative centre of the Haut-Rhin, a town which Voltaire, after a visit in 1753 and musing upon the contrarieties of its location in the disputed territory of Alsace, described as 'half German, half French and totally Iroquois'. Auguste Bartholdi, born there in 1834, cleaved to the Frenchness and sculpted the Statue of Liberty, presented by the people of France to America in 1866, to honour its century of liberty and independence.

The stage, classified as 'average mountainous', was considered by many riders to be 'altogether mountainous' because of the 'frightful Platzerwasel'. Incessant rain, wind and penetrating cold added to the misery of this *jour de merde*. The main contenders stuck together, and, braving the wretched conditions, the crowds lining the route were dense, demonstrating just how popular the Tour still is. The Australian-German rider Heinrich Haussler – his father is German – moved to Germany when he was 14, determined to become a professional bike rider. He loves the cold and the wet and, joint author of an attack 3km from the start, he eventually shed the last two survivors of the break to win handsomely by over four minutes. He crossed the line in tears, overwhelmed, overjoyed. Haussler it was who seemed to have the 2009 Milan–San Remo won until

Cavendish, engulfing his lead at phenomenal pace, robbed him by a tyre's width. Pellizotti took the 27 points left on the climbs by the breakaway and overtook Martinez – who struggled badly on the Platzerwasel and added only seven to his total – in the mountains competition. Cavendish ended way down the field and ceded green to the all-rounder Hushovd, who finished sixth.

On the col du Bannstein, 35km from the finish, Oscar Freire (Rabobank) and Julian Dean (Garmin) sustained minor wounds from airgun pellets, possibly fired by a hunter and not a malevolent attack, but the police were investigating. A Garmin spokesman casually dismissed Dean's injuries: 'He doesn't feel pain,' he said.

After the finish in Besançon, there were recriminations on two fronts. An escape of ten men, including the veteran Hincapie, had a lead of 6m 30s 20km from the line. Hincapie had started the day 5m 25s behind Nocentini, stubbornly retaining the yellow jersey, so that he was, effectively, 'leader on the road'. Moreover, Nocentini's Ag2R team, leading the chase behind, was tiring and getting no support. The Columbias, whose loyalty was divided between possible yellow for Hincapie and regaining the green for Cavendish, made no move. (Hincapie had worn yellow for one day in 2006.) Inexplicably, the Garmins now moved to the front to aid the flagging Ag2R pursuit. Since their sprinter Tyler Farrar was way out of contention for the points jersey, they seemed to have nothing to gain. Under the kite, the Columbias, as it were, programmed to the task, swept past and drove Cavendish through ahead of Hushovd.

Cavendish crossed the line and looked questioningly over his left shoulder, as Hushovd came up on his right, as if to say *what was all that about?* Hushovd rode by and gesticulated. Cavendish looked baffled. An appeal ensued, not instigated by Hushovd, apparently, but prompted by the race direction's acute concern to obviate accidents in the nervy and, often in the past, insensate dash for the line. Cavendish was accused of crowding the Norwegian into the barriers and relegated to last place, with the loss of the 13 points he'd taken. This was unduly harsh and, since Hushovd had not been so incommoded that he couldn't follow his rival in, the penalty should have been a switch in their places over the line. Sadly, it led to some bitter remarks from Cavendish – 'his green jersey is tainted . . .' etc. – which soured relations between the two men.

As to the Garmin intrusion and the subsequent denial of yellow for Hincapie, by a mere five seconds, their *directeur*, Jonathan Vaughters, defended the action: Wiggins had already once been caught out by a glitch in the timing of a gap in the finishing bunch and they were at pains to make sure it didn't happen again.

As the race traversed Wittelsheim, a woman of 60, 'imprudently' crossing the road, was knocked down by a motorbike of the Garde républicaine travelling at 90kph and killed. The bike slid on and struck two women spectators, one of 61 (who suffered a broken arm) and a second, 34 years old, holding a baby. The mother, who suffered concussion, had the presence of mind to push her child aside at the moment of impact. The *peloton* observed a minute of silence before the departure of the 15th stage. Boonen wasn't among them: suffering from a virus which had blighted him from the beginning, he called a halt and left the race. As they finally rolled out, the Archbishop of Besançon, in full ecclesiastical fig, waved an asperge in blessing from the side of the road. The asperge, a bunch of hyssop twigs, delivers a spray of holy water. Hyssop also works as a purge. A purge was on the way.

Out of season, the ski station at Verbier has little to recommend it as a destination and the road up to it is devoid of character, a holiday-coach highway to a village which craves snow for its being and purpose. That it served for a mountain-top finish in the 2009 Tour de France is possibly the only distinction it merits. All the top riders were together when, 5.6km from the finish, Contador took wing with an acceleration firmer and more concerted than the attack on Arcalis. No one followed. It was, in the terms of the Spanish corrida de toros, *l'estocada*, the lethal sword thrust delivered by the matador. Andy Schleck was the only man to reply, but then only after Contador had taken a lot of ground. Armstrong, clearly in some distress, had no answer and it was Klöden who now played the supporting role, offering his drafting wheel to the American. The younger Schleck was making no significant impression on Contador when, 2km from the summit, a small group, including Evans, Sastre, Fränk Schleck and the astonishing Wiggins, drew away from Armstrong and went for home. This move by the Briton took him into third place, nine seconds behind Armstrong, who finally could not follow Klöden and lost 1m 35s on his teammate Contador, now in yellow. The ambivalence of the Astana team strategy – 'the road will decide' – was now trounced. The road *had* decided. 'It was very hard,' said Armstrong, in a more placatory mood than he had yet shown. 'Alberto has truly shown that he was better. I suffered. I tried, but I couldn't follow . . . I limited my losses . . . When someone has shown he is stronger, it would be dishonest and contrary to the code of cycling to attack him.' He added, in tones more emollient than ever he has evinced before: 'If I could sign today to be second in the Tour, I'd do it, yes, yes.' Yet, in an interview the following day, he seemed to retrench his praise of Contador. Imagine, he said, if in 1999, when he was highly ambitious for a win in the Tour, Indurain had joined his team. Indurain, the legend, would, of course, have been leader. The case doesn't answer. The unlikely hypothesis aside, in 1999, Armstrong's Tour record was two stage wins. In 2009, Contador arrived as one of only five men, with Anquetil, Gimondi, Merckx and Hinault, to have won all three major national tours.

As ever, getting off a mountain-top at the end of a stage is a real problem. While his newly installed official team leader fielded the usual blitz of questions from the post-race media scrum, Armstrong and his bodyguards set off down the road on mountain bikes. Another shift in his comportment. Although he still has his own vehicle to whisk him to the hotel, eschewing the team bus, hitherto he routinely helicoptered off cul-de-sac summits.

After the second rest day, stage 16 began in Switzerland, in Martigny, home of a Musée et Chiens Saint-Bernard – a combined museum, kennels, gift shop (Valais products), garden and restaurant. Martigny is also a centre for a favourite local event, cow-fighting. Combats – cows with butch names like Bataille, Rafale, Vandale, Diablesse (Battle, Gust of Wind – hmm – Vandal, She-Devil), pushing, shoving, heaving – may last for up to 40 minutes and end when only one cow is left standing. Only in Switzerland . . . Only in Switzerland? Actually quite common hereabouts in France and Italy, too

The denouement came closer: two stages in the Alps, a time-trial and the final combat on Mont Ventoux, the day before the *Grande Arrivée* in Paris. From Martigny (547m) to the Grand-Saint-Bernard (2,473m) is a more or less a continuous climb, albeit the first 17km are fairly gentle before the gradient proper kicks in. There follow some 26km of gradually sharpening steepness, the last 5km rearing up at between 8 and 10 per cent. This is the pass Napoleon crossed with the Grande Armée in May 1800 on his way to drive the Austrians out of Italy. From the col, where stands a hospice recalling the original Carthusian monastery built for the succour of pilgrims and other peregrinators, runs a long descent into Italy and through the Valle d'Aosta to the foot of the Petit-Saint-Bernard (2,188m). The Pope, taking a summer break in the town of Aosta, didn't make a personal appearance but sent a papal Benedicite and Bonne Route.

The 31km descent to the finish in Bourg-Saint-Maurice suggested that any significant change in the overall standings was unlikely, but the Schleck brothers were anything but content to let things lie. A small group of riders opened a gap on the descent on the Grand-Saint-Bernard in pursuit of Pellizotti and Vladimir Karpets, of the new Russian team Katusha. They joined before the final climb and it was Pellizotti who crossed the summit in the lead, attended by Evans' teammate, the young Belgian Jürgen Van den Broeck, who had assumed the role of leader on the road in default of his nominal captain, already in difficulties on the climb. The Basque Mikel Astarloza and the Frenchman Amaël Moinard hooked on and they set off for the *Arrivée*. Behind them Fränk Schleck stirred the action. Andy joined him with Contador, Wiggins, Klöden and the Italian Vincenzo Nibali, who had begun to show real flair. Armstrong was dropped. However, as Fränk Schleck faltered, Armstrong clawed his way back and the pair of them gradually retrieved the lost ground to come in with the rest. Astarloza won the stage, only his second win as a professional – he took the Tour Down Under in 2003.

On the descent of the Petit-Saint-Bernard, the veteran *rouleur* Jens Voigt had a horrible crash – his back wheel slipped and flipped on the paint of a white line. It is a sight which gives any cyclist the shudders: the pain and distress of flesh scraped and abraded, bones broken, the fearful shock of the fall and the agonising slide along the asphalt. Luckily, the injuries looked worse than they were later reported to be – a broken cheekbone, concussion, severe lacerations, of course.

Stage 17. Bourg-Saint-Maurice–Le Grand-Bornand. 169.5km: cormet de Roselend (1,968m), col des Saisies (1,650m), côte d'Arâches (964m), col de Romme (1,297m), col de la Colombière

(1,618m) . . . four first category, one second.

I was in the Alps the week before the Tour came through, researching the second volume of a study of the mountains.[1] The photographer and I drove this Étape Reine. The col de Romme has never featured on the Tour nor is it obvious on the Michelin map. I had to consult a very large-scale walkers' chart to find it. In the ensemble of this day's climbing – five cols with very little in the way of valley between the foot of one and the next – the Romme, which leads directly onto the Colombière, is a pure climber's col, that is to say, a brute. It hurts from the very start – possibly the reason why someone has set a small shrine to the Virgin Mary (PPN . . . *priez pour nous*) into the rock of the sidewall a short distance up. The first three kilometres hit around 10 per cent, sheer rock to the left, the yawning abyss of the valley to the right. In the first village the gradient eases a little but then resumes at 10 per cent. After the village which names the col there is a false flat before the drop onto the final approach to the Colombière. No relief.

The col de Romme itself isn't marked but one of the residents of the village had constructed a cardboard and wood model of an uphill road topped with a small painted col sign on his front lawn. Other gardens were adorned with bikes, both real and made of flowers; window ledges, telegraph poles, barn doors, café entrances were hung with banners, garlands, polka-dot jersey, placards welcoming the Tour. In Reposoir, where the Romme melds with the Colombière, in the car park opposite the Mairie sat a number of campervans. I knocked on the door of one – an elderly couple sitting with cups of coffee, reading. Were they waiting for the Tour? They were. Six days to go. Now, I mean to cast no aspersions on the charms of Reposoir (means 'resting spot' but you will have to read my book to find out why). I received a kindly welcome in the Mairie office, my initial enquiry – about an enigmatic graffito on the Romme – sadly remains unanswered, but we were encouraged to visit the old Carthusian monastery nearby, and did so. However, Reposoir didn't *look* to have what you'd call a lot of immediate diversion on hand, no regular entertainment aside from what is almost certainly a decent restaurant and a perfectly unexceptionable bar. Shops: grocery, stationers', Missy Sports. The church. The monastery, now occupied by Carmelite nuns. It gives cogent testimony, therefore, to the ardour of your determined Tour fan that he and she should be happy to pass a week of repose in a place named for the pastime in expectation of a brief explosion of bike-race fireworks. There were still more campervans lined up on the Colombière, either side of the col and packing a large lay-by below it, where roadside attractions were even thinner on the ground. Perhaps they organise Scrabble tournaments.

The green jersey competition was inaugurated in 1953 to encourage those riders who had no hope of vying for either the yellow jersey nor yet the mountains prize. (The polka dots didn't come until 1975.) However, it was an era when most riders had to be all-rounders, *rouleurs*, if not at home in the mountains, at least adaptable to them. The unseemly spat between Cavendish and Hushovd pointed up a basic issue: whether the green should reward the best sprinter or, as in custom and usage, the most consistent finisher? Hushovd's actions on this queen of stages, designed to make sure of green in Paris, underlined the latter. He joined the first break of the day and was first to both the intermediate sprints – at the bottom of the Saisies and the Arâches – took the maximum 12 points and now led Cavendish by 30. All he had to do to ensure winning the points competition in Paris was stick to Cavendish.

On the Romme, the two Schlecks, Contador and Klöden were in the lead, following two spurts from the Luxemburgers, and at the col, they had an advantage of 1m 2s over Armstrong, Nibali, Wiggins and his teammate Christian Vande Velde. Vande Velde, fourth overall in 2008, had injured his back during the Giro and it was a marvel that he was riding so soon afterwards. That he rode with such application to support the man who had become de facto leader of the Garmin team was a great tribute to the team ethic and his own generosity. At the foot of the Romme, the time gap stood at 1m 20s and, on the climb, Fränk Schleck forced the pace. Now we must rely on *a posteriori* report. Contador says that about 1.5km from the summit, he asked Klöden if it was all right for him to attack, by implication 'can you follow?' Klöden, said the Spaniard, consented. Contador attacked. Neither the Schlecks nor Klöden answered. Contador looked round, saw that Klöden was dropped and waited for the Schlecks. They continued over the col, Contador checking for his teammate – down by 100m, then out of view. The yellow jersey pressed on with the Schlecks, doing no work, and Fränk took the stage in Le Grand-Bornand, then declared that he would now devote himself to keeping his brother on the podium.

Armstrong, 2m 6s down on the leaders when they topped the climb, now attacked and dropped Wiggins and Nibali near the top. (Vande Velde had peeled off, exhausted by his relaying effort.) Nibali rejoined him, they caught Klöden, and Armstrong and Nibali finished at 2m 18s on the leaders, Klöden at 2m 27s, Wiggins at 3m 7s. The overall standings read: Contador, A. Schleck 2m 26s, F. Schleck 3m 25s, Armstrong 3m 55s, Klöden 4m 44s, Wiggins 4m 53s.

The Astana hierarchy was not pleased. Contador's high-handed attack had compromised the chance of a podium finish for both Armstrong and Klöden. (On the testimony of their performance that day and the final overall, this was *not* feasible. And, since when was a yellow jersey required to help relay weaker members of his team?) The American said that he had 'always followed team orders' . . . he did, but then he was instrumental in framing them.

The time-trial, a 40.5km circuit of Lac d'Annecy, shuffled the top order further: Contador won the stage, Andy Schleck conceded 1m 45s but stayed in second place, Armstrong (who lost 1m 30s) moved to third and Wiggins (43s down) to fourth.

'Get me to the top of the col and I'll do it,' Cavendish told his team next morning. He referred to the l'Escrinet, 16km before the descent into Aubenas. They did. He did. On his wheel, Hushovd. (A split between the sprinting bunch containing Armstrong and the chasers allowed him to snaffle four extra seconds on his rivals.) Afterwards, Cavendish spoke with a magnanimity which overrode any animus. 'After what Thor did in the high Alps he deserves the green jersey, no one more. It made me feel humble. Everything I do is thanks to my team.' And, next day, they reached the summit of the fearsome Mont Ventoux together, laughing, merry as grigs, comrades in mutual respect.

The Ventoux fishes out many depths of emotion but rarely chuckling good humour. The Schlecks had made no secret of their intention to attack. Contador might still commit a decisive error – he had lost the Paris–Nice when seemingly assured of victory, by failing to eat properly and going down with the hunger-knock.

Both Armstrong and Wiggins were bound to fight all the way for a podium finish. The stage victory assumed secondary importance.

On the upper slopes of the bald mountain, Giant of Provence, Domain of the Angels, generator of the wind turbines which flay the region, Juan Manuel Garate and Tony Martin were heading for the finish, nearly two minutes ahead of the main scrap. Andy Schleck attacked four times and four times Contador went with him. Each time he accelerated, Andy looked behind him, not for Contador but to see if his brother was there. The aim, to haul him onto the podium. Had he pursued the attack, with Contador, who knows but they might have overtaken the leaders? But this was brother helping brother. Three times Fränk answered, the fourth time he could not and stayed with Armstrong, dogged by Wiggins. In the final act of the continuing drama of this Tour, the most exciting and elevating in years, Armstrong was magnificent and *L'Equipe*, for so long his remorseless gadfly, awarded him its headline next day: *Chapeau, le Texan.* For Wiggins, too, it was a heroic achievement. Finally unable to hold the American, he faltered. But this was the mountain on which Tommy Simpson had died and his photograph was on Wiggins' handlebars. 'I had an added force with me today,' he said. There was no doubt that he had the heart to ride himself into that oblivion beyond pain. That he also had the legs was what counted and, as he crossed the line, completely spent, he had held onto fourth overall by three meagre seconds over Fränk Schleck, the best placing by a Briton since Robert Millar's fourth in 1984.

(Garate heaved some extra speed out of himself to beat Martin by three seconds.)

If the conclusion of the Tour had not quite the tension of the 1989 showdown on the Champs-Elysées, when Greg Lemond snatched victory from Laurent Fignon by eight seconds, Ventoux had certainly produced a finale of epic grandeur. And the crowds up there were dense-packed.

There remained the arrival in Paris and the glory of the win on the Champs-Elysées. Inside 3km of the line, the Garmin team suddenly went onto the offensive, clearly determined to spoil the Columbia-Cavendish party. Vande Velde, Millar, Dean, Farrar launched to the front and drove the entire field at around 80kph, Millar shouting to Vande Velde to give it full gas. The American rode flat out for a kilometre, perhaps more, before pulling off to allow Millar to come through. Another stupendous effort, Columbia apparently caught up in the chase, mounting no challenge. But, as the red kite loomed, suddenly Hincapie broke clear down the opposite side of the road, followed tightly by Renshaw and Cavendish. It was superb: the three-man rocket going for home. But Garmin came back, Dean and Farrar cutting a line towards the final bend onto the long, long straight up the Champs towards the Arc de Triomphe. It was tight and they were going to cut it very fine, but as Hincapie – in considerable pain from a broken collarbone sustained in a crash on stage 19 but refusing to have an X-ray – swung clear, Renshaw took his own line for the apex, a tangent past the Garmin duo sliced closer than seemed possible. He and Cavendish, as if on a tandem, dizzy speed and, 100m from the line, Cavendish went, unstoppable, the following pack nowhere. So fast were they moving that Renshaw, the quickest lead-out man in the *peloton*, came second. Unheard of.

Six wins in a single Tour for Cavendish, the youngest winner of ten stages all-told since the war. Hushovd took green by ten points only – his alpine panache had been timely.

Pellizotti won polka dots, Andy Schleck won white as best young rider for the second year running. Wiggins, fourth overall. Armstrong, after a three years' absence, the oldest man on the podium since Poulidor (then 40) in 1976. Contador, second victory. Asked who'd been his toughest opponent, he replied, 'The hotel.' In blackly comic echo of the alienation he'd endured for most of the Tour, Contador, standing on the podium as victor, for several minutes had to listen to the strains of '*Der er et ynidgt land*' ('There is a lovely land'), the national anthem of Denmark and Rasmussen, the disgraced Dane who'd led the 2007 Tour (Contador's first win) before being booted out. The Iberian fans whistled their dismay until the organisers located the '*Marcha Real*', the wordless Spanish hymn.

Contador has said he wants to leave Astana, but Astana say they will hold him to the remaining year of his contract. Armstrong and Bruyneel will have a new team next year, sponsored by an American electronics retailer, RadioShack, and the American has said he will come back, stronger, to the Tour.

And, another comeback: no positive dope tests, so far.
This race was a triumph . . . *absit omen.*

NOTE
1. *Great Road Climbs of the High Alps* , complementing vol. I, *Great Road Climbs of the Southern Alps and Riviera,* to be published by Rapha Racing (www.rapha.cc)

CHAPTER TWENTY

2010

Hail and Farewell

The first time the Tour began on foreign soil, in 1954, the organisers chose Amsterdam in Holland as a mark of solidarity with the suffering of the Netherlanders during the German occupation. The great port of Rotterdam founded, like the Dutch capital, in the twelfth century, was nigh on obliterated by German bombing in 1940; the town was the birthplace of the humanist scholar Erasmus, and the 2010 Prologue route crossed the magnificent new bridge named for him spanning the Nieuwe Maas river. The Tour organisation is careful to honour the race's history, and 2010 marked the centenary of the Tour's first visit to the high cols of the Pyrenees. Advances in television technology meant that the strictly limited space atop the monster col du Tourmalet could accommodate a stage finish, and a possible showdown, three days from Paris.

Alberto Contador, emancipated from the malign chaperoning of Johan Bruyneel and Lance Armstrong in 2009, had won his second Paris–Nice and started as clear favourite to win. His Astana team was not only now declared loyal to his interests, it had been strengthened by the return of Alexandr Vinokourov, banned for doping in 2007. The Italian Ivan Basso was also restored to the *peloton* and had won the Giro d'Italia. Armstrong himself, who had ridden well in the tours of Switzerland and Luxembourg, was less ambiguous about his own ambitions this year. He felt stronger and in better form than in 2009, and he was unguarded in saying that this Tour de France, in which he was riding for the new outfit sponsored by the American chain store RadioShack, would be his last but that he aimed to win it. Andy and Fränk Schleck must surely have refined their tactics, somewhat ill-sorted last year, to prosper Andy's battle with Contador; Cadel Evans, always censured for timidity, had found a new aggression and, riding for a new team, was current world road-race champion. He'd won the rainbow jersey by a bold attacking move in Italy last autumn, fired, perhaps, by a blatant failure of technical help that had robbed him of the Vuelta a España a month before.

Of other men routinely mentioned as possible contenders for overall victory, none seemed in the same league as the top riders, but Bradley Wiggins, the surprise of 2009, was much bruited for a high placing. The new team for which he was riding, financed to a massive 11 million euros per annum by the Sky organisation and managed by the mastermind of British track successes in the past few years, Dave Brailsford, had a firmly stated ambition to win the Tour within five years. Wiggins had quit Garmin to join Sky, lured by a generous fee, but compounded what seemed to many to be a bad move by some shabby comments. Snootily dismissive of a team that had given him such sterling support in 2009, he said that he wanted to ride with a premier league club, a Manchester United as opposed to Wigan Athletic. The last British-sponsored team to ride the Tour came and went in 1987 and included the Australian Shane Sutton, now part of the Sky staff overseeing a team that fielded only three Britons: Wiggins, the Welshman Geraint Thomas, current British road champion, and Steve Cummings, riding his first Tour. The team was dedicated to Wiggins, but Brailsford was also hedging options: the Swede Thomas Löfkvist was in cracking form and would also be in contention for a high overall placing. The Sky management were certainly talking a good race and their near obsessive attention to detail is known. The team ethic is undeniably strong, but there was a certain naivety about their approach. They preached vacuous mantras like 'Ride the line' (whatever that means) and 'Pride, Passion, Commitment', as if riders needed to be reminded that they were competing in the greatest bike race in the world.

Brailsford, scanning the weather forecast ahead of the Prologue, elected to send out the ultra-quick time-triallist Wiggins early in the day to avoid the predicted rain. A sorry miscue. Wiggins rode the circuit in the wet and posted only a modest time. He shrugged off the disappointment: it was only seconds lost; they would not count in three weeks' time. It was a disturbing hint of a general and unhelpful casual acceptance of setback.

The Swiss Fabian Cancellara won the Prologue, as expected, and David Millar rode brilliantly to come third. Mark Cavendish's teammate the German Tony Martin came second and Armstrong fourth, 22 seconds down. Andy Shleck, who the week before had become Luxembourg time-trial champion, had much improved his riding against the clock, but not this day: over 8.9km, he lost 1m 9s to the winner and an unhealthy 42 seconds on Contador. 'I was really crap today,' he said, then added, 'In the third week, we won't be talking about these lost seconds any more.' Nemesis, the baleful goddess who punishes the folly of human pride, must surely have been listening. Those lost seconds might be said to have cost him the Tour.

The race route had much to commend it for variety. The first day ran across the Dutch polders, always prey to the offshore wind. Cyrille Guimard has compared bike racing to yachting in that dealing with winds is a vital skill. (Consider what trouble a brisk crosswind gave Contador in 2009.) A dead flat stage into Brussels and the *peloton* fragmented into echelons. Two stages across Belgium ended with 13.2km of the infamous cobbles, the *pavé* of the Hell of the North, the Tour visiting the classic terrain of the Flandrian one-day races. A number of lumpy stages, across the Jura and the southern edge of the Massif Central, only two days in the Alps, but, honouring their first inclusion, the Pyrenees hosted four days with two crossings of the Tourmalet. Nodding at the 1910 stage that ran 326km from Bagnères de Luchon to Bayonne over five mighty cols, the route crossed those same mountains in one stage from Luchon to Pau, a mere 199.5km by comparison. No team time-trial and only one long individual race against the clock. The aim was evidently to bring the final decision to the mountains, three days before the arrival in Paris.

Cavendish had brought opprobrium on himself – a thoughtless obscene gesture at a stage finish in the Tour de Romandie (which he passed off as being aimed at ignorant journalists, no one else) and careless riding in the Tour de Suisse that brought down Heinrich Haussler, Thor Hushovd's teammate (broken elbow), and Tom Boonen, both out of the Tour. Guimard was scathing: Cavendish is a track rider; he ought to be able to hold a better line. Cavendish had also had a miserable start to the season – emotional upheavals and serious dental surgery – but had declared his ambition to win the green jersey, by stage wins. Intermediate sprints are not his style. Alas, on stage one, riding in the big bunch, he mistimed a sharp right-hand bend 2.2km from the line, went down and took Oscar Freire and Jeremy Hunt with him. There were angry murmurs – Cavendish should show more respect – and *L'Equipe* dubbed him '*Le Pyromane*', fire-raiser, rabble-rouser. A ginger dog ran out into the road and felled Millar, Basso and Nicolas Roche, and the veteran Italian sprinter Alessandro Petacchi took his first Tour win since 2003, when he won four stages. Earlier in the day, a member of Cavendish's HTC-Columbia team, the Australian Adam Hansen, crashed and broke his collarbone. He rode on but did not start the next day.

Stage two, another flat course, passed by Tervuren, childhood home of the great Eddy Merckx. An escape, initiated by the Frenchman Sylvain Chavanel, went away some 190km from the finish in Spa. Chavanel, hit by a following car in the Liège–Bastogne–Liège, in April, suffered a fractured skull at the base just above the spine and severe facial injuries. Much feted in France but for no good reason of victories won, he now rides for a Belgian team and said that because of his accident he had come to the Tour fresher than he would normally do. At the foot of the col de Stockeu, 34km from the finish, in pouring rain, Chavanel cut loose from the breakaways. Perhaps the cars following him left a slick of oil or petrol on the wet road of the descent: the chasing *peloton*, split in two, the yellow jersey Cancellara in the lead bunch, Armstrong, Contador and the Schlecks behind, was further shattered by a succession of crashes on tarmac that someone described as being as slippery as wet bathroom tiles. Armstrong, Evans, Petacchi, George Hincapie, all went down. Christian Vande Velde, Garmin's contender for GC, was left with a severely contused and bloody left eye and, it transpired, two broken ribs. He did not start next day. The Schlecks went down, too, and were left stranded some

15km from the finish. Riding at the head of the *peloton* into Spa, Cancellara, their teammate, took charge. The yellow jersey told the organisers that the race had become too perilous to contest and that the leading riders would not be sprinting for second place behind Chavanel, who had taken the stage and yellow. Hushovd, eager to garner points for the green jersey, complied reluctantly with what became a group decision.

About the next stage, onto the cobbles, many riders had expressed disquiet. The Tour had no business on these roads, too many riders had no experience of them, there would be carnage. Hunter underlined the danger: 'See how much you guys like hitting the deck at 60kph.' Fränk Schleck did hit the deck, if not at that speed, and broke his collarbone. He was out. Armstrong punctured, was held up for a replacement and had to chase most of the way to the finish on his own. He lost more than two minutes to Andy Schleck, 55 seconds to Contador, who had ridden the cobbles on a recce in the spring and finished third in the Flèche Wallonne classic. The winner of that race, Evans, a former mountain-bike world champion, had a fine day, too. He finished third and moved up to third overall. Schleck himself took back 31 seconds over Contador and moved up to sixth overall. Hushovd won the stage and the green jersey, some recompense for the previous day's frustration, and Cancellara took back yellow. Wiggins redeemed his unworthy Prologue time by a performance of some merit and, 57th overall at the day's start, was now 14th. Thomas had ridden like a champion and was now second overall and in the best young rider's white jersey.

Armstrong, his right forearm bandaged, delivered a gnomic utterance: 'Sometimes you're the hammer, sometimes you're the nail. Today, I was the nail. I have 20 days now to be the hammer.' Bold words, closer aligned to the misplaced bravado of an odd belief that he really might win the race than a clear sense of the possible. Sean Yates, a *directeur sportif* with Sky, pointed out that the Texan's time-trials in the California and Swiss tours had been mediocre 'and the chrono doesn't lie'. Monsieur Paris–Roubaix, Roger de Vlaeminck, opined: 'On the *pavé*, it's a question of morale. Nothing happens by chance. The best riders never puncture.'

More than half the riders in the race had crashed. It was hoped that the fourth stage, Cambrai to Reims, across the battlefields of the First World War, might bandage the wounds. It certainly did nothing for Cavendish's wobbly confidence. Riding comfortably in the Columbia lead-out train down the left-side barriers, he saw Petacchi's chosen lead-out man, Danilo Hondo, surge at flat-out speed down the right-hand gap. It was a brilliant strike, a diversion that disrupted the opposition so completely that Petacchi had only to follow through and take his second win ahead of the Sky sprinter Edvald Boassen Hagen and Garmin's Julian Dean. Garmin's lead sprinter, Tyler Farrar, was riding with a probable broken wrist. Millar, having crashed three times on the stage into Spa and then caught fever and a stomach bug, was in a sorry state. He spent 180km on his own this day, which he described as one of his worst-ever days on a bike, saying, 'I [was] convinced I was going to abandon or be eliminated.' He survived, 42 minutes behind the winner.

Cavendish, seeing the sprint lost, petulantly sat up and threw away precious points in the green jersey competition, a sign of shaken faith, if not deserving of one journalist's jibe 'coward'. He said he was disappointed: his teammates had ridden so hard for him and he didn't finish it off. He made up for it next day across the Champagne region in scorching heat – one bike computer read 42°C. Bernhard Eisel and Mark Renshaw gave him the perfect lead-out and he repaid them. The relief was palpable; on the podium, he wept. He admitted that he had felt a terrible stress and in fact Petacchi had come up to him during the stage and told him that the problem wasn't in his legs, it was in his head. 'In the last few days, I came crashing down to earth very hard and it hurt,' he said. Accepting his vulnerability, he regained his strength of mind and, next day, on a long, undulating course, won again, lengths ahead of the pursuers, his true style. It was his twelfth Tour victory, bringing him level with his mentor, Erik Zabel.

Stage seven, up to the Station des Rousses in the Jura mountains, had a tough profile: six categorised climbs. Hondo and the French rider Jérôme Pineau, chasing points in the mountains prize, were a long time clear of the main bunch. Then a second breakaway, including Chavanel and Thomas Voeckler, caught them. On the final climb, a long, modest gradient ('like riding the rollers', said Chavanel), Pineau went ahead. Hondo could not respond, Chavanel chased and, after a brief conversation with his teammate – 'You've got the polka dots, I'm off for yellow again' – he dropped Pineau and took his second stage win and the overall lead. Sky's Boasson Hagen trailed in 18m 57s down, exhausted by the heat from both the sun and the high tempo of the race.

On the approach to the col de la Ramaz, one of two first-category climbs before the stage eight finish at the ski station of Avoriaz, Armstrong clipped a kerb with a pedal at 50kph and pitched over. The front tyre was ripped off, he skidded into another rider and his saddle broke. This was a rider who never used to fall. It was a sure sign of dwindling power. 'I've never been so unlucky,' he said, as if that explained the otherwise obvious. He was then nearly decked again by a Basque rider making a dog's breakfast of grabbing a musette and was cooked. He finished 11m 45s down and admitted that his race was over; he was going simply to enjoy his last Tour de France.

Supposedly to suppress an attack by Contador, the Sky team frittered precious energy on the Ramaz. This was perplexing. Juan Antonio Flecha drove them up at such a searing pace that their top men had little in reserve for the final climb. Wiggins, on a climb he'd have cruised up last year, cracked three kilometres from the top and 'had to back off so I wouldn't completely blow . . . damage limitation . . . I have to admit that I wasn't good enough today.' It was a worrying sign of laissez-faire. He was being coached by a sports psychiatrist to focus on the next challenge rather than to dwell on losses, as if such advice is revolutionary in the world of competitive sport. He might have done better to adhere to the grittier maxim put about by Stuart O'Grady: 'Harden the fuck up.'

Up ahead, Contador was struggling and the Saxo Bank *directeur*, Bjarne Rijs, spotted it. Five kilometres from the line, he told Schleck to attack. Schleck, sticking to his belief that the Pyrenees would decide the issue, refused, a caution that he must, surely, have come to rue. He did finally attack, under the red kite, one kilometre to go, and took ten seconds out of the Spaniard. Contador was being led up the slope by his man Dani Navarro, whom he praised roundly as 'a monster of generosity', but was finding it difficult to breathe – a combination of allergy and suffocating heat. Schleck had expressed doubts about Evans' ability, but the Australian had acknowledged that he needed to change his mentality and, although he couldn't follow Schleck's attack – a fall earlier in the day had discommoded him so that he couldn't pull on the handlebars – he did ride into the overall lead, the first rider to exchange rainbow for yellow since Greg Lemond in 1990. Now he was saying openly, 'I can win.' However, he'd sustained a hairline fracture in the elbow and, though a rest day followed and he did not broadcast the seriousness of his injury, his race was already compromised. Millar, not always at his best in the mountains, had nonetheless recovered and was in buoyant spirits again. He said that this was one of his best days ever in the Tour.

Stage nine: 204.5km, 66km of climbing, 4,000m of height gained, two first category climbs, one *hors catégorie*. Another French attack early on and Sandy Casar the third French stage winner at the finish in Saint-Jean-de-Maurienne. On the col de la Madeleine, 27.5km long, Schleck attacked Contador three times and three times Contador held his wheel. They agreed a truce, expressly not to take unnecessary risks on a tricky descent. An odd way to contest a Tour, turning it into an agreed duel, time and date fixed ahead. Jens Voigt, the human engine, had relayed Schleck most of the way up the Madeleine but was spent one kilometre short of the col. Had he been able to stay with his teammate, what work he might have done for him on the final straight. From the foot of the col, Contador and Schleck chased in tandem along the valley and very nearly caught the breakaways, among them the senior man of the *peloton*, Christophe Moreau, 39 years old, who had just announced that he would retire at the end of the season. Casar knew the finish well, the sharp left-hand bend and the short dash for the line. He attacked with smart timing. Schleck went into yellow and Anthony Charteau took over the polka dots from his compatriot Pineau.

Evans, who caved in on the Madeleine, collapsed in tears at the finish, his race and the yellow gone. Wiggins, however, was talking up his own chance of finishing on the podium in Paris.

On 8 July 1971, Luis Ocaña launched an attack on the vicious côte de Laffrey (7km at 9 per cent) out of Vizille that eventually put eight minutes into Merckx. This year, it presented the worst of the last day in the Alps. Vasil Kiryienka of Caisse d'Epargne and Sérgio Paulinho of RadioShack were the sole survivors of a break on the finish into Gap. They were both riding hard, with none of that tiresome jockeying for position that frequently mars such a face-off. Paulinho, former Olympic silver medallist on the road, outfoxed the Belarusian in the two-up sprint and thus took only the ninth ever Tour stage win by a Portuguese. Ten kilometres behind them, Roche had broken clear of a dawdling pack – 'They were all taking it fairly easy there and I didn't see why I should hang around' – and moved up to 13th overall. Wiggins dropped further, to 17th, and any talk of the podium looked whimsical. Pineau assumed the polka dots once more and Armstrong lost a further minute. Millar was suffering again, feeling even worse than before (two cracked ribs confirmed), but, as he put it, 'The pace was finally much lower and . . . in comparison to Tuesday it was a cakewalk.' Brave riding and a plausible mental toughness.

Cavendish won his third stage in Bourg-lès-Valence, going from 350m – 'the longest break of the day' he said – but Renshaw, his pilot fish, as the French call the lead-out man, was evicted. Hitting the front of the speeding bunch, as usual, he reacted ill when Dean rode up on his left elbow. A minor shove, maybe, but Renshaw leaned across and hit the New Zealander three times with his helmet. As Hondo later told me, once might have been ignored but three times risked a crash, and Dean had done nothing aggressive; he certainly hadn't forced Renshaw into the barriers, as the Australian claimed.

The two kilometres of plateau into the stage twelve finish at the aerodrome in Mende is preceded by a brutal hill three kilometres long at 10 per cent, the Montée Jalabert, after Laurent Jalabert's solo victory here in 1995, the year of his second overall green jersey. Vinokourov, riding for Contador, was nevertheless in the hunt for a stage victory. He went clear from the remnants of a break and, one kilometre from the summit of what is also called the côte de la Croix-Neuve, he dropped his sole companion, Kiryienka, angling to make up for his loss in Gap, and went for home. Back down the road, Contador, seeing Schleck in trouble, attacked. He caught Joaquim Rodríguez and the two Spaniards rode on past Vinokourov. Contador said nothing. Rodríguez, in his first

Tour, won the stage, Schleck lost ten seconds and Vinokourov was spitting: why had Contador relayed an opponent for such a meagre gain and deprived Astana of a stage win? Not for the first or the last time, Contador blamed a problem with his earpiece – he had no idea where Vino was. This is improbable.

For Farrar, the Tour was over. A slight fracture in his left hand and a badly hurt elbow meant that he couldn't support himself on his bike.

Vino's *directeur* told the press that 'he claims to have tired legs but his head is still hard, and when Vino is angry . . .' He was, for sure, angry, and on another day of torrid heat into Revel in the Haute-Garonne, he unleashed his fury on the final obstacle of a consistently hilly stage, the côte de Saint-Ferréol. Just under 2km long and a moderate 6 per cent, it was nonetheless enough to propel him into a lead that he held for the last 7.5km to win by 13 seconds. Cavendish, showing just how strong his self-assurance had become once more, despite the loss of Renshaw, rode the hill with ease and took the final bunch sprint ahead of Petacchi, who recovered green from Hushovd.

It was another day when the French had been on the attack, showing a welcome fiery spirit. They have no rider capable of winning the Tour, but this generation of professionals, a clutch of them all 31 years old, are fostering a habit of aggression, vital to any future prospect. Voeckler incarnates the spirit: he attacks, he says, not merely to attack but to win. The *baroudeur*, or opportunist, often sets off without a specific aim to win, hoping to stir up the action, to grab some publicity time for his sponsor. Thomas Voeckler, so often reeled in from what might seem to be futile sorties, speaks differently. It's an agreeable attitude. For too long, the French have felt sorry for themselves and dolefully shrugged their shoulders at their lack of success. Others have called it, rather, lack of enterprise, lame excuse. Chavanel has striven to buck this trend and has now thrown off any hint of caution in exchange for real boldness of action. It must be said, too, that whereas once around two-thirds of the Tour *peloton* was made up of French riders, in this global age there are but 35 of 198.

Tour tradition allots a curious celebrity to the *lanterne rouge*, the race's tail-ender. As the arch-*baroudeur* Jacky Durand once told me, better the queer fame of last man into Paris than the anonymity of the middle of the bunch. However, some things do not last, and Marc Madiot, twice winner of the Paris–Roubaix and now *directeur* of the Française des Jeux team, lambasted his man Anthony Roux, the current *lanterne rouge*, at a morning briefing. 'Last man in the Tour de France is shameful. I do not like *lanternes rouges*.' The implication was that Roux ought to follow, instead, the boisterous example of his teammate Casar.

Sunday, 18 July, Mirepoix
The Tour is due here, a medieval bastide with a pretty square of thirteenth- to fifteenth-century houses built over wooden arcades, at around 1.20 p.m. The photographer Gerard Brown and I set off from the sleepy town much earlier and head along the race route towards the Port de Pailhères: quiet, twisting roads out of the Aude into the Ariège, bright sun, not much sign of life, yet, in somnolent villages that will later wave the Tour through. The road finally quits open country and narrows into the Gorges de Saint-Georges and the Gorges de l'Aude, craggy stone cliffs crowding on either side. We join a swelling argosy of bikes and cars making for the big col. On the col itself, the procession slows into a cortège and eventually stalls. Crowds of people are already marking their pitch at the roadside and camper vans are squeezed into impossible gaps on the verges. Eventually, we creep up the first slopes of the climb to a junction where a gendarme is ordering cars to turn round and head back down the road: there is no more room further up. We reach the front of the queue and the gendarme beckons us through on the 'open sesame' of our blue press sticker.

On this climb, in 2003, Jan Ullrich very nearly broke Armstrong. It's 15.5km long, a punishing average gradient of 8 per cent, with some lifts of up to 10.5 per cent. By the time we find our spot, just below the summit, the sun is high and broiling. The bald cap of the mountain is thickly invested with fans, barbecues on the go, iceboxes to hand, people drifting aimlessly up and down the road, waiting, waiting for the bike race. It's 1 p.m. Airless heat. A massive crowd on a mountain-top that might be a convention of eccentric religionists drawn on promise of a divine manifestation. There is a sense that everyone here is in the know, shy to divulge but confirmed in their belief that something special is going to happen. A miraculous epiphany.

At nearly three o'clock, the caravan rackets up the narrow road to the pass. The usual cascades of objects and souvenirs fly to either verge, earnest foragers add to their stash. The shutterbug straps on his pouched accessories belt and makes for the col. I observe an Ag2R car draw up and its two occupants begin filling *bidons* with cold water for their riders, then, *bidons* packed into bags, walk up the road past the gendarmes spaced out to keep an eye on the spectators.

A hee-haw of klaxons down the mountains, the lead cars flit in and out of my view of sections of hairpin down the climb, and here is the Ag2R rider Christophe Riblon, by himself. He comes past, taut with effort but his face set. Over this vicious col, a 19km drop into Ax-les-Thermes and 8km up to the finish at Ax Trois Domaines. He's been away with nine others since kilometre twenty-four, and not far from the top of this ascent he shelled out the last of them. He later said that he'd seen a shooting star when he was a child and made a wish to be a racing cyclist, and although he wouldn't have bet a single euro on winning this day, here he was, going for it. After him, Carlos Sastre, winner on this stage in 2003, and other survivors of the break, still hanging on. And so we watch them all, lone riders, ones and twos, small knots and, at the back, the *sauve qui peut* bunch of sprinters and others who respond to the general alarm call '*grupetto*' (popularised in the '90s by the Italian rider Eros Poli) and ride at a pace just fast enough to beat the day's time limit. This year, it's the German and Austrian sprinters Hondo and Eisel who organise them.

The moment the gendarmerie *fin de course* wagon goes by, we are in the car and behind it, to get off the mountain before the madness of the general evacuation. Exhilarating, down the hairpins, running free, no traffic. Beeline for the escape route of the Ariège valley. At the foot of the climb, a young woman holds up a sign: 'RECHERCHE CYCLISTE A ADOPTER' (looking for a cyclist to adopt).

Riblon made it, another French victory; Contador and Schleck came in together with Denis Menchov, always more dangerous as the Tour proceeds and beginning to haunt the leaders. Wiggins, almost five minutes down and now, at 18th, leapfrogged by Löfkvist (16th), admitted, 'It's disappointing but it's the reality. I'm steady at middling. Last year it was a bit of a stroke of luck, but I'll be back again next year to try again.' One might say that his astonishing performance in 2009 was partly due to the way that Armstrong and Bruyneel clamped down so tight on Contador to stifle the race. As to the situation this year, mutterings: Shleck should be niggling at the Spaniard to destabilise him . . . Rijs had told him not to be drawn, only to sit on Contador's wheel . . . Contador is relying on the final time-trial and thought the final climb at Ax Trois Domaines not sufficiently steep to test the Luxemburger with an explosive attack . . . and next day?

Port de Balès
Voeckler, it's Voeckler in the tricolour jersey of French champion. He's dropped the rest of the escapees 8km down the climb and the man with a truffle hound's nose for an opportunity knows that once he is at the col he has a rollicking 21.5km downhill into Luchon. He'd nearly abandoned at Gap with a bad stomach. Had the wind blown from the side next day, he'd certainly have quit. Luckily, it was from the front so he could take shelter. He rides by, seething with energy and tenacity.

Some two kilometres from the col, Schleck in yellow comes to an abrupt halt; his chain has shipped and got stuck between freewheel and frame. He climbs off to free it. The neutral Mavic service car isn't allowed through to help – there's no space. Contador sees his rival in trouble and attacks along with Menchov and Samuel Sánchez. Had Schleck's brother been riding, he could have given Andy his bike. Suddenly, his absence has a calculable price, and it's 30 seconds, the time it takes for Andy to remount and set off in pursuit. Rage spurring his flight, he is only 17 seconds down at the col, but Contador and his two rivals are sharing the work ahead of him and in Luchon Schleck has lost 39 seconds. What thought, then, of those other seconds whose loss he discounted after the Prologue?

Voeckler rode across the line in an ecstasy, the first French champion to win a stage since Durand in 1994. When Contador appeared on the podium to pull on the yellow jersey, the crowd booed and jeered. He grinned and winked like a schoolboy who has got away with some devilry. He denied that he had seen Schleck in trouble, said that the attack was spontaneous, instinctive. Since the evidence of the film was plain to the contrary, he later retracted and sought out Schleck to apologise. As to the ethics of the attack, punctures and mechanical breakdown are part of racing, and Schleck might have fitted a chainguard (for an extra 50g), which some riders use to prevent just such mishap. And what of the general truce called into Spa by Schleck's teammate Cancellara? It was not an issue to vex any but the nit-pickers. What did grate, however, was Contador's disingenuity. Had he shown even a suggestion of embarrassment about accepting the golden fleece in questionable circumstances, there might have been no bad feeling. As it was, the equable Schleck said he would come back at the Spaniard, but, very soon, friendship was resumed and declared. Indeed, there was a curious lack of animosity between these two contenders for victory. Mutual respect does not rule out hostility, and Schleck's equanimity began to look too much like passive acceptance. When was he going to get stirred up about winning this race?

Out of Luchon next day, an attack went almost straight away on the lower slopes of the col de Peyresourde, including Armstrong, Roche, Sastre and a Garmin rider who was showing great promise, a future leader, no doubt, the Canadian Ryder Hesjedal. A number of French scrappers joined – Casar, Moreau, Pierrick Fédrigo – and Chavanel's Spanish teammate Carlos Barredo. We watched them cross the summit of the Tourmalet, from the east, in hot, bright sunshine, the group more or less intact, Moreau first over, the yellow-jersey group nearly four minutes back. They grab the daily handout Vittel newspapers from spectators to stuff under their jerseys. Before the race comes through, the gendarmes maintain a temporary compliance among the crowd. When the riders appear, however, the crowd responds to an unruly inner compulsion of excitement and the wide road becomes a narrow funnel through which the riders pass in a cacophony of shouting, cheering, whistles, hand-held horns and cowbells. I asked Hondo, during an interview next day in Pau, whether the riders find this din intimidating. No, not so much in the Tour, it lifts them, they hear their name being called out, it helps boost their effort, and for the sprinters that's good. Out of curiosity, I asked him whether they read the names painted and daubed on the tarmac. 'In the *grupetto* you do,' he said and smiled.

A lone Ag2R rider rolls up and stops short of the col. He grabs a bidon from his team man and stops for a quick chat and a breather before heading off.

Forty-four kilometres from the finish in Pau, Barredo jumped from the break and soon had a forty-five second lead. Over the humps and rolls of the final run, the lead shrank to eighteen seconds, but it seemed that he might, just, make it. Moreau led the pursuit and Barredo was caught with nary a kilometre to go. Armstrong had nothing left; the survivors shaped up for the sprint. Fédrigo denied his compatriot Casar a second stage win, but it was the sixth French stage victory, a good augury. Hushovd, leading in the bunch sprint at 6m 45s, regained the green jersey from Petacchi.

Pau. Rest day.
We mosey into town and loiter at the Quick Step team hotel. A mechanic cleaning a bike, special attention to the chain. Pineau returns from a short ride. Some teams go out *ensemble*; this Belgian outfit releases its riders to suit themselves. Pineau looks relaxed (he's dropped out of the mountains prize). He takes off his shoes and washes them, inside and out, sponge and bucket of detergent, power jet to rinse, its fine mist reminiscent of a botanical garden glasshouse. He ambles across to the barrier to oblige a fan who wants his picture taken with the star. Chavanel arrives. He doesn't clean his own shoes. The suntan stops on the line of the helmet strap round his cheek to his chin. Arms and legs bronzed, the front of his jersey is open showing the corpse-white flesh of his chest. We go round to the back of the team bus, the rear of its interior lined with bikes (Chavanel's yellow-framed machine for the days of glory), racks of spare wheels, lockers for spares, wheel bags. Inside one part is a washing machine and a side cupboard, below which is a line of paper bags with riders' names in black felt pen: JEJE (Pineau), KEVIN (Seeldraeyers), who arrives from his ride. They contain energy bars, biscuits and snacks. We talk to

Henk Schipper of Fast Forward Wheels, visiting to see how their new kit is performing. Some riders don't like to test equipment on the Tour; Chavanel is a techno nut and always ready to try new things. Riders train on clincher tyres (i.e. wired-on), but they are all racing on tubulars now – they're lighter and more comfortable to ride. It means a lot more work for the mechanics. We see one later levering and tearing a tub off, scraping dry glue off the rims, applying fresh glue, fitting the tyre, probably three, four times the time it takes to fit a clincher. But tubs are safer, too, these days: the fixing cement is much improved; in normal circumstances they don't come unstuck and roll off.

The atmosphere is calm, but there is a general sense that the riders are apprehensive – the showdown stage on the Tourmalet is next day – and looking for some way to fill their day after the essential loosener ride.

Hondo is waiting for us in the team hotel on Pau's périphérique. We spend nearly an hour with him; he's friendly, informative, intelligent, down to earth, helpful. The return to the top level in an Italian team, riding with Petacchi (both men are 36) and putting the wiles of experience to play against the irresistible speed of Cavendish have given him new enthusiasm. At Gerard's request, he rings Petacchi and the man comes down for a picture. Are these men so vain that they crave any chance to talk about themselves and have their phizogs captured on digital? No. They are near indifferent to the camera's inquisitive eye and happy to supply answers to questions that must become utterly banal by their sameness. It is the way most cyclists have always been with their fans, whether professional or amateur – receptive, unless provoked or harried. I wish Petacchi '*forza per la verde*'; we shake hands and leave.

Tourmalet

It's been raining all night and, up here, it's blowing a gale, sky as grey as squirrel fur, a freezing chill in the air. The race isn't due to arrive at the col from the west until past five in the evening and it's only one o'clock. Gerard has the harder task, a three kilometre walk from this side road above La Mongie, highest point of access for our car, to the col, there to wait. I have the easier walk up a short hill to the vast, unheated tent that is serving as a press hall – rows of tables, television screens, a man serving coffee, small packets of biscuits. I settle down to read back copies of *L'Equipe,* essential research for my work, and to watch the TV coverage.

The Tourmalet will decide. That is what Schleck has been saying and it is like a gauntlet for the scrap that will take place somewhere on the 19 kilometres of climbing from the valley at Luz-Saint-Sauveur. Schleck, 8 seconds down, needs upwards of another minute if he's to wrest the final yellow from Contador in Saturday's time-trial. The sudden prick of ire that drove him up the Balès is some evidence that he *can* match Contador's explosive acceleration when goaded. Perhaps a demon will enter his soul this day, a sprite of quicker temper out of the unwithered rock of this mountain. From Barèges, 12km from the col, the gradient teeters around 8 and 9 per cent. In the thickening mist that gathers at altitude, the riders will not see the gaunt projection of the massif lowering over the head of the valley as the road swings sharp left towards the first big ramp of the escarpment. Schleck and Contador have been looking each other in the eye on other climbs, testing reaction. They've been chatting inconsequentially in lulls of the racing and, unfeignedly polite, for the most part, talking of friendship, their mutual liking. At the start in Pau, they shake hands – 'may the stronger man win'. They even ride the same brand of bike.

A straggle of riders is already on the climb when the Tour's main contenders arrive on the nursery slope out of town. They ride together for a little under half the way, and at ten kilometres from the col Schleck launches his first sally. It's characteristic: a gear up, steady surge, full power, strong and fast. Contador matches it. No one else can. They ride at the new pace for another kilometre and a half and, without a glance, overtake the front man on the road, the Russian Alexandr Kolobnev. (To illustrate what a terrible moral shock it is to have the lead, and hope of a victory, snatched in an instant, Kolobnev eventually trailed in more than five minutes down.) More pressure from Schleck. Contador closes. At just under four kilometres from the line, Contador dances out of the saddle and attacks. Schleck counters and they are side by side once more. Whatever added effort either man applies now, they must both know the day is going to end at quits. The Tourmalet has decided: evens on the two best climbers in the race. The mountains prize is for the skirmishers and Charteau confirms his win today. But he, in his polka-dot jersey, and Moreau in second place in the competition, are way back down the climb, five and a half minutes behind these conquistadors of the high places, one in yellow, one in white.

It's almost sacred writ that the conclusion of such a hard-fought *ex aequo* contest must be that the yellow jersey allows the other man through to the win itself, even by a few centimetres, and so it is, Schleck first across the line. They ride on through, in the inspissated gloom of the mountain's foul weather, one arm across the other's shoulders, the joust drawn.

Hesjedal, the new revelation at Garmin, at 1m 27s, Wiggins, last year's Garmin star, at 23m 19s. Bare statistics can be eloquent.

We drive across the flat, sandy hectares of the Landes, the long stands of pines planted to contain the loose soil against the off-sea winds, but here are vast areas, too, denuded of trees, and enormous log piles awaiting collection at the roadside. In a small village, a sign reads 'ALLEZ FIGNON LACHE-PAS LE GUIDON' (Go, Fignon, don't let go of the handlebars). Fignon, stricken with cancer, is still commentating for French television, and his courageous battle with the deadly disease has drawn affection and huge sympathy from a public who admired him as a rider of extraordinary gifts and fiery spirit. Such messages of support are touching indeed.

Another, more acrimonious sign reads LA FORET ASSASSINEE referring to the depredation of the forest and, on a water tower where we stop on a long straight, another *cri de coeur*: SANS ARBRES ET SANS MEMOIRE BIENVENUE DANS LES LANDES (No trees, blanked memory, welcome to the Landes).

Gerard gets his side shot, first of a small break, then of the bunch, and we head for Bordeaux to see, on television, Cavendish take his fourth stage, once again by lengths. He has come back to startling form, even without Renshaw, and taken victory in what has always been an iconic venue for Tour sprinters, the city by the great river Gironde, coursing through the flatlands. Petacchi was third, Hushovd fourteenth, ceding green again to the Italian. Cavendish lay 16 points behind Petacchi in the competition. The win in Paris would garner him a maximum 35 points. Petacchi, therefore, would have to finish no lower than sixth to keep green.

The *Equipe* headline read '*Ouf*' (Phew). Schleck very nearly pulled off a remarkable reversal of prediction. On the morning before the time-trial to Pauillac, I bought a good bottle from that famous vineyard, together with another clutch of decent clarets, and rather agreed with a sideline in the paper: 'Andy, no more the angel.' Such uncomplaining acceptance of the way things are simply doesn't wash. Time to take the gloves off and get down and fight *à l'outrance*. And he did. He rode Contador to within seconds of losing yellow. The Spaniard had an awful day, presumably because he had not only been tested physically harder than ever before, by a man who was in the form of his life, but also shaken morally, stripped of that inner conviction that he could trounce Schleck against the clock and be secure in his focus on Paris. In the event, he scraped by, took 31 seconds out of Schleck and finished in a heap, his face suffused with tears of relief. Schleck, too, was spent, empty, worthy.

Fignon, interviewed by *L'Equipe*, was scathing. Schleck had talked much of taking Contador on, but he hadn't really done so. 'It will remain a Tour of lost opportunities,' he said. Contador had, effectively, succeeded in putting his opponent to sleep with all this 'we're pals' talk. It put Schleck psychologically on the back foot. As to that loss of 41 seconds in the Prologue . . . now he was going to lose the Tour by 39 seconds.

Fignon has never minced his words. I interviewed him once and was much impressed by his manner – forthright, brisk, warm – and, in all his utterances, by his manifest intelligence and good sense. If his censure of the amiable Schleck seems harsh, it must be taken in the context of winning, and losing, the Tour de France. Fignon lost (and, in my view, unjustly) the '89 Tour by eight seconds. Did he shake Lemond's hand? Did he hell. The disappointment was too bitter, the rage to win too molten.

Paris
Hondo joins the final break on the Champs-Elysées. He and Petacchi had talked a lot during the race about how they should ride the final run-in, and their objective this day was to preserve

the green jersey. A stage win wasn't important – Cavendish looked hot for that – but Petacchi needed to finish no lower than sixth to be sure of the points. By joining the escape and driving it close to the finish line, Hondo's job was to break their rivals' rhythm, to compromise the build-up to the final run and thereby to relieve Petacchi of as much pressure as possible. When Petacchi sprinted clear of the pack, riding down Hushovd, he did so from comfort at the front of the bunch. He couldn't match Cavendish's finishing attack, but he feinted deftly after him and rode across in second place. Job done. Although he has won the points prize in both the Giro and the Vuelta, Petacchi has only once before finished the Tour: that he took the green jersey and two stage victories says much for the tandem he makes with Hondo.

Cavendish reached five stage wins, and had he not sat up that day of Petacchi's second win, he might have taken the green jersey. But he has shown much greater maturity and true champions are those who know the depths of loss and mine their rich seams of self-knowledge without fear or caution.

For the other major British involvement in the race, Team Sky, a punishing disillusion. Brailsford confessed so. Where he had set his face against hiring any ex-rider who had been involved in the drugs scandals of the late '90s (Neil Stephens, for example), he now thinks this may be an unduly pietistic attitude. He will, perhaps, embrace the reality about which Wiggins spoke and rely more on men who know the rough business of the road than on the pleasing symmetries of finite calculation on the wooden boards. The Tour de France, as the most experienced of his *directeurs*, Sean Yates, said shortly after the *Grande Arrivée*, is like no other race. It is incomparably hard and pressurised, capricious and remorselessly exacting. It yields neither to money nor to fanciful ideation. In one of the sagest and most unforgiving maxims applied to bike racing: the road decides.

Contador, overall winner, without a stage win. Schleck . . . hardened ambition, maybe, for the more the victory costs, the less it counts what you have to pay for it.

As for Armstrong, suddenly popular with the French press now that he is leaving the race for good, he stepped onto the podium one last time, with RadioShack, to collect the team prize. *Ave atque vale.* Menchov overhauled Sánchez in the final time-trial to mount the podium in third place. Andy Schleck won the white jersey for best young rider for the second year running, an overall prize of 20,000 euros.

Envoi

On 31 August, Laurent Fignon succumbed to the cancer and died. An exceptional rider, a man of great spirit whom I liked and admired. His death adds a poignant and unlooked for note of sorrow to the title of this chapter.

CHAPTER TWENTY-ONE

2011

Racing, Old Style

In 1999, the Tour crossed the Passage du Gois linking the Vendée mainland with the tiny Ile de Noirmoutier for the first time. As many had predicted, it proved to be a disaster. (see pp. 215–16). This year, the narrow causeway, which is submerged twice daily beneath the sea, was used as a sort of processional for the 198 riders setting out on the 3,430km anti-clockwise journey round France. Each stage begins with a départ fictif (three kilometres or so of neutral zone) before the flag waves for the real start, and there was no action across the tide-washed rib of stone.

For the first time since 1967, there was no Prologue. As the general director of the race, Christian Prudhomme, explained: realistically only ten riders contend for the first yellow jersey in a short time-trial. Instead, the entire field could contest an opening stage of 191.5km, ending with the 2km climb of the Mont des Alouettes (Larkhill) – not particularly steep but a hard ascent at speed – at one end of the Collines Vendéennes. The point is taken, even if there are probably not many more than ten riders with the kind of strength needed to win on such a finish: the one-day Classics specialists, like the Belgian Philippe Gilbert, the first man to win all three Ardennes Classics (Amstel Gold, Flèche Wallonne and Liège-Bastogne-Liège) in one year, 2011, or the Norwegian hard man Thor Hushovd, current world champion, even a puncheur (a rider who can knock a field dead with a daring and all-out attack) like Thomas Voeckler, who was born in Alsace, grew up in Martinique but has made the Vendée his home.

Absence of a Prologue was but one of many radical changes. In particular the points competition, for the green jersey, was now designed to stimulate competition for stage wins and intermediate sprints. Whereas there had been two or three intermediate sprints on each stage, with a mere handful of points on offer – 6, 4 and 2, generally snaffled by men in a breakaway – now, there was only one, rewarding the first 15 men across the line with points from 20 down to 1. There were 20 points for the winner of a mountain stage, 30 for a hilly stage and 45 for a flat stage. In principal, this favoured the Manx Missile, Mark Cavendish, already winner of 15 stages since 2007. However, it also induced him to contest the intermediate sprints, something he has firmly eschewed hitherto. This stricter confine of the green jersey competition coincided with a more lucid assessment by Cavendish of what it was going to take to grasp a prize that had eluded him for two years. Tighter grip on effort.

Indeed, the entire shape of the course was evidently calculated to stimulate competition right to the finish, in Paris: a team time-trial early on, only one individual time-trial, a short course of 42.5km on the penultimate stage and four mountain-top arrivals, as well as a trio of evil uphill finishes and the notably arduous Arrivée on the summit of Super-Besse, at the end of a very lumpy day in the Massif Central. The Super-Besse is no mountain, but the accumulated effect of 189km of relentlessly undulating road, a minor col towards the end, and a vicious thump of around 8 per cent up a long, straight 1.5km climb to the finish was hard, indeed.

The 2010 winner, Alberto Contador, lined up, having won the Giro d'Italia for the second time. He had tested positive for clenbuterol* in a blood sample examined after his third Tour victory but pleaded innocence – he said he had eaten a piece of contaminated steak – and been exonerated by the Spanish cycling federation. Both the UCI (Union Cycliste International)

*Clenbuterol, generally prescribed as a bronchiodilator for asthma sufferers, is an organic substance (an amine) which speeds the metabolising of body fats and thus increases the proportion of muscle. Its use in cattle, to make the meat leaner, is forbidden by the European Union, but its occasional presence in beef is not unknown. It has been used as a performance-enhancing drug by athletes and cyclists.

and WADA (World Anti-Doping Agency) appealed against this decision but the hearing, at the Court for Arbitration in Sport (CAS), had been deferred to 1–3 August, a week after the 2011 Tour reached Paris.

Many French fans were outraged that Contador was allowed to ride the Tour, albeit the ASO who organise the race had no recourse but to accept his entry, pending the appeal. At the presentation of the teams in the fake Roman arena at the Puy-du-Fou historical theme park, he was as roundly booed and jeered as any gladiator who had shown cowardice in the Colosseum.

The riders themselves tended to be equivocal. Fränk Schleck, who crashed out of the 2010 race, said that it wasn't for the public to decide whether Contador should ride or not. Cadel Evans, twice second and expressing confidence that this would be his year, said that if the rules permitted Contador to be there, there was nothing to prevent his being there. And Contador was a great rider. As to whether he should be there, Evans guarded his opinion: his own objective was to beat the Spaniard. Twice second, Evans has frequently been accused of lack of enterprise, an unwillingness to drive himself beyond safety. His bromide reaction to Carlos Sastre in the 2008 Tour cost him the race, although he has said that he was so tired at the time that just getting out of bed was impossibly fatiguing. He has also suffered from bad luck, nasty falls and injury. However, at the 2009 World's Road Race in Mendrisio in Switzerland, not far from where he lives in Italy, he attacked with great courage and rode to a solo victory. The curse of the rainbow jersey – how many world champions win much, if anything, in the year of their reign? – seems, in Evans' case, to have been the jolt he needed. It gave him attitude. Neither a very charismatic nor elegant rider, he undoubtedly has exceptional class. Time, then, for him to show its full range. Andy Schleck, second in 2010 and for three years winner of the young riders' white jersey, declared that he was glad the Spaniard was riding: he wanted and aimed to win against the best man in the field. Much censured for his laid-back, amiable temperament and lack of what the French call fougue, people were asking whether he had the mental force to accept the responsibility of winning the Tour, not just being the best rival for Contador. The British rider, Bradley

Wiggins, whose sterling performance in 2009 (4th overall) had been controverted by a wretched showing in 2010, said, somewhat enigmatically, that Contador's presence was good for the race but bad for the sport. As to his own condition, Wiggins admitted that he had not comported himself well the year before. Too locked in himself, unwilling and ill prepared to take on the role of leader, his performance had been decidedly lacklustre. His propensity to cynical public utterance didn't help his cause, either. Nevertheless, he is a fine rider and has had to deal with a very difficult transition from brilliance on the track to performance on the road. The disciplines are so different: calculation of minute difference in the one, a constant bombardment of contrary circumstance in the other. The people from Sky, his team's sponsor, had pitched in, however, and he had clearly wedded a tougher mental composure to his physical brilliance as a rider. Proof of that: an impressive win in the Dauphiné Libéré, highly regarded by French riders and a natural warm-up race for the Tour. His win followed that of two other Britons, Brian Robinson in 1961 and Robert Millar, 1990, and he looked impressive. A strong time-trial, over the same course round Grenoble as chosen for the Tour, and solid containment in the mountains brought him to the Vendée in what his directors were calling the form of his life. The aim: a podium place.

Two men who had returned to the peloton after two-year bans were riding: Ivan Basso (winner of the 2010 Giro d'Italia, his second victory) and Alexandr Vinokourov, (stage winner in his comeback Tour, 2010, and victory in Liège-Bastogne-Liège in the same year). The Kazakh was set on wearing the yellow jersey once before his announced retirement. Neither could be considered realistic contenders but their mere presence added significant weight to the top order. Two members of Lance Armstrong's former team, Radioshack, were talked up as possible men for a high overall placing: Janez Brajkovic, the Slovenian who'd won the 2010 Dauphiné Libéré, and Chris Horner, tenth in the last Tour and winner of the recent Tour of California. Both would for sure be liberated by Armstrong's absence, though whether to great performance was merely speculative. The Euskaltel-Euskadi rider and Olympic champion Samuel Sánchez, sixth in 2008, fourth in 2010, discounted any thought of his winning the Tour, but he was certainly ambitious for a good placing. That said, he thought the race route did not favour him. The weaker outfits always suffer in the team time-trial – Sánchez reckoned they faced at least a 90-second deficit. Jürgen Van den Broeck, the highest-placed Belgian in a Tour (fifth in 2010) since Claude Criquielion's fifth in 1986, had never really matched the promise of his win in the World's junior time-trial ten years previously, but, given leadership of the Omega Pharma-Lotto team after Evans left for the American BMC team, he responded with a stage win in the Dauphiné. However, his Belgian team was less stirred by grand tours than by the classic races, and the presence of their big sprinter André Greipel, former teammate and now determined rival of Cavendish, as well as the classics specialist Gilbert, meant that Van den Broeck was not guaranteed the support of his team.

The Tour first crossed the Galibier, 'the monster of the Alps', in 1911 (see p. 39). To commemorate that singular event – one not much appreciated by the early riders – the race finished on its high summit one day and, next day, crossed it, but via the tunnel 90m below. Emile Georget, the very first man over (by way of the same tunnel) gave his own wry take on the fearsome experience:

> The men who dug the tunnel at the top of the col might have driven it through at the bottom. It would have been a little bit longer, no doubt, but it would have spared us a matryrdom. Between the tunnel of the Métro and the summit of the Galibier, well, I still prefer the Métro.

Henri Desgrange's eulogy probably did not impress him: 'Before this giant, one can but doff one's cap and bow very low . . . Devant ce géant, il n'y a plus qu'á tirer son bonnet et saluer bien bas.' The col finish this year marked the highest ever stage finish in a Tour.

The 98th edition of the Tour de France set out along the Passage du Gois on the same day, 2 July, as the 9th edition rolled out from Paris, in 1911. Since Prudhomme took over direction of the race, his aim has clearly been to ginger it up. There is much debate about the use of earpieces, the routine aspect of racing when riders seem more subservient to fear of risk of losing than to the true cavalier spirit of competition. A break goes clear, stays clear until a few kilometres from the finish, the peloton stirs itself and, lo, sprinters move in. The debilitating effect of Armstrong's seven-year domination, the aftermath of the drugs scandals, the injection of huge sums of money into teams by sponsors who want returns for their money – stage wins, prizes, high-profile performance – has, to an extent (and to how great an extent is a contentious issue), strait-jacketed racing and, in particular, the Great Bike Race itself. However, there is an apparent resistance to that astir, not only among many riders who want to show that cycling, the most-tested of any sports, is now clean, but also in the organisers who yearn for a less predictable shape to their races. The criticism of cynics who decry riders' timidity is not new. Fifty years ago, the Tour director Jacques Goddet fulminated:

> The competitors in this Tour [1961], Jacques Anquetil excepted, are dwarfs. Yes, ghastly, impotent dwarfs, utterly resigned, content with their mediocrity, quite happy to receive an honourable mention. Nonentities who, above all, are afraid to suffer . . . they no longer show any willpower. They calculate, they quibble, they forever analyse in the sense of limitation. They no longer think of hurling themselves into action at a venture. They prefer inertia.'

Similar accusations have been and are being made today. In twenty years, three riders have won fifteen Tours. One passionate deprecator of the modern race, himself an ardent fan of the great Eddy Merckx, the film-maker Olivier Dazat, is scathing: 'Everything seems to answer to an internal market logic, a logic of boredom.' This is an extreme view, but it points to a profound dissatisfaction with the way cycle sport has succumbed to commercial imperative, dull and managed, like Formula 1. There is always a hint of nostalgia for the heroic epoch in such critiques, the time when Anquetil climbed off his bike at the end of a time-trial looking as if he had aged 20 years, so ravaged by fatigue and exhausting effort was he. Nevertheless, there are riders dedicated to the very opposite style of the anodyne manner excoriated by the critics, men of the jusqu'au-boutiste, all or nothing mentality, and the shape of the 2011 Tour gave them not only a wide field of action but witnessed a glorious triumph of the great tradition of the race.

Gilbert had dyed his hair blond in confident expectation of collaring the first yellow jersey and this he did on the first stage, up the stiff incline to the Mont des Alouettes. That he was followed in, at handfuls of seconds, by Evans, Hushovd, the Spaniard José Joaquín Rojas (vying for the green jersey), Van den Broeck, Geraint Thomas, the feisty Welshman, full of hwyl, riding for the Sky team, and a whole bunch of Tour notables, was splendid. Thomas put on the white jersey of best young rider. As to Contador: misery. On the approach to Herbiers, nine kilometres from the finish, the Spaniard was caught up in a crash. A former Astana teammate, the Kazakh Maxim Iglinskiy, clipped a spectator who was bumbling about at the roadside, went down and caused a general pile-up, Contador included. Sixty-seven riders sped on in front and at the finish Contador had lost 1m 20s on all his rivals. Many of them, including the Schlecks, Basso and Wiggins, had also gone down but only 2.3 kilometres from the line. The rule is that no time can be forfeited within three kilometres, although this does not apply in a mountain finish. Strict application of the regulation, therefore, meant that Contador ended the first day with a significant deficit. That the organisers didn't practise lenience may suggest their undeclared feelings about his being there at all. As to the spectator who caused the crashed, 'the woman in yellow' (even Iglinskiy was convinced), she was eventually traced and turned out to be a plumpish 13-year-old boy in a yellow T-shirt.

The second-stage team time-trial went to Garmin-Cervélo and put Hushovd into yellow. David Millar, designated leader of the team, said that all riders fear an event that puts immense strain on each man in the drive to serve the team's combined strength. As the race develops, consideration has to be taken of weaker members, to avoid giving them too long at the front of the line, at the risk of losing time. The stronger men give extended pulls, the rest sheltering in the slipstream. Even the turbulence in a gap at the back of the line can make latching onto the rearmost wheel a trial. Coming out of a corner, the lead man has to remember not to step too hard on the speed because the back marker will be decelerating into the bend and must not be required to accommodate both the renewed acceleration and his own increasing speed merely to maintain position. It's a nervy, stressful ride at maximum effort from start to finish. Bernhard Eisel of Cavendish's HTC-Highroad team crashed in the first 500 metres and Contador's Saxobanks lost riders at around 10km, nor were they riding a good line. The losses to HTC meant little, but for a rider aiming at the overall victory, Saxo Bank's 28-second deficit meant that Contador was now 1m 42s off the lead.

At the intermediate sprint the next day, Hushovd moved across Cavendish's line and they rubbed shoulders. There was no apparent danger of a crash but both men were docked their points (10 and 9). Given the animosity that had soured relations between them two years ago and the cordial rapprochement which healed it, their reaction was pleasing. Indeed, the Norwegian asked to take full responsibility for the incident but was denied. On this 4 July, the American sprinter, Tyler Farrar, scored his first stage win for Garmin-Cervélo. On the Giro, his great friend Wouter Weylandt had crashed and died. Farrar left the race and was totally demoralised. But, with that astonishing resilience of these professional bike riders, a little more than a month later he had recovered himself and, as Jonathan Vaughters, the team manager said: 'You can see how unified the team is. Finally, it's clicking.' Team support and unity of purpose is vital to success, in every area of the Tour. Farrar, answering to the concord in his team, thus became the first American to win stages in all three grand tours. As for Cavendish: more woes. He was, he claimed, squeezed out by some 'kamikaze riding' by the French sprinter Romain Feillu as he himself was fending off the Spaniard Rojas. Tempers rise, the emotional pressure is high, sprinters do combat in a febrile state.

Into the finish on the Mûr de Bretagne, stage four, Contador attacked. There was little chance of making any useful time gains, but the psychological effect was, perhaps, more important. It meant he was still there, still ready to battle it out. Evans, way down the field, had a mechanical problem and had to race back, with the help of his team including the amazing George Hincapie, riding his 16th Tour – thus equalling Joop Zoetemelk's record, albeit Hincapie has had to abandon once, the Dutchman, never.

Evans, having 'no idea if I had anything left the tank' went into the overdrive of motivation. Alert for Contador's final burst, Evans pounced just before the line and, though the Spaniard, grimacing with grim satisfaction, raised his arm in triumph, the Australian took the win. It was workmanlike, but it showed a deeper resolve to fight for trifles. Wiggins, meanwhile, having conceded six seconds, reverted to the sort of insouciance he should keep to himself. Only a few seconds . . . won't matter in a week's time. Stuff. A Tour can be won or lost on such trifles. Give away seconds, you pare away morale.

Cavendish was already outside the top ten in the sprinters' competition, over fifty points behind Rojas. The three men leading the competition were up at the front scrapping for victory on the hard uphill into Cap-Fréhel, but Cavendish took his first win. He'd seen Thomas break for the front with some 200 metres to go – his usual moment for the final break. Not confident of a win, he needed to get some points. Robbed of his lead-out man, Mark Renshaw, who'd got caught up in the bunch somewhere, he reeled in Thomas, then Rojas and went through. Something of the frustration that they all face but which Cavendish articulates, often with less tact than is prudent, was stirred by more argy-bargy at the intermediate sprint. Rojas and Tom Boonen cut right across him towards the left-hand barriers and then Boonen wove back across to the right, for no evident reason. He was relegated, but such precipitate explosive changes of line can inject terrible jitters in a man travelling at high speed. As to Cavendish's want of diplomacy, his directeur, Allan Peiper, some while ago rounded on him: 'Fact is, you don't understand the job.' The youngster needed to shape up, take on more responsibility, do more for the team. The change has come, although Peiper concedes that the ace sprinter does need 'to live with hostility'. That's what fires him and as to his absorption of the team ethic, there is no question about that now.

There were more crashes, most seriously to Brajkovic, who had to abandon with a broken collarbone and cranial trauma. Boonen copped a badly bruised shoulder, Sylvain Chavanel, in the tricolour jersey of French champion, a dislocated shoulder, Contador, a strained back to add to an already bruised right knee. The Danish rider Nicky Sørensen went down when a motorbike snagged his bike and carried it off, 200 metres up the road, offering the bizarre spectacle of a rider sprawling on the deck and his bike nowhere to be seen. The motorbike was evicted.

Three Frenchmen, doing what they have been forced to do in recent years, for honour if not major reward, tried to carry an escape to the finish. Jérémy Roy and the arch baroudeur Voeckler struck out but were caught in the last kilometre.

On a drenching wet day in Normandy, Edvald Boasson Hagen gave Sky their first Tour stage win. Since Normandy takes its name from the Norsemen who settled here centuries past and Hushovd was still in yellow, this was a singular day for Norway's only two representatives in the Tour. Next day, the sky fell in on them.

When nearly 200 riders are striving to keep position on a narrow road, a directeur telling his men to get to the front may as well whistle at the wind. When the crash happened, 39 kilometres from the finish, Wiggins went down heavily. He'd broken his left collarbone. He was out. The entire team, Thomas in the white jersey, waited to ascertain whether he could ride on and by the time they set off in pursuit, they had lost their leader and almost certainly any chance in the young riders' competition. Also badly hurt in the accident, Chris Horner was carted off to hospital with a broken nose, a lacerated cheek and a contused wrist and Roy's Française des Jeux (FDJ) teammate Rémi Pauriol with a broken foot was out, too.

Up the road, a break including Chavanel and Vinokourov was reeled in and, three years after his first stage win in Chateauroux, Cavendish took his sixteenth victory in a town which, as part of Eleanor of Aquitaine's marriage to Henry, Duc de Normandie, later Henry II, in 1152, became a fief of the English crown and remained so until 1612. A nice symbol of reclamation.

The hoped-for scramble on Super-Besse was pre-empted by a lone break. Rui Costa took the first victory by a Portuguese rider since Joaquim Agostinho's time-trial win in 1973. Voeckler, true to his instinct, attacked 42 kilometres from the start in Issoire and, in company with five other riders, crossed the main hurdle of the day, the col du Pas de Peyrol, 99.5 kilometres out, with 3m 25s over the peloton. Some two kilometres down the col, a crash took down a number of riders, most gravely: Vinokourov, off the road into the side slope, helped back up with a broken femur, his racing career almost certainly finished, and Van den Broeck, with a broken shoulder blade. A number of other riders were also forced to abandon. The drama was not over.

On a stretch of road no wider than two cars through farmland, with Voeckler leading the break, Juan Antonio Flecha to his right, Johnny Hoogerland to his left, a France-Télévision car, one of 86 supernumerary vehicles on the course – apart from the 44 driven by directeurs – suddenly swerved to avoid a tree in the verge. It bundled Flecha off his bike and catapulted Hoogerland, bike and all, over a barbed wire fence. The race director had, minutes before, warned all such cars to give precedence to team vehicles and to stay well clear of the riders. The culprit was expelled, but the shots of the accident were surreal. Amazingly, both Hoogerland, his thighs, buttocks and calves torn by the barbs, streaked with blood and heavily bandaged, and Flecha, bruised but otherwise unhurt, rode on and stayed in the race. Flecha had ricocheted into Voeckler but the Frenchman kept his seat, looked back in disbelief and, as his compatriot Sandy Casar came up alongside him, discussed what was to be done. Nothing. Press on. So they did, together with Luis Léon Sánchez. Flecha rejoined them and, Voeckler driving the break with every sinew, the four men hurtled over the last of the wearying ups and downs across the Monts du Cantal, the extinct volcanoes of the Massif Central, into Saint-Flour, which the French poet Camille Gandilhon called 'the windy city'. Sánchez won the sprint over Voeckler, at five seconds, but, seven years after he had worn yellow, Voeckler once more took over the Golden Fleece.

Contador, having taken his third fall, lost more time and was now at 4m 7s from the lead. Evans and the two Schlecks lay third, fourth and fifth, Sánchez second overall. Hoogerland reached the finish nearly five minutes up on the grupetto and pulled on the Mountains jersey before going off to get thirty stitches in his lesions. Remarkable.

Dr Florence Pommerie of the Tour's medical service, who has dealt with other sportsmen and -women, commented on the fortitude of these professional bike riders:

They are outside the common mould of mortals. Cyclists exhibit an endurance, physical and mental, greater than any I have encountered. They are accustomed to prolonged and repeated exertion; their tenacity is unmatched. Cyclists are true athletes with but one objective, and to attain that they put everything else aside, including pain. Physical effort also provokes a secretion of endomorphine which helps them to suppress pain to a lower level. The body is well constructed. When Vinokourov fell he did not complain. All he said to me was, 'It hurts there,' even though a fracture of the femur is one of the most painful injuries. They also heal more readily. They possess a physiology which scars faster than with most people, a more rapid cellular turn-round. In addition, they have mental strength. They are in urgent haste to get better and they know how the body functions. This helps – just as hospital patients are encouraged to get out of bed and start moving as soon as possible after an operation to aid recovery. Cyclists have one goal: to get back on the bike as quickly as possible and resume the race. They even get angry with the doctors for urging caution, but . . . they come back to apologise. Because, as well as being resilient, they are adorable.

There is, too, a directness about them. I have spoken at length with Chavanel a couple of times this year, and when I wished him well in the Tour de Suisse he smiled and said, 'That's what we're paid to do.'

Saying that a stage is one for the sprinters, these days, means 'one for Cavendish'. The wide hill roads through the Lot and the Tarn and a downhill into Carmaux also favoured any rider who tried to slip free when many in the bunch were bent on saving energy before the Pyrenees, and six riders belted off the start to cover the first 51.6km in an hour. But the HTC chase moved in to peg their advantage to manageable proportion. Even so, the spirit of adventure was abroad and in the final run-in both the yellow jersey of Voeckler and the green now worn by Gilbert were off the front, going for victory. It was, as the French say, supertop. But not to survive. Too ripe a plum not to cull and the fast crew swept them aside. The HTC train was not there in full complement, though, wearied by having to galvanise the last-ditch pursuit and Greipel, Gilbert's teammate, took the win over Cavendish by little more than a tyre's width. Sweet for him, bitter for his ex-leader.

Vice-versa next day and Cavendish took green, too. Situation normal, all fired up. 'I told the team I'd win,' he said.

Stage 12. Cugnaux– Luz-Ardiden.
Distance: 211km. Hourquette d'Ancizan 1,538m, col du Tourmalet 2,115m, Luz-Ardiden 1,715m.

The Schleck brothers had it in their talent to begin a procedural dismantling of the race, to discomfort Contador, also to put Evans on his mettle and to leave the Pyrenees with an advantage to bolster further attack in the Alps. Their father, Johnny, has said that, in the saddle, their complicity is unquestioned, they ride for each other without bias of ego or envy, even if the two of them will bicker about the comparative size of fish they have caught with the venom of a couple of harridans. Fishwives, if you like. The younger, Andy, was clearly identified as the better prospect for the overall win, but who could tell? His own genial disposition seems ill fitted to the shouldering of a harsh responsibility, the ruthless decision making of all-out attack, no matter who stands in the way. And if his brother stands in the way? The same apparent 'it's OK' amiability of last year's putative duel with Contador? Was he, was either of them, ready to sacrifice the other? Fränk, somewhat obliquely, said that when someone talked of sacrifice it was like asking him to chuck his brother into the pit of a volcano. Whether extinct or active he did not specify.

In the event, Fränk did take the lead, attacking with some purpose on the final climb of the day. Earlier, Thomas and Roy had ridden hard up and over the Tourmalet, the two of them forging a massive break together, Roy (who went from the start) of 199km, the Welshman, 187km. Roy pipped Thomas on the Tourmalet to collect the prime of €5,000, but Thomas was awarded the day's combativity prize of €2,000. At one point, he was virtual leader of the Tour on the road, but the long break had worn both him and

Roy. They were overtaken by the big guns on the final climb.

The ascent to Luz-Ardiden is not punishingly steep, but it lasts for 13.3km. On the lower slopes, the Schlecks had something of a conversation – possibly in Luxembourgish, which, in the Francophone world of the Tour, serves as a sort of thieves cant, impenetrable to anyone else – and, plainly, decided that this was not the time to be making any firms decisions. The group rode on, Voeckler tucked in nicely at what is, for these men, a cruising pace, stoutly supported by his teammate Pierre Rolland, 24 years old, looking very strong.

Up the road, Sánchez and the Belgian Jelle Vanendert were going for the win; some way down the road, Contador, his right knee giving him gyp, was playing containment, only. Fränk Schleck attacks, is caught, he attacks again, is caught a second time. At three kilometres to go, he made the break and, although he reeled in the two leaders, Sánchez, cheered on by a mass of Basque fans, cut free and won by a sliver of seconds. Across the line, Voeckler draped one arm round Rolland's shoulders, yellow saved, his lead still 1m 49s over Fränk Schleck, 2m 6s on Evans, and so on. As for Contador, he said he thought it prudent not to react too violently to the Schleck attack, yet.

The title of this chapter evokes a cavalier attitude to racing which has been missing in recent years, a flouting of risk. But the past was not always charged with derring-do and gallant enterprise, as in some Arthurian twilight zone of heroism. At the Dauphiné, I asked Sean Yates, a known all-outer, about the difference in tactics between his days and now. He burst out laughing. 'We didn't have any,' he said. 'In the old days, when a guy went up the road, the rest would say, "OK, let's have an ice cream, we'll try tomorrow."' Prudence leaves out the ice cream.

Sánchez now led the mountains prize, Voeckler could hardly walk and Contador had conceded a further 13 seconds to his main rivals.

Europcar, the latest incarnation of the Vendean team managed by Jean-René Bernaudeau, is a second-division outfit. They'd not even been sure of a ride in the Tour. It was a joy, therefore, to see the forest green of the Europcar team riding together, shepherding their leader up the Aubisque, the day's major obstacle, controlling the race. Not so easy for some of them, who were riding the Tour for the first time. But Voeckler, to whom I talked back in April, is a man of infectious good spirits, a born leader. They are truly a band of brothers. He never gives up, said Vincent Jérôme. He's clear about things and when he has something to say, he says it. 'You just have to see what lengths he went to last winter to ensure that the team carried on. There are not many people in this milieu with such heart and spirit.' His teammates repay it with equal devotion and he finished, in Lourdes, with all the main contenders.

The indefatigable Roy, meantime, had been out on the attack again. By the end of this day, he had clocked up 650km of escape. He'd shed his companions and was alone at the 25km banner, 1m 25s up on the chasing pair of Hushovd and David Moncoutié. Hushovd against two Frenchmen. Should Moncoutié aid the chase or not? General feeling, next day, was that he should have sat on Hushovd's wheel. He did not and was roundly vilified by the French, naturally. At 5km, Roy held a slender 15-second lead, Hushovd dropped his willing helper, caught the luckless Roy 2.5 kilometres from the line in Lourdes and won by 10 seconds over Moncoutié, who had overtaken his compatriot. Roy had some recompense – king of the mountains (do we pun on roi? I think not) – but a stage win snatched from him, oh, sorrow.

On the three occasions that the Plateau de Beille has featured in the race, the winner here has won overall – Pantani in 1998, Armstrong in 2004, Contador in 2007. In 2004, Voeckler arrived there having saved the yellow jersey, against all prediction, by 22 seconds. On this day in 2011, 168.5km over the Portet d'Aspet, the col de la Core, the col de Latrape, col d'Agnès to the 15.8km ascent to the Beille, he not only preserved his lead, he rode like a true patron (boss) of the race.

Once again, Vanendert and Sánchez fought out the win and the Belgian took it, as well as the polka dots. However, the front-runners did little, to the delight of Voeckler and his lieutenant Rolland, who were girding themselves for a real fight, if it came, but in no wise ready to stir it needlessly. Voeckler, who was off the front on the final climb, driving them all as hard as he could, showing the yellow jersey at the head of affairs, behaving like a true champion, conceded a mere two seconds to Andy Schleck but came in equal with the rest. The willingness of the so-called hard men to ride so tamely behind him suggested that either they were genuinely discomforted or else marking time against a showdown in the Alps. Either way, they were leaving themselves a lot to do.

To gloss, further, the title of this chapter. As Voeckler told me, he trains hard, races around a hundred days per year, racing is what gives him most pleasure and he stresses the fact that he can't substitute the drive and sharpness which comes through racing with endless training. A rider like Contador can pick and choose, and he can win. That's not divisive – an élite class and hoi polloi – it's a matter of fact, the way things are. Sure, in the old days, the season was, de rigueur, much longer and Voeckler still prefers to race from February to October, but that's partly because he is not a rider for overall victory in most events. He isn't strong enough to specialise, so he needs to take the chances of victory that are offered. 'If I were capable of winning the Tour de France, I wouldn't ride so many races, but that isn't the case, so why waste energy bothering about it? Besides, I can't substitute racing for training.' And, better to win a stage than work like a slave merely to be the first Frenchman on GC. There is a risk that racing so much compromises a performance in the biggest race of all, but, as he puts it:

> This is my conception of the bike. The Tour is beautiful, but I take as much pleasure in riding the Four Days of Dunkerque [which he won] or the Tour au Trentin [one stage victory] because I am a competitor. It's important to win races [eight for him before the Tour] and the more so because we have a new sponsor.

It may be summed up as responsibility, the word that Cyrille Guimard puts at the centre of bike racing – a multi-faceted answering to all manner of demands but essentially full commitment at whatever price. For example, three kilometres from the finish on the Plateau, Voeckler rode up alongside Rolland and said, 'You're the strongest one here.' Rolland nodded resignedly, indicating that his legs felt very weak, but, as Voeckler put it, 'He didn't realise that the others felt much worse.'

The flat stage through acres and acres of vineyards to Montpellier, last chance of a sprinter's win before the finish in Paris, started for the first time in Limoux. Seek out Blanquette de Limoux, if you have never tasted it. A fruitous bouche of fizz, ideal for aperitif or summer picnics and a coupe d'honneur, though the habitual tipple of stage winners is champagne. Cavendish, of course, fourth-stage win. Sean Kelly, a noted sprinter, himself, said of the Manxman that his great strength is that he knows, as by instinct, the precise moment to launch a sprint.

> This may sound silly, put like that, but when you are riding at 60–65kph, your points of reference are limited. [He added that Farrar wasn't reading the run-in at all well. A problem he himself shared.] Cav, though, senses the moment. He sees the banner and it's as if he's making an ultra-fast calculation in his brain.

On the rest day, Vinokourov announced, from the hospital in Paris where he had been operated on, that, at 37 years old, he could not contemplate a return to racing. A sad exit.

The stage into Gap was tricky: a long haul into the foothills of the Alps, over a significant climb, the col de Manse, and a twisting, narrow, potentially treacherous descent into the first major town to welcome Napoleon on his return from Elba. Aptly enough, on the Ides of March, 1815. He had less than a hundred days to go. Gap has welcomed the Tour many times since 1931, but on Tuesday, 19 July, it was in a foul mood: pelting rain all day.

I watched the finish from the sterile, functional, emotionless press hall – Hushovd over his fellow Norwegian, Boasson Hagen – then ran out to the barriers on the last straight to see the immediate followers come in spurred on by the heat of applause and cheering: Evans off the front of the main pursuit, Contador hard behind, so, too, Sánchez and Voeckler, elder Schleck but no Andy. Forty-eight seconds down on them. He got stuck on the descent of the Manse. 'That's the most dangerous part,' he said.

A descent to the finish. It's not necessary to make the finishes like that. It's ridiculous. I had to stop and put my foot to the road when a rider in front of me slid. People want to see a race played out with pedals not with an ambulance. Sure, I lost big time today but my father said he was happy to see us both still in the race and not in hospital.

I saw him on that descent and thought, 'He's losing the Tour.' Easy to say, but there is no room for such timidity.

Contador took time out of Voeckler, who admitted that it had been a bad day for him, not helped by his spontaneous decision to try to match Contador's attacks on the Manse. There was no need to go just because he was on the Spaniard's wheel at the time. Besides, he is a brilliant descender and could probably have made up any gap on the way into Gap. Moreover, the Europcar team had taken a hammering – some of the riders were very tired and Anthony Charteau was sick. Nonetheless, Voeckler was still in yellow. It was for the others to take it from him, not for him to give it away.

Neither the col de Montgenèvre nor Sestriere is a particularly hard climb, more a long drag to the Italian border at the formless ski station, but, on the day before the Étape Reine, literally 'queen' but, colloquially, 'mother and father of all stages', finishing on the Galibier, the field was open to the chancers. The break went at 54km, 10 riders including the Sky rider Boasson Hagen, joined 2 kilometres on by Chavanel. The leaders stayed in the pack, no need for wasteful expenditure of energy.

The road from Sestriere into the Chisone valley gave the riders a fast descent of around 46km to the foot of the Colle Pra Martino. I saw them go through on the double hairpin at Fenestrelle. A local man in a lurid yellow gilet and Tyrolean cap with feather slouched on a stone parapet, occasionally stirring to remonstrate with an unruly member of the crowd impatient for the Giro di Francia to come through. The unruly members of the crowd either ignored him or obeyed his objurgation with polite reluctance. The caravan sped through in a welter of blaring music, klaxons, loudspeaker announcement, like a sonic force pump, scattering the usual manna of plastic gew-gaws, sweeties, hats, bags, lens cloths and key lanyards. An hour later, the leading group, then the chasers, slowing down on the switchback as if for a photocall – which they got – and out again into crazy speed.

The narrow Pra Martino road, 6.7km of woodland by-way, overhung with a leaf canopy, its descent towards Pinerolo a helter-skelter of blind corners, tight bends and jinking twists, had one rider off the verge into the trees, another into the courtyard of a house standing on a bend and, seconds later, Voeckler himself into the same impromptu safety run. With plausible calm, the yellow jersey circled the forecourt and rode back on, with the help of a bystander in a yellow shirt. Touché.

Nearly five minutes ahead, Boasson Hagen had gone clear of the escapers on the last climb – he and the Sky riders had reconnoitred it, most importantly, the descent, twice on a special trip. He'd programmed the difficult sectors and been able to ride at full economy of speed and safety, an extra boost to what was a determined attack. He took the stage. 'It is,' as he said, 'a formidable feeling to cross the line alone.'

No such luxury of recce for Voeckler – he was too busy riding races. Definitively 'old-style' racing calendar.

> I could see I wasn't going to get round the bend, but there was a safety route. That meant jumping over a step of around a metre in depth. I lifted myself up on the pedals and closed my eyes. When I opened them again, I was still on the bike. There was nobody there otherwise I'd have said, "Hello, ladies and gentlemen." Still, I might have been in an ambulance – it could have been a ravine or a wall. I was very, very lucky.

One of the factors which makes descending more perilous these days is the ultra-light weight and rigidity of the bike frames, most of them in carbon, the shortness of the wheel base (which raises the centre of gravity) and the lack of flexibility in the wheels, all designed for more speed, which they undoubtedly deliver. Poor bike handlers suffer, therefore, from finer tolerances on the behaviour of the machine at speed and tilt. Old-style steel frames coped better with the precipitate hurtling off high cols into the corkscrews of the descent.

Stage 18. Pinerolo– Galibier Serre-Chevalier.
Distance: 200.5km. Col d'Agnel 2,744m (23.7km of climbing), col d'Izoard 2,360m (14.1km of climbing), Galibier, 22.8km uphill from Briançon to the highest summit finish ever. A total of 4,662 metres of ascent. Actually more, because on the Izoard, the road drops into the bowl of the Casse Déserte before a steep climb up to the col, but, in the weight of such fearsome statistics, who's counting?

Having failed, or been unable, to exploit the opportunity of the Pyrenees, the Schlecks had to do something. Fränk to attack on the Izoard and Andy to finish the work? It seemed feasible.

Significantly, two of the Schlecks' teammates, Maxime Monfort and Joost Posthuma, joined the early break that set off near the foot of the Agnel. The Kazakh Maxim Iglinskiy dropped his fellow escapees and rode over the col alone, to be caught by most of his erstwhile companions at the bottom. The peloton was already over five minutes down. Iglinskiy went again on the Izoard, followed by four, only, of the original 16, Monfort among them. Posthuma pressed on, but he was riding to orders, for, when the chasing bunch was 15.5km from the col d'Izoard, Andy Schleck broke clear at purposeful speed. He rounded up the remnants of the break, but Posthuma was there, ready to help, putting all he had into relaying his leader up to the col before Schleck cut loose, once more on his own, only 1m 50s on Iglinskiy but with four minutes on the yellow jersey group. A short way ahead of him, Monfort waited his turn to help, by giving his leader a wheel to follow down the hairpins, thus nullifying Schleck's inadequacy as a descender. They caught the riders ahead, some 30 kilometres from the finish, and Schleck went through, on his own. Following him, standing up in the aperture of the sunroof of Prudhomme's red car, Eddy Merckx, cheering the Luxemburger on.

No more than 10.5 kilometres from the finish, Schleck, riding with great fluency, in no obvious distress, had an advantage of 4m 25s over the main contenders. He'd added two minutes up the valley from Briançon and was leader on the road, in company,

TOUR DE FRANCE

still, with Iglinskiy. A headwind was driving straight down towards Briançon. He seemed undeterred, although behind him his rivals were showing no willingness to take on both the chase and the added nuisance of the gusting breeze, despite Evans' haranguing them for some work. Why should Voeckler help Evans? The BMC team had not ridden for him. His job was to save the jersey if he could but, emphatically, not to hand any gifts to a rival. Rolland even asked whether Voeckler wanted him to ride. (The French 'rouler' suggests putting effort in, as in 'doing a ride'.) Voeckler told him not to. 'OK,' said Rolland. 'You're the boss.'

Some 11 kilometres from the finish, Evans took on the responsibility. He has ducked it in the past. Now he put talking the race, good or bad, aside and poured everything into the kind of all-out action that saves and wins Tours. On his own (sure, he complained about that later) he drove the chase, with unfailing strength and unwavering application. This was splendid: the buccaneering attack up ahead, the relentless pursuit behind.

Schleck crossed the line and the clock began its work: the sweep of the second hand sharpening the shears which would chop the yellow jersey off Voeckler's back and sever Evans' realistic chance of winning the race.

Contador cracked three kilometres from the col and was gone. Evans persisted, Fränk attacked out of his slipstream and rode up past Iglinskiy. At two kilometres, Voeckler pulled out his earpiece – it wasn't working well, crackling noisomely in his ear. He asked Rolland how much time Schleck had on them. Three minutes and 'some dust' (i.e. three minutes odd). Voeckler said, 'You need to put in a real drive.' Rolland, like Ariel, correspondent to command, did so, at the cost of the white jersey.

The Schleck brothers made history: first and second on the stage. Of Andy's ride, Merckx enthused, 'A great page in the history of our sport has been written today . . . Andy has revived a certain [style of] cycling, he raced the way the great names in cycling used to. Yes, he has imparted grandeur to the Tour de France.'

Evans brought in the chase, having stubbornly cut the lead in half; Voeckler saved yellow by 15 seconds, at what depth of suffering may be read in his tortured face as he crossed the line and raised his arm feebly in triumph. Asked whether he was moved to have preserved the jersey he said, no, he felt only pain.

The grupetto, 80+ riders, missed the time cut (Cavendish among them) but were reprieved: too many to boot out.

The leader board now showed the Schlecks at 15 and 18 seconds, Evans at 1m 12s and the next man, Damiano Cunego, 3m 46s. And tomorrow? Galibier again to the finish on l'Alpe d'Huez.

Contador refused to give in. For the first time, ever, facing defeat in a grand tour provoked in him just the sort of ride that a competitor of his mettle needed to deliver. On the slopes of the Télégraphe, he attacked and was hauled back by the Schlecks. An early break was already 2m 30s up the road, a group of riders of no danger to the overall standings grabbing the last chance for a swashbuckling stage win. Evans bridged the gap, Voeckler followed across, but he was plainly near his limit. Fränk Schleck joined, too, and then broke clear. This was what the two brothers might have done in the Pyrenees: a double assault. Voeckler suddenly exploded in anger, hurled his bidon to the ground, expostulating. The explanation for this unwonted blast of rage came later. 'The wind was in our faces, I was with Evans, Contador and Andy Schleck. A television motorbike draughted Contador for about 200 metres, it gave him enough rest to be able to jump clear of us. I couldn't get back.' Suddenly, Evans was dropped, victim of a mechanical fault, the rear mechanism locking up, finally a change of bikes. He remounted but had lost two minutes. Was he going to lose once more to bad luck?

Contador and Andy Schleck crossed the Télégraphe with 34 seconds on Voeckler and 1m 35s on the Evans group. The Frenchman hooked up with Jérôme Pineau, who'd dropped out of the break, the countrymen putting aside team loyalties briefly before Voeckler once more resumed his pursuit of the men threatening his jersey. That chase cost him a lot of energy and he admitted it was an error: he should have waited for Evans. Nevertheless, he was only 35 seconds behind Schleck, Contador and three of the escapees seven kilometres from the summit of the Galibier. Evans, who had no teammate with him, and a number of other riders, including Rolland and Sánchez, caught Voeckler four kilometres from the top and two kilometres on he attacked, in company with Rolland. Voeckler was finished. Rolland later recalled the exchange with his team leader in the moments before Evans attacked. Voeckler had told his men that he would hang on until he could no longer do so and that would be it. Now he said to Rolland, 'It's over for me, I want you to go after Evans, Schleck.' Sánchez was ahead of them too, in pursuit of the leaders.

Evans twice won the World's mountain bike series (1998 and 1999) and is a superb descender, as witness the 1m 9s he took out of Schleck on the col de Manse. On the long drop to Bourg d'Oisans both he and Sánchez caught Contador and Schleck, Rolland and the Canadian Ryder Hesjedal of Garmin-Cervélo comfortably with them, 25km from the finish. Voeckler had slipped back to 1m 20s. At 23.5km to go, Rolland attacked and only Hesjedal could, or would, go with him. Somehow, Voeckler dragged himself back up to the favourites near the foot of l'Alpe d'Huez, but, even as Rolland and Hesjedal were beginning the climb with a 50-second advantage, he faltered, again. From here on it was a dogged slog for him.

Contador now launched what must be his own final essay in the high stakes 12.5km from the Alpe's summit. He caught the leading pair and went past, Rolland reeled him in some 500 metres on, Hesjedal could not follow. Behind them, Sánchez sped away from the favourites and set off in chase of the leaders. Contador had dropped Rolland and five kilometres from the finish had a lead of 23 seconds on him and Sánchez, 40 seconds on Evans and Schleck, 2m 55s on Voeckler.

In the last four kilometres, Contador visibly weakened, paying for his audacity. The organisers had planted this short stage in the hope that it would encourage the climbers to attack from early on and so they had. (Oddly, they'd put the intermediate sprint just outside Bourg d'Oisans, when none of the contenders for the green jersey would be close. Why not in Valloire, between the Télégraphe and the Galibier?) Rolland and Sánchez caught him 2.5 kilometres from the top and Rolland, with remarkable poise, turned to consider the two Spaniards, once, twice, a look which said mine to do, yours to counter, if you can and attacked. He seemed to be in complete charge, of himself, of the road, of his rivals, mastering whatever physical distress he must have felt as he had done throughout in the mountains. He became only the second Frenchman to win on l'Alpe d'Huez, after Hinault in 1986, the year of his birth. He also took over the white jersey of best young rider, even as his leader surrendered yellow (by 3m 22s) to Andy Schleck. Evans came in with the Schlecks at 57 seconds and was now third overall. Andy took the yellow jersey. Sánchez (at 14 seconds) robbed Vanendert of the polka dots. Contador (at 23 seconds) lay fifth overall.

Evans, 4 seconds behind Fränk and 53 on Andy, went into the time-trial, a circuit of Grenoble, knowing that the race was his to take. The Schlecks had ridden the Tour de Suisse as a warm-up for the Tour, he the Dauphiné Libéré (second to Wiggins), which used the same course for this one individual race against the clock in the Tour. Since he had twice flunked the final time-trial – in 2007 and '08 – arguably giving away the Tour on both occasions, that reconnaissance served him well. But it was nerve he needed. The race against the clock is above all a test of how far a rider is prepared to push himself beyond reasonable tolerance, into a state verging on physical and mental collapse. On this day, Evans, who had ridden with such dogged insistence, in ungainly style, lying flat along the bike as if gnawing at the headset or out of the saddle with a look of abject misery on his face, but with unflagging power, on this day he rode with exactly the tyrannical force ultimate victory depends on.

He missed the stage win by seven seconds to Tony Martin but relegated both Schlecks by over two minutes. The yellow jersey and a triumphant ride to Paris next day. The stage set out from Créteil, home of the club to which Laurent Fignon had belonged. The Tour paid him homage.

Cavendish took his third consecutive win on the Champs-Elysées and the green jersey. If the emotion is still quick to rise in him, he has quelled the petulance and funnelled the cockiness into a hard-nosed assurance. He's now won twenty stages in four Tours. A staggering achievement.

For Evans, a triumph of self-belief, proof that Desgrange's dictum – head and legs – is as true now as ever it was. Quite simply, Evans got tough with himself.

The two Schleck brothers shared the podium with him, Andy second for the third year running, but for his astonishing example of spirit, this was Voeckler's Tour. The fledgling Europcar team had not even been certain of a ride, yet they came away with fourth overall, Rolland eleventh, ten days in yellow, the sole French stage win and the white jersey? Magnificent.

★

POSTSCRIPT

The appeal against Contador's acquittal on a doping charge by the Spanish Federation was postponed for a second time in late July and will probably be heard in November.

The Court of Arbitration for Sport said that it had been deferred at the request of the World Anti-Doping Agency with the 'unanimous agreement' of all parties.

A spokesman for Contador said that the delay suggested the case against the star Spanish rider was weakening.

CHAPTER TWENTY-TWO

2012

First British Winner

Liège in Belgium, ten times a Tour de France stage town, was awarded the Légion d'honneur for its heroic defence against the Germans in 1914. The siege held way beyond hope or expectation and helped save France from invasion and a triumphal procession of the German army up the Champs-Elysées. Some would say that the honour of hosting the Grand Départ of the *Grande Boucle* invests a city with more kudos than mere state baubles and Liège has once before received that accolade, in 1989, the bicentenary of the storming of the Bastille in Paris. After the Frenchman Bernard Thévenet wrested the yellow jersey from the seemingly invincible Belgian Eddy Merckx in 1975, a fan at the roadside waved a placard which read 'The Bastille has fallen' and that year the Tour made its Grande Arrivée on the Champs-Elysées for the first time.

Mark Cavendish had won on the Champs for the last three years and his ambition, naturally, was to extend the run. However, being part of a team dedicated to the support of Bradley Wiggins inevitably compromised his own agenda for stage wins. A team entirely committed to riding for a potential overall winner undertakes an enormous workload. What energy would, could, they have left to spare for the Manx Missile? I mooted the question with Sean Yates, Team Sky's *directeur sportif*, and in an interview with one of their riders, Chris Froome, at the Tour de Romandie in May. The answer was uncluttered: on the flat they'd ride for Cav; on the climbs, for Brad. But this needs to be glossed. Clearly, Cavendish would sacrifice stage wins. However, the first gold medal of the London Olympic Games would go to the winner of the road race, on the Saturday after the Tour reached Paris. The Great Britain team was, effectively, a Sky outfit (plus David Millar, of Garmin-Sharp). It seemed apparent that a tactical bargain had been struck: Cavendish would net what he could at the Tour in return for total backing at the Games, albeit he himself said that he would ride principally for the yellow jersey.

Wiggins came to Liège as joint favourite to win the race overall. He'd won three major stage races – the Paris–Nice in March, the Tour de Romandie in May, the Dauphiné Libéré (as defending champion) in June. His Sky team had ridden with an impressive dominance throughout, yet many critics, some inside the *peloton*, opined that Wiggins had peaked too early. However, the Sky discipline has been to ride always to win and their preparation for the Tour is quite different from that of other teams, which follow the traditional process of a gradual build-up to the main event. The Sky performance coach, Tim Kerrison, told me that, having come from a background in rowing and swimming in his native Australia, he had been quite ignorant about cycling when he joined the team two years ago. However, any top athlete, in whatever discipline, has the same goal: to train to win. The difference with swimmers is that they train at what's called 'the top end' – that is, for peak performance – all year round. They don't use races for training. They use training for races. This, in the typical regimen of professional cyclists, is a revolutionary principle. (Even Eddy Merckx said that his best preparation for the Tour was the Giro d'Italia. He won it five times, but *preparation?*)

Proof of the efficacy of this radical approach – coupled with long stints of training at altitude on Mount Teide in Tenerife – has been in the results the team has delivered, both in races and training. For example, their training for climbing is geared to a calculation not based solely on power output or acceleration but on a system of performance analysis initiated by Michele Ferrari, namely *velocità ascensionale media*, VAM, 'mean, i.e. average, ascent velocity', which focuses on stamina, sustained effort expressed as a ratio of speed and metres of elevation gained in an hour, taking into account a rider's power output per kilogram of body mass. (The common English version 'Vertical Ascent Metrage' is meaningless.) The average VAM for a big climb on the Tour last year was 1,400 or 1,500 metres per hour. Kerrison told me he'd supposed that Wiggins' egregious success in track racing (multiple Olympic and Worlds gold medals) pointed to an explosive strength in acceleration. This was not the case. In fact, pursuiting calls for sustained effort at absolute maximum power output for short periods only. So, they have worked very hard to develop in Wiggins the essential capacity to respond to acceleration, to be able, as Kerrison put it, 'to make it possible for him to unleash that explosive power under fatigue, digging deep for as long as 60 seconds'. The evidence of all the science, the analysis, the study, the cross-referencing is encapsulated here: to make the talents on hand more rounded. *L'Equipe* greeted the first sprint victory of Wiggins' career – in imperious style, on an uphill finish, stage two, Tour de Romandie – as a new dimension to his riding, 'extending his range'. This said, science cannot master the unpredictable on the road. The Tour cannot be reduced to statistics, however carefully they are collated, however deeply rooted in evident truth of physical capacity. Three weeks of racing imposes a huge toll on body, mind and spirit, and only extreme wariness can obviate a disaster, witness 2011 when Wiggins, 'in the form of his life' (his coach Shane Sutton's words), crashed and broke his collarbone.

The Australian Richie Porte, one of Sky's designated climbers, whose job is to ride with Wiggins up the cols, said that the moment when the team knew their preparation was on course to win the Tour de France came on the penultimate stage of the Dauphiné Libéré. On the tough ascent of the col du Joux-Plane, there were five Sky men together, climbing at about 1,700 VAM. The pace they've routinely set is so hot that none of their competitors, so far, has been able to do much more than hang on, let alone drop them. Significantly, another favourite for the overall Tour win, the 2011 laureate Cadel Evans, was also with them on the Joux-Plane but alone, isolated, every member of his team, climbers included, having been shelled out. Evans had also won the 2011 Romandie but this year was nowhere. The most telling aspect of his rides in the two events before the Tour: the fact that Wiggins had pasted him in the time-trials. Although Evans was talking a good race, he knew, inescapably, that unless he could open big gaps in the mountains he couldn't hope to match the Briton's superior power in the Tour's two lengthy individual 'races of truth'.

The Sicilian Vincenzo Nibali had beaten Froome into second place on the 2011 Vuelta a España, but only by virtue of the time bonuses on stage positions. (Wiggins had come third.) He's a strong climber but also one of the most audacious descenders in the current *peloton*. It's a skill that can deliver large time gains. On that score alone, he posed a threat to Wiggins, although he had little experience of the Tour and a much weaker team.

Of the other men who might have been strong contenders, Alberto Contador was still under suspension for doping (see p. 459) and Andy Schleck was out – he'd fallen in the individual time-trial of the Dauphiné, broken his sacrum and aggravated a knee injury. No other rider posed any real threat to Wiggins or Evans. Andy Schleck's brother, Fränk, was putting it about that he could win but this was fanciful: without his brother's support and given his own weakness against the clock *and* the disarray in his RadioShack-Nissan team,* the best he could hope for was a mountain-stage win.

The American George Hincapie, now 39, was riding his 17th Tour, one more than Joop Zoetemelk's 16. Hincapie had abandoned once, Zoetemelk, never.

Fabian Cancellara won the short Prologue in the streets of the city, equalling Bernard Hinault's record of taking the first yellow jersey five times. Wiggins came second, at seven seconds, and Sylvain Chavanel, the new French time-trial champion, came third on his thirty-third birthday. The French teams, not disposing of the massive budgets of the bigger set-ups, have long become resigned to having to snap up trifles where they can, chancing their luck, accepting the fact that they have no one yet capable of ending the extended Gallic drought since Hinault's last win in 1985. Chavanel is pre-eminent amongst French riders ever ready to ginger up the action, and this result augured well. Nibali lost

---

* Internal relations were strained. The directeur, Johan Bruyneel, was not at the Tour: he is implicated in the continuing case against Lance Armstrong mounted by the American Anti-Doping Agency (USADA) and three of the team's riders had reported to the UCI that they had not been paid since May 2011.

eleven seconds to Wiggins and Evans ten, but the Australian confessed himself unsurprised. 'It was a good start for me,' he said. 'I was impatient to get stuck in and 6.4km doesn't carry much weight against the 3,500km that lie ahead.' Millar had caught a sickening cold just before the start and had to miss the team presentation. He declared himself happy simply to be in the race. Another feisty French rider, Thomas Voeckler, had been given a rough time in the Belgian press and he was booed at the finish of the time trial, an abrasive reaction to the news that his Europcar team had been subjected to a doping investigation a year earlier.

The first stage, 198km from Liège to Seraing, finished on the same uphill of the spring one-day Flèche Wallonne, 2.4km of punishing gradient with a false flat exposed to buffeting winds. Local road-maintenance crews were out before the race arrived to lay some fresh tarmac over a surface in poor state. Since Flemish bike fans are quixotically attached to the dilapidated surfaces of their roads, a sly aggravation of other attendant hazards – cobbles, potholes, sharp corners on very narrow streets, intemperate heckling from behind the barriers – which make, in their view, for more exciting racing, this namby-pamby, Tour-schmour smooth blacktop was going to be scraped off soon after the race was in.

One of Evans' team mates, the local boy Philippe Gilbert, third in the 2012 Flèche and Belgian champion in the native mould of *flahutes*, all-day strong men, was keen to do something on a finish that was ideal for him. An early attack was eventually reeled in nine kilometres from the finish but the bunch was nervous, as ever in these opening sallies – several riders went down from touched wheels but an imbecilic spectator, stepping out into the road to take a photograph, decked Alejandro Valverde of Spain and Jean-Christophe Peraud of France. On the lower slopes of the Seraing hill, Chavanel raced free but it was clear from the anguish on his face that the savage steepness of the cobbles was too much. He faded to be overtaken by Cancellara, who opened a gap that held for a short distance onto the false flat where he was caught by the Slovak, Peter Sagan, Nibali's team mate, a Tour novice at 22 years old, and Edvald Boasson Hagen, a team mate of Wiggins'. As so often happens when Cancellara is on the front within a kilometre of the line, other riders refuse to do any work and it was Sagan who sprinted away to cross the line, performing a curious flapping action with both hands perched on his shoulders, as if to say 'I have wings'. He already has thirty-seven wins in the two and a half years since he turned professional and, asked whether he felt particular pressure, being a neophyte in the Tour, replied, with that bravado of youth: 'What pressure? It's a bike race.' As Eddy Merckx replied when asked if he'd set out on any day to win, 'I didn't set out to come second.' Froome had a bad day. A puncture 14km from the finish cost him 1m 25s.

Cavendish, who'd lost weight ahead of the Olympic road race, had already won 20 stages in the Tour. 'The sprint,' he said 'is my way of showing my love for the bike.' In conversation with the Tour Director, Christian Prudhomme, he said that, for him, the number 22 meant one name only: André Darrigade, the outstanding sprinter of his day. It is this absorption of Tour history that marks out the British riders. They are steeped in and respectful of the legend of the race. They didn't come to it because it's the greatest bike race in the world and therefore, hey, a good one to win. They grew up with the stories of the Tour's heroes, they feel a kinship with the small band of Britons who have graced the long tradition of the Tour with their courage and passion, they experience a special frisson just being part of it. Cavendish took the win on stage three, pipping his ex-teammate André 'the Gorilla' Greipel by a tyre-width. Stripped of team support, Cavendish had to pick other wheels to follow and, with a track rider's nerve and silky speed, shimmied through the hectic bunch, wheel after wheel, until he had Greipel's measure. Five kilometres from the finish, he'd told his constant companion on the road – they also share a room – Bernhard (Bernie) Eisel and Boasson Hagen that he would give it a go on his own, and his victory was in no small way part of his commitment to honouring the rainbow jersey of world champion.

More men hit the tarmac 166km into the next stage between Orchies – home to a museum to the blue chicory flower, the *écoubelle*, which grows in abundance there – and Boulogne-sur-Mer. Both Gilbert and Voeckler went down and Voeckler finished in a pitiable state – a knee injury had flared up again, on top of the bruises sustained in the crash. He got to his hotel at 7 p.m., was besieged by fans wanting his autograph, he lingered to oblige, the pain notwithstanding, before going up to his room. The French call that generosity *politesse* and bike riders – not all – are markedly endowed with it.

The last stretch flipped up and over a succession of five short but punishing hills. Chavanel had another try for victory on terrain where he had won the previous year's French road championship. He broke clear on the descent of the last hill, Mont Lambert, and held off the *peloton* for five kilometres, only to succumb within 450m of the line on another very sharp uphill. Sagan, already in the green jersey, shook off the rest of the field and took a second win – the first debutant to win two stages since Diedrich Thurau in 1977. Crossing the line, he varied his victory antics and mimicked Forrest Gump running . . . the message: 'I could run like the wind blows'. Behind him, Team Sky suffered a major blow: 52km from the finish, one of their principal climbers, Kanstantsin Siutsou of Belarus, crashed and broke his left shin bone. 'Kosta' was the first man to have to leave the Tour and, aside from the sadness over his departure, the loss probably had the effect of stiffening their resolve. As Yates put it later, the rest of the team had to step up to cover for the work he would have put in.

Greipel got his own back on stages four and five, and his Lotto-Belisol team was really alone in mounting a lead-out train. The general jostling, therefore, made 'the fright bigger, everyone is fighting to put his rider in the right place,' as Cancellara put it. Having seen Sky riding with such authority at the front so often this season, I was surprised that they hadn't yet hit the front, to impose themselves – not only in the interests of getting Cavendish to the fore but, vitally, of shielding Wiggins from mishap. On stage four, Cavendish and Eisel crashed when Robbie Hunter went down at some sixty kph only two kilometres out. Sean Yates reported that Cavendish was 'beaten up. He's covered in cuts, all over, on his back, legs, shoulders, hip.' Perhaps this jolted a change of tactic because, next day, Sky came to the front, at last.

Their manager, Dave Brailsford, had told them to 'stop dithering' and Yates admitted that 'up to this point we never really got it together for various reasons'. This was vague but the message was clear – as a unit they needed to be more present, to show that they were one of the best teams in the race and to use that power more confidently. Moreover, hitting the front, opening up, energised them. In the first week, many of the riders are making the jarring shift from training to urgent racing, the mood is febrile, the composure lacking and in the *peloton* they are cruising along at high speed but without anything either to do or think about. Result? They switch off. Bad thing. The effect of that was, in shocking form, demonstrated next day in what riders called the Metz Massacre.

Twenty-five kilometres from the finish in the old Alsatian fortress town of Metz, the *peloton* was streaking down a long descent in single file at between 65 and 70kph. 'It was crazy,' said Valverde. 'There was no control, what happened was bound to happen.' It seems that one rider was trying to stuff some overshoes into a team mate's back pocket and with only one hand on the brake hit a rider in front of him. Millar said that the ensuing crash, which took down some 30 riders, was the worst he'd ever been involved in – detached chains flying about, chain-wheels spinning like angle-grinders, no possibility of braking . . . Many factors contribute to the prevalence of crashes in modern racing: the skittish lightness of the bikes with sloping tubes and short wheel base, on which riders sit well above the centre of gravity. The carbon rims tend to snatch at the brake blocks and make a smooth stop near impossible. There is the frantic temper of the race, too, the desperate rush of nearly 200 riders trying to jostle and squeeze to the front and, a vexed question, that of the earpieces – *directeurs sportifs* rapping commands in a constant flow of aural interference. Some riders blame this clamour of extraneous noise squarely for the reduced lack of spatial awareness that makes travelling at wild speed in a tight-packed bunch so very parlous.

Millar's Garmin-Sharp team all went down. Ryder Hesjedal, winner of the recent Giro d'Italia, lost 13m 24s and was out of contention for a high overall placing. Several others were badly hurt and shocked – Tyler Farrar and Johan Van Summeren both lost consciousness briefly. As their *directeur sportif* Allan Peiper put it, their entire Tour had been shot. The official medical bulletin announced that no fewer than 27 riders were receiving palliative treatment.

Wiggins, fortuitously, had moved ahead of the bunch not five minutes before the pile-up. Richie Porte fell three times and lost a lot of skin from his back and legs, Greipel's shoulder dislocated but popped back in. Of the many other casualties, four had to abandon. Fränk Schleck, impeded by but not caught up in the crash, lost over two minutes on his rivals. His cause, never strong, became even frailer.

One of the rivals, Nibali, gave a lengthy interview to *L'Equipe*. The headline? 'Wiggins doesn't impress me.' His swagger was undoubtedly reinforced by the opinion expressed by Merckx that 'only Nibali seems to me capable of stirring up the Tour with the unexpected'. In truth, not an especially illuminating judgement. Improvising is not encouraged by sponsors who want a solid return for their investment, and strict control of a race is an essential to victory these days. Moreover, spontaneous attacks of any real moment by a potential winner have very little chance of success if his rivals are vigilant and, with *directeurs* in the following cars constantly on the case, they are.

Sagan, crossing the line with a Great Hulk roar, took his third win. Was it now that his boss promised him a Porsche if he could win on the Champs-Elysées?

La Planche des Belles Filles, a plateau close to the celebrated Ballon d'Alsace in the Vosges mountains, making its debut in the Tour, is named for a group of local women who, in 1635, during the Thirty Years War, committed suicide in the nearby lake rather than submit to violation by the Swedish mercenaries who had slaughtered the entire male population of the neighbouring Savoureuse and Rahin valleys. The ascent of six kilometres from 542m to 1,035m hits some gradients of 15, 20 and, at the very top, 28 per cent. The final stretch had been tarmacked for the Tour but smooth surface cannot a 1 in 5 slope easy make. This was the first of only three mountain top finishes on the route. Game on.

The early escapees – from lesser teams snatching every chance to brandish their sponsors' names on the television coverage – held out until the *peloton*, like a furious swarm of killer bees, scattered them. The hellish pace came from Sky, Michael Rogers, Porte and Froome at their head, Wiggins impassive on their wheel, the BMC team of Evans and the luckless Garmin-Sharps clinging on until resolve and strength petered out. Only Evans and Nibali persisted, solitary, uninvited guests, a straggle of chasers fading like the Cheshire Cat's smile. The Sky modus operandi is highly structured: Porte finishes his work and peels away, then Rogers, until his effort dwindles whereat Froome takes over and it's only the four of them, top-drawer, speed not dipping. Evans tried to accelerate clear but his sudden burst of pace popped, like a blown bubble, almost at once and, even as he faded, Froome, still leading, sped away to take the victory by a delicious two seconds from Evans and his leader Wiggins. If riders are and must be correspondent to command, that command can, on occasion, loosen and the reward this day was ample: Froome, stage win and the polka-dot jersey, Wiggins into yellow by 1m 50s on Cancellara.

That evening, at the press conference which the race leader is obliged to attend – official protocols that eat into recovery time add further stress to the weighty responsibility of the yellow jersey – a journalist (almost inevitably American) asked Wiggins to comment on sceptical remarks about the astonishing jump in the level of his performance. Wiggins reacted ill and let rip, but with good cause. 'I cannot be doing with people like that. It justifies their own bone-idleness because they can't ever imagine applying themselves to doing anything in their lives. It's easy for them to sit under a pseudonym on Twitter and write that sort of shit . . . Cunts.' He stormed out.

If it was not very polite, it was timely. This is a man who, from the first time he rode the Tour, has railed against doping cheats. And what would a doping offence cost him? 'Reputation, livelihood, family, house, everything I've achieved, Olympic medals, world titles, CBE.' So, there's a *choice*? He first signed for the French Française des Jeux (FDJ) team managed for the 15 years since its inception by Marc Madiot, twice winner of the Paris–Roubaix. Madiot is unstinting in his praise of his former protégé. 'He was,' he says, 'my Cancellara.' Madiot knows well what firmness of purpose it takes to win the Tour overall but that is not something his team can contemplate. They must hunt the lesser prizes and Madiot is an outspoken critic of the formulaic style of racing so at odds with the way he used to race. I spoke to him a while ago. 'Today we're in a *cyclisme* of calculation,' he said, with evident passion, 'evading risk, everything controlled, all controlled, all controlled, all controlled.' (I use the French *cyclisme* because it means so much more than simply 'cycling'.) The very repetition exposes the fervent antagonism against the neutralising of what is, for him, the essential spirit of bike-racing: riding to win and to hell with the risk. It's a view seconded by two other riders to whom I have spoken recently, Chavanel and Voeckler.

Madiot expands: 'Take the case of Cavendish. He wins all the sprints. Why do the other sprinters' teams ride with him? They're stupid. The only chance they have of beating him is not to ride with him, leave him in the shit [yes, *merde*] and take him on at the finish. But, no, they all ride with him. Frankly . . . [a long pause] they work on the principle that no one loses, and they get the placings *but* . . .' (And that '*mais*' triggers a fine Gallic shrug of the shoulders, a rise in tone that takes the notion to the edge of the roof from where it stares down into an abyss of absurdity.) He adds: 'Cavendish laughs, eh?'

Madiot is not alone in his passion for racing dictated by heart, impulse, spontaneity and enterprise: in sum, a more fiery, devil-may-care spirit. The last French Tour winner, Hinault, had such a cavalier attitude, but, then, his superior class made caprice less a gamble than a taunt of his rivals. It's the difference between thinking you might win and knowing that you will. For the lesser teams, risk is their best option, even risk tempered with cunning. But it will generally be opportunist and always laudable. If carried to fruition, doubly so. For the bigger teams, risk is not an option. Huge budgets have to be justified, and, for that reason, if no other, the element of precise, even regimented, governance of every aspect of the race is paramount. The riders who are paid top money have to deliver top results and their individual ambition must be subservient to the general goal. They know this when they sign the contract and whatever they are told during the race, through the earpiece – where in the past it was by the *directeur sportif* leaning out of the team car alongside them (although this does still happen, at the back of the race) – they will do. Simple. Madiot and others do not have this apparent luxury, so they say 'to hell with it, we scrap like men without hope of winning in the possibility of winning'. That there are still two such vibrant modes of attack in the Tour enriches its wider drama.

Madiot's riders have the heat of his passionate advocacy of going hell-for-leather at their back and one of them, the youngest man in the race, Thibaut Pinot, might not have been there at all. Madiot had wanted to blood him at the Vuelta. Pinot went to his boss, told him, after a good showing in the Tour de Suisse, that he was in roaring form . . . he wanted his chance *now*. And, given it, if reluctantly, he repaid. On the climb of the first category col de la Croix, 16km from the finish in Porrentruy, the closest Swiss city to Paris (there's a thing), Pinot raced away from a small group of riders, caught and passed the Swede Fredrik Kessiakoff, who had amassed enough points over a lumpy stage to rob Froome of the polka dots, and kept going all the way home. 'I had to take my earpiece out,' he said, 'because Madiot was shouting so loud,' and right behind him came his manager, hanging out of the team car window, thumping at the door in his wild delight, screaming with joy.

Jürgen Van den Broeck of the Lotto-Belisol team, tipped for a high overall placing, attacked from the *peloton* on the last of a succession of six nagging climbs. Evans chased and a slight gap opened but it was no more than a brief glimmer of daylight between them and the relentless closure by Wiggins, jealous of yellow. Nibali, who has been scathing about Wiggins' adeptness going downhill, zipped off from the col at wild speed but won no advantage. The Sky team men knew he would put them under pressure here and responded as to reflex. They ride, indeed, with the sort of superior indifference to attack that increasingly tetanises the opposition.

Time Trial, Arc-et-Senans to Besançon 41.5km
A relatively flat course which, in the way of their meticulous preparation, Yates, the Team Sky *directeur sportif* – a superb time-trialler himself – had reconnoitred carefully. Wiggins describes

himself as a time-trialler who can climb. The same might be said of Jacques Anquetil and Miguel Indurain, the man who most inspired the young Wiggins growing up in the London suburb of Kilburn.

The other overall contenders knew that they were in for a drubbing and Wiggins meted it out: Evans lost 1m 43s, Nibali 2m 7s and the general classification now put Evans second at 1m 53s, the astonishing Froome (who'd ceded only 35 seconds) third at 2m 7s, Nibali fourth at 2m 23s. Evans and Nibali, both with some claim to be men for the mountains, had, so far, been tentative, ineffectual in attack. The Alps, after a rest day, lay open to a show of their true mettle.

Stage ten crossed the Côte de Corlier (second category), col du Grand Colombier (*hors catégorie*, 'outside categorisation') and col de Richemond (third) before making a long descent into Bellegarde-sur-Valserine. A downhill finish sometimes encourages but rarely favours serious attacks, except by chancers who pose no threat to the overall standings. It nevertheless presented Evans and Nibali with an opportunity to exert some pressure on the Sky men. They couldn't.

On the lower slopes of the Colombier, Millar, Sagan, Yauheni Hutarovich of FDJ and Matthew Goss, winner of the 2011 Milan–San Remo and the lead sprinter in a new Australian team, Orica-GreenEDGE, went clear. The attack swelled in numbers, among the recruits Voeckler and Luis Léon Sánchez, a feisty solo break man. Behind them, Van den Broeck tried to accelerate away from the *peloton* several times but the Sky men, defending the yellow jersey, pounced instantly. Voeckler crossed the col in the lead with five minutes on the bunch.

Nibali, nickname 'the Shark of Messina', attacked, as expected, on the descent when Rogers punctured, got a minute gap and hooked up with his Liquigas team mate Sagan. But alone on the final short climb of the Richemond, with not much more than 20km to go, he was hauled in by the yellow-jersey group, fronted by Porte.

The lead group began the wind-up. The Belgian Dries Devenyns, a team mate of Chavanel, launched a trenchant attack some three kilometres out, the others hesitated, then Voeckler shot after him, caught him inside a kilometre and got stuck in for the last agonising brace of kilometres. Approaching the line, his erstwhile companions strung out in dribs and drabs behind him, Voeckler, will and legs drained to the lees, had not the strength to lift his arms in a victory salute. 'I suffered like never before,' he said. 'At first, I shut my eyes, thinking that I was 150 metres from the line when there were still 300 to go. I turned round and saw [Jens] Voigt, then Sánchez, then [Michele] Scarponi. I thought I had lost till five metres from the line.'

Stage win *and* he took over the polka-dot jersey and the ambition to carry it into Paris. Fourth last year, he was way down now because of the pain in his knee, but here was an unexpected prize that would get him onto the podium. Knee? What knee?

As for Evans, 'the do-nothing king' as he was being described, he said: 'Perhaps I should have followed Nibali.' A lame aside better left unsaid. It seemed that he had already surrendered to the reality that he could not take charge in the mountains themselves nor climb the psychological mountain that he'd surmounted to win the Tour the previous year.

Bothersome incident: the Cofidis rider Rémy di Gregorio was taken into custody for examination by a judge on the rest day, accused of injecting ozone and a transfusion of blood enriched with ozone and glucose. He denied everything, of course, but was immediately suspended by his team and conducted before a judge's tribunal in Marseille.

Ozone has been administered since the nineteenth century for its detoxifying virtues as well as being an anti-inflammatory and antiseptic. Glucose replenishes stocks of glycogen and works as a carburant. The fault seems to lie in the fact that Di Gregorio committed an infraction of the UCI's 'no needle' policy.

Stage eleven, Albertville – Les Toussuires, 148km col de la Madeleine 2,000m HC (hors catégorie), col de la Croix de Fer 2,067m HC, col du Mollard 1638m second category, La Toussuire 1,705m first.
An analysis of the day's work put in by the Sky riders is instructive. Boasson Hagen rode at the front for around 56km up and over the Madeleine, the German Christian Knees took over in the valley

and Rogers succeeded to ferry them over the Croix de Fer. Porte came to the front for a short stint before Froome and Wiggins made the tandem for the last 12 kilometres. Once more, Evans was without support, the BMC team alarmingly short of climbing strength. Nibali had no team mate with him either but he at least was showing something of the hauteur needed to disguise any misgivings he had about his prospects here.

Ahead of them, at not much more than a minute, Pierre Rolland, hero of a signal victory against the big hitters on l'Alpe d'Huez in 2011, had shaken off another survivor of the breakaway group, his compatriot Pinot, full of a new confidence and swagger. Rolland eventually pulled clear and came in by 55 seconds, another stage win for Europcar, Pinot second, another bouquet for FDJ.

Behind these two, an untoward slackening of team tactics that was quickly worked up into a case of *lèse-majesté*. Four kilometres from the top, Froome surged away from Wiggins. It looked like a deliberate attempt to drop his leader and put time into him. Responding to Yates' firm reminder that his duty was to defend the yellow jersey, however, Froome reined in. Wiggins came up to his wheel as Froome turned to look at him. Speculation seethed. What lay in Froome's backward glance? Reassurance? Impatience? They rode on, Nibali and Van den Broeck in attendance, and came in with Pinot. Evans conceded 1m 26s and second place overall to Froome. Wiggins' declaration from the steps of the team bus need not excite cynical doubt. Sky held the first two places overall in the Tour de France, he said, so what's to question? But interpretation of monitored policy statement is always open to question and tweaking. The analogy of the rocket may apply: only one man can reach the stratosphere but he needs the other men to launch him within reach, just as the expendable stages of the rocket propel the business end beyond the pull of gravity. Trouble is, Froome didn't show any sign of being expendable. In fact, he looked stronger on the climbs than Wiggins. This was undeniable. It was also, in the wider scheme, significant only as an indicator of the team's power. Maybe, as some claimed, Wiggins *had* asked Froome not to go too quickly. Froome, accordingly, slowed down. Wiggins explained further that he had eased off a little when Froome went ahead to eliminate a bit of lactic acid in his legs. There was also a lot of noise, making it difficult to hear in the earpiece, to know exactly what the situation was. Of course some journalists talked up the affair – it was Greg Lemond and Hinault in 1986 again (see p. 58f). But when a Sky man talks about lactic acid, it ain't no whimsical excuse – you'd better believe him.

The final day in the Alps bit hard early on – two first-category climbs over the col du Grand Cucheron and the col du Granier led to a long run-in of relatively undemanding 140km – I say *relatively* . . . there was a third category alpine hummock, the Côte d'Ardoix, some 26km from the end. It lay open to an opportunist attack and Millar, steeped in Tour legend like all the Brits, wanted it. It was the 50th anniversary of Friday, 13 July 1967, when Tom Simpson died on the slopes of Mont Ventoux. Homage was due. Millar paid it with a sweetly timed jump a short way out. He'd been part of an early break of 19 riders before the Cucheron. Eight fell away on the climb, the veteran David Moncoutié, riding his last Tour, crashed on the descent and had to abandon. A sad finish to the career of a man who has always ridden with heart.

The escape counted only five men off the Granier and on the last kilometres, all uphill into Annonay Davézieux, the Spaniard Egoi Martinez cut loose, followed by Jean-Christophe Peraud, another of Madiot's AG2R men. In December 1782, in the garden of their paper mill in Annonay, the Montgolfier brothers built their first hot-air balloon and gave it a successful public flight on 4 June the following year. Having latched onto Peraud's wheel, Millar got lift-off. It was a fine win and, recalling the reason for Simpson's tragic demise, Millar took it, he said, in expiation of his own doping.

The day was slightly marred by the idiocy of some oiks waving flares at the riders on the final climb. Wiggins copped a slight burn on his arm but it was not grave 'and we chucked a few bidons at them in retaliation'. Nice one. Bastille Day followed. Greipel crossed the line by a tyre from Sagan. A published interview – conducted in Italian – with Froome, probed the sentiments of a rider for whom team ethics might seem to be a spike of his own ambition. 'I can't lie,' he said. 'It's difficult, truly, but it's my job.' And since a win in the Tour promised substantial financial gain? 'I know that. I know it could change my life. For that reason it's a sacrifice, a big sacrifice.' And, so what? This is candour, not complaint. Team first. A woman once asked Fats Waller what rhythm was. 'Ma'am,' he said 'if you have to ask that question, you will never know.'

The Pyrenees arrived with a first inclusion of the Mur de Péguère outside Massat in the Ariège. It's a pig. Five kilometres of around 20 per cent. I've ridden it three times and am content to know that I'll never ride it again because I won't ever tell myself to ride it again. I'd texted Yates a while back to suggest a reconnaissance of the climb. He texted back: he and Wiggins had just come back from there. Snow on the top. Not this day of Pyrenean wet mist and bouts of rain. Instead, a huge crowd lining a very narrow road and a poltroon with a bagful of carpet tacks that he scattered over the road on the descent.

I knew the Péguère would be a zoo and counselled an earlier vantage, so we watched them come off the Port de Lers, the Sky train in control of the bunch chasing the escapees, hurtling onto the snaky decline at alarming speed on the wet surface, some riders plucking gels out of their back pockets, others with bidon nipples clenched between their teeth, rain tops flapping. Wonderful balance and poise. Amazingly, Cavendish was leading out the Sky group – rainbow jersey riding like a mountain *domestique*. As d'Artagnan says, 'All for one, one for all.'

We watched the *Arrivée* in Foix at a bar in the valley and only later heard the story of the day. Principal casualty of the nails – a miserable sabotage that also marred the second edition of the Tour in 1904 – was Evans, punctured three times. When this news was relayed to Wiggins at the head of the chase, the yellow jersey asserted the responsibility, and the *puissance*, of his leader's status and called truce, to allow his rival to rejoin. It was, as the French delightedly say, '*très* fair play' and it confirmed their opinion of the man they were now calling '*le Colonel*' (one up in rank on Simpson, who'd been 'the Major') as being a *gentleman*. (They use the English.) Rolland, apparently defying orders, actually rode off after the truce was declared and got a wigging for it, although he explained that he had not been aware what was happening behind him. And who is to impugn his veracity? He expressed his chagrin at even a suspicion of treachery – not his intention – and apologised.

More seriously, coming off the summit, the Croat Robert Kiserlovski, who'd given up a wheel to his Astana leader, Janez Brajkovic, was waiting for a replacement when Levi Leipheimer collided with him. The luckless Kiserlovski went down hard and had to quit with a broken collarbone. If the butcher's bill for the malice was mercifully light, the cost in new tyres, for bikes and cars, was heavy. The Tour organisation caught and took process of the culprit, to whom they referred as 'X'.

Luis León Sánchez won after leaving his companions of a sizeable escape and holding out for a brave lone sally of 11km, the sort of derring-do for which he is known. And, next day, from Samatan, famous for foie gras and its winter duck and goose marché au gras, another rider known for his audacity on breakaway wins, the FDJ rider Pierrick Fédrigo, took his fourth Tour stage win in Pau. This made him the most prolific French stage winner currently riding in the Tour. His 2011 season was blighted by the onset of Lyme's disease, a bacterial infection caused by a tick bite that induces crippling fatigue. If caught early, it can be cured, and if not . . . not.

Chavanel, who has won three Tour stages, succumbed to a debilitating fever and climbed off a short way into the stage. It was, he said, a terrible disappointment, sharpened by the possibility that it would also mean his missing the Olympic Games time trial.

For all their talk about taking on Wiggins in the mountains, Nibali and Evans had not even rattled him so far. Fränk Schleck, though he had lost too much time to be any real threat, must have nursed some belief that he could redeem his promise of some action. However, on the evening of the rest day in Pau, he was taken into custody and immediately expelled from the race by his RadioShack-Nissan team. A dope test on 14 July revealed traces of a diuretic, Xipamide. The drug has been around a long time, for the reduction of cardiac, renal and liver oedemas, but is abused in aiding artificial loss of weight by boxers, weightlifters, wrestlers and to mask the taking of other dope. The more rapid evacuation of urine flushes out traces of them. Sale of Xipamide has been withdrawn in France since 2006 but it is readily available elsewhere. Schleck denied guilt and went to the examining magistrate voluntarily.*

Wednesday, 18 July. Morning.
Our passage up the west flank of the Tourmalet was slow. We pass cyclists, walkers, people who have decided to park lower down rather than bank on a place on the upper slopes. Wisely. The upper slopes are chock-full, so, too, the basin below them, the leas on either side. Everywhere, a vast diaspora with nowhere to go. There are more cars, campervans, caravans, bikes, motorbikes and their owners parked on the side of this road than dead souls waiting on the near bank of the Styx hankering to cross over, a great multitude that no man could number, of all persuasions of team support, all manner of flags and banners to wave, all varieties of faintly ludicrous costume. All crazy for the Tour. The road is closed by gendarmes – most quite affable, it must be said, if stern of command – and we, like the rest of the traffic trying to go up there, must wait. A film crew up ahead, apparently. There are times when even a press sticker on the car's windscreen cannot unblock or bypass a tailback. We eventually cross the col – no place on the verge below it on the way up – go down a short way and, lo, a gap between two vehicles. Our niche. And so begins the long dalliance, the rather less than *dolce far niente*, until, at around 1.30 p.m., the publicity caravan careers through, scattering hats, foldaway backpacks (very useful), key rings, packets of mini saucisson or madeleines (better), sachets of washing liquid . . . and disco music at unsociable volume, the whole deafening fandango proceeded by a man piloting a daffodil-yellow Crédit Lyonnais motorised split bean pod. Overhead, high in the azimuth, circle the five transmitter planes, ghostly grey in the ethereal vapours, volleying the television signals back to the receivers, like buzzards waiting for their lunch to die on the rock platter below. At 3 p.m., Brice Feillu and Voeckler hurtle down with about five minutes' lead on their chasers. It's a daring move – cols d'Aubisque and Soulor

* As is routine, a second B sample was later checked by the laboratory used by the UCI and Schelck made a statement: 'The result of the counter test was positive but for me nothing changes: I just know that I did nothing wrong. I will therefore continue my search to find out how the substance could have entered my body.'

behind them, cols d'Aspin and Peyresourde in wait. Voeckler is in his green Europcar jersey again but obviously greedy for the peas, as the French call the polka dots (*maillot à pois*). He'd been out with some 38 riders 20km from the start, among them the Kazakh Alexandr Vinokourov, badly injured in 2011 but here for a swansong, not to retire in anonymity, as he put it. Kessiakoff was also there, in the mountains jersey. By the foot of the Tourmalet, this fugitive posse had five minutes on the *peloton* but the climb shredded them.

On the Peyresourde, Voeckler dropped Feillu and began the 22km descent into Bagnères-de-Luchon, where he'd won in 2010. It was his fourth Tour stage win, putting him level with Fédrigo. He'd crossed each of the day's cols in the lead – repeating Jean Robic's famous exploit in 1947 (from the opposite direction) – and now held the polka dots by four points over his Swedish opponent.

The descent of the Peyresourde is one of the swiftest in the Pyrenees: after the sweeping hairpins off the summit, the road straightens in an almost clear run to the finish. This was Nibali's chance and the Sky management knew they needed to counter, hold his wheel up to the summit, let him go, move in and close him down. He got 50 metres. That was it.

Evans, suffering with a stomach upset, was finished. He lost 45 seconds on the ascent of the Aspin, rejoined but faltered again on the Peyresourde when Nibali accelerated. Riding into Luchon, he reached out to thank Hincapie, who, despite being injured in a crash that day, had nursed him through the misery, and crossed the line having conceded nearly five minutes on the three overall leaders. He slumped to seventh overall, one behind his team mate, the young American, Tejay Van Garderen, whose lead in the best young rider's competition, if not unassailable, was commanding. The Frenchman Rolland held ninth and Pinot tenth. A huge encouragement for French cycling.

The young Belgian Jan Ghyselinck crossed the line just ahead of the broom wagon – which, sadly, no longer carries the besom fixed to the back door – four seconds outside the time limit. He was still on the ascent of the Peyresourde, 23km from home, when Voeckler crossed the line. The maximum time gap instantly dropped to 43m 34s. Ghyselinck was probably out. Over the summit, he had to weave through cyclotourists starting their own descent. Ten kilometres from the finish, he took a wrong turn in a village, had to turn round and lost more time. But the Tour can be as compassionate as it is cruel. He was reprieved. The Voice of the Tour, Daniel Mangeas, announced with glee in the *longueur* after the last of the field had staggered across the line, 'Great news, Jan can continue the Tour de France.'

Next day, we watched them go over the Port de Balès, penultimate climb of the day and the Tour. Voeckler had dogged Kessiakoff on every col, defending his jersey, poaching the points in the last metres. Not very sporting, he owned, but he had a duty to his team and that was to get the peas to Paris and the podium.

Forty riders had separated themselves from the main *peloton* at the bottom of the day's first obstacle, the col de Menté, near the corner on which Luis Ocaña had crashed in the blinding rain of a dark, fogbound Pyrenean storm (see p. 49). Among the group, Nibali and Valverde. The presence of the Italian inevitably jeopardised the life of the escape. They discussed this and made a deal, on what might be called a Sicilian handshake, whereat Nibali, thanked by the Spaniard, dropped out to wait for the following bunch.

Froome teased the conspiracy theorists again on the final ascent to the Peyragudes ski station, above the Peyresourde, its first inclusion in the race. Was he playing dark horse or not? Desperate to show his full power and reined in by a niggardly team plan? He was clearly going a lot faster than Wiggins as they neared the finish – Valverde a short distance up ahead. He opened a sizeable gap and then turned round to look at the yellow jersey, surely in response to the orders of Yates reminding him that the plan was to stay together, even if there was (as on Toussuire) a stage win to be contested. He surely did have the legs of the Spaniard, who was faltering, and might have caught and overtaken him. Surely it wasn't untoward to drop Wiggins by even as much as a minute, say, to do that? Wiggins did seem to be stalled, if not in trouble, but Froome stayed, Valverde took the win, by a mere 19 seconds, and the Tour was effectively won. But that, said Wiggins, is what had broken his concentration, the realisation for the first time that perhaps he had just won the Tour de France. After all the training, the preparation, the hermetically sealed concentration that it had taken to bring him to this final climb, in yellow, without serious rival to his victory, the sudden understanding of what he had just achieved and would, in Paris, three days later, celebrate, invaded his mind and feelings with stupefying force. No wonder he went into somewhat of a trance, even pedalling at the same 'hellish speed' that had crushed the opposition. That Froome was still in fettle, fine, but he had not the weight of victory, and a historic victory, bearing down on him. Another time for him. Yates elucidated: 'I told them to stay together. Froome didn't listen. This was maladroit, he lacked tact. A pity, a bit disappointing but, OK, he's new to this level, he has a lot to learn. He needs to get the sense of a race, the good feeling, but he'll learn that . . . it takes time.' This was part of an overarching strategy that could, as occasion demanded, send Cavendish, the world champion, back to the team car as a humble water carrier to load up with and ferry the bidons back to his team mates. And, outstanding rider as he is, Froome would readily acknowledge that he would not be at this level now were it not for being with the Sky set-up.

That same world champion at the team briefing next morning heard Yates tell them to take it easy for the day – husband energies, time trial on Saturday, Champs-Elysées on Sunday. Cavendish was, of course, itching for a chance and Wiggins said, 'Yes, let's go for it, for Cav,' and it was Wiggins who led them out on the approach to Brive-la-Gaillarde. Thrilling to watch, the yellow jersey at the head of the bunch riding at pursuit pace, Cavendish slipping through what seemed to be a very thicket of other riders and, with ecstatic speed, like a clay from a launcher, searing past. His 22nd victory in the Tour.

The time gaps of the final time trial into Chartres do little more than underline Wiggins' superiority in a Tour that might seem to have been planned for him. But, there is no such thing as a soft Tour de France and the fact is, for all the talk of giving him a hard time in the mountains, it didn't happen. He won the stage by 1m 16s from Froome, put 3m 38s into Nibali and 5m 54s into Evans, who'd been overtaken by his young team mate Van Garderen. Another Sky man, Porte, came fifth at 2m 25s from his leader – three of the Team Sky in the top ten, confirming the triumph of their holistic approach.

'Every lap of the Champs-Elysées was goose-pimple stuff,' said Wiggins, but added that 'we had a job to do with Mark today and we were all motivated to do that, so it made it go a lot quicker.' That job was to reel in the breakaways – tantalisingly late, it must be said – and to launch Cavendish. Wiggins under the red kite, streaking into the last kilometre, a back crosswind on them as they raced at mad speed into the final corner, 400 metres out, too far, surely too far, but Cavendish went, went with such joyous power, such exuberant delight, like a rebellious kid out of detention, and there was no one close, no one to rob him. Sagan came second but was wheels apart. This brilliant display of panache and sheer speed confirmed Cavendish's worthiness of the title *Roi du Sprint* (King of the Sprint) conferred on him by a panel of French experts, including Christian Prudhomme and Bernard Hinault.

Gerard Brown, the photographer, and I boarded the ferry in Calais on Friday evening having heard of Cavendish's win that day. When we disembarked in Dover, there was a double rainbow like a triumphal arch in the mottled blue-grey sky over a placid, sun-glazed Channel. Sign or what?

There is no such thing as a boring Tour de France, save in the eyes of bores who look only at the surface gloss, the statistics, to excuse their own lack of insight and enthusiasm. For them, the numbers show British riders taking seven stage victories and first and second overall; the French contingent, five stages, polka-dot jersey and two placings in the top ten (Rolland eighth, Pinot tenth), the white jersey (best young rider) an American, and the debutant from Slovakia dubbed Tourminator, the green for best finisher and a trio of stages. Behind that, this Tour was remarkable for its first-time British winner (and first-ever Olympic track gold medallist to win) and behind that victory a story of dedication, self-knowledge and a socking great mistake. But the man who never made a mistake never made anything. Sky came to the Tour in 2010 with the stated intention of producing a British win in five years. This was indiscreet if nothing worse and the immediate failure, both of execution and management, was acutely embarrassing. They admitted it. So, they took the whole strategy apart and rebuilt, they learnt what they needed to do, they applied themselves to the work. I have said elsewhere in this book that the transition from track star to road racer is hard and complicated – mentally and psychologically. As Henri Desgrange said, to win the Tour takes head and legs, and note the order. So, they assessed what work it required and set to. And, for as cogent an evocation of the moral change wrought in Wiggins as there could be, consider what he says on p. 362 of this book.

Through the course of the Tour, Wiggins expressed extreme, even irritated displeasure with the barrage of banal questions he was expected to answer day after day, the mundanities of journalists looking for copy. One sympathises, on both sides of the interrogation. I overheard a German commentator ambushing him at the start of the Samatan–Pau stage. Wiggins said he didn't speak German. *'Ja, aber alles in Ordnung*, I speak very good Englisch,' says the German and the poached interview rolled. 'England's gone cycling crazy,' he asks. 'What do you think of that?'

'No idea,' says Wiggins, 'I've been here.'

At the end of the race, Wiggins, hitherto inclined to prickliness but now more relaxed in the embrace of what he was achieving, maybe, became not only *'le gentleman'* but the embodiment of British cool. Why, they even loved the mod sideburns. And on the podium, when he was handed the microphone . . . oh, Lord, what now? But, ah, a brilliant stroke: 'I'm gonna talk in English [he speaks good French]. We're just goin' to draw the raffle, now.'

Chapeau.

FOOTNOTE

A tactical error by the Great Britain team robbed Cavendish of any tilt at a win in the Olympics Road Race, the Saturday after the end of the Tour, but Wiggins took gold, and Froome bronze, in the time-trial a few days later.

CHAPTER TWENTY-THREE

2013

100th Edition

PREFACE: LIVE STRONG? LIE STRONG

In January of this year, Lance Armstrong confessed that he had taken performance-enhancing drugs, including EPO, throughout his entire professional career. That he chose to come clean about not riding clean to Oprah Winfrey, queen of the kiss-and-tell, bruised-heart-on-the-sleeve, stricken-conscience talk show, may be construed as tugging on the emotional emergency cord, playing the sentimental card.

In the course of not very strenuous questioning by Winfrey, whose expertise in the matter of professional cycling has not, so far, been validated, Armstrong said that in his era all riders took dope just as they put water in their bottles, but also claimed not to know what other riders were doing. This non sequitur implied that he was more a victim of a doping culture than a proponent of it; however, it later emerged that he had conducted a draconian regime of drug-taking imposed on all riders who rode for him and with him when he dominated the Tour. His admission of guilt was compromised not so much by his ardent denials of miscreancy over a long, long time as by his relentless pursuit of those who accused him of it, to the extent of pressing libel cases, for which he was awarded substantial damages as an innocent.

Armstrong was stripped of his seven Tour titles, but the legacy of his deceit will be less easy to clean out than the Augean Stables: the man Hercules's mammoth dung-shifting operation in labour number five. The current generation of younger riders has to deal with all that excrement and horse shit of lingering doubt, accusatory journalism, a cynical mistrust of their integrity, a swill of discredit dumped on them by the infamy of drug cheats, now gone from the scene. It's damnable.

Armstrong capped his own infamy by declaring, just before the Tour arrived in Corsica, that no one would win the race *unless* they were taking dope. As if anyone was interested in his verdict on riders who compete without recourse to the rocket fuel he used.

THE 100TH

Corsica, dominated by lofty mountain peaks, has been called a mountain in the sea. Its strategic position in the Mediterranean – the term *Mare mediterraneum* was coined by the Roman geographer Solinus around 200 AD – has made it a prime target for conquest from the beginning. It sits like a stepping stone between the long spine of Italy and the southern coast of the European landmass, the large bay of Calvi offering an ideal anchorage.

The Romans drove the first occupiers, the Carthaginians, off Corsica and established it, with Sardinia, as a province. Under the Empire, Corsica, now a senatorial province separate from Sardinia, was often used as a place of exile. The younger Seneca – later tutor to the mad emperor Nero – spent eight years of banishment on Corsica, for his alleged adultery with the sister of the mad emperor Caligula, who was scandalously rumoured to have had his own way with her.

After the Romans came Vandals, Goths, Byzantine imperial governors from Ravenna, and Saracens, before the Genoese took over in 1383 and held sway over the island for four hundred years. They made Bastia their capital. In 1748, they welcomed a French expeditionary force that arrived on the pretext of helping them to quell unrest on the island. More likely is that the principal concern of the French was to prevent it from falling into English hands.

There followed over twenty years of toing and froing, Corsican partisans versus Genoese overlords, and periodic intervention and withdrawal of the French, until they came back in strength and settled the issue. The Genoese left for good. In 1770, the deputies of the general assembly of Corsica swore allegiance to King Louis XV and, after a brief intrusion by the English in 1794 – allegiance switched to George III – the island became definitively French in 1815. In that year, the Corsican Napoleon Bonaparte was defeated at Waterloo and the Congress of Vienna redrew the map of Europe. Napoleon was exiled to St Helena, a rocky island aswim far off in the Atlantic. He'd left his home in Ajaccio, Corsica's new capital, in 1769 to study at the military academy in Brienne.

In 2013, the Tour de France sent its own massive expedition to Corsica, the only one of the ninety-five French départements the race had never visited. (Actually *two* – the island is divided into *Haut-Corse*, 'upper', and *Corse-du-Sud*, 'southern'.)

This novelty is further evidence of the imaginative flair that the Tour's director, Christian Prudhomme, has brought to the race routes in the past few years. The France of Napoleon and the Grande Armée expanded across Europe, just as the *Grande Boucle* has done since 1906 when it probed into German-held Alsace. *Grands Départs* from Britain, Belgium, Germany, Holland, Italy . . . For this 100th edition of the race, there were other novelties, too, notably a double ascent of l'Alpe d'Huez on the same day. This called into play the Col de Sarenne, which approaches the alp from the east and has never been used before because, until the Tour homed in on it, the first few kilometres from the top were not paved. Prudhomme's administration has surfaced not a few dirt roads. There's probably a Tarmac Tour de France Inc. franchise.

The course in general favoured the contenders who could climb. There were four mountain-top finishes altogether and the final week was packed with high-altitude cols. The aim was patent: to engineer a final showdown in the Alps, where the penultimate stage ended on Semnoz, the ski station above Annecy. Before the riders reached its welcome haven and an end to altitude – the day before riding into Paris – they faced two hard days in the Pyrenees, the ascent of the fearsome Mont Ventoux and five brutal days in the Alps, including a mountain time-trial.

The 2012 winner, Wiggins, who has described himself as 'a time-triallist who can climb', had pulled out of the Giro with a chest infection and then declared, some weeks before the Tour, that he wouldn't be riding because of a knee injury. Except that he had started training again. With a bad knee. Given his dismal form in 2013, this withdrawal was not unexpected, although plainly the course of the race did not suit him at all. He also announced, with that injudicious throwaway style of his, that he couldn't imagine ever putting himself through the work and sacrifice required to win the Tour a second time.

His absence clarified matters in Team Sky. Without him, the man who was largely responsible for helping him to the win the year before, Chris Froome, who describes himself as 'a climber who can time-trial', now came as designated leader of the team. There are many who believe he could – perhaps even should – have won the 2012 tour as well as the 2011 Vuelta, in both of which he had been required to sacrifice his own ambitions to team orders and the task of succouring Wiggins.

Froome had pretty well come from nowhere. David Sharp's excellent biography *Va Va Froome* (Birlinn) charts his progress from immense but largely unfulfilled or stalled promise to the stellar performance of the last three years. Froome arrived in Corsica as the winner of the Tour of Oman, the Critérium National, the Tour de Romandie and the Dauphiné Libéré, in which he'd beaten Alberto Contador. After that race, he said he had got the measure of the Spaniard, who returned to the Tour after two years' suspension for doping. Froome had been beaten in only one stage race, the Tirreno-Adriatico, by the Italian Vincenzo Nibali, riding on home turf. Nibali, winner of the Giro, was not coming to the Tour.

Froome was gracious about the absence of Wiggins, saying that the team would miss 'his engine' in the race, but he was certainly going to be well served by a team devoted exclusively to his cause, especially by his particular friend and training partner, the Tasmanian Richie Porte.

Cadel Evans and Alejandro Valverde also lined up: strong riders, both, but, in truth, neither promised more than spoiling action. Valverde, winner of the 2009 Vuelta a España, had been suspended for two years in 2010 for involvement in Operacion Puerto (see p. 345) and was unlikely to be challenging in the last week of the race. He was, inevitably, bullish about his form and his ambitions and the strength of his team. Evans, having won the 2011 Tour had, on the evidence, lost that extra fire of spirit it takes to win the race a second time.

Stuart O'Grady participated for the 17th time, a record, and made no secret of the fact that he intended to celebrate the close of his 40th year by coming back for an 18th, and final, Tour in 2014. Then he confessed that he had taken EPO in the notorious 1998 Tour, so any further participation is now out of the question. This happily reflects a new openness in the *peloton*, a genuine candour and contempt for what has gone before, and is largely evident in the young generation of riders.

O'Grady was riding for the Australian outfit Orica-GreenEDGE (Green), which grabbed big headlines on stage one. The team bus got stuck when trying to drive under and through the gantry above the finishing line when the *peloton* was 10km away, hurtling towards it in the hunt for the first yellow jersey. A Tour first? A stage victory for a coach driver?

In the desperation to prise out the mechanised behemoth, the organisers radioed the riders to tell them that the race would now finish three kilometres from the official line. But, lo, some bright spark among the would-be bus-shifters suggested what they might have tried to begin with. The vehicle's tyres were deflated and it trundled out of danger. With five minutes to go before the improvised finish, the riders were told: *back to plan A*.

Whether this news triggered the jolt in concentration is not clear, but there was a big pile-up. Peter Sagan, defending Points laureate, went down; Mark Cavendish was held up; and one of his great rivals, the German Marcel Kittel, relatively newly emerged, riding only his second Tour, with Argos-Shimano (Argos), won the stage. As a concession to the discombobulated *peloton*, all the riders were given the same time, but the Points competition stood, to the disgruntlement of its main challengers.

One of Sky's strongmen, Geraint Thomas, a former teammate of Froome in the Barloworld team (see p. 383), also went down in the crash and an MRI scan showed that his pelvis had a hairline fracture. Despite his mother's pleas for him to stop, he took painkillers and rode on, if gingerly. He had to be helped onto his bike, but Froome was upbeat: 'He's Welsh. He'll survive.'

Stage two ran from Bastia to Ajaccio. In the past, riders have been apprehensive about hungry bears roaming the mountains. Now they contend with encroaching road furniture, lunatic spectators squeezing the road thin, and escaped livestock. Four kilometres from the finish, on the Route des Sanguinaires, a small white dog ran across road, hotly pursued by the hapless chump who owned it. Since the riders trying to bring their sprinters to the front are travelling at upwards of 60kph, this could have been a bloody disaster. Luckily, pooch and poppa scrambled clear in time.

The road is named for the four small Sanguinaires ('bloodthirsty') islands, which form an archipelago off the coast nearby. They are named either for the purple light of the dying sun that imparts a blood-red glow on the rocks or for two species of pink flowers – Sea Heath, the leaves of which turn to a brilliant red in autumn, and Acis.

From the crown of the Mur de Salario, the final, 12km descent towards the coast, Froome unleashed a dazzling acceleration that left the two riders with him – Evans and Nicholas Roche – for dead. Fifty seconds of momentous speed took him clear of the bunch. (Two riders had broken free earlier.) This was clearly to get a clear road and stay out of trouble. He later confirmed this: 'I knew the descent was tricky and dangerous. I was on the front with Richie [Porte] and thought it might be a good time to push on a little bit, get ahead and take the descent at my own pace and stay out of trouble . . . It's always good to keep people on their toes.'

A number of spirited attacks caused some late disarray in the chasing *peloton*. Jan Bakelants of Radioshack-Leopard (Shack), won the stage and took over the yellow jersey.

This was the veteran French rider Sylvain Chavanel's 34th birthday, which explained the bike with a frame the colour of a boiled shrimp, a present from the team members, Cavendish among them. Chavanel chose the colour.

The next day, Simon Gerrans (Green) took the win from Sagan by a tyre *and* the yellow jersey.

The entire carnival of the Tour, like a splendiferous royal progress that would have made Louis XIV's extravaganzas of monarchical publicity look parochial, crossed the water to Nice for the 25km team time-trial. This race, not routinely included, is a taut, excruciating affair for the riders (see p. 464). It is worth noting that the Tour's longest team time trial ran 153km (1978) and 100km in '83, and in '86, after a mere 56km, 12 riders were eliminated on time.

Normally, Sky would have been among the favourites to win, but Thomas had been effectively incapacitated, for the moment, at least. Garmin-Sharp (Gar) might have been expected to do well, but their leader, David Millar, an exceptional man against the clock in his day, was badly off form. He even apologised for letting the team down.

For some time, the Belgian Omega-Pharma-Quickstep (Oqs) team, for which Cavendish (to no great surprise) had signed after what had been an extremely frustrating year with Sky, sat on the leader board. Cavendish himself, a former track rider of prodigious strength, had worked spectacularly hard on the front to drive the train of his new colleagues. However, they were eventually pipped for the win by Green at 0.76 seconds, with an average speed of 57.8km, the record for any Grand Tour event (set at 57.6 seconds in the 2006 Vuelta). Not only that, but the golden fleece passed to one of their men, Simon Gerrans.

Sky came in third, and Sir Dave Brailsford, their manager, expressed delight at the result. They had not only wrung time out of Contador (six seconds) and Evans (23 seconds), but not taking over the yellow jersey relieved them of the responsibility to defend it. Thomas, with that capacity to elevate his effort above the levels where common sense and aversion to suffering pertain, rode well. He said that he had decided to think of the first 700m as a team pursuit final on the track. If he got through that, then he'd be able to stay. He did.

The fifth stage ran along the Côte d'Azur, in view of the sparkling lapis lazuli waters of the Mediterranean, from the resort of Cagnes-sur-Mer to Marseille, first colonised around 600 BC by Greek traders, drawn to its sumptuous natural harbour. The old fishing villages along the coast, many of them now chi-chi destinations for the beautiful people, still exude a particular charm, enhanced by the perfumes of the wildflowers, the baked smell of the garrigue, pine trees and lavender, the sizzling stridulation of the *cigales*.

A break went early and stayed out for 220km of the stage's 228.5km. As the chasing bunch approached the final uncategorised climb, some 12km from the finish, Cavendish recalled it from his very first professional race, the Grand Prix d'Ouverture la Marseillaise, in 2007. Perhaps it came as a sign. He knew the hill, any qualms about gradient were quelled, and he went through to take his 24th victory in the Tour.

He was met, on the line, by André Darrigade, winner of 22 stages, who congratulated him on his progress towards the absolute record of stage wins in the Tour, Eddy Merckx's 34. All Cavendish's wins have been on road stages, none, as with Merckx, in time-trial.

In conversation between the two men, Darrigade, 84 and still trim, and Cavendish, 28, the Briton said he knew what victories his predecessor had won.

'Oh, very good,' said Darrigade. 'Not many young riders know the *palmarès* of former racers.'

'Yes, plenty of them haven't studied their sport. They're interested only in their contract . . . For me, cycling is a unique sport and it's important to know its roots and to respect its history.'

It now transpired that Cavendish had been suffering from a slight bronchitis over the weekend. The team had kept this quiet. He was on antibiotics and coming back to form, though he said that he was 'still not 100 per cent'.

The sixth stage was marred by a massive pile-up 25km from the finish in which Cavendish was caught up, and none of his teammates was there to help him, even as Chavanel was driving the train at the front of the *peloton*. Some 40 seconds down when he got going again, it's admirable that Cavendish not only managed to rejoin the bunch but to be in for the sprint. His force was spent, of course. Chavanel is a celebrated lone escaper and not an ideal man to play a tame team role.

André Greipel, nickname 'the Gorilla', who has been Cavendish's nemesis more than once, took the stage, but the winner of the day was Darren Impey, Gerrans's teammate, who became the first South African to pull on the *maillot jaune*.

Sagan honoured his green jersey by taking the last stage before the Pyrenees when his Cannondale team upped the speed to the finish and catapulted him to the line, followed at 15 seconds by a bunch containing Cavendish, Greipel and Kittel.

Narrating a warm-up skirmish before the Carthaginian Hannibal's defeat by the Romans led by Scipio Africanus, Livy, in a long sentence, speaks of the early action, repeated flurries of stinging attacks and feints by the light-armed skirmishers – archers, javelin throwers and slingers – that wear down the enemy, much as the goading of *picadores* and *banderilleros* taunts and weakens the bull in the *corrida*. Livy then summarises the definitive action that signals the effective end of the engagement, in three menacing, leaden words: *tum legiones approprinquaverunt*. 'Then, the legions moved in.'

The mountains wait like the formidable professional infantry of the Roman military machine to put fear and threat of vanquishment into those who come against them. Here is the battlefield of any Tour, the ground on which the men riding to win overall must show their class, courage, strength and, not least, their powers of recovery.

The 195km of stage eight ran from Castres to the beastly climb of Ax-3-Domaines across the equally beastly Col de Pailhères. Perhaps it was apt, on this first day of intense scrutiny of true mettle, that the French Inquisitor Bernard Gui, the Dominican charged with the examination – and extirpation – of the Albigensian heretics and various other treacherous marginals such as Jews, sorcerers, fortune-tellers and summoners of demons, in the Languedoc in the early 1300s, lived for a while in Castres.

Froome, mild-mannered, softly spoken and extremely polite off the bike, without any sense, either, of being guarded in what he says, has a ruthlessness on the bike that, coupled with his astonishing staying power and éclat of withering turns of speed, laid down as definitive a challenge as any contender could.

The Sky team came, at last, to the fore and dominated the latter part of the stage leading to the Pailhères, where, on the steep slopes of the mountain, some 37km from the mountain top finish, the 23-year-old Colombian Nairo Quintana of Movistar (Movi) broke clear. This was, surely, too early, the result of inexperience.

Born at 3000m altitude into a very poor family, Quintana suffered severe bleeding as a tiny child and was, it's said, cured by a decoction made from nine trees. Light of frame, he started riding in his mid-teens and since his professional début in Europe (2010) has won a hatful of races. A climber of soaring force, he established a considerable lead over the Sky duo. Nevertheless, they did not stir to chase. It is one of the characteristics of their riding that they know how much wattage a rider is developing in order to ride at any given speed on the climbs and to adjust their tactics accordingly. That they also compete with glorious flair and panache when the time is right for attack counters any accusation of robotic riding.

On the descent of the mountain, Quintana showed his lack of technique, taking poor lines on the corners – it's often forgotten how vital a skill descending is. Froome, Porte, Peter Kennaugh – Olympic gold medallist of the team pursuit (with Thomas) – and Vasilli Kiyienka's tenacious pursuit pegged his lead at around a minute. At the foot of the final climb, Quintana had no more than half that.

Now Sky, at the front of the dwindling group, applied fearsome pressure to stun their opponents. Kennaugh, like Cavendish a Manxman, worked especially hard, showing that devoted application of selfless and ultimately exhausting support that is the lot – and the pride – of the very best *domestiques*.

Kennaugh, spent, fell away, and four kilometres from the summit of Ax, Froome was riding in tandem with his main support, Richie Porte. Suddenly, leaving Porte to dog Quintana's efforts, he attacked with such exorbitant power that he took both the stage and the yellow jersey. Porte, too, swept clear of the Colombian and took second place on both the stage and GC. Valverde lost 1m 8s, Contador 1m 45s and Evans an irretrievable 4+m.

Afterwards, Porte was a mite complacent about the mistake that Quintana had made and how the Sky strategy had worked perfectly. Next day he must have rued his apparent nonchalance because he was nowhere, and Froome had to ride most of the hardest part of the stage alone, unprotected. It was as severe a test of his moral power as of his strength.

The route crossed the Cols de Portet d'Aspet, Menté, Peyresourde, the ski station of Val Louron and the Hourquette d'Ancizan before a final rundown into Bagnères-de-Bigorre.

The day began with a series of furious attacks, stirred by Garmin, but Movi took over and led the way over the five first category climbs. Sky was badly diminished. First, Peter Kennaugh was nudged by Ryder Hesjedal (Gar) and pitched off the road on the approach to the first climb of the day, the Portet d'Aspet. He tumbled into a bush and scrambled back up to the road with a gashed elbow but was badly shaken and unable to give Froome any further aid. On the climb of the Menté, Porte was blown out, drained, and eventually lost 17m 59s on the day.

On the Ancizan, the final climb, Quintana, with a strong presence of both Movi and its leader, Valverde, and Contador's Saxo-Tinkoffs (Saxo), essayed several attacks on which Froome pounced immediately. 'Not easy,' Froome said afterwards, 'definitely not easy to follow the Colombian.' To the surprise of many, he did this not out of the saddle but sitting down and speeding up with no visible effort. This he has trained to do and refined in a wind tunnel, precisely because the more aerodynamic crouched position develops less drag. A marginal gain, maybe, but a gain.

Two kilometres from the top, Froome moved forward to half-wheel the united forces of his principal rivals, and their attempts to shake or distance him were over. At the same time, the Irishman Daniel Martin (Gar) attacked; Astana's Jakob Fuglsang went after and caught him. The pair held out all the way off the col and set out at main speed for the finish. Martin outsprinted his Danish rival across the line, to the obvious delight of his uncle, Stephen Roche, who once ran a cycling lodge/spa/hotel nearby. What his nephew said afterwards perhaps encapsulates something that the toxic years of suspicion and deceit have buried, to the great detriment of what many riders have called 'this beautiful sport'.

'We just wanted to have fun,' said Martin of the final duel with Fulgsang. 'We love racing bikes and making racing exciting. If we win, we win. If we don't, we make a good show.'

Froome's riding that day was courageous, powerful, nerveless. He did enormous honour to the yellow jersey and, with a sense of taste not always evident in the race these days, wore black shorts, instead of togging himself out like a honey mango. He reported later that this had been 'the hardest day I've ever had on a bike' and with admirable cool said, also, that he was riding within himself, avoiding overexertion, 'but they did go for me'.

The Sky team was further weakened by the ejection of Vasili Kiriyenka, who did not make the time cut, and, almost inevitably – oh, with what wearisome predictability the carping sceptics line up to join the sour-face party – questions were asked about the integrity of the Sky leader. Millar weighed in to lend them support.

They know they're riding clean, he said, they're just very defensive about their methods of training. 'If we had their numbers,' he added, 'we would be copying their training files and we'd know what to do to beat them.' But, they don't, thus (so far) they don't.

However, Sky had now been badly weakened. Suffering a crash could never be predicted, but losing a strong man to the guillotine hinted at serious miscalculation, although, necessarily, in a Tour, nothing is ever dependable.

Rest Day, Britanny
The admirable summary of head and legs as the two essentials ingredients in the composition of a Tour rider and/or winner, by Henri Desgrange, the father of the Tour, still obtains today. (He expressed little if any interest in races other than his. Why would he?) Between the action of the brain, the need to preserve a mental freshness, and the legs, moving with supple fluency at a cadence that will not bruise the muscles, much else happens, in heart, lungs, nervous system . . .

The physiology of a professional cyclist is startlingly different from what the French call *un lambda*, an ordinary mortal. Certain riders are capable of reducing the effects of pain more than others by secreting extra-large quantities of endorphins, a curious alchemy that cannot be explained scientifically. Endorphins are released by the pituitary glands and act as neurotransmitters that, under extreme duress of exercise, in excitement, orgasm or even the consumption of piquant, spicy food, release both analgesic (painkiller) and a sense of euphoria.

A rider's heart can pump around 34 litres of blood containing 63 per cent of oxygenated blood into the body at a rate of 190 beats per minute. A *lambda* will not top 22 litres. Some riders can raise their heartbeat, and hence the flow of oxygenated blood, to as high as 205 beats per minute, a level normally associated with heart attack.

The lungs supply oxygen, the source of the vital fuel for exercise. For every expiration, a rider can use 23 per cent for the work of pedalling. The rest will be dissipated in heat and various other biochemical reactions. The everyday proportion is around 17 per cent.

As to the power developed by the beautiful machine of a rider propelling that other beautiful machine, the bike, at high speeds, it has been calculated that in a flat-out sprint, Cavendish (for example) 1.75m tall, weighing 69kg, and turning the pedals at a cadence of 110 per minute, produces 1,500 watts of power, sufficient to lift two 45kg bags of cement.

A word about the watt, the unit of activity or power named for James Watt (1736 – 1819), who first made the connection between heat boiling water, the steam from which lifted the lid of a kettle and led to his invention of steam power. Imagine him transfixed by the rattling of the lid and thinking, I wonder . . . Energy, the power of doing work, produces heat as a side-effect. This is why we get hot when exercising. Think of a 250 watt light bulb – extremely hot to the touch. Most riders at full gas may develop up to around twice that. Therefore, the wattage of any rider's physical system measures the output of his – or her – power.

[From an analysis conducted by Fred Grappe, doctor of sports physiology and a trainer with the Française des Jeux team.]

After the transfer to Brittany, the race headed to what is known as the Emerald Coast into a headwind off the sea, down narrow roads that switched direction, twisting this way and that, the *peloton* stretching out in a long snaking line. This makes life at the back of the race very trying. The tail of the bunch inevitably goes slower into corners because the view is interrupted, and there is the same effect as in a slow-moving traffic jam. To chase back to the last wheels of the main body expends a lot of extra energy.

Froome rode near the front of the field, where there is less chance of mishap, guarded by the strongman Ian Stannard, while the rest of the team saved their legs for the next excursion into the mountains.

At the finish of this, the tenth stage, the sprinters jostling en masse, Cavendish lost the wheel of his lead-out man, Gert Steegmans, and had to come from behind in an attempt to get Greipel's wheel. Greipel had been ensnared in a stoppage some two kilometres back but had fought his way back. The closing straight was kinked by two sharp right-angle corners, the final turn yanking them left. Kittel, well positioned by his Argos teammates, led Greipel and Cavendish as the Briton tried to come through from behind. As the sprint swung to the left, Cavendish collided with Tom Veelers, the Dutchman who had taken Kittel through and was dropping back, drifting to the right. Cavendish, trying to swing left, bumped Veelers with his shoulder. Veelers went down and Cavendish was through but beaten to the line by Kittel, the first man to win two stages on the Tour.

The race judges exonerated Cavendish, but Veelers was, understandably, angry. Such spills are awful at any time, but in the middle of a group of men reaching such high speeds, the risk of grievous injury is real, the precipitate rush of adrenalin sickening.

Cavendish did not help his case by grabbing the Dictaphone of a journalist who'd asked him if the crash was his fault and disappearing with it into the team bus. The sponsors of the first post-Tour criterium, at Boxmeer, in Holland, removed Cavendish from their guest list, although it seemed that the Manx Missile already had an engagement for that day.

The 33km individual time-trial (one of only two in this year's race) took the riders from Avranches, where General George Patton set up his headquarters shortly after the D-Day landings in Normandy, to the ancient abbey of Le Mont-Saint-Michel, built on top of an 80m-high granite plug rising out of the sands and visible for miles around. The Mont was originally called Mont-Tombe, and like Tombelaine, a small tidal island off the coast some 3.5km away, was probably one of the sea-tombs of Celtic mythology to which the souls of the dead were ferried in an invisible barque.

The religious foundation, which had its own way with dead souls, was founded between 1020 and 1135, a great confection of architecture, predominantly in two styles: the Massive and, when it was extended during the fifteenth century, the Flamboyant. It is a grandiose flourish of both.

The current world time-trial champion, Tony Martin, had gone down in the horrible crash near the end of stage one and sustained road rash all down his back, with sundry gashes to his arm. It seemed not to faze him this day – I have seen examples of road rash that would have a fainter heart out of competition for weeks. He rode a brilliant race and took victory by a mere 12 seconds from Froome. Happy as he would have been to win, Froome could be content that he had put even more time into the men behind him in the overall order. The Dutchman, Bauke Mollema, riding for the new Dutch team Belkin (Bel, taking the place of the now defunct Rabobank) and keen to make a good showing for the sponsors, conceded 1m 53s. Valverde dropped 2m, Contador 2m 3s and Froome now led by over four minutes.

During his ride, Cavendish was doused with urine from the side of the road, an incident that shamed fans of the Tour, generally so enthusiastic, and spoke ill for partisan tempers.

A crash 2.5km from the finish in Tours, next day, deprived Sky of another very strong rider. The Norwegian champion, Edvald Boasson-Hagen, rode in across the line with his head bowed, one hand across his chest, as if he were bending to listen to his radio. Alas, he had broken his shoulder and was out. Kittel, assuming the role of chief tormentor of Cavendish, took his third stage victory, just beating his compatriot Greipel across the line.

The composer Arnold Schoenberg was so superstitious that he would have nothing to do with the number 13. He misspelled his opera *Moses und Aron* because the correct spelling (Aaron) would give the title 13 letters. Since he died on Friday the 13th, this evasion of divine retribution may be said to have had a spectacular climax. Or else it may simply say 'hoo-ha' to such touch-wood hesitancy. Stage 13, then.

The crosswinds were already blustering across the roads out of Tours as the Tour headed for Saint-Armand-Montrond, 173km away. Cavendish's Belgian team know all about such hazards and made an early strike to disrupt the field and force the riders into echelons. The effects of a *bordure* have already been described (see p. 385) but the first decisive move came at 60km when, seeing Kittel some way behind them, Cavendish and his teammates attacked and split the field in two – ninety riders in the lead, the tail severed, Kittel among them, with 113km left to ride.

The Omegas of Cavendish and the Argos of Kittel began a fierce scrap, and one unlucky victim of the phenomenally high speeds, Valverde, copped a broken wheel and had to watch as the Omega-driven train sped away, supported by Europcar, whom the Spaniard later vilified for their unconscionable support of the attack. He was gratified, at least, that their man Pierre Rolland soon punctured.

The Movi team car was way behind. Several members of the team, including Rui Costa (but not Quintana, who was already up the road with the leading bunch), rallied to Valverde's support, but a gap of 30 seconds had already opened and they could not get back on. Should Valverde have taken a wheel rather than wait for the team or the team car? Probably. As it was, having worked strenuously to close the gap on the leaders, the Movi men eventually conceded and were swept up by the Argos-driven chasers.

Some 31km from the finish, the wind gusted savagely across the open roads of the Cher department. One of Contador's team, Daniele Bennati, looked down the line of the front bunch and saw that Froome had left a small gap, perhaps from a momentary lapse of concentration. Saxo pounced and broke clear, taking with them Ten Dam, Mollema, Cavendish and two of his men, the points leader, Sagan, and the former road captain for Sky, Michael Rogers, his loyalties switched to the services of Contador.

At full pelt, such an attack will hit speeds of up to 55kph, somewhat in excess of what they had been riding at – the average for the day was 47kph – and the combination of wind across the gap and turbulence behind the escaping riders means that any attempt to ride across will need to develop an even higher speed. Since a chase will be in single file and the echelon has a formation that affords a minimal shelter against the wind, this is a tall order. As Cavendish, who had sprinted like a demon to clip onto the echelon, put it later: 'When an echelon forms, it's like falling through ice. You've got five seconds or you're finished.'

Froome and the depleted Sky outfit – Kennaugh, Stannard and Thomas – had not the strength to close the gap, no one else was interested in aiding them, and the yellow jersey lost 1m 8s on Contador and the two Dutchmen – a shame but not catastrophic, he said. Cavendish won the stage, to his joy and relief, and said that he had used more power to join the split than in winning the sprint.

Valverde's misery was compounded. Beginning that morning in second place, 1m 25s behind Froome, he finished at 12m 10s, and slumped to 16th place overall. Two of the Belkins profited:

Mollema was now third overall at 1m 44s, and Laurens Ten Dam at 1m 50s.

Stage 14, into Lyon, went to the Italian Matteo Trentin, Cavendish's teammate, one of his lead-out men and his regular roommate. It was the first Italian win in the Tour since 2010. Trentin had jumped out of a breakaway group of 18 riders that went clear early in the stage.

Rolland, winner of two Alpine stages in previous Tours, had targeted the mountains jersey won by his team leader, Thomas Voeckler, in 2012, and was accumulating points steadily. He took the polka dots on stage two, lost it briefly to Blel Kadri on the sixth stage but then took it back. He lost it to Froome on stage ten but took the jersey back on the 15th stage. He was laying down a good investment before the real bounty on offer in the final week.

Stage 15: Givors–Mont Ventoux, 242km. Bastille Day
The longest stage, the Bald Mountain, col of Tempests, torrid heat.

Plenty has been already said in this book about the Domain of Angels – another sobriquet of Provence's notorious mountain – which needs no rehearsing here. The riders know all about its reputation, and it's a mark of Froome's seriousness that he had spent a week riding the Ventoux in May, up and down, up and down, up, up and down, until he had familiarised himself with its most unlikeable character.

There had been no French victory yet, and this, their national day. When, on the lower slopes in the sparse shade of trees, the arch chancer, Voeckler, took out his earpiece – they could say nothing that he wanted to hear – it was as eloquent a sign as any of just what stress the riders had to endure, the French carrying the added burden of expectancy. Voeckler has delivered much in his career, but, having broken his collarbone in the spring classic, the Amstel-Gold, he had only recently returned to any kind of form, after victory in the four-day Route du Sud. Fans at the side of the road were even belabouring him with taunts – why wasn't he doing anything? As if they knew.

The Luxemburger Andy Schleck, winner of the Tour in 2010, after Contador had been disqualified for doping, was also just returning after serious injury and had little of his former strength and poise. He cracked early in the climb so completely that he rode into the gravel of the verge and nearly fell off. Evans had gone, any dream of featuring in the race vanished.

As the main contenders headed through the trees towards the exposed upper slopes, Quintana attacked – this was audacious – and gained 50 seconds. Sky gave chase. Kennaugh moved up to front the pursuit. His sterling work over the next four kilometres left him utterly drained and when he peeled off, for Porte to take over, he came to a dead stop. Of the main men, only Contador with his lieutenant Roman Kreuziger, the Spaniard Joaquim Rodríguez (Katyusha) and the two Belkins had been able to hold the Sky wheels.

As they emerged from the tree cover at Chalet Reynard (1440m) and the final six kilometres to the summit (1912m), the Sky duo driving the pace, Quintana now in sight, not far, Porte moved across to allow his leader through. As Froome reported afterwards, he'd said to himself, 'Now's the time, keep pushing, don't play any games . . .'

Suddenly, Froome went, a blazing attack, hunched over the bike, looking down at the frame, looking up, looking down again, face the same expression he always has, blank, somehow, shoulders apparently cramped, his pedals moving at a stupefying speed. He went clear. None followed. Froome paused only to change to a higher gear and soared past the Colombian, who held him, held him, the only man who had, so far in the race, been able to do so.

At two kilometres from the top, after another blistering acceleration, Quintana was weakening, he could not follow, and Froome was away on the buffet of a driving tail wind, away to a victory of giant proportions. Quintana came in 29 seconds adrift but took the white jersey of young rider. Rodríguez lost 1m 23s, Contador 1m 40s. Froome had his commanding lead back even as he was being given oxygen to recover from the punishment he had inflicted on himself. It was the first time the yellow jersey had been won on Ventoux since Merckx, in 1970, and with the sort of daring and all-out assault so common with the great Belgian. *And* Froome took over the polka dot jersey.

The acceleration he had been able to produce owes much to the training shaped by the Sky performance coach, Tim Kerrison.

As well as riding for protracted periods at a set limit of speed, just below the extended level of tolerance, they are then inured to sudden spurts of extreme acceleration for a short distance – exactly what Froome did on Ventoux – from around 350 watts of effort to a quite astonishing 650 watts before going back to 350. The best climbers have always been able to vary their pace and to accommodate brusque upping of their power output, but Froome's demonstration that day was in a quite different league: it was like the kick of a sprinter out of already explosive effort into the realm of speed where no reason obtains, only instinct and the driven will.

Froome spun the pedals so dizzyingly fast because he did not want to risk shifting gear, a move that would have given him more leverage but at risk, in such circumstances of extreme pressure, always at risk, of shipping the chain.

His style is odd: the bobbing head sunk between his shoulders, looking down, looking ahead in the fashion of a man who is not sure what gear he's in, and a certain ungainliness. He never *looks* entirely comfortable. Charly Wegelius, ex-professional, said of him: 'His style is clumsy to say the least. It's terrible to watch, it's a crime against cycling, but it's obviously effective.' One thinks of the American track runner, Michael Johnson – four Olympic, eight World championship, golds – of whom it was said 'he runs like a duck'. His riposte? 'Well, I was the fastest duck out there.' Touché for Johnson, touché for Froome.

Rest Day

To the wearingly inevitable probing insinuations about drugs at the press conference, Froome responded calmly enough, but his reply showed a certain mild irritation at the incessant niggling.
'I'm not saying it's not a legitimate question, but . . . there is a tinge of frustration. You're asking me how can I prove to you that I'm not doping. It's quite sad that we are sitting here the day after the biggest victory of my life, quite a historic win, talking about *doping*.' [My italics.] 'Me and my teammates have slept on top of volcanoes to get ready for this. We've been away from home for months, training together, working our arses off to get here, and I am being accused of being a cheat and a liar. That's how I feel.'
Brailsford added: 'We rack our brains every day, I assure you, [to

find] the optimal way to prove to you guys that we're not doping,' and later gave all Froome's results in training over the past three years to the UK Anti-Doping Agency as proof of his consistency, but, alas, these days, such testimony, even corroborated, means very little to the intractable disbelievers.

The 2012 Tour blatantly favoured the time-triallists, and Wiggins profited, accordingly. The mountains always count for much, but in 2013 they counted for far more than they have done in a long while, perhaps ever, in the modern era.

By comparison, therefore, of 2013 with 2012: the total kilometres spent climbing, 244 and 142; the aggregation of the height of all the categorised cols, 35,441m and 18,745m and of them, 35 categorised as against 22, and of *hors catégorie*, 2013 included six, 2012, three.

This, alone, made the Tour one of the, if not *the*, hardest post-war races.

After the Rest Day, five monstrous stages.

Tuesday took the riders to Gap, in the préfecture of the Hautes-Alpes, and views of a daunting horizon. A group of 26 riders went off the front in the brief quasi-lull before the horrible climbs in store. A few overall contenders slipped in, but when the *peloton* surged up to call in the truants, the break was given its head and, at 69.3km from the finish, their lead profited from a hold-up near Montéglin, when the *peloton* had to stop as the gates at an open level crossing dropped to allow a TGV to go through. Not the first time such a thing had happened (see p. 88).

There are several competitions on offer in the Tour, not least that for the best team overall, for which the prize is substantial. By this stage of the race, Contador's Saxo men wore the yellow numbers that indicate the lead in the competition, but, as an indicator of how all teams may profit for prizes along the way, Omega-Pharma had, to date, won around 284,000 (from stage victories etc) while lowly Cofidis had scooped a mere 24,000.

At 34km from Gap, two Frenchmen, Kadri (AG2R Mondiale) and Jean-Marc Morino (Soja), attacked, for national honour, and built a slight lead on the rest of the breakaway. There were 42

French riders in the field, the highest proportion, nationally but, so far, empty-handed.

Kadri and Morino were caught and dropped 7km from the final climb, the Col de Manse, and the group began to disintegrate on the steep pitch of the Manse. Costa, winner of the last two Tours de Suisse, Portugese time-trial champion, and currently tenth overall, saw his chance and attacked, knowing that if he could top the climb with a good gap he had a downhill run all the way *into* Gap, hosting the Arrivée for the 23rd time.

A headline in *L'Equipe* said that the French were concerned that the Tour would produce a *fanny*, a blank card, presumably from 'sweet Fanny Adams'. Cheering, then, that three Frenchmen – Jérôme Coppel (Cofidis), Arnold Jeannesson (FDJ) and Christophe Riblon (AG2R) fought valiantly in a thrilling sprint at the finish for second place.

In 2003 on a nasty bend in broiling heat, the Spanish rider Joseba Beloki fell and, in the way of the Tour's tendency to spook, this descent had a certain pall of dread hanging over it. A rider who can enjoy the whole road, solo, has a clearer chance to evade accident, and Costa rode all the way to victory.

Contador, insisting that he would take any opportunity to dislodge Froome, did exactly that, first on the climb when he and Rodríguez banged away to blow the *peloton* apart and discomfit the Sky rider. Porte once more came back at them and held the line. Contador tried again on the sinuous drop. He attacked once, twice, thrice, taking considerable risks, was hauled in by Froome and Porte, overcooked one corner and came off, momentarily impeding Froome, who went slightly off the verge and had to unclip his pedals to put the bike back on the tarmac and get going again. Quintana and Valverde, who had, by now, rejoined, immediately shot past their decked Spanish compatriot, to Contador's fury.

The effort of chasing had hurt Porte, and he was dropped as Kreuziger attacked. Froome reeled him in even as Porte fought back magnificently to rejoin his leader.

Afterwards, Froome lambasted Contador for his desperate risk-taking and inability to control his speed. This wasn't petulance. The Spaniard couldn't hope to win much time on a descent against determined pursuit, but, having nearly trashed Froome, he showed just how perilously close these riders always are to a crash that will signal disaster.

The mountain time-trial on stage 17, 32km from Embrun to Chorges, westwards under the loom of the beak-shaped peak of Le Mourre Froid ('Cold Nose'), 2994m, and one of the many Ponts du Diables (Devil's Bridge) in France, posed a technical dilemma. The route traversed two climbs, the Côte de Puy-Sanièères, 1173m, and the Côte de Réallon, 1227m, before a fast rundown into Chorges, once an important Roman staging post. A bike fitted for a climbing race against the clock is not best suited to downhill. Whether, therefore, to switch from the uphill to a profile (flat-out time-trial) machine at the risk of a loss of around 15 seconds, at least, for the change, or not to gamble on that and stay on the same machine?

(The day – *the day* – after he won the Dauphiné Libéré – Froome went off to recce the route of the stage 17 time-trial before heading to the Sky training camp in Châtel.)

Who can say if Sky's decision to swap bikes gave Froome the edge over Contador, who did not? It cannot be certain. However, Froome took the stage, his third of the Tour – and in the mountains – over Contador by nine seconds, Rodríguez at ten and Quintana at 1m 11s. Classy as the Colombian is on the slopes, he will have to do better against the clock if he is ever to challenge for the overall win, but he is only 23, time aplenty.

Stage 18
L'Alpe d'Huez twice in one day. Chew that one over. Plus a lumpy approach, a first category – Col d'Ornon – and another parlous descent, off the Col de Sarenne, the back door to the Alpe, with 64km still to ride.

Rain was forecast, and Froome, and others, petitioned the organisers to stop the race at the first ascent of the big one to avoid the real possibility of catastrophe on the Sarenne if it *did* rain. They demurred. The rain held off.

Nine riders went ahead at about halfway, hoping to build enough time advantage to make an ecstatic win on such a gargantuan stage possible. Gradually the strain whittled them down, leaving only the American Tejay Van Garderen (BMC) and the Frenchman

Christophe Riblon on the first climb of the Alpe. Riblon fell away and was rejoined by another escapee, the Italian Moreno Moser. The trio regrouped over the top. Van Garderen was dropped on the Sarenne with a mechanical problem. Riblon went off the road on a bend into soggy ground but came back to chase. Van Garderen clawed his way back, caught the pair, and they began the second ascent of the Alpe together. On the roundabout leading towards the start of the climb, the route bore right; Riblon bore left, saw his error and bunny-hopped over the central spine to rejoin. Cool.

On the Alpe itself, Van Garderen surged away and built a good lead, but in the last three kilometres, his power went. He was cooked. Behind him, Riblon was fighting, for himself, for his team and, mistake it not, for France. A bare two kilometres to go gave him sight of the ailing American and, with a slow-motion, lethal strike, he caught him, passed him and went on to the line. *L'Equipe*'s headline was, indeed, ecstatic: HEROIQUE RIBLON.

Contador and Kreuziger took a small lead – 20 seconds – on the descent of the Sarenne but had not enough to resist the determined pursuit of Kennaugh, Froome and Porte, and Quintana's Movistars, who took over the pacing for their man. The elite group of contenders, including Quintana and Rodríguez, began the final climb together.

Accelerations goad opponents into resistance or concession, and Contador slowly yielded. Eleven kilometres to go: Kreuziger cracked, Froome went clear, Quintana et al came back. Porte was dropped but – what bravery – not only rejoined but instantly exerted further pressure at the front to deaden any counterattack from Quintana and Rodríguez. Who knows what that effort cost him? It might be calculated on what he was called upon, and able, to do next.

At five kilometres from the summit, Froome faltered. He had run out of juice and needed to eat. Hypoglycaemia, the wolf, the bonk – whatever you call it – added tribulation. That he did not have an energy gel in his pocket was later explained: Sky's lead team car had pulled over – an ice box in the boot had burst and threatened the vehicle's electrics. Taking on food in the last 20 kilometres is prohibited, and on the traffic-crowded, narrow drop from the Sarenne, the second team car hadn't managed to come up to the riders in time. Froome asked Porte to go back for a gel; Porte returned with the vital sustenance, but Quintana and then Rodríguez seized their chance and went clear to take 54s and 57s apiece out of Froome and Porte. Contador lost 57s to Froome and kept second overall, just, from Quintana. Rodríguez moved up to fourth, just behind Kreuziger.

The crowds on the Alpe are always dense, most of them out of control, many of them drunk, the great proportion of them not fans at all but exhibitionists slavering for an image of themselves on the telly and instilled with a gormless belief that it is wonderfully encouraging to the riders to brandish arms, banners and flags in their faces and pull away at the last moment or else run frantically alongside bellowing balderdash; that crowding the riders into a tight channel, like a swollen gut into a corset, makes life more exciting for them; that a cacophony of noise at intolerable decibel levels distracts from the heat, the fumes of petrol from cars and motorbikes and the sheer strain of trying to get to the top in the shortest possible time. It is a wonder and a miracle that more accidents do not happen. Why, when Guerini was pitched off his bike in the upper, barricaded section (see p. 218), the road was pretty clear, save the idiot buffoon who was taking a frontal picture of him.

Some commentators suggested, after the incident of the missing gel, that now Froome knew what it was to have such stalwart support as he had given Wiggins, with overt reluctance (some said) in 2012. The case is different. Froome had shown himself, thus far, to be the strongest climber on a Tour fashioned for the climbers. A moot point, of course, but *not* a moot point is the fact that Wiggins had to be shepherded to the top of every climb in 2012 and didn't win a stage at altitude. Q, as they say, E D.

Although sending Porte back for the contraband energy syrup was a ploy to elude any penalty for Froome, both riders were docked 20 seconds, no more than a minor inconvenience and proof that the race rules are rarely suspended, save in circumstances of severe injustice.

Quintana had moved up to third overall, at 5m 32s, and Rodríguez into fifth, at 5m 58s, Contador, 5m 11s, and Kreuziger,

5m 44s in second and fourth respectively. The race for podium places was tightening.

Stage 19 Bourg d'Oisan – Le Grand Bornand 204.5km. Col du Glandon (HC), Col de la Madeleine (HC), Col de Tamié (2nd), Col de l'Epine (1st), Col de la Croix Fry (1st).
Rolland went off on his own determined to retrieve the peas, as the mountains jersey is sometimes known. In the upshot, he missed by a single point from Froome and it seemed entirely possible that the Briton might win both yellow and polka dots in Paris.

The escape, stirred by Hesjedal, was given its head, the rain finally broke, Costa took his second Alpine win, and the main contenders came in together, caring not to over-extend themselves before the final *combat à l'outrance*, chips-down face-off, the next day. Porte came in 11 seconds behind his leader, testimony to the level of work he had been doing.

The final stage in the mountains, the penultimate of the Tour, was not going to deliver the big showdown between two contenders for overall victory that the organisers plainly hoped to see, but it would serve up a tremendous tussle for second and third places. There would be no breakaways given any rope this day. There was too much at stake.

Rolland broke away as the *peloton* approached the real start in Annecy itself – every stage begins with a fictive start of a few kilometres to ease the riders in – and was off in quest of the 50 mountains points on offer. A new rule awarded double points for the final ascent and the polka dots that he wore because Froome, in yellow, couldn't wear them, might just, just, be his. He took most of the early points and was thus in the lead in that competition, but there was the Semnoz to come.

The Movi action at the front, led by Valverde and Costa, drove the pace high to the foot of the final climb, after a circuit of the country round Lake Annecy. A second category climb followed by three third, a first – Mont Revard – and the *hors catégorie* Semnoz, making its debut in the Tour. Eleven kilometres of an average of 8.7 per cent with a shot of 10.5 per cent on kilometre three, two kilometres of 9.5 per cent and 8 per cent further up and a final blast of 9.5 per cent just before the summit. As an envoi to the mountains, this rated harsh veering on extremely unpleasant.

The powerful riding of Costa and Valverde saw off all but a handful and Rolland was gone. With eight kilometres left to ride, Contador was visibly weakening. Quintana and Rodríguez saw it and went clear; Froome, like a squirrel away from threat, fizzed across the gap, and then there were three.

Another trio – of morons – performed the clumsy pantomime trick of playing bodyguard to the riders and, in a glorious moment of panache, Froome lamped one, who stumbled right into his two poltroon partners and the three of them went down like loose bottles in a crate. It's unlikely that they had been drinking the Vittel emblazoned on their T-shirts.

Froome made one last bid to clear himself of the Spaniard and the Colombian, but Quintana, on his national day, sensed that the man in yellow didn't have the legs he'd had on Ax-3-Domaines and Ventoux. Quintana countered and surged past the Briton, kept going and made sure of the stage victory, the young riders' white jersey and the King of the Mountains competition, 11 points ahead of Froome.

The Tour began as a publicity stunt and there is always an echo of that same opportunism on show by the side of the route – farmers marking out the name of a community with straw bales, banners puffing a cooperative in one town or another, the green meadows of France providing a festive advertising board on show for the helicopters overhead. The Savoie region is known for its *reblochon*, a creamy cheese made of cow's milk. By the side of the road on this stage, nearing Clusaz, a banner read: *Le reblochon fait pousser les nichons* . . . *Reblochon* enlarges breasts. This is, as yet, not proven scientifically, although the sumptuous cheese certainly does perform that service to the girth.

And so the Tour had only its finale to play out. Many speak of the final stage as being a ceremonial procession into Paris. It was not always so, but, recently, the truce is unspoken, and it leaves the stage clear for the last throw of racing: for the win on the Champs Elysées, taken for the past four years by Cavendish. He faced vehement opposition.

Sagan was secure in the green jersey, but, although the flat-out sprint is not his forte, he must have been hankering to crown his second year in green. (On this: many people remain puzzled that a winner of a competition can fail to win a single stage. The analogy with Formula One should explain this, where a driver can win overall without victory in a single Grand Prix race.)

The two Germans, Greipel and Kittel, had already shown that Cavendish was not at his dominating best. Cavendish himself, quite apart from the fact that he had won only two stages, a singular disappointment, loves the win in Paris above all others. However, he almost certainly blunted his finishing edge in the Giro, where he won five stages and the red jersey as points winner. This made him only the fifth person to win the points jersey in all three grand tours. (Rik Van Looy, Eddy Merckx, Djamolidine Abdujaparov and Alessandro Petacchi are the others.) There is, too, a suggestion that he doesn't have the same confidence in Steegmans as a pilot as he had in Mark Renshaw (now with Belkin), with whom he rode at Columbia-High Road. Word is that he has asked his team to recruit Renshaw.

The route took them from Versailles to arrive in Paris near nightfall and, for the first time, round the Arc de Triomphe instead of just short of it on the Champs. In the amble towards the finishing circuit, before the pace hots up, there's a genial holiday spirit in the *peloton* and, in a passage of the jokey hilarity that ripples through men who have made it to the last Arrivée, Rodríguez, whose nickname is *Purito*, cigarillo, took one cigar, handed another to Quintana and tried to light them, but the Zippo would not zip in the wind.

Cavendish punctured on the third (of seven) finishing circuits and, having managed to get back on, he found himself isolated – his team nowhere – in the rush to the line. Kittel was in command, the Manxman strove to follow and pass, but he had not the force and Kittel it was, his fourth stage victory. Cavendish was candid. Kittel had been faster. 'I did 1,500 watts, and usually when I do 1,500 watts, I win by a few bike lengths.'

Quintana, the 'revelation of the Tour', as the French have it, mounted the podium three times: for second place overall, for the young riders' white jersey and for the polka dots as King of the

Mountains. The last man to stand there in his début Tour was Jan Ullrich (who recently confessed to doping) in 1996.

Much could be said about Froome, the lad born in Kenya who has weathered the sort of difficulties that no home-grown British cyclist has had to deal with to reach the upper step of the grand dais in Paris. Read, therefore, the biography I have already mentioned. Perhaps the tribute paid by Stephen Roche – who, with Merckx, is the only man to have won Giro, Tour and rainbow jersey in one season (1987) – encapsulates his achievement: 'This is also the moment that the British cycling public probably realises that there is more to cycling than just Bradley Wiggins.'

A mere 34km from the line across the Champs, poor Lieuwe Vestra, of the Dutch Vacansoleil team, had to quit the race. He was ill; he could no longer hang on to the bunch even at gentle speed. A vignette of just how hard this race is, how cruel it can be, what efforts a man will make just to stay with it, despite all circumstances contrary to such a thing.

CHAPTER TWENTY-FOUR

2014

The Sicilian Shark

Back le Bid. Bring the Tour de France to Yorkshire. The campaign to bring the Tour to a Grand Départ in Leeds and a second day of racing was well-organised, vigorous, persuasive and hospitable. The ASO, organisers of the Tour, came to supper, stayed for lunch and tea, reconnoitred the proposed route, liked what they saw and said yes. They'd been amazed at the reception the start of the Tour had in London, 2007, but the people of the Yorkshire organising committee promised still more: this would be the grandest Grand Départ in Tour history.

Gardeners across the county were encouraged to plant yellow flowers to out-bloom the emblematic white rose of the house of York. In one of the towns on the proposed route, market day was switched from Friday to Thursday. Bike shops trumped the ostentation of the publicity caravan.

I went north the week before the Tour arrived. Everywhere you looked, knitted bunting adorned window sills, telegraph poles, lamp posts, anywhere that could support a string of hamster-size pullovers in yellow, green and polka dot. The work of an outsize knitting bee? So it proved. Local volunteer energy had swung into action. Not everyone approved. The town councillors of Masson pronounced a ban: in the event of rain, the minuscule woollen garments – so *many* of them, lawks a-doodle – would get heavy and could easily pull down a lamp post.

There's nowt so queer as folk.

Someone asked me why the first two stages had been classified as 'flat', given that the race was taking in some of the vicious gradients of the dales and moors of North and West Yorkshire. I've ridden the roads and flat they ain't. I explained that, hard as the climbing would be, there was no comparison with the Alpine and Pyrenean monsters. Minutes of uphill against in excess of an hour? I sympathised with the sense of mild affront, though. A poster in Harrogate station gave a blunt response to *flat*. It read:

'The French believe they have the toughest summits. Our view: it's all downhill after Yorkshire.'

The organisers had made a major change: they introduced one only intermediate sprint on each stage, instead of three. This would cant the interest in the green jersey competition towards consistency of placings on stage finishes, the original concept behind it, rather than diluting it with snaffled pickings along the way. Latterly, the green has been interpreted as the sprinters' race within a race. Now it reverts to a prize favouring the fast men who can also weather the draining toll of harder terrain. The same imbalance obtains in the Grand Prix de la Montagne, often won by a rider who is certainly *not* the strongest climber.

The Tinkoff-Saxo team came up with a novelty: a belt with pouches to carry water bottles. Why hadn't anyone thought of it before? An end to cold-*bidons*-stuffed-down-the-jersey misery for the domestiques ferrying drinks up to their team mates from the team car.

Chris Froome, defending his title, arrived as favourite after a far less encouraging preparation than in 2013. He'd missed races because of a chest complaint, shown no great form, early on, injured his back in a bad fall in the Critérium du Dauphiné but he insisted that the lay-off had done him good. He thought his principal rival would be a rejuvenated Alberto Contador, but there was also Vincenzo Nibali, the Sicilian, who's beaten Froome in Italy more than once.

Controversially, Bradley Wiggins wasn't in the Sky line-up, after a lot of dubious speculation about his real desire to race the Tour again and a wretched performance in the Tour of Switzerland. The whisper was that Froome – who'd helped give him an armchair ride to victory in 2012 – didn't trust him, even as a rider sworn to help his leader. Defending Wiggins's omission, Dave Brailsford, the Sky director, said: you win a race with a star team, not with a team of stars.

There were only four Britons in the race: Froome, Geraint Thomas, the Welshman, Simon Yates, 21 years old, and Mark Cavendish. Riding for the American Giant-Shimano team, Ji Cheng was the first Chinese entry in *La Grande Boucle* and Jens Voigt, now 42 years old, was riding his 17th Tour, equalling the record of Stuart O'Grady and George Hincapie, before retiring from the sport.

Stage one finished in Harrogate, where Cavendish's mother lives. Of course he wanted to win there, but not from filial duty – he might call it that later. On offer was the first yellow jersey as well as adding to his total of 25 stage wins to date.

The run-in was testing: in the very last kilometre of a hard 190.5km ride, one sharp hill, down into a dip and another sharp hill to the line outside the famous Betty's café – 'traditional hand-baked specialities and chocolates'.

A bee stung the Italian sprinter Alessandro Petacchi and kept him out of the sprint. Cavendish's Omega Pharma-Quickstep lead-out attacked with about three kilometres to go. It was too early. If the plan was to burn off the rivals, it had only a slim chance of succeeding. Cavendish, left to fend for himself on the final slope, lost poise and position. Trying, by his own admission, to 'get through a gap that wasn't there', he collided with Simon Gerrans, the Australian road champion. They both went down. Gerrans got up, Cavendish broke a collarbone and didn't. Victory went to the ace sprinter who utterly trumped the Manx Missile in 2013, the German, Marcel Kittel.

Stage two squashed flat any idea of 'flat'. There were nine designated climbs, 3000m of ascension, three 4th category, five 3rd and one 2nd, all given French titles: Côte de Blubberhouses . . . Côte de Greetland . . . Côte de Jenkin Road, a nasty 800m stretch of nearly 11 per cent, five kilometres from the finish. They passed Featherbed Top, too. Scarcely that.

As for the Côte de Holme Moss, Brian Robinson*, first Briton to finish the Tour and win a stage, has lived in Mirfield, near the route, man and boy, and still holds the record for the climb of the Moss.

The crowds were stupendous – an estimated 70,000 on the Moss itself – and a probable four million along the route on the two days of Tour residency of the White Rose county, an average of one person every ten metres of the 391.5km covered. Thousands of people walked miles to get to Buttertubs Pass, one of the redoubtable local climbs which has honed the muscles of many fine riders, and, by, lad, it were grand. Bernard Hinault said he'd never seen such crowds in forty years and 'when you said you'd deliver the grandest Grand Départ ever, it was the truth'.

The relentless battering of hills, strong headwinds on the exposed moorland, narrow, twisting roads and a high pace shredded the *peloton* along the way. The main contenders were in at the finish but Nibali pounced two kilometres from the line, took the stage, yellow and a two-second lead. The gain was slight, the message to his rivals clear: I intend to win this race and this is how I'll do it, by carrying the fight to you.

Stage three was incontrovertibly flat – Cambridge, Essex and the eastern approaches to London. In a bunch sprint on the Mall, Kittel, who'd found the hills of West Yorkshire so punishing, took his second stage. In an interview with *L'Equipe*, he offered some insights into his trade. 'Every sprint is different, but it never starts where you think it would start, in the final kilometres. For me, it begins at the morning briefing. That's where I visualise the finish. My focus and sometimes my nervous edge, begin then . . . in the sprint itself, all I have to do is follow Tom Veelers.' He was matter-of-fact about why he wins: his physical strength. 'It's not the man who's mentally strongest who wins, the head remains in service to the legs.' He added the somewhat nugatory remark that it's the fastest man who wins the sprint.

Kittel also let on that at one briefing, he asked his Giant-Shimano

* Tony Hoar, *lanterne rouge* in 1955, had been allowed to stay in the race, to keep Robinson company after the rest of the team had pulled out, albeit he'd finished outside the time limit on one stage. See my book *Brian Robinson, Pioneer*, publ. Mousehold Press.

directors to stop shouting into the earpieces close to the finish. It
served no purpose. The riders were best placed to see how the chase
for the line was evolving. It was agreed that for the final 15km
there'd be radio silence. If the tribute to his team mates was routine,
albeit sincere, Kittel said that his refusal to call himself the best
sprinter in the *peloton* last year (when he took four stages, including
the finish on the Champs-Elysées) would have been pretentious.
'It's obvious that I'm one of the best but I'm not alone. Humility
adds lustre to a victory.'

The Tour came back to France. Not far from the start in Le
Touquet, another rider clipped Froome's wheel. He went down.
Left wrist and hip – injured in the Dauphiné – took the brunt.

They rode the last 30km into Lille at a withering 60kph, but
Kittel, once more, hung on to outsprint the big Norwegian,
Alexander Kristoff, winner of this year's Milan–San Remo. The
route hadn't been significantly lumpy, and Kristoff, who's
very strong but lacks the raw speed of most sprinters, profits
from a hillier terrain – like that of the classic race to the Italian
Riviera.

Thomas Voeckler sustained a long break, first with Luis Ángel
Maté, then on his own. Reporting on his day in the sun, he said:
'I'd decided in the morning to make a move to dust off the engine.
I'm a diesel, I'm 35, I need to warm up. I had no illusions about my
chances to go all the way but I really enjoyed myself.'

The Tour goes into Hell

Commemorating the 100th anniversary of the start of the First
World War, stages five and six crossed many of the battlefields of
the Western Front, from Ypres to Arenberg, whose chateau and
grounds were occupied by Germans and Austrians during the
war. Next day from Arras, via the Chemin des Dames to Reims,
which was all but obliterated in Easter week, 1917, by a massive
bombardment of 25,000 shells.

Along the Chemin des Dames (The Ladies' Road), built for
Louis XV's daughters to ease their journeys between Compiègne
(where the 1918 Armistice was signed) and the Château de
la Bove (destroyed in the war), scene of particularly savage
fighting, the fields today abound with *bleuets*, cornflowers. In

1915, the French chose the *bleuet* to symbolise the men in the blue infantry uniform coats who never reached 20 years old. Out of respect, the publicity caravan did not throw out a hail of keyrings, packets of sausage, sachets of washing liquid etc but only cornflowers.

The route of stage five included nine sectors of the infamous *pavé*, the ancient cobbled roads originally laid by the Roman legions who fought, and conquered, the Belgae, described by Julius Caesar as the fiercest fighters they ever encountered.

Vast tracts of the north east of France had been ruined in the war, the forests and farmland of the Pas de Calais and Nord départements blasted into mud, a gaunt, prickly stubble of broken trees protruding. The first post-war Tour, 'the Tour of Regeneration', crossed this wasteland in 1919 and, that same year, the classic Paris–Roubaix race got its celebrated nickname: *The Hell of the North*.

Stiff carbon bikes exaggerate the harshness of cobbles and most teams adapted frames to soften the punishment: longer forks, slightly bigger clearance, tyres marginally softer than usual. Specialised frames had little inserts in the front forks and rear dropouts containing fluid to reduce the violent vibration as well as a rubber damper by the seat post.

Froome came to the start with his left wrist in a splint. The wrists and arms take a shocking strain in riding over cobbles and he was, understandably, very nervous. But so was everyone. Any rider not close to the front of the bunch entering the cobbles always faces a doubly hard job to rejoin. When both sides of the *pavé*, which forms a slight mound, are filled with mud and puddles, the riders have no choice but to ride in Indian file. Any attempt to overtake risks a crash.

Romain Bardet, the young Frenchman, said later that 'it was crazy, epic. In the first sector of cobbles the mud was three centimetres thick. I thought of stealing a spectator's mountain bike.'

Froome tumbled on the greasy tarmac before he even reached the broken surfaces – as did a number of other riders – rode on with his team in support for eight kilometres and then abandoned.

Scans later showed that both wrists were fractured. It was bitter: the reigning laureate climbing into the car.

Another Sky man, Xavier Zandio, a good climber, also abandoned with a suspected broken collarbone as did one of Contador's support climbers, Jesús Hernández.

In March, Alexandr Vinokourov, the Astana director, had excoriated the whole team for their lack of spunk. Now, however, they were showing great form. They'd come to Belgium for a master-class in riding the pavé from Peter van Petegem, winner of the Paris–Roubaix in 2003, runner-up in 2000. 'We wanted to set out on this stage with total confidence,' Vinokourov said.

Lieuwe Westra joined an early break to be on hand when Nibali rejoined and Nibali himself rode superbly, his first time on cobbles: concentration, balance, line, strength. At the start of his career he was rather erratic – suicidal breaks and poor tactical judgement. Now, however, he was evincing a calm and imperturbability which has prompted the man who's shared hotel rooms with him for eight years, Alessandro Vanotti, to say that you'd hardly believe he was riding the Tour, let alone wearing yellow. This serenity acts as a valuable screen to diminish the intense pressure which the yellow jersey brings to bear on any rider, doubly so for a favourite. His nickname is *Il Squalo da Messina*, The Shark of Messina.

Belgians call the cobbles 'baby's heads' and Nibali crossed them as if he wanted not to crush them. He didn't falter, his team men supported him all the way and Westra's forceful riding whittled the lead group to four: himself, Jakob Fuglsang and Nibali of Astana, Lars Boom of Belkin. Boom went clear and rode to victory, but the Astanas had one job only, to make sure Nibali got to the finish intact.

Contador's gears clogged with mud and seized up. He lost 2m 54s.

The Sky management, in part defending their decision to omit Wiggins, said that the loss of Froome was lamentable but that, as planned, leadership would pass to Richie Porte. He was in fine shape, he had a real opportunity to get himself onto the podium in Paris.

This was, in my view, unrealistic. His dramatic collapse in the Pyrenees last year (see p. 517) questioned his ability to make the huge psychological leap from lieutenant to leader. True, he'd been nominated leader for the team riding the Giro. The root problem lay in switching roles during a race.

The German rider, André Greipel, took the next stage. The Frenchman, Jérôme Pineau, and the Spaniard, Maté, sole survivors of a long break, were still out in front 19 kilometres from the finish when Maté cut loose. He was caught 7 kilometres on but scooped the day's prize for combativity. Pineau was furious. 'Maté's a rat,' he said. 'He contributes hardly any work.'

Peter Sagan, who'd finished in the top five on these opening stages, consolidated his hold on the green jersey but of course yearned for a stage win. He's not really a top-flight sprinter but he endured another disappointment next day on the race's second longest stage, 234.5km from Epernay into Nancy. Epernay is home to several famous makers of champagne, Nancy is known for macaroons, but there were no celebratory biscuits or fizz for Sagan: he lost by the width of a stick of celery to Cavendish's team mate Matteo Trentin. Immediately behind them, the American Andrew Talansky, surprise winner of the recent Dauphiné, took a heavy fall and even further back, his compatriot, Tejay van Garderen, considered by some as a contender for a high overall placing, was caught up in a spill with some 17km to go. Already 2m 11s down on General Classification (GC), he lost another 1m 3s, despite a brave effort to rejoin the *peloton*.

Incidentally, the true *macaron de Nancy* owes its renown to a secret recipe formulated by two lay sisters of the Community of Women of the Holy Sacrament in the town four hundred years ago. So there.

The benjamin of the Tour, Danny van Poppel, aged 20, withdrew, making Yates the youngest rider in the race.

The Vosges are going to hurt

This was the 22nd time the Tour had visited the mountains which form a natural barrier along the eastern frontier of France. Usually they come for two days. This year they were staying three and crossing sixteen cols and hills, five of them first category climbs. The Tour director, Christian Prudhomme, whose itineraries have shown such flair and enterprise since he took control in 2007, was counting on the Vosges to demonstrate, to public and riders alike, that the Alps and Pyrenees are not the only places where the Tour could be played out.

Many of the ascents are steep, the roads narrow, the descents twisty and what cyclists call 'technical' – that means scary.

The arch *baroudeur* – scrapper – Sylvain Chavanel set off on his own, 23km from the start on the first day, and was joined by a few others, including Yates, feisty and chipper, and Blel Kadri of the AG2R team. Their riders had taken Paris–Nice, the Critérium International, fourteen wins all told and now stood fourth in the UCI's overall team rankings. Kadri gave them another victory this day.

He and Chavanel alone were still out ahead with 25km to go when Chavanel attacked. Kadri reeled him in and dropped him to cross the last climb, 22.5km from the line. Descending with nerveless poise, Kadri held on and won the stage by 2m 17s from the chasing bunch. His director said it had been a 'blackboard day', all planned.

Stage nine was a brute: six categorised climbs one after the other, the last summit 40km from the finish in Mulhouse. Two riders, Tony Martin and Alessandro de Marchi, established a healthy lead early on. Twenty-eight riders – only Astana, Sky and Garmin weren't represented – gave chase and, at Markstein, 59km from Mulhouse, they had a lead of 5m 30s on the yellow jersey group.

Now Martin, a time-trial specialist, three times world champion in the discipline and current holder, dropped de Marchi, and pressed on alone, perhaps mindful of that 2013 Vuelta a España when he was caught two seconds from the line after a long break. In the following group, the Frenchman, Tony Gallopin, was already virtual yellow jersey and, when he crossed the line, the jersey became his by 1m 34s over Nibali. The exultant joy of taking the Golden Fleece was the greater because he'd be wearing it next day, Monday (usually a Rest Day), 14 July, anniversary of the taking of the Bastille in 1789. A Frenchman in yellow on the national day? Wow.

Nibali had no concerns. Loss of the jersey eased the pressure on his team to defend it on the next stage, another killer, finishing on

La Planche des Belles Filles (for the legend, see p. 491), a climb of only five kilometres but over savage gradients, with a stretch of 20 per cent at the top.

The Germans celebrated too, even though the German media still boycott the race because of the taint of doping: this was their fifth stage win of the Tour. (In Italy, only *La Gazzetta dello Sport* – printed on pink paper, hence the *maglia rosa* worn by the leader in the Giro d'Italia – reports on cycling.)

Contador is out.
Launched on the high-speed descent of the Petit Ballon, a road that twitches as if it's trying to scratch a persistent itch, Contador was taking an energy bar out of his pocket, and, one hand only holding on to the bike, he saw and then went into a large pothole. 'I completely lost balance,' he said, 'the bike went out of control and flung me off.'

He landed on his left knee. Although the medics bandaged up a deep gash, he rode on for only a short way before knowing that it was all up with him. An X-ray later showed that he'd fractured the shin bone. His director, Bjarne Rijs, said that Contador, in the form of his life, was 'mentally destroyed' by the abandonment. A whole season dedicated to riding, and winning, the Tour de France, lost.

Over a succession of seven climbs – categories 2, 1, 1, 2, 3, 1, 1 – Martin was out in front again, in the mountains prize jersey, driving the break and towing his team mate, the Pole, Michal Kwiatkowski, wearing the white jersey of best young rider (and, for a while, yellow on the road), to distance his nearest rival, the Frenchman, Romain Bardet.

Martin tired at last, peeled off and all but stalled, on the penultimate climb, the Col des Chevrères, 18km from the finish. The Spaniard, Joaquim Rodríguez, had already broken clear, but Kwiatkowski and two others caught him on the descent. With a little over five kilometres to ride, Rodríguez went clear again to attack the last climb, 1m 15s ahead of Nibali, Porte, Alejandro Valverde (another contender for a podium place), the French climber, Thibaut Pinot, and Bardet.

Three kilometres left. Nibali eased away at a speed none could match, caught Rodríguez at 1.2km, rode alongside him for a short distance and, once more, applied the turbo accelerator to win the stage and retake yellow.

Behind him . . . sensation: the crowd was chanting *Thi-baut Pi-not Pi-not Pi-not* and here came the Frenchman, past Rodríguez, who was spent, to take second place, only fifteen seconds from Nibali. Across the line, Pinot was assailed by a swarm of microphones, dictaphones, cameras. He pulled off his jersey, steam rising from his back. A soigneur wiped him down with a towel even as his director, Marc Madiot, 'with edge in his voice and a beefy shoulder', was shoving the journalists out of the way.

Gallopin knew he'd never hold on to yellow but, in the way of men who wear the jersey, he rode with great pluck 'on the worst day I've ever had on a bike. Four hours of suffering such as I've never known.'

And yet, after the Rest Day, Gallopin joined a break which included Kwiatkowski, Sagan and the amazing Martin, driving it till he fell away. Gallopin cut loose eight kilometres from the line onto the descent into Oyonnax*, hosting the race for the first time. He descended with remarkable skill but was caught when the road flattened. At three kilometres to go, he attacked again. Another kilometre and Sagan and Kwiatkowski might have ridden him down but Sagan renounced, unwilling to tow the Pole to the line. These dog-in-manger tactics are, to most outsiders, dumbfounding and they never make much sense to insiders, either. The Pole did chase but it was too late. Gallopin, surrendered yellow, won a stage.

Sagan afterwards said that he'd wanted to win 'but it's not easy when everyone is riding against you. They know that if they come with me, I'll beat them in the sprint,' which underscores the folly of *not* going for the win. So close to the line, you know you can sprint better, you don't go for it?

Next day, in Saint-Etienne, the sprinters' capital, he missed out again, second to Kristoff. Kristoff's lead-out, Luca Paolini, is known as *il barbone*, 'beardy'. How very odd surplus face-hair looks on a

* If you're looking for a Museum of the Comb and of the Plastics Industry, Oyonnax is your place.

cyclist. Mutton-chop sideburns? Remember Philippe Thys who shaved off a luxuriant walrus moustache to cut down on wind resistance (see p. 79).

First alpine stage. Finish at 1730m on Chamrousse, a climb of 18.2km, average 8 per cent.

Torrid heat. Nibali wins in magnificent style.

The day's early leader, de Marchi, soared over the Col de Palaquit, 1st category, 14km long, a fairly benign gradient, essentially part of the Col de Porte, but not named on any map I've seen. On the descent, Nibali's team mate Jakob Fuglsang was pitched off his bike by a stray bidon and badly cut and bruised. Nibali was close by. 'A few centimetres and it could have been me,' he said.

Nibali is superstitious. He wore only the two yellow jerseys he took on the podium throughout the race – one was washed in cold water each night. Nor does he wear yellow shorts, a custom (regrettable) of recent years, because, his trainer Paolo Slongo says, 'he doesn't want to appear arrogant . . . even though we have yellow shorts in the case'.

Indeed, his studious politesse, his natural spontaneity of manner, no artifice, have been compared to the gentlemanly comportment of another great Italian champion, Felice Gimondi (winner in 1965).

The Belgian, Lucien Van Impe, five times winner of the mountains prize, stressed how vital rhythm is on a climb. It's the buffer to gradient, the smoothness which irons out the furrows of stress, the soft coating which protects a rider from the rasp of extreme effort. However, abrupt acceleration is the killer weapon in the armoury of the very best climbers. Lesser riders cannot accommodate them: the shock of increased speed shatters rhythm, impinges on concentration, dents morale.

The Swedish *fartlek* method of conditioning – it means 'speed play' – combines continuous with interval training: continuous to strengthen the aerobic system, interval – short bursts of violent activity over the aerobic threshold – to strengthen the anaerobic. Various athletic disciplines have long employed this method but it was only recently that the practice became more general in cycling.

Froome's preparation for the 2013 Tour included specific work on sudden jumps in pace (see pp. 524–5).

It was just such a jolt of rhythm which slew Porte on Chamrousse.

De Marchi led onto this last climb with a small gap. The yellow jersey group arrived but a short way up, Porte slipped away and was left, in the parlance, grovelling. He simply disappeared, like the Cheshire Cat, to the amazement of Nibali and the rest.

Around 12km from the summit the tempo zipped up again and others spilled out like beans from a hole in a bag. Surprisingly, some managed to rejoin and Pinot broke clear but didn't get far. Then Leo König and Rafal Majka went away and got a lead. (Majka came to the Tour after a hard-won sixth place in the Giro.)

A kilometre or so further on, Valverde surged ahead, but got no further than 200 metres before Nibali and Pinot reeled him in. Behind them, the group was fragmenting again.

In the sort of heat that lizards love to bask in, Valverde was still driving hard. Nibali sat in for a kilometre or so before he changed gear and went, the Pinkerton hounding felons, fugitives from implacable justice. He caught them, sat on their wheels for a while, an exquisite form of torture. They knew the coup de grâce was coming and, with a bare three kilometres to go, Nibali delivered it. König and Majka knew they were racing for second and third place now.

Valverde and Pinot were chasing but couldn't catch them.

The GC order was shaken *and* stirred: Bardet moved up to third place behind Valverde and ahead of Pinot. Van Garderen was now fourth and Jean-Christophe Péraud* (37 years old, a former mountain-biking champion, silver medallist at the Beijing Olympics, who switched to the road) fifth. Porte lost nearly nine minutes, despite Thomas's valiant efforts to help him up the mountain, and slumped to 16th, overall. Sky later issued a bulletin: he'd been suffering from a virus. What a wretched time the Sky team was having. For the past two years, their team bus had been under siege before and after the race. Now it was deserted, noplaceville.

This 18 July marked the 100th anniversary of the birth of Gino Bartali, winner of the Tour in 1938 and 1948, and the death of

* Even the French press is undecided about whether he is Péraud or Peraud.

Fabio Casartelli in the Pyrenees in 1995. Nibali paid tribute to both fellow-countrymen on the Italian radio network RAI.

Pinot has, until now, been extremely jittery going down the mountains – he suffered agonies of fear, especially on the Pyrenean descents which tend to be more chancy than those in the Alps. Bear in mind that on the downhills, riders hit speeds of around 100kph – the Norwegian Thor Hushovd was once timed at 118kph. The bikes they all ride are ultra-light (they must weigh no less than 6.8kg). Frames, wheel rims, spokes, straight front forks all of carbon, make the machines very stiff and much trickier to handle on descents, more prone, too, to buffets of wind, whereas the older steel frames with slightly raked forks had much more flexibility and were better adapted to hurtling over the planes of gravity.

Pinot underwent a course of psychotherapy to confront and master his fear – this included driving a racing car. On the second alpine stage, he was not only in the lead break on the fearsome Col d'Izoard, he led the descent, through the Broken Desert of rock stacks – sinister, dry gulch country.

The apparently indefatigable Thomas was also in the group, riding at full effort for his Sky team mate, the Spaniard, Mikel Nieve, in hope of winging him to a stage victory on the summit of Risoul, climbed by the Tour for the first time. But, 11.1km from the finish, it was de Marchi who shook things up – he'd won here in the 2013 Dauphiné. Others followed and, in his first Tour, Majka took his first professional win. He and Rodríguez were now equal on points in the mountains competition.

The race was being fought with courage and enterprise all round. A debutant taking on the giants, breakaways succeeding, a fierce tussle for the white jersey, and the French, so long cowed by a sense that they'd been handicapped during the inglorious years of rampant doping when, as it was said, there were two speeds in the *peloton*, were showing verve and confidence. AG2R epitomised the new flourishing: they led the team competition.

Two riders, the New Zealander Jack Bauer, of Garmin (going for a stage win to make up for the loss of their leader, Talansky) and the Swiss national champion, Martin Elmiger, were out in front for 222km, the entire distance between Tallard and Nîmes, holding a steady gap on a *peloton* that seemed undecided about chasing them down. They rode in a deluge of heavy rain, the roads awash with water which renders white road markings so very treacherous.

Perhaps the mood was damp – the sprinters' teams were making no concerted effort. At the red flag, one kilometre from the line, pushed on by a strong tail wind, the breakaways still had a thirteen-second advantage. And then? Fatal error. As Elmiger said afterwards: 'We started watching each other for the sprint.' Bauer did jump clear, with a hundred metres to go, but the hesitation had cost dear. He lost to Kristoff by 25m.

The spectacle of the closing chase and capture was electrifying. Apt that the scene of their despatch should be in the shadow of the city's famous Roman amphitheatre, in the arena where gladiator put gladiator to the sword, where, in Federico García Lorca's famous phrase, there was blood on the sand.

The Rest Day was based in and around the old fortress town of Carcassonne, its very mediaeval profile – cone turrets, high walls, crenellated ramparts – the work of the architectural restorer, Viollet-le-Duc, in 1855. Pinot opted for an artificial Rest Day ride: he sat on the home trainer in the hotel.

In another hotel, the Chinese rider Ji Cheng was probably wondering what on earth had happened to him. Two weeks of horrendous work done, another week still to come. He was ensconced as *lanterne rouge*, to which attaches a curious celebrity.* Some will have none of that – notably Marc Madiot (see p. 447). Since he held the red lamp by more than 24 minutes over his nearest rival (and was four hours back on Nibali), he looked safe to bring it to Paris. His role in the Giant-Shimano team is as an 'escape assassin'. When an early break goes, he joins it, does no work, to slow it down, so that the team's sprinter, Kittel, will be better placed for a finishing sprint. Cheng says he loves the idea – 'that's my job'.

* Max Leonard has written an excellent study of the ethos of, and psychology which underpins, this perplexing distinction – being *last* in a race. *Lanterne Rouge*, Yellow Jersey Press.

TOUR DE FRANCE

Nibali, who remains cool despite the added media responsibilities imposed on the yellow jersey – upwards of an hour at the end of each stage before he's free to get to the hotel and the massage table, as well as a long round of interviews and press conference during the Rest Day – has also faced the routine challenges about doping. In the sulphurous post-Festina and, more significantly, post-Armstrong climate any marked superiority will be called into question. Nibali counters any veiled accusation by emphasising that he has always repudiated those who take drugs – 'they're brainless' – and asserts that those who know him have always considered him a standard bearer for anti-doping. Detractors may echo Mandy Rice Davies – 'he would say that, wouldn't he?' – but a cynic is a dog it's hard to stop barking.

Nibali was not always so cool. Relations between him and Slongo were, for a time, strained. Slongo: 'It was love and hate at the beginning. He didn't see the point of testing. Like all gifted champions, he goes on instinct. At one point, I told him to pack his suitcase and go home. We didn't speak for two days. It wasn't until after his victory in the 2010 Vuelta that we felt at ease with each other and thereafter he's given me total confidence. On my side, I strive to preserve his imagination, because I remain an old romantic.'

There's much of note to consider in the nurturing of ruthless efficiency without losing flair.

After the Rest Day, the slaughterhouse: an unholy trinity of forays over the Pyrenees. Stage 16, longest in the Tour, 237.5km, a brace of lesser cols before the fearsome Port de Balès . . . Stage 17, shortest in the race, 124.5km, Cols de Portillon, 1st category, (after a brief excursion into Spain), Peyresourde, 1st, Val Louron-Azet, 1st, Saint-Lary Pla d'Adet, outside category . . . Stage 18, two beyond-category climbs: Col du Tourmalet and a finish on Hautacam which means, somewhat prosaically, 'high field'.

On the approach to the Port de Balès, a break of 21 riders had nearly 12 minutes on the yellow jersey group. Some of the escapees were grumbling that not everyone was doing his share of work, only appearing to. This soft-pedalling is called, in the slang, glass-cranking.

The break splintered as soon as the gradient, tough from the start, between 8 and 14 per cent, broke the bad news: a sign at the side of the road read *Summit at 11.7km*. By about halfway up, five men had detached themselves: Vasil Kiryienka, hoping to give Sky a stage win, Michael Rogers, José Serpa, and two Europcar riders, Cyril Gautier and Thomas Voeckler, who'd crossed the Balès to solo wins in Bagnères-de-Luchon (twinned with Harrogate) on the Tour's last two visits, in 2010 and 2012.

The group concertinaed – one man dropped, fought back on, another pair off the back, hauled themselves up again, but it reconvened over the top and set off on what starts as a nasty succession of tight switchbacks.

It was clear that Rogers wouldn't share the work to help the two Europcar men and Voeckler scolded him for his lack of cooperation. Rogers pointed out that it was sometimes more difficult to win from a break of three than five. This was logical and Voeckler appeared to accept it. Then Europcar boobed. As the road evened out for the run-in to the finish three kilometres away, Gautier attacked and Rogers chased, knowing that Voeckler wouldn't move. But Gautier didn't get clear, Rogers flashed past him and the Australian, a former world time-trial champion, put his head down to make sure of victory.

He said afterwards that previously he'd been scared to try such moves from a fear of failure, calculating too much on the cost of losing. Now he'd 'stopped trying to live someone else's life'. As he crossed the line, he bowed jokily, like a ham actor.

At the finish, Pinot had put nearly two minutes into Bardet and took over the white jersey. There were now four Frenchmen in the top ten of GC. Both Bardet (3rd) and Pinot (4th) had a real chance of displacing Valverde, still second overall. Majka pulled on the polka dots.

Van Garderen lost four minutes on the climb and the reigning world champion, Rui Costa, who said he felt as if he'd been run over by a truck, abandoned before the start with bronchitis. Pulmonary ailments are common, provoked by the weakening effect of sustained extreme effort in thin air, overheating on the up, biting cold on the down, or triggered by an excessively cold drink at the finish, an icy air-conditioning in the hotel . . . these men have very little body fat and their resistance even to minor ailments is stretched very thin.

The loss of Contador had shaken the morale of the Tinkoff-Saxo team badly. The riders had to try to salvage something. Sponsors need good results. The Russian millionaire Oleg Tinkoff owns the team and is a cyclist himself. Indeed, he set out to ride the stages ahead of the race until he was reined in one day in the Vosges and told to dismount by one of that species of stonewall merchants, the French gendarme. Rogers's win, therefore, his first ever in the Tour, not only meant joy for him but also for the team and it was another team mate, the Pole Majka, who delivered the next great prize.

A new scoring system awarded double points for mountaintop finishes, to encourage the battle for the polka dot jersey. Thus Pla d'Adet was worth 50 points. Going into the stage, Rodríguez and Majka led the competition, both on 88. Majka, in a move both audacious and impressive, rode to solo victory and the jersey, the second Pole to win here after Zenon Jaskoula in 1993. Majka was fined 50 Swiss francs (£32) and docked ten seconds for grabbing hold of the television antenna on a motorbike for a moment's propulsion . . . in full view of another television camera. Daft. But, Tinkoff had promised Majka an Aston Martin were he to win two stages. Bingo.

One of the Movistar riders was evicted from the race: he'd taken prolonged shelter behind one of the following cars.

There had been little doubt for some time that Nibali was heading for victory in Paris: on Hautacam he secured it. But there were others who contributed to one of the finest days' racing the Tour has seen in recent years.

Several things were at stake this day: Nibali's grip on the overall lead, the decider in the competition for the polka dot jersey – Majka led with 149, Nibali second with 118, Rodríguez with 112. Fifty points on the last day in the mountains – only a small scattering of points lay ahead towards Paris – would give Nibali the mountains prize. Were the Italian to win, Majka needed to come no lower than sixth, which would give him 20 points, to retain the jersey by a whisker. Perhaps the most intriguing prospect, however, was the scrap for second and third place overall.

At the start of the day, Valverde was second, 5m 26s behind Nibali, Pinot (aged 24) third, at six minutes, Péraud at 6m 8s. Bardet (23) at 7m 34s was probably out of contention but the mountains can do terrible things to any rider. He surely hadn't given up hope.

Van Garderen had something to prove, too. He'd suffered some bad luck, a bout of bronchitis and a crucial weakening on the Port de Balès. He was in sixth place at 10m 19s. A podium place was almost certainly beyond him but there is the racing spirit to honour.

An early breakaway group, containing a number of practised chancers – Voeckler, Chavanel, de Marchi et al – got to the foot of the Tourmalet intact. Significantly, no member of the Astana team had joined the break to police it. Clearly Nibali had his eye on stage victory and his men firmly controlled the front of the main *peloton* to limit the time advantage of the escapees which didn't extend much beyond three minutes.

Chavanel was the first to jump clear. Kadri, one of several riders who have so gingered up French self-confidence of late, chased him. So, too, Mikel Nieve of Spain, a last-ditch attempt to give his Sky team some recompense for their miserable showing. Two overall victories followed by complete wash-out? A dreadful prospect.

The race swept off the Tourmalet and along the road which keeps company with the Gave de Pau, its fast-flowing course supplied by a number of sources springing out of the mighty ridge near Gavarnie marking the frontier with Spain. (Gave, a Gascon word, describes a Pyrenean torrent and Pau, as so many times in Tour history, had hosted the start that day.)

Valverde tried to drop Nibali. He made a daring plunge down the corkscrew bends of the abyss towards the valley, but never got far and succumbed. So to the final climb of the Tour, 13.6km of an average 8 per cent.

Kadri and Nieve were still in front with a lead of 1m 29s. Majka began to chase them down.

In the 2013 Vuelta, Chris Horner, then 41 years old, fought off Nibali to win the race. It appears that the Italian hadn't taken the American's chances seriously enough. Thus, when Horner made the first move, 10.5km from the summit, Nibali was quick to follow. They opened a small gap, the followers didn't react, assuming that Nibali was merely containing the attack. A kilometre on, Nibali produced a startling burst of acceleration and the rest were, for a short way, sucker-punched.

Kadri was on his own by now. Nieve hadn't the legs. At 8.4km, Majka made his move while further back, Nibali caught and passed Nieve at a speed which must have drained any morale the Spaniard had left plain away. Kadri reeled Majka in but, less than half a kilometre up the road, the Pole attacked again and was free. He slowly gained 29 seconds on the small group of pursuers.

It was Pinot's time to go if he was to take second overall. When he applied the pressure, some five kilometres from the finish, Valverde couldn't answer. Had he cracked? It seemed so. Péraud and van Garderen did respond, and battled on to rejoin Majka. And Valverde came back. What grit. The slope was so steep that they were even zigzagging for a short distance to make use of the camber. Rarely has there been such an extended scrap for placings on the podium among so many riders and here, on this mountain, fought without quarter.

The Shark of Messina steadily homed in on Kadri. The Frenchman had no more metres of gap in him. Nibali passed him as if he weren't there.

His triumph on Hautacam underlined his supremacy in this Tour. He'd held the yellow jersey for all but two days, and, riding with studied composure, had never given any hint of being troubled or even hurried. He conjured speed at will. His attacks had the timing of a superior fencer delivering a lethal stoccado.

Pinot came in second and moved up to second overall, Majka third and secured his polka dots, Péraud fourth and moved up to third, van Garderen fifth, a fine comeback. Valverde lost 49 seconds to Pinot and dropped to fourth overall, two seconds behind Péraud.

Friday's largely flat stage in the Dordogne carved through the Périgord, famous for *foie gras*, truffles, *confit de canard*, the sweet white wines of Monbazillac and the red, white and rosé vintages of Bergerac which hosted the finish. Cyrano de Bergerac, duellist and dramatist, was immortalised in a play by Edmond Rostand

(1868–1918). Cyrano vaunts his panache, a word that means plume and the link with bold action begins with Henri IV's famous cry in battle: 'Rally to my white plume,' the feather he wore in his helm. Panache is a quality much prized in the history of bike racing, too, the willingness to cast caution aside, to ride to the limit, even at the expense of failing. Friday saw some real panache.

It was the last chance for the pilot fish to outstrip the predatory killer whale that is the *peloton* and five duly obliged in filthy weather – rain bucketed down all day. Gautier, Elmiger, the Estonian, Rein Taaramäe, Tom Jelte Slagter of Garmin and Arnaud Gérard of the new Bretagne-Seche Environnement team worked well together, except for Gérard who didn't contribute to the relays yet seemed to draw no tongue-lashing from the others.

About 20 kilometres from home, the Garmin team car drove up and, under pretext of handing Slagter a gel, the director gave him instructions. The two-way radios that all riders carry, now, can be hacked into and secrets of tactical moves eavesdropped.

Slagter went ahead on his own, the others fell away and were swiftly absorbed by the chasing bunch. At 13km to go the route crossed the Côte de Monbazillac, a short climb of around 8 per cent but enough of an obstacle to deaden weary legs. It was on this hill that Slagter eventually ceded, but not before one of his team mates, Ramunas Navardauskas of Lithuania, had gone off the front of the *peloton*. This was odd. It risked dragging the rest of the field up to Slagter and killing the break. But, Navardauskas persisted even as Slagter was swallowed up. They call him 'Honeybadger'*. He opened a gap, widened it to over 20 seconds, the *peloton* wasn't organised.

Honeybadger rode with a rare hunger, the *peloton* shilly-shallied. Around 3 kilometres from the line, a crash brought down a number of riders, including Sagan whose lead in the points competition was unassailable but his chances of a stage win very slight, now.

Finally, the remnants of the bunch not caught in the crash began to wind up their effort and as Navardauskas neared the finish, they

---

* The Honeybadger, closer, anatomically, to a weasel than other badgers, has a taste for honey, is a skilled digger, and lives alone in self-dug holes. So, why the nickname? I don't know.

loomed behind him. Some extra force must have impelled the Lithuanian, a revenge for Bauer's last-minute demise a few days before. He made it, he held them off. It was pure happy ending and bravo to a cheeky opportunist attack and the nerve to bring it home.

Unusually, this Tour included only one individual time-trial, the traditional race of truth on the penultimate day, the grandstand showdown. Much hinged on the performance of the top order of riders over the 54km between Bergerac and Périgueux. Pinot, second, not very good against the clock, Péraud, third, and Valverde, fourth, both good, were separated by a mere fifteen seconds. Van Garderen, another classy solo rider, aimed at leap-frogging Bardet, in fifth.

Martin set off 68th in the field, rode a massive gear – 58x11 which delivers around four metres for every revolution of the pedals – and had to wait around for ages to have his win confirmed. Nibali, holding an advantage of over seven minutes – a massive lead such as we haven't seen since 1997 when Jan Ullrich led Richard Virenque by 9m 9s in Paris – came a respectable fourth.

Péraud moved into second, Pinot dropped to third, Valverde stayed in fourth. Van Garderen moved up into fifth, by two seconds, but only because poor Bardet punctured.

A touching moment before the time-trial: the camera showed Pinot offering best wishes to Péraud and the two men shook hands.

Into Paris

Jens Voigt took the intermediate sprint, 91km from the finish, a final flourish for an outstanding career, Ji Cheng was lapped on the Champs-Elysées and Porte launched an attack at 36km from the finish. It had a whiff of desperation about it. (Although Sky came seventh in the overall team classification, won by AG2R, they took home nothing.)

Péraud was knocked off with an hour to ride – 'they took me for a skittle' – but wasn't badly hurt and rode on.

For the second year running, Kittel took the final sprint and added an excited optimism to his own delight: seven stage wins by Germans, a much-needed boost to the popularity of the sport in their homeland. The perennial Voigt was retiring. A new generation was taking over and Kittel now has eight Tour stage wins. (He made his debut in 2012 but retired, sick, on stage five.)

Two Frenchmen from two French teams joined Nibali on the podium and for those blockheads who say that this wasn't a real Tour – in the absence of two favourites – I say 'Pah'. If Nibali's supremacy proved untouchable, nothing can efface the magnificent quality of the racing behind him. And not just for the GC. Many riders injected a sheer devilry of attacking spirit throughout the race, Yates showed that reputation need not daunt a bold youngster, AG2R won the overall team classification by over half an hour, Sagan, without a stage win, reclaimed the green, for the third year running, as the reward to the most consistent finisher, his nearest rivals, Kristoff and the bustling young Frenchman, Bryan Coquard, behind him by some 150 points.

The overall combativity prize went to de Marchi, although Elmiger had been out in front of the *peloton* for a total of 788.5km.

La Course

Before the men's race arrived, a field of women professionals rode 13 laps of the 7 kilometre circuit 25 years after the last *Tour de France Feminin* arrived there.

Women's cycle racing is underfunded, given very little airing in the media, and is, for the most part, largely invisible. This is galling. The competitive spirit, fiery tactics and excitement which characterised the women's road race in the London Olympics, 2012, outshone the bromide men's race by far.

At last, however, the prejudice against the women is waning.

Perception is what counts here. A counter to the shameful attitude betrayed some while ago, in a yearbook. On a page at the back, like a throwaway postscript, under the title WOMEN, the editor had written 'A bit of meaningless copy needed here'.

Marianne Vos, current Olympic and world road race champion, had told her team before the race to ride aggressively, not to seek to control the race, but to be bold. And so they were. The attacks kept coming.

The silver medallist in London, Lizzie Armitstead, was unlucky to be shunted into the barrier on the approach to the line. The race went to Vos.

Emma Pooley, former world time-trial champion, wasn't riding, but had been a leading proponent of the women's event on the same roads as the Tour. She said: 'This race is brilliant . . . I do feel it's the start of a redevelopment of women's cycling which currently is a massive missed opportunity.'

Amen to that.

The moto-camera diary
(Luke Edwardes-Evans, driver for Graham Watson, photographer)

St 1
On Buttertubs, warning lights on the panel flashing. Engine's overheating big time. Crawl to the top, pull off onto the verge to cool down, race flashes past. We roll downhill. Found out later – the fan wasn't plugged in.

St 3
Massive crowd in Cambridge, opposite King's College. G gets up on the foot peg to get a shot, bends it. I'd need a chunk of the *Bismarck* to make one strong enough. Drove the rest of the way with a wonky foot peg.

St 5
Huge crowd in Ypres. Bike wouldn't start. Tried to bump it, no joy. Embarrassing. Checked fuse – dead. Luckily I had a spare and we're off. Otherwise it's 'shit, we're going to lose a day'.

Looking forward to the pavé. Last rode it with G in '94. There's a charge about the cobbles so I'm excited, nervous, too. Thought we might not be allowed on but the bike's trail style – tourist-style machines ruled out. Cars are the problem – splashing through puddles, chucking mud all over the place. Not so much today – rain has washed it off. And no cars on the course except the Mavic service cars.

Missed a trick, though – left out most of the cobbled sections. Sometimes you get to the finish and think 'could have done better' but after a beer and a bottle of wine it doesn't matter. Tomorrow's a new day.

St 10

Headlight goes off. Pulled over by a gendarme, tells us to drop back behind all the other bikes, which is bad news. Managed to dodge round them, though, and got to the finish.

Fuses blowing every day. I'm nervous. If one goes when we're in the middle of the bunch, it'll be dangerous – us cruising to a stop – so in every town we get to I buy spares. No one charges – if it's for *le Tour*. Eight went all told. Last year, not one – someone smiled on me.

Rest Day

Garage in Mulhouse. Two young Suzuki mechanics put aside all their other work to check the bike over. The ignition switch had some grit in it. They charge me 100€. Headlight back on.

St 11

Get to the motor pool at the finish. G chucks his helmet on the ground. In a right grump. Bad day. Joked about it next morning.

End of the stage G has 2 hours' work in the press room, supplying pics to teams, mags, his website. Most nights we don't eat till 9, 9.30. Digital age slows it down – everything has to be done instanter. Old days, it was negs in the post.

St 19

Get to the hotel 8.45pm. Nice place, people on the terrace eating. Looks great. Dump the bags and go out for a meal. Waiter says dread French word *terminé*. No food . . . ? Chef'll do us a cold platter. Forget it. We drive off to the nearest town and have a fun meal in a rocker's resto.

(G shares bike with an Italian photographer so they cox and box driving the support car.)

At one modern hotel, the worst meal *ever*: dishes on plates under cellophane. You point, they microwave. Dis-gus-ting.

Laundry

Carried more underpants this year – only two major washes. The merino T-shirts are fantastic – no bad odour. In work clothes all day, the real treat is to get into shorts, if there's time to change.

The independents
Most of the bikes are under agency control – everything organised
for them. We're more like camp followers. G rocks up and, because
of his name, he's left to his own devices. No one checks me (I do
have accreditation). It's all a bit gimcrack – we fend for ourselves.
G books the hotels in the winter. It's a bit the same as it was for the
independent riders 100 years ago. That's us, last of the roustabouts.

Home
Three weeks on the road, no voluntary aspect, it's all business, and
when there's a lot going it's knackering. But, not so tired as last year
– took me a month to recover. We'll see.

FOOTNOTE
Brailsford was widely censured for leaving Wiggins out of the Sky team, an
opinion I didn't share. Wiggins himself confirmed why, at the start of the
Commonwealth Games in Glasgow, after the English quartet, of which he was
one, took silver in the team pursuit, having been trounced by Australia. In an
interview on BBC, he said: 'The last six or seven weeks since I've been back
on the track have just been really refreshing and a good distraction from all
that Tour de France nonsense.' He then referred to politics, back-stabbing and
unsavoury shenanigans in road racing. Well . . .

CHAPTER TWENTY-FIVE

2015

Showdown on the Alpe

Utrecht, a gracious old town whose medieval core is largely preserved, once sat by the river Rhine. The Romans named their settlement here Traiectum, 'crossing'. The U, from Old Dutch *uut*, downriver, was added later. The course of the river gradually shifted south and was canalised as the Oudegracht, 'old canal', which runs on a gentle curve through the heart of the city. Utrecht, which had never before seen the Tour de France, this year hosted the Grand Départ, a 13.8km individual time trial which skirted the water and finished near the railway station, next to the new bike park, which will eventually have space for 12,500 machines.

The race route favoured the climbers emphatically. One individual time trial only, three days in the Pyrenees, four in the Alps, five summit finishes and several on lesser heights, all to the detriment of the sprinters. However, the ambivalence about the green jersey points competition – is it for consistent finishers or pure speed merchants? – was now more heavily weighted to persistence. Intermediate sprints carried points for the first 15 men through, 20 to the winner, counting down to a single point.

A team time-trial at the end of the first week might be regarded by some as a gratuitous act of cruelty but if the riders don't much like it, the spectators do: they see almost continuous action for the entire stage.

The organisers made one innovation – time bonuses of ten, six and four seconds for first to third placing on each stage, time trials apart. All riders are timed by the day's clock and then the bonus time is deducted. This may lead to anomalies. At least one Grand Tour has been lost by a rider who, in real time, had won the race but lost it to a man who had taken more time bonuses for stage placings. On the other hand, it does, in some circumstances, encourage a fiercer contest.

One thing does not change. In a charming nod to Tour tradition, the slate on which the time gaps are displayed to a breakaway continues to feature. The young Breton woman who has the job at the moment perches on the back of a yellow motorbike, clad in yellow from top to toe, and holds up the *ardoise* on which she's chalked the current time gap to spur on – or warn – the escapees. Given the fact that all riders are kept in constant touch with the managers by two-way radio, the travelling blackboard is entirely redundant, of course, but a touching souvenir of less technocratic times.

It was, though, adieu to the Voice of the Tour, Daniel Mangeas. I spoke to him. He'd been at the finish of each stage since 1974 and he told me that his passion was fired when he was at school, and developed into a continuing fascination with the history of the race. He rejoices, too, in the friendships his involvement has brought him. When he began, he said, 'people told me I wouldn't keep the same enthusiasm, I'd get blasé, offhand, but I said, No no, the passion is *inoxydable* [rustproof, stainless, untarnished]. We grow old but the passion doesn't, it stays the same, it's the core of my life. Every evening at ten o'clock, I'm in bed, I drink very little alcohol, it's like a sportsman's life, even if it's not a physical performance. Even when I was so young, I listened to the commentary of the race on radio and that's what I wanted to do. I was inspired, by the sound of the commentator's voice and how the radio allowed me to travel, to imagine myself going round France with the Tour . . . I could do that, I thought.'

A man of sharp intelligence, great charm, encyclopedic knowledge and indestructible tonsils. He'll be missed.

The Frenchmen Jean-François Péraud, 2nd overall in 2014, Thibaut Pinot, winner of the white jersey, even Romain Bardet, 6th, were surely hoping to perform well but they now faced five identifiable contenders for overall victory: Vincenzo Nibali, the reigning champion, Alberto Contador, Chris Froome, Nairo Quintana and Tejay Van Garderen. After a markedly lacklustre start to his season, Froome had won the Critérium du Dauphiné Libéré with a sizzling, courageous attack on the last day to beat the leader, Vangarderen. Nibali had shown poorly in that race. Contador, winner of the Giro d'Italia, despite having to ride for several days with a hampering injury, was bent on winning the Tour–Giro double, for the first time since Marco Pantani in 1998. Quintana, winner of the Giro in 2014, took the early season stage race Tirreno–Adriatico.

The Australian rider Rohan Dennis, riding in support of the American Van Garderen, is a noted powerhouse and former World hour record holder. Having come to Utrecht after competing in the Tour of Belgium in June expressly to reconnoitre the course, he posted a time of 14m 56s, setting a record speed of 55.446kph for the race against the clock in the Tour, topping the original record of 55.152kph, held by Chris Boardman over half the distance. He then had to wait a long time to see if the time would hold. Tony Martin, for Ettix-Quickstep, came closest, at five seconds. Nibali beat his three main rivals to gain seven seconds over Froome, fifteen over Contador and eighteen on Quintana.

The later riders had to contend with a strong wind on the return half of the circuit and Geraint Thomas, one of Froome's lieutenants, summed it up. He was, he said, 'dying all the time'.

It then emerged that a number of riders read a distance of only 13.5km on their computers at the close of the stage. This restored the record to Boardman. Two records could not be in dispute: it was the hottest day ever in Utrecht and this was the sixth time the Grand Départ had been held in the Netherlands, more than any other country outside France's borders.

Next day, a 166km trajectory across northern Holland, on some roads below sea level, took the riders into Zeeland – Sea Land – through gusting wind and pelting rain until the sun broke through to see them in along a narrow causeway road over a dam to the finish. Zeeland's motto, *Luctor et emergo*, was apt for the day: 'I strive and rise up.'

Early on, the field had been dramatically split in two: some 60km from the line, a group of 25 riders broke clear, among them Froome and Contador and two particularly strong men for driving an escape: Fabian Cancellara and Peter Sagan. Nibali and Quintana missed it. So, too, Dennis all in yellow: bike, helmet, probably undervest.

Mark Cavendish was well placed for the sprint finish but was beaten by André Greipel, Sagan – who, by dint of an astonishing show of strength, had managed to rejoin after a puncture – and Cancellara. Cavendish, the ace sprinter, said he knew he was going too slow that day if he could be beaten by a non-sprinter like Cancellara. Reunited with his best lead-out man, Mark Renshaw, Cavendish had, clearly, expected this one, but Renshaw went too soon – at 500 metres – and peeled off, leaving the Manx Missile a long haul of some 300 metres, instead of the ideal 200. Worse, when he realised, within metres of the line, that he'd lost, he sat up. Greipel took the ten second time bonus and Cavendish's teammate, Martin, lost out on the yellow jersey by a single, galling second. Cavendish, uncharitably, lashed out with a cavilling criticism of Renshaw's incompetence. It was unsavoury.

In the closing metres, Froome took a further four seconds out of Contador. Way behind them, Nibali and Quintana lost 1m 28s. It was a sucker punch. Cancellara took yellow for the 29th time in what is almost certainly his last Tour.

The finish of Stage 3 on the Mur de Huy was a minor savagery: a mere 128m in altitude, it's 1.3km long, narrow, twisty and of cruel gradient, up to 26% on one hairpin. Seven chapels line the road.

Alas, in the hectic speed and a buffeting wind along the open roads, a touch of wheels sent one rider down and the subsequent pile-up was awful to behold. Riders catapulted into the verge, just short of a concrete stanchion, hurled like mail sacks onto the tarmac, tangled up in the breaker's pile of broken machines, bruised, abraded, some very badly hurt indeed.

So calamitous was the accident that the race organisers neutralised the race and the peloton was made to ride at funereal tempo, even, at one point, to stop for a while to allow a commissaire's red car through. Whatever criticism this decision provoked was ill-considered. Those riders caught up in the crash who were able to, rejoined, in various states of damage – including Cancellara whose back, injured early in the season, had clearly taken another serious hit. Adam Hansen, riding his twelfth consecutive Tour (a record), had earlier fallen and dislocated his shoulder. A teammate manipulated it into position so that he could continue.

Tom Dumoulin, the Dutch hopeful, Simon Gerrans, the Australian leader of the Orica-GreenEDGE team, who wore yellow in 2013, and William Bonnet of France were all forced to abandon and taken to hospital, miserable for them. (Cancellara, too, after the stage. A sad exit, indeed, for this great stalwart.)

Three short climbs preceded the finish. The race was restarted at the top of the first, but, having been held up for some 20 minutes, the riders' muscles and minds had cooled. It took some time for the pace to develop but when it did, with some 13km to ride, Richie Porte and Thomas of the Sky team were on the front doing what they do so well: laying down a withering speed to sap weary legs. The effect was to deliver Froome to the foot of the wall in chipper form. Nearing the top, as the sharpening gradient unpicked the leading bunch, Froome went for home. Joaquim Rodríguez, the Spanish specialist climber, latched on and overtook him, but Froome persevered with the surge and put more time into his main rivals: Nibali and Quintana at 11s, Contador 18s, climbers all, taking a firm slap. Contador said later that he couldn't follow Froome 'but I don't know why'.

Froome took the yellow jersey by one second from Tony Martin. To a doltish reporter who wondered whether it was really a bit early to be taking the race leader's golden fleece, Froome smiled and said: 'It's never too early to take yellow.' It was his 15th yellow jersey, a British record.

Behind him: Van Garderen third at 13s, Contador 36s back, Nibali 1m 38s down and Quintana 17th at 1m 56s. The Frenchmen who had shown so well in 2014 were already having a bad time: Bardet at 2m 54s, Pinot four seconds behind him.

The fourth stage, longest in the race, 223.5km from Seraing in Belgium to Cambrai in France, included seven sectors of the infamous cobbled tracks, the *pavé* of the Hell of the North, the last six of them, including the longest stretch of 3.7km, in the final 35 kilometres.

Here is where Froome had been forced out of the Tour last

year. Lacking in poise, his confidence jarred, very nervy, he'd lost all the aplomb he'd shown when he won the race. Now, however, the only one of the main contenders to have ridden the Paris–Roubaix, he demonstrated splendid power and equilibrium. Nibali, who'd walloped the field on these cobbles in 2014, looked almost ordinary this day. Quintana, who'd come expressly to recce the terrain in advance, held a good line and stayed in contention. Contador also stuck with it, and the leading group – including Cavendish, here to work for Martin with the aim of getting him the yellow which he'd forfeited to Froome by 6/100 second – emerged from the final punishment of the broken stones in a swirling cloud of thick dust, to race into a town which was all but wrecked in two successive world wars.

Martin punctured and took over a teammate's bike. Pinot punctured twice inside two minutes and, at one point, looked as if he was going to hurl his bike at a wall. The distress was profound. His race was doomed. He eventually came in 3m 23s down on the stage winner, Martin. The German was helping to drive the bunch hard at a scorching pace, much encouraged by the sight of Cavendish, at the front, working hard for a teammate as his teammates work so hard for him. At 5km from the line, Martin, three times World time-trial champion, sprang out of the pack, and went for home. With a ten second time bonus on offer, all he needed to do was to retrieve that measly fraction of a second. This he did and raised his arm in ecstatic delight as he crossed the line. He'd never worn yellow. Whilst he must have chafed at not taking yellow two days earlier, this solo victory must have delighted him far more than wearing it, thanks to a teammate's action.

It was a sweetly timed move. The chances of chasing him down were slender. Froome's loss of yellow released the pressure on his team of defending it and Martin is no climber: the 12 seconds he now held over Froome was a trifle.

Before the start in Arras, the Sky riders Froome and Peter Kennaugh, together with the race director, Christian Prudhomme, laid wreaths at the Anglo-French war memorials for the men who'd died here. The race route crossed land where a million troops had fought in the great conflict, past lines of graves in the cemeteries to the dead of several nations, and on to Amiens, famous for its macaroons, capital of the *département* of the Somme, a name redolent of the horrific slaughter in 1916.

Once again, Cavendish missed out. Tipped off his bike when a motorbike gendarme slithered and fell at the side of the road, Cavendish had to take a wheel change and then haul himself back to the lead group. Matteo Trentin, usually part of the Etixx-Quickstep lead-out train, was absent with a bruised shoulder, and, although Martin and Renshaw worked hard, somehow Cavendish came adrift, had to struggle out of the closing pack and followed Greipel across the line. More conciliatory, now, he admitted that the defeat on Monday had been due to a mistake. 'Today I was just beaten,' but added that his confidence was solid and dismissed the idea that he'd expended too much energy the day before, helping Martin. They'd won yellow, that's all that counted.

The luckless Australian rider Michael Matthews, struggling with damaged ribs, was awarded the combativity prize for his courage.

The run from Abbeville to Le Havre took the riders most of the way over Normandy's Pays de Caux (Chalkland) on the 128km of what's known as the Alabaster Coast, named for the high chalk and pebble-striated cliffs which plunge down into the Channel. Etretat, in particular, is famous for its spectacular arches and the needle of rock, l'Aiguille de Belval, that rises up out of the water. The coastline is punctuated by *valleuses*, miniature gorges which give access through the cliffs to the sea.

The MTN-Qubeka team, based in South Africa, is funded by the World Bicycle Relief's programme there. (Qubeka means 'to move forward'.) On Stage 6 Daniel Teklehaimanot, one of two riders from Eritrea in the team, made history. He became the first black African to win a major jersey in a Grand Tour – he'd won the mountains prize in the Dauphiné Libéré outright. Part of a break of three which broke very early in the stage, he took the polka dots (mountains) by a single point. This great achievement was somewhat vitiated by reports that the Africans had suffered some racial abuse – bad-mouthing and contumely. One of their tormentors had been compelled to donate a month's salary to the foundation in recompense. A shameful 'what are you guys doing here?' attitude was in evidence.

On the run-in to Le Havre, up a vicious 3km hump, disaster. Martin clipped a wheel in front of him and went down. He shattered his collarbone and, though his teammates eventually rode him in, he had to abandon. The accident took out both Nibali and Quintana. Nibali, believing that Froome had caused the spill by accelerating up along the barriers, flung a bidon at him. In fact, the British rider had narrowly avoided collision, veered across the road, both feet out of the pedals, and had a lighter prang. A broken wheel replaced, his knee gashed, he rode to the line. He went round to the Astana bus to have the matter out with Nibali. They watched the TV coverage and Nibali apologised. 'Did we clear it all up?' he said. 'Yes. We're cyclists, not footballers.'

The second yellow jersey had crashed out of the race and, while the UCI ruled that no one should wear the Golden Fleece next day, Froome, loyal to Tour tradition, had already renounced on wearing it, although he now led the race. He was, one French commentator said, 'as relaxed as a July holidaymaker lounging in a deck chair, the only thing picking at him is whether to have a beer or pastis for his aperitif'.

The race has gone a day without the yellow jersey on a number of occasions, comically, in 1949, when the Belgian Norbert Callens won the stage and took the race lead in Boulogne-sur-Mer. He left the jersey in the team lorry overnight and, next morning, went to fetch it but . . . the lorry had left. He had to wear a yellow pullover instead (he later abandoned) and only recovered the precious tunic in 1994, in a staged presentation when the Tour came back to Boulogne.

The three times cyclo-cross World champion, Zdenek Štybar, of Martin's team won the stage. It was some compensation.

Next day, into Fougères, Brittany, produced, as the French say, 'a royal sprint'. The entire field together, the line fully extended by the impetuosity of the speed, a small posse of elite sprinters at the head, Štybar's teammate, Cavendish, locked in, Greipel jumps for the line, following Alexander Kristoff, Sagan in the white jersey of best young rider latching on, Cavendish, model of cool, spins up on Greipel's wheel, slots through and takes his 26th Tour stage win, one behind Bernard Hinault.

Poor Greg Henderson, having bravely ridden on with two broken ribs, finally capitulated.

Another rider, Luca Paolini, was also out. He'd tested positive for cocaine, not performance enhancing – save in the social sphere – but banned. In 2014, he'd got a wigging for cruising along in the middle of the bunch texting from his mobile. What a clot.

The Mûr de Bretagne, the so-called l'Alpe d'Huez of Brittany, 2km, at an average gradient of 6.9% and some places at 15%, lies some distance out of the eponymous village. A sharp right-hand bend flings the riders onto a long, straight ramp of some 10% – the top is in plain view from the foot – so that position in the front group was vital. Contador, Froome, Quintana and Van Garderen were there, Nibali not in evidence. The pace quickened, several riders tried to spring out of the small pack and were ridden down, until the young Ag2R rider Alexis Vuillermoz, in his first Tour, made a decisive break, pursued by Daniel Martin whose Cannondale team had striven so hard for him in the closing kilometres of the stage. Alas, Vuillermoz was too strong. He took it, the first French winner of a stage in this Tour.

Nibali came in on his own, disconsolate, ten seconds down on his rivals. Greipel slumped badly, Sagan took over the green jersey as well as holding onto the white.

The team time-trial: 28km from Vannes to Plumelec, in the heart of Brittany . . . and Breton fans will tell you that here is where the true soul of cycling is to be found. The crowds gathered at the barriers gave some proof of that.

The course began flat but moved into a lumpier line and the final section, of nearly two kilometres, ran up a long drag of around 7% with a strenuous final stretch of 12%.

The current World champions in the discipline – introduced in 2012 – team BMC, hoped to put 13-plus seconds into the Sky men so that Van Garderen might wrest the yellow jersey from Froome.

Froome wore a closely tailored yellow skinsuit, made for him by a local seamstress, no detail overlooked to make his profile as aerodynamic as possible.

Quintana's Movistar team held the leader board for some time at 32m 19s. Contador's Tinkoff-Saxo faltered and lost 24 seconds. Astana faded, too, so that Nibali lost 35 seconds to the Colombian climber. Sky, equal with and then ahead of BMC at the two time checks, finally ceded by 6/100 of a second – poor Nicholas Roche cracked in the last metres and, as fifth man of the finishing group, his time was what counted. Interviewed afterwards, Porte said 'it was brutal. After 5km, it was agony.'

This was the first time that the Tour had included the approach to the Col de La Pierre Saint-Martin – 15km long at around 8% with a flatter run-in – from the French side. In 2007, its first inclusion, the route ran across from Spain.

The first day in the mountains is always a jolt. After nine days on the flat, turning big gears at high speed, the muscles have to acclimatise to a very exacting change of rhythm: twirling small gears on rising gradient into thinner air. This stage added the strain of 150km of fairly flat ground to the sudden shock of the final climb.

The pack began to loosen and disintegrate even as the climb snarled at them. On this Bastille Day, the Frenchmen Bardet, Péraud, Pinot and Thomas Voeckler began to slip behind, so too Andrew Talansky of America and the Sky rider Kennaugh, then even Rodríguez, a contender for the mountains prize.

Robert Gesink, who'd had concerns about his heart last year, attacked on his own at 11.2km to go and, not long afterwards, Nibali cracked. Movistar, who'd already expended a lot of needless energy driving the pace on the flat, now picked up speed, Alejandro Valverde and Quintana looking good. Froome and three Sky men were on their wheel, Froome playing a mild bluff – dropping back, surging on again – which may have prompted Valverde to accelerate away to put extra pressure on him. Porte and Thomas reeled Valverde in whilst behind them, smitten by this abrupt change of rhythm, Contador fell away, 6.8km to go. The Spaniard later said: 'I couldn't breathe. I couldn't turn my legs.'

Now Porte, Froome and Quintana were on their own at the

front. Suddenly, Froome sped away from them, the gap extending visibly as he spun his pedals at an astonishingly fast cadence. Within a kilometre, 5km from the line, he had a 27s gap on Quintana and, perhaps, saw the big banner with a photograph of him and the legend, part in Swahili: 'Lion of the Savannah, Simba wa nyika.'

The crowds on the upper reaches made passage exceedingly difficult, even perilous, crowding Froome and the leading riders so close, dense as weeds in a pond, running alongside, flapping flags, gesticulating, waving banners in the riders' faces. For a cyclist riding at the extreme of effort and focus, such behaviour is horribly disturbing. These are not fans. They're morons.

Porte dropped away behind Quintana even as his leader Froome was racing further and further ahead. But, somehow, Porte recovered and began to come back on Quintana.

Froome raised his arms in victory, two years to the day since his last mountain stage win, on Mont Ventoux. And Porte, having caught Quintana, put on a burst to finish second. A minute later, Thomas and Valverde arrived and, as they crossed the line, Thomas patted the Spaniard on the back. Thomas later said that the pair of them had sat on Van Garderen's wheel for several kilometres, unwilling to pass him and give him draught. When Valverde attacked, Thomas – who'd been 'very frustrated' – was released from police work and went with him.

The losses back down the field tell the rest of the story: Quintana had lost another 1m 4s, Van Garderen 2m 30s, Contador 2m 51s, Nibali, who confessed 'I'm not even the little brother of last year's Nibali', 4m 25s. The best Frenchman on this national day was Tony Gallopin, 2m 22s down. The rest were nowhere.

'Carnage' is a favourite cliché with some hacks. On this day, one may say the word earned its corn.

Froome said that he'd planned his attack here. He chose the last of the very steep section of the climb to launch it, then, as the slope evened out somewhat, he went into time-trialling mode, pedalling at the very rapid cadence on which he's worked so hard, 100 revs per minute on the ascents. The fast turning of the pedals, as when a car driver changes to a lower gear to overtake, puts far less strain on the muscles but does make heavier demands on the oxygen intake. The technique has to be developed with long and sustained repetition. Some riders have tried to master it but failed.

Every evening, the holder of the yellow jersey faces an additional toil of attending a press conference, which means he often doesn't get to the team hotel till well after his teammates have gone for their massage. Very often, there'll be people waiting just for a glimpse of him, even the chance of waylaying him for an autograph or, these days, a selfie. Such delays and calls on his patience take their toll. When Froome returned to the hotel in Pau, after the Rest Day conference, he greeted the reception staff and made for the lift, where a man with his little girl persuaded him to stop for a photograph. Then he pressed the button to call the lift. It took an age to come and the kitchen staff ambushed him for a further round of selfies. Full of enthusiasm, a number of them also relayed their opinion of how the stage had gone. Froome, ever polite, fielded this whilst glancing surreptitiously at the lights by the lift door as it descended, floor by slow, slow floor.

'So, Chris,' said one of the cooks, 'you could have attacked earlier, no?' as he leaned in for the pop of the mobile camera.

'Ah, I don't know,' said Froome as another of the men was advising him to 'attack again tomorrow'.

'Thanks for the advice,' said Froome as the lift doors opened and he was, at last, released to head for the haven of his room.

Perhaps they'd expected a show of euphoria – great attack, fine win, strengthening hold on the leadership of the race – rather than the quiet containment of a man doing his job.

Stage 11, 188km over the Cols d'Aspin and du Tourmalet, finished on the third-category ascent to Cauterets. It was unlikely that the main contenders would do other than ride it out, recover from their effort and conserve energy ahead of the third Pyrenean stage.

Contador's Tinkoff-Saxo team was badly in need of a morale boost – their leader trailing, Ivan Basso gone home for surgery on testicular cancer, Daniele Bennati, a strong rider for the mountains, suffering from what proved, this day, to be a suspected broken leg and forced to abandon. Their man Rafal Majka, the Pole who'd won the mountains prize in 2014, was, therefore, released to make his own attack. He succeeded, followed in by Daniel Martin, who rode with exceptional fortitude, first to bridge the long gap on a breakaway group and then forge away from them after the Pole.

Nibali lost another 50 seconds on the tame climb to the finish; Bardet, who was suffering from sunstroke, vomiting even as he rode, lost nearly 14 minutes; Péraud and Pinot (at over 22 minutes) were humiliated. Porte still wore the polka dot jersey actually held by Froome.

The best way to see the Tour de France is in terrain as close to its original setting as possible: a small mountain village. Massat, at the foot of the Port de Lers, is one such. The race swept up the wooded valley of the fish-replete river Arac, under a banner on the lead-in welcoming it to the Land of the Bear, swung across the tiny market square and, like icing in a confectioner's tube, squeezed through the twisting narrow street named for the col ahead, rue de Port.

I was there to watch them with a man who's done so much to foster interest in cycling in this lovely area, Nick Flanagan, to enjoy the essential aperitif to the arrival of the Grande Boucle in the community: a good lunch. And we join other fans at Le Maxil, now Massat's hub for cyclist visitors and the enthusiasm for and of two wheels. Dylan's the man. The shelves of his vibrant hostelry are lined with the library of cycling books he took over from Flanagan and, this day, the place is doing that wonderfully French thing, celebrating their Tour at the side of the quiet road they walk every day. No barriers. Just the entire population plus visitors cheering through the giants of the route as their ancestors did the first time the race came through here, before television, before the publicity caravan, before mechanical assistance, in 1910, the first year the Pyrenees were included. The excitement is tangible, like a village turning out to welcome a local hero back from the big city. The riders are so close, the pulse of their speed, the thrum of the spokes, the exotic flash of multi-coloured jerseys, the magnetism . . .

The break of three goes through, more than 11 minutes up on the main field and some distance from a chasing group. We wait. The town bates its breath and then they're on us, the big crowd, Sky on the front looking after the slight figure of Froome, Quintana locked on his back wheel, Nibali there, Contador and . . . too many to identify, they're past, trailing wonder, like the sun's afterglow.

The final climb of the day, Plateau de Beille, is a stinker and made worse this day by a heavy storm – hailstones as big as blueberries battering the road on the climb's upper reaches. The rain eventually eased even as the scrap for the win developed. It was Rodríguez who cut loose from the pursuers to overtake the breakaways. Michal Kwiatkowski, current World road champion but no climber, held on bravely to a diminishing lead until Rodríguez overtook him and, clearly in some distress himself, flogged his legs and body on to victory, his second of the Tour.

Behind him, Froome, accompanied by the seemingly indefatigable Thomas and Porte, fended off a succession of attacks. Contador, small gap, Porte stays calm, brings him in. Nibali next. Same reaction. Now Valverde, Sky men unfazed. Then, at 3.5km, Quintana, even as Porte, who'd spent his own reserves, slipped off the back. Now Froome himself blazed off the front. It didn't last and they stayed together, Van Garderen included – he's told a press conference that he's not in a position to attack, he's playing the long game – until, some 100 metres from the line, Valverde sprinted away, chased by an obviously weary Froome, who lost a mere second on the line.

Bardet had somehow recovered himself, was in the lead group and straggled in with them.

This had been a slugging match. The hard spoiling grounds of the Pyrenees handed over to those of the Alps. Not that the transition was in any way soft. An up and down excursus through the Tarn valley into the Aveyron led to three days of gruelling slog over four fourth-category, two third-category and three second-category climbs.

The first of these four stressful days was made tougher by blistering temperatures – nigh on 40 degrees – and claggy humidity. A break of six riders hit the road early on, the bunch content to let them go and conserve energy.

At about 60 kilometres to go, the hapless Péraud, perhaps ruffled by a fluke of the cross-wind, nudged a wheel and took a hideous fall. He tumbled, rolled, slid on the scorching tarmac and skinned his left arm, leg and upper thigh. The poor man, obviously deeply shocked and in considerable pain, nevertheless remounted and took off after the group, already some three minutes ahead of him. The race doctor patched him up even as he rode alongside the car and, showing great fortitude, the French rider chased, caught and came in with the main peloton.

The six escapees became three with about 20km to go, even as the bunch began to wind up to hound them with greater purpose. It was another of those bitter last-minute pounces. On the final steep 500-metre climb up to the cathedral above Rodez, they hove into view and swallowed the wilting men who'd been out alone for so long. The Belgian Greg van Avermaet pipped Sagan by a bike length. More chagrin for the Slovak, who'd come second on four stages now.

The Sky team had suffered verbal abuse from the side of the road – suspicions, of course, about their domination of the pace-making and Froome's electrifying spurts of acceleration. This day, Porte was actually clouted in the final three kilometres – 'I got a full-on punch,' he said. 'It was the same atmosphere on l'Alpe d'Huez two years ago.'

The Gorges du Tarn, a deep chasm which slices through the Cévennes, took the riders over four categorised climbs, the road nosing through archway galleries cut from the living rock, below them the twisting course of the river, above, the limestone Causses plateaux.

The lead group of some 20 riders got to the foot of the final climb, a nasty 3km haul out of Mende, average gradient around 10% with some stretches between 11% and 12% with time in hand. It was Bardet who made the first significant move. He rode hard for the summit from where a fast descent led onto the runway of Mende's aerodrome. Pinot slowly pulled away after his compatriot, bringing Rigoberto Urán with him. Urán faded, Pinot caught Bardet but, not far from the summit, the Englishman Steve Cummings, riding for the MTN-Qubeka team, celebrating Mandela Day with an orange flash on their helmets, rode up behind them. They hesitated, he did not and pounded on, flat out for the line, to give his team, a wild-card entry to the Tour, the honour of a stage win.

Behind them, the main contenders were at the front of the pack. Quintana went first, Froome didn't answer, Nibali and Valverde joined him, Contador sat on Froome's wheel. Such is Froome's glacial calm that he gradually brought Quintana back and, in the process, dropped Contador and Valverde. Nibali, too, had spent his effort as Froome and Quintana rode on together. The Colombian attacked again, Froome came back, Valverde dropped Contador at high speed and, nearing the line, Froome jumped past Quintana to lead him in for the gain of another second. Van Garderen lost second place overall to Quintana.

After the race, Froome reported that some 50–60km from the start, a man standing at the side of the road threw a cupful of urine at him and screamed 'Doped'. Sky's dominant style of riding doesn't endear them to a public deprived of a home winner since Hinault's fifth victory in 1985.

Jean-René Bernaudeau, director of Europcar (and once more in quest of a new sponsor), said that it was 'indecent to cast aspersions on Froome's performance' and Sylvain Chavanel, riding what may well be his last Tour, denounced the doubters, saying he felt no sense of unease about the Sky team in the peloton, implying that if the riders are satisfied that Sky are riding clean, then they are.

Cavendish (recovering from a bout of diarrhoea), Kennaugh and Péraud (the dressing of whose wounds took a painful 30–45 minutes each morning) came in with the autobus this day, as Greipel took his third stage win on the flatlands of the Rhône valley in Valence.

Before the second Rest Day, Stage 16 made a tough ride of 201 kilometres, largely uphill and over a couple of second-category climbs to the tricky descent from the Col de Manse (1,268m) into Gap, on which Joseba Beloki fell in 2003 (see p. 287). So nervous were the organisers of the possibility of melting of tarmac that they sent out two water bowsers to spray the road. Kennaugh, who'd been ailing for some time, didn't start.

A break of 23 riders went early and built a substantial lead, among them Sagan, still hunting for his first stage win since 2013, but, gathering intermediate sprint points, consolidating his grip on the green jersey which he's won three years running. Also there, the Frenchmen Voeckler, Pierrick Fédrigo, Christophe Riblon, all experienced opportunist winners, hoping to bring France some glory.

At 46km from the finish, their lead over the main peloton at 17-plus minutes, the former Australian time-trial champion, Adam Hansen, cut loose and swiftly built a gap before the group, really too big for efficient organisation, got its act together and cranked up its own speed. Then Hansen was joined by the Austrian road champion Marko Haller and they increased their lead to 46 seconds. Since the 9km, 6% climb of the Col de Manse was looming, they needed to build a solid advantage to give them any chance against the chase.

Nearing Gap, the road runs past the mighty natural citadel of the Montagne de la Grande Céüse, a flat-topped height with a ring of cliff ramparts beneath it and a slanting glacis at their foot.

The escape group came back together. Three MTN-Qubeka riders were there and, were they to preserve this large time gap over the bunch at the finish, the African outfit would dislodge Movistar in the lead of the team competition. (In the event, they didn't.)

A number of riders made tentative attempts to break free to go for a stage win, closely monitored by Sagan, but it was the 35-year-old Spaniard Ruben Plaza, in his 16th year as a professional, who finally got away. Although Sagan – an exceptional bike-handler – clawed back on the descent a goodly chunk of the 55-second time gap Plaza had at the col, he came second again but now held the green jersey by 89 points over Greipel.

Froome and company launched onto the descent of the Manse and Nibali attacked. He was scraping up seconds, but who knew what he might yet do in the Alps? On one corner, Warren Barguil took a dreadful line, lost control, sliced across the road straight into Thomas, who careered off, over a line of tapes, and cartwheeled 12 metres down the vertical bank, bashing a lamp-post on the way. It looked bad but he scrambled back up, remounted and was away. He lost only 38 seconds and kept his sixth position overall.

His teammate, Porte, had sagged from the main group some while before and so, too, Gallopin, certain, therefore, to lose his high placing. Another setback for the French contingent.

Nibali's attack garnered him 28 seconds, small change on the eight-minute deficit he was carrying.

Stage 17. Digne-les-Bains–Pra Loup. 161km.
Ushering in four tough days in the Alps, on a stage which duplicated a stage of the recent Dauphiné Libéré, a string of lesser climbs built towards the long drag of the Col d'Allos, at 2,250m, what's known as the roof of this year's race.

From the pass, the road swishes into a notoriously tricky descent of some 17km, at the bottom of which the route swings left onto a 6.1km climb to the ugly ski station at Pra Loup, the gradient at the top quite stiff. On this climb, on a stage which followed this same route, Bernard Thévenet ended Eddy Merckx's domination of the race in 1975 (see p. 43) and in 1980, another yellow jersey, Joop Zoetemelk also came to grief. Riding in the slipstream of the young champion of Holland, Johan van de Velde, Zoetemelk nicked the wheel – his fellow Dutchman had wobbled as his chain slipped – fell heavily but managed to remount and save the jersey, which he later took to Paris.

Today marked only the third time Pra Loup had featured in the Tour.

Halfway into the stage, on the lower slopes of the Col de la Colle de Saint-Martin, poor Van Garderen, sick and unable to go on, abandoned in tears.

An escape of 28 riders had cut loose early, among them two men from Movistar, two from Tinkoff-Saxo (Majka and Sagan), and Porte and Roche from Sky, with the clear objective of being available to wait for their leader if necessary. Some ten minutes back, the yellow jersey group consisted of 12 riders. Contador is a noted racer, with a fiery disposition and a taste for random attack. On this prelude to the Allos, he made just such an attack, got no further than 100 metres and was reclaimed without difficulty. At 75km from the finish, it was a worthless expenditure of energy, a pointless attempt at showing that he was in good form. It seemed, rather, an exercise in impatience.

On the Col d'Allos, riders started to cut loose from the lead group, without getting clear until Teklehaimanot managed to do so and then Simon Geschke, who overtook the Eritrean and built a substantial lead. Pinot, anxious to recover something from the rubble of his Tour, now set off at a blistering 24kph in pursuit of Geschke.

Obedient to team tactics, Porte let the rest of the breakaways forge on whilst he waited for Froome, who rode up behind Nibali as two Astana men forced the pace. Nibali, reckoned to be the best downhill man in the peloton, clearly intended to go hell for leather on the descent.

Porte, due to leave the Sky team at the end of the season, nevertheless continues to show an unswerving devotion to Froome and the team objective of overall victory. Men like him, the close support riders, demonstrate, through a force of will and sacrifice of personal ambition, the fidelity to cause of Achilles' Myrmidons.

Pinot crossed the col just over a minute down on Geschke but he's a very jittery descender. Thus his chase was compromised from the outset. On a nasty left-hand bend, his back wheel locked, he fell and, though he remounted at once, his nerves were shot and he continued to lose time. Indeed, he was overtaken by two other men from the breakaways, Andrew Talansky and the young British rider Adam Yates.

Contador, Froome, Porte, Nibali, Quintana, Valverde hit the descent, Froome close on Nibali's wheel. Contador goes down, his bike is damaged; Sagan, one of the escapees, has waited, hands him his bike.

Way ahead, Talansky tried to chase Geschke down but in vain. Geschke's win made it five for Germany on the Tour.

Under the red kite, on a very steep section – some 15% – Froome and company were still together after various sniping attacks aimed at dislodging him. Quintana and Valverde tried, Froome raced back. Again, Quintana burst clear, but Froome was on him. They accelerated away from the others and crossed the line together. Valverde came in 7s adrift, Nibali at 15s, Thomas – who'd fought his way back – 1m 2s (and into fourth position overall). Unlucky Contador, 2m 17s down, was now fifth overall.

Thomas's admission that he 'really had to grovel' might speak for them all.

There's been much suspicion about Froome's superiority, among sections of the French press, a prejudice fuelled by the pernicious legacy of Armstrong's lying. On the patent evidence of Froome's driving himself to the utter limit of his effort, there's no sense that he's a superman. Just very, very strong. Last year, when Nibali was so obviously in the ascendant? Not a peep. But the French riders were performing brilliantly.

The main climb of Stage 18, the Col du Glandon, is one of the nastiest in the area: a steady uphill of just over 30 kilometres from the valley of the Romanche, virtually no respite, and, although the slopes lower down are relatively mild, the upper level gradients push up to 11%.

The star attraction of the day, a new inclusion, was the zigzag stairway of the 18 hairpins, the Lacets de Montvernier, built between 1928 and 1934, 3.4km long, crooked as a firecracker or a coiled intestine, at upwards of 8–9%, from which the road drops into Saint-Jean de Maurienne, included for only the second time. It might be a squashed spiral staircase mounting from the ground floor of the Arc valley to the roof-top garden of Montvernier. So narrow is the road that spectators were barred and to see a climb bereft of bystanders was eerie, although there were knots of long-distance observers perched in eyries on the bare crags overlooking the ascent's tight loops.

A group went clear, lesser riders determined to try for a stage win as the race neared its conclusion. The yellow jersey group moved onto the Glandon more than three minutes down on the leaders and, inevitably, the attacks came, but they were jabs, not haymakers. Contador went and got nearly a minute clear, but incited no reaction from the six Sky riders at the front of the pack. In fact, given Contador's deficit on GC, it was for Movistar (Quintana) or Astana (Nibali) to challenge and Sky to tag along.

Bardet made an audacious move with some distance to go and went full out for the col. He crossed with around 40 seconds on his nearest pursuer and set off on what is a much more lenient descent than many.

Meanwhile, Contador flagged, the yellow jersey group was once more compact and making for the descent. The expected assault by the swooping Nibali didn't come, Froome and the rest held him with apparent ease and, although Valverde fell back at one point, he fought back on. From here on in, there seemed no chance of any serious split in this group, as Bardet raced on, held his lead, dancing up and over the *lacets* ('hairpins') and down into the town where his compatriot, Sandy Caspar, had won in 2010. Bardet's courageous ride moved him into tenth place overall, first Frenchman in the standings.

Froome and company came in together. Any mountain stage that finishes on a downhill offers less real chance of a lethal attack, unless from some way out and the cost in energy – and moral strength – this requires risks leaving the attacker at a disadvantage next day. With two uphill finishes to come, the opportunity for decisive duels was dwindling.

As for the sprinters and non-climbers, the four-day hammering of the climax to this race was a torment, the purgatory before they rode onto the Elysian Fields of the Paris boulevards. Cavendish, who was suffering from diarrhoea, said he also had a dose of chicken pox, in mock allusion to the splatter of red dots on the stage routes, marking the climbs.

The domestiques deserve at least collective mention. Their role is humble but crucial to the fortunes of the team and merely to finish the Tour is a remarkable achievement.

Stage 19 began straight onto the climb of the Col de Chaussy, a Tour debutant, and the Sky team was immediately reeling from a savage attack by Nibali and his team. At the top of the climb, Froome was isolated, his only supporting rider the Dutch climber Wouter Poels. But Nibali eased up, the race steadily coalesced and it was on the long slog of the Col de la Croix de Fer (which refers to the wrought-iron cross by the col, marking out a pilgrimage route) that the real fight started.

Although the French language gave us a number of words for decent behaviour – *politesse, courtoisie, galanterie, etiquette* – it's significant that it borrows an English expression for sportsmanship . . . *le fairplay*. It's a mark of Tour decorum that when the yellow jersey has a mechanical problem there should be no attack on him. However, nearing the top of the Croix de Fer, Froome had to stop to remove a small stone locking up his back wheel against the brake calliper. Nibali glanced across, saw him in trouble and attacked. He later denied that he'd seen Froome in trouble and that the attack – some two kilometres from the col as the gradient eased – was planned. Television showed him plainly looking at the yellow jersey. The stoppage cost Froome some 30 seconds.

Nibali was set on using the descent to make time and, riding with something like the verve he showed last year, he overtook Pierre Rolland, thus squashing yet another French hope of a stage win on the uphill of La Toussuire. Froome – who was spat at by a spectator in the last kilometres – and Quintana (at 44 seconds) raced in third and second respectively after the Colombian attacked the Briton and took 32 seconds out of him. Froome was clearly not impregnable. Nor, alas, Thomas, who paid for his sterling defence in the past few days: he finished 22 minutes down.

His words may speak for many of the riders: 'I was just empty today. It was always going to happen, I guess . . . As they say, sometimes you're the hammer, sometimes you're the nail. I was a cheap IKEA nail today. It was a tough start and when you've got nothing in your legs there's nothing you can do.'

The Frenchman Bardet had been going hard for mountain points and he finished three ahead of Froome, thereby taking the polka dot jersey. This had not been a good Tour for the French, ill luck and the sheer class of the top men had cost them dear, but not in spirit. Péraud was still there, his injuries notwithstanding, the Europcar team were doing all they could to push for screen time by joining the breaks, with the hope of winning a stage, and Pinot and Bardet with them.

Nibali's late throw of aggression had lifted him to fourth overall, at the expense of Contador, who was now fifth, but Froome confronted him about his sly attack. If the tone of his public declaration – 'that's not what you do to a leader' – was mild, reportedly his manner with the Italian was all but.

The finale on l'Alpe d'Huez promised a battle à l'outrance . . . without quarter, between Froome and his immediate challenger, Quintana, who had still not given up on overall victory.

And so it proved.

The Alpe is a merciless climb, not so much because of the road itself but for the wild press of the crowd shrinking the tarmac to a slender ribbon up which the riders must pass. And add to that the accumulated fatigue of three weeks' racing, bodily stress (Froome had, it transpired, been suffering from a debilitating chest infection since the second Rest Day), the steepness of the tight hairpins, the heat and thinning air, the exhaust fumes of cars and motorbikes, the battery of noise and frenzied movement of the crowd distracting and menacing them at such close quarters.

One of the tunnels which lie between the foot of the Col du Galibier and Bourg d'Oisans, at the foot of l'Alpe d'Huez, had collapsed so that the original route – which included the Galibier – had to be changed. The riders were now directed up the approach of the Croix de Fer down which they'd descended the day before, down the Glandon and round to the final climb.

It was for Movistar and their top men, Quintana and Valverde, to take the fight to Sky. They made their first move on the Croix de Fer. Froome's support men, all very tired from a manful defence of their leader, dropped away and, as the front men crested the col, Froome and Porte were alone. Perhaps through indecision or reluctance to take such an all-out risk so early, Quintana and Valverde didn't press their advantage and, bit by bit, the Sky support guard, Thomas, Roche and Poels, rejoined on the descent.

Ahead of them, Pinot, having cut loose from a small breakaway group, which included Quintana's Colombian climber teammate Winner Anacona, was building a solid lead of around three minutes into Bourg d'Oisans and the first of the famous 21 hairpins of the Alpe. Number 7 is the infamous Dutch corner where the men in orange scream, run alongside the bikes, waving arms and fists in the riders' faces, let off orange smoke flares – a veritable bedlam.

Froome, his men, Quintana and Valverde arrived. A mere 13.8km for Quintana to claw back 2m 38s. Anacona was somewhere ahead of him, ready to give him support.

For eight kilometres, the yellow jersey and Quintana rode together. At 5km from the finish, Quintana burst clear. He'd probably left it too late but would Froome's effort hold? Poels and Porte were still with him, then only Poels, sometimes going too fast – Froome saying 'slow down' – then too slow – Froome: 'up the pace' – report of Quintana's gains in his earpiece . . . increments of five seconds, ten seconds . . . he had nearly a minute, but the road was running out for him. Now he came up alongside Anacona. He had support.

Meanwhile, a man in a polka dot jersey leaned in towards Froome and spat at him. The torment of what Froome was going through at that point is barely imaginable. Two voices in his head: 'enough, no more of this, your body can't take it . . .' and 'don't give up now, you're too close, too close . . .' He later said that he'd been on his absolute limit, not knowing which way this was going to go. 'I felt I was dying a thousand deaths,' he said, 'but being with my teammates meant I had something left for the final kilometres when I was on my own.'

In that final kilometre he was holding, Quintana had taken all the time he was going to take. By some force of will, Froome drove himself on even as his overall lead dwindled second by second, but only second by second.

And Pinot . . . Pinot was close, too. On the run-in to the line, where the slope peters out onto a flat stretch, he turned round anxiously to see if there was any challenge. There, at the end of the finishing straight, he could see Quintana, but too far away. It was Pinot's day, lone Frenchman on the Alpe, a single stage but a massive victory.

Quintana came in 18 seconds down and waited. His only chance was if Froome cracked. He didn't. Obviously *in extremis*, he 'turned himself out' (in the parlance) and saved his yellow jersey by 1m 12s. There was a brief moment of mutual respect between the two men: Quintana, slumped on a chair, barely able to lift his arm, Froome, coughing, leaning down to shake his hand, both men exhausted.

Although Bardet surrendered the polka dots, he crossed the line in the jersey and hoisted himself into ninth on General Classification. His countryman Rolland, who finished a mere three seconds behind Froome, jumped to tenth. The French had a bad time this year, but these two young men delivered something of compensation on a very hard-fought race, from the very start in Utrecht. Bardet and Pinot also thrived in the competition for the white and the polka dots jerseys – top five in both.

Froome had also done something which only four other men

had done, in winning both the overall and mountains prize – Gino Bartali, Fausto Coppi and Merckx, twice; Federico Bahamontes, once. But his great triumph was this second victory, something no other Briton has done, and against three of the best stage racers in the peloton on surely the hardest course the Tour de France has covered in recent times.

From Sèvres, home of the famous porcelain factory, to Paris, the roads were awash with rain.

It was 40 years since the Tour first arrived on the Champs Elysées and, for the second year in succession, La Course, an 89km race for professional women, covered 13 laps of the finishing circuit hours before the Tour arrived. Unhappily, there was a succession of crashes on the slick wet cobbles. A heap of riders went down on the last lap almost in sight of the line. It was shocking bad luck, a huge shame that this new race should be so marred. Victory went to the Dutch time-trial champion Anna van der Breggen. Britain's Lizzie Armitstead, who crashed last year, came fourth.

As a result, the Tour organisation ruled that, once the race had reached the final circuit, all challenge for the overall jerseys would finish. Thus Froome in yellow and polka dots, Quintana in white (for the second time), Sagan in green (for the fourth year running) would be secure.

The sprinters had been offered very few chances for a win this year. (They grumbled.) Even the victory Cavendish took was not on a stage he'd earmarked as a strong possibility. Facing the last stage without two strong men on his team, Martin and Renshaw, who'd had to abandon, he might consider his chances much reduced. But his other win had come when he was on his own. His tactic must be to get a good wheel to follow.

Despite the neutralising of the race overall, attacks did come, as they always do on this great boulevard, a fine showcase, and the attacks were, one by one, snuffed out. A full bunch charged the finishing line and it was Greipel who made it four victories for this Tour, thrusting out of the pack for a convincing victory. A great race for him, the sixth German stage win of the race.

Froome and the Sky team rode across in line abreast, arms round shoulders and, from the winner's podium, Froome read from a speech he'd prepared, in riposte to the accusations that he and the team had suffered during the race. 'The *maillot jaune* is special, very special. I understand its history, good and bad, and I will always respect it, never dishonour it and I'll always be proud to have won it.'

This was not, could not be, enough for sceptics who have only their prejudicial suspicion to reinforce opinion. Those who call for the publication of data will probably not be convinced either: numbers can be manipulated. As someone once said, there are lies, damned lies and statistics.

Perhaps the most cogent proof that he – and his teammates in an outfit that declared from its inception that it would not tolerate even a hint of malpractice – rides clean is the sight of him, more than once, on the very edge of physical collapse. A team that dopes does not suffer such lapses. A rider who dopes does not lose 22 minutes in a single day, as Thomas did. One thing obvious about Froome's win is the man's enormous moral and mental strength. As Desgrange, the father of the Tour, said, to win it takes head and legs, and, note, he put *head* first.

Cycling is the one sport where a single individual wins a race and the whole team is credited with victory. Insight into how this ethic, puzzling to some, works came from Luke Rowe of Sky, speaking of Froome's riding in the 2014 Vuelta: 'There was one day where he was dropped time after time but kept drawing himself back into it, turning himself inside out. When you have a leader who's prepared to kill himself where other guys would throw in the towel, that's why you get eight guys prepared to put themselves on the line for him. He's a pleasure to work for.'

AFTERWORD AND
MYTHOLOGY

AFTERWORD

There used to be two types of rugby player: those who played the piano and those who shifted them. I have an idea there are two sorts of racing cyclist, too: those you'd want to spend time with and those you're happy to get no closer to than television allows. On 18 October 1997, in the tiny Pyrenean town of Oust, we're about to meet one of the former. I rode through here in July and have come back to the Ariège to ride some cols, go for walks with my daughter, Lucy, do some work and renew acquaintance with our hosts, Nick and Jan, cooks extraordinaire and cycling fans complete, who run a small guest house along the valley for cyclists and walkers keen to enjoy their special brand of support for Pyrenean Pursuits, the name of their enterprise.

Nick met us at Toulouse airport and we dropped in at Oust on the way home to enjoy half an hour of the Fête du Fan Club Frédéric Moncassin, a day of VTT (mountain bike) races on a circuit specially designed by Frédo. He's a big star, leading sprinter for the GAN team, a pal of Chris Boardman's, but a local boy, too. He lives in a hamlet below the crest of the col du Saraillé a few miles away – he couldn't imagine living anywhere else. Here he is, turning out for a day mixing it with local amateurs, semi-pros and a handful of other star names: Stéphane Barthe, Christophe Rinero, Henk Vogels – pals of his from the *peloton*, jobbed in to add frisson to the occasion. We park the car. Cyclists are everywhere, cruising idly or tinkering with the machines – a true cyclist is always tinkering, they say. Indeed, a pal of mine at school almost never had his bike, a very superior model, on the road: it was always in bits on the kitchen table, having its ballbearings massaged. Anyway, we found Moncassin changing an inner tube in his front tyre, chatting with a couple of bystanders. Nick went up – Frédo recognised him from a casual encounter a year ago – and they exchanged greetings, Moncassin autographed a couple of programmes – one for me – and we moved on.

There was nothing in it for Moncassin other than pleasing his fan club, drinking a *vin d'honneur* with the Mayor at 6 p.m. and chilling out at the dinner and knees-up with a local band later on, except for *amour du vélo* . . . love of the bike. It's what links us all, whether we're riding for fun or hitting the front of a jostling, jittery bunch at 60+kph, where a touch of wheels, a flailing elbow, a sideways rock of the frame can bring you down under a charge of wheels. You risk broken bones that put you out for the rest of the season, but routinely take risks for the glory of coming through ahead, winner of the stage. Moncassin missed out this year; second by four millimetres, stage four, a day of gruesome crashes, several riders out with injury, but he was there day after day. A slim-built guy, his father was a great sprinter, too: the power seems to come from the buttocks, the instinct from the family genes, the courage from somewhere under the jersey.

The Tour de France rode past Nick and Jan's house in 1997 and will do so again in 1998. The night before it passed in '97, there'd been a huge beano, of course: visiting cyclists from England, local enthusiasts, a trio of filmmakers from Liverpool Cycle Centre putting a short documentary together. Then came the big question: What were they going to paint on the road outside the house? Messages to the Wirral man, Boardman, naturally: Attack it, Chris. However, when it came to partisan advertising, Jan put her foot down: No, strictly *no*, Pyrenean Pursuits.

It is 4 a.m., dawn squeezing itself under night's black-out curtain, Nick and the graffiti team are out on the road scrawling the legends in white daub, when Simon O'Brien one of the inspirations behind the Liverpool Cycling Centre says:' 'How do you spell Pyrenean Pursuits?' Jan, fast asleep in bed, is what she terms a 'creative speller' and there was some doubt. But the legend is still there, and in the house a photo of the *peloton* ambling across it at a leisurely 32kph, the gaudy array of team strips offset by bunting in the trees, flags and miniature jerseys strung from the electricity poles. The Tour de France doing today what Desgrange's vision shaped nearly a century ago. Was he, come to think of it, inspired even a little by the imperial Persian horse-couriers of ancient times, the original Pony Express: 'Nothing in the world travels faster than the Persian horse-couriers, and it's a Persian invention, exploiting their network of imperial roads. A relay of horses and riders is stationed along a fixed route, one man and one mount for each day of the journey. Nothing stops them: not snow, rain, heat of the sun, or night-time.' (Herodotos, *Histories*).

On our autumn visit to Biert, Lucy and I walked up to the Queire de Massat – a majestic view along the valley of the River Arac towards the ranges hiding the col de Port, and home to a tiny woodland shrine to a Saint Branda, ignored by my hagiographies. We drove up to the col de Crouzette (I cycled it first: a bit of a facer, 5km of acute angle to round it off, which make you think twice about this 'love of the bike' stuff) and for four hours rambled through sweet chestnut and dwarf oaks, birch and beech trees to the crease of the valley, across the stream and up the other side. We passed ruined stone houses, home to recluses in the last century who weathered winter and summer up there, several hours trek from any source of food to augment what the woods could not provide. There are mushrooms in abundance for a few weeks of the year, every year, except that mushroom pickers tread the mulch at their peril these days: the hunting lobby have introduced *sangliers* (wild boar, favoured nosh of Obélix and Astérix) into the high woods and, for their own safety – from flying wild buckshot rather than wild tusk – the mushroom gatherers are denied.

There were wolves and the famous black Pyrenean bears here once, but although an occasional mountain man turns up in the village and town squares hereabouts to show what twinkly toes the local bruins have, the danger in these sauvage regions comes largely from the human species.

Lucy rode her first col – the Saraillé – first the gentler way; which had a Liverpool racer squealing: he's a sprint specialist and rode up in company with a few of his teammates and Nick and, at the first bit of identifiable gradient, was complaining. This prepared Lucy, 17 years old, veteran of one family-sponsored Tour de Holland and the one-off Calais–Cherbourg six-day ride, for the ascent from the steeper side and that feeling familiar to all serious bikies of: 'Sod this for a pot of japonica jam, I've *had* it.' Yet, for some reason best left to God and guesswork, carrying on anyway.

I rode the col de Péguère, 3.5km of one in five, a side turning after 7km of the col de Port. The first 500m or so out of the saddle I was thinking I'd definitely had it and any more of this and I'd turn into a puddle of something not quite kosher in the middle of the road. I decided I'd better sit down and give that a go. Surprisingly, it worked, and though it would be an exaggeration to say the climb was easy, it *was* short and the view from the top – reckoned to be amongst the finest in the Pyrenees – was ample reward. So, too, the valley leading up to the col d'Agnès – whose towering breastlike peak is macabre reminder of the grisly way she was martyred: punitive mastectomy – a 16km ribbon of peaceful riding to a marvellous panorama into the next valley at whose foot nestle the old Roman spa town of Aulus-les-Bains. I rode over names of riders long retired – a trio of Dutch aces: Breukink, the all-rounder, Rooks, the climber, Van Poppel the sprinter.

Did Robert Millar – the British rider with the best record in the Tour, mountains prize and fourth overall in 1984 – rejoice in the view when he led the Tour over in 1988? He never strikes me as a rider who really *enjoys* anything. His approach to journalists and the rest of humanity makes Fignon look like Mr Helpful; not so much love of the bike as 'sod off'. The ferruginous springs at Aulus continued to draw health-seekers in their droves till the craze waned and the splendiferous lodgements for the fashionable visitors, such as the Grand Hotel, empty, decrepit, forlorn, became grand only in destitution. The hydrotherapy is starting up again, though, and Aulus may see a kind of prosperity once more. Its original celebrity depended on the patronage of officers in the French army, home on leave from the war in Indochina, with the clap. Aulus provided chemical salt cures; they came in droves and Aulus thrived. Times have changed and the pox-ridden aristos of the French military have evanesced; the resorts clings on.

These are, without doubt, the most beautiful mountains I've

ridden. The July of my earlier trip, we rode from Bayonne east, criss-crossing from France into Spain and back. The first two full days were murder: plunging off the main itineraries on to lonely cols in the inner ranges, we hit one in fours, thick mist, roads that seemed to peter out into grit-encrusted mud. On the Sunday, we tackled the col de Marie Blanque, 10km only, but in torrid heat. I was expecting daily to hear the news of my mother's death – she'd been to the brink of death and back several times that year – and I got as close to capitulation on that climb as I have ever been. Nightmares followed by hours awake had smitten me physically; an appalling dread that she had died that very night reduced me mentally. John had warned me way back in January that – against our normal pattern of lead and follow – he'd be racing me up this ascent and when he appeared alongside me I very nearly caved in. I had not the heart nor the legs, it seemed, for competition. He drew ahead on his lower gears and I watched him go by. Gradually, I did reel him in but, as I drew level, I said: 'I'm finished in my head,' and I was. If ever I have been embroiled in what they call the Calvary of extreme physical and mental duresse it was then.

John stopped for a pee and I had not the courage, not the magnanimity, to stop and wait; had I paused I might never have started up again. I was nearly hallucinating with the effort of keeping going, however. Then something of salvation filtered into my head: the slight zigzag using whatever camber there was to ease the gradient. It didn't *look* steep but it was doing some terrible things to me. Slowly the torment lessened; I found a rhythm, precious rhythm. I even quickened and, as I did so, realised that the pain in my head had gone and I was riding free once more. Not fast but free, and suddenly I was there, the blessed sign reading 'col' popped out from behind the trees like a treat at a surprise party. Later that same day we rode most of the climb of the Aubisque, to Eaux-Bonnes (no towns offered on the far side) and the day after that over the Aubisque itself, down the corniche which skirts the adjacent range and up and over the col de Soulor, where Boardman crashed. That afternoon we crossed the Tourmalet. It was one of the experiences of my life to cycle that legendary giant of the Tour, to emerge from the long twists of the lower valley road and see that massive bulk of the first buttress ahead of me, the road cut into its flank rising steeply in the shelter of the rock to where it turned round the corner and out of sight. What beyond the bend?

You ride up and find that beyond the bend is another buttress, another long ramp of road, several kilometres, but by now you've got the experience not to be deterred; just ride on until you can see in the far distance, where the hairpins swishing like a snake's tail finally straighten into the final few hundred metres and the topside refuge which means you're there. After 18km nothing, you feel, could stop you. Locals on either side of the mountain claim that their approach is the worse for the riders; certainly the southern ascent, from Bagnères, is steeper in places; the longer ride from Barèges imposes its own difficulties.

A day or two later, we rode the Port de Bonaigua. It lasts 28km, but is characteristic of these mountains: wooded valleys folded into sinuous rock walls, roads winding graciously to the ridges and down again like downhill skiers swaying their hips in a lovely slide along gravity's runway. More human in scale than the Alps, less tonsured than the Dolomites, wilder and more remote than both, the pleated green-clad Pyrenean ranges, dinted with countless valleys, are cycling perfection.

Another day of the October visit I cycled down the valley of the Arac, through Oust and up the long but beautiful haul towards Guzet Neige, the ski station where Robert Millar rode in to his second solo victory (of three overall) in 1984 and where, four years later, in company with Giotti, he turned right past a traffic cop instead of left, 3km from the top, into the car park.

After a visit to the market town of St Girons, browsing round second-hand bookshops and antiquated backstreets, Jan suggested a trip to see the memorial to Fabio Casartelli, the young Italian rider killed in 1995. It was a sombre ride in the car up through the village of Portet d'Aspet, on to the col and down through the trees. I'd seen the accident – moments after it happened – on French television: Casartelli lying inert on the road, no indication whether he was still alive. Virenque, the winner that day, wasn't told what had happened until he was sitting in the caravan waiting to mount the podium. As we drove down, I was riding the descent in my mind: marking the way the camber seems to tip out towards the verge, to make the sinuous ledge you're riding on slope away from the mountain wall, so that the already sharp right-hander has an extra danger built in. And the long, open, serpentine twists of the road occasionally tighten to make rounding the bend an abrupt lesson in balance, nerve, judicious braking.

Suddenly, we saw the memorial ahead: it stands a hundred metres or so uphill from where he skidded. Is it just imagination that makes that sharp curve, like a kink in wire, look so dramatically steeper, more frightening, than the others? The stone that was at first thought to have killed him (no blood was found on it) is gone; a low wall fringes the verge and, at the spot, a makeshift shrine – plaque, flowers, ribbons. Till recently, there had been a similar wrack of old tubs to that I saw on Ventoux for Simpson; for ages a Motorola cap signed by every member of the team – a valuable collectable for anyone meretricious enough to purloin it. No one did. There are such people: the thief who walked into the museum of the Tolpuddle martyrs in the village of their birth (entry free) and stole Emmett's watch, a worthless *objet* on any market. A judge once sent a convicted thief to the gallows for theft of a watch: 'You snatched at Time,' he said 'and you caught Eternity.'

The memorial itself is a beautiful structure in white marble: a finely sculpted disc wheel merging at the back into wings, rough-hewn to suggest feathers; the leading rim is swathed in a banner, streaming back as if in wind, and etched with the five interlocked rings of the Olympic Games – Casartelli was Olympic Road-Race Champion in 1992. On the rock face opposite the unofficial shrine, someone has daubed, in white paint now fading from the weather: *HOMMAGE À UN CHAMPION*.

When the Tour rode up the Portet d'Aspet in 1997, the whole *peloton* stopped by this silent testimony to the panache and courage of a young rider bursting with enthusiasm for his chosen *métier*, to pay their respects. His wife was there, his father and mother. A fleeting pause, a re-echo of the terrible grief of that dreadful day, and the *peloton* rode on.

And how many heroes of this epic Tour have I not even mentioned. Homer would have found room for them, every one. The Dutchman, van Est, in yellow, who, like Rivière, plunged off the road into a deep ravine, on the Cirque du Litor, and, to general astonishment, was hauled back out on a rope made of tyres unscathed. Iron Willem, he became. And would Anquetil have won five times had Rivière survived to match him? And what of André 'Dédé' Darrigade, sprinter extraordinary, winner of 22 Tour stages, five of them stage one; first Bobet's and then Anquetil's right-hand man, particularly on the end-to-end holding of the yellow jersey; holder of the golden fleece himself, and outright winner of green. Yet, he said of himself: 'I was always thought of as a team man and I never pretended to be anything more.' A team man like Jos de Schoenmaker, Merckx's faithful lieutenant, out of that fateful '71 Tour with a broken femur sustained in the Midi Libre. What a difference he might have made; except that Merckx did it, after all. And the strong man, Van Springel, robbed of yellow in the final time-trial, 1968, by Jan Janssen, still riding at the age of 37, green jersey in 1973. How could I give so little space to Felice Gimondi, winner at his first attempt in 1965, of whom Merckx said: 'Gimondi is a complete rider: intelligent, brave. I admire his strength of character, his noble nature, his decency. He brings honour to our profession.' Or? . . . but that is a good note to end on.

MYTHOLOGY

God had just finished creating the world and, surveying His work, He saw France: such wonderful scenery, landscape of every description, food, drink, vegetation in abundance and rich variety – France had everything. No other country enjoyed half what France had in plenty and to spare. How unjust. So, to even things up, God created the French people.

It's a joke the French tell against themselves – add a dash of irony – and if trying to get to the heart of what makes the Tour de France unique ranks with analysing humour as unrewarding work, there's no doubt that France itself, herself, forms a large part of the equation. The country and the way its people think and feel about it. The French didn't invent patriotism – though Chauvin, father of chauvinism, was one of theirs – but they have cultivated it into a fine art.

'The most beautiful kingdom second only to heaven,' someone said of France, an earthly paradise of contrasts enough to fill an entire catalogue of holiday brochures *and* bags of room. Most of

France is rural and a traveller can still roam most of France in the kind of tranquillity and solitude which the automobile destroyed decades past in cramped and overcrowded England where the traffic jam has become a protected species. Half of England is road and half the roads of England are up.

The modern Tour navigates the hexagon clockwise and anti-clockwise alternately, along the self-same roads covered by the early race; better surfaces, but the same roads. And, if scenery doesn't figure high on the riders' preoccupations – now as then – stunning views of such a grand variety of landscape can make a difference, even subliminally; any distraction from sheer mileage, although the domineering character of the high mountains cannot be evaded. For the spectators, the impact of the Tour against its dramatic backdrop is, and was, stupendous. Consider the words regularly applied by French commentators to the Tour: legend, myth, epic, saga, exploit, heroic. 'The Tour passes through a truly Homeric geography. As in the *Odyssey*, this race is a voyage both of human endeavour and exploration to the far reaches of the land, every nook and corner.' Roland Barthes, *Mythologies, 1957*.

Mythology? Particularly in the early days it *seemed* unreal and yet there, before their eyes, palpable, true. In 1903, six years before Blériot's maiden flight across the Channel, bike riders whom people had only heard of, celebrated names and unknowns, emerged from the haze into remote villages in inner France, outlying hamlets, walled towns, and disappeared into the haze again; or into the darkness of night, their lamps like glow-worms in the distance. Vision or fact? 1997 and what has changed? Well, Blériot and his insect of a machine are ancient history but the Tour is still the Tour: fame on a bicycle, the heroes of the legend spinning through the provinces, the forgotten holes of regional France, the backwaters where television antennae angle for *télésport*, sweeping down the main street past the shops, the bar with the rusting publicity *affiche* on its side wall – St Raphaël, Anquetil's old team – and into the haze again, passing the black and white chequer sign on the garage – Peugeot, Merckx's first sponsor, Thévenet's, Tommy Simpson's.

It goes everywhere; they call it *La Grande Boucle*, 'the big loop' and everywhere it goes the people gather to gawp: they line the streets at siesta time, they hang over the garden gate, take picnics out to the verges of the long road meandering through the open wheatbowl, they crowd the tree-lined slopes of the narrow road snaking up one massif or another; roads the pilgrims took from Paris to Santiago across the Pyrenees, or to Rome across the Alps; roads laid by the Romans for their conquering armies; back-road circuits taken by Gauls on the run; secret roads the intrepid mountain guides took across the Pyrenean passes leading allied soldiers and airmen to neutral Spain; roads the young men with ambition tramped, to court and the cities, the cities paved with gold and walled about with fire; roads the troubadours ambled with poetry and music on their mind:

> They talked as they rode
> Towards the city
> At a fair speed,
> And beside the road
> The casual murmur
> Of a stream through rushes
> Over the gravel.
> > Jean Renart, twelfth century

And 800 years later, the song of the rider in distress: sprained ankle, dry water bottle, sun beating down, puncture, hollow stomach, sick and tired, trying to keep his spirits up:

> My God, where is the *peloton*?
> My God, where is the *peloton*?
> This Tour de France is unholy
> tour-ment
> A Tour too big
> This Tour's a pig . . .
> My God, where is the *peloton*?
> *Bon Dieu, où est ce peloton?*
> > Blaness, Fugain, Schmitt

The French passion for Le Tour has much to do with it being *their* Tour of *their* France in quest of *their* accolade. Cycling is *their* national sport, the sport they all follow in July. It was the first great bike race and still is the greatest. The first claim no one can argue about; the second only a fool would quarrel with. And it comes with passion, above all, in a country where passion is a legitimate plea against a charge of murder; passion both emotional and intellectual. It is the French way: frivolous in their amusements, serious and studied in their tastes. You enjoy wine: you find out precisely *why* you enjoy wine, because knowing adds to the pleasure and the pleasure is enhanced by discussing it.

The Absurdist playwright Ionesco remained unconvinced. He couldn't understand, 'The passionate desire of people wanting to lead a bunch of cyclists into Paris after a complete circuit of France . . . and a spectator overcome with joy because he'd spotted Poulidor's back flying past, three seconds in which to admire the lone passage of an escaped cyclist.' A very absurd opinion.

Roland Barthes, the philosopher, was fascinated by the extraordinary phenomenon of the Tour. In *Mythologies*, he suggests that in the Tour, myth and reality fuse and become indistinguishable: the combat both between rival men and men and Nature are idealised, the stuff of chivalric romance, say, but at the same time the men are flesh and blood, too, as never in any other myth. The resulting ambiguity perhaps goes some way to baring the secret of the Tour, its intrinsic fascination – superhuman heroes battling with titanic adversity, in their shadow the retainers, the humble *domestiques*. And then the natural elements, hidden forces of evil and good, the magic of good and bad luck, conspiring to advance or deny victory. Not so far-fetched to think of it in terms of the knight's journey through the Wasteland, across the Mountains of Despair, into the Valley of False Comfort, through the Forest of Foreboding and on over the Plain of Desolation, to reach the promised city, Paris, thousands of miles away. They even call the leader's yellow jersey 'the golden fleece', Jason and the Argonauts's mythic prize.

We unromantic Anglo-Saxon *rosbifs* see a great bike race and that's that. We might get sentimental about our plucky losers, but that hardly consitutes passion. The French see a great bike race, too, but there's nothing they can't and won't philosophise about, nothing behind which doesn't lurk the metaphysics. Barthes said the names of the champions become like algebraic symbols standing for moral qualities: Valour, Loyalty, Treachery, Stoicism, Noble Sacrifice.

And the Tour liberates passion, they are all agreed on that; a very French passion, giving expression to what Napoleon identified as central to the French character: 'When I hear of a nation that can exist without bread, I will believe that the French can exist without glory.' Glory, yes. And, after all the complication, the analysis, the philosophising and the intellectual passion for comparison, symbol, mythic truth and the penetralia of legend, the quest for the glory is simple: *La gloire . . . maillot jaune.* Interchangeable.

INDEX

Abdujaparov, Djamolidine 533
Acouturier, Hippolyte 22ff
advertising and publicity 17, 18, 87, 93, 102,
    155, 171, 172, 219, 281, 290, 484
Ag2R team 263, 347, 354, 427, 543, 548,
    556, 557
Agnel, col d' 409, 410, 477
Agnès, col d' 52, 311, 312, 313, 421, 472, 486
Aimar, Lucien 120, 127, 141, 159, 196, 239
Alavoine, Jean 80, 83, 98–9, 171
Allos, col d' 43, 44, 82, 182
Anacona, Winner, 583, 584
Anquetil, Jacques 7, 11, 36, 43, 46–7, 53,
    55, 56, 69, 88, 101–2, 103, 110, 111, 116,
    117, 118, 120, 121, 126–7, 128, 130, 131,
    132, 137–8, 139–41, 144–5, 154, 155, 156,
    158–9, 160, 166, 175, 187, 190, 191, 192,
    193, 210, 229, 273, 277, 307–8, 411, 422,
    429, 463, 490, 491, 495
Arâches, côte de 430, 432
Aravis, col des 82, 237, 361
Ares, col des 89, 405
Armitstead, Lizzie 557, 585
Armstrong, Lance 11–12, 13, 29, 40, 63,
    121, 160 , 214, 215, 216, 217–18, 219,
    220, 221, 222–3, 224, 225, 226, 227, 229,
    230, 231, 234–6, 237, 238, 239, 242, 243,
    247, 251, 252–3, 254, 255–6, 257, 258,
    259, 260, 261, 263–4, 265–6, 267, 268,
    269, 270–1, 272, 273, 274–5, 276, 277,
    279–80, 281, 282, 284, 285, 286, 287, 288,
    289–90, 291, 292–4, 296, 297, 298–9,
    300–2, 304, 305, 306, 307, 309, 310, 311,
    313, 314, 315, 316–18, 319–21, 322,
    323, 324, 325, 326, 327, 328, 329, 331–2,
    333–4, 337, 338, 339, 340, 341–2, 343,
    344, 347, 348, 352, 353, 354, 355, 367,
    370, 372, 374, 398, 413, 414, 415, 416,
    417, 418–19, 420, 421, 422, 428–9, 430,
    432, 433, 434, 435, 437–8, 439, 440, 441,
    443, 445, 447, 449, 450, 451, 456–7, 461,
    463, 472, 486n, 507–8, 580

ASO 371, 373, 385, 386, 387, 395, 397, 398,
    404, 413, 414, 417, 423, 460
Aspet, Portet d' 89, 92, 95, 106, 145, 157,
    250, 254, 266, 290, 338, 472, 488, 489
Aspin, col d' 27, 89, 91, 168, 176, 197, 223,
    250, 255, 354, 405, 422
Astana team 345–7, 372–4, 379–80, 385,
    392, 395, 398, 415–16, 419, 420–1, 429,
    433, 435, 437, 446, 464, 541, 553
Astarloza, Mikel 286, 430
Aubisque, col d' 27, 42–3, 50, 82, 84, 89,
    126, 135, 173, 197, 223, 234, 264–5, 334,
    392, 394, 472, 487
L'Auto 18–19, 20, 21, 22, 23, 24, 25, 27, 40,
    79, 85, 109, 112, 125
L'Auto Vélo see L'Auto
Avoriaz 443
Ax Trois Domaines 289, 293, 332, 448, 449
Azet, col d' 176, 197, 333
Azevedo, José 311, 315, 317, 319, 328, 348

Bagargui, col 295
Bahamontes, Federico 34, 102, 103, 115–16,
    139, 140, 142, 252, 285, 308, 585
Bakelants, Jan 512
Balès, Port de 390, 449, 453, 503
Ballon d'Alsace 26, 117, 181, 185, 327–8
Bannstein, col du 427
Bardet, Romain 540ff, 562, 565, 570, 573,
    574, 575, 580, 581, 582, 584
Barredo, Carlos 450, 451
Bartali, Gino 14, 54, 101, 105, 134–5, 136, 137,
    168, 172, 181, 182, 193, 216, 414, 547, 585
Barthélémy, Honoré 283
Barthes, Roland 491, 493
Basso, Ivan 277, 284, 304, 310, 311, 313,
    314, 315, 316, 317, 318, 319, 323, 324,
    325, 329, 331–2, 333–4, 339, 340, 341,
    345–6, 347, 355, 369–70, 371–2, 373, 437,
    440, 461, 464, 572
Bauer, Jack 548ff, 556
Beausoleil, côte de 417

599

Beille, Plateau de 266, 267, 268, 311, 313, 315, 316, 388, 472

Beloki, Joseba 236, 239, 247, 257, 258, 260, 262, 265, 266, 267–8, 270, 272, 275, 280, 285, 286, 287, 299, 302, 335, 346, 347, 357, 527, 576

Beltrán, Manuel 217, 286, 331, 404

Bennati, Daniele 522, 572

Beret, Pla de 354, 355, 357

Bernaudeau, Jean-René 59, 471, 576

Berzin, Evgeny 63, 64, 249

Bettini, Paolo 233, 285

Bidot, Marcel 7, 15, 65, 66, 69, 74, 75, 88–9, 90, 91–2, 93, 96, 98, 101, 117, 118, 130, 136, 193

Binda, Alfredo 94–5, 97, 121

Blondin, Antoine 166, 269, 353

Boardman, Chris 39–40, 67, 70, 114, 115, 149, 150, 153, 209–10, 214, 215, 217, 225, 298, 364–5, 366–7, 483, 484, 487, 563

Boasson-Hagen, Edvald 521

Bobet, Louison 65, 74–5, 100–1, 104, 105, 111, 116, 118, 120, 132, 134, 136, 137–8, 149, 155, 158, 172, 183, 207, 383, 400, 490

Bonnette, Cime de la 150, 409

Boogerd, Michael 214, 216, 269, 273, 274, 332–3, 355, 394, 395

Boom, Lars 541

Boonen, Tom 303, 305, 320, 324, 325, 326, 330–1, 349–50, 351, 352, 354, 359, 363, 378, 379, 380, 384, 387, 398, 417, 428, 440, 466

Bordeaux–Paris 53–4, 158, 166, 185

Botero, Santiago 236, 237, 260, 263, 264, 265, 270, 272, 273, 280, 285, 286–7, 292, 293, 329, 330, 369

Bottechia, Ottavio 84, 86–7

Boyer, Eric 63, 407

Brackeveld 81

Brailsford, Dave 438–9, 456, 490, 513, 525, 537

Brajkovic, Janez 461, 466

Brambilla, Pierre 107, 108, 138–9

Brochard, Laurent 114, 220, 269, 332–3

Bruyère, Jos 167, 197

Bruyneel, Johan 63, 64, 245, 253, 264, 266, 273, 294, 297–8, 301, 315, 316, 317–18, 319, 372, 398, 415, 416, 421, 422, 423, 435, 437, 449, 486n

Bugno, Gianni 69, 275, 316

Buret, col de 405

Buysse, Lucien 89, 90, 414

Callens, Norbert, 568

Cancellara, Fabian 301, 302, 375, 376, 378, 381, 385, 390, 400, 402, 406, 409, 412, 416–17, 419, 421, 439, 440, 441, 450, 486, 492, 564, 565

Casagrande, Francesco 71, 72, 306

Casar, Sandy 305, 332, 338–9, 351, 384, 394–5, 444, 581

Casartelli, Fabio 156–7, 254, 255, 488, 489, 548

Casper, Jimmy 256, 282–3, 350

Cavendish, Mark 121, 375, 377, 378, 379, 381, 383, 399, 403, 404–5, 408–9, 417, 418–19, 420, 422–3, 426, 427, 432, 433, 434–5, 439–40, 442, 445, 446, 452, 454–5, 456, 459, 462, 465, 466, 467, 469, 470, 474, 479, 481, 483f, 488ff, 492, 499, 504f, 511, 513, 514, 519, 520, 521, 522, 533, 537, 564, 566, 567, 568, 576, 581, 585

Chambre Arbitrale du Sport 417

Champs, col des 43

Charteau, Anthony 444, 454, 475

Châtenay-Malabry 343, 367, 368, 370

Chavanel, Sylvain 292, 293, 294, 312, 338, 392, 404, 412, 440, 441, 442–3, 446, 450, 451–2, 466, 467, 469, 475, 486, 489, 495, 500, 512, 514, 543, 553, 576

cheating 22, 25, 26, 27, 167, 221, 374

Cheng, Ji 537, 549, 556

Chiapucci, Claudio 69, 70, 217

Chioula, col du 250

Christophe, Eugène 28, 78–80, 87, 173–4, 179

Cipollini, Mario 71–2, 94, 215, 224, 228–9, 242, 263, 273, 283, 302, 305, 307, 324–5, 379, 403, 409

Clerc, Patrice 386–7, 395

Cofidis team 231–2, 244, 282, 309, 402

Colombière, col de la 237, 274, 361, 381, 430–1, 432

Columbia team 398, 399, 408, 417, 418–19, 422–3, 427, 434–5, 440, 442

Contador, Alberto 373–4, 382, 389, 390, 393, 394, 395, 398, 400, 415, 416–17, 418, 419–21, 422, 428–9, 430, 432–4, 435, 437–8, 439, 440, 441, 443–4, 445–6, 448–50, 453–4, 455, 456, 459–61, 464, 465, 466, 468, 470, 471, 472, 473, 474, 475, 478, 479–81, 482, 486, 513, 516, 517, 521, 522, 524, 526, 528, 529, 530, 532, 536, 541, 544, 552, 563–6, 569, 570, 573, 574, 576, 578, 579, 580, 582

Cooke, Baden 275–6, 283–4, 288, 296, 298, 303, 324

Coppel, Jérome 527

Coppi, Fausto 14, 53, 54, 101, 105, 118, 121, 132–7, 142, 149, 156, 193, 206, 252, 280, 298, 585

Core, col de la 266, 290, 313, 472

Cornet de Roselend 328, 382

Cornet, Henri 25, 73

Corsica 508–9

Costa, Ruí 467, 522, 527, 531, 551

Coudons, col de 250

Couraduque, col de 334

Croix de Fer, col de la 58, 73, 75, 134, 139, 175, 359, 409, 496f

Croix Fry, col de la 317
Cucheron, col du 46, 120
Cummings, Steve 438, 575
Cunego, Damian 323, 348–9, 358, 406, 409, 479

Darrigade, André 24, 80, 88, 121, 296, 340, 488, 514, 542
Dauphiné Libéré 53, 68, 121, 158, 175, 193, 209, 223, 243, 256, 267, 280, 281, 289, 297, 315, 382, 401, 406, 461, 481, 484f
Dean, Julian 427, 434–5, 442, 445
Defraye, Odile 28, 80
Dekker, Erik 230, 232, 233, 235, 239, 248, 249, 350
Delgado, Pedro 57, 151, 161–2, 188, 189, 261, 273, 370
Delisle, Raymond 43, 142, 143, 144
Demarbaix, Sebastian 232
Dennis, Rohan, 563, 564
Denson, Vin 185, 187
dérailleur gears 33, 99, 124, 172, 181
Desgrange, Henri 8, 20, 21–2, 23–4, 25–6, 27, 28, 61, 77, 79–80, 82, 83, 84–6, 87, 89, 90, 91, 92, 93, 95, 97, 98–9, 100, 105, 109, 110–11, 112–13, 123, 124, 130, 133, 135, 148, 153, 161, 167, 172, 173, 182, 212, 281, 314, 383, 462, 481, 506, 518, 586
  as world record holder 18
Dessel, Cyril 354, 355, 360, 363, 410
Devenyns, Dries 495
Dewaele, Maurice 91–3
Dick, Nigel 8, 387, 424
diet 134, 137, 159, 162
Di Gregorio, Rémy 496
Dion, Comte 17, 18–19
Discovery Channel team 245, 325, 328, 329, 342, 372, 373, 382, 395, 415, 416, 419
Dreyfus affair 17–18
drugs 62, 159, 160–8, 186–7, 195–6, 197, 201, 202–4, 205–6, 207–10, 211–13, 220, 221, 223–4, 225, 229, 238, 239, 240, 241–2, 243, 248–9, 280, 299, 301, 302, 309, 366, 367, 368, 372, 380, 381, 385–6, 396, 398, 399, 456, 463
Dueñas, Moisés 407
Dufaux, Laurent 203, 209, 273, 291
Dumoulin, Tom, 565
Durand, Jacky 230, 232–3, 234, 244–5, 249, 254, 260, 268, 305, 336, 356, 402, 446–7, 449

Eisel, Bernhard 442, 448, 465, 488f
Elmiger, Martin 548ff
Envalira, Port d' 102, 421
epitestosterone 367, 368
EPO 165, 201, 202, 203, 204, 208, 211–12, 213, 219, 220, 222, 240, 249, 269, 271, 286, 299, 301, 307, 308, 344, 345, 349, 370, 371, 395, 398, 404, 408, 510
Escartin, Fernando 217, 218, 234, 237
Evans, Cadel 336, 348, 355, 358, 373, 382, 389, 393, 395, 400, 404, 405, 406, 407, 409–10, 411–12, 416, 419, 421–2, 428, 430, 438, 440, 441, 444, 460, 462, 464, 465–6, 468, 470, 471, 474, 478–80, 481, 485, 487, 492, 494ff, 499, 502, 504, 510, 512, 513, 516, 523–4

Faber, François 27, 88, 121, 125, 126, 261
Farrar, Tyler 418, 427, 434–5, 442, 446, 465, 490
Faure, Benoit 24–5, 95, 97–8, 124, 173
Fédrigo, Pierrick, 357, 450, 500, 577
Feillu, Brice 420
Feillu, Romain 402, 403, 420, 465
Ferrari, Michele 243, 253, 307, 372–3
Ferretti, Giancarlo 277, 314
Festina team 71, 201–2, 207–8, 229, 235, 239
Fignon, Laurent 55–6, 108, 118, 154, 229, 242, 256, 258, 297, 299, 382, 402, 403, 412, 434, 454, 455, 457, 481, 486
First World War 82, 162, 442
Flanagan, Jan and Nick 311, 338, 389, 573
Flandres, Tour des 68, 184, 324, 349, 379
Flecha, Juan Antonio 309, 443, 468
Flèche Wallonne 350, 379, 441, 458, 487
Fontan, Victor 91–2, 94, 109
Françaises des Jeux team 205, 209, 221, 394, 424, 447, 467
Frantz, Nicolas 87–8, 90, 91–2, 121, 123–4, 261
Freire, Oscar 262, 263, 354, 403, 412, 427, 440
Frigo, Dario 260, 274, 330
Froome, Christopher 483, 488, 492, 495ff, 503ff, 536ff, *2013 passim, 2015 passim*
Fuente, de la David 355, 358
Fuente, Eufemiano 345, 346, 348, 369
Fuglsang, Jakob 517, 546
Futuroscope 224, 227

Gachet, col de la 339
Galdeano, Gonzalez de 257, 263, 267
Galibier, col du 28, 39, 40, 56, 58, 74, 78, 82, 84, 88, 95, 97, 100, 104, 106, 108, 111, 112, 113, 116, 117, 120, 121, 122–3, 126, 127, 128, 129, 135, 139, 149, 175, 181, 182, 217, 236, 273, 277, 286, 329, 330, 359, 360, 383, 384, 409, 410, 462, 475, 477, 479, 480
Gallopin, Tony 543, 545, 571, 577
Garin, Maurice 19, 22–5, 254
Garmin-Chipotle team 398, 409, 412
Garmin-Slipstream team 398, 417
Garrigou, Gustave 27, 125–6
Garzelli, Stefano 260, 358
Gaul, Charly 74, 120, 124, 142, 146, 155, 183, 184, 252, 253, 261, 404, 492

Gautier, Cyril 551, 555
Géminiani, Raphaël 74, 102–3, 105, 120,
    137, 139, 155, 158
Georget, Léon 22, 23
Gérard, Arnaud 555
Gerdemann, Linus 381, 382–3
Gerrans, Simon 512, 513, 537, 565
Geschke, Simon, 578, 579
Ghent–Wevelgem 65, 158, 305
Ghyselinck, Jan 502
Giant-Shimano team 537–9, 549
Gilbert, Philippe 340, 458, 462, 464, 469–
    70, 487, 489
Gimondi, Felice 35, 42, 44, 45, 117, 118,
    187, 200, 206, 280, 429, 490, 546
Giro d'Italia 42, 43, 59, 69, 94, 120, 132,
    158, 213, 228, 242, 260, 279, 302, 323,
    336, 343, 358, 369, 398, 399, 400, 414,
    416, 437, 459, 461, 484, 563
Glandon, col du 40, 50, 58, 65, 66, 72, 73,
    76, 100, 103, 134, 139, 146, 249, 251, 317
Goddet, Jacques 20, 47, 66, 105, 159, 168,
    169, 187, 195, 198, 463
Goddet, Victor 20
Godefroot, Walter 197, 257, 261, 288, 314,
    323 347
Goss, Matthew 495
Grand-Bornand 430, 433
Grand Cucheron 498
Grand Prix des Nations 56, 137, 158
Grand-Saint-Bernard 429, 430
Granier, col du 120, 498
green jersey 33, 54, 118, 245, 257, 261, 266,
    274, 275, 276, 283, 284, 296, 303, 320,
    324, 331, 340, 341, 349, 350, 365, 380,
    387, 400, 401, 412, 417, 418, 422, 426,
    427, 432, 433, 440, 441, 442, 445, 451,
    456, 459, 464, 480, 481, 490
Greipel, André 399, 462, 470, 488f, 491,
    514, 519, 521, 533, 542, 564, 567, 568,
    569, 576, 577, 585
Grosse Pierre, col de 327
Guerini, Giuseppe 217, 218, 219, 274, 313,
    331, 338, 530
Guerra, Learco 94–8, 110
Guimard, Cyrille 53, 55, 68, 142, 143, 300–1,
    323, 342, 354, 370, 382, 422, 439, 440, 473
Guzet Neige 52, 188, 488

Hagen, Edvald Boasson 442, 443, 467, 474,
    475, 476, 488, 496
Hamilton, Tyler 223, 262, 282, 283, 286,
    289, 294, 295–6, 298, 299, 300, 304, 306,
    309, 310, 313, 369
Hansen, Adam, 440, 565, 577
Haselbacher, Rene 284, 305
Hauptman, Andrej 229
Haussler, Heinrich 426–7, 440
Haut de la Côte, col du 250

Hauteville 382
Heras, Roberto 237–8, 243, 247, 251, 265,
    266, 267, 270, 304, 310, 317, 328, 329,
    348, 369
Hernández, Jesús 541
Herrera, Luis 58, 272, 284
Hervé, Pascal 202, 237
Hesjedal, Ryder 450, 454, 480, 490, 516, 531
Hinault, Bernard 7, 15, 35, 52, 53, 54,
    55–60, 61, 64, 65, 66, 68–9, 111, 118, 121,
    144, 160, 167, 168–9, 174–5, 191, 196,
    219, 221, 225, 252, 255, 262, 268, 273,
    274, 277, 300, 304, 316, 319, 325, 338,
    340, 341, 342, 343, 356, 378, 382, 384,
    400, 417, 429, 481, 492, 498, 505, 538, 569
Hinault, Sébastian 337, 394, 576
Hincapie, George 80, 265, 319, 328–9, 333,
    340, 343, 348, 349, 350, 351, 354–5, 358,
    376, 403, 419, 423, 427, 428, 435, 440,
    465, 486, 502, 537
Hoban, Barry 80, 118, 119, 185, 187, 188,
    403, 405
Honchar, Serhiy 351, 354, 363, 384
Hondo, Danilo 442–3, 445, 448, 450–1, 452,
    455–6
Hoogerland, Johnny 468
Horner, Chris 461, 467, 553
Huez, l'Alpe d' 30, 32, 33, 34, 35, 36, 38, 40,
    41, 50, 56, 58, 65, 70, 71, 72, 103, 111,
    114, 142, 145, 167, 174, 177, 200, 218,
    219, 249, 251, 253, 273, 284, 286, 293,
    316, 327, 338, 357, 358, 409, 410, 416,
    479, 480, 481
Hunter, Robert 385, 441, 489
Hushovd, Thor 260, 262, 271, 275, 288, 303,
    306, 320, 324, 326, 331, 340, 341, 349, 350,
    365, 379, 392, 401, 403, 420, 422, 426, 427,
    432, 433, 435, 440, 441, 446, 451, 454,
    456, 458, 464, 465, 467, 472, 474, 548
Hutarovich, Yauheni 495
Huysmans, Joseph 48, 126, 127

Iglinskiy, Maxim 464, 477, 478
Impey, Darren 514
Indurain, Miguel 12, 15, 52, 61–3, 64, 71,
    72, 118, 121, 149–50, 157, 160, 214, 225,
    263, 267, 275, 277, 429, 495
Iseran, col d' 100, 101, 106, 383
Ivanov, Serguei 229, 248–9
Izoard, col d' 79, 82, 84, 90, 91, 106, 132,
    134, 135, 136, 138, 142, 145, 146, 148,
    149, 159, 170, 171, 182, 198, 357–8, 477

Jacquelin, Edmond 22
Jacquinot, Robert 81–3, 98
Jaksche, Jörg 372, 394
Jalabert, Laurent 63, 203, 205, 207, 212–13,
    228, 229, 230–2, 234, 245–6, 247, 254–5,
    261, 262, 263, 265, 266, 269, 273–4,

276–7, 285, 289, 318, 337, 402, 445
Jalabert, Nicolas 318
Janssen, Jan 43, 108, 490
Jaskuła, Zenon 552
Jau, col de 250
Jeannesson, Arnold 527
jerseys worn by competition leaders 29–30
Jimenez, Jose Maria 234–5, 237
Jimenez, Julio 102, 126–7, 128, 186
Joux-Plane, col de 361, 485
Julich, Bobby 214, 215–16, 217, 351

Kadri, Blel 522, 526, 527, 543, 553, 554
Karpets, Vladimir 320, 323, 430
Katusha team 430
Kelly, Sean 33, 55, 70, 80, 118, 119, 153, 215, 303, 325, 359, 364, 474
Kelme team 236, 237, 255, 285, 299
Kennaugh, Peter 515, 522, 524, 529, 566, 570, 576
Kerrison, Tim 484f, 524
Kessiakoff, Fredrik 494, 503
Kessler, Matthias 351, 352, 357, 358, 379
King of the Mountains 30, 106, 113, 228, 229, 232, 236, 237, 260, 269, 276, 339, 355, 373, 417
Kirchen, Kim 401, 403–4, 405, 406, 423
Kiryienka, Vasil 445, 517, 551
Kirsipuu, Jan 215, 247, 263, 283, 303, 306
Kiserlovski, Robert 500
Kittel, Marcel 511, 514, 519–20, 521, 533, 537ff
Kivilev, Andrei 248, 253, 255, 257, 280, 289
Klöden, Andreas 313, 314, 316, 317, 318, 319, 323, 324, 326–7, 328, 329, 332, 336, 349, 351, 355, 358, 359, 360, 361, 364, 365, 373, 376, 379, 383, 389, 416, 428–9, 430, 432–3
Knees, Christian 496
Koblet, Hugo 104–5, 130–1, 155, 158, 329
Kohl, Bernhard 409, 410, 411–12
Kolobnev, Alexandr 453
König, Leo 547
Kreuziger, Roman 524, 527, 528, 530
Kristoff, Alexander 539, 545, 549, 557, 568
Kubler, Ferdi 74–5, 168
Kuiper, Hennie 142, 145, 167, 172, 251, 316
Kwiatkowski, Michal 544, 545, 574

Laffrey, côte de 26, 47, 112, 113, 182, 444
Lambot, Firmin 73, 79–80, 171, 414
Landis, Floyd 317–18, 319–20, 329, 348, 351, 352–3, 355, 356–7, 358, 359, 360–2, 363, 364, 365, 366, 367–8, 369, 370, 373, 391, 396, 399, 400
Lapébie, Roger 182–3
Lapize, Octave 27, 28, 39, 79, 125
Larrau, Port de 392
Latrape, col de 290, 313, 472

Lautaret, col de 108, 357, 358
Lavenu, Vincent 348
Leblanc, Jean-Marie 152, 205, 207, 212, 213, 219, 229, 241–2, 244, 246, 249, 255, 256, 258, 262, 281, 306, 310, 316, 319, 347, 374
Leducq, André 91, 95–7, 98, 103, 109, 110, 111, 121, 124, 172
Lefèvre, Géo 20, 22, 25
Leipheimer, Levi 282–3, 304, 349, 351, 355, 363, 373, 389, 393, 395, 416, 426
Lelangue, John 356–7, 360
Lemond, Greg 7, 15, 56–8, 59, 108, 111, 118, 121, 152, 153, 154, 174, 175, 239, 241, 252, 259, 297, 300, 307, 325, 337–8, 339, 434, 444, 455m, 498
Lers, Port de 311, 313, 499
Les Deux Alpes 206, 218, 272
Lévitan, Félix 168, 169, 182, 198, 255
Liège–Bastogne–Liège 65, 158, 178, 233, 300, 401, 440, 458, 461
Liggett, Phil 62, 327, 345, 346, 347
Livingston, Kevin 223, 237, 243
Llorente, Pascual 237, 299
Löfkvist, Thomas 438, 449
Lombarde, col de 409
Londres, Albert 85–6
long-distance road races 19–20, 25
Lourdes Hautacam 61, 134, 233, 293, 405, 472
Luitel, col 167, 253
Luz-Ardiden 250, 256, 290, 292, 293, 308, 470, 471

Madeleine, col de la 69, 72, 100, 114, 206, 236, 249, 250, 273, 317, 329, 444, 496
Madiot, Marc 205, 424, 447, 492ff, 545, 549
Maertens, Freddy 7, 33, 34–5, 94, 142, 143, 146–7, 168, 273, 379
Maes, Romain 88, 182, 244
Maes, Sylvère 54, 106, 132, 170, 182
Magne, Antonin 91, 95, 96, 98, 102, 106, 109–10, 111, 182, 214, 364
Magne, Pierre 95–6, 109
maillot jaune 11, 29, 87, 140, 141, 232, 237, 306, 312, 387–8, 494
Majka, Rafal 547ff, 572
Mancebo, Francisco 235, 312, 315, 323, 329, 345–6, 347, 348
Mangeas, Daniel 503, 562
Mapei team 240
Marchi, Alessandro de 543ff
Marie Blanque, col de 57, 234, 354, 392, 487
Martin, Daniel 517, 569, 573
Martin, Tony 175, 423, 434, 439, 481, 520, 543ff, 563–8
Martinez, Egoi 309, 329–30, 425–6, 427, 498
Massi, Rodolfo 205–6
Massif de la Chartreuse 27, 120, 134, 156

Mate, Luis Angel 539, 542
Mattan, Nico 234
Matthews, Michael, 567
Mauvezin, col du 250
Mayo, Iban 280, 285, 286, 291, 293–4, 298,
    302, 303–4, 310, 312, 313, 315, 328, 340,
    354, 382, 389, 395, 398
Mazan, Lucien 27
McEwen, Robbie 215, 226, 261, 262, 274–6,
    283, 284, 296, 298, 303, 305–6, 310, 316,
    320, 324–6, 331, 340, 349–50, 351, 354,
    365, 375, 377, 379, 383, 407, 408–9
McGee, Bradley 257, 261, 275, 282, 283,
    284, 288, 301, 302, 305, 341
McQuaid, Pat 368–9, 386–7, 393, 395, 398,
    407
Menchov, Denis 348, 351, 355, 358, 359,
    373, 394, 400, 406, 409, 410, 411, 416–17,
    419, 448, 449, 457
Mengin, Christophe 326
Menté, col de 49, 142, 250, 266, 290, 291, 503
Mercado, Juan-Miguel 354
Merckx, Axel 272, 293, 308–9, 332, 337,
    356, 358, 359–60, 395
Merckx, Eddy 7, 12, 34, 35, 37, 42–50, 52,
    53–6, 59, 62, 65, 71, 82, 94, 110, 111,
    117–20, 121, 130, 132, 142, 146, 149, 153,
    154, 159, 160, 161, 170, 175–6, 177, 178,
    193, 195–7, 200, 218, 222, 225, 242, 253,
    255, 260, 264, 267, 268, 270, 271, 273–4,
    277, 304, 307, 325, 340, 342, 343, 353,
    356, 361, 429, 440, 444, 463, 477, 478,
    483f, 491, 514, 533, 534, 578, 585
Merviel, Jules 96, 97
Milan–San Remo 42, 53, 94, 131, 132, 134,
    153, 173, 185, 190–1, 426–7
Millar, David 115, 229–31, 235, 236, 243–4,
    245, 248, 250, 260–1, 263, 264, 268, 269,
    270, 275, 281–2, 283, 285, 286, 288,
    294–5, 297–8, 301, 305, 309, 315, 349,
    351, 360, 362, 370, 375–6, 377, 382, 385,
    387, 389, 392, 394, 395, 398, 399, 412,
    417, 419–20, 423, 434–5, 439, 440, 442,
    444, 445, 464, 484, 487, 490, 495, 498,
    513, 517
Millar, Robert 70, 131, 175, 188–9, 190, 298,
    363, 434; 461, 486, 488
Moinard Amaël 430
Mollard, col du 359
Mollema, Bauke 520, 522
Moncassin, Frédéric 483–4
Moncoutié, David 309, 330, 472, 498
Montford, Maxime 423, 477
Montjuic 420
Mont Ventoux 74, 75, 120, 155–6, 176, 177,
    178, 185–6, 187, 193–6, 199, 200, 223,
    235, 236, 237, 239, 247, 269, 270, 271,
    272, 308, 429, 433–4, 439
Moreau, Christophe 235, 236, 237–8, 239,

243, 244, 260, 263, 272, 291, 328, 338–9,
    341, 348, 354, 360, 361, 381–2, 384–5,
    388, 444, 450, 451, 454
Moreni, Cristian 363, 393–4, 398
Morino, Jean-Marc, 526, 527
Mortensen, Leif 46, 47
Morzine 238, 240, 285, 361, 362, 363, 370
Moser, Francesco 44, 53, 56
Moser, Moreno 528
Motta, Gianni 197–8
mountains
    categories 33
    challenge 33–4, 38–9, 114
    climbing qualities 114
    conciliation magistrates 14
    included in Tour for first time 26
Muravyev, Dmitriy 416
Museeuw, Johan 63

Navardauskas, Ramunas 555–6
Nazon, Jean-Patrick 231, 233, 283, 284, 293,
    298, 303
Nencini, Gastone 155, 156, 239
Nibali, Vincenzo 430, 432, 433, 486, 491,
    494ff, 502ff, 510, 536ff, 562ff
Nicholson, Geoffrey 142, 166–7
Nieve, Mikel 548, 553, 554
Nocentini, Rinaldo 420, 427
Noval, Benjamin 304, 355, 416

Ocaña, Luis 37, 46–50, 142–3, 144, 170,
    189, 254, 260, 266, 274, 325, 358, 361,
    444–5, 503
O'Grady, Stuart 233, 245, 246, 247, 248,
    249, 257, 258, 261, 262, 274, 275, 283,
    298, 303, 305, 310, 320, 324, 325, 326,
    340, 376, 383, 400, 409, 443, 510, 537
Olano, Abraham 214, 217, 230, 246
ONCE team 203, 205–6, 213, 228, 230,
    231–2, 246–7, 257, 262, 263, 264, 280
Opperman, Hubert 81–2, 125
Osquich, col d' 89, 354
Otxoa, Javier 234–5, 236, 237

Padini, Luca 545
Padrnos, Pavel 294, 306–7, 340
Pailhères, Port de 289, 331, 389, 447
Pantani, Marco 52, 62, 71–3, 124, 197, 205,
    206, 213, 218, 220, 228, 231, 234–9, 242,
    253, 259–60, 269, 270, 280–1, 316, 363,
    472, 563
Parc des Princes 18, 19, 23, 24, 53–4, 80,
    111, 112, 298
Paris–Brest–Paris 19, 25, 79, 81, 125, 185
Paris–Nice 54, 101, 118, 158, 159, 190, 196,
    242, 280, 342, 356, 373, 422, 433, 437
Paris–Roubaix 19, 65, 119, 132, 158, 197,
    248, 296, 324, 349, 375, 378, 383, 390,
    409, 424, 441, 447, 566

Parra, Fabio 284
Paulinho, Sérgio 416, 445
Péguère, col de 65–6, 486
Péguère, Mur de 499
Peiper, Allan 403, 466, 491
Pélissier, Charles 34, 94, 95, 96, 97, 100, 109, 111, 216, 273
Pélissier, Francis 84–6, 91, 165
Pélissier, Henri 82, 83, 84–6, 165
Pellizotti, Franco 338, 425, 427, 430, 435
Peña, Victor Hugo 284–5
Peraud, Jean-Christophe 487, 498, 547ff
Péraud, Jean-François, 562, 570, 573, 574, 576, 582
Perche, col de la 89
Pereiro, Oscar 329–30, 333, 334, 336, 338, 341, 356, 359, 360, 361–2, 363, 364, 365, 368, 373, 400, 410, 422
Perjuret, col du 156
Perty, col de 357
Petacchi, Alessandro 283, 284, 302–3, 305, 306, 325, 409, 440, 442, 446, 451, 452, 454–6, 533, 537
Petit-Saint-Bernard 430
Pévenage, Rudy 315, 323, 324, 347, 363
Peyresourde, col de 27, 83, 89, 91, 98, 223, 250, 255, 290, 291, 333, 354, 390, 405, 450, 502f
Piil, Jakob 275, 287–8, 305
Pineau, Jérôme 442–3, 444, 445, 451, 479, 542
Pingeon, Roger 117, 145, 193, 220
Pinot, Thibaud 494, 497, 505, 544ff, 562, 565, 566, 570, 573, 575, 579, 582, 583, 584
Pla d'Adet 143, 144, 172, 250, 255, 332, 334
Plateau de Beille 266, 267, 268, 311, 313, 315, 316, 388, 472
Platzerwasel, col du 426–7
Poels, Wouter, 581, 583
Pollentier, Michel 34, 35, 167–9
Pooley, Emma 558
Popovych, Yaroslav 329, 337, 340, 341, 355, 373, 382, 416
Port, col de 89, 181, 250, 266, 389, 421, 485, 486
Port de Lers 311, 313
Porte, col de 46, 47, 68, 120, 284, 285
Porte, Richie 485, 491f, 504, 510, 515, 524, 527, 529, 530, 531, 541, 544, 547, 556, 565, 570, 571, 573, 574, 575, 577, 578, 579, 583
Portet, col du 290
Portillon, col du 143, 223, 250, 254, 290, 354, 355
Pottier, René 22, 23, 24, 25, 26, 130, 216, 328
Poulidor, Raymond 11, 35, 43, 46, 80, 101, 102–3, 108, 110, 111, 117, 118, 126–7, 131, 139–41, 143, 144–5, 159, 166, 175–6, 186, 188, 193, 198, 200, 307–8, 352, 382, 411, 422, 435, 493
Pozzato, Filippo 306, 379, 385, 408

Pra-Loup 43, 44, 170
Prato Nevoso 409
Prudhomme, Christian 347–8, 368, 386, 392, 395, 397, 400–1, 408, 423–4, 458, 462, 477, 488, 505, 509, 542, 566
psychology 178
Puy de Dôme 44, 53, 135, 140, 307, 411
Puymorens, col de 89, 106
Pyrenees 26–7

Quintana, Nairo 515–16, 517, 522, 524, 527, 528, 529, 530, 532, 533, 563ff

Rabobank team 215, 332–3, 348, 355, 373, 382, 386, 393, 394, 398, 399, 400, 427
RadioShack team 435, 438, 445, 457
Ramaz, col de la 285, 443
Rasmussen, Michael 311, 312, 327, 328, 329, 334, 339, 341, 355, 359, 360, 373, 374, 382–3, 385–91, 393, 398, 399, 435
Renshaw, Mark 423, 435, 442, 445, 446, 454, 466, 533, 564, 567
Riblon, Christophe 448, 527, 528–9, 577, 585
Riccò, Riccardo 404, 405, 408
Rigat, col 89
Righi, Daniele 360
Rijs, Bjarne 61–4, 71–2, 156–7, 197, 203, 205, 212, 262, 276, 289, 295–6, 313, 314–15, 347, 371–2, 391, 410, 411, 417, 443, 449, 544
Ritter, Olé 45
Rivière, Roger 116, 137, 156, 158–9, 489–90
Robic, Jean 7, 65, 104–5, 106–8, 138, 157–8, 160, 168, 404
Robinson, Brian 75, 141, 183, 461, 538
Roche, Nicolas 440, 445, 450, 512, 570, 578, 583
Roche, Stephen 69–70, 71, 115, 118, 151, 273, 303, 517, 534
Rodríguez, Joaquim 189, 445–6, 524, 527, 528, 529, 530, 532, 533, 544, 545, 548, 552, 565, 570, 574
Rogers, Michael 522
Rojas, Joaquín 464, 465, 466
Rogers, Michael 351, 370, 383, 423, 492, 551–2
Rolland, Pierre 471, 472–4, 478, 449–82, 497, 499, 505, 521, 522, 532, 582, 584
Romandie, Tour de 484f
Rominger, Tony 63, 64, 149–50
Romme, col de 430, 431, 432
Roussel, Bruno 201–2
Rowe, Luke 586
Roy, Jérémy 467, 470–1, 472
Rubiera, José Luis 265, 266, 268, 286, 294, 316, 328, 336
Rujano, José 361
Rumsas, Raimondas 271, 275, 276, 277–8

Sagan, Peter 487, 489, 491, 495, 498, 505, 511, 514, 522, 532, 542, 545, 555, 557,

564, 568, 569, 575, 576, 577, 579, 585
Saint-Martin, col de la Pierre 392
Saisies, col de 237, 361, 430, 432
Saíz, Manolo 213, 264, 345, 373–4
Sánchez, Luis Léon 422, 468, 471, 472, 474, 479, 480–1, 495, 500
Sánchez, Samuel 282, 449, 457, 461–2
Sastre, Carlos 355, 359, 360, 361, 362, 364, 373, 381, 389, 400, 406, 409, 410, 411–12, 414, 416, 419, 428, 448, 450, 460
Savoldelli, Paolo 328, 336–7, 342, 355–6
Saxo Bank team 417, 419, 443, 465
Scarponi, Michele 496
Schleck, Andy 400, 406, 409, 410, 412, 416, 417, 420, 428, 430, 432–4, 435, 438, 440–1, 443–4, 445–6, 448, 449–50, 453–4, 455, 456—7, 460, 464, 468, 470, 471, 473, 474, 477–9, 480, 481, 486, 523
Schleck, Fränk 358, 381, 382, 389, 400, 406, 409, 410–11, 412, 416, 417, 428, 430, 432–3, 434, 438, 440–1, 449, 460, 464, 468, 470, 471, 474, 477, 478–9, 481, 486, 500f
Schlucht, col de la 326, 426
Schoenmaecker, Jos de 43, 490
Scholz, Ronny 318, 363
Schumacher, Stephen 401, 402–3, 404, 412
Sciandri, Max 189, 269
Scieur, Léon 77, 174
Sentinelle, col de la 357
Sept-Frères, col des 250
Serpa, José 551
Serrano, Marcos 337
Sestriere, 217, 218, 293
Sevilla, Oscar 255, 273, 332–3, 334, 336, 345, 347, 363
Sherwen, Paul 114, 190, 191, 192, 289–90, 327
Simeoni, Filippo 307, 318–19
Simon, François 249, 253, 255, 284
Simon, Régis 192
Simoni, Gilberto 260, 279–80, 286, 287, 290, 291, 304, 306, 317
Simpson, Tom or Tommy 7, 54, 115, 126–8, 141, 157, 183, 184–8, 190–1, 195–6, 198, 199, 235, 380, 434, 489, 491, 498
Siutsou, Kanstantsin 489
Sinkewitz, Patrik 351, 361, 383, 384, 399
Sky team 443, 464, 536, 547, 553, 556 passim 2012, 565, 566, 573, 576, 578, 580, 581, 583, 585, 586
Slagter, Tom Jelte 555
Slongo, Paolo 546, 550
Soler, Mauricio 383, 389, 393, 403, 407
Sørenson, Nicki 425–6
Soudet, col de 295, 354
Soulor, col de 39, 158, 176, 223, 334, 335, 487
Spandelles, col des 334
Speicher, Georges 110, 171, 172
Spilak, Simon 423
Squinzi, Giorgio 240

Stablinski, Jean 131, 390
Stapleton, Bob 399
Steegmans, Gert 351, 378, 519, 533
Steels, Tom 216, 224, 230–1, 263
Steinès, Alphonse 26
Stephens, Neil 456
Štybar, Zdenek, 568
Superbesse 401, 403

Taaramäe, Rein 555
Talansky, Andrew 542, 548, 570, 579
team tactics and ethics 60–1, 71, 81, 92, 98, 133, 230, 336, 422, 438
Teklehaimanot, Daniel 567, 578
Télégraphe, col du 58, 96, 97, 100, 103, 104, 126, 139, 217, 329–30, 359, 383, 479, 480
Telekom team 62–3, 197, 203, 215, 226, 228, 231, 247, 251, 257, 275, 276, 280, 322, 347, 371–2, 381, 384
Ten Dam, Laurens 522
Terront, Charles 19, 185
testosterone 201, 345, 366–8, 369, 379, 393–4
Thévenet, Bernard 37, 43–6, 50, 69, 132, 143, 144, 145, 161, 167, 170, 175, 177, 251, 271, 274, 340, 483, 515, 578
Thomas, Geraint 375, 378, 392, 394, 438, 441, 464, 466, 467, 470–1, 511, 512, 513, 522, 537, 547, 548, 563, 565, 570, 571, 574, 577, 579, 582, 583, 586
Thurau, Diedrich 489
Thys, Philippe 28, 79, 87, 171, 546
Tignes 382
time-trials 30, 34, 35, 46, 55, 64, 65, 88, 91, 107, 108, 115, 125, 133, 141, 154, 156, 159, 162, 176, 217, 224–5, 227, 229, 239, 246–7, 249, 253, 257, 262, 263, 279, 284–5, 288, 296–7, 302, 304, 316–17, 319, 323–4, 325, 340, 342, 343, 351, 363–4, 375–6, 395, 400–1, 402, 418, 419, 433, 457, 459, 461, 464, 467, 481, 490
Tinkoff, Oleg 552
Tinkoff-Saxo team 536, 552
Tirreno-Adriatico 418
Tonkov, Pavel 115, 214, 215–16, 218
Tossato, Matteo 363
Totschnig, Georg 332
Tour des Flandres 68, 184, 324, 349, 379
Tour de France 13, 17, 20–4, 90, 93, 104, 105–6, 109–10, 122–3
  commercialism 93, 109, 155, 207–8, 342
  conditions 39, 65
  earnings 92–3
  fatalities 88
  night riding 81–2
  points systems 26
  repairs 81
  rules 27, 30, 47, 92, 96, 154, 241–2, 304, 347
  substitute riders 91
  technical developments 82, 94, 124, 171–2

time-trials 30, 34, 35, 46, 55, 64, 65, 88, 91, 107, 108, 115, 125, 133, 141, 154, 156, 159, 162, 176, 217, 224–5, 227, 229, 239, 246–7, 249, 253, 257, 262, 263, 279, 284–5, 288, 296–7, 302, 304, 316–17, 319, 323–4, 325, 340, 342, 343, 351, 363–4, 375–6, 395, 400–1, 402, 418, 419, 433, 457, 459, 461, 464, 467, 481, 490

Tour de Suisse 242, 416, 440, 469, 481

Tour Down Under (Australia) 415, 430

Tour of Lombardy 53, 56, 94, 132, 198

'Tour of Regeneration' 540

'Tour of Suffering' 88

Tour du Var 191

touristes-routiers 81, 93, 95, 98, 130, 173, 188

Tourmalet, col du 15, 26–7, 39, 42–3, 78, 82–3, 89, 112, 118, 125–6, 173, 176, 182, 184, 197, 223, 250, 255, 265, 291, 292, 309, 354, 405–6, 422, 437, 439, 450, 452–4, 470–1, 501

Toussuire 359

Trentin, Matteo 523, 542, 567

Trousselier, Louis 26

Trueba, Vicente 30, 95–6, 113

UCI 168, 203, 204, 207–8, 209, 213, 214, 241, 289, 307, 323, 325, 344, 346–7, 358, 367, 368, 370, 373, 374, 384, 385–7, 392, 393, 395, 397–8, 405, 407, 413, 423, 459–60, 568

Ullrich, Jan 55, 62, 71–2, 152–3, 160, 197, 203, 206–7, 212, 217, 218, 227–8, 229, 231, 234–5, 236, 237–9, 242, 243, 245, 247, 251–2, 253, 255–6, 257–8, 259, 260, 261–2, 275, 280, 285, 286, 288–9, 291, 292–4, 296–8, 299, 301–2, 304, 310–11, 313, 314–15, 316, 317, 318, 319–20, 322, 323–4, 326–7, 328, 329, 331, 332–4, 339, 341–2, 343, 345, 347, 363, 364, 372, 381, 447–8, 533, 556

Urán, Rigoberto 575

Val-Louron-Aspet, col de 250, 329

Valverde, Alejandro 323, 329, 331, 349, 350–1, 356, 373, 382, 400, 401, 404, 405, 406, 409, 410, 487, 490, 503, 510, 516, 517, 521, 522, 527, 531, 544ff, 570, 571, 574, 576, 579, 580, 583

Van Bon, Leon 232

Van den Broeck, Jürgen 430, 462, 464, 468, 494ff

Vande Velde, Christian 247, 248, 406, 409, 410, 412, 432, 433, 434, 440

Van Garderen, Tejay 502, 504, 528, 529, 542ff, 563, 565, 569, 574, 576, 578

Van Impe, Lucien 34, 35, 44–5, 48, 80, 115–16, 142–4, 172, 175, 252, 259, 285, 308, 546

Van Looy, Rik 533

Vanotti, Alessandro 541

Van Petegem, Peter 541

Van Poppel, Danny 542

Vansevenant, Wim 391, 413

Van Springel, Herman 47, 108, 490

Van Summeren, Johan 490

Vars, col de 79, 91, 135, 136, 169–71, 174, 182, 198

Vasseur, Cédric 176, 337, 384

Vaughters, Jonathan 216, 223, 256–7, 266–7, 268, 395, 398–9, 409, 428, 465

Veelers, Tom 519–20, 538

Veikkanen, Jussi 419

Le Vélo 17, 18, 19, 24

vélocipède 15

Verbruggen, Hein 214, 386

Verbrugghe, Rik 258, 263, 357

Verheyen, Geert 233

Vestra, Lieuwe 534

Vietto, René 106–7, 124–5, 132, 172, 179

Ville, Maurice 165

Vinokourov, Alexandr 257–8, 280, 285, 286, 287, 289, 291, 293, 294, 302, 313, 323, 324, 326, 328, 329–30, 331, 332, 333–4, 339, 341, 345–7, 372–3, 379–81, 382, 383, 384, 385, 386, 388, 389, 390, 391, 395, 398, 415, 437, 445–6, 461, 467–8, 474, 502, 541

Virenque, Richard 62–3, 71–2, 114, 116, 124, 156, 197, 202, 203, 204, 205, 211, 212, 213, 214, 215–16, 217, 218–19, 220, 228, 234, 237–8, 269–70, 271, 273–4, 285, 286, 290, 291, 296, 308–9, 311, 317, 488–9, 556

Visentini, Roberto 69–70

Voeckler, Thomas 305, 309–14, 316, 320, 324, 337, 341–2, 363, 382, 402, 404, 419, 422, 442, 446, 449, 458, 467–8, 469–70, 471–5, 476, 478–80, 481–2, 487, 489, 495f, 501, 503, 522, 539, 551, 553, 570, 577

Voet, Willy 201, 211–12

Voigt, Jens 230–1, 232, 248, 257, 315, 316, 328, 330, 356, 400, 406, 409, 430, 444, 496, 537, 556

Vos, Marianne 557

Vuelta a Castilla y Léon 415

Vuelta a España 43, 118, 208, 243, 262, 314, 343, 369–70, 372, 438, 510

Vuillermoz, Alexis 569

Wadley, J.B. 'Jock' 79, 139

Wagtmans, Marinus 47, 48, 49, 119–20

Walkowiak, Roger 73–4, 239

Watt, James 519

Weening, Pieter 326–7

Wegelius, Charly 375, 417, 525

Westra, Lieuwe 541

Wiggins, Bradley 360, 362–3, 375, 376, 380, 388, 392, 394, 405, 417, 419, 421, 423, 428–9, 430, 432, 433, 434, 435, 438–9,

441, 443, 444, 445, 448–9, 454, 456, 461,
  464, 466, 467, 481, 509–10, 530, 534, 536,
  541 *passim 2012*
world hour record 20, 43, 70, 101, 132–3,
  149, 156, 158
World Road Race Championship 34, 94,
  131, 142, 146–7, 154, 460
Wright, Michael 185, 188
Wüst, Marcel 229, 232, 233

Yates, Sean 70–1, 80, 115, 176, 189, 191,
  196, 289, 363, 381, 406, 441, 456, 471,
  483, 489, 494, 504
Yates, Simon 537, 542, 543, 557
Yorkshire 535–6, 538

Zabel, Erik 33, 203, 215, 216–17, 226, 232,
  233, 239, 245, 257–8, 261–2, 263, 273,
  274–5, 276, 283, 296, 303, 320, 323, 350,
  354, 371–2, 380, 381, 391, 418, 442
Zabriskie, David 324, 325, 352–3, 375, 419
Zandio, Xavier 541
Zberg, Markus 231
Zoetemelk, Joop 44, 45, 48, 49, 54, 59, 80,
  143–4, 154, 167, 168, 169, 175, 188, 325,
  365, 465–6, 486, 578
Zubeldia, Haimar 289, 298, 313
Zülle, Alex 157, 203, 204, 209, 214, 216,
  217, 218, 224–5, 228, 231, 234, 239, 261